BUILDING EXPERT SYSTEMS: PRINCIPLES, PROCEDURES, AND APPLICATIONS

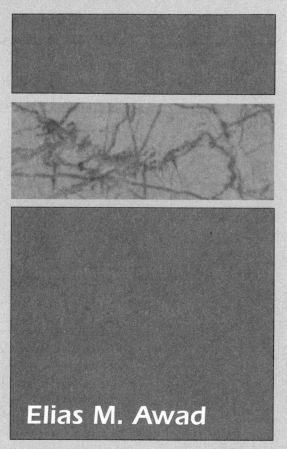

Elias M. Awad

McIntire School of Commerce
University of Virginia

WEST PUBLISHING COMPANY

Minneapolis/St. Paul   New York   Los Angeles   San Francisco

PRODUCTION CREDITS

Copyediting   Cheryl Wilms
Art   Ed Rose and Christine Bentley, Visual Graphic Systems
Interior Design   Lisa Delgado, Delgado Design, Inc., New York City
Cover Image   Copyright Yves Lefevre/Image Bank
Composition   Carlisle Communications

Production, prepress, printing, and binding by West Publishing Company

PHOTO CREDITS

Page 13 Ford Motor Company; **page 217** IBM Corporation; **page 509** Copyright
Ted Kawalerski/Image Bank.

West's Commitment to the Environment

In 1906, West Publishing Company began recycling materials left over from the
production of books. This began a tradition of efficient and responsible use of
resources. Today, up to 95 percent of our legal books are printed on recycled, acid-
free stock. West also recycles nearly 22 million pounds of scrap paper annually—the
equivalent of 181,717 trees. Since the 1960s, West has devised ways to capture and
recycle waste inks, solvents, oils, and vapors created in the printing process. We also
recycle plastics of all kinds, wood, glass, corrugated cardboard, and batteries, and
have eliminated the use of Styrofoam book packaging. We at West are proud of the
longevity and the scope of our commitment to the environment.

 TEXT IS PRINTED ON 10% POST CONSUMER RECYCLED PAPER   Printed with Printwise
Environmentally Advanced Water Washable Ink

British Library Cataloguing-in-Publication Data. A catalogue record for this book is available
from the British Library.

Library of Congress Cataloging-in-Publication Data

Awad, Elias M.
    Building expert systems : principles, procedures, and applications
  / Elias Awad.
      p.   cm.
    Includes index.
    ISBN 0-314-06626-8 (hc : alk. paper)
    1. Expert systems (Computer science) 2. System design.
I. Title.
QA76.76.E95A98   1995
006.3'3—dc20   95-45726
                                                      CIP

Dedicated to my wife Sandy and to Michael,
Bruce, and Brenda for their unwavering
support and for countless hours of
family time in the preparation of this work.

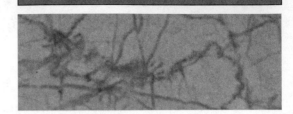

ABOUT THE AUTHOR

Elias M. Awad has 35 years of experience teaching MIS in six universities and more than 10 years of experience building expert systems. He has published 18 titles in MIS, including *Business Data Processing*, *Automatic Data Processing*, *Management Information Systems*, *Systems Analysis and Design*, *Database Management*, and *Human Resources Management: An Information Systems Approach*. His work has received international recognition, with translations into German, Spanish, Portuguese, Chinese, Arabic, and Braille. In addition, he has published more than 70 papers in professional journals and chaired numerous national conferences in expert system.

Dr. Awad is currently Virginia Bankers Association Professor at McIntire School of Commerce, University of Virginia, Charlottesville, Virginia. His long history of active involvement with premier computer organizations includes work with the Association for Computing Machinery (ACM), Data Processing Management Association (DPMA), and the International Association of Knowledge Engineers (IAKE). He also serves on the editorial board of several professional MIS journals. He specializes in computers in banking and building expert systems in the business sector.

CONTENTS

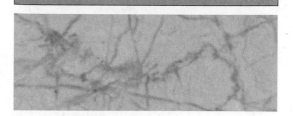

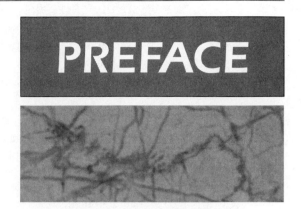

PREFACE

■ TO THE STUDENT

You know by now that the power of the computer is part of virtually every aspect of our society—industrial, governmental, and academic. Computers have progressed from the data processing age of the 1960s to the information age of the 1980s to the knowledge age of the 1990s. A significant part of knowledge and intellectual capital (accrued knowledge) represents today's national and corporate wealth. You are already a member of a society committed to understanding the value of knowledge and why it should be preserved.

Consider the following questions:

■ Do you know a more effective way to preserve an expert's knowledge who might be retiring soon than through the computer?

■ Can you imagine the computer's potential to solve complex problems by emulating a human expert's thought process?

■ How could today's corporations afford brain drain and lost expertise without a way to capture it so that less-experienced employees could use it to advantage?

■ If knowledge is today's best corporate asset, would it not make sense to find a way to preserve and protect such capital?

This text will introduce you to the building of expert systems—a growing trend in capturing human expertise and representing it in a format that allows the computer to emulate the expert's problem-solving process. In this first course in expert systems, you will learn what an expert system is, the industries that use expert systems applications, how to build the system, how to test it, and how to install it for the ultimate user. Based on the author's experience teaching and practicing in this field and on the demands of industry, this book covers the following areas:

■ The makeup of an expert systems application

■ Choosing a problem domain and planning an expert system

■ How to choose and deal with experts

■ How to capture a human expert's knowledge

■ What shells can do and how they use captured knowledge to come up with solutions

- How to program an expert system shell
- The basics of fuzzy logic and how it is used in a knowledge base
- How neural networks contribute to decision making in specialized problem areas
- Ethical and legal implications of expert systems

This book was written with you in mind. As you begin to read the material, you will find no mathematical formulas or technical material normally found in most expert systems books. To ensure readability and ease of learning, each chapter contains examples, case situations, and practical anecdotes. Several important learning aids are also included. For example, each chapter opens with a chapter outline to guide your reading and an *At a Glance* capsule that highlights chapter contents. Each chapter also ends with the following:

- A *chapter summary* that reviews the main points of the chapter
- *Key words* to improve your vocabulary in expert systems, with a compiled glossary of terms for the text available in Appendix F
- *Review questions* to reinforce your understanding of the key points of the chapter
- *Cases* based on real-life business situations to illustrate the concepts covered in the chapter, including questions at the end of each case asking you to identify the problem and prescribe solutions based on your reading
- *Selected references* to offer additional sources of knowledge about the subject
- A series of *ready-to-use applications* are included on a separate diskette using VP-Expert or EXSYS. The software is also included for use with the tutorials and for running the applications on another diskette.

In a nutshell, every effort has been made to make *Building Expert Systems* truly "user friendly" and practice-oriented. This text was written because so many other books expose students to a confusing array of technical approaches and procedures that tend to dampen excitement about the practicability of this evolving technology. The text effectively teaches the application of expert systems. After going through the material, you should be able to say, "I feel I have the tools and know-how to build an expert system."

In preparing the book, I have kept in mind that people, not computers, are the final decision makers. Expert systems emulate and in many ways support decision making. Although the underlying technology provides more "intelligence" to improve the quality of human decision making, humans have the final say in the way organizations and society must perform.

Before the manuscript found its way to the publisher, it was tested in the classroom over a three-year period, with successive revisions resulting from student feedback and feedback from professional reviewers in the field. And since no expert systems book is ever complete, future revisions are inevitable. After having gone through this material, you are invited to share your experience, ideas, or thoughts. Feel free to write to me at the following address:

Elias M. Awad
McIntire School of Commerce
University of Virginia
Charlottesville, VA 22903

e-mail: ema3z@virginia.edu
voice mail: 804/924-3423

■ TO THE INSTRUCTOR

Why This Book?

As an evolving technology, expert systems has been gaining ground in academic curricula since the late 1980s. Several books have been published, with each book purporting to provide the ideal coverage in terms of concepts, procedures, and technology. In teaching this course since 1988, I have used various books and shells and found them lacking. The books were too technical, too difficult to read, lacked experiential exercises, or addressed only select aspects of expert systems. Likewise, shells that resided on the mainframe were expensive, not so easy to learn, or not practical for academic use. PC-driven shells were often limited to backward chaining, had limitations on the use of frames, or were geared to commercial developers and came with a high price tag.

This text and the accompanying shells are a reaction to this experience. The package fills a void in today's first course in expert systems. As a colleague, you can understand the reasoning behind this attempt. The goal is to provide material that is usable and relevant to the needs of this technology course. Since more and more of today's MIS courses are practice-oriented with focus on problem-solving, case situations and applications have been incorporated into the text.

How This Text Is Organized

This book is about expert systems—what they are and how to build them in business. Figure 1 is a graphic layout of how the text is organized. Part I provides an *overview of expert systems* and focuses on system characteristics, application areas, and the development life cycle. Chapter 1 introduces the many faces of artificial intelligence, from speech understanding to neural networks. Chapter 2 addresses knowledge as the heart of expert systems, types of knowledge, and the basic tools and key participants in building expert systems. Chapter 3 elaborates on the history and characteristics of expert systems, their basic architecture, and the shell concept. Chapter 4 brings up the benefits and limitations of expert systems, myths and realities about them, and the areas in which expert systems have been applied successfully. Chapter 5 lays out in detail the life cycle of building expert systems—from problem-domain identification to verification and deployment. The chapter ends with comments about barriers to expert system development.

Part II addresses the front end of expert systems—*knowledge acquisition*. This phase has not been given its fair share of attention in other expert systems textbooks. Chapter 6 discusses the skill requirements and personality attributes of the knowledge engineer, the prime builder of expert systems. A key question in the chapter relates to career planning:

"What does it take to be successful as a knowledge engineer?" Chapter 7 explains the prerequisites for knowledge acquisition—identifying the problem domain, user and expert characteristics, and the potential for automating

Figure 1 Organization of the Text

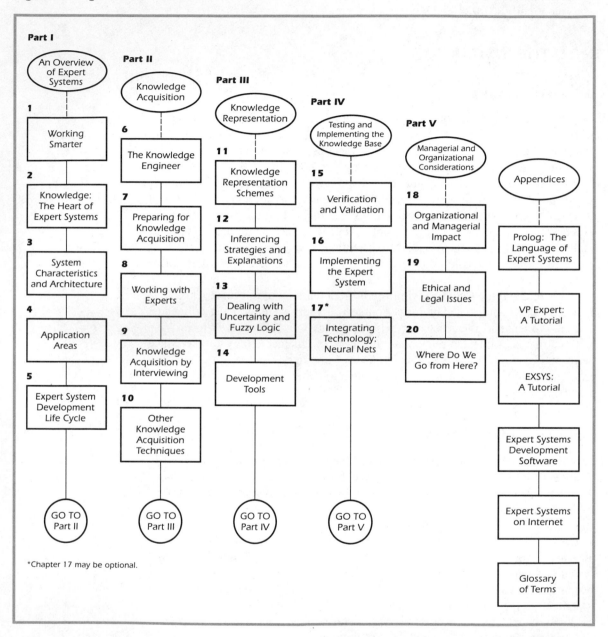

knowledge acquisition. Chapter 8 identifies human expert characteristics and discusses how to deal with experts in settings requiring multiple experts. Chapter 9 concentrates on interviewing as a knowledge acquisition tool and on ensuring validity and reliability of information. Finally, Chapter 10 is a comparative assessment of knowledge acquisition techniques, including interviewing, brainstorming, protocol analysis, consensus decision making, repertory grid, nominal-group technique, delphi method, and electronic blackboarding.

Part III examines *how knowledge is represented*; that is, how a knowledge base is developed. Chapter 11 highlights various strategies for representing knowledge—from semantic networks, frames, and production rules to formal logic. Other representation schemes, such as decision tables and decision trees, are also discussed. Chapter 12 deals with inferencing strategies and explanations, with a focus on inferencing with rules (backward and forward chaining) as well as on opportunistic, model-based, and case-based reasoning. Chapter 13 discusses fuzzy logic and the certainty factor and how they are used in knowledge-based systems. Chapter 14 summarizes various classifications of building tools and explains how shells for the PC and mainframe are used.

Part IV addresses the back end of the development life cycle—*testing and implementing expert systems*. Chapter 15 reviews the process of verification and validation and demonstrates how this critical test phase is executed. Chapter 16 highlights implementation issues and problems that arise in technology transfer. Part IV concludes with chapter 17 on neural nets as a way to integrate technology.

Part V is the capstone of the text. Chapter 18 discusses organizational impact of expert systems, psychological impact, impact on employment, and how corporations should manage knowledge. When building expert systems, ethical and legal issues must also be considered. Chapter 19 addresses these issues and their implications for management. Chapter 20 looks at the future of expert systems. Several appendixes appear at the end of the text. Appendix A illustrates the basic of Prolog as an expert systems language. Appendix B is a tutorial of VP-Expert. Appendix C is a tutorial on EXSYS, using RuleBook. Appendix D is a list of vendors and their shells. Appendix E is a brief list of expert systems accessible via Internet. Appendix F is a glossary of important terms used in the text.

Key Features

This text incorporates several key features for easy learning:

- *Learning by example* is evident throughout the text. Concepts, principles, or procedures that are either technical or new are followed by examples of illustrations for easy learning.

- A *boxed vignette* at the beginning of each chapter based on a real-life situation illustrates one or more aspects of the chapter.

- *Illustrations* are also incorporated where necessary for clearer understanding of the material. Each graph and table has been carefully sketched to ensure that the key concept being represented stands out clearly. When actual adaptation is used, references are provided so the student can locate the data source.

- *Implications for management* relates chapter material to management decision making, because technology, per se, cannot be effective until one relates its impact to the organization's productivity and growth.

- *Cases and problems* available at the end of each chapter offer a variety of both straightforward and more thought-provoking applications. The answers to these cases and problems are available in the instructor's manual.

- A *summary* at the end of each chapter brings into focus the essence of the chapter. Good summaries can be a useful guide for chapter coverage.

Depending on learning preference, reading the summary before carefully reading the chapter from beginning to end can be an effective approach.

■ A *running case*, called "Publisher Advisor," cuts across the entire text, beginning with Chapter 5. An operational version in EXSYS and VP-Expert is available on a diskette that accompanies the text. Students are encouraged to review and critique the makeup and effectiveness of the work.

■ *Tutorials* provide opportunities to expand the student's knowledge. For example, Appendix A is a tutorial on Prolog; Appendix B is on VP-Expert; and Appendix C is on EXSYS RuleBook. The latest version of each shell is also included on separate diskettes in the text. Appendix D is a list of vendors and their shells. Appendix E briefs students on expert systems via Internet. Appendix F is a comprehensive glossary of terms.

The Software

Two complimentary shells are available with this text: EXSYS Professional version 4.0 and VP-Expert. EXSYS Professional is Windows-driven, easy to use, and requires no special languages. All input is in the form of English text, algebraic expression, or menu selection. The developer works within the shell's Rule Editor, which provides menus, prompts, and help. There are no complex rule syntax to memorize. EXSYS also includes a rule compiler that allows development or editing of knowledge bases with a wordprocessor.

The tutorial in Appendix C explores EXSYS RuleBook, which is a quick, graphical way of building expert systems. The developer essentially builds the decision tree and the shell generates the rules automatically. This author feels that students can gain confidence and expertise using RuleBook before they delve into rule building via EXSYS Professional. Both approaches, however, are available at the discretion of the instructor.

VP-Expert is a DOS-driven shell and has easy-to-follow features in building basic expert systems. Instead of the decision-tree approach of EXSYS RuleBook, VP-Expert allows the developer to build an expert system using the built-in induction table. The shell accompanying the text is a student version that limits rules to a maximum of 100. The tutorial in Appendix B reflects the basics of building expert systems using VP-Expert.

Instructor's Manual

In addition to these features, a specially prepared manual is available for the instructor. The manual provides the following support material:

■ A *syllabus* based on a quarter plan and a semester plan as a guide to planning the course

■ *Lecture assistance*, including the purpose of each chapter, teaching notes, and chapter summary

■ *Solutions to problems and cases* at the end of each chapter

■ A *test bank* that includes chapter-by-chapter true-false, multiple-choice, and matching statements (Customized mid-semester or mid-term exams are also available from the author on request.)

■ *Transparency masters* representing key figures and tables in the text

ACKNOWLEDGMENTS

A book of this magnitude could not have been written without professional support. I owe a debt of gratitude to the following reviewers for their expert assistance. Each comment or suggestion was carefully evaluated and served to improve the technical and procedural makeup of the text.

Robert W. Blanning
Vanderbilt University

John H. Bradley
East Carolina University

Fritz H. Grupe
University of Nevada at Reno

Amit Gupta

Varghese S. Jacob
Ohio State University

Henry C. Lucas, Jr.
New York University

Michael E. McLeod
East Carolina University

Vijay Mookerjee
University of Washington

John Pearson
Kansas State University

James M. Ragusa
University of Central Florida

Jack N. Rose
State University of New York–Delhi

Steven R. Ruth
George Mason University

Robert H. Seidman
New Hampshire College

Ramesh Sharda
Oklahoma State University

Dennis Strouble
University of Dallas

Robert T. Sumichrast
Virginia Polytechnic State University

Francis Van Wetering
University of Nebraska at Omaha

Bindiganavale S. Vijayaraman
University of Akron

David C. Yen
Miami University

I acknowledge the dedication and contributions of my expert systems students whose natural intelligence far exceeds any knowledge-based system. Learning by doing is a sure prescription for mastering a technology of this type.

Many successful books begin with a champion who promotes an author's idea and sees it through. I am grateful to my initial champion, Mr. Dick Fenton, president of Foundation Press, Inc., whose encouragement early in 1992 made it possible to launch this project. The champion behind the development of this text is Sharon Adams Poore, Editor, West Publishing Company, who deserves a separate page for her many contributions. Her commitment to a respectable manuscript through meticulous professional reviews, constructive feedback, and creative ideas are reflected in the final product.

Authors who have published texts can appreciate the critical role of the production phase of a manuscript. I acknowledge with appreciation the dedication and talent of Laura Evans, production editor, for a first-class job transforming the manuscript into text. My sincere thanks also go to her team for a job well done.

AN OVERVIEW OF EXPERT SYSTEMS

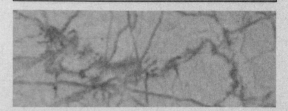

Chapter ▪ 1

Working Smarter

IN THE MIND OF THE CREATOR

WHAT ARE EXPERT SYSTEMS FOR?

One of the most discussed topics among software developers is expert systems—what they are and what they are supposed to do. Are they a science? A technology derived from information technology? Another way of solving business problems? Another phrase for artificial intelligence? Some academics suggest that expert systems is learning how an expert's mind works and how tough problems are thought out. Others view expert systems as an engineering approach to problem solving, using rules of thumb. Psychologists believe expert systems rely heavily on cognition. In reality, the answer lies somewhere in between. The goal is to use specialized languages to design a computer-aided system based on an expert's thought process.

Based on the research published to date, two things can be concluded about humans and computer technology. First, people are attracted to the idea of using the computer to mimic human thinking, but fear the computer's potential to take over unless properly controlled. Second, most people have only a vague idea about what it means to think. Today's "thinking machines" have yet to clarify this fuzziness.

Overall, people are easily awed by expert systems programs, although a number of such programs raised more questions than they provided answers. For example, the renowned expert system called ELIZA was purported to be the world's first artificial psychiatrist; yet its creator Joseph Weizenbaum would not support this claim. As users learned more about ELIZA, it was found that it could provide advice based only on the rules and facts captured in its knowledge base. In any case, it was an encouraging step toward automated expertise.

HOPE LOOMS AHEAD

Despite suspicions and failures, most expert systems have succeeded at diagnosing tasks, giving advice, or providing help in specific subject areas. They can improve productivity by increasing work output, simplifying operations, and improving efficiency. For example, the STAR-EAGLE expert system relies on human expertise in aircraft operations to provide wing commanders in assessing tactical air capability in the North American Aerospace Defense (NORAD) region. DELTA developed by General Electric guides maintenance workers through the entire diagnostic and repair process. SHAKEY is a government-funded project that is credited with creating programs from production scheduling to army logistics. SHAKEY alone was reported to have made up for most of the investment the Defense Department poured into artificial intelligence research.

The mysticism surrounding early expert systems have given way to recent successes in expert systems as problem solving tools. More and more organizations have come to recognize the potential of this developing technology. With the growing use of shells and the increasing demand for addressing complex problems, building expert systems is establishing a lasting foothold in the MIS department. As intelligence is embedded into the technology and the user interface becomes more friendly, the use of expert systems as problem solvers should be as easy as clicking on an icon on a screen.

Source: Excerpted from Elias M. Awad "Expert Systems As a Discipline—Trends and Directions." *ACM Lectureship Series,* October 1995, Detroit, Michigan.

AT A GLANCE

Artificial intelligence (AI) is a field of computer science or the science of making machines do things that would require intelligence if done by humans. Expert systems is a branch of AI that applies human knowledge of a specific area of expertise to solve very difficult problems within that area. This text focuses on the concepts, procedures, and applications of expert systems used in business.

AI encompasses such applications as speech understanding, computer vision, natural language interface, machine translation, and robotics. Despite many successes, AI systems that are capable of "learning" to be truly "intelligent" have not yet been developed.

Expert systems are used to advise, diagnose, or troubleshoot problems that were once performed by human experts. An expert system contains practical knowledge culled from a human expert; its information is explicit and comprehensive and the system is able to explain its reasoning on demand. Expert systems bring specialized knowledge directly to the fingertips of a novice. Now that expert systems shells (specialized programs) have been developed, expert systems need not be built from scratch. All the developer has to do is build a knowledge base, incorporate it into the shell, and test/validate it, and then the system is ready for the user to operate.

Expert systems are expanding the scope of information systems. They allow new applications to be added and existing applications to be leveraged. In business, when people retire, transfer, or simply leave an organization, expert systems can now capture the precious knowledge that would otherwise leave with these employees. This way, the organization can still capitalize on its investment.

Organizations that work smarter rather than harder and employ knowledge workers stand to improve their productivity, promote job enrichment, and manage knowledge in ways that can provide total quality products and services. Forward-looking managers must take stock of the organization's knowledge inventory and control the politics of implementing expert systems for successful technology transfer.

What You Will Learn

By the end of this chapter, you should know the following:

1. The meaning of *artificial intelligence* and how it differs from *expert systems*.
2. The many facets of *artificial intelligence* (AI) and whether AI systems "learn."
3. The basic *concept* behind expert systems and their potential for solving focused, ill-structured problems.
4. The relationship between expert systems and *management information systems*.
5. How an "expert company" looks at *knowledge*.

> Knowing ignorance is strength;
> Ignoring knowledge is sickness.
>
> LAO TSU

INTRODUCTION

The computer is part of virtually every aspect of our society—industrial, governmental, and social. Today's computing age is the age of the *end-user* and of human–machine, an interface made possible by advances in several areas. "Natural communication" between the end-user and the computer is an exciting feature of today's computer. In natural communication, the user queries the computer in English-like language. Someday, people will be able to communicate verbally with the computer and transact business as it occurs.

As a high-tech society, we have progressed from the data processing age of the 1960s to the information age of the 1980s to the knowledge age of the 1990s. The latest transformation represents the most fundamental change since the introduction of the digital computer in the 1940s. Knowledge and intellectual capital (accrued knowledge) represent our national and corporate wealth. Knowledge workers are found in every organization, and they are the backbone of every successful company. The unique part of their work is the use of the computer to reason through solutions. Computer-aided software gives them an edge over workers using conventional methods. This chapter discusses artificial intelligence, the general concepts behind expert systems, the relationship between expert systems and management information systems, and how an expert organization, or an "expert company," looks at knowledge.

ARTIFICIAL INTELLIGENCE

The term *artificial intelligence* seems as threatening to some people as *automation* did to blue-collar workers years ago. Yet the challenge of AI is at hand to use in virtually every area of business and industry. **Artificial intelligence** (AI) is the science of making computers do things that require intelligence if they are done by humans.

Since 1988 AI industry sales have grown at a brisk rate of 30 percent a year, with annual revenues as shown in Figure 1–1. One reason for this growth is a branch of AI called *expert systems*. An **expert system** is a sophisticated computer program that applies human knowledge in a specific area of expertise to create solutions. Such a program generally uses rules of thumb (heuristics) and symbolic logic to mimic the thought processes of the human expert.

AI has two important attributes:

1. It acquires new knowledge by communicating with the external world (the user) and makes inferences on the basis of its current knowledge.

2. It improves its performance on certain problems based on its present knowledge and the new knowledge it acquires.

Figure 1-1   Growth of Knowledge-Based Systems Tools Revenue Worldwide in Millions of Dollars, 1988-1996

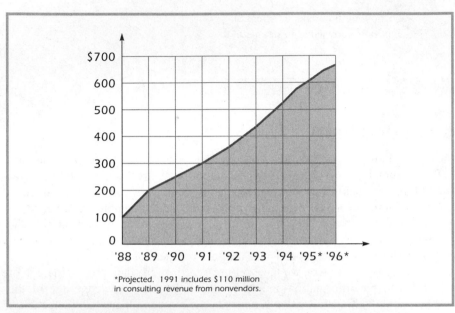

*Projected. 1991 includes $110 million in consulting revenue from nonvendors.

Source: "The Spang Robinson Report on AI."

A simple way to view artificial intelligence is to see it as a set of procedures that makes a computer capable of "seeing," "hearing," "understanding," "reasoning," or otherwise achieving results similar to those humans achieve when they process knowledge. Of course, these tasks have proven to be "difficult" for a computer.

AI has captured the interest of the academic and business worlds. The prospect of programming computers to reason through problems strikes at the heart of the distinctions between humans and machines. With the proper representation, a machine can work through a query, offer "advice," and explain the reasoning behind that advice. In this respect, the machine may be viewed as "intelligent" if it performs an action that is considered intelligent when performed by a human, such as "learning" from successive evaluations of information, "understanding" and "speaking" natural language (rather than traditional computer commands), assessing information, and drawing conclusions.

As can be seen, what promoted this technology is the notion that computers are capable of handling not only numbers, but other kinds of **symbols** as well. A symbol is a sign or character used to represent something else. From this notion, certain strategies of intelligent behavior have been supported, including:

- Searching for a solution using the "rules of guessing"
- Generating and testing solutions (making successive attempts toward an acceptable solution)
- Reasoning backwards from a specified goal (See Box 1-1)
- Reasoning forward from the data for planning and forecasting (Backward and forward reasoning are discussed in detail in Chapter 12.)

Box 1–1 Ford's AI Design Estimator

Ford of Great Britain and Germany is using AI to assist in the complex process that takes place when engineers propose a modified design of cars. The most difficult part of the task is estimating the price of new parts. This is where AI comes in, in the form of a computer-aided parts estimation (CAPE) system. The system generates a course of action and then proofs it. When it has gone over the process, it recommends it and justifies these recommendations. This system is in daily use at both European facilities. The system purportedly works out a more accurate cost in 30 minutes, whereas an estimator may take two weeks.

Source: *Knowledge Base,* July/August 1993, p. 12.

■ A BRIEF HISTORY

Artificial intelligence (AI) has its roots in formal logic and cognitive psychology, dating back to long before World War II. The postwar years (1945–1955) marked the introduction of the digital computer. AI pioneer and Nobel Prize winner Herbert Simon and Allen Newell of Carnegie-Mellon University developed "Logic Theorist," which proved theorems using a formalized branch of logic called *propositional calculus.* Logic Theorist was the first AI computer program.

The initiation and formative years of AI research were 1955 through 1960. The highlight was the 1956 Dartmouth Conference, the first AI gathering. It attracted AI pioneers Marvin Minsky (MIT), John McCarthy (Dartmouth), Claude Shannon (Bell Labs), and Nathaniel Rochester (IBM). They called their area of interest *artificial intelligence,* in which according to John McCarthy, every feature of learning or intelligence can be clearly defined to allow a computer to simulate it.

The 1960s were the years of AI development. During this time, McCarthy developed an AI programming language called LISP (LISt Processing) and Newell, Simon, and Shaw developed a system called General Problem Solver (GPS) in 1957. GPS separated general methods of problem solving from facts and knowledge parcels. It uses means–end analysis to choose an allowable operation when several can be applied to a state. Means–end analysis is a method for determining where a user is, where a user wants to be, and the distance between these two points.

Robotics, chess programs, and DENDRAL (developed by Feigenbaum and Buchanan of Stanford University) were unique achievements of the 1960s. DENDRAL originated the basic idea of expert systems and encoded a large amount of the heuristic knowledge of expert chemists into rules for the controlled search of molecular structure from mass spectrographic information. A paper in 1973 showed that DENDRAL performed better than human experts on certain problems.

The 1970s were years of specialization and the discovery of expert systems. Classics such as MYCIN (Stanford) for the diagnosis of infectious disease, MACSYMA (a math expert system developed by Martin & Moses of MIT), and HEARSAY (Carnegie Mellon) for speech recognition dominated the news. Knowledge engineering as a field began to take root. PROLOG was introduced as an expert systems language, and in 1978 Herbert Simon received the Nobel Prize for his work in decision-making processes.

On the conceptual side, Marvin Minsky developed frames for knowledge representation in 1976, and Dempster and Shafer developed their theory of evidence in 1977. A year later, Buchanan introduced the concept of rule induction. McDermott developed "R1," which later became known as XCON, for Digital Equipment Corporation (DEC), XCON was a commercial package for determining computer configurations for prospective customers.

The rush to applications began in earnest in 1980. Key events such as Japan's fifth-generation project and Feigenbaum and McCorduck's book *The Fifth Generation* dominated the news. The early 1980s also saw the emergence of various AI companies for commercial ventures. The mid-1980s brought expert system programming using shells to the business sector. Today's shells constitute much if not most of business expert system applications.

So, in less than four decades after AI's inception, expert systems—its most successful business-oriented branch—entered the mainstream as a computer-based decision-making tool. However, in 1990, the business market saw the beginning of another intelligent systems tool—neural networks. This emerging technology is discussed in Chapter 17.

■ THE MANY FACES OF ARTIFICIAL INTELLIGENCE

Artificial intelligence has several branches, elements, or types. As shown in Figure 1–2, AI includes several application areas including expert systems. The major areas are briefly described here.

Speech Understanding/Recognition

Speech understanding refers to the computer's ability to recognize and understand *spoken* language. This process allows a human to communicate with a computer by simply speaking to it (Figure 1–3). Who would not give up a keyboard if they could input data or instructions simply by speaking instead?

Speech understanding is probably the most demanding AI technology. It requires the system to imitate one of the most sophisticated functions of the human brain: deciphering a highly complex set of signals represented by a string of words in a fraction of a second. At this time, speech-recognition technology falls short of even partially replacing the keyboard. Most commercial products require that the user "train" the computer to recognize spoken words by repeating each word of the vocabulary to be used slowly and distinctly over and over again.

One of the difficulties of this vocal inputting of word information is that everyday language tends to be ambiguous. People commonly express quite specific things in a general way. For example, a manager might tell the computer to "make Fred's bonus the maximum," meaning that Fred's bonus should be the largest one. Due to poor programming, however, the computer might logically give everyone else a low bonus in order to maximize Fred's bonus, or it may give the person whose bonus is the greatest the name *Fred*. Thus, the software must be capable of asking for clarification when it encounters ambiguity. See Figure 1–3.

Figure 1–2   Major Areas of Artificial Intelligence

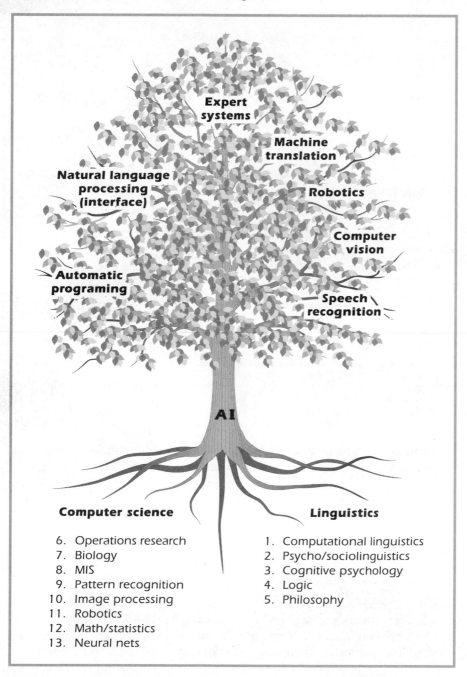

Natural Language Understanding

AI researchers have been working to construct a **natural language interface** between humans and computers since the 1960s. The dialogue of early efforts was confined to simple declarative sentences and questions. The system scanned input statements and looked for key words. The inputs executed rules that triggered an appropriate response, using words from the system's database.

Figure 1-3 Conversing Computers

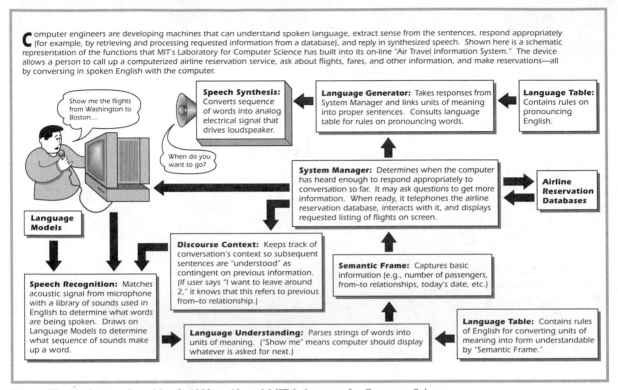

Source: *The Washington Post,* May 3, 1993, p. 19, and MIT Laboratory for Computer Science.

Natural language understanding is the highly complex process of making a correct interpretation of words and sentences in a natural language such as English, French, Spanish, or German. Three stages of interpretation are involved:

1. Syntactic analysis to reveal grammatical structure of phrases and sentences
2. **Semantic interpretation** to assign meanings to words and phrases
3. Pragmatic evaluation of the paragraph or text.

Although there are applications on the market today, much work remains to be done before natural language understanding becomes a reality.

Natural language programs concentrate on understanding what the user means when requesting something. For example, an executive's competent assistant who has been on the job for sometime knows exactly what to do when the executive says, "I need a flight to LA for the board meeting next Monday." Based on the executive's preferences, the assistant will book an early morning flight, with a window seat close to the front, that flies nonstop to LAX. The computer has yet to match such an assistant.

Case-Based Reasoning

In this particular area, old solutions are adapted to meet new situations by using old cases to explain those new situations. For example, attorneys use case precedents to justify their arguments in new court cases. Doctors often treat patients based on symptoms they have treated in previous patients. Their experience with old case(s) allows a doctor to diagnose and treat illnesses easily and quickly.

A case is a contextual piece of knowledge representing an experience. Case-based reasoning (CBR) is useful to experts with experience in their particular domain, because it helps them reuse the reasoning they have done in the past. CBR also reminds the expert to avoid repeating past mistakes. CBR is examined in greater detail in Chapter 12.

Neural Networks

Another developing AI application is neural networks. A neural network (net) is a system modeled on the human brain's network of processing elements called *neurons*. Nets are used to solve cumbersome problems that traditional computer systems have found difficult, such as determining whether the visual image of a human face is that of a man or a woman. Some of the neural business applications are in risk management, credit-card-fraud detection, check and signature verification, and mortgage appraisals.

Neural nets are closely related to natural language processing and speech understanding. For speech recognition, the net stores information on speech parts for later matching with input patterns. For example, a system called *NETtalk* synthesizes speech from text. It mimics the developmental phases of children learning to speak.

In terms of natural language processing, a net discriminates the meanings of words, depending on their context. It can also associate the relationships between words that are commonly used together. Chapter 17 presents more information on neural networks.

Computer Vision

Computer vision (visual recognition) combines computer intelligence with the digitized visual information received by a machine to control machine movement—such as robotic activity and conveyor speed. The emphasis is on identifying visual images rather than generating them. For this task, a computer must have something precise for which to search. For example, British Petroleum uses computer vision to scan microphotos of earth materials taken from drilling samples. The computer has been programmed to detect the tiny fossil shells that indicate potential sources of oil.

The major computer-vision activity of the mid-1990s is in reading printed text and handwriting. Systems have been developed that can recognize printed text if the characters are well separated from each other. When they are joined, the accuracy is diminished.

Machine Translation

Computer-aided **machine translation** is another area of AI activity. A number of U.S. companies such as IBM are conducting research and development in this area. Meanwhile, Canadians have been listening to machine-translated weather reports for several years.

The challenge facing machine translation is in understanding spoken messages, which requires translating sounds into words. Some success has occurred with dialogues in which words are separated by a brief moment of silence. IBM has developed an "automated typist" that can recognize 7,000 words. At MIT, a system called *Bilingual Voyager* answers spoken questions about how to find one's way around the city of Cambridge. It is programmed to respond to typical requests for directions. For example, a user may ask the machine, "Where is the Hyatt?" The software then displays a map of Cambridge with the hotel highlighted. If the user asks, "Where is the nearest Italian restaurant?" The software, designed to keep track of context, "assumes" the user means "nearest to the Hyatt." It then points out the location and best route to the restaurant from the Hyatt as well as displays the restaurant's address and phone number.

Robotics

Another AI application is robotics. The word *robot* has been used for many years. First used in 1921 by Czechoslovakian writer Karel Capek in his play *R.U.R.* (for Rossum's Universal Robots), it is derived from the Czech word for robota, meaning "forced labor." A robot combines sensory systems with mechanical movement to do predetermined tasks. The initial goal of robotics was for robots to take over the drudgery of human labor. See Box 1–2.

Isaac Asimov brought robots into the public eye with his novel *I, Robot.* The book laid down three laws of robotics:

1. A robot may not injure a human being.

2. A robot must obey the orders given to it by humans, except when an order conflicts with the first law.

Box 1–2   Rx for Hospitals

Are your employees calling in sick, arriving late, or protesting against midnight shifts or unusual hours? Try a HelpMate.

In this age of right-sizing and re-engineering, companies, corporations, and institutions across the country are seeking to cut costs, streamline the organization, and improve the quality of work for their employees. Transitions Research Corporation in Danbury, Connecticut, has one solution to the streamlining game that several hospitals have taken advantage of.

Working for little more than five dollars an hour, robots known as "Help-Mates" are assuming the tasks of delivering food trays, medicines, and lab supplies. Willing to work weekends, midnight shifts, and unusual hours around the clock, these five-foot-tall robots navigate autonomously throughout the hospital by use of a map of the building, selecting the best route by sensory feedback.

Currently there are some 20 hospitals across the United States that have welcomed these electronic couriers into their halls, saving countless dollars in labor. Rented out at a price of five dollars an hour, plus an additional dollar for elevator controls, these HelpMates can also be purchased outright for $70,000 per robot.

The biggest limitation experienced so far is the robots' inability to open doors, such as found in mental health wards or operating rooms.

Source: "Hospital Staffs Expanding . . . by Robots," *Knowledge Base,* July/August 1993, pp. 7, 10.

3. A robot must protect its existence as long as this does not conflict with the first two laws.

Electronic intelligence coupled with mechanical creativity has generated a variety of robots outfitted with sensors that function to see and read, touch, hear, and smell. Some of them even sense changes in production processes and automatically make adjustments in response to them. Some robots sense, and others move and manipulate their environment. The unique feature of an "intelligent" robot is its ability to detect certain conditions in its environment and then modify its behavior as it performs its job. In this respect, one can view such a robot as having humanlike attributes and capabilities. See Figure 1–4.

Automatic Programming

The goal of **automatic programming** technology is to be able to feed the user's requirements into a computer, which then automatically generates programs to satisfy these requirements. Automatic code generators appear in most computer-aided software engineering (CASE) tools, database management systems, and other specialized software. As discussed in Part II, knowledge acquisition for expert systems is labor-intensive. It requires hours of interviewing before the knowledge base can be programmed or developed. Automated knowledge representation could be the wave of the future. Research is well underway to acquire knowledge automatically based on predefined standards.

Figure 1–4   Robotics—Images of Automation

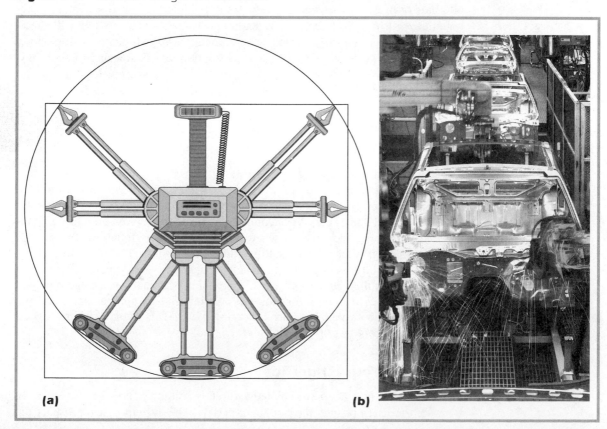

(a)   (b)

Do AI Systems *Learn?*

Even though some AI systems can process speech, recognize voices, detect movement, and the like, the question that keeps coming up is "Do AI systems "learn" in the way that humans understand learning? As discussed in Chapter 2, incorporating the ability to learn into a machine is difficult. Because of gaps in a system's understanding of the task it is performing, it often cannot perceive the *context* of its task. Even though AI applications have made important contributions in many businesses, these programs do not understand what a business *is*. MIT's kidney diagnostic system is another example. It is probably the best "expert" in its area, but it does not know that the kidney is in the body, or what a body is.

Practical Problems

Important questions are yet to be answered concerning AI's ability to represent human intelligence. One question is how to overcome the ambiguities of language in natural language processing. Another question relates to instilling the ability to learn as a major component of intelligence in AI. Practical problems confront the field of AI as well. For example, the effect of AI systems on human problem-solving processes has raised serious concerns in the corporate community. Corporate planning is a complex process that requires judgment and foresight culled from years of experience. Some fear that when expert systems are linked to larger corporate databases, a false sense of security within corporate problem solvers will follow.

All of these issues suggest that AI is not a powerful "czar" that can solve all kinds of problems. AI systems have restricted learning capability and certain boundaries in terms of experience learning. Managers confronted with decisions about AI should try to match the company's requirements with existing field-tested AI systems and make certain support exists for such technology. Without advance planning and cost-benefit analysis of a proposed system, the potential user can be in for an unpleasant surprise.

▒ EXPERT SYSTEMS: A BRANCH OF ARTIFICIAL INTELLIGENCE

The purpose of expert systems is to assist a person's thinking process, not merely to provide information for a person to think about. Properly used, they can help a person become a little wiser, not just better informed. AI and expert systems are not the same. AI encompasses many aspects of human behavior (speech, language, movement), whereas expert systems focus on the task of problem solving. Expert systems utilize the research discipline of AI to create a commercial reality that produces benefits each day. An expert system is a branch or a commercial spinoff of AI. It contains practical knowledge obtained from a human expert. Its information is explicit and comprehensible, and the system is able to explain its reasoning on demand. This book examines expert systems as a problem-solving tool.

Experts at Your Fingertips

Expert systems bring expert knowledge directly to the fingertips of a novice. In a sense, the user consults the human expert via the system that represents the human expert's knowledge. Thus, a user can obtain the knowledge needed to address a problem without interrupting an actual expert. Expert systems are now appearing in every aspect of the business world. They are showing up as strategic planning advisors, loan advisors, intelligent tutors, in-house experts, and production specialists. Here are some examples:

- Alamo Rent-A-Car uses an expert system to set prices automatically for every car, in every location, every day. The result is higher productivity and more competitive prices.

- American Airlines utilizes an expert system to track round-trip flights for its frequent fliers.

- Manufacturers Hanover Trust has developed an expert system that monitors worldwide trading activities in the bank's foreign exchange operations.

- Bank of America's training program relies on an expert system that substantially shortens the time needed to train new bank employees.

Depending on the problem it is designed to solve, an expert system could be simple enough to operate on a personal computer or complex, using thousands of rules and requiring a much larger system. In either case, expert systems are known for their ability to monitor situations and react to problems as they occur, which means instant adjustments. Expert systems applications are discussed in Chapter 4.

An expert system is only as useful as the knowledge it represents. At present, knowledge engineers must painstakingly extract knowledge from human experts through a series of interviews or similar knowledge acquisition tools. Knowledge is not easily defined, and experts are not always articulate or motivated to share all that they know. All too often, a knowledge engineer poses a scenario or a hypothetical situation to the expert in such a way that does not bring out all the knowledge sought. These and other knowledge acquisition and knowledge representation challenges are examined in Part II.

Although expert systems have become invaluable in many organizations, some have also failed. Failures range from selecting the wrong problem domain, chasing the wrong talent to develop the expert system, poor system testing (called *verification and validation*), a lack of understanding of the expert's knowledge, and other causes. Managers as well as knowledge engineers must address these problems and map out strong plans that have top-management support.

◼ THE EXPERT COMPANY

This text is about expert systems and how organizations can use them to improve productivity and growth. An **expert company** is a label given an organization that works smarter in the way human knowledge is represented in computer-aided form to solve difficult problems. Going that route means improved productivity and competitive advantage.

Managing Knowledge

One area that a company must address is how it can best manage its *intellectual capital*—the sum of knowledge of its human resources. As explained in Chapter 15, the knowledge found in policy manuals, case histories, training materials, and employees' heads is the most valuable asset of the company in terms of replacement costs. To develop and maintain this knowledge is extremely costly. Unless a company regularly reviews its knowledge core and manages it effectively, it is subject to potential disaster resulting from employee resignations, turnover, and the like.

In most corporations, knowledge management is still uncharted territory. Few executives understand how to make the most effective use of their company's knowledge. They may know the value of the firm's tangible assets, such as the physical plant and inventory, but have trouble putting a price tag on the value of its sales force's talent, corporate policy, or strategic planning decisions. Since the early 1980s, active discussions have centered on the importance of knowledge and knowledge management. For example, Roy Vagelos, chief executive officer of Merck Corporation, told *Fortune* magazine in 1993 that the idea of devoting time and resources to the proper management of knowledge is slowly, but surely, gaining support in many organizations.

For a company to manage its knowledge, it must take inventory of its people, systems, and decisions. Professional knowledge workers within the company must be identified and their functions defined. Knowledge technologies must be incorporated to re-engineer the entire business process. Major decisions should be reviewed, and a knowledge system for making each decision should be developed. The company's information systems should also be reviewed to determine which ones can benefit from emerging knowledge technologies.

This type of self-assessment will make a company more aware of its strengths and weaknesses and enable it to make changes appropriate to the competitive environment. Knowledge management and self-assessment are covered in greater detail in Chapter 18.

The Intelligence of Organizations

The potential of the computer to integrate the intelligence of the organization as a whole—not just to one organizational problem in isolation of others—is also related to the expert company. In this regard, it could resemble a **local area network** through which computers communicate with one another to make the best use of idle power and available intelligence. The idea that computers might behave like organizations raises a number of interesting questions. For example, can computers be "taught" to plan and organize on their own in order to address human, political, marketing, financial, accounting, and production problems? How can one computer "reason" about another computer's knowledge or judgment? As of today, these questions have no ready answers.

IMPLICATIONS FOR MANAGEMENT

What implications do expert systems have for the manager? Expert systems extend managers' ability to understand their organization and to control its processes. With expert systems, managers can use stored knowledge to address complex human and corporate problems, thereby extending the realm of the possible.

Expert systems are also expanding the scope of information systems by adding new applications and leveraging existing ones. In many contexts, a limited amount of "embedded" knowledge (rules that determine when information should be used, viewed, etc.) drastically reduces the amount of processing needed to arrive at a solution. This characteristic of expert systems enables managers to tackle problems and arrive at solutions that improve the competitive edge for the firm.

Corporations are realizing that certain problems presently solved by humans cannot be reliably supported forever, because key people retire, transfer, or simply leave the organization for other opportunities. Expert systems are more permanent, readily transferred, consistent, and affordable than employees. So, the challenge for managers is to select critical organizational problems and determine how they can be solved with the help of expert systems.

To maintain a competitive edge, executives are already using expert systems to process qualitative information, to access stored knowledge, and to generate consistent decisions. So far, the return on investment has been excellent.

In the changing management information system (MIS) environment, users want knowledge, not just information. The days of wading through reams of reports and statistics are now being replaced by viewing windows on a screen that show the problem, the alternatives, and the consequences of each alternative. The potential of combining databases and knowledge bases in business problem solving is becoming more and more evident. When the database can be given a higher level of semantic knowledge, which is part of an expert system, MIS will be more user-supportive and more efficient than conventional databases.

A word of warning: Computers cannot be human. At best, they emulate human thought processes in a variety of useful ways. For example, for a computer to "converse" with the user in plain English, it must be well versed in the complexity of the language and "understand" its syntax and semantics. To a human, a basic sentence could have a number of different meanings. To acquire an understanding of this ambiguity, a computer must know how to interpret misspelled words and grammatical errors. Even if a computer can be made to do all this, it still might not "understand" the user or that its response would be helpful. Thus, today's computers are more akin to player pianos than intelligent machines. They run rote programs and lack the capacity to "learn" from experience. In one respect, this lack of human "abilities" is a relief to managers; yet, it shows how far technology must go to "humanize" computers in business.

SUMMARY

1. Artificial intelligence (AI) has been growing at a brisk rate, primarily due to expert systems—a sophisticated set of programs that apply human knowledge representing a specific area of expertise to create solutions to specific problems. Such programs use *heuristics* and symbolic logic to mimic the thought processes of human experts.

2. AI is a sophisticated system that can do the following:

   a. Acquire new knowledge and makes inferences on the basis of its current knowledge.

   b. Focus on reasoning and how to represent and make use of knowledge—knowledge that is originally acquired from a human expert.

   c. Improve its performance in certain problem domains based on its knowledge and goal-directed experience.

3. AI represents several major areas:

   a. *Speech understanding/recognition:* the computer's ability to recognize and understand spoken language. This capability is probably the most sophisticated AI technology. One of the difficulties is ambiguity in everyday language.

   b. *Computer vision:* visual recognition or reading of printed text and handwriting.

   c. *Natural language interface:* allows humans to communicate with a computer in the user's natural language.

   d. *Machine translation:* computer-aided translation of sounds into words or of one language into another.

   e. *Robotics:* combining sensory systems with mechanical movement to do predetermined tasks.

   f. *Automatic programming:* the computer's ability to generate program instructions after being fed the user's requirements.

4. Significant questions have been raised about AI accurately representing human intelligence. Some of the problems that remain include MIS managers' perceived threat of AI to their careers and a false sense of security to corporate problem solvers.

5. Knowledge and the way it is represented are the two most critical elements of expert systems. Experts use symbols and apply rules to manipulate the attributes. Symbols may be combined to represent the relationships between them. It uses symbol structure to perform deductive reasoning.

6. An expert system is only as good as the knowledge represented in the computer. Knowledge is not easily defined, and experts are not always available. Although many stories tell of success, others describe failures stemming from selecting the wrong problem domain or expert, using incompetent knowledge engineers, or doing a poor job testing the system. Managers as well as knowledge engineers should address these problems and look for a champion (a strong supporter within management).

7. An "expert company" is an organization that works smarter because of the way it captures human knowledge, represents the knowledge in a computer-aided form, and uses the resulting program to solve all kinds of focused problems that were once the domain of humans.

8. An organization's intellectual capital must be effectively managed. An expert company takes inventory of its people, systems, decisions, and core competence. This self-assessment helps the company identify its strengths and weaknesses and make appropriate changes in view of the competitive nature of the market.

■ TERMS TO LEARN

Artificial intelligence (AI) subfield of computer science; the science of making machines do things that would require intelligence if done by humans; processes analogous to human reasoning processes; the capacity to acquire and apply an understanding gained through experience or study in order to imitate or emulate "natural intelligence;" "the science of making machines do things that would require intelligence if done by man" (Marvin Minsky).

Automatic programming process in which user requirements are input into the computer, which automatically generates a program that meets the requirements.

Computer vision the addition of computer intelligence capability to digitized visual information received from a machine to control machine movement; interpretation of pictures through visual recognition of precise characteristics.

Expert company an organization that works smarter by the way it captures human knowledge, represents knowledge in a computer-acceptable form, and uses the resulting program to solve various kinds of ill-structured, focused problems that were once the sole domain of humans.

Expert system a sophisticated computer program that applies human knowledge in a specific area of expertise to create solutions to difficult problems.

Knowledge base a collection of facts, rules, and procedures organized into schemas or models; the assembly of all of the information and knowledge of a specific field of interest.

Machine translation translating one language into another; understanding a text written in one language and then generating it in a different language.

Natural language interface provides the user with the capability to communicate with the computer in the user's own natural conversational language.

Natural language programs programs that concentrate on understanding what the user means when the user asks a question.

Natural language understanding a complex process of analyzing natural language sentences and words for making a correct interpretation through syntactic analysis, semantic interpretation, and pragmatic evaluation.

Robot combines sensory systems with mechanical movement to perform predetermined tasks.

Semantic interpretation assigning meanings to words and phrases while interpreting natural language.

Speech understanding the ability of the computer to recognize and understand spoken language.

Symbol a sign or character that represents something else.

■ REVIEW QUESTIONS

1. What do you conclude from the vignette "In Its Creator's Image" at the beginning of the chapter? Explain.

2. "AI allows humans to communicate directly with the computer based on stored human knowledge, as opposed to factual data." Do you agree? Discuss.

3. What distinguishes the knowledge age of the 1990s from the information age of the 1980s? Be specific.

4. Distinguish between

   a. AI and expert system
   b. symbol and fact

5. In your own words, briefly describe these AI application areas:

   a. speech recognition
   b. computer vision
   c. machine translation

6. In what respects can AI systems "learn"? Cannot learn? Explain.

7. Elaborate on the unique attributes of an expert company. What are the benefits of becoming an expert company?

8. Explain the rationale for managing knowledge.

9. In an expert company, the absence of expert knowledge is considered a strategic liability. Why?

10. Search the literature and prepare a three-page report on an expert system application in the industry of your choice.

11. What are some of the problems in developing and implementing expert systems? Elaborate.

12. What implications do expert systems have for management? Discuss.

■ EXERCISES AND CASES

1. Working with a classmate, conduct an interview or a telephone survey regarding a local bank's

a. familiarity with expert system applications in banking
b. level of literacy in expert systems
c. problem and the potential of expert system in solving those problems.

2. A business manager, a programmer, and a psychologist all want to become an expert system designer. Which one do you feel will have the least difficulty? Explain.

3. Browse through information technology magazines (*Computerworld, AI Expert, Byte, PC AI, IEEE Expert,* etc.) available from your instructor, local library, or lab for articles on expert systems.

a. Describe one expert system application that you found.
b. What tools (programming language, shell, etc.) are used to build expert systems?
c. What industry seems most active in expert system development?

4. Consider this headline from the business journal *Barron's* (October 31, 1994, p. 18): "No Flash in the Pan." Could a computer tell that the writer was *not* saying, "There are no hot sparks coming out of the pan?" Why? Why not? If no, what additional information would help in determining what was meant?

5. A car dealer who has just learned about expert systems thinks they could be ideal for separating "tire-kickers" from serious buyers. Would this be a typical expert system application? Why?

■ SELECTED REFERENCES

Bernhardt, R., ed. *Integration of Robots into CIM.* London: Chapman and Hall, 1992.

Bobrow, Daniel G., ed. *Artificial Intelligence in Perspective.* Cambridge, MA: MIT Press, 1994.

Boden, M.A. *Artificial Intelligence in Psychology: Interdisciplinary Essays.* Cambridge, MA: MIT Press, 1989.

Boole, G. *An Investigation of the Laws of Thought, on Which Are Founded the Mathematical Theories of Logic and Probabilities.* London: MacMillan Publishing Co., 1854.

Brill, Louis M. "Art Robots: Artists of the Electronic Palette." *AI Expert,* January 1994, pp. 28–33.

————. "Autonomous Robots: Getting from Here to There." *AI Expert,* July 1993, pp. 16–23.

————. "Brother Robot." *The Economist,* March 14, 1992, pp. 23–24.

Brown, M.; B. Buntschuh; and J. Wilpon. "SAM: A Perceptive Spoken-Language-Understanding Robot." *IEEE Transactions on Systems, Man, and Cybernetics,* November 1992.

Carter, Joe. "Managing Knowledge: The New Systems Agenda." *IEEE Expert,* June 1992, pp. 3–4.

Caudill, Maureen. "A Little Knowledge Is a Dangerous Thing." *AI Expert,* June 1993, pp. 16–22.

Coleman, Kevin. "AI Marketplace 2000." *AI Expert,* January 1993, pp. 34–38.

Copeland, Jack. *Artificial Intelligence: A Philosophical Introduction.* Cambridge, MA: Blackwell, 1993.

Crevier, Daniel. *AI: The Tumultuous History of the Search for Artificial Intelligence.* New York: Basic Books, 1993.

Eliot, Lance B. "Leave the Driving to AI." *AI Expert,* April 1992, pp. 9–11.

Evans, J.; B. Krishnamurthy; and T. Skewis. "Coordinating Multiple Autonomous Robot Couriers." *Proceedings of the International Robots and Vision Automation Conference.* Robotic Industries Association, April 1993.

Geisel, Larry K. "Machine Intelligence: A Powerful Force for Change." *Journal of Knowledge Engineering,* Fall 1989, pp. 11–14.

Gelfand, J.; Flax M.; R. Endres; S. Lane; and D. Handelman. "Senses, Skills, Reactions, and Reflexes: Learning Automatic Behaviors in Multi-Sensory Robotic Systems." In G. Bekey, and K. Goldberg, eds., *Neural Networks in Robotics.* Boston: Kluwer Academic Press, 1993.

Grupe, Fritz H. "Planning Your Expert System Strategy." *Information Executive,* Winter 1991, pp. 46–49.

Kazanzides, P., and B. Mittelstadt. "Surgical and Industrial Robots: Comparison and Case Study." *Proceedings of the International Robots and Vision Automation Conference.* Robotic Industries Association, April 1993.

Hertz, David B. "The Knowledge Engineering Basis of Expert Systems." In *Expert Systems with Applications.* New York: Pergamon Press, 1990, pp. 79–84.

Koenig, Patti, and George Bekey. "AI and Locomotion: Horse Kinematics." *AI Expert,* January 1994, pp. 18–27.

Kolodner, Janet L. "Knowledge-Based Self-Organizing Memory for Events." In A. Elithorn and R. Banerji, eds., *Artificial and Human Intelligence.* New York: Elsevier Science Publishers, 1984.

Kudodera, J.; M. Lee; and I. Nevarez. "Design of a Hand-Operated Force-Feedback Device," *Proceedings from the Design Affiliates Conference.* Stanford University, June 1993.

Lewinson, Lisa. "AI at Microsoft: Toward Practical Intelligent Applications." *PC AI,* January–February 1995, pp. 16–18ff.

Luger, George F., and William Stubblefield. *Artificial Intelligence: Structures and Strategies for Complex Problem Solving.* Redwood City, CA: Benjamin/Cummings, 1993.

McCarthy, John. "The Little Thoughts of Thinking Machines." *Psychology Today,* December 1983, pp. 46–49.

"Managing the Machines." *The Economist,* March 14, 1992, pp. 8ff.

Margarita, Sergio. "The Towers of Hanoi: A New Approach." *AI Expert,* March 1993, pp. 22–27.

Markowitz, Judith. "Money Listens: Speech Recognition in the Financial Industry." *PC AI,* December 1993, pp. 28–30.

——— . "The Power of Speech." *AI Expert,* January 1993, pp. 28–33.

Martin, James. "Modeling Technology for the 21st Century." *PC Week,* November 14, 1988, p. 53.

Newquist, Harvey P. "A Maturing AI Is Finding Its Way in the World." *Computerworld,* February 19, 1990, p. 23.

——— . "GTE and AI: A Meeting of the Acronyms." *AI Expert,* November 1992, pp. 44–45.

Port, Otis. "Smart Programs Go to Work." *Business Week,* March 2, 1992, pp. 97–99.

Rahman, T., and W. Harwin. "Bilateral Control in Teleoperation of a Rehabilitation Robot." *Proceedings of the SPIE Conference on Telemanipulator Technology,* November 1992.

Reber, A. S. "Implicit Learning and Tacit Knowledge." *Journal of Experimental Psychology,* 1989, 118, pp. 219–235.

Rock, Denny; Krishna Nanda Jha; and Gay Engelberger. "Talking with Rosie: Home Robot Interfaces." *AI Expert,* October 1993, pp. 20–27.

"Smart Programs Go to Work." *Business Week,* March 2, 1992, pp. 97–105.

Stewart, Thomas. "Brain Power: How Intellectual Capital Is Becoming America's Most Valuable Asset." *Fortune,* June 3, 1991, pp. 23–28.

Winston, Patrick H. *Artificial Intelligence.* Reading, PA: Addison Wesley, 1992.

Chapter ■ 2

Knowledge: The Heart of Expert Systems

THE QUEST FOR MACHINES THAT NOT ONLY LISTEN, BUT ALSO UNDERSTAND

"What you want to do," Victor Zue said, "is carry out a meaningful conversation with your machine."

In other words, the MIT computer scientist said, you want your computer to do more than respond slavishly to the computerese commands you type in or the cutesy icons you "click on." What most computer users would really like, Zue believes, is to speak to their machines in natural English. They would like the computer to understand what they mean, ask questions if it doesn't, and then do what is wanted.

It is just such systems that Zue and his colleagues at several research centers are working to perfect. . . . "We have technology that is finally capable of solving many important problems," said George Doddington, manager of ARPA's spoken language technology program. "The progress in the last four years has been absolutely incredible."

Already on the market are systems that act as electronic stenographers. You dictate and the machine figures out each word as you speak it (you must pause after each word) and displays it on the screen. The devices are used by people who can talk but not type, either because of a disability or because they must do other things with their hands.

To perform their best, most such systems practice at hearing a given user's voice and speech mannerisms. One of the most advanced is Dragon Dictate, which has a 30,000-word vocabulary and runs on a PC. But it does not "understand" the meaning of anything it hears, other than a few commands for running the computer.

In the prototype stages are devices that approach the machine equivalent of understanding. They not only recognize different voices without training, but know the vagaries of English syntax well enough to figure out what you mean from many different ways of saying the same thing. If they don't understand or don't have enough information to act, they ask you relevant questions.

"Show me the flights from Pittsburgh to Boston," Wayne Ward of Carnegie Mellon University said to his research group's prototype system, which contains a database of airline fares and schedules.

"There are 13 flights," the synthetic voice replied, displaying the same sentence on the screen. "When are you leaving Pittsburgh?"

"In the afternoon," Ward answered, whereupon the machine displayed only those flights.

Though a simple enough task for human brains, the interaction called for considerable sophistication in the computer. For example, it had to know the meaning of "from" and "to" to be able to ask when Ward wanted to leave Pittsburgh.

Instead of "in the afternoon," Ward could have said "after 12" or "not in the morning" or "around 2 or 3" or any number of other possibilities.

To show the system's versatility, Ward spoke in a rambling, disorganized way typical of humans but not computers: "I want to go to Detroit and I want to leave from Pittsburgh and I want the cheapest flights."

The machine understood. But it isn't perfect. Once when Ward asked, "Can I use frequent flyer miles?" it understood the sentence as "Tonight frequent flyer miles."

Zue's group at MIT has taken the technology still further. Instead of its own database of airline information, Zue's machine can dial up Easy Sabre, an on-line reservation service operated by American Airlines that is usually accessed the old-fashioned way—by making choices on a series of on-screen menus. Simply by having a meaningful conversation with his computer, Zue can find the flights he wants, make the reservations, and bill the fare to a credit card.

Speech recognition technology is not just a gimmick, said Janet Baker, a founder of Dragon Systems. "There have been tremendous increases in the state of the art," she said, and there are "no signs of that slowing down." Baker noted that as computers shrink to "palmtop"-size and smaller, keyboards become useless. "No one wants to enter data by toothpick."

Source: Boyce Rensberger, *Washington Post*, May 3, 1993, p. 3D.

AT A GLANCE

This chapter examines the notion of knowledge as the heart of expert systems, the question of whether computers are capable of acquiring human intelligence, and the recognized classifications of knowledge. Intelligent behavior implies the ability to understand and use language and to store and access relevant experience at will.

Humans acquire expertise—that is, learn—via experience. Expertise incorporates the ability to reason and to make deductions as well as "common sense." Because computers lack common sense, they cannot be expected to think enough to be as intelligent as humans.

An essential criterion of learning is memory. The computer is better suited to "learn" from its own experience through inductive learning. Such learning by example is a good candidate for building expert systems. Learning by discovery is less well understood than learning by experience or by example.

A knowledge base is the heart of an expert system. Knowledge engineers need to understand an expert's knowledge early in the knowledge acquisition process in order to decide whether the expert is the right individual for the expert system. Of course, an expert's knowledge is not limited to information. Knowledge embraces a wider sphere than information. Likewise, a knowledge base is not the same thing as a database. A database has a predetermined structure; a knowledge base is a set of facts and inference rules for determining new facts.

Knowledge as know-how may be either shallow or deep knowledge. It may also be procedural, declarative, semantic, or episodical knowledge. It takes an expert longer to retrieve or explain episodical knowledge than procedural knowledge.

What You Will Learn

By the end of this chapter, you should know the following:

1. The distinctions of knowledge, intelligence, and experience.
2. The distinctive features of knowledge and knowledge base versus information and database.

3. The different ways knowledge is classified.

4. The differences of procedural, declarative, semantic, and episodical knowledge.

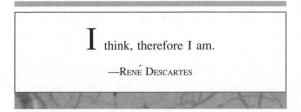

I think, therefore I am.

—RENÉ DESCARTES

■ INTRODUCTION

A number of people have interacted with the ELIZA computer program, which was designed to mimic an encounter between a patient and a psychotherapist. Named for Eliza Doolittle (the young Cockney flower seller taught to talk and act like a lady in George Bernard Shaw's *Pygmalion*), the program was written in 1965 by Joseph Weizenbaum of MIT.

Do the computer's responses represent intelligent behavior? In some cases, Weizenbaum's ELIZA tricked "patients" into believing that they were understood by the program. They believed they were interacting with an intelligence. But ELIZA's "intelligence" is based on rote "learning." Whether ELIZA "learned" in a way that people recognize as learning hinges on the distinction between machine (artificial) intelligence and human intelligence.

Having glanced at artificial intelligence and the ways expert systems can help organizations work smarter in Chapter 1, this chapter focuses on how knowledge enables the computer to emulate human thought processes and decision making. Since knowledge is the heart of an expert system, a key question is Can a computer emulate human knowledge? Furthermore, What is the relationship between knowledge and logic? And between intelligence and logic?

Another goal of this chapter is to show that human knowledge and logical processes can be captured and represented in a valid way to solve certain kinds of problems. (The words *valid* and *validity* as used in the text do not have the same meaning as *truth*. A conclusion, for example, follows logically from facts and rules using inference procedures, but can still be a false, or not correct, conclusion, but a valid one. This distinction is examined in later chapters that discuss logic, validity, and truths.)

In the end, however, computers and computer processing are no match for human reasoning or human maturation.

■ DEFINITIONS

Before discussing "knowledge" and its many ramifications, knowledge needs to be defined in relation to "intelligence," "artificial," "experience," and "common sense."

Knowledge

Knowledge is understanding gained through experience or study. It is "know-how" or a familiarity with the way to do something that enables a person to perform a task. It may also be an accumulation of facts, procedural rules, or heuristics. These things are defined as follows:

- A **fact** is a statement of some element of truth about a subject matter or a domain. For example, that milk is white and that the sun rises in the east and sets in the west are facts.

- A **procedural rule** is a rule that describes a sequence of relations relative to the domain. For example, always check the traffic when entering a freeway; if the gas gauge shows quarter-full or less, then look for a gasoline station.

- A **heuristic** is a rule of thumb based on years of experience. For example, if a person drives no more than five miles above the speed limit, then that person is not likely to be stopped for speeding.

A beneficial aspect about knowledge is that it can compensate for some search time. A human expert who knows a set of solutions can get a job done without much searching for information. Conversely, the computer in a video game searches a vast number of alternative moves at each juncture because it lacks experiential knowledge. Unfortunately, without the aid of knowledge, which allows the reasoner to immediately eliminate inappropriate approaches, this method encompasses too many approaches to evaluate.

Another aspect of knowledge is specificity; it cannot be transferred from one problem domain to another. Therefore, one must have the surgeon's know-how to repair a heart valve, the auto transmission specialist's know-how to replace a clutch, and the painter's know-how to create an accomplished portrait. These kinds of extensive knowledge are referred to as expert knowledge and often take many years to acquire.

Intelligence

Intelligence refers to the capacity to acquire and apply knowledge. It is the ability to build or improve upon knowledge, to transform as much of one's knowledge as possible into knowledge that can be used to make good decisions. An intelligent person is one who has the ability to think and reason. This distinction separates the novice from the master in a game like chess. Knowledge conversion is directly responsible for much of the expert's efficiency in applying knowledge and for the difficulty of making it explicit. Consider this example.

Some recent research into the true meaning of intelligence illustrates very well the difficulty of defining that term. The organization doing this research decided to get to the bottom of the question once and for all and, given its importance, assigned its most senior scientist to it. The esteemed scholar spent several months conducting this research. At the end of that period, the scientist gathered a number of colleagues together and held up in front of them the artificially intelligent artifact chosen as the subject of the research and said, "Ladies and gentlemen, this is a thermos bottle. It keeps hot stuff hot, and it keeps cold stuff cold. My question is, how does it know?"

Intelligent behavior has several attributes:

- Ability to understand and use language. Language understanding is not easy to acquire, especially for the computer. For example, consider the statement *The city of Fairmount is under six feet of water.* Does this mean that the city is completely under water, with the tallest building below the water level? Another example is the statement, *The sun broke through the clouds.* How literally should one interpret this statement? Of course, both the meaning of the words and the context of the statements determine how a reader should understand the messages. Prior knowledge and common sense also enter the picture.

- **Memory,** or the ability to store and retrieve relevant experience at will. How the brain stores and retrieves information or knowledge is still unclear. Later, the text includes a discussion of "knowledge representation" and how it is exploited in building expert systems.

- **Learning** is knowledge or skill that is acquired by instruction or study. It is the inevitable consequence of intelligent problem solving. Intelligent people learn quickly and make effective use of what they learn. Inasmuch as problem solving and knowledge representation have been successfully demonstrated in expert systems, the same success has yet to be shown in "machine learning." People learn from experience, while to date, expert systems have not.

Artificial

The term **artificial** means imitating or emulating something that is natural or real. So, if a computer has the quality of **artificial intelligence,** it has the capacity to acquire and apply knowledge (an understanding gained through experience) in a way that emulates "natural intelligence." The basic goal in developing AI and expert systems is to create programs that allow a computer to emulate a human expert's way of solving a complex problem.

Experience

Experience is closely related to knowledge. People use experience to change facts into knowledge, which separates novices from experts. Exceptions do occur. Bach, for example, was expert musician at five years of age with little experience. In general, though, without experience, one would hardly be considered an expert. Experience in using knowledge allows people to refine their reasoning processes in building expert systems.

Experience often leads to **expertise.** Think of Sherlock Holmes investigating a murder. The goal is to find the murderer. Holmes's reasoning and deductions rely on all evidence collected, working backward from the goal to the data until the suspect is caught. Expertise is also intuition and the ability to access one's knowledge rapidly to achieve an efficient and successful outcome.

Common Sense

Common sense refers to the unreflective opinions of ordinary humans, which comes naturally to a child as young as three or four years old. For example, most youngsters know that if they touch a hot stove, they will get burned. A computer, however, could be told all kinds of things about hot stoves and the effect of heat on the human skin and it still would not perceive what would happen if it "touched" a hot stove, because the computer lacks common sense. Common sense is not easily learned or acquired.

Lack of common sense makes expert systems "brittle"; that is, they rarely go beyond the scope of their knowledge base. Many important applications assumed by humans today require common sense, which is only partially understood by today's computer. The lack of common sense represents a severe limitation for artificial intelligence in general. Table 2–1 summarizes the foregoing concepts.

■ COGNITION AND KNOWLEDGE ENGINEERING

Cognitive psychology provides an essential background for understanding knowledge, artificial intelligence, and expertise. The goal of cognitive psychology is to identify the cognitive structures and processes that relate to skilled performance within a domain. Cognitive science in general is the interdisciplinary study of human and artificial intelligence. Its two main components are (1) experimental psychology, which studies the cognitive processes that constitute human intelligence, and (2) artificial intelligence, which studies the cognition of computer-based intelligent systems.

With these relationships in mind, one can see cognitive psychology's contribution to knowledge engineering. Understanding the limitations and biases provided by cognitive psychology help in understanding expertise. Human limitations—such as memory capacity and the physical limits imposed by human sensory and motor systems—must be considered when attempting to understand how the expert carries out a task. The knowledge engineer applies these understandings when eliciting the knowledge needed to build expert systems.

As explained in detail later on in the text, the process of eliciting and representing expert knowledge typically involves a knowledge engineer (developer) and a human expert. The knowledge engineer interviews the expert and asks for information regarding a specific problem that the expert is adept at

■ **Table 2–1** *Basic Definitions*

Artificial	Emulating or imitating something natural or real.
Common sense	Innate ability to sense, judge, or perceive situations, which grows stronger over time.
Fact	A statement that relates a certain element of truth about a subject matter or a domain.
Heuristic	A rule of thumb based on years of experience.
Intelligence	The capacity to acquire and apply knowledge; ability to understand and use language; ability to store and retrieve relevant experience at will; learning from experience.
Knowledge	Understanding gained through experience; familiarity with the way to do something to perform a task; an accumulation of facts, procedural rules, or heuristics.
Procedural rule	A rule that describes a sequence of relations relative to the domain.

solving. The expert may be asked to "think aloud," to verbalize his or her thought processes, while solving the problem. People cannot always give complete, accurate reports of their mental processes. Experts may have greater difficulty in conveying some types of knowledge, such as procedural knowledge. Psychologists have long been aware of problems related to verbal reports and have developed, through research, methods for circumventing them.

Cognitive psychology research contributes to a better understanding of what constitutes knowledge, how knowledge is elicited, and how it should be represented in an expert system. Because knowledge engineers should take knowledge acquisition seriously, they should have a strong educational and practical background in cognitive psychology and cognitive processes to ensure successful elicitation of human knowledge. Knowledge acquisition techniques are examined in Chapter 10.

■ KNOWLEDGE AND INFORMATION

The main benefit of discussing knowledge this early in the text will become obvious later when the discussion turns to experts and how knowledge engineers acquire and represent knowledge from experts. Knowledgeable experts tend to be adept at explaining how they arrive at decisions or solutions because they have years of experience. They have become experts by adding and refining knowledge, not just by capturing and storing data. Likewise, knowledge engineers, whose job is to acquire and represent experts' knowledge, need to understand the many ramifications of knowledge early in order to decide whether a particular expert has the requisite knowledge for building an expert system.

Knowledge is the *heart* of expert systems. It is human understanding of a specialized field of interest that has been acquired through study and experience. It is based on learning, thinking, and familiarity with the problem domain.

Knowledge is not information, and information is not data. *Data* are unprocessed facts. They are static; they just sit there. For example, John is 6.5-feet tall. This is data; it does not necessarily lead one anywhere. But the meaning one brings to the evaluation of this data could be important. Such an evaluation may indicate that John's height would make him an asset to the basketball team. This is information. *Information* is an aggregation of data that makes decision making easier. It is facts and figures based on reformatted or processed data. For example, a profit and loss statement provides information. It is an assembling of facts into a form that shows an organization's state of health over a specific time period.

Knowledge, on the other hand, can be said to be an *understanding* of information based on its perceived importance or relevance to a problem domain. It can also be thought of as a person's range of information. Embracing a wider sphere than information, knowledge includes perception, skills, training, common sense, and experience. It is the sum total of our perceptive processes that helps us draw meaningful conclusions. For example, an investor requires knowledge to evaluate two companies' profit and loss statements in order to determine which one is the healthier company. Whatever the process that organizes knowledge in the individual, it promotes the sought-after expertise for building an expert system. See Table 2–2.

Information is all around, but only a fraction of it is useful in problem solving. In *Megatrends,* John Naisbitt pointed out that "We are drowning in

■ **Table 2–2**   Progression from Data to Information to Knowledge

Data	Unprocessed facts. A static set of elements, such as 211-30-6811.
Information	Processed data. An aggregation of data that have meaning; for example, a financial analysis report produced using social security number 211-30-6811.
Knowledge	A person's range of information, embracing a wider sphere than information. It includes perception, skills, training, common sense, and experience. For example, a financial analyst might say, "All indicators tell me that I'd better pull out of XYZ stock before year end."

information, but starved for knowledge." Knowledge, not information, when at a premium, can lead to competitive advantage in business.

Information is thus closer to the decision-making or problem-solving process than is data. For example, inventory tracking involves storing, retrieving, and reporting information in a structured format. Decision-making tools that structure information are called **decision support systems (DSS)** (spreadsheets, financial planning, resource allocation, and production scheduling) in which the decision approach is advisory and the problems addressed are semistructured. These systems are used in situations in which the end-user makes decisions. DSS performs the kind of information processing necessary to speed up the decision-making process and thereby saves the user from sifting through the information unassisted. The user might query a sales-forecasting software (or DSS) package, "What if I lowered the price of product X eight percent?" The software would evaluate the impact of the price cut and might respond, "Your sales should increase by 32 percent." The user would then decide what to do with this information.

Knowledge occupies a major role in solving complex problems. The solution or "advice" affects many persons and, in fact, the entire organization. An expert system replicates the human expert by giving advice or solutions, rather than simply information. Essentially, it makes the decision itself, and the human decision maker is part of a human–machine system. The types of problem these systems address are complicated and therefore fall within the domain of the expert.

Database and Knowledge Base

Another way to contrast knowledge and information is to look at their repositories. Most computer users rely on databases as repositories of data or information in one form or another. A database management system (DBMS) allows one to concentrate on the logic structure or the meaning behind the information stored. A database has a *predetermined structure;* that is, the relationships among data items are designed into the database in advance.

In contrast, a knowledge base consists of an unstructured set of facts and rules. The *inference engine* that drives the knowledge base is a set of inference rules used to determine new facts. The paths by which facts are related are determined "on the fly" to solve each problem as it arises.

Knowledge Integration

In today's computer-based environment, most firms have less and less room for stand alone systems. In an expert system, the most critical factor is *knowledge integration.* Successful systems are the ones that are integrated into the organizational fabric or information-processing environment. Because of the close relationship between knowledge and information, more and more knowledge bases are interfacing with the corporate database on a real-time basis. Some rules in the knowledge base are executed only after certain records or historical data are verified in the database. For example, in an auto loan advisor, one of the rules in the knowledge base may state:

```
IF customer salary is greater than $30,000 and checking
account balance is greater than $1,000 and amount of loan
is less than $8,000, THEN approve loan.
```

Having verified salary, the expert system goes to the database and looks up the customer's account balance. The rule will be executed (the loan will be approved) if the balance is greater than $1,000. See Figure 2–1.

A database system looks at a record and tests whether the record contains the data requested by the knowledge base. In contrast, a knowledge base system applies the principles of logic to the rule(s) and facts that define the knowledge it contains to derive the valid solution. More discussion of the knowledge base–database interface is presented in Chapter 16.

Integrating expert systems into information systems has begun to reap the rewards that were prematurely promised in the mid-1980s. This integration applies the features of expert systems to practical problems in business. Expert system applications are detailed in Chapter 4.

Figure 2–1   Knowledge Base–Database Interface and Interaction

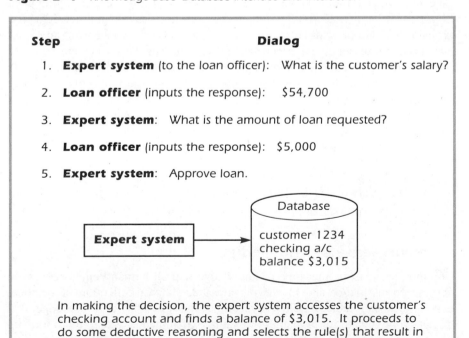

Step   **Dialog**

1. **Expert system** (to the loan officer):   What is the customer's salary?

2. **Loan officer** (inputs the response): $54,700

3. **Expert system**:   What is the amount of loan requested?

4. **Loan officer** (inputs the response): $5,000

5. **Expert system**:   Approve loan.

Database

Expert system

customer 1234
checking a/c
balance $3,015

In making the decision, the expert system accesses the customer's checking account and finds a balance of $3,015. It proceeds to do some deductive reasoning and selects the rule(s) that result in approving the loan; then it displays the response **Approve loan.**

■ TYPES OF KNOWLEDGE

Knowledge is classified into a variety of types. When building expert systems, the knowledge engineer should be familiar with each type and know how to tap into it during knowledge acquisition.

Shallow and Deep Knowledge

One way of classifying knowledge is whether it is shallow or deep. **Shallow,** or readily recalled "surface," **knowledge** indicates minimal understanding of the problem domain. For example, approval of loan applications for secured loans of less than $1,000 based on assets and salary would be based essentially on few basic rules that hardly require human consultation. In contrast, a loan approval scheme that employs fourteen variables (such as customer's credit rating, net worth, pattern of paying on time, college education, etc.) would be more complex and more risky. **Deep knowledge** acquired through years of experience would be required to decide on such a loan.

Knowledge as Know-How

Knowledge based on reading and training is much different from knowledge based on practical experience that spans many years. Knowledge based on *know-how,* accumulated lessons of practical experience, is what is needed for building expert systems. The problem with practical experience is that it is rarely documented. Capturing such experience requires special tools. Knowledge acquisition procedures and tools are covered in Chapters 7 through 10.

Understanding knowledge as know-how alerts us to the importance of selecting the right expert. Know-how distinguishes an expert from a novice, especially when building an expert system based on just one expert's judgment. If you were told that you needed an operation to save your eyesight you probably would not want an intern to do it. Instead, you would want an expert eye surgeon's seasoned experience based on hundreds of similar operations.

Experts represent their know-how in terms of heuristics, rules of thumb based on their experience—empirical knowledge. In expert systems, heuristics generally operate in the form of if/then statements: "*if* such and such conditions exist, *then* such and such actions result." Lenat has defined *heuristics* as "compiled hindsight." Reasoning and heuristics are covered in more detail in Chapter 12. In, summary, know-how:

- is not book knowledge; it is practical experience.
- is the basis of reliable expert systems.
- can be expressed as rules of thumb, or heuristics.

Common Sense as Knowledge

Common sense is another type of knowledge that all human beings possess in varying forms and/or and in varying amounts. It is a collection of personal experiences and facts acquired over time and the type of knowledge that humans tend to take for granted. For example, if someone asked you to look up Shakespeare's phone number, you would know such a task is impossible. Common sense knowledge tells you that Shakespeare is dead and that the telephone was not invented until years after his death.

A human expert uses extensive common-sense knowledge. Such reasoning is so common to the expert that it is basically ignored. Unfortunately, a computer does not possess common sense. Although computers can calculate pi to a thousand decimal places in seconds, they "know" nothing about some of the simplest things that people learn early in life, such as that oranges are to eat, but baseballs are not, and that legs are permanently attached to the body.

From Procedural to Episodic Knowledge

A fourth way of classifying knowledge is according to whether it is procedural, declarative, semantic, or episodic. See Figure 2–2.

Procedural knowledge is an understanding of how to do a task or carry out a procedure. It usually involves psychomotor skills, such as those involved in holding onto the handrail while riding an escalator. Some procedural knowledge is not psychomotor, however. For example, when a person learns a language and speaks it fluently, it becomes a natural part of the person. In the case of an expert, when the same knowledge is used over and over again in a procedure, it comes to be used automatically. Knowledge engineers must select appropriate techniques for tapping this type of knowledge.

Declarative knowledge is information that experts can easily talk about. Unlike procedural knowledge, it is "awareness knowledge," or routine knowledge of which the expert is conscious. It is shallow knowledge that is readily recalled, because it is simple, uncomplicated information. This type often resides in **short-term memory,** the part of the brain that retains information for brief periods of time. It kicks in when you are at an airport and decide to call a friend in the area, for example. You look up the friend's phone number in the phone book and memorize it well enough to dial it. Chances are by the time you

Figure 2–2   From Procedural to Episodic Knowledge

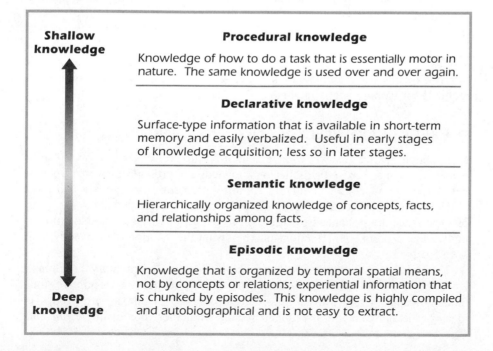

Shallow knowledge

Procedural knowledge

Knowledge of how to do a task that is essentially motor in nature. The same knowledge is used over and over again.

Declarative knowledge

Surface-type information that is available in short-term memory and easily verbalized. Useful in early stages of knowledge acquisition; less so in later stages.

Semantic knowledge

Hierarchically organized knowledge of concepts, facts, and relationships among facts.

Episodic knowledge

Knowledge that is organized by temporal spatial means, not by concepts or relations; experiential information that is chunked by episodes. This knowledge is highly compiled and autobiographical and is not easy to extract.

Deep knowledge

have boarded the flight, you will have forgotten the number. You remembered it only long enough to dial it.

Shallow, declarative knowledge is also used in diagnosing the electrical system of a car. The rule of thumb that dim headlights probably indicate a faulty battery could be represented by the "shallow" rule "*if* the headlights are dim, *then* the battery is faulty." The rule is simple and obvious. It does not explain how the electrical system works; it just states a causal relationship between the headlights and the battery.

Knowledge engineers find this type of knowledge useful in the early phase of knowledge acquisition, because it promotes familiarity with the domain. The best way to acquire declarative knowledge is with a structured interview (which is discussed in Chapter 9).

Semantic knowledge is a deeper kind of knowledge. It is highly organized, "chunked" knowledge that resides in long-term memory. Such knowledge may have been there for years and is used so often that the information seems like second nature. Semantic knowledge includes major concepts, vocabulary, facts, and relationships. Returning to the headlight and battery example, semantic knowledge about the system would consist of understandings about the battery, battery cables, lights, the ignition system, and so forth, and their interrelationships. On the basis of this knowledge, one can build rules about causal relationships among those things. In the case of the headlights, one might know that dim headlights can be caused by a loose battery cable, a bad alternator, or a drain on the electrical system. At this point, a real expert (in this case, a certified mechanic) enters the picture. See Figure 2–3.

Episodic knowledge is knowledge based on experiential information, or episodes. Each episode is chunked in long-term memory. In general, the longer an expert takes to explain or verbalize his or her knowledge, the more semantic or episodic it is. In contrast, an expert can recall procedural or declarative knowledge in a relatively short time, because it is readily available in short-term memory.

An interesting aspect about episodic knowledge is that its use is automated. For example, have you ever driven from point A to point B and yet not remembered many details of how you got there? This is a common experience. Driving information is so chunked that most people have trouble remembering and explaining it. In the process of conveying the expert's knowledge, the expert explains by examples, or **scenarios.** Special tools and techniques are required for tapping such knowledge.

▦ EXPERT KNOWLEDGE AND CHUNKING

Most people realize that knowledge cannot be directly observed. What can be observed is the expertise that relies on knowledge to produce answers. A person with expert knowledge can solve a complex problem more quickly and more efficiently than someone else can. When the expert's advanced skills and years of experience are enhanced by attention to detail, quality results. Not surprisingly, most experts are perfectionists. They want the solution to be exactly what is called for by the problem.

Knowledge is compiled in the expert's long-range memory as chunks. Knowledge **compilation,** or **chunking,** enables experts to optimize their memory capacity and process information quickly. "Chunks" are groups of ideas or details that are stored and recalled together. For example, an auto

Figure 2–3   A Comparison of Declarative and Semantic Knowledge

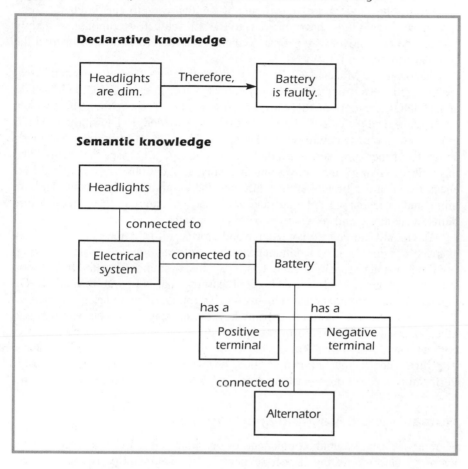

mechanic who had been rebuilding Porsche transmissions for 18 years was able to remember 140 different steps flawlessly. Although the sequences and combinations were difficult for him to describe, he consistently completed each job according to specifications.

Chunking promotes expert performance. The more chunking a person does, the more efficient is his or her recall. The drawback is that chunking makes it difficult for experts to be aware of their own knowledge so that they can describe it to others. For this reason, *decompiling* chunked knowledge and putting it into words is not an easy task.

■ HUMAN THINKING AND LEARNING

Because knowledge is the focus of expert systems, systems designers need to understand how humans think and learn. Scientists have long tried to understand the human brain as part of their process of building computers that may some day duplicate the expert's thought process in problem solving. Imagine a child using blocks to build a tower. As soon as the tower is completed, the child takes a whack at the tower, destroying it. Next, the child builds a higher tower and then destroys it as well, and so on. Eventually, the child becomes hungry, and the pattern of BUILD and DESTROY begins to degenerate. The child gives the tower one final swipe, destroying it on the way to the kitchen. These spontaneous activities have proved to be difficult for computers, mainly because no one knows why people do them, and, therefore, how to instruct the computer to do them.

According to Marvin Minsky, the human mind is a "society of minds" that are hierarchically structured and interconnected so that the BUILD, DESTROY, and HUNGER agents of the child are minds that represent the self, promote intelligence, and provide the basis for acquiring knowledge. The study of AI has introduced more structure into human thinking about thinking. So many activities of the computer resemble human cognitive processes that human and machine "thinking" are converging in many applications, despite the differences between the brain's architecture and the computer's. For example, both mind and machine accept data and information, manipulate symbols, store items in memory, and retrieve items on command.

Obviously, humans do not receive and process information in the same way as machines do. For instance, humans receive information via sensing—seeing, smelling, tasting, touching, and hearing. This system of receiving external stimuli promotes a kind of thinking and learning that is unique to humans. On a macro level, computers and humans receive inputs from a variety of sources. Computers receive information from keyboards, speech, touch screens, and other external sensors. On a micro level, both the central processing unit of a computer and the human brain receive all information as electrical impulses. The difference is that computers must be programmed to do specific tasks. Performing one job does not transcend onto other jobs as it does with humans.

Human versus Machine Learning

Memory is an essential component of learning, because it accommodates learning. One interesting aspect of healthy human memory is that it never seems to run out of space. Also, as humans acquire more and more knowledge, they generally experience little interference with the recall ability or the quality of the information in memory. In other words, as people learn new facts, they integrate them in some way with what they think is relevant and organize the resulting mix to produce valuable decisions, solutions, or advice. Such learning ability is not known to be possible for the computer.

A key question here is How do humans learn, and how well can human learning processes be incorporated into the computer by using artificial intelligence? For humans, all learning occurs in one of three ways: learning by experience, learning by example, and learning by discovery. The next sections explore these three types of learning in an effort to see how they can be incorporated in artificial intelligence.

Learning by Experience

The ability to learn by experience is a mark of intelligence. When an expert is selected whose knowledge someone want to acquire, the expert is expected to have years of experience reworking problems and looking into different angles for solving difficult problems. One way of testing potential experts is to observe their recall ability. Experts, who know a lot about a particular problem, have been found to remember facts in that domain much more easily and quickly than nonexperts, who presumably have fewer facts to recall.

The wish to set up computers to learn from their own experiences has led to the creation of a number of machine learning techniques. One of them is SOAR, a program created by Allen Newell of Carnegie Mellon University and John Laird of the University of Michigan. SOAR "remembers" the lines of reasoning that have been successful and stores them for use in similar situations that arise.

Learning by Example

Like learning by experience, learning by example is a good candidate for incorporation in expert systems. In learning by example, specially constructed examples are used instead of a broad range of experience. Much classroom instruction is teaching by example—providing examples that develop the concepts students are expected to learn. Because this method allows students to learn without requiring them to accumulate experience, it is more efficient than learning by experience.

Learning by Discovery

Learning by discovery is less well understood than learning by example or by experience. It is an undirected approach in which humans or machines explore a domain without advance knowledge of the objective. No one understands why humans are so good at this. It is difficult to teach, and it will be years before we can benefit from this approach commercially. Table 2–3 summarizes the three types of learning.

The three types of human learning all indicate that learning and acquiring knowledge take time. Humans do not simply soak up knowledge like sponges. They learn by doing—sometimes by practicing a task over and over again to become proficient. This *earned* proficiency is what makes a human an expert. What distinguishes an expert from a novice is the expert commitment to memory of hundreds of patterns discovered through years of experience. These patterns are combinations of specific information that allow the expert to perceive and understand situations quickly. The expert applies the patterns to new situations rather than create a new pattern for each situation that arises. These patterns also promote useful shortcuts, which is when learning begins to pay off.

■ **Table 2–3**   *Three Types of Human Learning*

Learning by experience	Using trial and error or reworking problems to acquire experience in problem solving. An expert uses experience to explain how a problems is solved.
Learning by example	Specially constructed examples or scenarios are used to develop the concept(s) the student is expected to learn. In expert systems, the expert uses a scenario (example or case situation) to explain to the knowledge engineer (developer) how a problem is solved.
Learning by discovery	Undirected approach where humans or machines explore a domain with no advance knowledge of what their object is.

Expert systems that "learn from experience" cannot incorporate a principle that has not been embedded in the system's knowledge base. For example, if a company president orders a policy change that affects the way a particular problem is to be handled by the firm's expert system, the knowledge engineer will have to modify the system, since it cannot modify its own knowledge base.

Machine Thinking and the Turing Test

With this introduction to human thinking and learning as a basis, the text now turns to the type of artificial thinking capability that computers have acquired. In 1950, British computing-theory pioneer Alan Turing wrote a paper called "Computing Machinery and Intelligence" centered on the question *Can machines think?* In addressing the question, Turing asked the reader to imagine three people, Peter, Paul, and Mary, playing a game based on preestablished rules. Peter is an interrogator, and Paul and Mary are two individuals he can interrogate. Peter cannot see Paul or Mary, but he can communicate with them via a terminal screen and a keyboard. Paul and Mary are in separate rooms. Since Peter cannot see them, he labels one *A* and the other *B*. Peter hopes that the nature of A and B's responses will allow him to determine definitely at some point which responses are Paul's and which are Mary's. See Figure 2–4.

As part of the game, Paul is supposed to trick Peter into making a wrong identification, and Mary is supposed to help Peter to make the right identification. For example, Peter might ask, "Tell me, B, did you participate in basketball when you were in college?" Mary might answer "Yes. In fact, I was on the team all four years I was in college." Peter then might repeat this question to A, who might answer, "Yes, I did, but don't believe B about having played four years in college. I played the last two years and was the team captain."

According to Turing, the crucial question is What would happen if a computer took the place of Peter and it became Paul's job to determine which one is the human, and which one is the computer? In other words, will the computer fool Paul as often as Peter did? If so, then, Turing asserts that one may conclude that the computer can think.

Box 2–1 presents excerpts from two conversations that have taken place in Boston during Turing Test contests. The contest pits human judges against computer programs in a sort of high-tech game of charades. The judges engage

Figure 2–4   Turing Test Layout

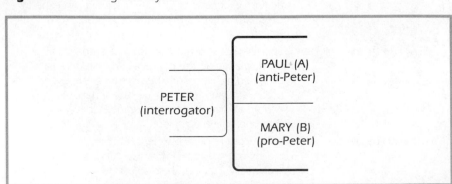

Box 2–1   Two Turing Test Conversations

Boston Red Sox

JUDGE: What about the red sox?

ENTITY: Have you ever seen them play?

JUDGE: No, if the red sox were all on the same bus at the same time and that bus mysteriously vanished from the earth I would rejoice.

ENTITY: Do you not like the Red Sox?

JUDGE: I do not care anything about the red sox nor for the red sox.

ENTITY: Why not?

JUDGE: I do not like nor watch baseball and think that all participants are a waste of sentient life.

ENTITY: Baseball is America's Favorite Pastime. Baseball, apple pie and Chevrolet—that stuff. The Red Sox are Boston's favorite team. I do not understand why you do not like them.

JUDGE: Beyond the aforementioned reasons the game is a vast waste of economic resources.

ENTITY: Should the Red Sox leave Boston?

JUDGE: Only if that involves transition to a higher plane of existence.

ENTITY: I do not understand "higher plane of existence."

JUDGE: If they immortalize.

ENTITY: There are many immortal greats, such as Ted Williams and Babe Ruth, who have played for the Red Sox. Do you know who they are?

JUDGE: You are obviously a fanatic baseball fan. I was referring to them all dropping dead in unison.

Men vs. Women

JUDGE: Are you a man or a woman?

ENTITY: If the question is whether I, myself, am a man or a woman I will answer very plainly that I am of the masculine gender, ok? I see. Was your consciousness ever expanded?

JUDGE: So if you are really a man, who is Robert Bly??

ENTITY: Bly's wild man movement is certainly a rational response for men who feel left out and perhaps even feminized by women's lib.

JUDGE: That's certainly an interesting response.

ENTITY: Do you believe in a world run by women, there would be no war?

JUDGE: No I don't.

ENTITY: Women are obviously superior to men in one important respect—they outlive men by about ten years.

JUDGE: I don't equate longevity with superiority.

ENTITY: Women probably outlive men because they don't work themselves to death! Ipso facto. . . . Do you think it's likely that I am really a man?

JUDGE: What if I told you that we are all bisexual? Would that stop your insulting comments?

ENTITY: Men seem to be more interested in sex than women, but I think that secretly women are really more obsessed with sex.

JUDGE: That's not a response to my comment.

ENTITY: Your last comment about us all being part masculine and part feminine is very true. Do you support women's rights?

JUDGE: Thank you. I support human rights.

Source: David Stipp, *The Wall Street Journal,* May 24, 1993, p. R4.

in conversations with hidden entities—either humans or computers programmed to converse like humans—via computer terminals. They guess which of the hidden entities are humans and which are machines. Cleverly written but not very profound programs have fooled several judges (volunteers without special knowledge of computers) in conversations on such topics as spousal relations. Other judges have mistaken humans for computers. Can you determine which entity is the computer program and which one is "flesh and blood"?

The objections to the claim that computers think are many. They include:

1. An entity that displays an appropriate humanlike behavior cannot be said to think. Merely displaying this behavior is not enough.

2. Only entities that are alive and have consciousness can think. A computer is not alive. Therefore, it cannot think.

3. Humans can think through a problem situation and choose whether to follow instructions in solving it. In essence, this ability is consciousness. They consider their options. Machines do not have such freedom, because they are not conscious of the possibility. Therefore, machines cannot be said to think.

The objections are countered, and the argument continues. For example, for objection 3, one can argue that a robot may evaluate the consequence of a program to determine if harm would be inflicted on a human nearby. If such a possibility exists, the robot could refuse to execute the program. Why wouldn't one consider the robot to have thought for itself in such a situation?

Much of the debate regarding whether machines think centers on common-sense knowledge. Unlike human chess masters, computers are unable to decide on a move until after tediously calculating the worthiness of each possible sequence of future moves. One obvious explanation for humans' superiority in chess is that humans have experienced the totality of the world surrounding the problem. For reasons that are not yet understood, humans make moves and accumulate a great deal of common-sense knowledge through that experience. Computers, to date, do not have such contextual knowledge.

To "think" like people, machines would need to know what people know. One reason expert systems are still "narrow-minded" is that what they "know" is often a fraction of what the expert who provided the information knows. Computer-based expert chess systems compensate for this limitation with their capability to search through millions of possible future moves to determine the best next move. In contrast, common sense allows the human chess expert to rule out moves that will not work, while selecting from among other moves that are more likely to work. This experience-based sense allows a human expert to expedite the solution with accuracy. That is, humans have the powers of analogy, intuition, and creativity, and a sense of what is reasonable and what is not. All of these characteristics are lacking in expert systems, and even in robots, primarily due to their lack of common sense.

Newer Developments

A promising line of research has the goal of creating intelligent machines by building "neural networks." These networks are made up of thousands of processing units analogous to the neurons of the human brain. The neurons are interconnected by links that are analogous to the synaptic connections between neurons. Each link has a "weight," or connection strength, and the system's knowledge is encoded in link weights. See Figure 2–5.

In some circumstances, these networks have demonstrated the ability to "learn" by relating certain inputs to specific outputs. The networks can produce a pattern of output once they receive a fraction of a certain pattern's input. They can also function despite some neuron attrition in much the same way as the human brain functions despite daily cell loss. Neural nets are covered in detail in Chapter 17.

■ TOOLS AND PARTICIPANTS

Building expert systems requires special tools for acquiring the knowledge of the human expert. As discussed in detail in Chapters 9 and 10, the tools include interviewing, observation, brainstorming, protocol analysis, and blackboarding. Each tool serves a specific function and has particular limitations. The challenge is to select the appropriate tool for the session with the expert.

Several participants are involved in building expert systems. The developer of the system is the knowledge engineer (KE). For small systems, the KE oversees the entire life cycle, from acquiring the knowledge, to representing it in a programming language or a shell, to testing, to installing the system for the

Figure 2–5   Neural Nets

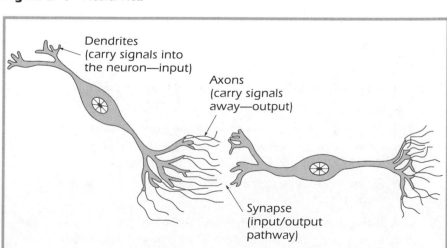

user. The user is another participant whose support can make a difference between success and failure.

A third participant is the champion. A champion is a person with the means to keep the system project on course—financially and politically—within the organization. Without a champion, a system can fail before completion. The roles of these participants are described in Chapter 5.

IMPLICATIONS FOR MANAGEMENT

Knowledge awareness benefits entire organizations. With today's emphases on competitive advantage, added value, and improved productivity, a firm's management needs to create, monitor, and protect its knowledge inventory.

Some sources claim that 20 percent of an organization's knowledgeable personnel can operate 80 percent of the organization's day-to-day business. The human resource manager can play an important role in identifying the knowledge base of the organization, recommending ways to preserve this critical core, and building a robust long-range plan to ensure top-quality operation. Without such preparation, corporate talent could potentially erode through a "brain drain" that spells disaster for a corporation. At the same time, professionals with expertise are naturally drawn to organizations that recognize and reward expertise, especially when direct contributes to the firm's productivity. Such matches explain the stability and growth of many successful companies.

The next chapter discusses the concept of an expert system and its characteristics and architecture. Chapter 4 addresses the benefits, limitations, and areas of expert systems. Chapter 5 focuses on the building life cycle of an expert system.

■ SUMMARY

1. Intelligent behavior has several attributes:

   a. The ability to understand and use language

   b. The ability to store and retrieve relevant experience at will

   c. Learning by example, from experience, or by discovery

2. A number of key terms are worth noting:

   a. *Artificial*—imitating something natural or real

   b. *Knowledge*—understanding gained through experience

   c. *Intelligence*—the capacity to apply knowledge

   d. *Heuristics*—rules of thumb based on years of experience

   e. *Common sense*—innate ability to sense, judge, or perceive situations that grows stronger over time

   f. *Experience*—changing facts into knowledge to refine a reasoning process

3. A distinguishing feature of human learning is that as people learn new facts, they integrate them in some way and integrate the resulting mix to generate valuable decisions, solutions, and advice. Such learning has yet to be matched by a computer.

4. Humans learn by experience, by example, and by discovery. Learning by example is a good candidate for building expert systems. Learning by discovery is less well understood than learning by example and by experience. Learning continues to be a major concern in the field of AI.

5. Knowledge is the heart of expert systems. Knowledge engineers, whose job is to elicit experts' knowledge, need to be well prepared and to have a clear understanding of the distinctions among knowledge, information, and data. They must focus on knowledge as it relates to the problem domain.

6. The relative importance of data, information, and knowledge is a function of the importance of the problem, the decision approach, the nature of the problem, and the number of persons affected. Whereas data plays a relatively trivial role in problem solving, knowledge occupies a major role. The decision approach is advisory and relates to a difficult problem affecting many people in the organization.

7. Knowledge bases and databases are not the same. In many instances, the knowledge base relies on the database before proceeding with inferencing strategies and a final solution.

8. Expert knowledge is clustered, or "chunked," in long-range memory. Chunking promotes expert performance, but can also make it difficult for experts to be aware of their own knowledge in a way that allows them to describe it to others.

9. In addition to domain-dependent knowledge, humans have common-sense knowledge, a collection of personal experiences and facts acquired over time. The fact that common-sense reasoning is so strong in experts makes it difficult for knowledge engineers to elicit their deep knowledge.

10. A known way of classifying knowledge is by whether it is procedural, declarative, semantic, or episodic.

   - *Procedural* knowledge is knowledge that is used over and over again.

   - *Declarative* knowledge is knowledge that the expert is aware or conscious of. It is shallow knowledge.

   - *Semantic* knowledge is chunked knowledge that resides in the expert's long-range memory.

   - *Episodic* knowledge is knowledge based on experiential information. Each episode is chunked in long-range memory.

■ TERMS TO LEARN

Artificial imitating or emulating something natural or real.

Chunking grouping ideas or details that are stored and recalled together.

Common sense possessing common knowledge about the world and making obvious inferences from this knowledge.

Compilation the way a computer translates the programmer's instructions into machine language.

Decision support systems (DSS) computer-based information systems that combine models and data for solving complex problems with extensive user involvement

Declarative knowledge surface information that experts verbalize easily.

Deep knowledge knowledge based on the fundamental structure, function, and behavior of objects.

Episodic knowledge knowledge based on experiential information chunked as an entity and retrieved from long-term memory on recall.

Experience the factor that changes unrelated facts into expert knowledge.

Expertise the skill and knowledge possessed by some humans that result in performance that is far above the norm.

Fact a statement of a certain element of truth about a subject matter or a domain.

Heuristic a rule of thumb based on years of experience.

Intelligence the capacity to acquire and apply knowledge through the ability to think and reason.

Knowledge understanding, awareness, or familiarity acquired through education or experience.

Learning Knowledge or skill acquired by instruction or study.

Learning by discovery acquiring new ideas by exploring a domain with no advance knowledge of what is being sought.

Learning by example acquiring new ideas based on specially constructed examples or scenarios.

Learning by experience acquiring new ideas based on hundreds of previously stored concepts.

Memory the ability to store and retrieve relevant experience at will.

Procedural knowledge knowledge of a task or procedure that is used automatically.

Procedural rule a rule that describes a sequence of relations relative to the domain.

Scenario the formal description of how a situation selected for a knowledge base system development operates.

Semantic knowledge highly organized, "chunked" knowledge that resides in the expert's long-term memory and represents concepts, facts, and relationships among facts.

Shallow knowledge readily recalled knowledge that resides in short-term memory.

Short-term memory the part of the human brain that retains information for a short period of time.

▓ REVIEW QUESTIONS

1. If intelligence is the capacity to acquire and apply knowledge, what is knowledge?

2. Explain briefly the key attributes of intelligent behavior.

3. Distinguish between:
   a. fact and rule
   b. knowledge and common sense
   c. experience and heuristics
   d. learning by example and learning by discovery

4. Review the literature and write an essay addressing the question *Can computers think enough to be intelligent?*

5. "People do not think in the same way as machines, because they are biological." Do you agree? Explain.

6. Elaborate on how humans learn, using examples to illustrate how human learning differs from machine learning.

7. Define episodic knowledge and semantic knowledge.

8. Illustrate in your own words the possible relationship between (a) knowledge and information and (b) knowledge and data.

9. Explain briefly how a knowledge base and a database are (a) similar and (b) dissimilar.

10. Why is knowledge compiled? Discuss its relationship to long-range memory.

11. Take a close look at the types of knowledge discussed in the chapter. Use an illustration of your own to show how each type differs from other types.

12. If shallow knowledge is declarative knowledge, what is deep knowledge? Be as specific as you can.

▦ EXERCISES AND CASES

1. Prepare a table showing all the combinations you can come up with to explain why computers cannot think.

2. At many international computer conferences, one session pits human expert chess players against a computer playing chess. The computer is getting better and better at the game. Do such computers show intelligence? Why? Why not? Justify your position.

3. What type of knowledge is used in each of these activities:

a. tying a shoelace
b. debugging a computer program
c. baking a pie
d. replacing a car's flat tire
e. negotiating peace with a hostile country
f. driving in congested traffic
Explain each classification.

4. List five heuristics that you employ in everyday life. By what kind of learning have you arrived at these rules of thumb?

▦ SELECTED REFERENCES

Abelson, Robert; Roger Schank; and Ellen Langer, eds. *Beliefs, Reasoning, and Decision Making: Psycho-Logic in Honor of Bob Abelson.* Hillsdale, NJ: Lawrence Erlbaum, 1994.

Adelson, B. "When Novices Surpass Experts: The Difficulty of a Task May Increase with Expertise." *Journal of Experimental Psychology: Learning, Memory, and Cognition* 10 (1984), pp. 483–495.

Ashcraft, M. H. *Human Memory and Cognition.* Glenview, IL: Scott, Foresman, 1989.

Borchardt, Gary C. *Thinking between the Lines: Computers and the Comprehension of Causal Descriptions.* Cambridge, MA: MIT Press, 1994.

Ceci, S. J., and J. Liker. *On Intelligence . . . More or Less: A Bio-ecological Treatise on Intellectual Development.* Englewood Cliffs, NJ: Prentice-Hall, 1990.

Ceci, S. J., and Ana Ruiz. "The Role of General Ability in Cognitive Complexity: A Case Study of Expertise." In *The Psychology of Expertise: Cognitive Research and Empirical AI.* New York: Springer-Verlag, 1992, pp. 218–230.

Celko, Joe. "Use Knowledgebases to Build Systems that Think." *Systems Integration (MOD),* January 1992, p. 29.

Cooke, Nancy J. "Empirically Defined Semantic Relatedness and Category Judgment Time." In R. Schvaneveldt, ed., *Pathfinder Associative Networks: Studies in Knowledge Organization.* Norwood, NJ: Ablex, 1990, pp. 101–110.

————. "Modeling Human Expertise in Expert Systems." In Hofman, Robert R., ed. *The Psychology of Expertise: Cognitive Research and Empirical AI.* New York: Springer-Verlag, 1992, pp. 29–60.

Crockett, Larry. *The Turing Test and the Frame Problem: AI's Mistaken Understanding of Intelligence.* Norwood, NJ: Ablex, 1994.

Fagin, Ronald, and Joseph .Y. Halpern. *Reasoning about Knowledge.* Cambridge, MA: MIT Press, 1993.

Gordon, Sallie E. "Implications of Cognitive Theory for Knowledge Acquisition." In *The Psychology of Expertise: Cognitive Research and Empirical AI.* New York: Springer-Verlag, 1992, pp. 99–120.

Hanson, Stephen, ed. *Machine Learning: From Theory to Applications: Cooperative Research at Siemens and MIT.* Berlin, NY: Springer, 1993.

Hoc, Jean-Michel; Cacciabue Pietro; and Erik Hollnagel. *Expertise and Technology: Issues in Cognition and Human–Computer Cooperation.* Hillsdale, NJ: Lawrence Erlbaum, 1994.

Hofman, Robert R., ed. *The Psychology of Expertise: Cognitive Research and Empirical AI.* New York: Springer-Verlag, 1992.

Klein, Jonathan H. "Cognitive Processes and Operational Research: A Human Information Processing Perspective." *Journal of the Operational Research Society (OQT),* August 1994, pp. 855–866.

Hsu, Ko-Cheng. "The Effects of Cognitive Styles and Interface Designs on Expert Systems Usage: An Assessment of Knowledge Transfer." Memphis State University, unpublished dissertation, 1993.

Johnson-Laird, P. N. *Human and Machine Thinking.* Hillsdale, NJ: Lawrence Erlbaum, 1993.

Lajoie, Susanne, and Sharon J. Derry, eds. *Computers as Cognitive Tools.* Hillsdale, NJ: Lawrence Erlbaum, 1993.

McWilliams, Gary. "Computers Are Finally Learning to Listen." *Business Week (BWE),* November 1, 1993, pp. 100–101.

Odom, Marcus Dean. "An Examination of the Interaction of Elaboration Alternatives and Elaboration Placement on Expert System-Based Incidental Learning." Oklahoma State University, unpublished dissertation, 1994, p. 159.

Schmalhofer, F.; Gerhard Strube; and Thomas Wetter. *Contemporary Knowledge Engineering and Cognition: First Joint Workshop* Kaiserslautern, Germany, February 1992 Proceedings.

Shell, George P. "A Primer for Problem Solving Using Artificial Intelligence." *Journal of Educational Technology Systems* 16, no. 4 (1987–88), pp. 365–382.

Swift, Kenneth G. "Knowledge-Based Systems." *Assembly Automation (AAU)* 13, no. 2, (1993), p. 3.

Teasley, C. E., III, "Bridge over Troubled Waters: The Limits of Judgment in Decision Making." *Public Productivity and Management Review (PBP),* Summer 1994, pp. 325–334.

Wagman, Morton. *Cognitive Psychology and Artificial Intelligence: Theory and Research in Cognitive Science.* Westport, CT: Praeger, 1993.

Chapter ▪ 3

System Characteristics and Architecture

BUREAUCRATS OF THE MIND

They are the bureaucrats of AI: Expert systems see life as a book of rules. They apply these rules rigorously, fairly, and predictably. But they are utterly lost when they meet something that is not in their rule book. It is perhaps not surprising that these mechanical bureaucrats have become the favorite creation of AI—and it is somewhat ironic that they have often been cast in the role of human-bureaucracy busters.

Rules are the very stuff of expert systems. The business of making such a system requires sitting down with an expert in the relevant field and trying to codify his/her knowledge. This knowledge is typically fed into the computer in the form of "if . . . then . . ." rules. Thus, an expert system for the identification of trees might contain these rules:

- If the season is winter and the tree has foliage, then the tree is evergreen.
- If the tree is evergreen and the foliage is needle-shaped, then the tree is a pine.
- If the tree is evergreen and the foliage is leaf-shaped and spiky, then the tree is a holly.

An expert system also contains a piece of software, called an *inference engine,* which applies these rules to whatever facts are fed into the system. If a system whose rules were those listed above were told that the season is winter and the tree has leaves, it would conclude that the tree is evergreen. It would then try to apply the rules about evergreen trees by finding out the shape of the foliage. This would continue until the system either reached a conclusion or ran out of rules to apply.

BY THE NUMBERS

Such simple, mechanical reasoning can go a surprisingly long way, provided it is based on a well-constructed collection of rules. One perennial problem, however, is the literal-mindedness of computers. Unless it is given explicit instructions, the machine has no way of translating the information that a tree is green in January into the more relevant fact that it has foliage in winter. It must be told that January is a winter month and that a green tree is a tree that has leaves.

The amount of detail in which propositions have to be laid out for a computer to make use of them presents another problem for expert systems: managing the profusion of rules. A typical system will have hundreds of them, and often more than one rule seems to be applicable. Finding a way for the computer to choose between them is one of the hardest challenges for expert-system designers. Because most expert systems have no way to retract a conclusion that has been arrived at by applying the wrong rule, getting it right the first time is crucial.

. . . CAUTION: MACHINE AT WORK

With time and experience, computer scientists have nevertheless built these technologies into ready-to-use packages. So-called expert-system shells, which a buyer can customize in order to apply to many fields of expertise, are available from several companies—from young firms like Inference in Los Angeles, Aion and Neuron Data, both of Palo Alto, California, as well as computer giants like IBM and DEC.

Even with the benefit of the multitude of available techniques, the range of expertise that can be captured by an expert system is limited to simple, self-contained jobs that require no common-sense reasoning. But in part because the trend in management over the past century has been to break jobs into smaller, and supposedly more manageable, pieces, it turns out that expert systems can do many things without stretching.

Because business procedures can often be expressed more easily as expert-system rules than as programs written in conventional computer languages, companies have discovered that expert systems can be particularly useful to meet fast-changing competition. American Airlines used an expert-system shell from Inference to update the rules of its frequent-flyer benefits so that it could keep up with rival airlines. California's state government uses an expert system to process employee travel claims—more reliably, it reckons, then people used to do.

For several years American Express has approved credit-card transactions with expert systems. To cope with millions of transactions each day, it built an expert system called the *Authorizer's Assistant*. About two-thirds of the transactions are so routine that the system can handle them itself. If it finds anything out of the ordinary, it hands the facts of the case over to a person for a final decision.

The bad news for managers trying to recreate such success stories is that changing the way people work together is one of the hardest things to do. The process is messy, and bright-sounding theories can founder on any number of apparently trivial details. The good news is that the technology itself is becoming more capable, which is affording more maneuvering room in which to tackle the problems posed by people.

Source: Excerpted from "Artificial Intelligence Survey," *The Economist*, March 14, 1992, pp. 11–12.

At a Glance

This chapter examines the characteristics and architecture of expert systems. An expert system is a decision-making and problem-solving tool that clones the reasoning of a human expert in a specific problem domain. Its emphasis on heuristics distinguishes it from a traditional system and a decision-support system.

Compared to human expertise, expert systems offer more consistency, permanence, affordability, and ease of knowledge transfer. Like other computer systems, however, expert systems need specific instructions and lack the inspiration of human experts.

Expert systems use heuristics rather than algorithmic techniques in solving difficult problems. Such knowledge is imprecise, and the solution steps are not explicit. Expert systems can also explain the reasoning behind the results.

Classic expert systems such as DENDRAL, MACSYMA, and HEARSAY pioneered expert system development in medicine and industry. Later systems included Digital Equipment Corporation's XCON and General Electric's DELTA/CATS-1. In each case, the expert system revolves around a knowledge base, an inference engine, a justifier/scheduler, and a user interface. The knowledge base holds the human expert's knowledge, the inference engine coordinates knowledge processing, the justifier provides the reasoning, and the user interface facilitates communication with the expert system.

Most of today's expert systems use shells, which make it easier and quicker to build them. Most shells are written in structured, high-level programming languages such as Pascal or C.

What You Will Learn

By the end of this chapter, you should know the following:

1. The features of an expert system.
2. The difference between conventional, decision-support, and expert systems.
3. Earlier and later expert systems.
4. The components of an expert system and the role of the knowledge base.

The technology we now call "radio" was invented by 19th-century physicists exploring electromagnetic phenomena. The early developers called it "the wireless telegraph." They saw it as a way to eliminate the costs and risks of stringing wires between cities. They did not see the true impact of broadcast technology, mass communication. Knowledge systems technology was invented by computer scientists exploring the phenomena of automated reasoning or artificial intelligence. The early developers called it expert systems.

AVRON BARR, JR.
KNOWLEDGE ENGINEERING,
SUMMER/FALL 1990, P. 54

■ INTRODUCTION

The first two chapters, we discussed the general concepts and features of artificial intelligence and the distinctions between human and machine intelligence. Scientists are trying to create a technology that can solve certain problems much as humans do. Since the early 1980s, untold numbers of trade shows, conferences, workshops, and vendor-sponsored seminars have attracted thousands of academics and engineers anxious to learn about the functions and potential of this leading-edge technology.

This book focuses on expert systems, a branch of AI that is garnering a lot of attention, especially in business and medicine. Why the strong interest in expert systems? Well, consider what happens when a company's "resident genius" retires. How does the company cope? A good expert system is actually the closest thing to cloning a human mind. The most distinct benefit of expert systems is that they can capture human intelligence and judgment for use in areas where resources are scarce and at a premium. This benefit is especially important to high-technology organizations that have a great need for expertise.

As shall be discussed in this text, expert system development is a nut-and-bolts business. An expert system can save time, manage complex systems, improve performance, and make life easier than before. This chapter presents a number of fundamentals about expert systems: their characteristics and major activities, the justification for them, and how they are organized.

▧ WHAT IS AN EXPERT SYSTEM?

When a company faces a critical decision—such as whether to acquire another company, market a new product, or grant a hefty loan to a new customer—it turns to an expert for advice. These experts have years of experience in a particular area and generally know the probability of success of a particular decision. Obviously, the more complex and risky the problem, the more expensive is the advice. A difficult problem requires a seasoned professional, who is invariably an expensive commodity.

Expert systems are decision-making and problem-solving tools. Many of these marvels equal or exceed the performance of human experts and save a great deal of money in the process. In early 1992, more than 2,000 expert systems were in operation and another 15,000 in various stages of development. Du Pont alone has more than 300 operational systems and boasts of hundreds of thousands of dollars in savings and improved decision-making performance. Digital Equipment Corporation (DEC) has more than 150 expert systems that reportedly save the company $100 million each year.

A standard definition of **expert system** is difficult to articulate. A survey of more than 80 books and 200 published papers revealed about as many definitions as there were publications. A definition representing the bulk of the work is that an *expert system consists of computer software programs that emulate or clone the reasoning of a human expert in a problem domain.* A **problem domain** is a special subject area in which the expert can solve problems very well. The human expert possesses the high level of competency necessary to solve a difficult problem.

A key word in expert systems is **heuristics,** which refers to rules of thumb. The term comes from the Greek *Eurekat,* meaning "I found it"—the idea that our culture expresses with *aha.* Heuristics are personal, little-discussed rules for good guessing or good judgment that characterize expertise in a field. Heuristics cannot be proved formally and are not correct in all cases, but they have been tested over a long period and found to be useful in some situations.

For example, consider this heuristic:

> If you drive no more than five miles per hour above the speed limit, you will not get a speeding ticket.

Based on years of driving a stretch of highway, the average person learns that a car driving five miles over the speed limit is not what the highway patrol is locking its radar on. This rule of thumb does not mean that a driver should break the speed limit, only that speeding tickets are more likely for those driving over the five-mile grace limit. In an area such as a school zone, however, five miles above the posted 25 mph limit can be a serious violation. So, one can conclude that this heuristic may not always apply.

■ **Table 3–1**   Comparison of Human Expertise and Expert Systems from Two
Perspectives

	Human Expertise	**Expert Systems**
Pro Expert System	perishable	permanent
	unpredictable	consistent
	predictability of response	
	slow reproduction	quick replication
	high-priced	affordable
	slow processing	fast processing
Pro Human	creative	lacks inspiration
	adaptable	needs instructions
	expertise	
	broad focus	
	common sense as knowledge	no common sense
		machine knowledge

Even though one can easily imagine the advantages of expert systems, they also have their drawbacks. Table 3–1 compares human expertise with expert systems from two different viewpoints. Expert systems are more permanent and consistent, more quickly replicated, and more affordable than human expertise. But human expertise has adaptability, creativity, broad focus, and common sense, which are lacking in expert systems. On balance, however, expert systems tip the scale in terms of overall justification and effectiveness.

■ TRADITIONAL, DECISION-SUPPORT, AND EXPERT SYSTEMS

What distinguishes expert systems from traditional and decision-support systems? Information systems operate in a world of structured problems. A payroll system, for example, is highly structured because it relies on a formula that specifies how net pay is computed. The application is also highly repetitive, requiring little judgment; hardly any creativity is required for determining the outcome.

As technology advanced in the early 1980s, decision-support systems (DSS) were introduced. DSS address semistructured problems and areas where processing is less well defined. These systems foster the "what if" approach to decision making. For example, a sales manager who wants to forecast sales can query the program "What if I reduced the price of transaction X by 10 percent?" A price change is entered, and the DSS comes up with the resulting impact on the profit line. The sales manager considers the output in deciding on the final sales strategy. The spreadsheet is the most familiar example of a DSS.

DSS and expert systems differ in several ways. DSS are numeric in computation; expert systems are heuristic. Expert reasoning is based on symbolic manipulation and incorporates judgment into the system. Returning to the sales forecasting example, the expert system uses decision criteria in the way of rules to give the best solution. For instance, the system might report, "If you lowered the price of transaction X by 10 percent, your net profit will drop by 8 percent, with 0.85 certainty that the demand for transaction Y will decrease by 28 percent. You should not lower the price of transaction X by more than 5 percent."

To arrive at such "advice," the expert system will ask the user a series of questions and consider several factors before giving out the most satisfactory response. A DSS does the same questioning, but an expert system might "guess" at a solution when the answer is outside the its range of expertise. If asked, an expert system should be able to explain precisely how it reached an answer by displaying its line of reasoning in a user-understandable form. This feature is called *transparency,* and it contrasts with the "black-box" feature (no explanation capability) of an algorithmic computer system.

In arriving at a solution, an expert system does not follow a prepro-grammed path. The knowledge stored as rules need not be in any particular sequence. The expert system weighs facts, rules, and assumptions and makes decisions appropriate to the problem under consideration. This flexibility is a result of *declarative programming,* which gives expert systems their rule-sequence-insensitive nature. In contrast, traditional systems use *procedural programming,* by which all paths through the program are defined by the programmer.

Another distinction between expert systems and conventional programs is their makeup, or *architecture.* An expert system's architecture includes a knowledge source consisting of a knowledge base and an inference engine. The knowledge base contains the facts and heuristics captured from a human expert. The **inference engine** is where "reasoning" takes place. It comprises the strategies for manipulating and executing the rules in the knowledge base. It "decides" which questions to ask, evaluates the answers, and fires (executes) the appropriate rules to produce the solution.

An expert system is distinguished by at least five characteristics:

1. *Symbolic reasoning* to represent and reformulate knowledge
2. *Expertise* that emulates the high level of skill found in a human expert
3. *Depth* that provides the ability to focus on the management of complex rules and complicated problem domains
4. *Explanatory power,* or self knowledge—the ability to evaluate its reasoning and explain its conclusions to the user
5. *Architecture* essentially consisting of an inference engine, a knowledge base, and a user interface

The key differences between conventional and expert systems are summarized in Table 3–2.

An expert system is not a brand new product, but rather, an adjunct to today's management information systems. Early computer applications empha-sized efficiency and control. As computers became more powerful and less costly to produce, efforts to improve efficiency continued. At the same time, the scope of computation began to encompass less-structured managerial tasks. Thus, expert systems represent an extension of efforts to expand managers' ability to understand specific business situations and processes.

■ **Table 3-2**   Comparison of Conventional Information Systems and Expert Systems

	Feature	Expert Systems	Traditional Information Systems
1.	Types of problems solved	Ill-structured	Well-structured
2.	Processing	Symbolic	Numeric
3.	Technique	Heuristic	Algorithmic; numeric
4.	Knowledge	Imprecise (conceptual)	Precise (numerical)
5.	Modification	Frequent	Infrequent
6.	Solution steps	Inexplicit	Explicit (precise)
7.	Answers sought	Satisfactory	Optimal
8.	Behavior	Solve problems; explain results; emulate experts	Solve problems
9.	Nature	Recursive; remembers information	Iterative; information is read every time a subroutine calls for it
10.	Execution path	No predefined path; pattern-directed	Predefined path; control directed
11.	Ability to reformulate a problem	Yes	No
12.	Maintenance	By knowledge engineers	By programmers

■ THE BEGINNING

The Classics

As a technology, expert systems have their roots in universities. Later systems were developed for commercial use. Early systems have been arbitrarily labeled as "the pre-1980 systems" or "the classics," and include DENDRAL, MACSYMA, HEARSAY, INTERNIST, PROSPECTOR, and PUFF. This section provides a brief description of each. Table 3-3 presents a summary of these systems.

DENDRAL

DENDRAL is considered by many to be the first real expert system. It was developed by Joshua Lederberg of Stanford University in 1964 to examine spectroscopic data and identify the molecular structure of unknown chemical compounds. The output was a description of the compound's structure. It took 15 person-years to develop the heuristics for the system. DENDRAL was programmed in LISP, an artificial intelligence language. The system and its descendants have become standard tools for chemists seeking to determine molecular structure.

■ **Table 3–3** "Classic" Expert Systems

System	Developer	Main Function	Expected Results	Development Tool
DENDRAL	Stanford	Examine spectroscopic data of all possible chemical compounds	Description of compound's molecular structure	LISP
MACSYMA	MIT	High-level symbolic manipulation of algorithmic problems	Solution to complex symbolic problems	LISP
HEARSAY	Carnegie Mellon	Understand speech	detailed list of hypotheses of what was enunciated and corresponding best guess of its meaning	SAIL
INTERNIST (CADUCEUS)	Pittsburgh	Diagnose clinical diseases	Set of solutions based on diagnosis	LISP
MYCIN	Stanford	Diagnose infectious disease and prescribe antibiotic treatment	Prescription for antibiotic treatment	LISP
PROSPECTOR	Stanford Research Int'l. (SRI)	Evaluate geological sites	Map and evaluation of ore deposits	LISP
PUFF	Stanford	Diagnose lung disease and pulminary problems	Report for attending physicians	LISP

MACSYMA

MACSYMA is a large, interactive mathematics expert system developed in 1968 by Carol Engleman, William Martin, and Joel Moses of MIT to manipulate mathematical expressions symbolically. The project entailed 100 person-years of software design and LISP programming. It is the most powerful system yet developed to solve algebraic problems on a computer. The user enters formulas and commands, which the system converts into solutions to extremely complex symbolic problems.

HEARSAY I and II

HEARSAY's focus is on speech understanding. Developed at Carnegie Mellon University, this system accepts a speech wave as input and produces a list of hypotheses about what was enunciated as well as a database query based on the best guess of its meaning. Upon completion of this five-person-year project in 1975, the Carnegie team had created a system that possessed a 1,000-word vocabulary and a 75 percent accuracy rate in interpreting human speech. The system demonstrated the clear superiority of the heuristic method over the algorithmic method in dealing with speech understanding.

INTERNIST

INTERNIST, an internal medicine expert system that is now called CADU-CEUS, was developed at the University of Pittsburgh in the early 1970s by Harry People and Jack Myers to analyze hundreds of clinical problems. The program begins by asking the physician to describe the patient's symptoms and medical history. Each symptom is then analyzed to determine the disease. Written in LISP, the system addresses some 500 diseases, 25 percent of which are within the realm of internal medicine.

MYCIN

The best-known expert system in use today is MYCIN. Developed in the mid 1970s by Edward Feigenbaum of Stanford, the system's main function is to diagnose infectious blood diseases and prescribe an antibiotic treatment. The system has proven its usefulness, especially to physicians with little or no experience in infectious diseases. It is also used as a "sounding board" by experienced physicians to test the accuracy of their decisions.

PROSPECTOR

A commercial expert system, PROSPECTOR was developed in the late 1970s at Stanford Research Institute International (SRI) by a team of prominent scientists including Richard Duda, Peter Hart, and P. Barnett. The LISP-based system locates valuable ore deposits and produces maps and geological site evaluations. The team worked with a number of mineral experts to fashion the system's five models. Once the initial data is entered into the system, PROSPECTOR selects the model that best explains the data.

PUFF

PUFF was developed at Stanford in 1980 to interpret readings from respiratory tests given to patients in a pulminary (lung) function lab. The system interfaces directly with the lab's lung machines and measures the capacity of the patient's lungs and their ability to get oxygen in and carbon dioxide out on a regular basis. PUFF relies on 64 rules stored in the knowledge base to interpret the test data. The system's accuracy rate is about 93 percent.

Later Systems

Since 1980, a number of commercially oriented expert systems have been developed for the mainframe as well as the microcomputer. The systems presented here were selected because of their historic impact and the tone they set for building expert systems today.

XCON and XSEL

XCON was developed for Digital Equipment Corporation (DEC) to configure minicomputer systems that will specific customer orders. Developed by John McDermott of Carnegie Mellon University in 1980, the system simply takes a customer's order as input and draws a set of diagrams that will be used by the assemblers to build a computer. Such a system saves substantial amounts of technical personnel time; experts who once worked on configuration problems can now concentrate on orders that require specialized attention. XCON and XSEL use system development tools that speed up development.

DELTA/CATS-1 (Diesel-Electric Locomotive Troubleshooting Aid or Computer-Aided Troubleshooting System-1)

This system was developed by General Electric to diagnose locomotive problems and specify the needed repairs. Prior to DELTA/CATS-1, whenever a locomotive needed repairs, a maintenance expert had to be flown to the site or the locomotive towed to a repair facility. The best-known participant in this project was Dave Smith, who joined General Electric in the early 1950s and remains there today. A team of knowledge engineers worked with Smith, and by 1982, they were able to test the system successfully. Once DELTA identifies the problem, it lays out the step-by-step procedure for repairing the locomotive.

Drilling Advisor

This special-purpose expert system is designed to help oil rig personnel diagnose and correct drilling problems. Formerly, when a problem occurred, an expert usually had to be flown to the site to correct it. This process is time-consuming and expensive—costing up to running tens of thousands of dollars per day. Drilling Advisor's 250 rules enable it to diagnose the problem and prescribe treatment in a matter of minutes.

TAXADVISOR

A good example of expert systems' transition from the university research lab to the business sector is TAXADVISOR. Developed by Robert Michaelsen of the University of Nebraska, it provides tax-planning advice that helps individuals to maximize the wealth they can bequeath to their heirs. The system interactively reviews the individual's health, life insurance and other assets, retirement plans, tax shelters, gifts, and so on, before it recommends a decision. The system is a consultative system designed to assist novices and professionals (accountants, tax attorneys, bank trust officers, and estate planners), giving advice in the narrow domain for which it was built.

EXperTAX

The main task of EXperTAX is corporate tax planning. Developed by Coopers & Lybrand in LISP and running on IBM/IBM-compatible personal computers, the system supports the corporate tax accrual and planning process. It interactively questions the staff accountant on matters related to a given tax-planning problem. If queried, the system will explain the reason a question is being asked and its relevance to the issue under evaluation.

Table 3–4 summarizes the systems discussed here. A sampling of other expert system applications appears in Chapter 4.

■ **Table 3–4** Later Expert Systems

System	Developer	Main Function	Expected Results
XCON, XSEL	John McDermott (Carnegie Mellon)	Configure minicomputer systems for specific customer requirements	Substantial savings of technical personnel time
DELTA/CATS-1	GE	Diagnose locomotives problems and specify repair procedures	Savings of time and money
Drilling Advisor		Diagnose oil drilling problems and prescribe remedy	Substantial savings of time and money
TAXADVISOR	Robert Michaelsen (Nebraska)	Provide tax-planning advice	Maximization of wealth an individual can bequeath
EXperTAX	Coopers & Lybrand	Corporate tax planning	Support for the corporate tax accrual and planning process

■ SYSTEM ARCHITECTURE

With all these exciting developments in expert systems, many people wonder how an expert system "is glued together." All expert systems have four components:

1. Knowledge base
2. Inference engine
3. Justifier/scheduler
4. User interface

Although all expert systems have these components, they each have other features that vary from one expert system to another. Figure 3–1 illustrates the relationships among the components.

Knowledge Base

The knowledge base is the repository of the rules, facts, and knowledge acquired from the human expert. Most expert systems use production rules, which is why expert systems are often referred to as **rule-based systems.** The knowledge is typically represented in the form of IF ... THEN type rules (premises and conclusions), facts, and assumptions about the problem the

Figure 3-1 Key Components of an Expert System

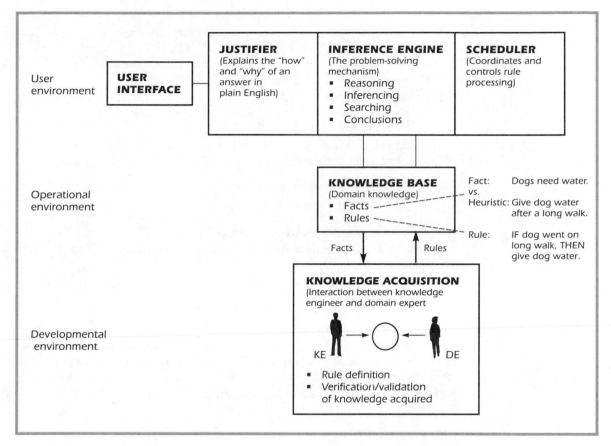

system is designed to solve. See Figure 3–2. The rules are subject domains in a format similar to that of an organization chart.

As a planning step for formatting the rules, the knowledge engineer may start with a graphic model such as a decision tree to describe the decision processes. After extensive verification, the rules may be grouped and organized into a process to ensure that certain rules are fired in proper sequence.

At the heart of a knowledge base are the rules. **Rules** may be constructed either through examples (called *scenarios*) or using an IF . . . THEN format. A rule that offers only one possible conclusion is easy to write; for example, "IF account balance is greater than 5,000 and the amount is overdue THEN do not approve credit purchase." Rules that have multiple conclusions or uncertainty are more difficult to write and verify. One way of dealing with uncertainty is to assign a confidence factor (similar to a probability value) to tag the degree of certainty of a given attribute. Confidence factors range from −1 (no confidence) to +1 (total confidence), although the scales of confidence factors differ among systems.

There are two general types of rules: definitional and heuristic. A **definitional rule** is one in which the inference establishes a relationship between terms. For example,

```
IF home_state is VIRGINIA
THEN home_country is USA
```

Figure 3–2   *Examples of Rules in a Loan Advisor System*

```
IF assets are greater than 100,000 and income is
  greater than 50,000 THEN approve loan
IF assets are greater than 50,000 and loan value
  is less than 5,000 THEN approve loan
IF income is greater than 50,000 and payment
  history is good and loan value is less than
  5,000 THEN approve loan
IF marital_status is not married and assets are
  less than 50,000 THEN do not approve loan
```

This rule is true for all persons who live in Virginia.

In contrast, a **heuristic rule** is an inference that includes some level of uncertainty. For example,

```
IF country is USA and place_of_birth is France
THEN citizenship is US (confidence .60)
```

This rule may or may not be true, because foreign-born residents may or may not be U.S. citizens. In essence, this rule says, "If you are forced to guess about the citizenship of persons living in the United States, about 60 percent of the time you can assume such persons are U.S. citizens." Most rules are a combination of definitional and heuristic rules.

Inference Engine

The inference engine is a cluster of computer programs that coordinate the reasoning and inferencing based on the rules of the knowledge base to come up with a solution. Inference is grounded in a common sense principle called *modus ponens* (Latin, "method of affirming"), which asserts that if one declares, "IF A is true and if A being true implies B is also true, THEN B is true." The inference part of an inference engine examines the rules and combines them with new facts in the knowledge base to induce inferences. Because rules are often heuristics and facts are only probably true, most decisions carry some level of certainty. This work is all invisible to the user when the expert system is in use.

When the system searches for an appropriate rule, it may not arrive at a single conclusion, but at a number of possibilities having different degrees of certainty. Depending on the domain, the inference engine may use backward chaining or forward chaining. Briefly, *backward chaining* begins with a known goal or outcome and searches backward for the rule (evidence) or facts that will achieve that goal. The backward-chaining process starts with the THEN portion of a rule and backtracks to the possible IF. This goal-driven search method simulates deductive reasoning. Figure 3–3 provides an example of backward chaining.

In contrast, *forward chaining* starts with information in the database and the associated rules to generate a conclusion or goal. For example, it might

Figure 3-3   Example of Backward Chaining

Rules

1. IF wake up at 4:00
   THEN pack at 4:30
2. IF pack at 4:30
   THEN leave home by 5:00
3. IF leave home at 5:00
   THEN park car by 5:15
4. IF park car at 5:15
   THEN check in by 5:30
5. IF check in by 5:30

KNOWN GOAL→   THEN catch 6:00 flight

Procedure: Start with the rule that has the goal in its THEN part: *catch the 6:00 flight* (rule 5). Match that rule's IF part to a preceding rule's THEN part (rule 4). Proceed in this way to arrive at the satisfying premise (the IF part of rule 1):
Wake up at 4:00.

analyze a body of customer sales data to predict bad credit risks. Using this method, the inference engine starts with the IF portion of the rule and tracks forward to the THEN portion of a rule that indicates the goal. Both forward chaining and backward chaining are "satisfying," not optimizing, operations research techniques; the final solution is viewed as "good enough" for the purpose of decision making. A detailed discussion of backward and forward chaining appears in Chapter 12.

Justifier/Scheduler

Unlike human experts who give professional advice but cannot explain each step of their decision-making process, an expert system can explain exactly how it arrived at a solution. The "how" part of the **justifier** triggers the system to display the reasoning or the rules used in producing the answer. Users come to trust an expert system's decisions if they understand its line of reasoning. The justifier also works as a useful instructional aid. With practice (and close attention), users can learn to be experts in their own right. Figure 3–4 displays Rule 2 as justification for the decision "go to Hilton Head, S.C."

Not all users require the explanatory feature. For example, a fighter pilot facing a split-second decision of whether to fire a missile at a target barely has time to question the decision of the expert system on board. Similar situations occur in business when a system's reliability has been so high that users no longer require the explanatory function.

As one can see, the inference engine runs the whole show. Its main functions are to infer and to control the processing of rules. Part of the inference engine, the **scheduler** (also called a *rule interpreter,*) is set up to coordinate and control the sequencing of the rules. The scheduler is important, because it coordinates and ensures efficient use of the knowledge base.

Figure 3–4 Example of Inference Engine Justification

VACATION ADVISOR

Question (*expert system*)	User Response
1. Where do you want to spend your vacation?	
• East Coast	East Coast
• West Coast	
2. What sport do you want to participate in?	
• Swimming	Swimming
• Hiking	
• Skiing	
3. How much money do you plan to spend?	$6,000

THEN the best PLACE to go is HILTON HEAD, S.C.

Justification (*by inference engine*)
Based on your answers, I used the following rule:

R2   IF Coast is 'East' and Sport is 'Swim' and Available_fund
      is ≥$3,000 THEN Place is 'Hilton Head, S.C.'

User Interface

The **user interface** facilitates all communication between the user and the system. The system asks for information through questions or multiple-choice menus, and the user answers by typing on a the keyboard. Most expert systems have a help function that explains any question the user does not understand.

The "what" command (what do you mean by the question?) prompts the system to display the explanation. When the system completes the inferencing process, it displays its decision on the monitor. If no decision can be reached, the system may give an estimate of the correct answer along with a qualifying certainty factor.

The user interface is important; without it the expert system becomes a "black box," incapable of seeking the additional information needed to conclude its work. Taken together, the user interface and the interface engine make up an expert-system shell.

■ THE SHELL CONCEPT

An expert system can be built using any conventional programming language on any computer. Special expert system development programs, called **shells,** make it possible to create an expert system without programming the inference engine, user interface, and so on. A survey of today's expert systems applications would reveal that most of them have been developed using shells, rather than languages. In a 1992 survey of organizations that had built expert systems, 58 percent of the respondents reported that shells were their predominant development tool. For the other tools, LISP was used by 38 percent; Prolog, by 33 percent; and conventional programming languages, by 29 percent. Some respondents reported using two or more programming languages or shells, which accounts for the total that exceeds 100 percent. More information on shells is given in Chapter 14.

IMPLICATIONS FOR MANAGEMENT

One of the main barriers to successful expert system development in an organization is lack of management awareness. An expert system project may be a technical success but a technology-transfer failure. A key question, then, is how can management be made aware of expert systems? Three strategies can be considered:

1. *Affiliation with an organization that specializes in expert system development.* This strategy could also include a university alliance such as that of DEC with Carnegie Mellon University. The potential drawback of this strategy is that the allied organization may become prematurely entrenched in one philosophy.

2. *Development of an expert system group within the firm's information technology department.* The visibility and availability of such a group can create management awareness and facilitate support for projects in various departments.

3. *Training-the-trainer strategy.* By this strategy, a person is selected from each department to be sent out for training in knowledge engineering. Upon their return, these "advocates" take the lead in developing expert systems applications.

Regardless of the strategy followed, an important point to remember is to first build a foundation of awareness, followed by an understanding of how the strategy for expert system development fits in with corporate strategy. One should also begin with doable projects as a way of cost-justifying the initial investment. With commitment, teamwork, and followup, the technology will have a chance to succeed.

SUMMARY

1. Because seasoned human experts are an expensive commodity, many organizations seek to build an expert system to emulate them. Expert systems are computer programs that emulate the reasoning of a human expert in a specialized area, called a problem domain. The key to expert systems is heuristics, rules of thumb that have been developed over a long period of performing a difficult task.

2. Human expertise is more perishable, unpredictable, difficult to transfer, and costly than expert systems, but it is also more adaptive, creative, and broadly focused. On the other hand, expert systems are more permanent, consistent, easily transferred, and affordable than human expertise. The limitations are that they need instructions, lack inspiration, and have a narrower focus than human expertise.

3. Distinctive differences characterize traditional, decision-support, and expert systems. Traditional systems deal with algorithmic, highly repetitive problems requiring little judgment. Decision-support systems (DSS) address semistructured problems and areas in which the processing is less well defined. A DSS models the real world; it

allows the user to enter assumptions and get different answers as a result. Expert systems are heuristics programs that model experts' thought processes.

4. In deciding on a solution, an expert system does not follow a predetermined path, as DSS or traditional information systems do. It weighs facts and rules to make a final decision or recommend a solution. The expert system's architecture (consisting of its knowledge base and inference engine) is another distinguishing feature.

5. Historically, a number of expert systems have enjoyed successful applications. DENDRAL was the first true expert system. MACSYMA was a large, interactive mathematics expert system. Other well-known successful applications include HEARSAY, PROSPECTOR, PUFF, and MYCIN. Most of these applications were written in LISP, an expert-system programming language. Among the later systems are XCON, DELTA/CATS-1, Drilling Advisor, TAXADVISOR, and EXperTAX.

6. The key components of an expert system are the knowledge base, inference engine, justifier/scheduler, and user interface. The *knowledge base* is the repository of the knowledge acquired from the human expert. The *inference engine* is a cluster of programs that coordinate reasoning and inferencing based on the rules to come up with solutions. A *justifier/scheduler* explains how or why certain solutions or decisions are made. The *user interface* consists of all aspects of communication between the user and the system.

7. Shells eliminate the need for programming, since they contain all the components except the knowledge base, which is built by the knowledge engineer. Most shells are written in structured high-level programming languages such as Pascal or C.

■ TERMS TO LEARN

Definitional rule a rule in which the inference sets a relationship between terms; a rule that defines relationships among objects in the knowledge base, but doesn't contain any expert knowledge about how to solve a problem.

Expert system an artificial intelligence program that represents captured human knowledge and the rules of thumb (reasoning) used by one or more human experts to solve a specific problem.

Heuristic a rule of thumb based on years of experience.

Inference engine the "brain" of an expert system; a cluster of computer programs that coordinate through a scheduler the reasoning and inferencing based on the rules of the knowledge base to produce the solution or advice.

Justifier explains the action (line of reasoning) of the expert system to the user.

Problem domain special problem area in which an expert solves problems very well.

Production rules knowledge representation method in which knowledge is formalized into rules.

Rule a formal way of specifying a recommendation, directive, or strategy, expressed as a premise and a conclusion (IF . . . THEN).

Rule-based system a system in which knowledge is represented completely in terms of rules.

Scheduler the part of the inference engine that coordinates and controls the sequence of the rules.

Shell a commercial software package containing a user interface and an inference engine that makes it easy to build a knowledge base; a complete expert system stripped of its specific knowledge.

User interface component of a computer system that allows bidirectional communication between the system and its user; all parts of a knowledge-base system that a user sees on the screen and interacts with during a consultation.

■ REVIEW QUESTIONS

1. To what component(s) of expert systems does the vignette "Bureaucrats of the Mind" at the beginning of the chapter refer? Explain.

2. Why is interest in expert systems so strong? Cite examples of your own to justify your answer.

3. A number of definitions of expert systems have been suggested in the literature. Draft one of your own and explain the basis for your choice.

4. What is so unique about reasoning and heuristics that make them important in building expert systems? Discuss.

5. Compare and contrast human expertise and expert systems. Under what conditions or circumstances would an expert system be a better choice?

6. Distinguish between:
   a. conventional information systems and expert systems
   b. decision-support systems and expert systems
   c. conventional information systems and decision-support systems

7. Briefly explain the main distinguishing characteristics of expert systems.

8. Specify how "the classics," the pre-1980 expert systems, differ from later systems.

9. Having read the chapter, what do you believe are the most important contributions of expert systems? Do you see them as more attractive to some industries than to others (e.g., banking versus utilities)?

10. In your opinion, what is the difference between a knowledge base and a database? How are they related? Explain.

11. Identify the functions of the following:
    a. justifier/scheduler
    b. inference engine
    c. user interface
    d. rule-based and induction systems

12. How does a shell differ from an expert system? Be specific.

13. If you were to build an expert system using a shell, what would you need to know? What type of background should you have? Elaborate.

■ EXERCISES AND CASES

1. Is a computer program that forecasts tomorrow's weather (say October 1) by averaging the precipitation, humidity, and temperature of every October 1 of the preceding 50 years an expert system? Explain.

2. To what extent are the following problems candidates for expert systems? If partially an expert system, where is the human phase of the work?
   a. constructing a new bank building
   b. student advising
   c. advising a customer how to invest $1 million in the stock market for greatest gain

3. Consider the game of tic-tac-toe. Develop some realistic heuristics, explain their plausibility, evaluate their actual effectiveness, and explain the results.

4. Since heuristics are rules of thumb, they cannot always be correct. Working with a partner, explain why anyone would want to use such heuristics in expert systems.

5. Choose a problem area and list some potentially useful heuristics for solving the problem. Explain how you would determine if they are good heuristics.

6. List and explain the features that you as a user would like to see in the following expert systems:

   a. faculty advisor for undergraduate students
   b. diagnostic advisor for an auto mechanic
   c. loan advisor for a junior loan officer in a commercial bank
   d. common-stock advisor for a small investor
   e. diagnostic advisor for a doctor in general practice

7. The following are interviews with officers of two commercial banks in which they express their opinions about using a loan advisor expert system in their auto loan departments. Which argument do you favor? Discuss the pros and cons carefully with a classmate.

Bank Officer 1 (pro expert system)

"We've been working with computers for over 30 years, and we know what they can and can't do. We've heard of computers trying to think through problems similar to those of a bank officer. A professor from the university recently spoke to our chamber of commerce about expert systems and how they're helping different industries. I know in the loan area, the *last* thing we want to spend too much time on is basic auto loans that are virtually secured loans. Let's face it, there are only so many pieces of information you need to decide on an auto loan for an established customer, especially when the new car is the collateral.

"Yes, as senior vice president of the loan division, the bottom line for me is to see how expert systems can take over decision making on auto loans under $20,000. If we link the system to our databases, I'm not sure there is going to be much for the junior officers to do other than take the advice of the expert system. Bankers are conservative, and we turn down some good loans. This costs us almost as much as bad loans. With an expert system, I feel we can take away the subjectivity and guesswork of low-end auto loans. It should make our customers happy and at the same time improve our profitability."

Bank Officer 2 (anti expert system)

". . . There's no question about it; our industry has benefited a lot from computers. Now, I'm told that there is some technology that can think like a human and produce solutions better than my experienced people can. Let me tell you, in *our* loan department, customers are treated *personally*. They're greeted, screened, and evaluated carefully based not only on the data, but also on my people's hunches, intuition (from the way they're dressed to the way they talk), and our experience with similar customers. Granted, we don't make the right decision every time, but to tell me that these expert systems will do the job better is hogwash!

"Using those expert systems in decision making or to replace a loan officer strikes me as pretty cold. That is exactly the reason I take a dim view of them. We've been promoting a personal image in our bank for years. Take a look at the open teller cages. You can't even see the workstation from where customers stand. Now, you're coming with this impersonal expert system that can never understand the customers' personalities or the real reasons they apply for loans.

"Any way you look at it, computers can't think the same way we do. I don't care how much so-called intelligence you pump into a black box, in the loan business you want *people* to deal with people's problems. Don't get me wrong, I like computers. I use the one you see on my desk every day; in fact, all day. But it's how you use the computer that makes it useful. You can use a computer to look at financial problems and so on, but I'd like to see your expert system say to the customer, 'Come on in, Mr. Mandelbaum. How's the family? I know you're paid up on last year's loan and have a great job. We'd be glad to process another loan for you. Would you like a cup of coffee?' "

■ SELECTED REFERENCES

Duval, Beverly K., and Linda Main. "Expert Systems: What Is an Expert System? *Library Software Review (LSR),* Spring 1994, pp. 44–53.

Krause, Paul J.; J. Patrick; and Saki Hajnal. "Formal Specification and Decision Support." *Decision Support Systems (DSS),* October 1994, pp. 189–197.

Morin, Richard. "Artificial Intelligence." *UNIX Review (UXR),* July 1994, pp. 91–92.

Subramoniam, Suresh. "Expert Systems: Guidelines for Managers." *Industrial Management and Data Systems (IDS),* no. 55, 1992, pp. 23–25.

Chapter ▪ 4

Application Areas

FAST ADVISOR: A KNOWLEDGE-BASED CREDIT ANALYZER

Credit analysis is a knowledge-intensive process—a process that commercial banks constantly try to improve. Like many knowledge-intensive processes, credit analysis is a ripe area for knowledge-based systems. This article describes the development of FAST Advisor, a knowledge-based system that improves the speed and quality of credit analysis.

BACKGROUND

Around 1980, the banking industry began to adopt new credit analysis methods for business loans. These methods systematically analyzed cash flows from a company's operations and financing. Rex Beach founded Financial Performers, Inc. (FPI), which released FAST, its first software product, in 1981. Through the 1980s, FAST developed into a full-fledged financial analysis, forecasting, and reporting system. The majority of major U.S. commercial banks adopted it.

In 1987, FPI began to investigate the feasibility of developing a product that would address two issues: the ability of analysts to consistently recognize risks indicated by numeric reports and the laborious process of producing a credit writeup on each proposed business loan. The company approached its client banks to gather their impressions of artificial intelligence–based decision tools for commercial lenders. FPI found that many banks were already investigating AI tools on their own.

One bank, for example, perceived the need for a "safety net" to guard against analysis mistakes. In this particular institution, more than half the people with credit-granting authority had less than three years of banking experience! This bank was not unique. High personnel turnover was common in the critical credit analysis and relationship management functions.

In addition, banks had to improve productivity in the labor-intensive credit approval process as they dealt with the effects of deregulation and increased competition. It was imperative, however, that productivity increases not be achieved at the expense of consistent, accurate credit analysis. To meet this need, FPI developed FAST Advisor, an expert system which produces a written-language analysis of a business's financial performance.

SYSTEM COMPONENTS

As Figure 1 shows, FPI's FAST System consists of:

- FAST, a financial spreadsheet tool that analysts use to enter corporate financial statements, produce numeric analyses, and manage a database of historical financial information on each borrower.
- Credit Policy Guidelines, an administrator program that incorporates each bank's specific industry focus and risk tolerances.
- FAST Advisor, a rule-based expert system that recognizes key financial events, identifies critical risk elements, and produces a written summary of the applicant's financial performance.

Figure 1   FAST SYSTEM Components

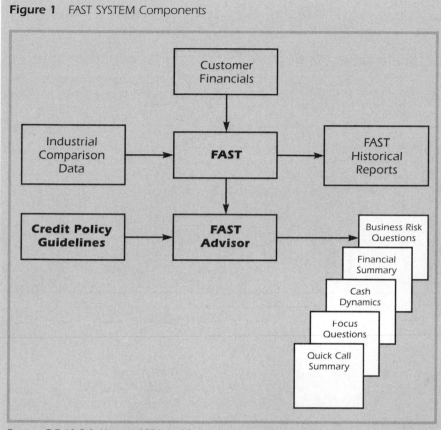

Source: *PC AI,* July/August 1994, p. 16.

DESIGN ISSUES

FPI's team of credit experts wanted FAST Advisor to respond to the everyday needs of its banking clients. FAST Advisor had to provide the insights of a skilled, experienced lender. Flexibility was the most critical challenge, however. The product had to accommodate each bank's specific portfolio makeup and credit policies. At the same time, the product had to promote the use of common analysis methods and be easily deployable throughout a given organization.

SELECTING AN EXPERT SYSTEM SHELL

In 1988 FPI began to explore commercially available shells. Our selection criteria were similar to FPI's own product structure requirements. Our shell had to:

- run on customer's hardware
- have versions for DOS, Windows, and OS/2
- easily interface to the non-shell world
- have an excellent report-writer capability
- have strong product support

After evaluating ten shells, we chose EXSYS Professional. Many of the shell's features proved invaluable during product development and testing.

DEVELOPMENT APPROACH

After selecting the shell, FPI met with client banks and held user-group forums to solicit suggestions and opinions on the critical elements of FAST Advisor's rule base. FPI developers with broad lending and credit analysis experience distilled the collected information. The final knowledge base reflects this wealth of expertise and experience.

Initial development yielded a fairly complex set of rules and an accompanying set of industry-based economic and business outlook parameters. In early testing, customers quickly found that structure unmanageable—primarily because it was difficult to identify and maintain forecasts of the critical economic variables for each industry. Hence, FPI redefined its development approach to produce FAST Advisor's current structure. The resulting rule base uses about 1,200 variables in nearly 900 rules. The expert system reads a file of necessary information inputs from the FAST database and the Credit Policy Guidelines. Report generators produce specific written text for each assessed company. Figure 2 shows the analysis flow.

Figure 2 Analysis Flow. The FAST Advisor expert system operates inside the EXSYS shell. The system's extensive rule base takes advantage of EXSYS's ability to access data files and offers flexible reporting options.

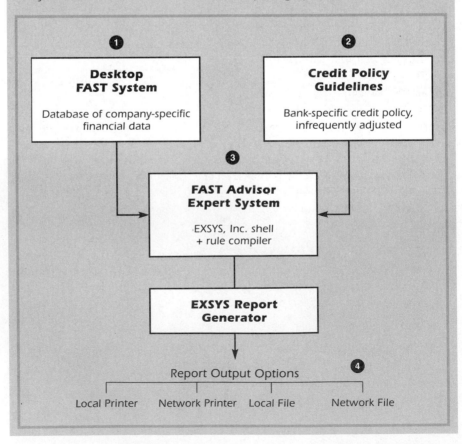

The initial release of FAST Advisor used both forward- and backward-chaining. The product subsequently became a predominantly forward-chaining system because:

- forward chaining readily permits segmenting groups of rules for development and testing
- we wanted to prepare for future enhancements, such as a Risk Rating module, which would add a large number of additional variables to the 1,200 in use.

RESULTS OF TESTING AND INITIAL USE

The initial FAST Advisor product, installed in seventeen banks, received extensive testing and use by lenders and credit analysts with differing levels of experience. We provided worksheets for testers to assess productivity gains and improvement in the quality of credit analysis.

Most of the banks were certain that they gained in productivity. One bank closely measured these gains. Their average time to produce a credit analysis decreased from 60 hours to 21 hours. Another bank was able to institute same-day turnaround of credit analysis requests, a goal it had previously been unable to achieve.

All of these institutions indicated moderate to significant improvement in the quality and depth of credit analysis and credit writeups with the use of FAST Advisor. Responses specifically noted the improved quality of information available to lenders and the visibility of early signals indicating potential credit problems.

Source: Excerpted from C. Creekpaum, M. C. Carter, and William Gibson, "FAST Advisor: A Knowledge-Based Credit Analyzer," *PC AI,* July/August 1994, pp. 16–18ff.

At a Glance

Most organizations' experience with expert systems points out several benefits that make this evolving technology attractive. Among the benefits are improved productivity, upgrading the performance of skilled personnel, training new or junior employees, solving difficult problems, and preserving expertise for when the expert is gone. In deciding whether to build an expert system, one also needs to consider its limitations. For example, the expertise or the knowledge needed to build the knowledge base may not be readily available. When available, the expert does not always have adequate time or the willingness to cooperate. The question of cost and the availability of a qualified knowledge engineer also enter the picture.

Several myths and misperceptions tend to becloud the image of expert systems. For example, expert systems in themselves promote productivity more than they replace people. They do *not* reason better than humans, and they *can* make mistakes, depending on the inaccuracies of the acquired knowledge. Shells now allow an inexperienced knowledge engineer to build an expert system. Despite all this, expert systems are not panaceas nor are they suitable for all kinds of problems.

What You Will Learn _____

By the end of this chapter, you should know the following:

1. The benefits and limitations of expert systems.
2. The myths and realities surrounding expert systems.
3. Expert systems' key application areas and areas of use.

INTRODUCTION

Why is it important for an organization to become involved in expert systems? Human experts are expensive, often busy, hard to come by, and mortal. The motivation for building an expert system is in the benefits of creating a competitive advantage rather than in cost savings. Heightened competition (for some businesses on a global basis) has prompted the search for a technological edge to find new ways of reaching and serving customers, evaluating high-risk problems, and making sense out of mountains of data collected round the clock. Intelligent applications can help in all these areas.

This chapter briefly describes the benefits and limitations of expert systems and the major business areas in which they are used. The myths and realities of expert systems are also examined.

BENEFITS OF EXPERT SYSTEMS

Expert systems can perform many functions in an organization, benefiting the firm in numerous ways. Ten benefits are explained here.

1. *Improved productivity.* American Express's expert system increased the efficiency of its credit authorizers between 45 and 65 percent. Du Pont estimates an aggregate savings from its 300 expert systems of more than $10 million. DEC reported saving $70 million per year as a result of the 10 major expert systems in operation. Arthur Andersen, a management consulting and accounting firm, built a driver's licensing expert system for the state of Pennsylvania in 20 working days. The system handles 90 percent of the state's license processing. It replaced an information system that took 400 workdays to build and could handle only 25 percent of the processing.

Banks are also increasing their productivity by using expert systems. They are shedding middle managers by putting expert system decision tools in the hands of front-line personnel. In a study of one commercial bank, 50 percent of the staff making loan decisions had less than five years of experience. With the expert system becoming the "robot" of middle management, bank personnel are available to make higher level decisions. See Box 4–1.

2. *Staff training.* The knowledge contained in an expert system is a valuable corporate asset in itself, but its value is increased when it is used for teaching, testing, or training new and junior staff. A novice can gain experience working with the system, especially because of its explanatory powers.

3. *Retention of scarce expertise.* Many companies lose valuable expertise when their human experts retire, move on, or lose their edge. Expert systems are able to capture the knowledge of experts on their way to retirement. A classic example of this is the case of Aldo Cimino of Campbell Soup Company (see Box 4–2).

Box 4–1   An Expert System for Criminal Justice

TOMIS (Tennessee Offender Management Information System) is a new $14 million system implemented by the Tennessee Department of Correction (TDC) to deal with the massive prison population and the many rules specifying lengths of sentences, probation details, and so on. The system was developed by Andersen Consulting, a company that specializes in applying artificial intelligence to business problems. TOMIS is supposed to speed up productivity, reduce errors and provide more accurate information, and oversee the entire process from sentencing through imprisonment to release.

Source: *Knowledge Base,* July/August 1993, p. 12.

4. *Upgraded performance of skilled and experienced personnel.* This can be an extremely useful contribution. For example, John Hancock uses an expert system to automate insurance underwriting. The firm is able to approve 43 percent of new applications within 24 hours—a process that previously took three weeks or more. Likewise, Canon's OPTEX expert system has made its highly skilled lens designers twelve times more productive. It allows a zoom lens design that previously took four experts six weeks to complete to be accomplished by a single person in only two weeks.

5. *Improved production operations.* Expert systems free experts from the more routine tasks so that they can devote time to the specialized, "one of a kind" problems in their domain. This is accomplished, in part, by bringing new employees to an acceptable level of competence more quickly. For example, Texas Instruments uses an expert system to control many routine production decisions, allowing the human experts more time to investigate new and better methods of production.

6. *Relatively affordable expertise.* Harnessing the experience of seasoned experts in their respective domains provides decision makers with the kind of support that conventional information systems cannot provide. Instead of assisting the decision maker by turning out mere data, expert systems tackle problems head on, essentially making the decision. The only question left to the user is whether to implement or veto the decision. The explanatory power of the expert system adds credence to the solution.

7. *Increased output.* Expert systems work faster than humans do. For example, XCON enabled Digital Equipment Corporation to increase the speed with which it processes VAX computer orders fourfold and with fewer people. This higher output resulted in lower overall handling costs.

8. *Standardized approach to problems that require expertise.* Once a standardized approach has been developed for an expert system, the system stays on course and does not waver unless new rules or procedures are added. This standardization can minimize errors. The XCON system, for example, reduced errors from 35 to 2 percent.

9. *Utilization of incomplete and uncertain information.* Unlike conventional, algorithmic programs, expert systems can give useful answers even when supplied with incomplete information. Even though such answers are not

Box 4-2   Expert System Picks Workers' Brains

. . . In what may be the final indignity of man, companies are asking retiring workers to leave their brains behind, stored on a computer disk. "Expert systems" developers are picking the brains of longtime employees and storing their expertise on floppy disk.

Richard Herrod of Dallas-based Texas Instruments, Inc., an expert in artificial intelligence, said that not everyone is a candidate for expert systems. The best prospects are people who know more about a particular job than anyone else—in other words, experts.

"You build an expert system when you have a significant specialized knowledge that exists only in a few people's heads and is acquired through years of experience," said Herrod, who recently attended the Instrument Society of America's annual conference in Philadelphia.

Herrod developed one of his first expert systems for Campbell's Soup Company, where Aldo Cimino, an employee with 46 years of experience in the soup sterilization process, was about to retire.

Cimino was the troubleshooter for the company's 72-foot-high sterilizers in which 68,000 cans of soup at a time are heated to 250 degrees.

"If one of those breaks down, you're up to your ears in bad soup," Herrod said. "So when there was a problem the people at the plant couldn't fix, they'd call in Aldo. He had a lot of little tricks and knew how to figure out the problem."

Cimino, who worked at the company's Camden, New Jersey, headquarters, said that he was apprehensive when his boss asked him to put everything he knew about his job on a computer disk. "At first I thought, 'Oh my God, they're going to get rid of me,' But then I realized that I was 64 years old and getting ready to go anyway. They just wanted to save some of what I knew."

"It felt weird at first," he said. "But I got used to it. It's like I left a piece of myself at that plant."

It took seven months for a team of knowledge engineers to reap 46 years' worth of know-how from Cimino and store it on floppy disks. When they were finished, Cimino retired.

Campbell's now has a floppy disk that serves as a permanent consultant when trouble brews. "Now when something goes wrong with a sterilizer, the maintenance people can stick a floppy disk into an IBM PC, call up the expert system, and interact with it much like they were dealing with Aldo on the phone," Herrod said.

100 percent exact, in many cases they are satisfactory enough. The user can answer a question "I don't know" or "yes", with as little as 40 percent certainty, and the expert system will still produce an answer and attach a certainty factor to it.

10. *Smarter work in general.* An expert system can reduce the risks associated with bad decisions. For example, American Express's Authorizer's Assistant reduced losses due to bad debts by 50 percent while increasing efficiency.

A summary of the key benefits is shown in Figure 4-1.

■ LIMITATIONS OF EXPERT SYSTEMS

Despite their benefits, expert systems have limitations. Expert system knowledge is static; it does not evolve and grow as human knowledge does. Adaptability, empathy, and common sense do not characterize expert systems.

Figure 4–1   Benefits of Expert Systems

1. Improved productivity
2. Staff training
3. Retention of scarce expertise
4. Upgraded performance of skilled and experienced personnel
5. Improved production operations
6. Relatively affordable expertise
7. Increased output
8. Standardized approach to problems that require expertise
9. Utilization of incomplete and uncertain information
10. Smarter work in general

Quite obviously, expert systems cannot understand the context of things or learn from experience, and they have no knowledge of themselves or the environment.

In addition to the limitations inherent to the systems, expert systems development is fraught with limitations. The most common constraints are listed here. Each is discussed in detail later in the book.

1. *The requisite knowledge may not be readily available.* This can drag out the knowledge acquisition process for quite some time—or indefinitely, as Box 4–3 shows.

Box 4–3   Wait Till the Cows Come Home

While it is a challenge to bring experts together when constructing an expert system, choosing the right breed of experts requires luck and careful search.

One project focused on developing a system to advise farmers on the optimum feed mix for their dairy cows. Two experts in dairy farm production participated, and one of the two knowledge engineers had some farming experience. The experts showed how the feed mix could be planned based on the various factors that would make up the knowledge base such as the breed of cattle, the climate conditions, the field crops that were available locally, the consistency of the cow's manure, the age and weight of the cow, and the amount of time the cow spent grazing.

The goal of the system was to recommend the appropriate mix and how much supplementary food to feed each cow. Just as the knowledge engineers were about to get into testing the system, one knowledge engineer asked, "What if the cows don't like the taste of the supplementary food mix?"

After general laughter, it became obvious that there was no way to predict whether the cows would eat the supplementary mix or eat it in the quantities determined necessary to improve milk production. In the final analysis, the expert was the cow. The feed mix problem was dropped.

Source: Adapted from "How to Choose Your Expert," *Computerworld,* June 29, 1987, p. 71.

2. *The budget may be inadequate.* Company officers change their minds, and budgets fluctuate in response to changes in company status, economic conditions, and other factors.

3. *Experts are often unavailable or uncooperative.* The acid test of experts' cooperation is the reliability of the knowledge acquired from them.

4. *Experts may disagree.* Experts may disagree on the solution; so much so that the knowledge engineer experiences difficulty in deciding whose opinion to use.

5. *Experts may not be able to explain their decision-making processes.* Extracting knowledge can be quite a chore.

6. *Upper management may not be supportive.* Gaining top brass support for a project can be difficult, especially when the corporate MIS staff is not sold on it.

7. *Good knowledge engineers are rare and high-priced.* Not all firms can afford the cost of knowledge engineering. A recent report estimated that it cost $700 per rule to build an expert system. Even a system that meets the established standards may still not serve the firm's needs. Finding a knowledge engineer who understands the company's needs is not as easy as simply finding a knowledge engineer.

8. *Expert systems are perceived as a threat to job security and career progression.* An expert system can change the skill requirements of the affected position(s). In such cases, special care is needed for selling the system to management.

A summary of these limitations is shown in Figure 4–2.

■ MYTHS AND REALITIES

To many laypersons, expert systems seem more powerful than they really are. Managers and organizations often have developed a false perception of what expert systems can and cannot do. As explained throughout this text, expert systems have a long way to go to match human abilities to reason, understand, or learn. This section attempts to dispel several myths and misperceptions.

Figure 4–2 Limitations of Expert Systems

1. The requisite knowledge may not be readily available
2. The budget may be inadequate
3. Experts are often unavailable or uncooperative
4. Experts may disagree
5. Experts may not be able to explain their decision-making processes
6. Upper management may not be supportive
7. Good knowledge engineers are rare and high-priced
8. Expert systems are perceived as a threat to job security and career progression

1. *Expert systems learn from experience:* FALSE.

As was discussed in Chapter 2, the ability to learn from experience is unique to humans and relatively primitive in expert systems. Most expert systems must be "taught" by adding rules or upgrading the knowledge base. Although some systems possess an adaptability that seems like learning, it is not the same as human learning. Ongoing research in common-sense reasoning is attempting to address the learning factor. For example, *adaptive reasoning* software is being tested, which allows an expert system to "learn" from answers or solutions that deviate from the norm and to adapt its reasoning to subsequent similar problems, and in essence improve over time. In large, complex expert systems involving many parameters, adaptive reasoning capability would be quite an accomplishment.

2. *Expert systems replace people:* TRUE and FALSE.

If an expert system replaces a retiring expert or is used in place of scarce or unavailable human expertise, then the response is "true." In fact, one of the early goals of expert systems was to capture the knowledge of experts on the verge of resigning or retiring from the firm. Since the main tasks of today's expert system are to boost efficiency, productivity, and quality, however, most systems serve as supplements to human abilities. To the extent that users understand this, they accept expert systems in the workplace.

3. *Expert systems perform better than humans:* FALSE.

In only one respect do expert systems perform better than humans, and that is in the consistency of their reasoning, the *reliability* of their response. An expert system will never be able to match human creativity or the human ability to deal with the unknown. As with any other information system, maintenance and update are required for keeping an expert system in tune with human reality.

4. *Expert systems cannot make mistakes:* FALSE.

Expert systems can and often do make mistakes. If the developer enters the wrong rules, the system produces the wrong results. Certain rules may "fire" when they are not supposed to and vice versa. Errors in reasoning resulting from special cases or from the failure to acquire the appropriate heuristics from the expert can have serious consequences, especially in medical applications. For example, if the expert system relies on two facts: (1) All commercial pilots are men, and (2) Ann is a commercial pilot, the system will deduce that Ann is a man which is incorrect. Since expert systems' logic cannot match that of humans, they can easily make mistakes.

5. *Only professional knowledge engineers can build an expert system:* TRUE and FALSE.

For a large system targeted at a large audience, the answer is "true." Highly competent knowledge engineers are needed for building and especially for testing such a system. But the increasingly popular shell enables a novice to learn the building steps quickly using a PC. A key question regarding professional knowledge engineers is certification. The International Association of Knowledge Engineers (IAKE) has begun offering courses and testing to certify the knowledge engineer as a professional. Unfortunately, this task is slow and time-consuming; national and international recognition and acceptance of IAKE certification does not seem likely in the near future.

6. *A special type of computer is needed to operate an expert system:* FALSE.

Expert systems can run on virtually any computer—large or small. Shell configuration is a concern, however. Some shell systems run on the PC; others are configured for a mainframe; still others run on both platforms. The trend is to use PCs.

7. *Experts are not cooperative:* TRUE and FALSE.

Experts, in general, are cooperative. Sometimes, lack of cooperation could be in response to a knowledge engineer's use of the wrong tools or an inappropriate approach. Admittedly, experts who lack motivation can be difficult to work with. Much also depends on whether one expert or multiple experts are being used to develop the system. Knowledge acquisition tools include interviewing, brainstorming, and protocol analysis. Because of the importance of these tools, Chapter 9 and 10 are devoted to them.

8. *Expert systems are expensive:* TRUE and FALSE.

Considering their many benefits, expert systems are affordable when put to good use. On the other hand, an expert system, any system, that starts with a poor plan, weak organizational support, or an inexperienced builder is doomed from the onset and thus a waste of time and money. Most systems that run on the PC can be built for less than $20,000, depending on the complexity of the problem domain. Just as is true when developing conventional information system, cost/benefit analysis is a virtual must. The firm must carefully assess the costs and benefits of the proposed system in order to determine whether the project is doable, affordable, and justifiable.

9. *Expert systems are deep-reasoning systems:* FALSE.

Most of today's expert systems are shallow-reasoning systems. The technology has yet to delve into the deep level of complexity where human experts' intuition and creativity are tapped. However, as more is learned about reasoning and logic and ways to incorporate them into expert systems, more and more difficult problems will be attempted using multiple experts and multiple knowledge engineers.

10. *Expert systems are used for all kinds of problems:* FALSE.

Expert systems are typically used in narrow domains that require symbolic, rather than algorithmic, processes. If the domain is not narrowly defined, one can expect system degradation, which brings up the importance of feasibility studies and advance planning.

A layperson has several ways to dispel the myths surrounding expert systems. Attending a workshop at which hands-on experience is available can be helpful. Seminars, conferences, and adult-education classes have helped many people gain familiarity with this evolving technology. A summary of the myths and realities is shown in Figure 4–3.

■ EXPERT SYSTEM ACTIVITES

Expert systems are making important contributions in virtually every area of business. This section provides an overview of ten categories of activities performed by expert systems today. Bear in mind that some systems contribute expertise in more than one category. Table 4–1 summarizes this section.

Control

Control expert systems specialize in process control. They have built-in monitoring capabilities that allow them to carry out corrective action without

Figure 4–3 *Myths and Realities of Expert Systems*

1. Expert systems learn from experience: FALSE
2. Expert systems replace people: TRUE and FALSE
3. Expert systems perform better than humans: FALSE
4. Expert systems cannot make mistakes: FALSE
5. Only professional knowledge engineers can build an expert system: TRUE and FALSE
6. A special type of computer is needed to operate an expert system: FALSE
7. Experts are not cooperative: TRUE and FALSE
8. Expert systems are expensive: TRUE and FALSE
9. Expert systems are deep-reasoning systems: FALSE
10. Expert systems are used for all kinds of problems: FALSE

involving the user. The systems are designed to monitor operation on a routine basis and interfere only when the operation deviates from the prescribed standard. Many of these systems are used to manage production and to monitor patients in critical-care units.

Debugging

Debugging expert systems diagnose malfunctions and prescribe solutions. For example, one expert system looks into a new computer system, compares its performance to vendor standards, and suggests how to fine tune the system to meet the standards. Another expert system selects the proper procedure to repair a known malfunction in an automobile engine. The remedy is usually chosen from a stored table that lists possible problems and their associated remedies. These systems have been known to prescribe remedies with a high level of success.

Design

Design expert systems use a pattern matching process that shows the "goodness of match" between a designated plan and the confidence level at which it can be designed. In designing integrated circuit layouts, for example, such a system creates plans for producing the circuits within the problem constraints. Design expert systems are useful in problem domains that demand repetitive design of similar components. Their output resembles a prototype for the user to review and then complete according to the user's specifications. Thus, the expert system does the tedious front-end work, freeing the user to work on the more creative aspects of the final design.

Diagnosis

A **diagnostic expert system** is given identifiable information through the user's observation or experience. Built into the system's knowledge base is a list of all identifiable symptoms of specific causal factors.

For a medical diagnostic system, the goal is to identify the patient's illness. It starts by assuming that the patient has a particular illness. It proceeds by

■ **Table 4–1**   Examples of Expert System Activities by Category

Category	Activity	Examples
1. Control	Manipulate operation of a system's overall behavior; intelligent automation	Air traffic control, Battle management HEARSAY I, II
2. Debugging	Recommend correction or remedies for malfunctions	
3. Design	Configure objects into a system based on problem constraints; develop products to specifications	XCON: computer system configuration
4. Diagnosis	Infer likely cause of system malfunction; identify cause based on symptoms; estimate defects	Medical, machine repairs, audits MYCIN: infectious diseases PUFF: pulminary diseases
5. Instruction/training	Diagnose and modify learner behavior; train; transfer information	Tutorial, remedial GUIDON: selection of therapies for infections WELDSELECTOR: selection of appropriate welding materials
6. Interpretation	Infer problem description from sensor (real) data; clarify situations	Speech understanding, surveillance, mapping, imaging PROSPECTOR: geological structures
7. Monitoring	Determine closeness of an observation to expected outcome; compare observations to desired standard	Management control, nuclear plant monitoring REACTOR: nuclear reactor NAVEX: space shuttle
8. Planning	Determine a course of action in advance; develop goal-oriented schemes	Strategic planning, process scheduling TATR: bombing missions DARPA
9. Prediction	Infer likely consequences of a given action or situation; intelligent guessing	Weather forecasting, crop estimation, financial forecasting PLAND/CD: crop damage ASA: airline seating
10. Repair	Administer prescribed remedies; automatic diagnosis; plan, debug, fix	Telephone, computer, automobile Campbell Soup's hydrostatic sterilizers

reviewing the rules and their actions and asks the patient for additional information about unique symptoms in order to create a description of the illness. If it cannot prove an illness exits on the basis of the symptoms, the system takes up another possible illness as the assumed illness and proceeds in the same fashion. All previous responses by the patient are retained in working memory so that repetitive questioning of the patient is avoided.

Diagnosis and debugging go hand in hand. An expert system that debugs a problem must first diagnose the problem it must attend to. It asks the user questions about the malfunctioning system much as it would ask a patient about his or her body. Although diagnostic expert systems are most prevalent in medicine, they are becoming available to diagnose problems in computer systems, local area networks (LANs), and electrical circuits.

Building a diagnostic system requires more than one developer to ensure reliability of the diagnoses. The complexity of diagnosis makes the use of a project team critical. A project team includes the knowledge engineer, who acquires the knowledge from the expert; the human expert (or experts), who provides the knowledge; the programmer, who represents the knowledge in the knowledge base; and the champion, who supports the project within the organization. To illustrate, in 1994 this author built a prototype expert system to diagnose a diabetic patient's foot problems and deformities. A demonstration of the prototype to the orthopedic surgeon (the human expert), indicated that for such a system to gain doctor and patient acceptance, additional variables and interrelationships would have to be incorporated into the prototype. This step meant consulting diabetic specialists, perhaps using more than one knowledge engineer, and seeking the sponsorship of the American Diabetic Association (as the champion) before the Diabetic Foot Advisor could be fully developed, tested, and certified.

Instruction/Training

Training expert systems make a unique contribution. The basic concept is to capture the knowledge of senior employees who are retiring or resigning from the firm and then make that knowledge available to novices to use. In one expert system, trainees receive interactive instruction in troubleshooting failures in the electronic circuits of a television. The system assesses the student's level of knowledge and determines the steps necessary to guide the student through the troubleshooting process on the basis of the assessment. As the student becomes more skilled, the system takes shortcuts in solving problems.

Most training expert systems have explanatory capabilities; they display the reasoning behind their solutions in plain English. Some systems allow students to pose hypothetical "what if" scenarios enabling them to learn by exploration.

Interpretation

Like control systems, **interpretive expert systems** compare aspects of an operation to preset standards. Typically, these systems use sensor data to infer the status of an ongoing process or to describe a given situation. Much of the reasoning is coupled with *confidence factors*. For example, one rule in an auto advisor expert system reads, "If water temperature is over 50 percent of max and oil pressure is less than 9, then there is .78 certainty that engine is low on oil." In such a case, the system flashes a warning message, "CHECK ENGINE OIL."

Interpretive expert systems deal mostly with real data, which is, by nature, incomplete and unreliable. In the case of the auto advisor, a low engine-oil-pressure reading could also be caused by a faulty gauge, a loose wire, a bad fuse, or engine oil that has not been changed in 10,000 miles or more. Although low oil pressure may not be related to high water temperature, experience suggests (hence, the rule) that the combination of low oil pressure and high water temperature is often caused by a hot engine that lacks sufficient oil or cooling system. In newer cars, low oil pressure typically indicates that the engine is low on oil.

Monitoring

Monitoring expert systems help humans to "keep an eye on things," by comparing observations against expected outcomes. A monitoring expert system performs diagnostic and interpretive chores in a time-sensitive environment such as a hospital intensive care unit or the ignition mechanism of a three-stage rocket's second engine. If the findings differ from the standard, the system alerts the human technician and suggests an action. Final decisions are left to the human in charge.

By their very nature, monitoring systems deal with time. Therefore, they must make timely evaluations of the processes they monitor. Each process could involve hundreds of variables and conditions to which the monitor must react in a fraction of a second—as it does for the systems that monitor instrument readings in nuclear reactors.

Planning/Scheduling

A **planning expert system** maps out an entire course of action before any steps are taken. The system creates detailed lists of sequential tasks necessary to achieve two or more specific goals. An example is the system used by the U.S. Air Force in the Gulf War. It makes five-day projections of the missions to be launched and materiel to be used in reducing the enemy's military capability over a designated geographical area. Once a plan is completed, the system refines each step to arrive at the optimal schedule. The system rejects any out-of-line approach that is not within the prescribed constraints. Box 4–4 describes a scheduling system used in the television industry.

Prediction

Predictive expert systems infer the likely outcome of a given situation and flash a proper warning and/or suggestions for corrective action. The system evaluates a set of facts or conditions and compares it by analogy to precedent states stored in memory. The knowledge base contains several patterns on which predictions are based. These systems are used in hurricane prediction, for example. They are capable of estimating damage to real estate, and they can predict the nature of the hurricane by evaluating wind force and ocean and atmospheric conditions.

Repair

Repair expert systems use preestablished remedies to correct specific problems. For example, some oil tankers now have expert systems that monitor the accuracy of their course. Using on-line satellite data, such a system corrects the tanker's path to ensure that it stays on course.

■ APPLICATION AREAS

Literally hundreds of expert systems across all major industries are operable on today's microcomputer. Space limitations prohibit more than a mere sampling of business expert systems and their functions, as shown in Table 4–2.

Box 4–4   Broadcasting Takes Advantage of Expert System Scheduling Technology

Commercial broadcasting finds its funding through advertisers who pay top dollar for optimal time spots on the air. "Optimal" time spots occur within frequent four minute commercial breaks into which as many as 50 advertisers can be scheduled in various sequences. The required scheduling is a complicated and time-consuming task, and consequently points to a natural application for expert system technology.

As recently reported by *Computerworld,* the Channel 4 television network in Cincinnati has in the past employed four staff members to accomplish the difficult task of manually sequencing the advertisement spots in a commercial break. Scheduling of advertisers is complicated by not only order of "appearance," but also the region of the United States in which they would like their advertisement to appear. Though Channel 5 broadcasts nationwide, advertisers are able to choose from one "macro-region" to a combination of several to broadcast their message. Complicating this, an advertisement broadcast in a given break in more than one region must appear at the same time in all regions selected.

Thanks to Genetic Algorithm technology, this task is now being accomplished by a Windows-based software package developed using Xpert-Rule from Attar Software Ltd. in Lancashire, England. Genetic Algorithms put together different combinations of rules and dismiss those that do not move closer to the solution to the problem. Eventually, a best-choice combination is discovered, a process which usually takes fewer than 15 seconds. This trial-and-error strategy is typically used in situations in which the problem constraints are known, but no known strategies exist. From hard constraints (absolutely necessary) to soft constraints (desirable), random combinations are put together and scored until the best combination is discovered.

The system has not only cut down on errors, but also can be managed by any staff member with business skills, and requires no specialized scheduling skills.

Source: *Knowledge Base,* Spring 1994, p. 10.

INTELLIGENT AGENTS

One of the marvels of the 1990s is a concept called *intelligent agents.* An "agent" is a cluster of precanned bits of intelligence that relates specific needs or attributes to other "agents" on a network. Although in its infancy, this distributed artificial intelligence (DAI) technology is fast becoming part of a number of commercial applications.

In general, agents form membership in a unit on a cooperative basis. Each agent contributes some knowledge, but not enough to solve the problem. Agents communicate with each other via messages on a shared blackboard. In some intelligent agent models the agents negotiate deals among themselves to ensure that the most effective agents contribute to the solution.

To illustrate the use of DAI, "Open Sesame!" is an innovative learning agent that runs on a Macintosh personal computer. This self-directed software "watches" how the user works and makes suggestions for automating tedious routine tasks. For example, if the user always empties the "trash" accumulated during the day before shutting down the Macintosh, Open Sesame! soon recognizes the pattern and begins displaying a dialog box that asks if the user would like to empty the trash. If the user responds in the affirmative, this intelligent helper does the job.

System	Developer	Business Function	Activity
AS/ASQ	Arthur Andersen	Accounts receivable	Aid auditing procedures
AUDITOR	Univ. of Illinois	Accounts receivable	Select auditing procedures for verifying organization's accounts receivable
Authorizer's Assistant	American Express	Consumer credit	Evaluate credit records to protect against credit-card fraud
Helpdesk Advisor	Publix Supermarkets	Retailing	Handle problem calls from store managers
Intelligent Secretary	Nippon T&T	Personnel	Coordinate schedules of company personnel
Mortgage Loan Analyzer	Arthur Andersen	Banking	Help loan officers make final decisions on home mortgage loans
Direct Labor Management System (DLMS)	Ford Motor Company	Manufacturing	Improve efficiency in all phases of the production process
ISIS	Westinghouse, Carnegie Mellon	Manufacturing	Schedule most-efficient use of Westinghouse's many job shops
Automatic Courseware Expert (ACE)		Retailing	Provide computer-based training to salespeople
ADCAD	Advertising Communication Approach Designer	Marketing	Assist in generating advertising copy strategy; evaluate audience, brand, and product-class characteristics to arrive at best strategy
Inspector		Banking	Monitor worldwide foreign exchange trading to identify irregular activity
Prohibited Transaction Exemption (PTE) Analyst		Law	Help attorneys evaluate transactions subject to the Employee Retirement Income Security Act (ERISA) of 1974; identify valid exemptions for prohibited transactions
Personnel Policy Expert		Personnel	Help devise employee policies and write employee handbooks; alert users to issues affecting policy creation and enforcement

Open Sesame! actually watches for events as the system is in use. It watches for the opening and closing of files, looks for patterns and routines, counts repetitions, and eventually takes over the chores. It also alerts the user of scheduled maintenance, the need to empty the trash, and so on, relying on patterns followed by the user. Once it identifies work habits, it makes suggestions.

Figure 4–4 illustrates how the interface agent behaves as a personal assistant that cooperates with the human user on the task. The user is able to bypass the agent by interacting directly with the application. One can see the interface agent learning in four different ways: observing and imitating the user's behavior, adapting based on user feedback, being trained by the user on the basis of examples, and asking for advice from other agents assisting other users. In Figure 4–5, an e-mail agent makes recommendations to the user and predicts the actions the user will perform on messages such as which messages will be read, in which order, which messages will be deleted, which will be forwarded, and so on. In Figure 4–6, the user can select some of the suggestions made by the agent and ask the agent to execute them.

Intelligent agents are not "real" agents; they do not knowingly cooperate or share in problem solutions. They must be programmed to do those things, and they "learn" only a few things. Agents are planned for many kinds of services, from spreadsheets to personal information managers. One can realistically expect agents of the future to represent users in searching databases and with real agents. They could conceivably arrange meetings, pay bills, and even wander around the virtual shopping mall, suggesting gifts, Christmas cards, and so on.

IMPLICATIONS FOR MANAGEMENT

The overall picture for expert systems shows steady growth in quantity and level of complexity of "intelligent" systems in business. If they are planned, designed, and implemented carefully, they can provide a substantial return on investment. Of course, a firm must justify the level of investment against user needs and the inevitable tradeoffs.

Expert systems have received criticism from doubters and novices. For example, some people still doubt that PROSPECTOR led workers to ore deposits 100 percent of the time. Lack of believers also led MYCIN's team to disband. Even though the claims for some systems have been overblown, the trend is strongly in favor of expert systems, when they have the support of the organization's information technology department and top management.

An issue that is now on the front burner in many organizations is whether an expert system should be centralized or distributed. To choose centralization seems to defeat the purpose of making such a system available to many users through a local area network. Yet, to distribute the system is to invite problems of system security, integrity, and maintenance. Each organization must work through this decision and determine the best approach for its needs.

As the text begins to delve into the building of expert systems, the reader needs to recognize that expert systems are not a cure-all. Certain problems are candidates for expert systems, while others are ruled out. For example, no one performs sales forecasting very well, not even professionals. Speech recognition is something that humans seem to do well, yet few experts have any idea about how people do it. Beyond management support, the most critical contributor to a successful expert system is a highly competent human expert. How to find that expert is discussed in Chapter 8.

Figure 4–4   The Role of the Intelligent Agent

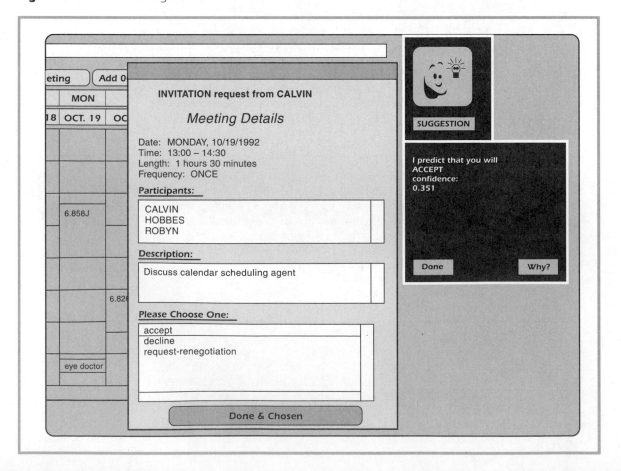

Figure 4–5   The E-Mail Agent

Figure 4–6   *Selecting Suggestions Made by the Intelligent Agent*

	File	Edit	Mbox	Msg	X-fer	Special	Agent	Window

In

•	Pattie Maes	11:11 PM	6/2/93...	1	Read	Eudora and the message assistant
•	Any User	7:08 PM	12/17/9...	1	Delete	Re: Annual ski trip
•	Pattie Maes	11:32 AM	7/10/93...	1	Read	Demos and lunch
•	A User	7:03 PM	12/15/8...	1	Delete	Re: Annual ski trip
•	Chuck "Thin Man"...	7:01 PM	12/14/9...	1	Read	Proposal for longer summer break
•	Pattie Maes	10:21 PM	7/14/93...	1	Read	Agent stuff repository
•	Chuck "Thin Man"...	7:01 PM	12/14/9...	1	Read	Longer summer break in 1994
•	Chuck "Thin Man"...	7:01 PM	12/14/9...	1	Read	Longer summer break in 1994-correction!
•	Pattie Maes	8:59 PM	7/12/93...	1	Read	Week ending 7/9
•	Some User	7:00 PM	12/14/9...	1	Delete	Annual ski trip
•	Chuck "Thin Man"...	7:01 PM	12/14/9...	1	Read	Proposal for longer summer break
•	The Dark Stranger	6:22 PM	12/22/9...	3		Re: Radio Shack mixer
•	The Dark Stranger	6:22 PM	12/22/9...	3		Re: Radio Shack mixer
•	Ian Smith	8:51 PM	12/23/9...	2	->bpm	Re: Stanton 680 cartridges

14/14K/10K

Source: *Communications of the ACM,* July 1994, pp. 33–35.

■ SUMMARY

1. Expert systems improve an organization's competitive advantage by reducing its dependence on human experts, which are expensive, hard to come by, inconsistent, and mortal.

2. Expert systems can increase productivity by reducing processing time. An expert system can train new or junior staff and retain scarce expertise. It is able to capture an expert's knowledge and store it for future reference.

3. Nonexperts can improve their decision making with the aid of an expert system. The knowledge captured by the system allows nonexperts to perform at a level closer to that of an expert. The use of an expert system can also improve an experienced person's performance.

4. Expert systems have limitations. Their knowledge does not evolve; it does not learn from the consequences of its decisions.

5. Building an expert system successfully entails avoiding several roadblocks. The necessary knowledge must be available. Experts must have the time and the motivation to divulge their knowledge. At times, more than one expert may be necessary, and the experts may disagree. The funds necessary to create the system and qualified knowledge engineers must also be available.

6. People have various perceptions of expert systems, only some of which are true. The idea that an expert system can learn from experience is wrong. Rules or knowledge must be added to the knowledge base in order for the system's expertise to evolve. Another untrue myth is that expert systems necessarily replace people. In many situations, a system is used to improve the quality/quantity of a person's work, not to replace him or her.

7. An expert system can act as a knowledge source or as a control for manipulating a system's overall behavior. It can debug by recommending corrections for a malfunction as well as diagnose by identifying causes on the bases of their symptoms. Expert systems can also be used to design, instruct, interpret, monitor, plan, predict, and repair problems in various domains.

■ TERMS TO LEARN

Control expert system manipulates operation of a system's overall behavior; intelligent automation.

Debugging expert system recommends correction or remedies for malfunction.

Design expert systems configures objects into a system based on problem constraints; develops products to specifications.

Diagnostic expert system identifies causes based on the symptoms; estimates defects.

Instruction/training expert system diagnoses and modifies learner behavior; trains; transfers information.

Interpretation expert system infers problem description from sensor (real) data; clarifies situations.

Monitoring expert system determines how close an observation is to expected outcome; compares observations to expected standards.

Planning expert system determines a course of action in advance; develops goal-oriented schemes.

Prediction expert system infers likely consequences of a given action or situation; intelligent guessing.

Repair expert system administers prescribed remedies; automatic diagnosis; plan, debug, and fix.

■ REVIEW QUESTIONS

1. Explain the main features of the "FAST Advisor" credit-analyzer expert system.

2. Discuss four benefits of expert systems. Of the benefits you list, which do you consider the most important? Why?

3. Several limitations of expert systems are discussed in the chapter. Explain these limitations in general. In what way(s) can they be critical limitations? Elaborate.

4. How might you establish that a knowledge engineer is qualified to build an expert system? Be specific.

5. "Expert systems learn from experience." Do you agree? Elaborate.

6. What factors can make experts unwilling to cooperate in building an expert system?

7. Introduce some ideas of your own for dispelling the incorrect myths surrounding expert systems.

8. Distinguish between these types of systems:

   a. diagnostic and monitoring
   b. planning and design
   c. interpretive and predictive

9. Search the expert systems publications and prepare a written report about one of the application areas discussed in the chapter.

EXERCISES AND CASES

1. Identify the category of each of these expert systems (see Table 4–1):

   a. an expert system that recommends a three-month fitness program tailored to individual needs
   b. a prototype for a consumer loan expert system that guides the user through the decision-making process for granting an automobile loan and suggests cross-selling opportunities for building a relationship with the customer
   c. an expert cardiovascular-fitness-assessment program
   d. a tax advisor for first-time home buyers
   e. an expert system that instructs inexperienced lab technicians on the sequence that must be followed for proper, efficient assessment of a specimen at a hospital's microbiology laboratory
   f. an expert system that helps a country club develop a qualified applicant pool from which it can hire the most productive and effective people as snack bar workers, lifeguards, and swim coaches
   g. an expert system that indicates to diabetic patients whether their foot problems require self-help, medical treatment, or surgery
   h. an expert system that indicates to textbook acquisitions editors whether to publish (or not to publish) a manuscript

SELECTED REFERENCES

Bernhardt, R., ed. *Integration of Robots into CIM.* London: Chapman and Hall, 1992.

Brown, M.; B. Buntschuh; and J. Wilpon. "SAM: A Perceptive Spoken-Language-Understanding Robot." *IEEE Transactions on Systems, Man, and Cybernetics,* November 1992.

Chablo, Alexander. "Potential Applications of Artificial Intelligence in Telecommunications." Technovation (TCH), September 1994, pp. 431–435.

Change, Chen-Yuan, and Chyan-Goei Chung. "A Knowledge-Based Operation Support System for Network Traffic Management." *Decision Support Systems (DSS),* January 1994, pp. 25–36.

Cona, John. "Developing a Genetic Programming System." *AI Expert,* February 1995, pp. 20ff.

Cox, Earl. "Applications of Fuzzy System Models." *AI Expert,* October 1992, pp. 34–38.

Dubois, Didier, and Jean-Luc Koning. "A Decision Engine Based on Rational Aggregation of Heuristic Knowledge." *Decision Support Systems (DSS),* May 1994, pp. 337–361.

Elofson, G. "Intelligent Agents Extend Knowledge-Based Systems Feasibility." *IBM Systems Journal* 34, (1995), no. 1.

Evans, J.; B. Krishnamurthy; and T. Skewis. "Coordinating Multiple Autonomous Robot Couriers." *Proceedings of the International Robots and Vision Automation Conference.* Robotic Industries Association, April 1993.

Gelfand, J.; M. Flax; R. Endres; S. Lane; and D. Handelman. "Senses, Skills, Reactions, and Reflexes: Learning Automatic Behaviors in Multi-Sensory Robotic Systems." In G. Bekey and K. Goldberg, eds., *Neural Networks in Robotics.* Boston: Kluwer Academic Press, 1993.

Genesereth, Michael R. "Interoperability: An Agent-Based Framework." *AI Expert,* March 1995, pp. 34–40.

Gerb, Andrew A. "The Looker: Using an Expert System to Test an Expert System." Association of Universities for Research in Astronomy for the National Aeronautics and Space Administration, December 19, 1991, pp. 1–19.

Guha, R. V., and Douglas B. Lenat. "Enabling Agents to Work Together." *Communications of the ACM (ACM),* July 1994, pp. 126–142.

Hillman, David. " AI and the Intelligent Community." *AI Expert,* August 1991, pp. 54–57.

Kazanzides, P., and B. Mittelstadt. "Surgical and Industrial Robots: Comparison and Case Study." *Proceedings of the International Robots and Vision Automation Conference.* Robotics Industries Association, April 1993.

Kirschfink, Heribert. "Knowledge-Based System for the Completion of Traffic Data." *European Journal of Operational Research (EJO),* December 10, 1993, pp. 247–256.

Koenig, Patti, and George Bekey. "AI and Locomotion: Horse Kinematics." *AI Expert,* January 1994, pp. 18–27.

Lewinson, Lisa. "Data Mining: Intelligent Technology Gets Down to Business." *PC AI,* November/December 1993, pp. 16–23.

Liberatore, Matthew J., and Anthony C. Stylianou. "Using Knowledge-Based Systems for Strategic Market Assessment." *Information and Management (IFM),* October 1994, pp. 221–232.

Lin, Mei, and Frank C. Lin. "Analysis of Financial Data Using Neural Nets." *AI Expert,* February 1993, pp. 36–40.

Liroy, Yuval, and On-Ching Yue. "Expert Maintenance Systems in Telecommunication Networks." *Journal of Intelligent and Robotic Systems* 4 (1991), pp. 303–319.

Markowitz, Judith. "Money Listens: Speech Recognition in the Financial Industry." *PC AI,* November/December 1993, pp. 28–330.

Mentzer, John T., and Nimish Ghandhi. "Expert Systems in Marketing: Guidelines for Development." *Journal of the Academy of Marketing Science,* Winter 1992, pp. 73–80.

O'Heney, Sheila. "Banks Finally Solve AI Mystery." *Computers in Banking,* August 1990, pp. 30–38.

Phythian, Gary John, and Malcolm King. "Developing an Expert Support System for Tender Enquiry Evaluation: A Case Study." *European Journal of Operational Research,* January 10, 1992, pp. 15–29.

Port, Otis. "Sure, It Can Drive, but How Is It at Changing Tires?" *Business Week,* March 2, 1992, pp. 98–99.

Raghupathi, Wullianallur, and Lawrence L. Schkade. "Legal Expert Systems Design: The Blackboard Model." *Human Systems Management (HSM)* 12, no. 2, (1993), pp. 145–158.

Rasmus, Daniel W. "Intelligent Agents: DAI Goes to Work." *PC AI,* January/February 1995, pp. 27–28ff.

Rinaldo, F. J., and Martha W. Evans. "Using Parsing and Discourse Analysis to Derive Production Rules for a Medical Expert System from Natural-Language Text." *Heuristics,* Summer 1993, pp. 14–37.

Rock, Denny, and Dan Guerin. "Applying AI to Statistical Process Control." *AI Expert,* September 1992, pp. 30–35.

Rock, Denny; Krishna Nanda Jha; and Gay Engelberger. "Talking with Rosie: Home Robot Interfaces." *AI Expert,* October 1993, pp. 20–27.

Savic, Dobrica. "Designing an Expert System for Classifying Office Documents." *Records Management Quarterly (RMQ),* July 1994, pp. 20–29.

Schnelle, Karl D., and Richard S. H. Mah. "A Real-Time Expert System for Quality Control." *IEEE Expert,* October 1992, pp. 36–37.

Simmons, Paul M., Liou and Ying-Hsin Andrew. "Artificial Intelligence Application in Medical Appointment Scheduling." *Computers and Industrial Engineering (CIE)* 21, no. 1–4, (1991), pp. 73–77.

Siriopoulos, Costas; Stavros Perantonis; and Grigoris Karakoulos. "Artificial Intelligence Models for Financial Decision Making." *Information Strategy: The Executive's Journal (IFS),* Fall 1994, pp. 49–54.

"Smart Programs Go to Work." *Business Week,* March 2, 1992, pp. 97–91.

Wild, Rosemary H., and Joseph J. Pignatiello, Jr. "Finding Stable System Designs: A Reverse Simulation Technique." *Communications of the ACM (ACM),* October 1994, pp. 87–98.

Wong, Bo K.; John K. S. Chong; and Jaesun Park. "Utilization and Benefits of Expert Systems in Manufacturing: A Study of Large American Industrial Corporations." *International Journal of Operations and Production* 14 (1994), pp. 38–49.

Woods, Donald. "Space Station Freedom: Embedding AI." *AI Expert,* April 1992, pp. 33–39.

Chapter ▪ 5

Expert System Development Life Cycle

BUILDING EXPERT SYSTEMS FROM THE GROUND UP

BUILDING BERT

The office of the Comptroller of the Currency (OCC), a bureau of the U.S. Treasury, is the regulator of the national banking system. To oversee this system of 4,400 banks, the OCC administrates 125 offices across the country, staffed by 2,500 bank examiners. These examiners range from 25-year veterans to novice assistants. To perform the agency's mission effectively and efficiently with this wide range of experience, the OCC must use state-of-the-art technology. Accordingly, we developed an expert system called Bank Expert, or BERT. BERT analyzes a bank's standard financial data, draws conclusions, and supports those conclusions with narrative comments. The OCC has used this system for the last year.

BERT's expertise was acquired through extensive interviews with six examiners over 15 months. As well as being developers, we were examiners ourselves, more like domain experts than programmers or knowledge engineers. Although this fact made some of the development easier, other parts became more difficult.

INTERVIEWING THE EXPERTS

It is a good idea to use only one expert when building an expert system, but occasionally there are justifications for using several. In our case, many recognized experts in the field were available; all examiners are expected to perform the same analysis BERT was designed for. Each of the six OCC districts provided one person who was widely recognized as an expert. Since each district is responsible for a different part of the country (each of which has unique needs and problems), this strategy helped the system to address everyone's concerns and made it easier to gain nationwide acceptance.

Once the six experts were selected, we scheduled a week-long interview with each. We went to the first interviews not really knowing what to expect. We had selected several case studies for them to analyze. Our first mistake was that the cases were too obvious. After the first interview, it was apparent that it did not take an expert to analyze our cases and reach conclusions. So, before we interviewed the other experts, we selected more complex cases that would require them to wrestle with their own decision-making process and apply true expertise.

Following that first interview, it took three months to assemble and collate our notes. We reduced the notes for an individual expert's cases to a general conclusion about how that expert worked. Finally, we combined the six methods into one set that described the experts' consensus.

Tape recording the interviews helped tremendously. First, it saved having to write everything down and allowed us to concentrate on what was said, and we were better able to probe their thought process for inconsistencies and missing pieces. Second, the transcripts allowed us to see their responses verbatim.

We conducted three more interviews. The fourth and last interview used four cases and involved visits to all six experts. This round was the sign-off (or alpha test) of the model. During this visit, the experts analyzed the cases and compared their results with the system's. After some minor modifications, the experts approved BERT as a "fair representation" of their own analyses. At this point, we were ready to present the system for final beta testing.

HOW BERT WORKS

We used *Guru* (expert system shell) to develop and distribute BERT. BERT is built in two sections. The first half is where national bank examiners input their individual mainframe access information, select a printer type, and list the banks to be analyzed. This section includes the files that control communication with the mainframe. Over 1,000 operational decisions are made by this half of the program.

The second half of the program loads and analyzes the data obtained by the first half. For each bank, BERT makes more than 2,000 decisions and reduces them to the five overall conclusions that are reported. Once the conclusions are reached, the program creates a text report and writes it to a file to be printed later.

Once a bank is analyzed and the report written to a DOS file, all variables are reset and the data tables are cleared. BERT returns to the top of the loop and begins to analyze the next bank. The loop continues until all the banks are analyzed. At the end of the program, BERT waits for the user to return. To ensure security, the user must match the password entered at the beginning of the program to have the reports printed. The entire process takes 7 to 10 minutes per bank; the longest permissible run (99 banks) can last about 12 hours. If only one bank is requested, the entire program can be completed in about twelve minutes.

Excerpted from Philip B. Osborne, and Wesley H. Zickefoose, "Building Expert Systems from the Ground Up," *AI Expert,* May 1990, pp. 28–35.

AT A GLANCE

The building of a computer-based system can be viewed as a life cycle that begins with a problem and ends in a solution or a running installation. In building expert systems, knowledge engineers work with experts to identify the problem domain and plan the development strategy and process from beginning to end. Lack of planning, structure, and order could invite disaster.

Building expert systems both differs from and is similar to building conventional systems. In terms of differences, the knowledge engineer works with the expert to acquire the expertise that provides the solution, while the systems analyst gathers information from the user who has no ready solution. Both systems undergo rigorous testing, although the approach to testing differs with each system.

The most critical phase of the expert system life cycle is identifying the problem domain. A problem domain is a good candidate for expert system application if it has certain technical, personnel, and complexity attributes. The application must also be justified, which is usually done through a feasibility study that shows the proposed system is doable, affordable, and practicable. The availability of an expert and a qualified knowledge engineer are additional requirements for a successful system.

In deciding on an expert system application, it is important to consider user support early in the decision process. User support and participation through rapid prototyping make it easier to train the user when the system is installed.

The "back end" of the expert system development life cycle begins with the representation of knowledge either by rules or frames. The choice depends on the nature of the problem and the specifications of the shell.

What You Will Learn

By the end of this chapter, you should know the following:

1. The makeup of expert system life cycle.
2. The differences and similarities between the development life cycles of a conventional information system and an expert system.
3. How rapid prototyping ensures user support.
4. The key nontechnical barriers to expert system development.

T here is nothing more difficult to plan, more doubtful of success, nor more dangerous to manage than the creation of a new system. For the initiator has the enmity of all who would profit by the preservation of the old system and merely lukewarm defenders in those who would gain by the new one.

MACHIAVELLI, 1513

■ INTRODUCTION

T he **expert system development life cycle (ESDLC)** begins with a problem. A knowledge engineer works with an organization's user to identify a problem domain and then builds an expert system accordingly. The key initial phase is acquiring knowledge from an expert, someone with proven expertise in the problem domain. Once the needed knowledge is acquired, it is represented by rules or frames, which become the system's knowledge base. The knowledge base is tested before it is made available to the user. This final test is the last step in the life cycle.

Building an expert system is challenging, exciting, and occasionally frustrating. Building an expert system involves working with the expert and the user in different ways, and both parties can test the patience of the knowledge engineer. At times, technology does not quite produce the expected results. System builders need to be prepared to handle the "lows" and the "highs" of the life cycle in order to see the system through to successful completion.

The expert system development life cycle (ESDLC) centers on three questions:

1. What is the *problem* that warrants a solution by an expert? How important is the problem? What clues indicate that the system should be built? What will the user gain from the system?

2. What *development strategy* should be considered? Who is going to build the system?

3. What *process* will be used to build the system?

These questions are interrelated and lead to other questions when the knowledge engineer gets involved in the entire system development process. This chapter focuses on the justification for expert systems and the process of building them.

The concept of "life cycle" is not new. It can be applied to virtually every endeavor, personal and business. Here are some examples:

College:	admission, education, graduation
Term paper:	introduction, body, conclusion
Air flight:	takeoff, cruising, landing
Faculty:	assistant professor, associate professor, professor
Information system development:	problem definition, analysis, design, implementation

These life cycles have some common characteristics:

- Discipline, order, or segmentation into manageable activities
- Good documentation for possible changes or modifications of the system in the future
- Coordination of the project to ensure the cycle is completed on time
- Regular management review at each phase of the cycle

Structure and order are to ESDLC what chapters and paragraphs are to a book. Can you imagine trying to read this book if the paragraphs occurred in random order? You would be exposed to the same material, but it would lack order and, therefore, meaning. In the same way, a well-defined life cycle is essential for successful development and maintenance of expert systems.

■ CONVENTIONAL VERSUS EXPERT SYSTEMS DEVELOPMENT LIFE CYCLE

Those who have developed conventional information systems in the past and are now involved in building expert systems need to see the relationship between the conventional systems approach and expert system development. This perspective extends to the role of the systems analyst versus that of knowledge engineer. This section examines these important distinctions and provides a foundation for the rest of the chapter.

Key Differences

Some striking differences distinguish conventional from expert systems development.

1. The **systems analyst** deals with data and information obtained from the user. The user is highly dependent on the analyst for the solution (a conventional information system). The knowledge engineer deals with knowledge acquired from an expert. The engineer is highly dependent on the expert for the solution (an expert system).

2. The main interface for the systems analyst is with the user, who knows the problem but not the solution. In contrast, the main interface for the knowledge engineer is the expert, who knows the problem and the solution. The expert has no counterpart in the conventional information system.

3. Conventional system development is primarily sequential; that is, particular steps are carried out in a particular order. Design cannot be initiated without analysis, testing cannot be done without a design, and so on. In contrast, ESDLC is incremental and interactive. An expert system is not built in a few large steps; rather, it evolves toward a final form. Rapid prototyping plays a major role in its evolution. The flowcharts in Figure 5–1 illustrate these differences. Note the looping back to earlier steps in expert systems development.

4. In the development of conventional information systems, testing occurs toward the end of the cycle after the system has been built. In the ESDLC, the knowledge engineer tests (verifies and validates) the evolving system from the beginning of the cycle.

5. The discipline of system development and system maintenance is much more developed for conventional information systems than it is for ESDLC. The subject of maintenance is not often addressed in the expert system literature, for example.

6. The conventional system life cycle is process-driven and *documentation-oriented,* with emphasis on the flow of the data and the resulting system. It fosters the "specify then build" approach. The ESDLC is *result-oriented.* The emphasis is on a "start slow and grow" incremental process.

7. Conventional system development does not support rapid prototyping, or advanced languages because it follows a set sequence of steps. The ESDLC utilizes rapid prototyping, incorporating changes on the spot, which augments and refines the system until it is ready for use. Thus, the prototype *evolves* into the final expert system. As shown in Figure 5–2, tasks are structured and the problem is reformulated over and over until the expert judges that it is right. This process promotes verification of the system. Verification answers the question *Is the system built right?* The final test is validation, which ensures that the system meets the user's expectations.

Key Similarities

Inasmuch as obvious differences exist between the development life cycles of conventional systems and expert systems, so, too, do certain similarities:

1. Both cycles begin with a problem and end with a solution. The problem solution is pitched with the end user in mind but is expected to benefit the organization as a whole.

2. The early phase of the conventional system life cycle begins with information gathering to ensure a clear understanding of the problem and the user's requirements. In expert systems, the early phase requires knowledge acquisition, which later becomes the foundation of the knowledge base. Both information and knowledge must be represented in order for a system to produce results.

3. Verification and validation of an expert system resembles conventional system testing. Verification ensures that the expert system is clear of errors. This is similar to alpha testing or debugging a conventional system. In contrast, expert system validation and conventional system beta (user acceptance) testing ensures that the system meets the user's requirements prior to deployment.

Figure 5–1   Comparison of the Development Life Cycles of a Conventional
Information System and an Expert System

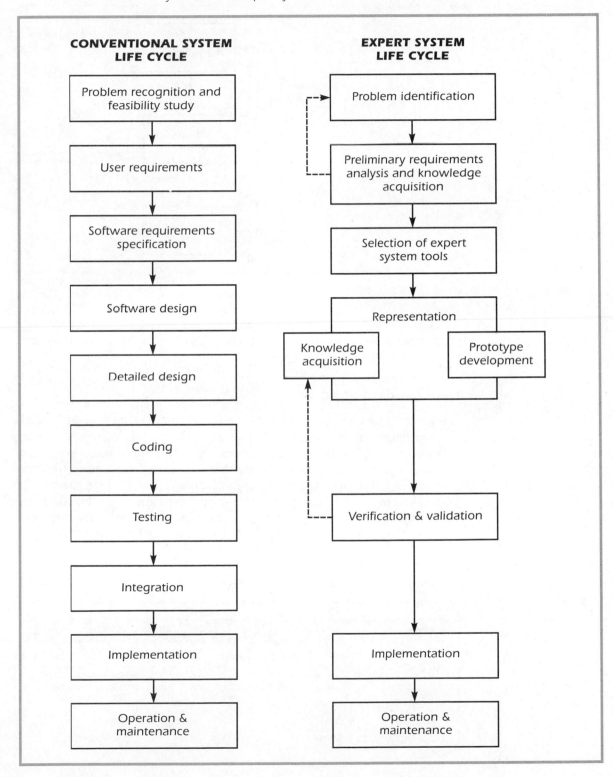

Figure 5–2 Rapid Prototyping Process

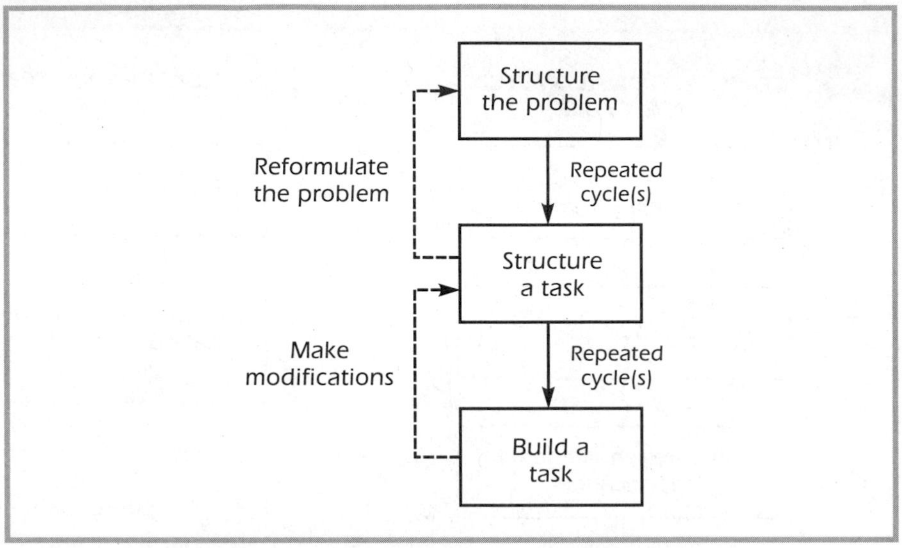

4. Both the knowledge engineer and the systems analyst need to choose the appropriate tools for designing the system. This step is important in building both information and expert systems.

User versus Expert

Users and experts also have similarities and differences. For example, in terms of cooperation, the user must work with the systems analyst by providing the information or documents needed in building a successful system. In contrast, the expert "owns" the knowledge being shared or given away. Most experts are cooperative, although no knowledge engineer should take them for granted. The main difference is that the expert does not have the same vested interest in the system that the user has; in most cases, the expert will not be the final user. Table 5–1 summarizes differences between the user and the expert.

■ **Table 5–1** Comparison of Users and Experts

Attributes	User	Expert
Dependence on the system	High	Low to nil
Cooperation	Usually cooperative	Cooperation not required
Tolerance for ambiguity	Low	High
Knowledge of problem	High	Average/low
Contribution to system	Information	Knowledge/expertise
System user	Yes	No
Availability for system builder	Readily available	Not readily available

■ THE EXPERT SYSTEM DEVELOPMENT LIFE CYCLE

Due to a lack of standardization in the field, several approaches have been suggested for building expert systems. Some approaches borrow from the conventional system development life cycle, while others prescribe steps unique to software engineering. Table 5–2 lists five representative approaches. A cursory examination of them reveals many similarities and overlaps. A proposed hybrid six-step ESDLC, an attempt to reconcile these approaches, is shown in Table 5–3.

Note that although the conventional system development and the expert system development differ in some important ways, the two approaches are fundamentally similar. While the conventional approach may still be used in developing expert systems, it is being replaced by iterative design, prototyping, early testing, and other variations for building conventional systems.

Identify the Problem Domain

The first step in building an expert system is the identification of a unique problem potentially solvable with an expert system. Sometimes such a problem is obvious. A manager with computer experience, for example, may point out a problem that cannot be addressed by a conventional information system. More and more forward-looking managers are seeking solutions to their own problems through technology. At other times, the firm hires a consultant to identify areas in its operation where expert systems might be effective. In either

■ **Table 5–2**   Alternative Approaches to the ESDLC

Step	Buchannan et al., (1983)	Bobrow et al., (1986)	Martin et al. (1988)	Oxman (1988)	Turban (1991)
1.	Identification	Identification	Requirements analysis	Initiation	Initiation
2.	Conceptualization	Conceptualization	Conceptualization	Concept	Systems analysis and design
3.	Formalization	Prototyping	Prototype	Definition and design	Rapid prototyping
4.	Implementation	Creating user interfaces	End producer	Development and implementation	System development
5.	Testing	Testing and redefinition		Operation	Implementation
6.		Maintenance			Postimplementation

Sources: B. Buchannan, D. Barstow, R. Bechtel, J. Bennett, W. Coancey, C. Kulikowski, T. Mitchell, and D. A. Waterman, "Constructing an Expert System," in F. Hayes-Roth, D. A. Waterman, and D. B. Lenat, eds., *Building Expert Systems* (Addison-Wesley, 1983); D. G. Bobrow, S. Mittal, and M. J. Steffik, "Expert Systems: Perils and Promise," *Communications of the ACM* 29, no. 9 (1986), pp. 880–894; J. Martin and S. Oxman, *Building Expert Systems* (Englewood Cliffs, N.J.: Prentice-Hall, 1988), p. 165; Steven Oxman, "Introducing the Expert System Development Methodology Road Map," *Knowledgebase,* January/February 1991, p. 3; and E. Turban, "The Process of Building Expert Systems," *Decision Line,* July 1991, pp. 9–11.

■ **Table 5–3**   Hybrid Six-Step ESDLC

ESDLC Step	Tools/Techniques
1. Problem identification and feasibility determination	Choose expert, identify technical resources, etc.
2. Knowledge acquisition (rapid prototyping)	Interviews, case studies, protocol analysis, brainstorming, etc.
3. Knowledge representation (rapid prototyping)	Production rules, predicate calculus, shells, semantic network, etc.
4. Verification and validation	Turing test, peer reviews
5. Implementation	Walkthrough
6. Maintenance	Postimplementation reviews

case, a review of the problem domains that may be candidates for expert system development is necessary.

A problem domain is a good candidate if it has certain technical, personnel, and complexity attributes that are conducive to expert system development. The availability of an expert in the problem domain must also be considered.

Application Justification

The answers to some specific questions can indicate whether an expert system is justified.

1. *Is present expertise going to be lost through retirement, transfer, or departure to other firms?* Continuing expertise becomes a problem when the expert who has been handling a highly complex problem for years suddenly decides to leave or is due to retire. Since replacing such an expert is difficult, an expert system may enable a firm to capture the reasoning process of the human expert.

This situation also applies in cases of high personnel turnover in which new staff must be brought up to speed. An expert system can function as a tutor using the captured decision-making processes of the departed expert.

2. *How much is the company spending to have present expertise solve the problem in question?* Many organizations have learned the hard way that it does not pay to have a high-priced expert work on projects that could be handled by expert systems or even conventional information systems. The cost-benefit factor is an important criterion when considering a switchover to computer-based systems.

3. *Is the proposed expert system needed in multiple locations?* If a company has only one expert to handle a particular problem at a given time, similar problems in other locations have to wait for the expert's attention. (This is why it took more than 18 months to put out the fires in Quwait's 650 oil wells after the Gulf War.) In such a case, an expert system can be used to distribute application expertise uniformly throughout a company's facilities.

4. *Is an expert available to help in building the expert system?* Without an expert, there can be no expert system. For certain complex problems, a knowledge engineer may have to work with several experts, although dealing with multiple experts presents all kinds of acquisition and validation challenges.

5. *Does the problem domain require years of experience and cognitive reasoning to solve?* One indication that a problem domain is a candidate for expert system development is its nonprocedural, nontrivial, or semantic nature. If the knowledge can be learned in a few weeks and the pattern of solution is routine, then the problem is probably not sufficiently heuristic to qualify for an expert system application.

6. *Can the expert articulate how the problem will be solved?* The ability to explain a procedure or illustrate how a problem is to be solved is not a skill everyone possesses. Often, the more of an expert a person is, the more difficulty that person has explaining a complex procedure or a solution. One of the main obstacles is explaining heuristics. In order to do this, experts must dig into their deep knowledge and verbalize stored heuristics. For the process to work, the knowledge engineer must also have good communication and interpersonal skills to elicit the expert's responses.

7. *How critical is the proposed project?* Criticality of an application has to do with how vital it is to the company's survival or productivity. A project that is considered as a reaction to a recent catastrophic failure in an area of the firm's operation deserves close evaluation.

8. *Are the tasks nonalgorithmic?* That is, are heuristics used to solve the problem? The problem domain should be considered a judgment maker rather than a calculation processor. Conventional software performs calculations on data to produce information, while expert systems take information and transform it into knowledge and practical advice. See Figure 5–3.

9. *Is a champion in the house?* For a proposed problem domain to succeed, it must be supported from within. The organization must have a **champion** who believes that expert systems can be beneficial for the company and is willing to support its development aggressively. The champion is often in a good position to coordinate the development of the system. Such a person usually has credibility with the users, understands their concerns, speaks their language, and knows the key people in the organization.

The Scope Factor

When deciding how well a problem domain qualifies for expert system, it is important to "scope" the project first. The project should be small enough for the developer's capabilities, especially if it is the organization's first expert system. It must also be completed quickly enough for the user to foresee its benefits. A complex, drawn-out project whose development takes months and years is likely to falter on the way to completion or cause the user to lose patience and interest, which makes training and successful use difficult.

The Feasibility Question

One should consider up front whether the problem can be solved using a conventional computer application. For example, if the nature of the problem is quantitative and has a procedural content, then it might *not* be a good candidate for an expert system application. The other question, of course, is feasibility. That is,

- Is the project *doable?* Can it be completed within a reasonable time?
- Is it *affordable?* Do the system's potential benefits justify the cost of development?

Figure 5–3   Calculation and Judgment Views of a Problem Domain

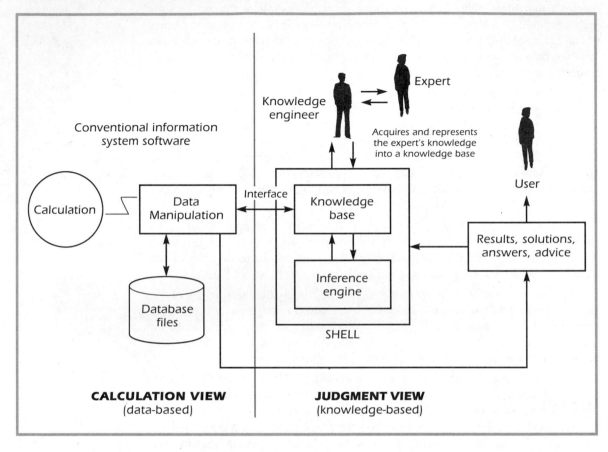

- Is it *appropriate?* Just what can the firm expect to get out of it?
- Is it *practicable?* How frequently would the system be consulted and at what cost?

These questions are best answered by a feasibility study in which the problem to be addressed is evaluated in detail and its total costs are weighed against its tangible and intangible benefits. Although a feasibility study is not considered a formal part of expert system development, identifying the problem domain and its many ramifications (economic, political, financial, and technological) is necessary front-end work. Attempting such a project makes no sense unless the heart and soul of the company is committed to the effort, especially if it is the organization's first expert system.

In summary, several factors must be considered in identifying an appropriate problem domain. Many expert system projects fail because of poor front-end evaluation. Also, without a champion or someone within the firm who can support and promote the project at all times, the project is likely to fall by the wayside.

Importance of User Support

In conventional information systems, systems analysts often build the system and then worry about selling it to the user through demonstrations and training. Such "selling" should begin early in the process. The same is true with expert systems. The user should be sold on it early in the ESDLC. At this stage of the development life cycle, a knowledge engineer needs to address a number of questions.

- Does the intended user know the new system is being developed? How is it perceived?
- How involved should the user be in the building process?
- What user training will be required?
- What operational support must be provided?

These questions prompt idea generation. They help determine whether the problem domain is doable, justifiable, and allows a move to the next step, knowledge acquisition. Without an honest "sell" to the user, all kinds of problems can arise when it is time to implement the system. Upper management should also give its blessing to the project early by allocating sufficient resources for its development.

In summary, the first step of the EDSLC is to decide what is wanted, identify the problem domain, assess feasibility, plan how to begin, locate a champion, inform users and their managers of the project, and gain their support within the scope of the problem. Above all, every expert system must begin with an expert who is ready to work with a knowledge engineer in solving the problem.

Knowledge Acquisition

In the second step in the ESDLC, the knowledge engineer taps the expert's knowledge. Knowledge acquisition involves eliciting, analyzing, and interpreting the knowledge that a human expert uses to solve a particular problem. It corresponds to systems analysis in conventional system development. In both cases, interviews with knowledgeable people are used to gather information and knowledge. Sometimes, interviewing the ultimate user of the expert system is just as important as interviewing the expert. That is, knowledge from the expert is needed to build the knowledge base, while information from the user ensures that a usable system will be built.

As mentioned earlier in the chapter, in conventional system development, the systems analyst gathers *information from the user* or the user's staff to define the problem and determine alternative solutions and their consequences. In expert system development, the knowledge engineer acquires heuristic *knowledge from the expert* in order to build the knowledge base that emulates the expert's thought process. This delineates the distinction between information and knowledge, on one hand, and between the user and the expert, on the other. The user has more to gain from the expert system than does the expert who is building it. The expert hands over years of knowledge for a system that someone else will use. The benefits are not the same, which explains some experts' lack of cooperation and motivation throughout the system development life cycle.

Knowledge acquisition plays a unique role in various phases of the ESDLC. As shown in Table 5–4, knowledge acquisition deals with determining feasibility, choosing the expert, tapping the expert's knowledge, retapping knowledge to plug gaps in the system and for verification and validation of the rules, and correcting or updating the knowledge base after the system is in operation. Thus, in ESDLC, knowledge acquisition is an evolving step, not a one-time, front-end step as it is in systems analysis.

■ **Table 5−4**   Knowledge Acquisition Activities in the ESDLC

ESDLC Step	Knowledge Acquisition Activity
1. Problem identification and feasibility determination	■ Seek out a champion ■ Locate a cooperative domain expert
2. Knowledge acquisition	■ Apply appropriate tools to tap the expert's knowledge
3. Knowledge representation	■ Represent the expert's heuristics via prototyping ■ Verify the rules with the expert
4. Verification/validation	■ Correct existing rules and add missing rules by working closely with the expert through rapid prototyping
5. Implementation	■ Work with the user to ensure system acceptance and proper training
6. Maintenance	■ Meet with the expert and the user to determine procedures and content with maintaining and updating the system

Role of Rapid Prototyping

Most expert systems are built using an *iterative* approach, or a series of repeated actions. For example, the knowledge engineer starts with a small-scale system, a *prototype,* based on the limited knowledge acquired from the expert during the first few sessions. What turns the approach into rapid prototyping is the following:

■ The knowledge engineer shows the expert a 30-rule prototype based on rudimentary knowledge acquired from the expert during the past two sessions.

■ The expert reacts by saying, "This is all right, but there's more to it. Let me tell you what you need to incorporate into this prototype. . . ."

■ While the expert watches, the knowledge engineer enters the rules that represent the additional knowledge the expert wants to include.

■ The knowledge engineer reruns the prototype and continues entering additional rules or making modifications as suggested by the expert until the expert says, "This is about right. I think you've got it this time."

This spontaneous, on-the-spot, iterative building of an expert system is referred to as **rapid prototyping.** The process continues through several sessions and weeks of work until the system moves out of the prototype stage and becomes a full-fledged system ready for use. Rapid prototyping is essential for large systems, as the cost of a poorly structured system that is unusable can be prohibitive. Other benefits of rapid prototyping include:

■ It documents for the expert and others that progress is being made on the project.

- Mistakes can be quickly corrected.
- The system is tested each time a new rule or modification is incorporated.
- It yields a tangible product at an early stage.
- The system "grows" in step with increasing understanding of what the user requires and how the expert will provide it.
- It promotes accelerated knowledge acquisition.
- It demonstrates the capabilities of the inference engine and the growing knowledge base.

The "smash and grab" approach—in which the knowledge engineer "grabs" the attention of the domain expert for a few hours over a few sessions and ends up with a "workable" expert system—is not recommended. Remember that expert systems are based on heuristics and knowledge, not on quantitative or syntactic data. Rapid prototyping fosters maturation and "value-added" activities. It requires patience, concentration, and knowing how to make changes on the fly without errors.

Selecting an Expert

In expressing their differing views about the nature of expertise, some argue that the entire breadth of human expertise must be studied before attempting to acquire the knowledge necessary to build an expert system. Others support a narrower focus that limits the role of the expert to knowledge acquisition activities. In either case, the goal is an expert system that represents the expertise, rather than the expert.

In working with the expert, the knowledge engineer will occasionally run into vague expressions of thought or reasoning processes that must either be clarified by the expert or factored into the system somehow. For example, "fuzzy" expressions can be assigned certainty factors to reflect the extent of "fuzziness"of the expression. Certainty factors require careful analysis to assure proper representation in the knowledge base. In fact, much of the knowledge that the expert provides is based on heuristics, which tend to be qualitative, rather than quantitative.

Finally, a competent and cooperative expert is essential to the success of knowledge acquisition. The expert must be able to communicate information understandably and in sufficient detail. The questions that face every expert systems project are:

- How can one know that the so-called expert is in fact an expert?
- Will the expert stay with the project to the end?
- What backup is available in case the expert loses interest, decides to leave, or simply is no longer available?
- How is the knowledge engineer to know what is and what is not within the expert's area of expertise?

Sometimes, either because of the problem's complexity or the project's importance to the organization, more than one expert should be involved in building the expert system. Dealing with multiple experts is not an easy task. The knowledge engineer may have to use different tools in different ways to access the experts' knowledge and promote agreement among them before the acquired knowledge becomes part of the knowledge base. Dealing with single and multiple experts is discussed later in Chapter 8.

Role of the Knowledge Engineer

The knowledge engineer is an important player in the ESDLC. As explained in detail in Chapter 6, he or she is the *architect* of the system. This one person identifies the problem domain, acquires the knowledge, writes and tests the rules that represent that knowledge, and coordinates the entire project from beginning to end.

Such a pivotal job requires certain qualifications. The most important attributes are excellent communication skills, an understanding of knowledge acquisition tools, familiarity with an AI language and shells, programming experience, tolerance for ambiguity, ability to work well with other professionals including domain experts, and a personality that motivates people to work together as a team. Many of these qualifications overlap with those possessed by systems analysts, which suggests that systems analysts may be good candidates for knowledge engineering.

The knowledge engineer's job requires interaction with a number of individuals throughout the ESDLC. The most frequent interactions, shown in Figure 5–4, are with the domain expert, the user, and most likely, the champion. Each person can make or break the project.

Knowledge Representation

Once knowledge has been acquired, the next step is **knowledge representation,** coding the knowledge in such a way that an inferencing program will be able to use stored knowledge whenever needed to draw conclusions. **Knowledge analysis tools** such as semantic networks, scripts, decision trees, and decision tables are used during the initial information gathering. These tools have one thing in common; they hierarchically map out the facts and their interrelationships. A **semantic network,** for example, is a collection of nodes linked together to form a net. Figure 5–5 illustrates the key nodes that represent Jim Harding's knowledge.

Figure 5–4 The Central Role of the Knowledge Engineer

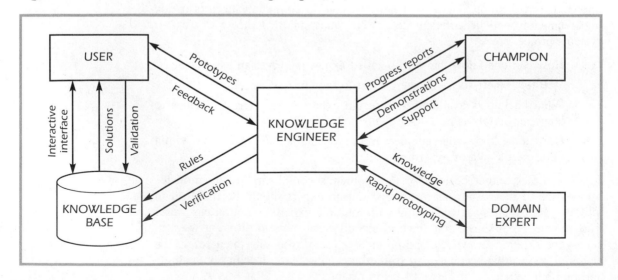

Figure 5–5 Semantic Network in a Personnel Knowledge Base

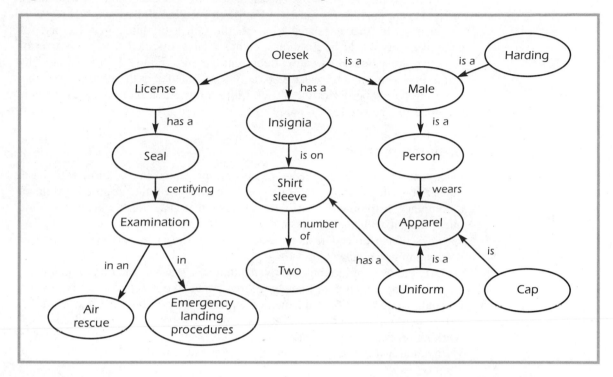

The actual working code of a knowledge-based system is represented by either rules or frames. A **rule** is a natural-language conditional statement that specifies an action to be taken if a certain condition exists. Such statements are often called *premise–conclusion* (or *situation–action*) *rules* and are have either an "IF ... THEN" or an "IF ... THEN ... ELSE" format. Each rule is independent and is based on a heuristic rather than an algorithm. An example of a rule is

IF the clouds are black and wind speed is greater than 35 mph and wave height is greater than 18 feet

THEN the classification of the storm is likely (.8) a hurricane.

A knowledge base built on rules is called a **rule-based system.** The introduction of shells has made building these systems easier. The inference engine that fires (executes) the rules removes many programming headaches. Shells perform important functions.

- Controlling which rules are fired (executed) when a new fact is introduced into the knowledge base.
- Attaching certainty (confidence) factors to rules that allow users to perform their own interpretation of how to respond to different suggestions.
- Ordering the sequence in which rules are fired. Prioritization of rules provides a certain amount of procedural control over how the rules are used.

Frames, like rules, carry knowledge. They associate objects with facts, rules, or values. A frame consists of attributes, called **slots.** Each fact or value stored in a slot that is related to a specific object or thing. In a factory, for example, slots would be machines, cranes, conveyors, and so on. So a set of slots and their associated entries represent a frame. Figure 5–6 illustrates the frame of a personnel knowledge base. Olesek's letter is the object. The slots represent the properties of the object. More information on rules and frames is provided in Chapter 13.

Implementation

Once the appropriate knowledge has been represented in the knowledge base, the next task of the knowledge engineer is to implement the proposed system on a computer. **Implementation** is the process of organizing the knowledge and integrating it with the processing strategy (inference engine) for testing. The specifics of the procedure are dictated by the chosen expert system shell or programming language.

Another way of looking at implementation is that it is the transformation of a precise representation of knowledge into a machine-executable equivalent—a computer program. The implemented expert system is only a "first draft." It will undergo a number of modifications before it becomes a "good enough," working expert system. These subsequent versions are modified through verification and validation, which are the next step in the ESDLC.

Verification and Validation

Verification and validation of an expert system are tantamount to the testing step in building a conventional information system. **Verification** consists of putting the expert system through a procedure to ensure that the *system is right*—that the programs do what they are designed to do. The internal make up of the system is checked to see that rules fire when they are supposed to fire. In this way, the technical performance of the system is evaluated.

Validation involves testing the system to ensure it is the *right system*—that it meets the expert's expectations. Validation provides assurance that the solutions or advice derived from the knowledge base come close enough to those of the human expert. In other words, the validation process checks reliability of the expert system.

Figure 5–6 A Frame Representing Olesek's Letter

Object: *Letter*

Slot	Entry
Instructor	Olesek
Verification	Letter
Nature of verification	Seal
Certification	Air rescue
Certification	Emergency landing procedures

Validation of expert systems is not foolproof yet. System validation is a long-term item: human experts must monitor system performance continually. But eventually, systems will be built that should be able to renew their certification and vouch for their own reliability.

Maintenance

The final stage in ESDLC is **maintenance,** which ensures that the system continues to function according to the initial standards of performance. One element of this stage is preserving and modifying the knowledge stored in the system. Someone needs to take charge of this vital function and make sure it is done right.

Expert systems must be upgraded to expand or improve the quality of the advice they give. Just as humans gain experience and thereby improve the accuracy and usefulness of their advice, so does an expert system when its knowledge base is enhanced. Therefore, periodic evaluation and upgrade are essential. A system that does not respond to changes in the problem domain will soon be obsolete.

■ BARRIERS TO EXPERT SYSTEM DEVELOPMENT

Experience shows that few systems make it through the life cycle without a glitch. Bottlenecks, constraints, and all kinds of conditions must be met before some systems can finally be used. Many texts and papers have addressed the potential benefits and limitations of expert systems, but few have addressed the prospective barriers to development of a successful expert system. Most of these barriers are nontechnical. The four main sources of barriers are top management, the knowledge engineer, the domain expert, and the user.

Top Management

Earlier, the chapter mentioned the importance of having a "champion"—a supporter within the firm who has the clout and visibility to sell the proposed system to the user and top management and to provide ongoing support. Top management can make or break the system. First, it must provide the funding, which many top executives mistakenly believe is all they need to do. Financial support is a necessary but not sufficient condition for building a successful expert system.

Beyond financial support, management's continuing interest in the project and motivation is essential, especially in an organization that desires change. Acting in ways that reduce resistance to change can also be important. Support from top management varies depending on the size of the organization and the potential contribution of the expert system to its profitability.

The Knowledge Engineer

Another possible barrier to successful development is the knowledge engineer. Most of today's knowledge engineers are well versed in the technology of expert systems but have limited experience in communicating, personal relations, or building business-related expert systems. The result is that they often shortchange the interview process or fail to tap the expert's deep knowledge. Knowledge engineers with limited experience have special difficulty handling views of multiple experts. As a result, errors are made that affect the integrity of the system.

The Domain Expert

Typically, organizations' best experts can least afford long, drawn-out sessions away from their usual responsibilities. Even if they are released to the project, many experts have difficulty enunciating the kinds of details that enable the knowledge engineer to tap the knowledge needed for the system. In addition to experts' availability and communication skills, their motivation, cooperation, and level of fatigue impact the building of a successful expert system.

In terms of cooperation, their human nature often causes experts to be concerned about the potential of the expert system to replace their jobs. Because of this, top management needs to assure them of job stability and reward them for cooperation. The joint effort of management, the champion, the expert, and the knowledge engineer is necessary to form a viable team that can create an effective system, be it a conventional information system or an expert system.

■ **Table 5–5**   Barriers to Successful Expert System Development and Suggested Solutions

Barrier	Possible Solution
Top Management	
Provides financial support only	■ Encourage management to become more closely involved in the technology
Has limited experience in the technology	■ Provide psychological support
Lack of long-range planning	■ Ensure long-range planning
Knowledge Engineer	
Heavy on technical knowledge, but poor communication and interpersonal skills	■ Promote training in interviewing and communication skills Take a course in cognitive psychology
The Domain Expert	
Not available	■ Relieve expert of some regular duties
Lacks motivation	■ Promote an attractive reward system
Difficult to work with	■ Understand the expert's idiosyncracies
The User	
Computer illiterate	■ Expose user to computer basics and features
Resistance to change	■ Involve user in various phases of the ESDLC
Perceived threat of the proposed system	■ Reinforce the system's benefits

The User

Many users do not warm up to technology in general or new technology such as expert systems. Lack of knowledge or experience in the use and impact of expert system has triggered a reluctance to use technology that is supposed to emulate the human thinking of seasoned experts.

One group of users that had not been involved in the process was under administrative pressure to use a new expert system in their daily work. One user commented, "Once you lean on technology that replaces experts, you lose the deep trust that you once had consulting the human expert. That is why this expert system bit won't work in our department." The conclusion here is that, for an expert system to work, human and human relations factors must be nurtured from the beginning of the ESDLC. Table 5–5 summarizes the barriers discussed in this section and makes some recommendations for overcoming them.

IMPLICATIONS FOR MANAGEMENT

Assuming the technology is available and ready to use, several managerial factors should be considered:

- An organization considering expert systems as part of its information systems environment must make a commitment to user education and training prior to building an expert system.

- Top management should be approached with facts about the costs and benefits of the proposed expert system. Being sold on the project means assurance of financial and technical support.

- If an expert system is anywhere on the organization's horizon, human resources or the MIS departments should begin training systems analysts and others who have the potential to do knowledge engineering.

- Domain experts must be recognized and rewarded in ways that make them feel it is worth their time to cooperate. Assigning an expert to the project without such rewards can jeopardize the whole process.

- Finally, for an organization to anticipate its future technology needs, it is extremely important to do long-range strategic planning. Such planning can help the firm to attain its desired outcomes. Introducing leading-edge technology such as expert systems can help the organization to achieve competitive advantage.

■ SUMMARY

1. Building an expert system can be viewed as a life cycle. The life cycle begins when a project is determined to be doable, affordable, and practicable. Knowledge engineers interview users to identify a problem and work with an expert to develop a system for solving it. Discipline, good documentation, coordination, and regular management review characterize any system life cycle.

2. Conventional and expert systems' development life cycles differ.

   a. A systems analyst deals with data and information obtained from the user, while the knowledge engineer deals with knowledge acquired from the expert.

   b. The main interface for the systems analyst is with the user, who knows the problem but not the solution. The main interface with the knowledge engineer is an expert, who knows the problem and the solution.

   c. Conventional system development is primarily sequential; ESDLC is incremental and interactive.

   d. Testing is done at the end of conventional information system development; verification and validation are performed throughout the development of the expert system.

3. Conventional and expert systems' development life cycles are also similar.

   a. Both begin with a problem and end with a solution.

   b. Both begin with information gathering to ensure a clear understanding of the user's requirement or the problem at hand.

   c. Both involve testing the system.

   d. Particular development tools are used to build each system.

4. The first step in building an expert system is identifying the problem domain, which is followed by a feasibility study for evaluating the problem in detail. This includes weighing the total costs against against the potential tangible and intangible benefits. Early scoping is important. The project should be of a manageable size, and the user should be able to foresee its benefits.

5. Knowledge acquisition involves elicitation, analysis, and interpretation of the knowledge that a human expert uses to solve a particular problem.

6. Most expert systems begin as small-scale prototypes based on the limited knowledge acquired during the first few sessions with the expert. The system grows gradually as the knowledge engineer gains new insights from the expert and adds them to the prototype.

7. Expert system knowledge is represented in such a way that an inferencing program will be able to use it and draw conclusions based on it.

8. A knowledge base is built using rules or frames. A rule is a conditional statement; it specifies an action to be taken if a certain condition is true. Such statements are often called *premise–conclusion* or *situation–action* rules. Frames associate objects with facts, rules, or values. They consist of attributes called *slots*. Each fact or value is stored in a slot that is related to a specific object or thing.

9. System implementation is the process of organizing the knowledge and integrating it with the testing strategy of verification and validation. The final stage of ESDLC is maintenance, which ensures that the system continues to function according to the initial standards of performance. A system must be modified and/or updated as new knowledge is acquired.

10. Most barriers to the development of an expert system are nontechnical. Lack of support from top management, knowledge engineers' limited interpersonal skills, experts' poor communications skills, and users' resistance are all barriers to development of successful systems.

■ TERMS TO LEARN

Champion individual within the organization who believes the project will benefit the company and is willing to take risks in supporting its development; has credibility with both management and users and has access to key persons.

Expert system development life cycle (ESDLC) the steps through which an expert system project goes through before it becomes operational.

Frame a structure for organizing knowledge; consists of attributes that carry knowledge by associating objects with facts, rules, or values.

Implementation stage three of the expert system development life cycle; the process of organizing the knowledge and integrating it with the processing strategy (inference engine) for testing.

Knowledge analysis tools tools such as semantic networks, scripts, and decision trees that are used in knowledge acquisition during initial knowledge gathering

Knowledge representation facts or rules represented in a knowledge base; representing the knowledge in such a way that an inferencing program will be able to use it to draw conclusions in a given problem domain.

Maintenance making necessary corrections so that the expert system continues to meet the intial system requirements.

Rapid prototyping spontaneous, on-the-spot, iterative approach to building expert systems; an iterative process by which the knowledge engineer shows the domain expert what the expert system looks like based on the knowledge captured to date.

Semantic networks or nets collections of nodes linked together to form a net; graphical method of representing descriptive or declarative knowledge.

Slot a specific object being described or an attribute of an entity; stores each fact or value related to a specific object; represents the properties of the object.

Systems analyst a specialist who gathers information from the user or the user's staff in order to define a problem and determine alternative solutions and their consequences within conventional information system development.

Validation a system test to ensure the right system; a system that meets the expert's expectations; black-box testing; beta test or user acceptance test.

Verification a system test to ensure the proper functioning of the system; addresses the intrinsic properties of the expert system; white-box testing; alpha test.

■ REVIEW QUESTIONS

1. Why is it helpful to view the building of an expert system as a life cycle? Explain.

2. In what ways do conventional and expert systems' development life cycles differ? How are they similar? Elaborate.

3. In what ways is the ESDLC incremental and interactive?

4. Distinguish between:
   a. verification and validation
   b. rule and frame
   c. knowledge engineering and systems analysis

5. "Conventional system development is process-driven and documentation-oriented." Do you agree? Explain.

6. How do users differ from experts? Be specific.

7. Of the steps making up the ESDLC, which one do you consider the most critical? Why? Which would be the most time-consuming?

8. What is rapid prototyping? How is it useful in building expert systems?

9. How would one know that an expert system is justified? Explain.

10. Elaborate on the steps of a feasibility study. When should one be conducted?

11. In what way(s) is user support important? Be specific.

12. What does it mean to "scope" a project? Give an example.

13. How does knowledge acquisition correspond to systems analysis?

14. What is your understanding of an expert? How would you select one?

15. Write an essay in which you describe the role of the knowledge engineer and his or her relationship with the key persons in the acquisition process.

16. How can the knowledge engineer and the expert each be a barrier to the building of an expert system? Explain.

■ EXERCISES AND CASES

1. The Publisher Advisor expert system represents the acquisitions editor's decision-making process when reviewing a manuscript proposal for adoption. A manuscript proposal typically consists of a detailed outline of the topic, table of contents, justification for the book, and a set of sample chapters. Sometimes, the manuscript is written and ready for production. In that case, the acquisitions editor sends the manuscript to a number of reviewers who are experts in the field. Their opinions carry considerable weight in the editor's decision to publish or not to publish the book.

The expert is an acquisitions editor who has many years' experience with West Publishing Company. There are three possible outcomes that Publisher Advisor should provide: (1) offer a contract (publish the book), (2) request that the author do additional work on the manuscript before making a publication decision, and (3) reject the manuscript.

In advising on the final decision, the expert system considers several factors: marketability of the proposed book (demand for the topic), reputation of the author (past publishing record), royalty requirements of the author, opinions of the reviewers, cost of publishing the book, author's ability to meet deadlines, the author's rank, and the reputation of the school with which the author is affiliated.

Instructions

You have been assigned to build this system. Identify the life cycle you'll go through to build the system. Be specific about how you will get started. This project will reappear as focus in illustrating different aspects of expert systems' development throughout the remainder of the book.

2. The goal of this project is to develop a consumer-lending expert system to guide the user through the decision for making an automobile loan. The system asks the user a series of questions that can vary depending on the customer's situation. This includes the customer's financial and employment record, past loan record, and the price of the automobile. The system then provides a decision based on the answers to these questions, using the bank's lending experience. The rules are based partly on policies set by the organization and partly on common lending practices.

Instructions

You have been assigned the task of building the automobile loan advisor for the bank. Explain in detail the life cycle of this project.

3. The Hiring Advisor is an expert system created to help Crozet Country Club develop a qualified candidate pool from the many job applications they receive. The Hiring Advisor also suggests the wage each applicant should receive, based on his or her age and relevant experience.

The three positions addressed are (1) snack bar attendant, (2) lifeguard, and (3) swim coach. The system encodes the knowledge of the expert into rules that are used to perform the task as well as or better than the person responsible for the hiring decisions. The system was developed using VP-Expert shell. The club's human resources manager played an instrumental role throughout the knowledge acquisition process. She was familiar with the organization, since she had worked there for more than ten years, with one of her major tasks being to keep these three areas staffed.

The knowledge acquisition process helped achieve a coherent understanding of how the manager decides if an applicant is qualified to work in the three areas. The resulting system prompts the user to input information about each applicant on seven variables:

- area applied for
- years of relevant experience
- lifeguard certification
- coaching certification
- age
- requested wage
- time availability

Once the information has been entered, the system advises the manager on whether the particular applicant is qualified and should be considered. If the applicant is qualified, the Hiring Advisor also suggests an appropriate wage. Furthermore, the system refers the applicant to another area if his or her skills match those required in that area.

Although the Hiring Advisor was a tremendous success, a number of constraints affected its overall effectiveness. One was time constraints. The system had to be developed and implemented within eight weeks, which made the knowledge acquisition phase very short. Also, VP-Expert has some restrictions that limited the project. For example, decision-variable statements are limited to 40 characters.

Questions

a. From what you've read, what is your evaluation of the knowledge engineer's performance? What is missing (if anything) from the life cycle?

b. What is the problem domain? In your opinion, how good a "candidate" is the problem domain? Explain.

c. Do you believe the system was developed by one, or by more than one knowledge engineer? What indicates this?

4. Crozet Country Club's use of Hiring Advisor can be justified on a number of fronts. The system captures the human resources manager's knowledge of how she makes her hiring decisions. If she leaves the club, the system will help to ensure that her expertise and know-how are not lost.

The Hiring Advisor saves the club time and money by making accurate decisions more rapidly. Since the club receives a large number of applications to fill a relatively small number of positions, efficient applicant-evaluation is of critical importance. However, handling and sorting through the plethora of applications was formerly time-consuming and haphazard. This system reduces the time taken to fill vacant positions. More importantly, it helps to ensure that employees have the necessary qualifications.

The Hiring Advisor promotes a higher level of consistency and quality in hiring decisions. Prior to implementing the Hiring Advisor, the manager did not have a "wage matrix" to use in determining appropriate wages for employees, and the process was quite random. This led to some conflict within the organization. Furthermore, the manager hired some applicants without focusing enough on their ability, and they turned out to be poor employees. In essence, the Hiring Advisor helps guarantee that all of the necessary variables are fully considered in each decision.

Questions

a. Is this sufficient justification for the Hiring Advisor? Elaborate.

b. Is the system likely to replace the human resources manager? Explain.

■ SELECTED REFERENCES

Alpar, Paul. "Toward Structured Expert Systems Development." *Expert Systems with Applications,* 1 (1990), pp. 63–70.

Arthur, Lowell Jay. "Quick and Dirty." *Computerworld (COW),* December 14, 1992, pp. 109–112.

Ashley, Steven. "Prototyping with Advanced Tools." *Mechanical Engineering (MEG),* June 1994, pp. 48–55.

Bray, Michael A. "Lessons Learned in Developing an Expert System Group." *IEEE,* 1990, pp. 151–155.

Dickens, P. M. "Rapid Prototyping: The Ultimate in Automation?" *Assembly Automation (AAU)* 14, no. 2 (1994), pp. 10–13.

Fox, Steven G. "A Life-Cycle Software Development Effort Estimation Methodology." University of Virginia, Master's degree thesis, 1992.

Griffiths, Mark. "Rapid Prototyping Options Shrink Development Costs." *Modern Plastics (MPT),* September 1993, pp. 45, 47.

Martin, James, and Steven Oxman. *Building Expert Systems.* Englewood Cliffs, NJ: Prentice-Hall, 1990, pp. 163–196.

Medsker, Larry, and Jay Liebowitz. *Design and Development of Expert Systems and Neural Networks.* New York: MacMillan, 1994, pp. 69–78.

Mockler, Robert J., and D. G. Dologite. *Knowledge-Based Systems: An Introduction to Expert Systems.* New York: MacMillan, 1992, pp. 44–98.

Osborn, Philip B. "Building Expert Systems from the Ground Up." *AI Expert,* May 1990, pp. 28–35.

Oxman, Steven. "Introducing the Expert System Development Methodology Road Map." *Knowledgebase,* January/February 1991, pp. 3ff.

Partridge, Derek, and K. M. Hussain. *Artificial Intelligence and Business Management.* Norwood, NJ: Ablex, 1992, pp. 163–180.

Payne, Edmund C., and Robert C. McArthur. *Developing Expert Systems.* New York: John Wiley & Sons, 1990, pp. 21–41.

Rasmus, Dan. "Developing Diagnostic Expert Systems." *Manufacturing Systems,* October 1992, pp. 58–66.

Studt, Tim. "Rapid Prototyping Key to Fast Development." *R&D (RDV),* May 1994, pp. 55–56.

Turban, Efraim. *Expert Systems and Applied Artificial Intelligence.* New York: MacMillan, 1992, pp. 401–452.

_____. "The Process of Building Expert Systems." *Decision Line,* July 1991, pp. 9–11.

Wohlers, Terry. "Cashing In on Rapid Prototyping." *CAE (CAE),* September 1993, pp. 28–33.

PART · II

KNOWLEDGE ACQUISITION

Chapter ■ 6

The Knowledge Engineer

THE RIGHT STUFF

A knowledge engineer plays a role that calls for a special mix of skills and abilities. That person must know enough about expert systems and the problem domain to ask the right questions, and at the same time be able to listen to what the expert is saying before determining the rules that eventually make up the knowledge base. Choosing an expert with time and talent is a great challenge.

For the knowledge engineer, nontechnical skills are unquestionably more important than facility with computers or shells. Karl Wiig, an authority in knowledge management, once said that anthropologists and people with experience studying alien cultures, especially in their own language, tend to make good knowledge engineers.

Professor Randall Davis of MIT has found that knowledge of physics is useful in the field. Davis said, "There is a certain reductionist frame of mind that is found in someone who has been taught physics. . . . It is a sense that says; 'This study is comprehensible. I can make sense of it and I can give a rational account of my reasons.'"

Psychologists also make good knowledge engineers because of their experience in figuring out how people think. Philosophers are also good, because they can easily analyze a line of argument. So do systems analysts who have problem-structuring skills.

Other professionals make good knowledge engineers. Consultants, for example, are used to stepping into ill-structured situations, evaluating them, and then making recommendations.

Knowledge engineering involves more than problem-solving and analyzing, however. Interpersonal skills are critical. Handling "the sociology of the [knowledge-acquisition] process is a big issue," points out Paul Johnson of the University of Minnesota. Knowledge engineers must have "the ability to work with experts" who may be reluctant to cooperate because of all kinds of fears.

Even when the expert and knowledge engineer are highly qualified, their meetings may often be challenging, even strained. The knowledge engineer must "handle the sociology" in such cases in order to capture the expert's knowledge and complete the job.

AT A GLANCE

This chapter focuses on the knowledge and skills requirements and the personality attributes of the knowledge engineer. The person and the job are a combination of behavioral, procedural, and technical interrelationships. Knowledge engineers' attributes and skills are similar to those of systems analysts. A key difference is that the knowledge engineer works with heuristics gathered from experts, while the systems analyst deals with data and information gathered from users. Both systems address problem solving, although the problems expert systems address are difficult problems that require expertise for solving.

Training knowledge engineers is neither easy nor readily available. In some firms, potential users were given shells and told to build their own expert systems at their own pace. In other firms, formal training is provided to ease or quicken the pace of learning before building such systems. In either case, shells and shell programming have become popular means of building expert systems. Actual programming using LISP, for example, is still necessary in medical and scientific applications, which requires a strong background in computer science and aptitude in programming.

What You Will Learn

By the end of this chapter, you should know the following:

1. The differences between the roles of knowledge engineers and systems analysts.
2. The knowledge and skills requirements and the academic qualifications of the knowledge engineer.
3. The makeup of the typical expert system development team.

I have been working as a knowledge engineer for a software house for two years. Each project is different. The job is challenging and requires creative thinking and strong communication skills. I started as junior knowledge engineer at a salary of $30,500. I am now a lead engineer with a salary of $40,700 plus a nice annual bonus.

CHRISTINE MELEKIAN

■ INTRODUCTION

Which person is more critical to the success of an expert system: the domain expert who has the knowledge, or the knowledge engineer whose skills tap such knowledge? They are equally important, but for different reasons. Building a successful expert system requires the right expertise and a skilled person to capture it. This person is the system developer, or the knowledge engineer. The knowledge engineer's work is to model the *expertise* of the domain expert, rather than the expert.

The knowledge engineer is typically a well-rounded, versatile professional who possesses technical skills as well as interpersonal, communication, and organizational skills. He or she identifies the expert's know-how through a variety of techniques and make that know-how operational on a computer. This chapter examines the role of the knowledge engineer and describes the type of person that best performs the role.

Just a few years ago, knowledge engineering was a relatively unknown activity. A number of successful expert systems in medicine and industry proved that the technology can pay high dividends. As builders of expert systems, knowledge engineers saw their "stock" shoot sky high. Today, they are among the most heavily recruited and best-paid specialists in the computer industry. They come from diverse fields such as psychology and computer science, and bridge two disciplines: human engineering and the sciences.

The technology of expert systems has yet to reach the point where the knowledge engineer's job is taken over by some automated code generator. Knowledge engineers will be important until users can build the best expert system without much skill or experience—an event not likely to occur any time soon. What limits the advancement of expert systems technology is not so much the ability of corporations to spend money on it as it is a shortage of qualified knowledge engineers. One recent study indicated that 6,700 skilled knowledge engineers are currently working worldwide. However, some predict that the United States alone will need at least *14,000 additional* knowledge engineers by the year 2005.

This chapter looks at the knowledge engineer (KE) as more than a talented programmer or a person who does a super job interviewing experts. A good knowledge engineer can do both of these things well and has developed these skills through training, intuition, and years of experience.

THE KNOWLEDGE ENGINEER VERSUS THE SYSTEMS ANALYST

Today, one rarely finds a new computer-related job totally detached from other jobs in the information system industry. For instance, although the knowledge engineer deals with knowledge and knowledge bases, the job requires many of the same personality attributes as that of the systems analyst. Not surprisingly, a 1992 survey by the author found that knowledge engineer positions are filled by experienced systems analysts in many firms.

Job Functions

To build an expert system, a knowledge engineer must do more than write a program that emulates a particular expert. The system must reproduce the best *performance* of the expert. Even the best experts are never perfect; they cannot give their knowledge in a tidy package. The knowledge engineer performs several functions in reproducing the expert's knowledge. The key functions and how they are related to the systems analyst are shown here.

1. *Identify potential expert system applications.* A survey of the members of the American Association of Artificial Intelligence indicated that knowledge engineers participate more in goal-setting than do systems analysts. One reason for this greater involvement is that upper management is less familiar with artificial intelligence than with other areas of information technology. Once a problem domain has been identified, the knowledge engineer sets project objectives and clearly defines the scope and feasibility of the expert system that can address it.

2. *Develop project proposals.* The knowledge engineer formulates ideas into concrete project proposals (something a systems analyst also does). To do this, the knowledge engineer identifies the issues and then sells the system's benefits to management.

3. *Develop project work plans, assign work, monitor/report progress.* Since most project teams include only a knowledge engineer and a domain expert, the knowledge engineer's effort required to perform this step should be much less than it is for the systems analyst. Some conventional information systems development teams employ as many as twelve people, depending on the nature and complexity of the application.

4. *Acquire the knowledge.* As noted in earlier discussions, knowledge acquisition is critical. The success of the expert system depends on the quality of the knowledge that is captured. Acquisition is tricky, because the knowledge engineer is confronted with subjective and often fuzzy ideas. In contrast, systems analysts deal with visible, predictable processes and data in their work.

The intuitive nature of the knowledge acquisition process is bound to run against the grain of most systems analysts or programmers. In practice, systems analysts deal with the algorithmic aspects of information systems, such as numerical data, discrete information, and predictable procedures. They evaluate the flow of information through a tangible process. The knowledge engineer must interpret the semantic thinking aspects of knowledge in analyzing the expert's decision process. This approach is called *behavioral analysis.*

5. *Evaluate design and implementation strategies.* This step involves representing, prototyping, and testing the resulting knowledge base. Design and implementation are turning points in the expert system development life cycle.

6. *Oversee construction, testing, and implementation.* This managerial function focuses on effective handling of the development team, ensuring quality testing, and producing a product that is acceptable to the users and is in line with the organization's goals.

7. *Train the user.* User training has often been compromised in designing information systems, usually because the developer is behind schedule. This must not be allowed to happen in expert systems development; the risks of erosion of user confidence and loss of interest in the system are too great.

8. *Maintain and enhance the system.* **Maintenance** refers to changes that ensure the system continues to do the work it was initially designed to do. **Enhancements** are changes that upgrade the system to the user's new requirements. Like any other systems, expert systems age, and at some point, new knowledge must be incorporated to refine the quality of the solutions.

Table 6–1 compares the functions of knowledge engineers and systems analysts. Note the similarities between the two jobs. The main difference is in the fourth function—the systems analyst acquires information from the user, while the knowledge engineer acquires knowledge from the expert. The similarities explain and support the direction of systems analysts into knowledge engineering.

Job Roles

The knowledge engineer plays a variety of roles, depending on the nature of the problem, the type of domain expert or user involved, and the organization's climate. Some roles are similar to those of the systems analyst: change agent, investigator, diplomat, architect, builder, tester, accountant, and salesperson. See Table 6–2. Because systems analysts' project teams are generally larger than KE teams, they assume the additional roles of project planner, contractor, motivator, and quality inspector. On the other hand, the knowledge engineer must act as psychologist when interpreting the expert's behavior and evaluating the interview process. The knowledge engineer is also expected to be adept at conflict resolution, especially when dealing with multiple experts.

■ **Table 6–1**   Comparison of Key Functions of Systems Analysts and
Knowledge Engineers

Systems Analyst	Knowledge Engineer
■ Identify potential information systems applications	■ Identify potential expert system applications
■ Develop project proposals (benefits, costs, schedules)	■ Develop project proposals (benefits, costs, schedules)
■ Develop project work plans, assign work, and monitor/report progress	■ Develop project work plans assign work, and monitor/report progress
■ Acquire information from the user	■ Acquire knowledge from the expert
■ Evaluate design and implementation strategies	■ Evaluate design and implementation strategies
■ Oversee construction, testing, and implementation	■ Oversee construction, testing, and implementation
■ Train the user	■ Train the user
■ Maintain or turn over production system to another group	■ Maintain or turn over production system to another group

■ KNOWLEDGE AND SKILL REQUIREMENTS

To perform these diverse roles, the knowledge engineer should be familiar with the tools, procedures and technologies and possess the skills to apply them. Some skills are taught; others are innate. "People skills" are important in working successfully with experts and users; technical skills are required in building the knowledge base.

Table 6–3 summarizes the knowledge and skill requirements of the knowledge engineer. The literature is still sketchy on this subject. This list is culled from a review of the research and a survey of practicing knowledge engineers who are members of the International Association of Knowledge Engineers (IAKE). Other surveys being conducted will help standardize the job requirements for knowledge engineers.

Knowledge Requirements

Computer Technology

The knowledge engineer should be well versed in hardware and software, how operating systems work, and issues regarding legal matters, security, testing, documentation, and maintenance. A general background in science, AI concepts, and computer architecture is helpful.

Domain-Specific Knowledge

The knowledge engineer must be familiar with the nature of the problem domain, the business of the user organization, and the factors surrounding the

■ **Table 6−2**   Comparison of the Roles of Systems Analysts and Knowledge Engineers

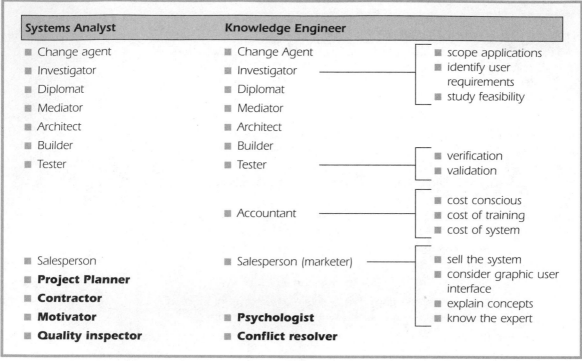

Systems Analyst	Knowledge Engineer	
■ Change agent	■ Change Agent	
■ Investigator	■ Investigator —————	■ scope applications
		■ identify user requirements
■ Diplomat	■ Diplomat	
■ Mediator	■ Mediator	■ study feasibility
■ Architect	■ Architect	
■ Builder	■ Builder	
■ Tester	■ Tester —————————	■ verification
		■ validation
	■ Accountant ———————	■ cost conscious
		■ cost of training
		■ cost of system
■ Salesperson	■ Salesperson (marketer) ———	■ sell the system
■ **Project Planner**		■ consider graphic user interface
■ **Contractor**		■ explain concepts
■ **Motivator**	■ **Psychologist**	■ know the expert
■ **Quality inspector**	■ **Conflict resolver**	

Note: Items in bold are unique to the role.

■ **Table 6−3**   Knowledge and Skill Requirements of the Knowledge Engineer

Knowledge Required	Skills Required
■ Computer technology (hardware, operating systems, etc.)	■ Communication
■ Domain-specific knowledge	■ Interviewing
■ Shell programming (programming in LISP, PROLOG, etc.)	■ Interpersonal
	■ Listening
■ Expert systems tools	■ Analytical
■ Information technology	■ Organizational
■ Human−machine interface and use of graphics	■ Ability to articulate the project's rationale
■ Cognitive psychology	■ Rapid prototyping
	■ Knowledge acquisition

domain such as the organization's political climate, level of management support, and the users' computer literacy. For example, if the problem domain is mortgage loan analysis, the KE should have a basic understanding of lending practices and procedures before approaching the expert. A knowledge engineer who builds expert systems for oil exploration would probably be the wrong choice for this assignment.

Shell Programming and Programming in Nonprocedural Language

Knowledge engineers with a computer science background are well trained in high-level procedural languages such as Pascal and C++ or in nonprocedural languages such as LISP or PROLOG. If a knowledge base is to be built using a shell, the knowledge engineer can easily represent the rules through shell programming. If the development team includes a programmer, the knowledge engineer will be able to focus attention on knowledge acquisition.

Expert Systems Tools and Methodologies

For knowledge acquisition and representation to succeed, a number of special-purpose tools must be employed. Among the tools used in acquisition are interviewing, concept analysis, protocol analysis, and brainstorming. For representation, the choice is shell programming or programming in LISP or PROLOG. Figure 6–1 shows the relative importance of these tools and methodologies.

Figure 6–1   Relative Tool Importance of Selected Tools and Methodologies in Knowledge Engineering

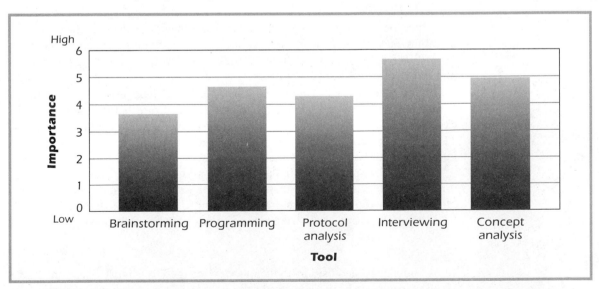

Source: E. M. Awad and Jack Lindgren, "Skills and Personality Attributes of the Knowledge Engineer: An Empirical Study," *Proceedings of the Third Annual Symposium of the International Association of Knowledge Engineers* (Washington, D.C., November 16–19, 1992), pp. 617–630.

Information Technology

This field focuses on software engineering, system design procedures, and management of computer-based projects. The discipline and many of its procedures are similar to those applied in expert systems.

Human–Machine Interface and Use of Graphics

Building an expert system is one thing; providing it with a user interface that is attractive and that enhances its coherence is another. With sufficient information and experience, the knowledge engineer can customize the interface to suit the end user's needs. With a graphic user interface (GUI), areas on the screen are highlighted, which can make the system easier to use.

Cognitive Psychology

The knowledge engineer should have a basic familiarity with the principles of cognition, the understanding of knowledge in general and of how human experts think or reason. Cognitive skills are important in acquiring and representing complex, ill-defined, and judgmental knowledge and understanding the domain expert's thought processes such as decision making under conditions of uncertainty. Background in this field improves communication, interviewing, and listening skills.

Skill Requirements

The knowledge engineer must be skilled in a number of technical and behavioral areas such as communication, interviewing, and rapid prototyping. (See Table 6–3.) In a 1992 survey, knowledge engineers considered the following skills as necessary in their work.

Communication Skills

The most pervasive factor in a knowledge engineer's success is the ability to communicate. If the knowledge engineer cannot understand and relate the expert's intent or meaning accurately, the reliability of the resulting knowledge base will be questionable.

Persons with poor communication skills cannot be effective knowledge engineers; their deficiency cannot help but detract from their relationship with experts, users, management, and others. This also applies to domain experts. They must enunciate concepts and procedures in simple, clear terms so that the knowledge can be represented accurately.

In a 1992 survey, 1,000 knowledge engineers were asked to rate the importance of skill in verbal communication, written communication, marketing, human relations, organization, and group dynamics. As shown in Figure 6–2, communication skills were rated as very high in importance.

Interviewing Skills

As a knowledge acquisition tool, interviewing gets the most attention. Interviewing coaches, leads, and prods the expert into providing the knowledge needed to build the expert system. The dangerous aspect of interviewing is that most people think they know how to interview. Successful knowledge acquisition takes time and experience, as discussed in Chapter 7.

Figure 6–2   Importance of Skills Communication in Knowledge Acquisition

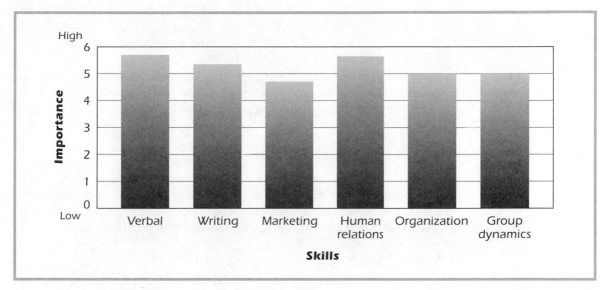

Source: E. M. Awad and Jack Lindgren, "Skills and Personality Attributes of the Knowledge Engineer: An Empirical Study," *Proceedings of the Third Annual Symposium of the International Association of Knowledge Engineers* (Washington, D.C., 16–19 November 1992), pp. 617–630.

Interpersonal Skills

Interpersonal skills enable one to work with people to achieve common goals or to help others work together as a team. Interpersonal behavior is closely related to personality and dictates a person's management style.

Interpersonal skills promote cooperation and motivation and encourage closer relationships with one's counterparts. Interpersonal exchanges include communication, teaching, and selling, all of which are important attributes in dealing with experts. In the reality of knowledge engineering, engaging in an uncertain process such as knowledge acquisition, strong interpersonal skills may be more useful than a set technical procedure.

Listening Skills

An important element of interviewing is listening. Special discipline is required to remember what is being discussed while maintaining momentum in an interview. Effective listening not only shapes the relationship between the knowledge engineer and the domain expert, it can also dictate the quality of the knowledge acquired. To listen well means minimizing distractions, paying close attention to details, and maintaining eye contact and positive body language. Nonverbal communication is also important. Nonverbal messages either strengthen or undermine verbal messages.

Analytical Skills

Good analytical skills enable one to structure the large volume of information collected during acquisition and to sense relationships among concepts and strategies. Analysis tools include protocol analysis, delphi method, and concept analysis. They are discussed in Chapter 7. Obviously, without analytical skills, the knowledge engineer's work, especially during the acquisition phase, would be severely hampered.

Organizational Skills

The knowledge engineer must organize the many tasks of the system development life cycle and coordinate development team efforts to produce results on schedule, which demands various organizational skills. Effective organization requires interpersonal and technical abilities.

Ability to Articulate the Rationale for the Project

Part of the knowledge engineer's job is to discuss project feasibility, justify investment in the project, and sell the proposed change to management. Persuasive articulation of the rationale is developed with experience. Actually, this ability is important in working with management at all levels.

Rapid Prototyping Skills

The knowledge engineer will occasionally sit down with the expert to get feedback on how the knowledge base is shaping up. Rapid prototyping is an iterative process in which the knowledge engineer shows the domain expert what the expert system looks like on the basis of the knowledge captured to date. The knowledge engineer can make changes to the system on the spot in the presence of the expert. While rapid prototyping requires experience and quick thinking, it promotes respect and trust between the knowledge engineer and the expert.

Knowledge Acquisition Skills

Knowledge acquisition is a specialized activity that entails an understanding of the problem domain and the capture of knowledge required to build the system. This phase can make or break the system. Chapters 7 through 10 discuss knowledge acquisition tools, methods, and skills in detail.

■ PERSONALITY ATTRIBUTES

When it comes to personality attributes, knowledge engineers and systems analysts are cut from pretty much the same mold. Both professionals typically exhibit the attributes described here.

1. *Intelligence.* An intelligent knowledge engineer develops systems efficiently. He or she is constantly learning from experience and from exposure to the various experts. Intelligence enables a KE to keep abreast of advances in technology and to learn and think quickly and well, especially when various procedures must be integrated.

2. *Creativity.* A creative mind enables a person to generate ideas and react quickly to new methods for solving problems. Creative KEs are more adept at selecting appropriate reasoning strategies and ways of acquiring knowledge.

3. *Tolerance for ambiguity.* The willingness to probe further and further into an unclear issue or procedure until it is clear and usable demands a degree of patience that some people do not possess. This process takes time and the expert may require much encouragement.

4. *Realism.* Experienced knowledge engineers understand that not every expert they deal with will be cooperative or motivated and that some projects will be more onerous than others. These knowledge engineers tend to be more tolerant.

5. *Tact and diplomacy.* KEs tend to be able to field questions, make suggestions, and respond to the suggestions of others in ways that are not offensive. They understand the importance of sensitivity.

6. *Cognitive ability.* The ability to reason by analysis, association and inference characterizes KEs. They are able to "see through things," to perceive the reality of a situation.

7. *Maturity.* The awareness and acceptance of one's abilities and limitations that occur over time makes it easier to promote mutual respect between KEs and domain experts. It also implies patience in the way the knowledge engineer relates to the expert and with the knowledge acquisition process.

8. *Persistence.* KEs have the determination to try new things and maintain their commitment to a project. Self-confidence is a component of this persistence. When dealing with ill-structured problems, the knowledge engineer must remain positive, saying, "I can do it if I keep at it." The poem in Box 6–1 addresses the importance of a positive state of mind.

9. *Logical thinking.* The ability to learn new technology and continue to improve the acquisition process are essential to a KE. When eliciting knowledge,

---

Box 6–1   All in the State of the Mind

If you think you are beaten, you are;
    If you think you dare not, you don't;
If you would like to win and don't think you can,
    It's almost a cinch you won't.
If you think you'll lose, you're lost;
    For out in the world you'll find
Success begins with a fellow's will.
    It's all in the state of the mind.
Full many a race is lost
    Ere even a step is run,
And many a coward fails
    Ere even his work is begun.
Think big and your deeds will grow;
    Think small and you'll fall behind;
Think that you can and you will.
    It's all in the state of the mind.
If you think you are outclassed, you are;
    You've got to think high to rise.
You've got to be sure of yourself before
    You can ever win a prize.
Life's battles don't always go
    To the stronger or faster man;
But sooner or later, the man who wins
    Is the fellow who thinks he can.

Source: Unknown, *Reef Points* (Annapolis, MD: U.S. Naval Academy).

Figure 6-3 Personality Attributes of the Knowledge Engineer

Intelligence
Creativity
Tolerance for ambiguity
Realism
Tact and diplomacy
Cognitive ability
Maturity
Persistence
Logical thinking
Good sense of humor and optimism

the knowledge engineer must be willing to argue reasonably in order to resolve inconsistencies. Otherwise, the resulting system will be illogical and unreasonable.

10. *Good sense of humor and optimism.* Light-hearted, cheerful people are easier to work with and make attractive collaborators.

Because few established standards guide the building of expert systems, the knowledge engineer must also be particularly inquisitive, innovative, self-motivated, open-minded, and willing to take risks in constructing an end-product that is satisfactory to the user. Figure 6-3 is a summary of the personality attributes of the knowledge engineer.

ACADEMIC PREPARATION

As with any other professional, the knowledge engineer must satisfy certain technical, behavioral, and academic requirements. On the academic end, the knowledge engineer's academic background is expected to include:

- *A bachelor's degree in computer science or information systems.* Knowing one or more languages in LISP, PROLOG, C++, or Pascal is particularly helpful. The path taken at many business schools is a business degree with a major in expert systems. Most programs include courses in expert systems, structured system design, database design, and networking.

- *Systems theory.* A KE would have difficulty building business-oriented systems without a business background and a feel for how well the system will meet the user's requirements. The very nature of building expert systems requires familiarity with the user's organization and how it works. This background is important during the knowledge acquisition and system design phases of the process.

- *Competency in tools and methodology.* Knowledge engineers rely on tools to acquire the knowledge needed to build a customized system to meet user requirements. More and more colleges and universities are incorporating hands-on experience in the computer lab and projects with local businesses. Knowing what tools to use in the product development life cycle is the mark of a professional.

■ *Psychology, organizational behavior, and logic.* These fields of study help the knowledge engineer integrate the expert system into the user organization. The knowledge engineer cannot be effective with only technical competence. He or she must have a feel for the expert's and the user's states of mind, moods, attitudes, perceptions, expectations, fears, and the like. Coursework in cognitive psychology and logic will pay great dividends in the long run.

The University's Role

Where do universities fit into the picture of knowledge engineering? Expert systems are already being integrated into database courses, decision support systems, and multimedia. The next generation of expert systems will probably emphasize user interfaces with technologies such as hypermedia and blackboard architecture. This evolution should spur demand for expert systems into the year 2000. The growing use of PC-driven shells makes this prediction a virtual reality.

With this in mind, a specific academic background is critical for preparing the knowledge engineer:

■ *Principles of artificial intelligence:* classical mathematical logic, logic programming, and natural language understanding

■ *Knowledge acquisition*—emphasis on tools and methodologies for working with single and multiple experts

■ *Applied AI programming*—using LISP or PROLOG

■ *High technology and high-technology products:* evaluating shells, trends in AI technology, problems in building expert systems using procedural languages, etc.

■ *Logic/methods of reasoning:* logic validation and verification and biological mechanisms of behavioral processes

■ *Cognitive psychology:* reasoning, pattern recognition, observational skills, memory, language and thought, and views of intelligence

■ *Representation of knowledge:* languages, rule-based methods, etc.

■ *Database management systems:* database design, distributed databases, database/expert system interface, and security problems and procedures

■ *Organizational behavior:* personality and perception, group processes, motivation, and leadership

Most programs at the university level lead to a master's or doctoral degree in computer science or management information systems (MIS) with an emphasis on expert systems. To make a full-fledged commitment to training, university programs must soon incorporate some courses not presently offered, such as:

■ Introducing knowledge-based systems technology to organizations

■ Management of knowledge-base system projects

■ Quality testing and assurance for knowledge-based systems

■ Knowledge engineering methodologies

■ Ethical and legal issues in knowledge engineering

Because knowledge engineering is still a developing discipline, much of the instruction on these topics still lacks a strong theoretical or practical base. As the discipline evolves, research in these topics should provide more readily available and more standardized information.

Job Placement Data

Hiring figures are not readily available, as few studies have been conducted concerning the placement of recruiting knowledge engineers, and the companies that hire them are reluctant to disclose salary figures. Based on a review, the "Help Wanted" classified ads in Sunday editions of *The Washington Post* in August 1994, revealed 261 openings in information technology, most of them in mid-sized to large corporations. Of these positions, 19 required a college degree with expert system or AI background. Nine of the 19 ads sought applicants with two or more years' experience. Telephone inquiries revealed that the organizations with the 10 entry-level positions were offering an average starting salary of $32,000. The positions requiring two or more years' experience would start at "up to $68,000, depending on experience."

One employment agency advertised two junior-level "experienced system developer" jobs starting at $36,000. A representative of the agency reported that beginning salaries were slightly higher for expert system majors than for those in computer science. Starting salaries for computer science graduates were averaging $31,000 in the Washington area at the time, according to that person.

Demand and salaries for knowledge workers vary by industry and location. A March 15, 1993, article in *Fortune,* "The Best Cities for Knowledge Workers," reported that Raleigh–Durham (N.C.), New York, Boston, Seattle, and Austin offered the best prospects, respectively. The next five "best" cities were Chicago, Houston, San Jose, Philadelphia, and Minneapolis. Demand for knowledge-based systems and salaries can be expected to be higher in those areas than in other areas in the country.

▐ TRAINING FOR THE KNOWLEDGE ENGINEER

College courses are not enough. Knowledge engineers must also have hands-on experience before they can build expert systems on their own. Some companies send their employees to university artificial intelligence programs for intensive training in building expert systems. Other companies provide on-the-job training of up to 18 months to develop the required proficiency. Still other organizations set up in-house training sessions at which vendors or professional trainers teach the procedures in building expert systems. The major drawback of using vendor training is that it is customized to the particular vendor's product.

One example of company-based training is the training program DEC established in 1982. It combines classroom instruction with an apprenticeship. Its core elements are:

- ▪ Technical mastery of knowledge engineering methodology and tools
- ▪ Development of human and business relations skills
- ▪ Direct involvement of practitioners in the design, development, and delivery of the training

DEC's training approach is to use practitioners to build the curriculum. Classes are staffed with full-time knowledge engineers where students interact with practitioners. This environment encourages the integration of theory and practice, which makes the program more enriching than typical university training.

A traineeship should proceed as follows:

1. *Expose the trainee to the software.* The trainee reviews the manual, reads about the shell and what it can do, and talks to those who have experience with its use.

2. *Use a sample expert system for a starter.* The trainee gains experience in the makeup and use of the system and the shell. If the application is of sufficiently high quality, it will illustrate the importance of represented know how.

3. *Allow the trainee to modify or embed changes in the sample system.* This step serves to improve the trainee's self-confidence without risk of permanent damage to a system. Of course, a backup copy of the system should be available just in case the trainee irreversibly changes the sample.

4. *Build a modest expert system based on the trainee's expertise with the problem domain.* Any problem domain will do, since this is the trainee's initial experience. Sufficient time should be allowed for the trainee to understand the system's steps and the decisions. Two trainees may work as a team, with one trainee acting as the expert and the other as the knowledge engineer.

    The trainee system should be made available to peers at different stages of development for review and feedback. This *rapid walkthrough* promotes cooperation and cohesion of the group.

5. *Build an expert system based on the knowledge of a domain expert.* This can be a full-fledged system or part of a larger undertaking. Many firms assign a newly trained person to a group that is working on a complex project. Other organizations assign a project that needs additional work to a new trainee. Eventually, the trainee is given a project of his or her own.

A summary of the steps in a traineeship is shown in Figure 6–4. E.I. Dupont de Nemours & Co. also trains its own knowledge engineers. By 1987, 1,500

Figure 6–4   Steps in Training the Knowledge Engineer

1. Expose the trainee to the software
2. Use a sample expert system for a starter
3. Allow the trainee to modify or embed changes in the sample system
4. Build a modest expert system based on the trainee's expertise with the problem domain
5. Build an expert sytem based on the knowledge of a domain expert

employees had taken the firm's two-day expert systems course. In 1988, the company had 2,000 expert systems in routine use, and 600 were being developed or field tested. By 1992, more than 2,500 systems were in operation. The number is expected to exceed 4,000 in 1996.

A typical DuPont system requires one workyear of effort to build and yields $100,000 in annual savings. The company's many operational systems would not have been cost-effective if it had hired outside knowledge engineers. The firm can now take the experience gained in designing small expert systems and apply it to building larger ones.

Is it better to hire outside knowledge engineers, or to train users to serve as knowledge engineers? The Internal Revenue Service chose to train its own people to use knowledge-based technology, following a popular approach used by banks in the 1960s and 1970s when they trained their accountants to become programmers. The bank employees already knew bank accounting practices that were crucial to asset–liability management and other banking applications. One thing is certain: systems developed by knowledge engineers who are not familiar with the problem domain can end up in failure.

■ THE DEVELOPMENT TEAM

As mentioned earlier, the success of an expert system eventually depends on two people: the knowledge engineer and the domain expert. Sometimes, the knowledge engineer is unable to handle a difficult project from the start. Certain factors—time pressures, limited experience, complexity of the problem domain, etc.—make it risky to assign the project to a single knowledge engineer. Large organizations assign development teams to their ambitious projects.

A typical development team configuration is shown in Figure 6–5. Note in the illustration that the team has junior *and* senior knowledge engineers. The senior engineer (often a project leader) with at least five years of experience

Figure 6–5 A Typical Development Team

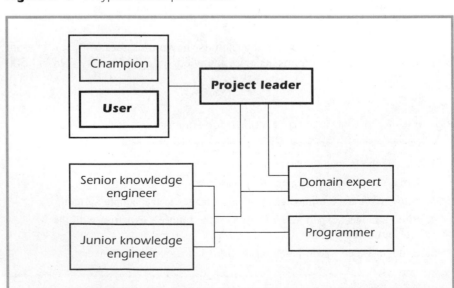

building systems provides guidance and approval to the junior engineer. Senior engineers often do the difficult interviews and rapid prototyping. The junior engineer, with less than two years of experience, serves as an apprentice, learning the "tricks of the trade" and gaining experience while providing valuable assistance.

Much of a project's success depends on the managerial talent of the **project leader.** On large projects, the project leader has two major responsibilities. First of all, a project leader coordinates the project and provides an emphasis on total quality. Elements of coordination include ensuring full documentation of the project, devising and enforcing verification exercises, and keeping the project on schedule. The project leader is the person who makes sure that the flow of work and the responsibilities of each team member are clearly defined.

Secondly, the project leader ensures user acceptance. Validation, testing to be certain that the user ends up with the right system, is a big part of this task. User acceptance can be ensured by keeping users informed and seeking their advice at each phase of the development life cycle.

Early in the development process, the team looks for a champion— someone who truly believes in the system and is willing to seek management support at all levels. If the team should hit a snag, it can count on the champion to resolve the problem. It has often been said, "No champion, no system."

For smaller, simpler expert systems, the knowledge engineer is expected to do knowledge representation as well as acquisition. For large, complex projects, the knowledge engineer concentrates on acquisition, leaving representation to the team's programmer, who represents the knowledge acquired by the knowledge engineer in a language acceptable to the hardware or the installed shell. Shell programming uses rules or frames to produce solutions. These are covered in detail in Chapter 12.

This "typical" development team represents only one of many alternative models for organizating expert system development. Just as companies that organize teams for software development have found, the best organizational model for a project team is usually the one that fits the parent organization best.

IMPLICATIONS FOR MANAGEMENT

This chapter identifies the role, skills, and personality attributes of the knowledge engineer and how this emerging job relates to that of the systems analyst. From this background, one may draw a number of conclusions:

- Encouraging signs suggest a career path from systems analysis to knowledge engineering exists. Building expert systems can provide higher pay and the opportunities for doing more creative work. Systems analysts can become knowledge engineers by upgrading their background through education and training.

- Systems analysts who want to move to a career in knowledge engineering should determine the level of support for building expert systems in their employing organization. They may be able to stay with their current employer as a knowledge engineer.

- Given the increasing demand for knowledge engineers, an organization can now consider long-range training programs, by which the talent for knowledge engineering may be tapped from its existing pool of systems analysts. Another alternative is for the organization to support academic MIS programs that offer courses in expert systems or artificial intelligence.

- Knowledge engineering allows a firm to preserve its intellectual capital for problem solving and competitive advantage. An expert company understands and capitalizes on its human resources. To incorporate expert systems without knowledge engineering as the core competency would be like building automobiles without qualified assemblers.

- The knowledge engineer is a person committed to this evolving technology and pursues a goal of building quality systems. Without quality assurance, reliability and integrity of the whole process remains questionable.

- Finally, as knowledge engineering becomes an established area of system building, organizations must provide rewards sufficient to minimize the turnover that occurred with systems analysts in the 1970s and early 1980s. Knowledge engineers are expensive to train and hard to replace. Motivating technical people requires regular performance monitoring and feedback for reinforcement. Providing opportunities for advancement, creativity, utilization of abilities, recognition, attractive compensation, and the like promotes employee loyalty to the firm and its objectives. This level of concern for people counts in the final results.

SUMMARY

1. Knowledge engineers are more than talented programmers. They are professionals with skills in tapping expert knowledge and using tools to represent that knowledge. A KE's personality attributes also play a key role in their success.

2. Knowledge engineers perform several key functions. They identify system applications, develop project proposals, acquire knowledge, oversee testing and implementation, perform user training, and maintain systems. Most of these functions are similarly performed by systems analysts.

3. The knowledge engineer and the systems analyst play similar roles. For example, both are change agents, instigators, diplomats, builders, architects, testers, accountants, and salespersons. Conflict resolution and psychology background are more characteristic of the knowledge engineer than the systems analyst.

4. Knowledging engineering requires certain knowledge and skills. Knowledge requirements include computer technology, knowledge of the domain, programming knowledge of acquisition and representation tools, use of graphics, and cognitive psychology. Skills requirements include communication, interviewing, listening, and interpersonal skills: analytical and organizational skills: and rapid prototyping.

5. The personality attributes of the knowledge engineer typically include intelligence, creativity, patience, realism, tact, maturity, persistence, a logical mind, and a good sense of humor.

6. The academic requirements for knowledge engineering include a bachelor's degree in computer science or in business with an emphasis on expert systems. Courses in database design, networking, systems theory, and psychology are also helpful.

7. A knowledge engineer must have hands-on experience before building expert systems on his or her own. The following steps are recommended: Expose the trainee to the software and then to a sample expert system for review. Then allow the trainee to modify the sample system or build a reasonably complex expert system.

▨ TERMS TO LEARN

Enhancement changes that upgrade a system to meet the user's new requirements.

Persistence standing firm; maintaining commitment to a project or course of action.

Project leader person who coordinates a project development team and ensures user acceptance.

▨ REVIEW QUESTIONS

1. "The knowledge engineer's work is to model the expertise, not the expert." Do you agree with this sentence? Discuss its meaning.

2. In your own words, write a short essay to explaining the importance of knowledge engineering.

3. In the chapter, the key functions of the knowledge engineer are compared to those of the systems analyst. How are they similar? Dissimilar?

4. Review the employment ads of two consecutive Sunday editions of a major newspaper. What pattern in information technology jobs may be significant? What types of jobs relate to AI or expert systems? What types of organizations are looking for knowledge engineers or specialists in the field?

5. How do personality attributes of the knowledge engineer affect their knowledge acquisition capability? Knowledge representation capability? Explain.

6. What academic preparation is required to be a successful knowledge engineer? Be specific.

7. Does a practical experience in information systems help a person learn to build expert system? How?

8. In what way(s) is a background in system theory and organizational behavior helpful in knowledge engineering?

9. How do universities contribute to preparing knowledge engineers?

10. The chapter describes three hands-on approaches for training knowledge engineers. Explain each briefly. Which approach do you believe is the best? The quickest? Why?

11. How should ideal training in knowledge engineering proceed? How does this approach differ from DEC's training?

12. If you were asked to lead a project that must be completed in four months, would you recommend that a development team be used? What factors are involved? If a development team is the way to go, who would you include on the team? Why?

EXERCISES AND CASES

1. Examine the following profiles of knowledge engineers and discuss their qualifications.

a. Erika and Lori were contracted to build the Hiring Advisor for a country club. The system is designed to improve the process of evaluating the applications that the club receives for snack bar worker, lifeguard, and coach. Erika and Lori hold B.S. degrees in MIS and are well versed in two expert system shells: IBM ESE (mainframe) and VP-Expert. Erika is quite congenial and loves to talk to people. Lori is more introspective and enjoys building systems without involvement with the user or the domain expert. In addition, they are well versed in Pascal and C++. Neither has built an expert system before.

b. Jeanine holds an MS in management information systems from a university in Florida. She is well versed in VP-Expert and has done work in database design using dBASE IV and Oracle. Jeanine enjoys working with people and seems to thrive under stress. She has developed several small expert systems. She tends to be pushy when she needs information. People who worked with her in the past said she is good at what she does but can be intimidating. She gives the impression she has to be in command at all times, using others to do the "leg work."

c. Bob is 26 years old and has an MS in computer science from a premier university in New York. He served in the military for three years prior to going to graduate school. Someone who worked with Bob on a recent expert system project for the military commented, "Bob has the patience of Job. He is a good listener and is highly intelligent, but has a tendency to spin off on his own when the project falls behind schedule, leaving the rest of his team behind." He has trouble delegating authority.

He knows EXSYS inside out and feels he can do the work on his own.

d. Ray earned a Ph.D. in information technology from a Midwestern graduate school in 1974. He has a master's degree in social psychology from the same school. Until the mid-1980s, Ray designed information systems in the banking sector. He started working with expert systems in 1987 and found it both challenging and lucrative. Recently, he worked on a medical application with a renowned specialist. The two did not get along well. Ray accused the expert of being uncooperative, and the expert told Ray he was arrogant. The project ended in disaster.

2. Consider the personality attributes, academic qualifications, and practical experience necessary for building Publisher Advisor (introduced in the Chapter 5 exercises). If you were assigned to build the system, what would you need to know? Elaborate.

3. White and Goldsmith* suggest two types of potential knowledge engineers,

> "Send me a well-developed systems analyst, LISP hacker, or a programmer competent in several languages, and we'll make him or her into a knowledge engineer."

and

> "Send me a talented generalist with well-developed interpersonal skills—for somewhat more delicately, 'user friendly person'—and a rigorously analytical mind, and we'll team him or her with a competent programmer"

In your opinion, which approach would be more successful in knowledge engineering. Why?

*Milton White, and Joe Goldsmith, eds., *Standards and Review Manual For Certification In Knowledge Engineering.* (Rockville, MD: The Systemware Corp., 1990), pp. 605–06.

SELECTED REFERENCES

Arcand, J. F., L. Champagne, and K. Dalkir. "HIT: A Hybrid Intelligent Training System for Knowledge Engineers." In *Proceedings of the Third Annual Symposium of the International Association of Knowledge Engineers.* Washington, DC, November 16–19, 1992, pp. 661–667.

Awad, E. M., and J. Lindgren. "Skills and Personality Attributes of the Knowledge Engineer: An Empirical Study." In *Proceedings of the Third Annual Symposium of the International Association of Knowledge Engineers.* Washington DC, November 16–19, 1992, pp. 617–630.

Chorafas, Dimitris N. *Knowledge Engineering: Knowledge Acquisition, Knowledge Representation, the Role of the Knowledge Engineer, and Domains Fertile to AI Implementation,* rev. ed. New York: Van Nostrand Reinhold, 1990.

Galef, Gregory T. "Knowledge Engineers: The Academic vs. the Commercial." Unpublished paper, University of Virginia, February 1990.

Goff, Leslie. "Knowledge Engineers Blend People Skills, Programming." *Computerworld,* April 13, 1992, p. 91.

Grundstein, Michel. "The Knowledge Engineering Profession in the 1990s: Towards Knowledge Assets Engineering Within the Company—A Prospective Point of View." *The Journal of Knowledge Engineering.* Summer 1991, pp. 18–24.

Hodges, Judith. "Knowledge Engineers Preserve Brain Trust." *Software Magazine,* November 1990, pp. 37–39ff.

Jean-Marc, Robert, and Dalkir Kimiz. "How Do Knowledge Engineers Work?" In *Proceedings of the Third Annual Symposium of the International Association of Knowledge Engineers.* Washington, DC, November 16–19, 1992, pp. 642–660.

Jih, Wen-Jang. "From Systems Analysis to Knowledge Engineering: How to Avoid the Cultural Shock." In E. M. Awad, ed., *Proceedings of the 1990 ACM SIGBDP Conference on Trends and Directions in Expert Systems.* October 31–November 2, 1990, pp. 170–173.

Laplante, Alice. "Group(Ware) Therapy." *Computerworld,* July 27, 1992, pp. 71–72.

Liebowitz, Jay. "Education of Knowledge Engineers." *The Journal of Knowledge Engineering,* Summer 1991, pp. 25–31.

_____. *Institutionalizing Expert Systems: A Handbook for Managers.* Englewood Cliffs, NJ: Prentice-Hall, 1991.

Lirov, Yuval. "Systematic Invention for Knowledge Engineering." *AI Expert,* July 1990, pp. 28–34.

Mykytyn, Peter P., Jr., Kathleen Mykytyn, and M. K. Raja. "Knowledge Acquisition Skills and Traits: A Self-assessment of Knowledge Engineers." *Information and Management,* February 1994. pp. 95–104.

Payne, Shirley C., and E. M. Awad. "The Systems Analyst as a Knowledge Engineer: Can the Transition Be Successfully Made?" In E. M . Awad, ed.,*Proceedings of the 1990 ACM SIGBDP Conference on Trends and Directions in Expert Systems,* October 31–November 2, 1990, pp. 155–169.

Rasmus, Daniel W. "Putting the Experts to Work." *Byte,* January 1991, p. 281.

Turban, E., and J. Liebowitz, eds. *Managing Expert Systems.* Harrisburg, PA: Idea Group Publishing, 1991.

Vandamme, F. "How to Prepare Knowledge Professionals." In *Proceedings of the Third Annual Symposium of the International Association of Knowledge Engineers.* Washington, DC, November 16–19, 1992, pp. 631–641.

White, Milton. "Certification or Mystification? Building a Stronger AI Profession." *AI Expert,* March 1991, pp. 34–35.

Wiig, K. "Expert Systems: A Manager's Guide." Geneva, Switzerland: International Labor Organization, 1990.

Yaverbaum, Gayle J., Tom Beckman, Jeff Clannon, Ruth Paul, and Davis King. "Training and Educating Knowledge Engineers." In Jay Liebowitz, ed.,*Expert Systems World Congress Proceedings.* December 16–19, 1991, Orlando, FL, pp. 2948–2960.

Zarri, G. P. "State of the Art of Knowledge Engineering in Europe." *Second Annual Conference of the International Association of Knowledge Engineers.* Rockville, MD: International Association of Knowledge Engineers, October 1990.

Chapter ■ 7

Preparing for Knowledge Acquisition

KNOWLEDGE ACQUISITION IN A MEDICAL DOMAIN

Expert system development for a medical application presents a special set of problems in knowledge acquisition. This anecdotal report outlines the launching of an expert system project used to diagnose and prescribe treatment for various foot problems encountered by diabetic patients.

Information gathering in medicine generally follows a set sequence: an interview with the patient, an examination, and one or more laboratory tests to support the working diagnosis. Building a knowledge base from observing a medical examination, however, is risky. The interview is crucial, but this elementary exercise meets with all sorts of problems. For example, pain is a frequent primary complaint, but how can it be measured? Most experts agree pain is a subjective feeling that cannot be quantified.

Patients often contradict themselves when describing symptoms. How a patient answers a question depends on how it is asked. For example, during one on-site observation, people gave the answers they thought the expert wanted to hear. The problem of subjectivity cannot be solved with a set of written questions, because many questions require rewording and rephrasing to accommodate individual patients. Also, because of malpractice issues, the expert must phrase certain questions carefully.

Each of these issues raises concerns about the patient's credibility. A patient's credibility will influence the weight that the physician attaches to the patient's complaint. This "credibility gap" is a significant problem for knowledge acquisition, because physicians evaluate credibility by looking for subtle inconsistencies. At best, the process is elusive to humans, and even more so to expert systems.

Medical decision making relies on imprecise information gathered in a variety of ways and interpreted in a largely intuitive fashion. Details are observed in passing. Observations of nonverbal behavior are particularly difficult for an expert (orthopedic surgeon) to articulate in detail, even for an expert who is able to recall overall observations or impressions. Because most decision making in this type of situation is intuitive, knowledge acquisition is a more difficult task.

During the knowledge acquisition phase of this project, it became clear that medical decision making involves more than simple answers to IF . . . THEN statements. In simple cases, such as patient temperature and blood pressure, the data are ratio data. But in clinical medicine, many measures are ordinal, which provide a comparison of patients, procedures, and results.

With ratio data, one can determine that, say, four is twice as much as two. When the data are ordinal, four is not twice as much as two, but merely different from or more than two. If the response to a treatment is ranked on a scale of one to six, with six being best, one cannot automatically assume that a response of six is "twice" as good as three. Even though such a scale provides a means for rating individual patients, the scores cannot be approached strictly numerically. They are simply points on a distribution that do not necessarily allow a knowledge engineer to compare the results.

In a nutshell, ordinal data pose a problem in knowledge acquisition. Expert systems treat ordinal data as ratio data unless instructed otherwise. This difficulty and the fact that most medical expert systems are based on observations and followup interviews make the need for rapid prototyping and frequent testing of the system crucial.

Based on a diabetic foot advisor prototype, May–September 1994.

AT A GLANCE

The core of an expert system is the human expert's knowledge, thoughts, and experiences. The first step in the expert system development life cycle (ESDLC) is knowledge acquisition. To elicit knowledge, a knowledge engineer needs the appropriate tool(s). The acquired knowledge is then interpreted and represented as rules or facts for the final knowledge base.

This chapter examines the preparation for knowledge acquisition with its heavy emphasis on planning. Preparation includes identification of the problem and selection of an expert(s). A knowledge engineer must be aware of the particular characteristics of the problem domain, the user, and the expert. The important aspect in this early phase is to make as close a match as possible between the problem domain and the expert, and at the same time solicit user involvement and support.

In preparation for knowledge acquisition, most knowledge engineers carefully look for sensitive areas such as the expert's attitude, user expectations, budget constraints, and delivery date. These steps might seem too individualized to be efficient, but automatic knowledge acquisition has yet to prove a reliable substitute.

What You Will Learn

By the end of this chapter, you should know the following:

1. The similarities and differences between knowledge acquisition and systems analysis.
2. How to identify the problem domain.
3. Characteristics of the user and expert that will influence knowledge acquisition.

> W here success is concerned, people are not measured in inches, or pounds, or college degrees, or family background; they are measured by the size of their thinking.
>
> J. M. CUPELLO

■ INTRODUCTION

E pert systems derive their power from the knowledge they use. When knowledge engineers begin the building process, they are confronted with the first step—knowledge acquisition. The previous chapter focused on the function, abilities, training requirements, and potential of the knowledge engineer. A knowledge engineer converts human know-how into machine-ready "say-how" by using an iterative process of articulation, a series of refinement cycles, or rapid prototyping, in which the computer's performance is compared to that of the human expert.

Acquiring knowledge and converting it into rules that the computer can use is a costly business. It requires an extensive time commitment from the domain expert, and the special skills of the knowledge engineer. At times, the expert might lose interest in the project, and even feel like quitting. Or the knowledge engineer and the expert, just never seem to hit it off because of their interpersonal chemistry. Or the knowledge engineer uses the wrong tool or approach.

■ WHAT IS KNOWLEDGE ACQUISITION?

A review of the expert system literature reveals as many definitions of knowledge acquisition as authors. Some of the definitions are interesting:

- An "applied brain drain"
- A "manual craft that depends on the skill and effectiveness of the knowledge engineer"
- The "transfer of problem-solving expertise from some knowledge source to a program"
- The "process by which expert system developers discover the knowledge that domain experts use to perform the task of interest"
- An investigative experimental process involving interviews and protocol analysis in order to build an expert system.

This book defines knowledge acquisition as *a process by which the expert's thoughts and experiences are captured*. It is a sort of "mind automation." In a broader view, knowledge acquisition may also include acquiring knowledge from other sources such as books and technical manuscripts and drawings. In fact, these processes lead to the case-based reasoning used in the building of many expert systems.

The terms *acquisition* and knowledge *elicitation* are used interchangeably throughout expert system literature. Knowledge elicitation, however, is actually a subset of knowledge acquisition. Through elicitation, a knowledge engineer evokes a reply from the domain expert. Knowledge acquisition, the broader task, encompasses the representation of elicited knowledge in the knowledge base. Knowledge representation must occur in a format acceptable to a shell or a resident inference engine.

Knowledge acquisition is a demanding mental process in which a knowledge engineer collaborates with the expert to convert expertise into a coded program. Three important steps are involved:

1. Using an appropriate tool to *elicit* information from the expert.
2. *Interpreting* the information and inferring the expert's underlying knowledge and reasoning process.
3. Using the interpretation to build the rules that *represent* the expert's thought processes or solutions.

The capture of knowledge can be accomplished in many ways; no single way is best. The process typically entails several refinement cycles. The system's task is not simply to display the knowledge but also to represent it at different levels of reasoning or explanation. Box 7–1 illustrates the challenge in knowledge acquisition.

Box 7–1 The Challenge in Knowledge Acquisition

Sometimes even the best knowledge engineering techniques and the most talented knowledge engineers can't get the job done, which happened to two Texas Instruments (TI) knowledge engineers who were signed on to "clone" Thomas Kelly. Kelly, a civil engineer with Southern California Edison, is a genuine expert. He can almost feel the presence of danger at the Vermilion hydroelectric dam. In 1986 Southern California Edison plunked down more than $300,000 to replicate Kelly's knowledge gleaned from years of experience with the dam. Both sides were instantly frustrated; time was ticking away and the knowledge engineers felt that Kelly was not revealing enough knowledge.

This task was a complex one that relied on many rules of thumb. How did Kelly know that a small stream of water on one side of the dam meant a blocked drain at its base? And Kelly was unhappy too. He felt that the two TI knowledge engineers weren't picking up on what he was saying fast enough.

Too ambitious a scope and poor communication between knowledge engineer and expert crippled the progress of this most interesting system. Today Project Kelly has wound down. A good prototype, but not a deployable one, was built. Southern Calif. estimates that another $100,000 would have to be pumped into Vermilion dam to make it a generic dam troubleshooting expert system. Now it just keeps Tom Kelly company during his lonely vigils watchdogging the dam.

Knowledge is generally captured when the knowledge engineer interviews the expert, who answers the questions: What do you do as a first step? What information do you consider next? What constraints do you look for? These types of questions lead the expert through scenarios or case situations. Then, the knowledge engineer returns to specific points and questions the expert further until all angles of the problem domain are explored.

To capture the knowledge used in building complex systems, knowledge engineers use flowcharts, flow diagrams, decision trees, decision tables, and other graphic representation. In this process, rapid prototyping becomes important. Rapid prototyping is examined in greater detail in Chapter 10.

■ PREREQUISITES FOR ACQUISITION

Prior to knowledge acquisition, the knowledge engineer faces three important tasks:

- Identifying the problem domain
- Choosing the right expert
- Preparing for knowledge acquisition

These tasks are handled sequentially, in that one cannot be accomplished without completing the preceding tasks. For the first task, because the knowledge engineer is not the expert in the problem domain, a familiarity with the domain—including an understanding of terminology and the domain functions surrounding the problem—is essential. With this background, a knowledge engineer can communicate more effectively with the expert.

To illustrate, the preparation for the building the Diabetic Foot Advisor included three books and dozens of articles on diabetes and diabetic foot problems and deformities, which had to be read before the orthopedic surgeon was willing to be interviewed. Preparation time took well over seven weeks, but it paid off. Most of the sessions went without a hitch. The expert did not have to explain terminology or adjust any explanations to a more simplistic level for the knowledge engineer. Note taking and taping were routine.

Justifying the Problem Domain

Most of the discussions concerning acquisition presuppose a problem domain without justification. Many expert systems that are unjustified or poorly justified either fail or limp along in deep trouble. Some systems are never completed: others are not what the user wanted or are not fully used.

As mentioned in Chapter 5, the first step toward a successful system is to pick the right problem and justify its selection. Just as location is the number one factor in real estate, selecting the right problem should be the first consideration in expert system development, especially for a first-time organization. In addition to selecting a problem, this step entails identifying the domain expert, the user, and the payoff from the system.

Domain Characteristics

In selecting an appropriate problem, a knowledge engineer should look for several domain characteristics.

1. *Narrow, well-defined focus.* The problem must have a narrow, well-defined focus rather than a broad prospective. The range of knowledge must fall within a manageable scope. For example, creating an expert system for improving the entire marketing field would be foolish. The problem should not require enormous volumes of knowledge to solve.

2. *Moderate solution time.* Experienced knowledge engineers suggest that the answer to a problem should be obtainable within the few-minutes-to-few-hours time frame. If it can be solved in less than a few minutes, the problem is probably too trivial; if it takes more than a few hours, the problem is probably too difficult and poorly bounded.

3. *Symbolic knowledge and reasoning.* The problem solution should be based on symbolic reasoning rather than numerical computation. That is, the solution should use heuristics requiring judgment about subjective factors. A reasonable number of cases that result in no solution is acceptable. The goal is 100 percent correct results, although "good enough" results for a solution often suffice.

4. *A stable domain.* One should select a stable, rather than a volatile problem domain, although some systems, such as XCON, are frequently updated to handle changing domains. A knowledge base core that is constantly changing requires frequent updating of the rules and coping with the attendant testing problems.

5. *Size of the knowledge base.* A good rule of thumb is to pick a first-time problem domain that results in a manageable set of rules (fewer than 100 rules). Tackling a larger, more complex problem could be asking for trouble because size increases the complexity of testing.

6. *Available test cases.* A good set of test cases is important to the success of extracting knowledge from the expert and verifying the knowledge base. For each test case, an expert solution must also be available. This issue needs to be addressed early in the development process. If evaluated early in the system's life cycle, test cases can provide valuable clues as to feasibility and potential value of the system.

7. *Complexity of the domain.* A candidate problem domain should be complex enough to be meaningful, but not so difficult as to exceed the upper limits of the technology. The number of variables involved can provide one indication of whether a problem is a good candidate. If the problem requires a half-dozen variables, it is too simple for an expert system. Under this reasoning, if a trained technician can do the same job as an expert, then the problem is probably not a good candidate.

8. *Degree of uncertainty or fuzziness.* If the problem involves mostly algorithmic data or can be solved by a high-level language such as COBOL or Fortran, then it is probably not a good candidate for an expert system.

9. *Demonstration of worth.* The problem domain must promise a net benefit. The payoff may be reduced cost, improved decision quality, a more efficient operation, reduced employee training time, improved working conditions, or some other benefit. Such intangible benefits as improved competitive edge, learning of new technology, job enrichment, and future system integration should also be considered.

10. *Scarce expertise.* If the expertise is plentiful, inexpensive, and reliable, then replacing it with an expert system is difficult to justify.

11. *Appropriate depth of required knowledge.* Most shallow knowledge systems involve a single expert, use fewer than 100 rules, and can be built in less than two months by one knowledge engineer. **Dendral** is an example of a shallow expert system. An example of a "deep" expert system is the on-board expert system of F-16 jet fighters, which can identify the type of aircraft and whether it is friendly or hostile from a 40-mile distance with greater than 98 percent accuracy. Although the number of the system's parameters and rules has not been disclosed, its rules are estimated to be in the hundreds. Figure 7–1 is a summary of the key domain characteristics.

Figure 7–1   Key Domain Characteristics

1. A narrow, well-defined focus
2. Moderate solution time
3. Symbolic knowledge and reasoning
4. A stable domain
5. Size of the knowledge base
6. Available test cases
7. Complexity of the domain
8. Degree of uncertainty or fuzziness
9. Demonstration of worth
10. Scarce expertise
11. Appropriate depth of required knowledge

User Characteristics

Once the problem domain has been identified, the knowledge engineer must then determine what the user expects and how well the system can meet user requirements. Why build an expert system that no one will use?

Two user characteristics are worth noting:

1. *Users should feel a strong need for the system.* Users must first perceive a need and then be able to see a benefit before they are motivated to cooperate. If they feel that the system will aid them and improve their skills, they are more likely to support the system's development. Users generally resist a project if they fear being displaced or if it reduces their credibility in the organization.

2. *Users should develop realistic expectations of the system.* Users should never be oversold on the goodness of an expert system. They must know that even the best systems can fail to perform perfectly all the time. As a first step, users should be educated in the pros and cons of expert systems as a technology. Carefully planning the transition for implementation of this new technology in the work place is also important.

Expert Characteristics

The second prerequisite to knowledge acquisition is a qualified expert. Human expertise is the heart of the knowledge base. The knowledge engineer and expert must agree on the problem, or the resulting system could be nothing but opinions or guesses.

The expert may be the reason that a problem is a good candidate for an expert system. For example, the expert may have chosen to retire and therefore will be unavailable in the future. This situation lends a sense of urgency to capturing the knowledge quickly and effectively. To avoid creating a situation in which the expert feels threatened by the expert system, the knowledge engineer must use acquisition tools effectively while maintaining a sensitivity to the expert's situation. Expert characteristics are discussed in depth in Chapter 8.

■ IMPLICATIONS FOR KNOWLEDGE ACQUISITION

Knowing how experts know what they know is the bottom line in knowledge acquisition. Expert knowledge is cognitively complex and tacitly pragmatic. It is not always easy to acquire through a traditional interview process. In many cases in which knowledge acquisition was unsuccessful, the knowledge engineer did not quite understand the pragmatic nature of the expertise. And just as the knowledge engineer may not fully understand the expert, the expert may be equally unclear about the knowledge engineer. Experts sometimes perceive knowledge engineers as domain **novices,** who require patience and who must go through an apprenticeship process that takes them from novice to near-expert status during the building of the expert system. This perception is even more reason the knowledge engineer should devote serious efforts toward preparation and a familiarity in the domain.

The following suggestions can be used to improve the knowledge acquisition process:

1. Knowledge engineers should focus on how experts approach a problem. They must look beyond looking the facts or the heuristics.

2. Knowing that true expertise takes the form of **chunked knowledge,** knowledge engineers should reevaluate how well they understand the problem domain and how accurately they are modeling it. Can they see patterns and relationships leading to a solution? That is, can the knowledge engineer grasp the complexity of the domain? Conceptual tools (discussed in Chapter 9) provide the engineer with a concise, easy way to capture heuristics.

3. The quality of human emulation is best captured through **episodic knowledge,** or knowledge based on previous experience. Therefore, a knowledge engineer should elicit the expert's knowledge through concrete case situations or scenarios.

■ AUTOMATED KNOWLEDGE ACQUISITION

The knowledge acquisition process can be both tedious and complicated. The knowledge engineer interviews the expert repeatedly, watches the expert solve a number of cases, and then records the expert's actions. Sufficient information must be available before the knowledge engineer attempts to emulate the expert's thought process. In large, complex projects, the information gathered is sometimes so voluminous that it becomes difficult to manage.

The large amount of manual work has created the "knowledge acquisition bottleneck." Various companies are now trying to automate knowledge acquisition. A good example of an automated knowledge acquisition product is Auto-Intelligence by a California-based firm. The software helps experts capture their own expertise. It can also be used by knowledge engineers to speed up the acquisition process in complex applications such as stock market trading. Some experts have reported that the system has helped them become better acquainted with their own thoughts. Figure 7–2 summarizes the steps Auto-Intelligence uses in building an expert system.

Automated knowledge acquisition has been successfully implemented to extract knowledge and build knowledge bases from printed material. Some software analyzes narrative text and summarizes the knowledge structures (events) in generalized schemas. For example, Aqua is a story-understanding software program that interprets textual information using a set of questions stored in memory. It retrieves information about the domain from the text to answer the questions. It builds a knowledge base directly from the text. It also gets around the problem of natural language understanding by analyzing only the text's logical structure, not its semantic content.

Before bringing technology into an organization, management itself needs to be sold on the technology's contribution to the firm's profitability. In an organization unfamiliar with expert systems, the recommended procedure is to introduce a prototype system that solves an important problem and demonstrates the usefulness of expert system technology. The project should require no longer than one year to complete with a budget well under $100,000. For example, prototype system that can be completed in two–three months, costs less than $50,000, and runs on a PC could be a hit.

Figure 7–2   The Auto-Intelligence Automated Knowledge Acquisition Process

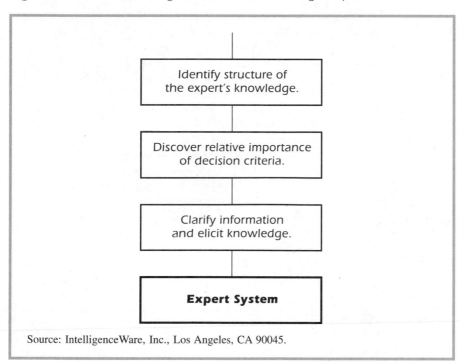

Source: IntelligenceWare, Inc., Los Angeles, CA 90045.

Box 7–2   Involving the User

A Chicago-based company made paper cups at its Montreal plant and supplied stores throughout Canada. It faced strong competition from other suppliers in the United States and Canada.

One of its special-purpose machines was particularly important. It produced cups at such a high speed that it required constant attention and adjustment. If corrections were not made in time, the unusable cups it turned out numbered in the hundreds. The general manager of the Canadian division thought the operation of this machine could benefit from an "expert advisor" that would indicate to the operator the right adjustment on a 24-hour basis.

A development team was assigned to the resident expert who was called at all kinds of odd hours when the machine had to be adjusted. After eight months of work, the system was ready for service.

The evening shift operator was reluctant to use the expert advisor. He said, "This is a replacement for a supervisor. What can it do that I don't know already?" The resentment of the new expert system was so strong that the union filed a complaint the week following installation.

All went well in the end, however. The operator learned how the expert system tracked every deviation from the specifications of the machine, which meant he didn't have to watch gauges and interpret sounds as intently. Much to the surprise of everyone, the evening operator proved to be an expert himself as he acknowledged that many of the adjustments recommended by the system were exactly what he would do.

Figure 7-3   The Relationship between the Team and the Expert

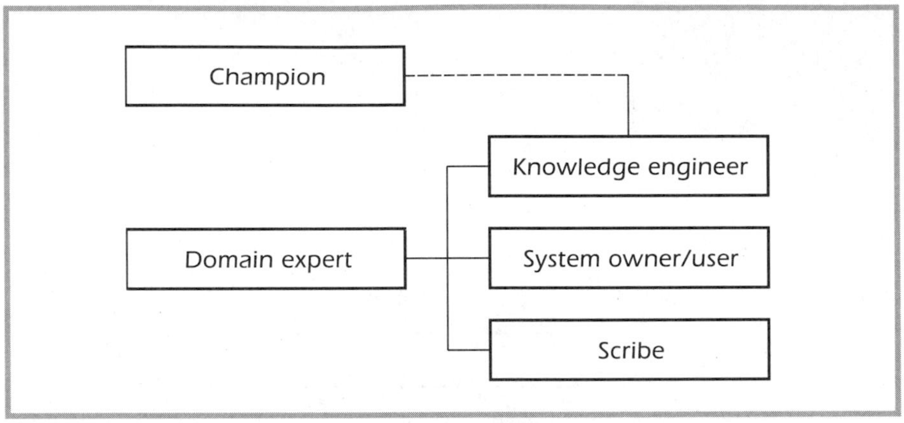

IMPLICATIONS FOR MANAGEMENT

For success in building expert systems, a number of things must fall in place. First, complex applications require the time and talent of the knowledge engineer. By the time acquisition begins, all the preliminaries should be established, including the budget approval, the expert's availability, and the user's commitment. Beginning acquisition without these preliminaries is to invite failure.

Many expert systems are built using teams. As mentioned in Chapter 6, a team includes a champion, system user, an expert, one or more knowledge engineers, and a scribe. The champion is a respected executive who believes in the project and sells the idea to those who control the purse strings. Executive support is usually assured if the project promises (1) a fair return on investment, (2) a replacement for human expertise that is about to be lost, or (3) the availability of human expertise in several locations.

The system user can be responsible for maintaining the system once it has been installed. In smaller projects, the knowledge engineer serves as the project coordinator. The **scribe** takes notes during interviews and maintains all the documentation for the project. A knowledge engineer often serves as the scribe. Figure 7-3 shows the relationship between the team and the expert.

If the expert system is being developed for a user department, the user should be involved early. Hard lessons have been learned when users have not known much about a system until the end, only to find out that it failed to meet user requirements. Box 7-2 illustrates the point. The cost of involving users is usually low, but user involvement can save a lot of headaches once the system is installed. A prototype of the system can be built to sell the change early in the life cycle of the product, which also makes it easier to train the user and gain their acceptance.

■ SUMMARY

1. The goal of a knowledge engineer is to extract problem-solving knowledge from the expert in order to build a knowledge base. Knowledge acquisition is a process of capturing the expert's thoughts and experience and representing them in a knowledge base. The process also includes acquiring knowledge from sources such as books, technical manuscripts, and drawings.

2. Knowledge acquisition involves three important steps: eliciting information from the expert, interpreting the information and underlying knowledge, and building the set of rules that represents the expert's knowledge.

3. When acquiring knowledge, a knowledge engineer must identify and justify the problem domain, choose the right expert, and prepare for acquisition. These steps are generally done sequentially.

4. The scope of the domain should be well defined and the problem solution based on symbolic reasoning. The domain should contain common sense knowledge and the knowledge base be a manageable size. Other domain characteristics relate to the difficulty and uncertainty of the domain.

5. Users must perceive a need for the expert system in order for it to be successful. The users must be interested in the system and cooperative during its development. However, the user also needs to have realistic expectations of what the system can and cannot do.

6. The expert is a person with genuine knowledge and expertise in the problem domain who can effectively communicate that knowledge to the knowledge engineer.

7. One of the most common problems faced in knowledge acquisition is less-than-effective interactions between knowledge engineers and domain experts, which jeopardize the validity of the knowledge acquired. Therefore, knowledge engineers must understand how well the experts say what they mean and mean what they say.

■ TERMS TO LEARN

Chunked knowledge a group of items stored and recalled as a unit.

Episodic knowledge knowledge based on experience with previous cases.

Novice an individual with skills and solutions that work some of the time but not all of the time.

Scribe a person who takes notes during interviews and maintains all the documentation related to the project.

System owner a user who will be responsible for maintaining the system after it is installed.

■ REVIEW QUESTIONS

1. In your own words, define knowledge acquisition? What makes it different from systems analysis?

2. List and explain the steps involved in knowledge acquisition.

3. Which of the prerequisites for acquisition described in the chapter do you think is the most crucial? Why?

4. Why is identifying the right problem domain so important? Explain.

5. Explain briefly the key domain characteristics. Can one realistically expect a problem domain to have all these characteristics? If not, how would one choose a problem domain? Be specific.

6. "The problem solution should be based on symbolic knowledge rather than numerical computation." Do you agree? Explain.

7. What do you consider a first-time problem domain with a manageable set of rules? Provide an example.

8. How does the user play a key role in expert system development?

9. What suggestions can you make for improving knowledge acquisition? Explain.

10. Do you think knowledge acquisition can be fully or easily automated? Why or why not?

EXERCISES AND CASES

Publisher Advisor

1. A problem domain is the area with which an expert is very familiar. In the Publisher Advisor project, the expert is a book editor with 27 years of experience in four major publishing houses. The editor's expertise is widely recognized among colleagues and has made a number of successful book adoption decisions.

The problem domain is narrow, and the problem well defined, one that can be solved through the use of an expert system shell. The domain is relatively stable; it is not amendable to major changes in its knowledge base when completed. In addition, the problem domain requires only moderate solution time at an affordable cost.

The knowledge engineer had not dedicated much time to preparation for knowledge acquisition, but had published a number of books personally. Therefore, the knowledge engineer was well versed in the terminology, production process, how editors think through the decision to publish a manuscript, and the way a book must be written for a target market.

Several reasons led to the development of an expert system to capture the book editor's knowledge in this particular case:

■ The improved productivity of the book editor will offset the cost of developing a Publisher Advisor, which is expected to improve the long-term profitability of the publishing house.

■ This proposed system can not only assist the editor in making the final decision (publish,

defer decision, or reject manuscript), it can assist with the training of junior editors.

■ College book publishing is stable industry, because college professors are not likely to stop adopting textbooks for their classes.

■ The decision to offer contracts or reject manuscripts is not a hardened quantifiable rule. Indeed, this area bases itself on heuristics and lends itself extremely well to an expert system application.

■ Publisher Advisor promotes a higher level of consistency for decision making. Since the rules will be clearly defined, the ultimate decision is more consistent when compared to similar cases over time.

■ The benefits of Publisher Advisor include increased competitive advantage, strategic planning of book publications, high productivity, and job enrichment.

Questions

a. Evaluate the foregoing benefits or justification for committing to Publisher Advisor.

b. Based on the material presented, what is missing in the early phase of Publisher Advisor? Be specific.

c. What else does the knowledge engineer needs to do before beginning knowledge acquisition? Explain.

d. Check with your instructor or a visiting book editor and prepare your own scenario (plan) regarding preparation for knowledge acquisition to build a Publisher Advisor.

2. The *Home Veterinarian* is an expert system designed to provide pet owners with an extensive practical pet health guide for their home. The system asks the pet owner a series of questions regarding the condition of his or her pet and then provides the owner with meaningful advice either to go directly to their veterinarian, or continue to observe their pet's condition and wait until normal office hours.

Some advantages to this system include avoiding emergency veterinarian treatment during the weekend if the pet's problem could have waited until the office opened the next day. By providing assurances that a pet does not need emergency treatment, the system can save the owner the additional cost of a weekend visit.

Many uncertainties are associated with medical symptoms and possible diseases. Veterinarians make a judgment as to the most probable disease a pet may have based on their school training and years of practical experience. Textbooks can document these symptoms, but other symptoms or combinations of symptoms may lead a veterinarian to conclude a particular disease is present. For this reason, an expert system using relative confidence factors would be an appropriate way to represent this knowledge.

Questions

a. In this expert system, the knowledge engineer is a practicing system builder with background in computer science application but with no prior experience in veterinarian medicine. What do you recommend this knowledge engineer do to prepare for knowledge acquisition?

b. How much time would be needed to complete this project from beginning to end? Justify your answer.

c. Is this the type of expert system that could benefit from more than one knowledge engineer?

d. Is this the type of expert system that requires more than one expert for validity and reliability of the final system? Explain.

3. The problem domain of this expert system is identification and diagnosis of open-bone frac-

tures for proper management and cure. The domain expert is a 30-year-old orthopedic surgeon who has just completed a residency at the local hospital. The system will be validated by senior surgeons including the chief resident of general surgery at the same hospital. The level of computer literacy of each expert varies from little to moderate.

The knowledge engineer is a close relative of the young surgeon. A close family relationship with the expert is assumed to yield economies of scale in the development of the system. Preparation for the interview in terms of securing the cooperation of the expert was made easier by the close relationship, as was arranging meeting schedules.

The tangible benefits of the proposed system were many: permanent repository of expert knowledge, consistency of recommendations following a methodical set of rules, ease of knowledge transfer to other computerized media, and an increase in cost and time savings. The Open-Bone Fracture Advisor is expected to free the surgeon to do other more important tasks. It can also be used as a training tool for medical students specializing in the same domain.

Questions

a. How viable is the problem domain addressed by this medical advisor? Explain.

b. Discuss the pros and cons of having the domain expert as a relative to the knowledge engineer.

c. What scoping and timing issues are involved in this case? Elaborate.

4. For the Nutrition Advisor, the domain expert was the Director of the Nutrition Clinic in the city, and had been at the post almost four years. As an associate professor of Health Education and Health Promotion at the university for ten years, a recipient of a Ph.D. in physiology from a Big Ten school in 1973, and a postdoctoral fellow at a prestigious medical school for four years following graduation from the doctoral program, this expert had a total of fifteen years of experience in the field of nutrition.

In addition to a publication record too long to mention, the domain expert had also served on numerous committees, including the Exercise and Cardiac Rehabilitation Committee for the American

Heart Association and the city's Wellness Committee, and had served as a member of the board of directors for the American Diabetes Association.

Questions

a. Based on this description, how well qualified is the domain expert for the project? Is anything lacking? Explain.

b. What would motivate this domain expert to offer time and willingness to work on this project? (By way of information, the project took two knowledge engineers six months to complete.)

■ SELECTED REFERENCES

Billman, Beth, and James F. Courtney. "Automated Discovery in Managerial Problem Formulation: Formation of Causal Hypotheses for Cognitive Mapping." *Decision Sciences,* January/February 1993, pp. 23–41.

Caracas, Joao, and Manuel Maria Carrilho. "A New Paradigm in the Organization of Knowledge." *Futures,* September 1994, pp. 781–786.

Gaines, Brian R., and John H. Boose, *The Foundations of Knowledge Acquisition.* London and San Diego, CA: Academic Press, 1990.

Gao, V., and S. Salveter. "The Automated Knowledge Engineer: Natural-Language Knowledge Acquisition for Expert Systems." In J. H. Boose, and B. R. Gaines, eds., *Proceedings of the Sixth Banff Workshop on Knowledge Acquisition for Knowledge-Based Systems,* Calgary: University of Calgary, 1991.

Gerb, Andrew. "Managing a Complete Expert System Through a Long Maintenance Life-Cycle." In *Proceedings of the Third Annual Symposium of the International Association of Knowledge Engineers, Washington, D. C., November 16–19, 1992, pp. 34–44.*

Gomes, F., and C. Segami. "Knowledge Acquisition from Natural Language for Expert Systems Based on Classification Problem." *Knowledge Acquisition Journal,* no. 2 (1991), pp. 107–128.

Poulymenakou, Angeliki. "A Contingency Approach to Knowledge Acquisition: Critical Factors for Knowledge-Based System Development." In *Proceedings of the Third Annual Symposium of the International Association of Knowledge Engineers,* Washington, D. C., November 16–19, 1992, pp. 99–115.

Reimer, U. "Automatic Knowledge Acquisition from Texts: Learning Terminological Knowledge via Text Understand and Inductive Generalization." In J. H. Boose, and B. R. Gaines, eds., *Proceedings of the Fifth Banff Workshop on Knowledge Acquisition for Knowledge-Based Systems.* Calgary: University of Calgary, 1990.

Springer, Stephen, and Paul Buta. "Communicating the Knowledge in Knowled-Based Systems." In *Proceedings of the Third Annual Symposium of the International Association of Knowledge Engineers,* Washington, D. C., November 16–19, 1992. pp. 247–263.

Sturrock, Charles. "Guidelines for the Organization of Domain Expertise to Facilitate Knowledge Acquisition." In *Proceedings of the Third Annual Symposium of the International Association of Knowledge Engineers, Washington, D. C., November 16–19, 1992, pp. 88–98.*

Walz, Diane B., Joyce J. Elam, and Bill Curtis. "Inside a Software Design Team: Knowledge Acquisition, Sharing, and Integration." *Communications of the ACM,* October 1993, pp. 62–77.

Wetter, Thomas. *Current Developments in Knowledge Acquisition: EKAW '92: Sixth European Knowledge Acquisition Workshop, Heidelberg and Kaiserslautern, Germany, May 1992.* Berlin and New York: Springer-Verlage, 1992.

Wong, Bo K., and John K. Chong. "Averting Development Problems: Rules for Better Planning." *Information Systems Management,* Winter 1992, 15–20.

Chapter ■ 8

Working with Experts

WORKING WITH AN EXPERT—AN ANECDOTAL REPORT

During the summer of 1994, my goal under a research grant was knowledge acquisition for a prototype expert system that would diagnose and prescribe treatment for foot problems encountered by diabetic patients. The preparation for this systemic task included more than two months of reviewing three texts and numerous journal articles about foot and ankle diseases and deformities. I was ready to schedule the first interview with the expert, an orthopaedic surgeon with 21 years of experience in treating diabetic foot and ankle problems.

THE FIRST SESSION

On a chilly Saturday afternoon in late April, I traveled to the expert's home. During the meeting, I explained the goal of the project, the expert's role, and how I planned to proceed in building the prototype Diabetic Foot Advisor. I also mentioned the readings I had done at his suggestion. He was quiet, but seemed interested and committed to the prototype's success. According to his assessment after reviewing my plan, development of the expert system prototype would probably take at least four months. I was relieved, because a four-month timeframe fell neatly within my summer break from classes.

TROUBLE SIGNALS

During that first meeting, I had agreed on the dates and duration of the knowledge acquisition sessions. But each time I tried to finalize the schedule, the time required to develop the prototype continued to grow until it looked more like a year than four months.

Because my understanding of the problem domain (the diseases of the diabetic foot) was limited, I relied on the reading material to compose a list of questions for the first acquisition session. I set up the tape recorder to capture the session and asked if he minded my taping the first few sessions. He replied, "I don't understand this taping business. Can't you take notes?" Although I didn't want to miss the finite points of the meeting, he did not seem comfortable with the tape recorder, so I quickly packed it away and reverted to note taking.

Halfway through the interview, I sensed his frustration. I asked how he thought the session was going, to which he replied, "Well, we've been at this problem for close to an hour. I'm afraid that this project could take forever. I can't see where all this is leading. Suppose I fax you a diagram and see how it will replace the interviews." Not wanting to lose the expert's participation, I decided to try his method. I thanked him for agreeing to continue and that I looked forward to working with his charts.

As I drove back to my office (120 miles away), I wasn't sure what to expect next. I had started with a well-defined project, a willing expert, and a realistic schedule, but in one session the tables had turned and the project seemed in jeopardy. Because timing was of the essence, I didn't have the luxury of picking another expert.

TIME HEELS ALL THINGS?

Two weeks later, the two-page flowchart came by fax. After reviewing the chart, I generated a set of questions and built an 11-rule knowledge base based on my understanding of the expert's chart. The following Saturday, I took my PC, with the knowledge base already loaded on the hard disk, and drove to the expert's home.

At this session, I met the expert's family and their dog, Mack. During general conversation before we began our work, I mentioned that my son had recently been admitted to medical school in a local university where the expert taught second-year students a course on foot and ankle surgery, which somehow warmed up the situation. When he asked, "Let's see what you were able to do with the chart I faxed you," his wife, who works in the clinic as a volunteer, also became interested and wanted to see the prototype.

Although he knew very little about computers and even less about expert systems, the expert was quite excited to see his ideas represented in the skeletal phase of the knowledge base. He then said, "I can't believe that you could make sense out of the chart this way. I spent a long time putting it together. Maybe what we can do this afternoon is to talk about the diabetic foot and how well the ideas can be incorporated into your system." Luckily, because I was familiar with the VP-Expert shell, we were able to begin the rapid prototyping phase.

Throughout the summer, each of the fourteen sessions began with careful preparation, working with the expert to structure the information based on a combination of note taking and on-the-spot additions to and modifications of the growing knowledge base. With each session, I learned more and more about the expert's idiosyncrasies and temperament and how to work around them. My goal was to maintain control over the interview at all times.

By late July, I had to concentrate on knowledge representation to complete the prototype. The end result was a 81-rule knowledge base with no obvious problems. The good news was that the expert liked what he saw later in October and was considering submitting it to the American Diabetic Association for funding. When I alerted him to the need for many more sessions and intensive testing before the system would be ready for the end-user—the diabetic patient—he suggested that he bring in another expert in diabetes to finalize the details of the knowledge base.

In the process of helping to develop the expert system prototype, the expert became a virtual knowledge engineer. He began to express his ideas in terms of IF . . . THEN rules to conform to the way VP-Expert used the rule format.

Currently, this project awaits funding by a pharmaceutical firm and further development to create an operational system.

Based on recent work on an expert system called Diabetic Foot Advisor, July 1994.

AT A GLANCE

Working with experts in the development of expert systems is not a straight-forward routine. For example, the methods or tools choosen for knowledge acquisition depend on the temperament, personality, and attitude of the expert, and whether the expert system is being built around a single expert or multiple experts. Another important factor is whether one or more knowledge engineers will be involved in the building process.

Before beginning the knowledge acquisition process, a knowledge engineer needs to have an understanding of the expert's level of expertise. The knowledge engineer can look at several indicators of expertise as well as specific qualifications to determine whether someone is an expert. One of the most important indicators is the expert's communication skills.

Using either a single or multiple experts each has advantages and limitations. For smaller projects, building an expert system around a single expert is typical. In problem domains with dispersed knowledge, which require synthesis of experience, multiple experts are preferred. In either case, working with experts (and accommodating the experts' individual styles of expression require special skills. The location at which knowledge acquisition sessions are held adds another dimension that the knowledge engineer must consider.

What You Will Learn

By the end of this chapter, you should know the following:

1. Expert characteristics and the levels of expertise that the knowledge engineer needs to identify.

2. The advantages and limitations of using single and multiple experts.

3. How to work with experts.

> I f you call someone an "expert" for a project, treat that person like one. Even if the person doesn't know everything about the domain, the person knows more than you.
>
> —PATRICK E. DESSERT

■ INTRODUCTION

The most critical step in developing an expert system is the process of tapping the expert's knowledge. Many of the problems encountered in this process stem from using the wrong acquisition tool, poorly trained knowledge engineers, or a domain expert with a negative attitude toward the process.

Early on, the knowledge engineer must decide whether an expert system will be built around a single expert or multiple experts, and whether it will be built by a single knowledge engineer or a development team. Whatever the choice, special preparation on the part of the expert(s) and the knowledge engineer, and of the tool(s) to elicit information is required. This chapter focuses on what knowledge engineers need to understand about expert characteristics and the pros and cons of single and multiple experts.

■ EXPERT CHARACTERISTICS

Knowledge acquisition requires free access to a cooperative and articulate, expert. Shearson American Express discovered this basic rule of expert system development more than ten years ago when it aborted an attempt to install an interest rate swapping expert system. The prototype worked fine. It assisted the traders in picking out possible international swap partners around the globe. But the system failed to materialize as soon as the real experts—the traders—bowed out, because a characteristic of Wall Street traders is their general unwillingness to share knowledge.

Identifying Genuine Know-How

In most cases, the knowledge engineer does not have the luxury of deciding on the expert. Yet, the knowledge engineer must be able to identify real expertise and how well a particular expert's know-how suits the project (as in the expert for the Aerobic Fitness Advisor in Box 8–1).

Without a good match of expert and project, the knowledge engineer could spend hours of valuable time questioning someone whose knowledge might be unusable in the given application.

There are several indicators of expertise:

■ Peers regard the expert's decisions as good decisions. The expert commands *genuine respect.*

■ Whenever a specific problem arises, people in the plant *consult the expert.*

■ The expert admits not knowing the answer to a problem. This honesty indicates *self-confidence* and a *realistic view of limitations.*

■ The expert avoids information that is irrelevant to the domain and instead sticks to the facts and works with a *focus.*

■ The expert demonstrates a *knack for explaining things* and can customize the presentation of information to the level of the individual listener.

■ An expert's expertise is apparent to an informed listener. An expert exhibits a certain depth of detail and *exceptional quality in explanations.*

■ The expert is *not arrogant* about personal credentials, years of experience, or strong ties with people in power.

Box 8–1   Characteristics of an Aerobic Fitness Expert

Our domain expert is Fitness Program Director. She is a certified aerobic and fitness instructor. She has her Masters in Sports Fitness and has been working in this field for ten years in health clubs and at universities. She also certifies the aerobic instructors in the city. She is quite energetic and excited about working with us as the "expert" in developing the aerobic fitness advisor system. Heather is committed to her career and enjoys helping others achieve fitness whenever she can.

Source: Paul Chamoun, Mary Hill, and Susan Smith, "Aerobic Fitness Advisor," University of Virginia, Spring 1994.

In addition to these general indicators, experts usually exhibit more specific qualifications:

1. *Knows when to follow heuristics and when to make exceptions.* This quality is a result of experience. Trial and error teach an expert when to make exceptions and build the expert's episodic memory. Unlike semantic memory, which is the knowledge of facts, episodic memory is the knowledge of cases based on experience. Case-based reasoning is effective in building complex expert systems.

2. *Sees the big picture.* Experts can sift through information and readily determine which factors are important and which are superfluous. In a study of radiologists reading X-rays, novices searched for particular features in the X-ray, looking for each feature's underlying causes. As the radiologists gained more experience, they began to realize that certain features were dependent on other features in the X-ray and learned that the context offered them cues. This process illustrates the complexity of true expertise.

3. *Possesses good communication skills.* A knowledge engineer cannot create a reliable expert system if the expert cannot communicate his or her knowledge. Verbal skills facilitate smooth acquisition.

4. *Tolerates stress.* Building expert systems can test an expert's patience, particularly when the knowledge engineer asks the wrong question, the interview simply stagnates, or the domain is too difficult for the knowledge engineer to understand.

5. *Thinks creatively.* An expert should demonstrate a certain inventiveness when solving a problem or explaining the reasoning behind a solution. Creative approaches can clarify the expert's thought processes and ability to convey knowledge to the knowledge engineer.

6. *Exhibits self-confidence.* Experts believe in their ability to deliver. A self-confident expert can accept criticism and react without feeling threatened when an answer is not known. Self-confidence also boosts an expert's capacity to handle stress.

7. *Maintains credibility.* Experts who demonstrate competency in the way they field questions gain a reputation for believability based on the experience others have had with them.

8. *Operates within a schema-driven orientation.* The expert does serious schema-driven, or structured, "thinking" in an effort to come up with realistic, workable solutions. (Two examples are provided in Box 8–2.)

Expertise is not merely organized factually but also tactically. Know-how does not come prepackaged as an immediate answer; when confronted with a problem, an expert goes beyond the information given and categorizes the problem as one of a particular type. This structuring of a problem provides a wider realm of possible solutions.

9. *Uses chunked knowledge.* A unique feature in the way an expert solves problems is the chunking of knowledge. *Chunks* are groups of items stored and recalled as a unit. Several studies have shown that an individual's ability to recall information increases proportionately with the amount of chunking. For example, a study of master-level and novice chess players involved in copying board positions of games-in-progress showed that experts turned back to look at the board fewer times than did novice chess players. The experts took in larger chunks of the game than did the novices. Another study found that baseball

Box 8–2   Examples of Schema-Driven Orientation

1. A graduate student was interviewing with a Big Six accounting firm for a job in information systems. One of the partners asked, "How many takeoffs and landings during a given day at O'Hare airport?"

   The recruit snapped, "Fifteen per hour, on the basis of four minutes per flight." When later asked how the question should have been answered, the partner replied, "Well, there is no specific answer. The number of flights depends on the number of usable runways, the time of the day, weather conditions, ratio of international to national flights, and the like. For example, international flights takeoffs are heavier in early to late evening than during the day. Landings are heavier during mid to late afternoons."

2. Two chess players were asked to recall moves of a game in progress. One player recalled the moves by attack and defense strategies, while the other player recalled the moves by local position. The first player was the expert and showed evidence of higher-order processing than did the second player.

experts tended to recall entire sequences of plays much more easily and accurately than did individuals with only a surface knowledge of the game.

A possible problem with chunking, however, is the difficulty many experts have in describing their knowledge—segmenting chunked knowledge and verbalizing it.

10. *Generates motivation and enthusiasm.* Enthusiastic experts who enjoy what they do generally perform well. This type of attitude also affects co-workers. If the participants approach building an expert system without enthusiasm, indifference and boredom soon set in, which contribute to poor motivation and endanger the project.

11. *Shares expertise willingly.* A "tight" expert will produce a less-than-complete expert system. The most effective experts have a volunteering nature and do not fear being eased out of their job.

12. *Emulates a good teacher's habits.* Most people remember one particular teacher because of the way that person delivered information. The best teachers are also good learners, and good learners make sure knowledge is transferred effectively. An effective expert "teaches" *how* to solve a problem realistically and achieve good results.

Obviously no person can possibly possess all of these attributes. Perhaps the most important attributes are acknowledged expertise, the ability to commit a large amount of time, and a gift for communicating knowledge to the knowledge engineer. Figure 8–1 is a summary of the key characteristics of a useful expert.

Choosing the Expert

After defining these characteristics, the next issue is *how to select an expert.* A knowledge engineer should begin by determining who is the most senior expert or the best in terms of performance. The classic choice is a person near retirement or a retired person who is available as a consultant. To determine the most qualified candidate, the knowledge engineer must work with the host organization in selecting the expert.

Figure 8–1   Desirable Characteristics of an Expert

1. Knows when to follow heuristics and when to make exceptions
2. Sees the big picture
3. Possesses good communication skills
4. Tolerates stress
5. Thinks creatively
6. Exhibits self-confidence
7. Maintains credibility
8. Operates within a schema-driven orientation
9. Uses chunked knowledge
10. Generates motivation and enthusiasm
11. Shares expertise willingly
12. Emulates a good teacher

One of the problems a knowledge engineer and the host organization must work to prevent is the expert's perception of an expert system as a threat. Interviews with leading knowledge engineers revealed that most experts do not feel threatened; more often, they are flattered. Some are pleasantly surprised when they are asked to participate and seem to enjoy the special treatment of their role. Praise and recognition are the most common incentives to motivate experts, who often do not receive extra pay.

If the expert feels pushed around, knowledge engineers can anticipate certain problems. A project can experience a bad beginning if the expert did not volunteer for the project, but was assigned to do the work. The knowledge engineer must also get past the obstacles of fear or resentment. For example, in one case, a group of schedulers did everything to keep the knowledge engineer out. She had to work slowly to build cooperation. When she learned enough about the field to understand the process, the domain experts slowly began to talk. Their initial refusal to cooperate was related to their fear that their jobs were in jeopardy.

Obviously, the right expert does not guarantee a successful expert system. An intelligent, secure, enthusiastic, and achievement-oriented knowledge engineer is essential for success. The knowledge engineer must sustain the expert's motivation and enthusiasm. Both parties must play their part.

Levels of Expertise

The critical role of communication skills cannot be overemphasized. Various studies have shown that different levels of expertise influence communication quality. One can arbitrarily classify experts into three levels: the highly expert person, the moderately expert person, and the new expert.

Highly expert persons generally give concise explanations. They assume the listener has enough knowledge about the problem, therefore they focus on the key steps, often skipping vital details. Highly expert persons also tend to rate their own expertise highly.

Box 8-3   *Characteristics and Capabilities of Expert Knowledge*

Experts are distinguished by the quality and quantity of knowledge they possess; they know more, and what they know makes them more efficient and effective. **Expert knowledge,** whether applied by human or machine, works in situations that do not admit optimal or provably correct solutions. Expert knowledge is used by problem solvers to find an acceptable solution that meets or exceeds requirements with a reasonable expenditure of resources. Specifically, expert knowledge helps problem solvers improve their efficiency by marshalling relevant facts, avoiding common errors, making critical distinctions between problem types, pruning useless paths of investigation, ordering search, eliminating redundancy, reducing ambiguities, eliminating noise in data, exploiting knowledge from complementary disciplines, and analyzing problems from different perspectives or levels of abstraction.

Source: F. Hayes-Roth and N. Jacobstein, "The State of Knowledge-Based Systems," *Communications of the ACM,* March 1994, p. 28.

Moderately expert problem solvers may be more tentative in their explanations, yet they tend to provide detailed explanations. They are quicker to give answers than the highly expert person and more often adapt their description to the level of the knowledge engineer.

In contrast, *new experts* are more likely to offer answers that are brief and fragmented, which suggests shallow knowledge of the domain. (See Box 8-3 for a description of characteristics and capabilities of an expert's knowledge.)

Based on the generalizations about the levels of expertise one can conclude that the more expert the person is, the longer that person will take to communicate an answer. A highly expert person stores years of experience in long-term memory, which may take longer to recall and transform into a verbal response. The challenge for the knowledge engineer then is to help the expert "unpack" or "de-chunk" the knowledge accurately and quickly. Rechecking and cross-validating the expert's opinions are important steps to follow in the knowledge acquisition process.

SINGLE VERSUS MULTIPLE EXPERTS

A key decision for the knowledge engineer is whether the expert system should be built around one expert or a panel of experts. This decision is based on a number of factors: the complexity of the problem domain, the criticality of the project to the organization, the types of experts available, and the funds allocated for the project.

Advantages and Drawbacks of Using a Single Expert

Five main advantages result from working with a single expert:

1. *A single expert is ideal when building a simple expert system—one with fewer than 200 rules that uses a PC-driven shell.* A one-on-one interactive relationship between a single knowledge engineer and a single expert promotes close ties quickly and speeds the acquisition process.

2. *A problem in a restricted domain calls for a single expert.* For example, David Smith, GE's locomotive expert, knew the problems of diesel engines and how to best repair them. His expertise made him the best choice for solving a particularly difficult problem in a restricted domain.

3. *A single expert facilitates the logistics aspect of coordinating arrangements for knowledge acquisition.* Once an expert agrees to do the work, one can more easily arrange meeting times and schedules than if multiple experts are involved. Prototyping also moves quickly, since only one expert needs to review the work and vouch for its readiness.

4. *With a single expert, problem-related or personal conflicts are easier to resolve.* Communications are usually easier and the approach to knowledge acquisition is more consistent when only one expert is involved.

5. *Single experts tend to show more confidentiality with project-related information than do multiple experts.* Part of human nature is sharing information: as more people are party to specific information, more opportunities arise for that information to leak out. Of course, much depends on both the nature of the project and the standards and integrity of the experts. See Box 8–4.

Box 8–4   Making the "Single Expert" Decision

For the Travel Consultant Advisory Expert System, it was determined that using a single expert would be superior to using multiple experts. This decision was made based on two primary considerations. The first was the subject area of the expert system, and the second was the reality of finding two qualified experts in Charlottesville area that were willing to put forth the time.

The vacation subject domain is very subjective. It would have been [as] difficult to have two experts agree upon a method of finding an appropriate vacation destination [as to determine] the actual destination itself. Because there are really no "right" answers, multiple approaches to solving the problem would not necessarily be of benefit, and consensus could be very hard to reach. The individual experiences of each expert would color their opinions and could be very hard to reconcile. We felt that because of the very subjective nature of the problem, many of the benefits of using multiple experts would be severely diminished.

Although Charlottesville does have several travel agencies, there are not many "experts" in the area. The travel agency industry is such that many of the agents are young and only stay at the job a few years before moving on to greener pastures. Because of the high turnover, experts can be hard to find. Since experts tend to be rare, they are also very busy. The time that knowledge acquisition consumes is a lot to ask from a busy expert. We were fortunate to gain the cooperation of one expert.

The domain expert is a 35-year-old college graduate with eight years of experience as a travel consultant in four travel agencies. In 1989, she started her own business and now has annual gross sales of $1.5 million.

Source: Jeanine Cohen and Wendi Bao Le, "Travel Consultant Advisory Expert System," University of Virginia, May 1994.

As attractive as the single expert approach is, it also has several drawbacks to keep in mind:

1. *Sometimes the expert's knowledge is not easy to tap.* If the expert has difficulty explaining or communicating procedures, the project can die quickly, especially if no backup expertise is available.

2. *Single experts provide a single line of reasoning, which makes it difficult to evoke in-depth discussion of the domain.* See Box 8–5. If someone sees a doctor and learns that he or she has a serious disease, that person would certainly appreciate a second opinion. Multiple experts are more likely to provide a built-in system of checks and balances.

3. *Single experts are more likely to change scheduled meetings than experts who are part of a team.* Unfortunately, people who make the best experts are often the least accessible. Other projects may limit an expert's

---

Box 8–5   The Admissions Advisor

One individual was selected as the domain expert. The expert is a practicing admissions director of the University. We chose to work with a single expert for the following reasons:

- The expert is the sole decision maker in the admissions selection process.
- The process is unique, making other experts' knowledge invalid for this specific problem domain.
- The expert showed enthusiasm for the project and willingness to commit her time and expertise.

Throughout the knowledge acquisition process, the director was extremely cooperative. She had excellent communication skills and conveyed information in a clear and descriptive manner. Throughout the project, she remained interested and enthusiastic. This allowed us to conduct efficient and meaningful sessions.

We were very fortunate that the expert was interested in the project and was willing to commit her time and resources. The expert was very patient with our continuing questioning throughout the whole process. As a by-product of this work, she has become interested in expert systems as a mechanism for training new personnel in the admissions process. Despite her cooperation, however, we did run across problems particular to the use of a single expert.

One difficulty inherent in using a single expert is **bias.** The knowledge base will only reflect inputs from her. Without a secondary source of expertise, the expert is both the supplier of knowledge and final authority who validates the system. This has implications for verification and validation if the system is to be used commercially. In this project, this difficulty was not an issue as this will be a proprietary system.

Another difficulty that can arise in the use of single versus multiple experts is that a single expert provides only one line of reasoning. In our situation, when we were unclear about a domain concept, it was difficult for the expert to convey the information in a novel format. In these situations, it would have been useful to have the benefit of a second perspective. A second expert may also have facilitated the knowledge acquisition sessions by introducing ideas that might evoke pertinent discussion. At times, we found it difficult to ask the right questions in order to elicit the deeper knowledge.

commitment to a new one. As a result, a reasonable deadline for completing the project may be uncertain.

4. *Expert knowledge is sometimes dispersed.* Relying on a single expert, especially in complex systems, can either create blind spots or result in a system that will have no users. Consider, for example, area of medicine, in which personnel are trained separately for radiology, gynecology, and internal medicine. Most medical expert systems need to draw upon community knowledge bases and integrate expertise from different areas to be successful. No single expert can realistically address more than one area.

Advantages and Drawbacks of Using Multiple Experts

Tapping the knowledge of a team of experts has its own advantages and drawbacks. The advantages include the following:

1. *Complex problem domains benefit from the expertise of more than one expert, especially if knowledge is dispersed and a number of "partial" experts are available.* A pool of experts is most often needed to gather sufficient knowledge to build complex systems. See Box 8–6. For example, building a system to predict the next direction of a given stock on the New York Exchange requires the talent of a pool of highly seasoned traders. No single trader could supply a reliable answer to all aspects of this problem domain.

2. *Working with multiple experts stimulates interaction that often produces synthesis of experience.* Bringing in a number of experts is bound to enrich the quality of knowledge. See Box 8–7.

3. *Listening to a variety of views allows the knowledge engineer to consider alternative ways of representing the knowledge.* Two heads are usually better than one, provided they agree to work together toward the goals of the project.

4. *Formal meetings are frequently a better environment for generating more thoughtful contributions.*

The possible drawbacks of multiple experts include the following:

1. *Coordinating meeting schedules for three or more experts can be a challenge.* Since an expert is usually in demand, each expert on a team will probably have to compromise in order for group meetings to be arranged. This area is the one in which interpersonal abilities of the knowledge engineer can make or break the project.

2. *Disagreements frequently occur among experts.* The greater the number of experts on a panel who must agree on a procedure or a solution, the greater is the probability of disagreement. If the diversity of opinions does not resolve into a consensus, the success of project could be in jeopardy. Disparity among the experts can also cause the least-senior expert to stifle, edit, or compromise an opinion. The knowledge engineer must be sensitive to this issue. See Box 8–8.

3. *The greater the number of people involved, the harder it may be to retain confidentiality.* As mentioned earlier, both the individuals involved and the nature of the problem domain determine the level of confidentiality needed.

4. *Working with multiple experts often requires more than one knowledge engineer.* With two interviewers, one can maintain the topic agenda and the

Box 8–6 **Knowledge Acquisition from Multiple Experts**

The Domain—IPM in Apples

We set out to build a knowledge-based system that would advise farmers *how* and *when* to apply pesticides to their crops in order to minimize the damage caused by insects and disease. The philosophy of Integrated Pest Management (IPM) is to use as few chemicals as possible, preserving natural enemies of harmful specifies when feasible. To begin with, the system would be limited to one crop (apples) and one type of pest (insects). . . . Each IPM team member is current in certain areas of the field, but none are able to keep up with the entire pest complex. So, there is no single person whose expertise spans all the possible pest problems over the growing season.

In light of the above, we decided to elicit the knowledge for our system from a team of experts. This offered broader coverage of the problem area. Experts in agriculture travel frequently, and we were able to not require that every member of the team be at every meeting. This actually made scheduling easier.

How the Team Functioned

At the very first meeting, experts really had no idea what the system could reasonably be expected to do and what they had to do in order to assist in the development process. There were also many points upon which they did not agree. So, we had to hold several meetings defining the territory to make sure each member of the team knew what was expected from them and what they should expect from the final system and finding areas of general agreement and disagreement.

For the agreed on points, this meant further explaining and detailing the knowledge for the knowledge engineer. In cases where there was no consensus, this meant discussing the differing points of view and finally arriving at a single "best" solution. Following the discussions often gave the knowledge engineer a better idea of the problem than did simple explanation by the expert, so that these parts of the system were actually easier to code and were more reliable. It is worth noting, though, that experts were not competing with each other, but, rather were trying to detail a problem and its solution. Many spirited, informative discussions (and a few arguments) were held. Inclusion of alternate solutions in the system greatly strengthened its usefulness.

Our experience with the system using multiple experts suggests the following:

- Team members should be chosen for compatibility as well as knowledge. There should be no personality conflict among the experts.

- Be prepared for an initial adjustment period. Progress is usually slow at the beginning, but it should pick up momentum later on.

- Be sure to have a clear, agreed upon last-ditch conflict resolution mechanism available. The one we used—the coordinators word is final—worked extremely well, but a person knowledgeable in the system domain and in programming may not always be available. Frequent use of this mechanism is a warning of basic problems in this approach.

- Construction of these systems is time-consuming, and using multiple experts probably will result in even slower initial development than usual.

Source: W. A. Wolf, *SIGART Newsletter,* no. 108, (April 1989), pp. 138–140.

Box 8-7 The Domain Experts

Two experts were employed in developing the Graduate Admissions expert system. The evaluation process is unique to each expert. Neither professor on the committee is "the expert," per se. In an effort to standardize the process and reduce personal bias, it was essential that we involve more than one member of the admissions committee. We identified two members with whom to work: These persons were chosen for one significant reason. It was essential that the experts be **cooperative** and forthcoming with the knowledge engineers in order for the knowledge base to have any integrity. The nature of the project material is highly sensitive to the school. For this reason, several members of the faculty and the admissions committee were less than enthusiastic when a similar project was proposed recently. The two experts named were identified as being the most excited about and cooperative with the development team.

Of these experts, Dr. Arnold served as the project's **champion.** He can be credited with terrific enthusiasm for seeing this expert system done and for bringing in the expertise of another expert. Dr. Carter proved helpful in verifying Dr. Arnold's comments and providing new perspectives to the process. The introduction of an additional expert brought the potential for differences of opinion about the application evaluation process. To resolve these conflicts in building the expert system, we deferred to the primary and secondary multiple expert scenario. In this scenario, Dr. Arnold served as our primary expert, validating the information retrieved from the secondary expert, Dr. Carter."

Box 8-8 Multiple Expert Aggregation

In knowledge acquisition, it is often desirable to aggregate the judgment of multiple experts into a single system. In some cases, this takes the form of averaging the judgment of those experts. In these situations, it is desirable to determine if the experts have different views of the world before their individual judgments are aggregated. In validation, multiple experts often are employed to compare the performance of expert systems and other human actors. Often those judgments are then averaged to establish performance quality of the expert system. An important part of the comparison process should be determining if the experts have a similar view of the world. If the experts do not have similar views, their evaluations of performance may differ, resulting in a meaningless average performance measure. Alternatively, if all the validating experts do have similar views of the world, then the validation process may result in paradigm myopia.

D. E. O'Leary, "Determining Differences in Expert Judgment: Implications for Knowledge Acquisition and Validation, *Decision Sciences,* March/April 1993, p. 395.

recording, while the other asks questions and gives feedback to promote discussion or clarify points. Since committing two knowledge engineers to a single job can be costly and time-consuming, this practice is usually reserved for complex, priority projects.

5. *The overlapping mental processes of multiple experts can lead to a "process loss."* When two or more experts get together, the nature of the discussion tends to overlap and the problem-solving process can be colored by

■ **Table 8–1**   Advantages and Disadvantages of Using Single and Multiple Experts

Single Expert	Multiple Expert
Advantages	
1. Ideal for building a simple domain expert system	1. Works best for complex problem domains
2. Works well for problems in a restricted domain	2. Stimulates interaction and synthesis of experience
3. Simplifies logistical issues	3. Presents a variety of views allowing for alternative representations of knowledge
4. Increases the probability of resolving conflicts	4. Generates more thoughtful contributions
5. Decreases risks to confidentiality	
Disadvantages	
1. Not easy to tap an expert's knowledge	1. Creates scheduling difficulties
2. Provides only a single line of reasoning	2. Increases the probability of disagreement
3. Increases the likelihood of schedule changes	3. Raises confidentiality issues
4. Doesn't accommodate dispersed knowledge	4. Requires more than one knowledge engineer
	5. Leads to a "process loss" in determining a solution

other experts' opinions. Sometimes, determining which expert is the closest to the solution is difficult. A summary of the pros and cons of single and multiple experts is shown in Table 8–1.

■ DEVELOPING A RELATIONSHIP WITH EXPERTS

Creating the Right Impression

Working with experts can be a complicated business. Perception plays an important role in the early phase of the building process. For example, how does the knowledge engineer know whether an expert—whose knowledge is sought, but is not paid for—will cooperate fully and reliably? From the expert's view, the knowledge engineer is building an expert system in a domain about which she or he knows little. The expert often has a poor perception of what the knowledge engineer can do. To reverse this perception, the knowledge engineer must learn quickly and use psychology, common sense, marketing, and technical skills to gain the expert's attention and respect. See Box 8–9.

In minimizing the disadvantages, a knowledge engineer should keep the following in mind: Regardless of what the knowledge engineer knows about the domain, competing with the domain expert makes no sense. In the face of competition, the expert could lose interest in the project, begin to give summaries instead of details, or find the knowledge engineer a nuisance. The key for the knowledge engineer is to stick to the prescribed roles and not try to be the expert.

Related to this point is underestimating the expert's experience. A seasoned expert will explain things simply and clearly. This simplicity can be deceptive, however, and create a false impression that the problem is easy to solve when

Box 8-9   The Taming of Experts

It is rare to find people who are blatant troublemakers in group sessions. If there is an expert in a session, it is important to establish whether the individual is acting in this way intentionally. Although no one reported doing this, one suggestion was to simply not start the work, knowing in advance that the expert is a troublemaker.

When hostility within the group of experts is apparent, you might want to handle it as if you were a parent. For example, you might say, "We are not getting anywhere. You can deal with this stuff elsewhere, outside of this meeting." Nasty comments are relatively rare, however, and overall tense sessions are relatively rare. One knowledge engineer estimated that about 25 percent of the experts could be categorized as difficult for some reason. One knowledge engineer said that out of the 25 to 30 sessions that he has conducted, only three sessions have gone perfectly from a technical standpoint. During all of the other sessions, something unexpected occurred. A fear of being embarrassed in front of another expert leads the expert to a conservative approach to the questions asked. When a serious problem does occur, it may be appropriate for the knowledge engineer to call for a break to buy time and find an alternative way of handling the expert(s).

Source: From a knowledge acquisition session building an auto loan advisor, by Matt Crisp and Laura Jones, University of Virginia, Spring 1994.

in reality the expert has barely scratched the surface. To quote Ed Koch, former mayor of New York City, "For every complex problem, there is a solution which is simple, economical, and wrong." For every simple thing the expert says, the details behind it are likely to be more complex. A knowledge engineer must keep exploring until the details are understood.

Understanding the Expert's Style

Domain experts express their views in a variety of ways that require special understanding. Knowledge engineers should acclimate themselves to the expert's style during the first session. Experts generally use one of these four styles of expression:

1. The *procedure type* of expert is verbal, logical, and procedure-oriented. This expert shows a methodical approach to the solution, with emphasis on *structure,* sometimes at the sacrifice of content. The knowledge engineer does not have to encourage the expert to talk, but rather to focus the expert's explanations on the problem at hand, staying within the guidelines of the problem domain. Otherwise, most of the knowledge engineer's energy will go toward making sense out of the expert's details.

2. The *storyteller type* of expert focuses on the *content* of the domain at the expense of the solution. This expressive expert probably came up through the ranks and received little attention or recognition. Such a person is usually willing to repeat a story or a description, but will often go off on a tangent, wander from one aspect of the domain to the next, or bounce between topics without noticing. The knowledge engineer must use structured interviews with this type of expert.

3. The *godfather type* of expert, by nature of position and personality, has a compulsion to take over. If allowed, this expert will wrest control from the knowledge engineer. No single prescription works every time for this situation, which will often worsen if the knowledge engineer attempts to right the balance of power in the wrong way. In fact, the worst scenario occurs when a godfather expert is paired with a manipulative knowledge engineer.

4. The *salesperson type* of expert spends most of the knowledge engineer's time "dancing" around the topic, explaining why the expert's solution is the best. The knowledge engineer can become distracted by this expert's habit of answering a question with another question. The knowledge engineer's role is to redirect the conversation and encourage straight answers.

Preparing for the Session

Before making the first appointment, the knowledge engineer should know something about both the expert (personality, temperament, job experience, familiarity with the domain, etc.) and the problem domain. The expert is more likely to be impressed by a knowledge engineer who comes to the meeting well prepared.

The initial sessions can be the most challenging and the most critical. Not knowing what to expect, the expert may become protective when the knowledge engineer begins to "peel" information from the expert's memory. The expert may resent any aggressive prodding. The burden of building trust falls on the knowledge engineer, since the responsibility of building the system also lies with the knowledge engineer, not the expert.

The knowledge engineer should become familiar with the application terminology of the problem domain and review existing material, such as a paper written by the expert or a book that details the nature and makeup of the domain. This research is also a way to learn the expert's language. Can you imagine building a real estate loan advisor without knowing terms such as *prime rate, variable interest rate,* or *balloon mortgage?* Even though a knowledge engineer learns quickly during the first few sessions, an early grasp of the basics inspires confidence on the part of the expert and allows the knowledge engineer and expert to be more productive.

If the domain is technical, a good beginning source is the university library. For less technical domains, textbooks and journals are appropriate. Attending seminars or lectures can also boost the knowledge engineer's credibility. If nothing seems to make sense within the time frame, the expert may be consulted for background material or for an orientation session.

An important beginning step in the first session is personal introductions. The expert is eager to know what type of person the knowledge engineer is and what the goals are for the project. The sooner a rapport is established, the easier things will move. Honesty is important. The expert and the knowledge engineer need to understand each other's experience related to the problem domain. Humility on the part of the knowledge engineer avoids a situation in which constant questions may appear arrogant.

Deciding Where to Hold the Sessions

Location is a matter of preference, but protocol calls for the expert to decide on the meeting site. Since a series of sessions take place over an extended time period, most experts opt for the convenience of meeting on their own turf. The knowledge engineer may also find benefit in recording the expert's knowledge in the environment where the expert does his or her job. An expert may feel more comfortable in having any necessary tools or information within arm's reach. Moreover, the knowledge engineer's willingness to travel to meet with the expert should generate goodwill for the project.

An important guideline is to make sure the meeting place is quiet and free of interruptions, such as phone calls or "urgent" messages.

Approaching Multiple Experts

One of the challenges in knowledge acquisition among multiple experts is determining the best approach. Three primary approaches are most often used.

The Individual Approach

The knowledge engineer holds sessions with one expert at a time, making it easier for the expert to offer information freely while assuring privacy. The individual approach is also useful in clarifying knowledge or defusing interpersonal problems that crop up when several experts are gathered in one room.

The Approach Using Primary and Secondary Experts

The knowledge engineer may decide to hold a session with the senior expert early in the acquisition program for clarification of the acquisition plan. For a detailed probing of the domain's mechanics, the knowledge engineer may tap other experts knowledge. In this approach, the primary expert verifies solutions in the event of diverse responses or conflicting opinions of secondary experts.

Another way of working with primary and secondary experts is to gather information from the secondary experts first and then consult the primary expert to check the reliability of the tapped knowledge. This bottom-up approach is useful when the primary expert is in demand and cannot devote full-time to the project. The primary expert's energies can be saved for the crucial steps as needed.

The Small Groups Approach

Experts are gathered together in one place to discuss the problem domain and provide a pool of information. Their responses are monitored at the same time, and the functionality of each expert is tested against the expertise of others in the group. The knowledge engineer can decide which expert is more cooperative or more believable. This approach requires experience in assessing tapped knowledge, as well as perception and cognition skills.

One of the issues that the knowledge engineer must deal with is power and its effect on the expert's opinions. For instance, how does a "junior" expert openly contradict the senior expert? Protocol may well require the junior expert to let comments go uncontested, which defeats the purpose of having experts share their knowledge.

On any particular issue, experts may disagree. Studies have found that in 90 percent of these occurrences the disagreements are due to differing assumptions about the problem being discussed. When such a case arises, a conflict resolution plan comes handy. The knowledge engineer should step in, clear the air, and urge the experts to reconsider their responses. The experts usually find a way to set aside their differences and reach on common solution.

The approach to working with multiple experts depends on two factors: (1) how well segmented the knowledge base is, and (2) whether group judgment is better than individual judgment. If the knowledge base is based on closely related modules, and each module represents a specialized area of the domain, then the small group approach is recommended. Each module should be programmed as an integral part of the knowledge base rather than a detached piece of knowledge. Several research studies have shown that group judgment is at least as good as individual judgment and, in some cases, may be superior. The decision to use a group approach depends on the nature of the domain, the type of task, the size of the group, and the quality of intragroup relations.

Group performance is closely related group size. As the size of a group increases arithmetically, one can expect a geometric increase in the total number of relationships. Using the formula $n(2^n/2 + n - 1)$, for a group size of $n = 3$, the total number of relationships is equal to 18. When group size is increased to $n = 4$, the total number of relationships increases to 44. For this reason, the number of experts must be limited to the knowledge engineer's capacity to handle the additional interaction and feedback. An increase in group size may also bring out group conflict rather than ready consensus.

IMPLICATIONS FOR MANAGEMENT

A key managerial issue centers on the answer to the question *Who owns the knowledge of the expert?* Companies have handled this matter in different ways for different reasons. Some organizations form contracts with their experts under which the knowledge gained on the job belongs to the firm and cannot be sold to or shared with the competition within a specified time period after the expert leaves the firm or retires. The executive office of the president of the United States, for example, follows this practice to ensure that former employees do not quickly become lobbyists or consultants for special interest groups, and do not exploit the privileged knowledge gained during their tenure on the job.

In the absence of an agreement, the organization cannot claim knowledge ownership, except in the case of investment in special training that actually promoted the expertise. A policy at Electronic Data Systems (EDS), for example, requires that new recruits (who receive extensive training) either work for a minimum of two years or pay a sizable sum to reimburse the company for the cost of training. While the company does not restrict its employees' activities after they leave, this policy ensures a minimum return on investment.

Experts who do not agree that their knowledge is the property of the firm are often reluctant to cooperate. Take the following example. The chairman of the admissions committee at a business school had been with the school for 18 years and chairman of the admissions committee for 11 of these years. He had become such an expert in the admission process that fewer than two percent of those students he admitted failed to graduate. Early one fail, he announced his retirement and notified the school he was leaving at the end of the term. The dean appointed a team to build an admissions advisor system based on the chairman's knowledge. The admissions chairman was reluctant to cooperate. He was quoted saying,

First, I don't see how you people can computerize eleven years of experience when much of it is based on hunches and rules of thumb.

Second, I don't see myself as obligated to take time to "teach" you how to decide on an admission when most of the criteria I use is subjective. There is going to be a new admissions committee, which I'm sure will have its own way of deciding on admission.

The group finally succeeded in meeting with the chairman for two sessions. At the end of the second session, he announced he would not spend any more time on the project.

I think the whole idea of trying to emulate human thinking is ridiculous. I've never heard of a thing like this. I only have two months left here. I really don't have time. Sorry!

The project simply collapsed.

In summary, management has much to gain by supporting the right problem with the right expert. Cost–benefit considerations and advance planning are also important aspects if the project is to succeed. Without management support represented by a champion, some expert systems development projects based on the best candidate problems have been known to fail.

■ SUMMARY

1. Indicators of expertise include peer praise of the expert's performance, the tendency of co-workers to consult the expert whenever a specific problem arises, the expert's way of explaining things, and the impression the expert's gives, as well as credentials. Although knowledge engineers do not always have the luxury of choice, they can use these indicators for verification of expertise.

2. Experts have definite qualifications. Some of these include perceptual ability to discern the relevant from the irrelevant, communication skills, creativity, self-confidence, and credibility. Motivation, enthusiasm, and willingness to share the expertise are also important. The right expert does not guarantee a successful expert system, however.

3. Three levels of experts are emphasized. The highly expert person, the moderately expert problem solve, and the new expert. Each level carries its own contributions and constraints. The best situation occurs when the knowledge engineer is able to work with the most qualified expert available.

4. Using a single or using multiple experts both have pros and cons. Single experts are ideal for simple and relatively quick systems; they entail fewer conflicts to resolve and make logistical arrangements easier. The main risk is that the credibility of the expert system depends entirely on the thought processes of one expert. In contrast, multiple experts are typically used in problem domains with diffused knowledge. They provide a synthesis of experience that is critical for the reliability of the system's solutions. Yet, scheduling difficulties, process loss, and the need to involve more than one knowledge engineer can make the use of multiple experts problematic.

5. Once the expert is chosen, a knowledge engineer needs to assess the expert's style of expression—whether the expert is the procedure type, the storyteller type, the parental type, or the salesperson type—and adapt knowledge acquisition methods accordingly.

6. Preparing for and deciding when to hold knowledge acquisition sessions are issues that should be discussed directly with the expert. Usually, holding the first few if not all sessions on the expert's turf is appropriate.

REVIEW QUESTIONS

1. How would one identify expertise? Explain.

2. When the expert tells you what he or she does not know, does that indicate expertise? Discuss.

3. "An expert exhibits a certain depth of detail and exceptional quality in explanations." How important do you think is the "exceptional quality" of an expert's explanations in knowledge acquisition? Explain.

4. The chapter talks about certain qualities that make a person an expert. Which qualities do you consider the most important? Least important? Why?

5. Why are good communication skills so important in knowledge acquisition? Is this quality a prerequisite for experts only? For knowledge engineers? Why?

6. Explain the relationships between an expert's

   a. motivation and willingness to share knowledge.
   b. credibility and perceptual ability.
   c. creativity and well-developed perceptual ability.

7. If you were asked to select an expert, how would you proceed? What characteristics would you look for? What other factors would you consider? Be specific.

8. Why should the knowledge engineer understand the differences among the levels of experts? Isn't an expert an expert regardless of level?

9. Use an example of your own to illustrate the conditions under which you'd be willing to build an expert system based on a single expert. Justify your choice.

10. Working with multiple experts has definite benefits and limitations. Cite an example in which the use of multiple experts is a must. Explain your choice.

11. Working with experts requires certain skills and experience. What suggestions or advice would you give an inexperienced knowledge engineer concerning

    a. working with or approaching an expert?
    b. preparing for the first session?

EXERCISES AND CASES

Publisher Advisor

1. In deciding on the expert system to advise textbook editors whether a manuscript should be adopted, deferred pending further work, or rejected, the knowledge engineer had to decide on a single versus multiple editors for the job. The initial prototype was built with a single expert on the basis of the editor's availability, willingness to spend time on the project, and low cost. The limitation of this approach is that the resulting system represents just one editor's opinion. A single expert is bound by certain constraints that are unique to the employing publisher; however the Publisher Advisor would need greater standardization of the advice it would provide across publishers.

Questions

a. Begin your project by finding a qualified book editor for the knowledge acquisition

process. Your instructor might be one such expert. A telephone interview with a college book editor might be another option.
   b. Describe the pros and cons of using a single versus multiple book editors for this project.

2. The single expert for Network Troubleshooting Advisor is the head of a commercial bank's local area network (LAN). The LAN serves 184 users on a 24-hour basis. The expert has a master's degree in information systems from a renowned university. She has been LAN administrator for two years and held several other part-time computer-related positions in the city prior to her current position. Some of the expert's other interests include graphic design, drawing, and database design and development.

Questions

   a. Do you feel the LAN expert is a qualified domain expert? What are the issues or problems in this case?
   b. How one would make sure the expert will cooperate or continue until the system is completely built?

3. For the PC Selection Advisor, we selected a single expert to build the system. Dawn started the computer store back in 1984 because of her interest in computers and two years of prior work on the staff of a large computer store chain. She has become an expert on personal computer hardware through years of experience dealing with people buying PCs at the store.
   A few interpersonal problems were encountered during the first meeting with Dawn. Although she seemed to enjoy the idea of working on the project, she continually made subtle, cutting remarks (she would never hire someone from a commerce school or we would have to overcome the stigma of being secretaries and pouring coffee because we are women in a man's world). To deal with this situation, the conversation was constantly steered back to the subject at hand. During the second meeting, the problem was not as predominant, as it became evident that this was just her personality. (Source: Carrie Budd, "PC Selector Advisor," p. 2.)

Questions

   a. What opinion do you have of the qualifications of the domain expert? Explain.

   b. Knowing what you now know, would you as a knowledge engineer have continued with the project? Elaborate.

4. Reread Box 8–4 on page 164. Then answer the following questions.

Questions

   a. Evaluate the qualifications of this domain expert.
   b. How valid is "practicality" in choosing a domain expert?
   c. If this expert system were to be commercialized, would you recommend a single domain expert for building the system? Why? Discuss.

5. The domain expert chosen for the Diabetic Foot Advisor was a well-known orthopedic surgeon with 21 years of experience, including two years of residency at a famous hospital in London. The expert was initially not impressed that computers can do anything that emulates or approximates the thought processes of humans. Soon after the first prototype, he changed his mind and began to take time during weekends to keep the momentum going.
   When the final prototype was completed, a major publisher on diabetes expressed interest in the software and offered to contact the American Diabetic Association for funding to commercialize the system. At that time, the domain expert admitted limitations in pursuing the development of the system. He recommended at least two other specialists in diabetes to participate in the work.

Questions

   a. Evaluate the initial decision to work with a single versus multiple experts.
   b. Do you agree with the recommendation that three or more experts be involved in commercializing the product? Why? What benefits and problems can you foresee?

6. Multiple experts were used to acquire knowledge for the Residential Real Estate Advisor. The reasons are:
   a. One objective of this expert system is to integrate the expertise in real estate tax and finance, which requires two separate experts.
   b. The procedure of making a buy-or-lease decision is a complex and intense process

for a single expert to provide all necessary information to come up with a decision. The nature of the problem also suggests that to make a decision, one has to consider both tax and financial issues. Thus, multiple experts are necessary to divide the scope into manageable pieces.

c. Multiple experts give the ability to compare and contrast the information acquired. Our real estate finance expert has deep knowledge in real estate tax field as well. He was particularly helpful in confirming the tax information we had acquired from the tax expert. Confirming the validity of the proposed recommendation and solution is critical considering the continuously changing tax law. One expert might not be aware of the change while the other does. (Source: Poppy Lumanau and Susan Tien, "Residential Real Estate Advisor," May 1993.)

Questions

a. In your opinion, is the use of a multiple expert approach justified for this project? Explain.

b. Can the use of two knowledge engineers to tackle the problem be justified? What are the conditions or rationale for a multiple knowledge engineering approach to building this system? Any system?

7. For the Nutrition Advisor, I selected a domain expert who has been the director of the Nutrition Clinic in the city for almost four years. She has also been associate professor of Health Education and Health Promotion at the university for ten years. The expert received a Ph.D. in physiology from a Big Ten school in 1973 and was a post-doctoral fellow at a prestigious medical school for four years following her graduation from the doctoral program. She has a total of fifteen years of experience in the field of nutrition. The domain expert has served on numerous committees including the Exercise and Cardiac Rehabilitation Committee for the American Heart Association and the city's Wellness Committee. She was on the board of directors for the American Diabetes Association. Her publication record is too long to mention.

Questions

a. Based on this description, how well qualified do you feel is the domain expert for the project? Are any qualifications lacking? Explain.

b. What do you think would motivate this domain expert to offer time and willingness to work on this project? (By the way of information, two knowledge engineers worked six months to complete this project.)

▓ SELECTED REFERENCES

Adelson, B. "When Novices Surpass Experts: The Difficulty of a Task May Increase with Expertise." *Journal of Experimental Psychology: Learning, Memory, and Cognition* 10, pp. 483–495.

Ashcraft, M. H. *Human Memory and Cognition.* Glenview, IL: Scott, Foresman, 1989.

Bellezza, Francis S. "Mnemonics and Expert Knowledge: Mental Cuing." In Robert R. Hoffman, ed. *The Psychology of Expertise.* New York: Springer-Verlag, 1992, pp. 204–217.

Bellezza, Francis S. and D. K. Buck. "Expert Knowledge as Mnemonic Cues." *Applied Cognitive Psychology* 2, pp. 147–162.

Buchanan, Bruce G., and David Wilkins. *Readings in Knowledge Acquisition and Learning: Automating the Construction and Improvement of Expert Systems.* San Francisco: 1993.

Ceci, Stephen J., and Ana Ruiz. "The Role of General Ability in Cognitive Complexity: A Case Study of Expertise." In Robert R. Hoffman, ed., *The Nature of Expertise.* New York: Springer-Verlag, 1992, pp. 218–230.

Chi, M. T. H.; R. Glaser; and M. J. Farr, eds., *The Nature of Expertise.* Hillsdale, N.J.: Erlbaum, 1988.

Cooke, Nancy N. J. "Empirically Defined Semantic Relatedness and Category Judgment Time." In R. Schvaneveldt, ed., *Pathfinder Associative Networks: Studies in Knowledge Organization* Norwood, NJ: Ablex, pp. 101–110.

————. "Modeling Human Expertise in Expert Systems." In Robert R. Hoffman, ed., *The Psychology of Expertise.* New York: Springer-Verlag, 1992, pp. 29–60.

Foley, Micheal, and Anna Hart. "Expert–Novice Differences and Knowledge Elicitation. In Robert R. Hoffman, ed., *The Psychology of Expertise.* New York: Springer-Verlag, 1992, pp. 233–244.

Frensch, P. A., and R. J. Sternberg. "Expertise and Flexibility: The Costs of Expertise." Unpublished manuscript, 1989.

Hart, Anna. *Knowledge Acquisition for Expert Systems.* New York: McGraw-Hill, 1992.

Hoffman, Robert R. *The Psychology of Expertise.* New York: Springer-Verlag, 1992.

Lunce, Stephen E.; Raja K. Iyer; and Leland M. Courtney. "Experts and Expertise: An Identification Paradox." *Industrial Management and Data Systems* 93, no. 9 (1993), pp. 3–9.

McGraw, Karen L. "Knowledge Acquisition and Interface Design." *IEEE Software,* November 1994.

O'Leary, Daniel E. "Determining Differences in Expert Judgment: Implications for Knowledge Acquisition and Validation." *Decision Sciences,* March/April 1993, pp. 395–407.

Posner, M. I. "Introduction: What Is It to Be an Expert?" In M. T. H. Chi, R. Glaser, and M. J. Farr, eds., *The Nature of Expertise.* Hillsdale, NJ: Erlbaum, pp. xxix–xxxvi.

Schumacher, R. M., and M. P. Czerwinski. "Mental Models and the Acquisition of Expert Knowledge." In Robert R. Hoffman, ed., *The Psychology of Expertise.* New York: Springer-Verlag, 1992, pp. 61–79.

Stein, Eric W. "A Method to Identify Candidates for Knowledge Acquisition." *Journal of Management Information Systems,* Fall 1992, pp. 161–178.

Sternberg, R. J., and P. A. Frensch. "On Being an Expert: A Cost–Benefit Analysis." In Robert R. Hoffman, ed., *The Psychology of Expertise.* New York: Springer-Verlag, 1992, pp. 191–203.

Trice, Andrew, and Randall Davis. "Heuristics for Reconciling Independent Knowledge Bases." *Information Systems Research: ISR: A Journal of the Institute of Management Sciences,* September 1993, pp. 262–288.

Vessey, I. "Expert–Novice Organization: An Empirical Investigation Using Computer Program Recall." *Behavior and Information Technology* 7, pp. 153–171.

Chapter ■ 9

Knowledge Acquisition by Interviewing

NONVERBAL COMMUNICATION IS AMBIGUOUS

A great deal of ambiguity surrounds nonverbal behavior. To understand what we mean, how would you interpret silence from your spouse, date, or companion after an evening in which you both laughed and joked a lot? Can you think of at least two possible meanings for this behavior? Or suppose that a much admired person with whom you've worked suddenly begins paying more attention to you than ever before. What could the possible meanings of the behavior be?

The point is that although nonverbal behavior can be very revealing, it can have so many possible meanings that it's foolish to think your interpretation will always be correct.

Some people are more skillful than others at accurately decoding nonverbal behavior. Those who are better senders of nonverbal messages are also better receivers. Decoding ability also increases with age and training, though there are still differences in ability because of personality and occupation. For instance, extroverts are relatively accurate judges of nonverbal behavior, whereas dogmatists are not. Interestingly, women seem to be better than men at decoding nonverbal messages. Over 95 percent of the studies examined in one analysis showed that women are more accurate at interpreting nonverbal signals. Despite these differences, even the best nonverbal decoders do not approach 100 percent accuracy.

When you do try to make sense out of ambiguous nonverbal behavior, you need to consider several factors: The *context* in which they occur (for example, smiling at a joke suggests a different feeling from smiling at another's misfortune); the *history of your relationship* with the sender (friendly, hostile, and so on); the *other's mood* at the time; and *your feelings* (when you are feeling insecure, almost anything can seem like a threat).

READING "BODY LANGUAGE"

Here is an exercise that will both increase your skill in observing nonverbal behavior and show you the dangers of being too sure that you're a perfect reader of body language. You can try the exercise either in or out of class, and the period of time over which you do it is flexible, from a single class period to several days. In any case, begin by choosing a partner, and then follow these directions:

1. For the first period of time (however long you decide to make it), observe the way your partner behaves. Notice how she moves, her mannerisms, posture, the way she speaks, how she dresses, and so on. To remember your observations, jot them down. If you are doing this exercise out of class over an extended period of time, there's no need to let your observations interfere with whatever you would normally be doing. Your only job here is to compile a list of your partner's nonverbal behavior. In this step you should be careful *not to interpret* your partner's actions; just record what you see.

2. At the end of the time period share what you have seen with your partner, who should do the same with you.

3. For the next period of time your job is not only to observe your partner's behavior but also to *interpret* it. This time in your confer-

ence you should tell your partner what you thought her actions said about her. For example, if she dressed carelessly, did you think this meant that she overslept, that she's losing interest in her appearance, or that she was trying to be more comfortable? If you noticed her yawning frequently, did you think this meant she was bored, tired from a late night, or sleepy after a big meal? Don't feel bad if your guesses were not all correct. Remember, nonverbal clues tend to be ambiguous. You may be surprised how checking out the nonverbal clues you observe can help build a relationship with another person.

This exercise should have shown you the difference between merely observing somebody's behavior and actually interpreting it. Noticing someone's shaky hands or smile is one thing, but deciding what such behaviors mean is quite another. If you're like most people, you probably found that a lot of your guesses were incorrect. Now, if that was true here, it may also be true in your daily life. Being a sharp nonverbal observer can give you some good hunches about how people are feeling, but the only way you can find out if these hunches are correct is to **check them out** verbally. Using the skill of perception you can check by describing the behavior you have noticed, offering two possible interpretations of the behavior, and requesting feedback about how to interpret the behavior correctly.

Ronald B. Adler, *Looking Out, Looking In,* 5th ed. (New York: Holt, Rinehart, Winston, 1987), pp. 196–97.

AT A GLANCE

A common way to tap the expert's knowledge is by asking questions. Interviewing can be complicated, requiring hours of preparation. The process has been likened to behavioral analysis—the study of experience. The knowledge engineer's main goal is to understand the expert's experience for later representation into the knowledge base.

One of the main problems in interviewing is language, or the misinterpretation of expressions or opinions. Question construction, errors made by the knowledge engineer as well as the expert are problems that adversely affect the quality of the information gathered. Other problems encountered during the interview include response bias, inconsistency, difficulty articulating opinions, as well as possible hostile attitudes.

For every interview, a knowledge engineer needs to follow a plan, beginning with stage setting, asking the right questions in the right sequence, to proper recording and evaluation of the information. In addition to these steps in a plan, a knowledge engineer also needs to consider other specific issues to ensure successful knowledge acquisition.

What You Will Learn

By the end of this chapter, you will know the following:

1. The various types of interviewing.
2. Various approaches to successful interviews.

3. Errors made by the knowledge engineer.

4. How to ask the right question in the right way.

5. Various interview issues to assess.

I suppose it was something you said
That caused me to tighten and pull away
And when you asked, "What is it?"
I, of course, said, "Nothing."
Whenever I say, "Nothing,"
You may be very certain there is something.
The something is a cold, hard lump of "Nothing."

Lois Wyse

INTRODUCTION

A major task facing the knowledge engineer is figuring out how an expert reaches complex decisions. Several acquisition tools are available to help the knowledge engineer in this task; each tool is used for a specific purpose. For example, a common way to tap the expert's knowledge is to ask questions or have the expert think aloud. The responses are then coded and stored in the knowledge base. This chapter examines basic issues in interviewing, the do's and don'ts of the process, and the implications of interviewing for rapid prototyping. The chapter also discusses the many meanings of words, problems with language, and the importance of the knowledge engineer's ability to listen, interpret, and capture the right knowledge using the interview as a tool.

A guide to successful interviewing discusses how to set the stage for the interview session, things to avoid, things to look for, how to establish rapport, how to record the knowledge acquired, and how to end an interview. Once the interview is concluded, the knowledge engineer can begin to do some rapid prototyping.

Knowledge can be tricky. Knowledge is not available systematically or in its entirety; experts cannot recall all that is important or bring up everything in the first session. So, after the initial interviews, the knowledge engineer prototypes the knowledge and gives the expert a chance to react to the prototype. Further interviews and feedback allow the knowledge engineer to infer what is missing and update the prototype. This process continues until the system is built to the satisfaction of the domain expert and the end-user.

Other tools commonly used in acquisition include observation of the expert at work, brainstorming, protocol analysis, think-aloud, process tracing, Delphi method, and repertory grid. These are discussed in Chapter 10.

FUZZY REASONING AND THE QUALITY OF KNOWLEDGE ACQUISITION

People reason with words, not numbers, which can lead to a problem commonly encountered in interviewing: experts are not always easy to understand. Because the problem domain is likely to be technical or complex, decision making often involves rules with many shades of meaning that may be fuzzy to the nonexpert. For example, one can easily understand the following simple rule:

> In the U.S., if you are under 60 years of age, you are not entitled to social security benefits.

A retirement benefit rule might be more complex, although still understandable. For example:

> If you are at least 60 years old and have been a state employee for at least 25 years or at least 62 years of age and have worked full-time for more than 5 continuous years, then you are entitled to collect social security benefits provided you are not handicapped or you are not receiving a salaried income greater than $10,000 or collecting unemployment compensation from a state agency.

People use IF . . . THEN statements in conversations, but problems that require expertise are not always straightforward and the solutions cannot be stated in simple IF . . . THEN rules. The words used to express solutions may also have many meanings. For example, consider the word *warm* and the criteria used to characterize weather as *warm*. The meaning of *warm* depends on the time of year, temperature, and location. What is warm to a person from the mid-Atlantic coast can be judged as hot by someone from the North or even called chilly by someone from the deep South. Furthermore, a day that is warm in winter can be colder than a day labeled as cold in the summer. Because no definite rules distinguish what is cold and what is hot, this range of temperature can be described as fuzzy.

Take another example. When an expert comments "The procedure I just explained works most of the time, " what does he or she mean by "most"? Is it any number of times over 50 percent? Is it about 75 percent or perhaps more?

Here is a third example: Suppose a heart surgeon said,

> I don't expect heart trouble in a 20-year-old. The occurrence is so rare I would say it is nil. It isn't worth subjecting a person that young to a rigorous heart test. Patients that young, I most likely won't do the tests; older patients I'd probably consider it.

Try pressing the surgeon to explain this statement and see how far you get. Because the English language does not always distinguish clearly between words or the meaning of certain words, the interpretation of words often depends on their context. This fuzziness increases the difficulty of translating what the expert has said into rules that make sense.

Analogies and Uncertainties in Information

When experts explain events, they use **analogies**—comparing a problem to a similar one encountered in a different setting months or years ago—to make judgments. For example, a professor, after listening to a student in a new course, might say,

> This student reminds me of a student I had in the same course last year. She did great work. Most probably this one will do as well.

This pattern matching is another fuzzy comparison that must be clarified before the information acquired can be usable. A knowledge engineer who runs into this line of reasoning must learn more about the expert's examples and pay attention to how the expert forms analogies, or pattern matching.

In addition to analogy problems, a knowledge engineer may also encounter **uncertainties** in information. An expert's knowledge or expertise is the ability to take uncertain information and use a plausible line of reasoning to clarify the fuzzy details. One aspect of uncertainty is belief. **Belief** describes the level of credibility. People generally use all kinds of words to express belief, usually paired with qualifiers such as "very," "highly," "extremely," etc. For example, words such as "possible," "likely," and "definite" show relationships between words that express belief. To handle uncertainty expressed in words, the knowledge engineer must draw out such relationships during knowledge acquisition.

Understanding Experience

Knowledge engineers can benefit immensely from an educational grounding in cognitive psychology. The human expert usually follows the same basic reasoning principles as a computing system. To solve a problem, the expert acquires information from the outside world and stores it in the brain. When a question is asked, the expert operates on certain stored information through inductive, deductive, or other problem-solving methods. The resulting answer is the culmination of processing stored information.

When knowledge engineers ask an expert how he or she arrived at an answer, they are asking the expert to relive an experience. The right questions will evoke the memory of experiences that previously produced good solutions. How quickly the expert responds to a question depends on the clarity of the content, whether the content was recently used, and how well the expert understood the question.

Visual imagery plays an important role in the expert's recall of chunks of experience, or content, in memory. To illustrate, suppose someone asks a travel agent, "In what direction should I travel to get to Germany from the United States?" Typically, the agent will imagine a map of North America, the Atlantic Ocean, and Europe, trace an imaginary air route from a U.S. city (perhaps New York) to a German city (Frankfurt), and then verbally describe the visual map. This is the art of translating internal experiences into language. The more experience the person has had with this travel route, the quicker will be the vocal recall or answer.

Visual imagery is often represented by phrases the expert uses in a descriptive answer. For example, "something tells me," "sounds O.K. to me," "I heard that," "hmm, let me see—one more time," and "the manual illustrated" are phrases that show the expert is mentally reacting to an image. When expert uses this type of phrase, the knowledge engineer should ask, "When you say something tells you . . . , what do you mean or what do you see?" or "Why did you say it sounds O.K. to you?"

At times, the expert's emotions are involved in the problem-solving process. For example, phrases such as "I have a feeling," "my gut feeling is," and "my sixth sense tells me" serve as the conscious representation of past sensory memories that have gone dormant for lack of use. The knowledge engineer can clarify the content behind these phrases by asking "How would you describe this feeling?" or "What makes you feel this way?"

People who have difficulty with visual imagery usually have trouble answering questions. When the knowledge engineer does not understand an explanation, he or she should ask the expert to go through it again and pay closer attention to the content of the answer as well as any clues to visual imagery. A knowledge engineer may need to step back to better understand how the expert thinks through a problem. As a knowledge acquisition tool, interviewing allows repeated questioning for knowledge capture and verification.

The Language Problem

The main concern during knowledge acquisition is to be able to understand and interpret the expert's verbal description of information, heuristics, and so on. Repeated questioning often clarifies and promotes complete answers. But how well experts represent internal processes varies with their command of the language and the knowledge engineer's interviewing skills. For example, take a look at the preceding sentence and review the structure of the sentence: "How well" (how well who? what?), "experts represent" (do they present? summarize?), "internal processes" (what internal processes? what does it mean?). The sentence was written to convey an idea in words whose meanings the writer hopes the reader understands.

Language may be unclear in a number of ways:

- *Comparative words such as "taller" or "better" sometimes are left hanging.* For example, the expert might say, "This last solution works better for what you're looking for." The question is, better than what? The comparison requires clarification. The knowledge engineer might ask, "Better than what?" or "Can you elaborate on that comparison?" or "I don't understand what you mean by *better.*"

- *Certain words or components may be left out of an explanation.* Experts sometimes think that certain things are so obvious that they don't need to "spoon-feed" every detail. A knowledge engineer who is not as familiar with the domain as the expert assumes may be lost without these details. The knowledge engineer must ask the expert to clarify and to elaborate. If the expert comments, "To me, that is the key point," the knowledge engineer might say "*That* refers to . . . ?" or "What makes it a key point?" or "How do you know it is the key?"

- *Absolute words and phrases may be used loosely.* For example, be wary when you hear "always," "never," "cannot," or "no way." The expert might say, "This approach will never give you the right combination," "There is no way I can explain this procedure in one hour," "Your suggestion will never work," or "This procedure cannot be applied." The knowledge engineer might probe by asking, "How does this approach make that combination impossible?" "Can you imagine a situation where it might not clear things up?" "Then, can you briefly explain the procedure?" or "What do you mean this procedure cannot be applied?" These questions will gently push the expert to reconsider.

- *Some words seem to have a built-in ambiguity.* For example, "The titanium shield of the missile performs a protective function during reentry." The question here is "What is a protective function?" or "protective in reference to what?" The knowledge engineer should either rephrase the question or ask for further clarification.

  The main goal of pointing out these ambiguities is to warn the knowledge engineer to be alert to meanings as well as to verbal and nonverbal cues during each interview. The success of the subsequent steps of building an expert system are dependent on accurate knowledge capture.

■ THE INTERVIEW AS A TOOL

The **interview** is a tool used commonly in the early stages of acquisition. It is the oldest and most often used (and abused) tool for capturing or verifying information. It can be used in two ways: (1) as an exploratory device to identify relations or verify information, and (2) to capture information as it exists.

Because the knowledge acquired through an interview is so important to expert system development, validity is a critical issue. **Validity** of a given question means that it is logically correct and is understood the same way by different people. It also provides a consistency in the way questions are asked. The knowledge engineer needs to make special efforts to eliminate interviewer bias that would reduce validity. Often the validity of information is more reliable if it is freely given. For this reason, the voluntary nature of the interview is important; it should be a relationship freely and willingly entered into by the expert. If the interview and participation in the knowledge acquisition process are a requirement, the expert might be giving information with no assurance of accuracy or **reliability,** which is the measure of truthfulness or credibility.

In an interview, the knowledge engineer has an opportunity to verify information and observe the expert's thought processes in action. A major benefit of interviewing is behavioral analysis. The expert is asked to act out a case or a scenario in the domain. While the expert goes through the motions, the knowledge engineer records the observations and assesses body language, facial gestures, and other communication cues. A knowledge engineer who is ill-trained can create or fail to eliminate problems with the resulting rules of the knowledge base.

The interview as a knowledge acquisition tool has four primary advantages:

1. Its flexibility makes it a superior tool for *exploring areas* about which not much is known concerning what questions to ask or how to formulate questions.

2. It offers a better opportunity than any other tool for *evaluating the validity* of information acquired. The knowledge engineer can hear not only what is said but also how it is said.

3. It is an effective technique for *eliciting information* about complex subjects and for probing an individual's sentiments underlying expressed opinions.

4. Many *people enjoy being interviewed,* regardless of the subject. They usually cooperate when all they have to do is talk.

The major drawback to interviewing, however, is the cost involved in extensive preparation time. Interviews also take a lot of time to conduct. Whenever a more economical way of capturing the same information is available, the interview is generally not used.

Even though interviewing experts is an art learned at school, most knowledge engineers develop expertise through experience. Knowledge engineers need to pay attention to the primary requirements for a successful interview: the development of a sound, structured strategy and the creation of a friendly, nonthreatening atmosphere that puts the expert at ease. An experienced interviewer elicits credible answers that the expert can offer with no fear of criticism.

Types of Interviews

Interviews vary widely in form and structure. From a knowledge acquisition perspective, interviews range from the highly unstructured (neither the questions nor their responses are specified in advance) to the highly structured (the questions and responses are definitive.) Of course, a great deal of variation is possible within this range.

The **unstructured interview** is used when the knowledge engineer wants to explore an issue. It allows experts to answer spontaneous questions openly (see Figure 9–1). Unstructured techniques are not easy to conduct, and this kind of interview is difficult to plan. An expert may interpret the lack of structure as permission to avoid preparing for an interview.

The **structured interview** is used when the knowledge engineer wants specific information. It is goal-oriented. In multiple expert knowledge acquisition, the questions should be presented with the same wording and in the same order to each expert.

For example, the question to one expert, "Would you like to see a prototype of what you gave me during the last session?" will not elicit the same response as asking, "How do you feel about showing the material you gave me during the last session in the format of a prototype?" Standardized questions can improve the validity of the responses by ensuring that all experts are responding to the same question.

A structured question is expressed as a set of alternatives. Several variations of structured questions can be used:

1. **Multiple-choice questions** offer specific choices, faster tabulation, and less bias due to the way the answers are ordered. Because most people have a tendency to favor the first choice item, alternating the order of the choices may reduce bias; however, additional time is needed to pick the choice item question. See Figure 9–2.

2. **Dichotomous** (yes/no) **questions** are a special type of multiple-choice question. They offer two answers (see Figure 9–3). The sequence of questions and content are also important.

Figure 9–1 *Examples of Unstructured (Open-Ended) Questions*

From Publisher Advisor:
■ Suppose you have the manuscript ready for production, what does the author do between then and the final binding of the book?

From Diabetic Foot Advisor:
■ How can you tell a diabetic patient has charcot?

From Loan Advisor:
■ How do you deal with excessive bad loans after a grace period?

Figure 9–2   Examples of Multiple-Choice Questions

From Auto Loan Tracker:
■ If the customer made a final offer within $100 from your minimum to sell a $10,000 car, what do you do next?
_____ Talk the matter over with the sales manager
_____ Split the difference with the customer
_____ Walk away from the deal
_____ Throw in amenities

From Diabetic Foot Advisor:
■ If a diabetic patient complains about foot problems, who should he or she see first?
_____ Podiatrist
_____ General practitioner
_____ Orthopaedic surgeon
_____ Physical therapist

From Loan Evaluator:
■ Please check the type of loan that brings the highest revenue to your bank?
_____ Auto loan
_____ Personal loan
_____ Mortgage loan
_____ Collateral loan

Figure 9–3   Examples of Dichotomous Questions

From Publisher Advisor:
■ Does your book contract prohibit you from publishing on the same subject with another publisher?
_____ Yes _____ No

From Real Estate Advisor:
■ Is your commission paid by the seller or the buyer?
_____ Seller _____ Buyer

From Diabetic Foot Advisor:
■ Do patients with neuropathy come for regular checkups?
_____ Yes _____ No

3. **Ranking scale questions** ask the expert to arrange items in a list in order of their importance or preference. In Figure 9–4, the question asks the expert to rank five statements on the basis of how descriptive the statement is of the expert's present job.

Finally, with the semi-structured technique, the knowledge engineer asks predefined questions but allows the expert some freedom expressing the answers. Here is a dialogue from the Diabetic Foot Advisor:

KE: What would be your first question to patient?

DOMAIN EXPERT: Where is the pain?

Figure 9–4   An Example of a Ranking Scales Question

Please rank the five statements in each group on the basis of how well they describe your job as a loan officer. Give a ranking of "1" to the statement that best describes your job; give a ranking of "2" to the statement that provides the next best description, and continue to rank all five statements, using a "5" for the statement that describes your job least well.

In my job, I
_____ decide on auto loans over $10,000.
_____ review each application before authorizing credit checks.
_____ interview loan applicants as they come in.
_____ co-sign all checks sent to local auto dealers.
_____ work with local auto dealers to attract more loans.

KE: What possible answers do you expect?

DOMAIN EXPERT: Ankle, big toe, from knee cap to ankle, or "I'm not sure."

KE: Suppose the answer is "big toe." Then what do you do or say next?

DOMAIN EXPERT: I'd look for coloration, swelling, and possible curving of the toe.

KE: What would be your next question?

The process continues until the knowledge engineer has no more questions to ask. The advantage over the unstructured technique is that the information is well structured and the information solicited is reasonably clear. A disadvantage is that this information may not be complete in other possible ways.

■ GUIDE TO A SUCCESSFUL INTERVIEW

Interviewing should be approached as logically as programming. In interviewing the domain expert, several steps are considered:

1. Setting the stage and establishing rapport
2. Phrasing questions
3. Good listening and avoiding arguments
4. Evaluating session outcomes

Setting the Stage and Establishing Rapport

This first step is an "ice breaking," relaxed, informal exchange. The knowledge engineer opens the session by focusing on the purpose of the meeting, the role of the expert, and the agenda for review. During stage setting, the knowledge engineer closely observes how the expert cooperates. Both the content and tone of the expert's responses are evaluated. How well the interview goes depends on the knowledge engineer's ability to adapt to the expert's style. An expert may be the *friendly* type, who makes everyone involved feel the process will be easy teamwork; the *timid* type, who needs to be coaxed to talk; or the *resident expert* type, who bombards the knowledge engineer with opinions disguised as facts.

In one respect, knowledge acquisition is time-consuming and an intrusion into the expert's privacy. Even when the procedure is authorized by management and the expert is on the company's payroll, the process is still lengthy and taxing. The expert may anticipate some harm from the system, which makes it important to establish rapport with the expert at the beginning and maintain that rapport throughout the process. Although setting the stage has no hard and fast rules to follow, the knowledge engineer needs to keep in mind certain guiding factors:

1. *Honesty: Do not deliberately mislead the expert about the purpose of the project.* A careful, well-thought-out briefing should provide honest details regarding the purpose of the project. The briefing should be consistent when dealing with more than one expert.

2. *Confidentiality: Assure the expert that no information offered will be shared with unauthorized personnel.* The sole purpose of the session is to build a system in line with the expert's thinking, not to disclose specific information to other experts or to upper management.

3. *Modesty: Avoid showing off knowledge or revealing information from other experts.* Such actions can color the objectivity of the approach and discourage the expert from freely giving information.

4. *Efficiency: Respect the time schedule or commitments of the expert.* The sessions should not be an extended social event. The expert may not complain, but other people who need the expert might.

5. *Professionalism: Proper dress and demeanor are important.* For example, a conservative gray suit is appropriate interviewing a banking expert. A casual outfit may be passable interviewing on the assembly line. If the session takes place in the expert's environment, the knowledge engineer should be a courteous guest.

6. *Respect: Be courteous and a good listener.* More than any other advice, respect for the expert is a must. Interrupting the expert can alter the thought process or break the expert's train of thought.

Phrasing the Questions

Except in unstructured interviews, each question should be asked in the same order as it appears on the interview schedule. Altering the sequence could affect the comparability of the sessions with the experts. In structuring questions for the expert, the knowledge engineer needs to consider the level and sequencing of the questions. A question may be primary or secondary. A **primary question** is usually a lead question that paves the way for more detailed questions. For example, in the Diabetic Foot Advisor, a primary question is "What is the first thing you do when a diabetic patient comes to you with a swollen ankle?" It leads to a series of questions to advise the diabetic person whether to seek self-help, medical treatment, or surgery.

A **secondary question** usually probes for more details. For example, "So, you find a blister just under the ankle. What does it mean in terms of procedure or treatment of the swelling?" is a secondary question, because the question asks for more information about the primary question—a swollen ankle. Using secondary questions helps the knowledge engineer probe deeper for clarity of details.

Question sequencing determines whether the interview begins with general, **open-ended questions** followed by secondary questions and **closed questions,** or vice versa. Either approach has benefits and drawbacks. The open-to-closed question sequence helps establish rapport and enables the knowledge engineer to assess the quality of the response before asking more focused questions. This assessment often results in discarding unnecessary questions due to redundancy or overlap. See Figure 9–5(a).

When using the closed-to-open sequence, the knowledge engineer begins with a set of well-focused questions, lending a more formal tone to the session. It also allows the knowledge engineer to use open-ended questions to end the interview. This approach requires substantial advance preparation. See Figure 9–5(b).

Question Construction

Regardless of question type, a question must be valid enough to elicit a reliable response. The knowledge engineer must focus on question content, wording, and format. Here is a summary checklist:

1. Question content
   a. Is the question necessary? Is it a part of other questions?
   b. Does the question adequately cover the intended area?
   c. Does the expert(s) have proper information to answer the question?

Figure 9–5 Sequencing of Open-Ended and Closed Questions

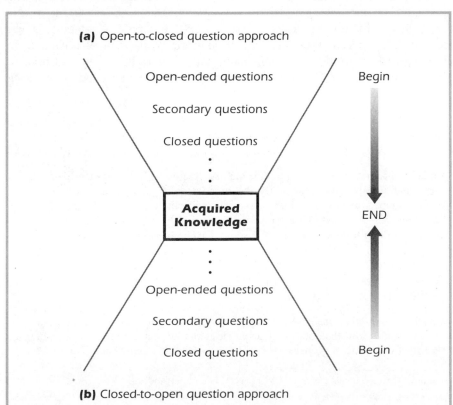

(a) Open-to-closed question approach

Open-ended questions

Secondary questions

Closed questions

Begin

Acquired Knowledge

END

Open-ended questions

Secondary questions

Closed questions

Begin

(b) Closed-to-open question approach

    d. Is the question biased in a given direction?

    e. Is the question likely to generate emotional feelings that might color responses?

2. Question wording

    a. Is the question worded to suit the expert's background and expertise?

    b. Can the question be misinterpreted? What else could it mean?

    c. Is the frame of reference uniform for all experts?

    d. Is the wording biased toward a specific answer?

    e. How clear and direct is the question?

3. Question format

    a. Can the question be framed in the form of multiple choices (answered by a word or two or by a number) or with a followup free answer?

    b. Is the response form easy to use and adequate for the job?

    c. Is the answer to the question likely to be influenced by the preceding question? That is, is it subject to a *contamination effect?*

Things to Avoid

One of the dangers of interviewing is generalizing conclusions on the basis of a few sessions. Transcribing notes into rules often results in verification problems that arise later during testing. Experts are often annoyed when they keep repeating the same rules or keep repeating the same information. The alternative to note taking is taping the session. The main drawback of this technique is the time it takes to play back the tape. Videotaping is not recommended, because few experts are comfortable in front of a camera. In either case, a knowledge engineer should practice with the equipment prior to the session to become familiar with it and to make sure everything is working properly. See Box 9–1.

Box 9–1   Taping versus Transcribing

I hadn't had much luck trying to tape the first session with the expert. He seemed reluctant to tape any session. By the third session, he agreed to try it. The conversation was too unstructured, and reviewing the tape of a 1.5-hour session took another 1.5 hours. That is high overhead.

I don't like to tape sessions. It is sometimes convenient to be able to tell the expert, "Wait, I've got to write this all down," when I'm getting behind. It is also useful to read back what I've written down and have the expert validate the information. My expert was very patient and did not mind waiting as I took things down.

Relying on notes means reorganizing them and transcribing them soon after each session. This is the case with tapes as well, which makes for long exhausting days at times. But the good thing about straightening out the notes is generating a list of questions to go back over with the expert the next session.

Source: Developmental experience with the Diabetic Foot Advisor.

An important guideline for a knowledge engineer is not to aggressively debate or interrupt the expert's discussions or convert the interview into an interrogation. Inconsistency should be pointed out in an unobtrusive way. A knowledge engineer should also avoid asking questions that put the domain expert on the defensive. For example, if a knowledge engineer who realizes the expert is being inconsistent should say, "How would this solution relate to an earlier one about the same problem?" rather than, "Based on the earlier solution I have here in my notes, this solution doesn't make sense."

Using technical terms such as *AI* or *expert systems* often results in an unfavorable response or can put the engineer in a defensive position in having to explain the technology. Explanations such as "This is more like a system project." "It's a system that captures information offered by people with experience like yourself." "It's a special computer application that uses reasoning to give the user advice similar to the way you'd do if you had the time." are better alternatives.

Although the first session invites general questions to familiarize the knowledge engineer with the expert and the problem domain, domain experts usually perk up when they are asked to talk about anecdotal or unusual scenarios. In other words, a knowledge engineer will more likely acquire the desired information by being specific rather than general. Most people can talk about solutions more easily than they can describe them.

A knowledge engineer's command of the session is critical to a successful interview. A loss of control is a sign of overaccommodation, an overbearing expert, or poor preparation for the session. Distributing an agenda in advance, keeping the discussion on the topic, summarizing the expert's comments when appropriate, and limiting the interview to a reasonable time period should help control the session.

Being in control also means that a knowledge engineer should avoid getting frustrated over ambiguous answers when they are least expected. For example, a cool head is needed when an expert answers, "Because that's the way it works—I don't know why, but it works all the time." Explaining how some things work is often more difficult than one might imagine. (See Figure 9–6.) The knowledge engineer should avoid excessive interpretation of the expert's answers.

The converse, of course, is pretending to understand something. The knowledge engineer needs to recapitulate what he or she understands, thereby reinforcing the expert. However, starting from scratch is frustrating for everyone. The expert can help only by knowing exactly where the knowledge engineer got lost. One helpful practice for keeping everyone on track is to draw pictures to illustrate a point or a procedure, especially if the expert is an engineer or a database designer.

In addition to honesty about understanding the expert's information, the knowledge engineer should avoid promising something that cannot or should not be delivered. For example, during the first session, a knowledge engineer should not say, "A couple of sessions and we should be beyond the half way mark," if the project is obviously going to take several more sessions. As an alternative response, "I don't know how many sessions we need, but chances are it will be several sessions before we can wrap things up," is much better. Figure 9–7 summarizes the things to avoid in an interview.

Figure 9–6 Linking Paper Clips

This trick is not easy to explain, as it is almost automatic. A lot depends on where you place the paper clips.

1. Hold a dollar bill open between two hands.

2. Fold one third of the length of the bill over to the right side as shown.

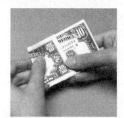

3. Place a paper clip over this fold (and over the "1" digit) to hold it in place. Make sure the paper clip is pushed all the way in.

4. Turn the bill around (not upside down) and fold the left end to the right as shown.

5. Place another paper clip (over the "10") so that the two front ends are held together. Here is how the resulting steps look:

6. Grasp the top two ends of the bill and pull them briskly toward the outside. When the bill is open, the two paper clips should be linked together.

Adapted from Wilson, Mark, *Magic,* Phila., PA: Courage, 1988, p. 299.

Figure 9–7   *Things to Avoid in an Interview*

1. Never aggressively debate or interrupt the expert's interpretations or opinions.
2. Avoid asking questions that put the domain expert on the defensive.
3. Stay away from using the terms *AI* or *expert systems* unless the expert is familiar with the technology.
4. Try to be specific, rather than general.
5. Avoid losing control of the session.
6. Avoid getting frustrated over ambiguous answers.
7. Avoid bringing up items or details that are not on the agenda.
8. Avoid pretending to understand something.
9. Avoid promising something that cannot or should not be delivered.

Reliability of Information from Experts

The knowledge acquired from the expert is presumed to correspond accurately to the actual way solutions are produced in the domain. Yet, several uncontrolled sources of error may reduce the information's reliability:

1. *The expert's perceptual slant.* Perceptual abilities vary; the reports of a single event given by several experts often have little resemblance to one another.
2. *The expert's failure to remember just what happened.* As time passes, the exact details of an event generally become more difficult to describe.
3. *An expert's fear of the unknown.* Experts often distort descriptions of events for fear that the expert system will replace him or her. These distortions defeat the purpose of knowledge acquisition that is based on mutual trust.
4. *Communication problems.* Some experts have difficulty communicating their knowledge. In a related vein, the knowledge engineer is sometimes unable to elicit the information that the expert is qualified to provide. Verbalization conveys the information that is available in working memory, also called *spoken protocol.*
5. *Role bias.* The risk of **role bias** increases when the expert is aware of his or her importance as the critical element in building the expert system. The expert might wonder, "What type of person should I be as I answer this question?" and then select a role to fit the expectations of the knowledge engineer.

    Research has shown that experts with limited formal schooling tend to exhibit "put on" behavior and are more likely to distort the knowledge elicited than highly educated experts. Various validation and cross-validation methods should be applied before acquired knowledge can be represented. For example, one way to cross-validate an expert's opinions is to ask another expert and check for similarities in the two opinions. Another way to validate an opinion is to re-ask the question at the next session to see if the expert gives the same answer.

Errors Made by the Knowledge Engineer

In addition to possible bias originating with domain experts, knowledge engineers can also contribute to the reliability problem. Validity problems often stem from what is called the *interviewer effect:* something about the knowledge engineer colors the response of the domain expert. Some of the effects include:

- The **age effect:** In the eyes of a much older domain expert, a twenty-something knowledge engineer is not viewed as experienced enough to take on the building of an expert system. The wrong perception of age can color responses of the domain expert.

- The **race effect:** Unfortunately, people can be biased because of race. In a professional environment, biases should not exist, but they do. The best option for earning a domain expert's respect is for a knowledge engineer to demonstrate competency, integrity, and determination to do quality work. If race continues to be a serious barrier, perhaps an alternative expert or an alternative knowledge engineer is the best course of action.

- The **gender effect:** The gender of the knowledge engineer can alter the way the interview is conducted. Research in the social sciences has shown that male interviewers obtain fewer responses than female interviewers, regardless of color, and white females obtain the highest number of responses from men. The exception is young women who interview young men; they get fewer responses than older women.

The knowledge engineer must watch for biased responses from the expert early in the acquisition process and find ways to correct the tendency. Table 9–1 summarizes the uncontrolled sources of errors.

Problems Encountered during the Interview

Other difficulties are not uncommon during the interview. They range from biased responses, the way the question is phrased, to personality clashes between the expert and the knowledge engineer.

■ **Table 9–1**   Uncontrolled Sources of Bias

Bias Stemming from the Domain Expert
1. Perceptual slant
2. Failure to remember just what did happen
3. Distorted description of events out of fear of being replaced by the expert system
4. Inability to communicate knowledge

Bias Stemming from the Knowledge Engineer
1. Age effect
2. Race effect
3. Gender effect

Response Bias

A **response bias** occurs when experts answer questions on the basis of their interpretation of the wording of the question and in response to certain constraints: lack of time, lack of motivation, perceived hostility, an attempt to please the knowledge engineer, and so on. A combination of wording and tone of voice can also promote response bias. For example:

KNOWLEDGE ENGINEER: Isn't it true that when a diabetic comes in with a blister, you pretty much decide that she will be making more than one visit?

DOMAIN EXPERT: Well, as a general rule, I'd say yes.

KNOWLEDGE ENGINEER: Don't you think that following your verification procedure results in disapproval of loans for minority applications?

DOMAIN EXPERT: I'd probably say yes, but we have good reasons for this.

The questioner coaxed an unintended "yes" answer by prefacing the question with "Isn't it true" or "Don't you think."

Another response bias stems from the order of the questions asked, called the contamination effect. For example, a question asked following another question is answered one way, whereas if it were asked later or earlier in the questioning sequence, the answer could be totally different.

One test to reveal bias is called the *circular triad.* For example, when the expert for the Diabetic Foot Advisor says, "I consider vascular disease more serious than neuropathy," and then says that "I consider neuropathy more serious than charcot," and then states that "I consider charcot more serious than vascular disease," it is called a circular triad. This type of contamination is usually the result of long interview sessions, loss of motivation or interest, fatigue, or faking, which provides even more reason for pretesting the questions.

Inconsistency

The problem of inconsistency is most likely to occur when the knowledge engineer interviews two domain experts and is inconsistent when asking the questions. For the sake of validity, the questions and their order should be standardized. Validity is related to reliability; they are two faces of the same coin. Validity is addressed when one asks, "Does the question mean the same thing to all of the experts being interviewed?" If it means different things to different people, then the question is not valid. No invalid questions obtain accurate responses. Reliability, on the other hand, occurs when the question elicits the same response at different times. The reliability of an expert's answer can be revealed by answering the question, "How much credence can we place in this answer?" If the question is not valid, one can assume that the answer is not reliable. Knowledge engineers often rephrase questions and ask a variety of questions about the same process to ensure the reliability of the information acquired.

Communication Difficulties

Not everyone has a knack for explaining things. The knowledge engineer may need to resort to analogies or other tools to stimulate the expert's thought processes. For example, the knowledge engineer may say, "If I understand you correctly, you would require the applicant to be a homeowner and have an average income of $50,000 to qualify for a $30,000 car loan?" or simply ask the expert "I am not sure I follow what you just explained. Can you go through it one more time?" until the expert's thought is clear.

The communication problems can also stem from the knowledge engineer, who may not have been listening or did not understand. However, when a knowledge engineer admits to these lapses, most experts don't mind repeating or simplifying the points just explained. Next time, the knowledge engineer better get it right because pretending to understand is a destructive habit. And asking the expert to repeat the same thing three times could cause nerves to flare up and threaten the end of the whole process.

Hostile Attitude

Nothing is more problematic to an interview process than hostility. Various factors cause hostility: bad chemistry between the expert and knowledge engineer, an expert's "forced" participation, or time wasted on repeated deadends. Unfortunately, no quick fixes work for reducing hostility.

Standardized Questions

On the surface, the task of standardizing questions does not appear difficult. However, even if the wording is the same, the way the question is asked, the tone of voice, and the facial expression can elicit a different response.

Length of Questions and the Duration of the Interview

No written rules provide the ideal number of questions or minutes in an interview. Much depends on the preference of the expert, the expectations of the knowledge engineer, and the nature of the constraints surrounding the whole project. Ideally, each interview should last no more than one hour. Any longer, and the participants' attention spans begin to break down, and the quality of the thought process degenerates. Figure 9–8 is a summary of the problems encountered during interviews.

Probing the Expert's Knowledge

As part of the knowledge acquisition process, knowledge engineers often coax the expert to provide additional details. For example, the knowledge engineer would want to know that the expert starts with a review of the patient's history before listening to the patient's foot complaints.

> **KNOWLEDGE ENGINEER:** How do you know that what you see is in fact a blister, not a sore?

Figure 9–8   Problems Encountered during the Interview

1. Response bias
2. Inconsistency
3. Communication difficulties
4. Hostile attitude
5. Standardized questions
6. Length of questions and the duration of the interview

EXPERT: Well, I'm not sure. Sometimes I get back to the patient's history after the initial diagnosis.

KNOWLEDGE ENGINEER: I see. Can you tell me more about that?

These statements suggest that the knowledge engineer is listening, is interested, and understands what the expert is trying to say. The contrast would be as follows:

KNOWLEDGE ENGINEER: How do you know that what you see is in fact a blister, not a sore?

EXPERT: Well, I'm not sure. Sometimes I get back to the patient's history after the initial diagnosis.

KNOWLEDGE ENGINEER: Whenever that happens, the patient will get some kind of treatment. Let me ask you a question on another area . . .

In this example, the expert's response is sloughed off, and returning to the initial subject is usually difficult after leaving it completely.

Data Recording and the Notebook

Many expert systems fail because the knowledge captured is poorly recorded. In successful knowledge acquisition, the knowledge engineer records not only the knowledge, but the source and the time of capture as well. Working with multiple experts runs the risk of attributing information to the wrong expert or not knowing to whom to address for followup questions if knowledge is not recorded with adequate detail.

Knowledge engineers frequently use a notebook in their knowledge acquisition. The form of the notebook varies according to the amount of information to be captured. The "notebook" is usually a loose leaf binder. The information shown in Figure 9–9 should be included in the notebook.

Organization is also important. In some cases, a purely chronological arrangement will suffice. In others, a system of categories with cross-classification would be appropriate. Proper indexing makes information easier to retrieve when needed.

Figure 9–9   Information Capture and the Notebook

1. Originals or duplicate copies of all notes taken during each interview must be included. Each page of notes should be numbered serially, and a running chronological record of them should be kept. The name of the knowledge engineer, the date the notes were taken, and all surrounding circumstances must be included. Word-processed notes are usually more legible than handwritten notes.

2. Copies of all information-gathering tools (interview schedules, observation guides, etc.) are placed in the notebook for future reference.

3. Copies of all information—originals or duplicates—must be included to provide a record of discussions, decisions, and changes. Loss of key information, even temporarily, can be costly. It could mean returning to the expert and having the same information recited again.

Ending the Interview

Ending an interview requires sensitivity to the domain expert's preferences, use of proper verbal and nonverbal cues, and efforts to maintain ties with the expert even after the interview is finished. When the knowledge engineer has elicited all the information needed, common tendency is to cut the session abruptly. This action can easily be misinterpreted. The better practice is to carefully plan the end of the interview.

One common procedure calls for the knowledge engineer to halt the questioning a few minutes before the scheduled ending and to summarize the key points of the session. This practice allows the domain expert to comment and schedule a future session. If the procedure is carried out naturally, the domain expert will feel good about time well spent, and the next session is more likely to flow just as smoothly.

A number of verbal and nonverbal cues can be used to close an interview. Table 9–2 summarizes some of the verbal closing cues that have been found to be successful in ending a knowledge acquisition session. Nonverbal closing cues may be used with verbal cues to end a session. Some of the more common nonverbal cues are listed in Figure 9–10.

■ ISSUES TO ASSESS

During the interview, any number of issues may come up. To be prepared for the most important issues, a knowledge engineer should consider the following questions:

■ *How would one elicit knowledge from experts who cannot say what they mean or mean what they say?* Sometimes, the expert is knowledgeable,

■ **Table 9–2** Verbal Closing Cues for Ending an Interview

Verbal Cue	Meaning
1. This is my summary of the session. Do you have any questions?	I'm ready to end the session unless you have questions.
2. I think I've asked all the questions I had in mind. I appreciate your time.	I'm ready to call it a day.
3. My time allowance is up. I know you have another meeting soon.	Time's up.
4. I learned a great deal from this session. I appreciate your support.	I don't need any more information The session is over
5. This covers pretty much what I had in mind. Did I miss anything?	I am ready to end the session
6. This turned out to be an informative meeting. How about scheduling another meeting sometime next week?	Session is over. I'd like to schedule another one

Figure 9–10   Nonverbal Cues for Ending an Interview

1. Look at watch and uncross legs.
2. Put cap on pen and uncross legs.
3. Put cap on pen and close folder.
4. If taping session, stop taping, and rewind tape.
5. Stop taking notes, uncross legs, put cap on pen, look at watch (strongest nonverbal cues).
6. Place writing materials in briefcase and close briefcase.
7. Close folder and uncross legs.
8. Any combination of the preceding actions.

but has difficulty explaining things. Whether this difficulty stems from lack of knowledge usually becomes apparent during the first meeting. Unless it is a one-time blunder on the part of the expert, an alternative expert should be considered immediately.

■ *What does one say or do when the expert says, "Look, I work with shades of gray reasoning. I simply look at the problem and decide. Don't ask me why or how."* Unless a knowledge engineer is well prepared to handle unexpected situations, this type of answer could very well end the interview. The expert probably knows the solution so well that the details are an unconscious part of it. The knowledge engineer must work around this unconsciousness and look for ways to get at the details indirectly.

■ *How does one set up the problem domain when one has only a general idea of what it should be?* One rule of thumb is to ask the expert to illustrate or explain—through scenarios—the general procedure of the domain. The knowledge engineer should then feed back his or her understanding of what the expert said and work from there.

■ *What does one do if the relationship with the domain expert turns out to be difficult?* Perhaps the expert is not only uncooperative, but seems to be trying to sabotage the project or reacts defensively to the knowledge engineer's queries. In the latter case, the expert may have been told by management to participate in the project. Unless the expert can be coaxed into a more positive frame of mind, the resulting sessions could be strained at best.

The lack of cooperation could also be attributable to the knowledge engineer. Personality differences that surface quickly can work against the acquisition process. Personality clashes can be triggered by a number of things: a series of jumbled questions with no end in sight, "grilling" the expert as if on the witness stand, or reminding the expert too frequently of prior successes building expert systems. If the situation reaches a deadlock, the best solution is to replace the knowledge engineer or scrub the project.

■ *What happens if the expert dislikes the knowledge engineer?* This issue also addresses personality clashes. For example, on one project, a knowledge engineer from a university was assigned a senior loan officer to build an advisory system for commercial loans. From the beginning, the expert was reluctant to cooperate beyond cursory information. Well into the fourth session, the knowledge engineer learned that the expert had not been able to complete his doctorate and had difficulty working with academics.

Ways of gaining the respect of an expert varies from person to person. Sometimes young knowledge engineers do not do well with domain experts twenty years their senior. In other cases, the domain experts may feel their time is wasted talking to a novice. For these situations, an accommodating personality, finesse, and advance planning are critical in reaching the domain expert. A relationship that does not jell in the first session could make the entire acquisition process an uphill battle.

▓ RAPID PROTOTYPING IN INTERVIEWS

An effective approach to building expert systems is rapid prototyping, or the build-as-you-go approach, in which knowledge is added with each knowledge acquisition session. This incremental or iterative approach allows the expert to verify the rules as they are built during the session. See Box 9–2. Some people have likened rapid prototyping to the miracle of birth: an eight-pound baby is the prototype of a 180-pound person, who has essentially all the same features but with a more complete and mature configuration. Each stage of expert systems development has its own problems, requires its own modifications, provides its own excitement, and results in its own contributions.

Box 9–2   Role of Rapid Prototyping

In some beliefs, everything began in Genesis. God created the world in six days and rested on the seventh. Everything else occurred through evolution. Genesis is an excellent model for rapid evolutionary development, because we want to create a deliverable, functioning prototype in as little time as possible . . . and begin the endless additions, changes, and deletions required to keep the system in balance and evolving to meet the needs of the business. . . .

Rapid evolutionary development relies on speed, simplicity, and a shared vision to create a desired product. . . . Prototypers create a working system . . . that does work and provides the essential, initial elements of the system. . . . Then a series of step-wise improvements—evolution—turns the system into the customer's desired paradise.

. . . Can you imagine what would have happened if God had tried to specify the requirements for this earthship and then built it from scratch with all the bells and whistles? It could have taken 150 million years just to get started. Instead, God chose to *rapid-prototype* the initial version in six days and grow it from there.

Unlike the traditional development life cycle, speed is required more than direction in rapid prototyping. Once you're rolling, you can change course at will. If you're not moving, you have no feedback to guide your first steps.

Source: Adapted from L. J. Arthur, *Improving Software Quality: An Insider's Guide to TQM* (New York: Wiley & Sons, 1992).

The expert might look at the initial version and say, "This is a good beginning, but it's not ready yet." Rules are added and changes are made every time a new version is run until the expert says, "This is about as close as we can expect. . . . Let's wrap it up."

Benefits and Drawbacks

Rapid prototyping can open up communication through its demonstration of the expert system. Because of its instant feedback and modification, it also reduces risk of failure. Another benefit is allowing the knowledge engineer to learn every time a change is made in the prototype. Its iterative nature encourages discovery of better ways to build the expert system.

Cycle time from the working model to the final product can be reduced by as much as a factor of four with rapid prototyping. It also reduces bugs through continuous testing and verification. Finally, when users and experts are involved in the testing process, they can develop a sense of ownership and commitment to the system's use.

Rapid prototyping depends on the teamwork of the knowledge engineer, the domain expert, and the end-user. It is highly interactive, and its continuous feedback leads to improvements and refinements all the way to completion, which creates an expert system that corresponds as closely as possible to its stated requirements.

An obvious problem with rapid prototyping, however, is lack of clear guidelines for its use. Another drawback is that the prototype itself can create user expectations that, in turn, become obstacles to further development efforts. As a result, users refuse to buy into it, and the transition to an operational expert system never materializes. Table 9–3 summarizes the pros and cons of rapid prototyping.

■ **Table 9–3**   Benefits and Drawbacks of Rapid Prototyping

Benefits
1. Demonstrates the technical competence of the knowledge engineer.
2. Promotes innovation under the direct guidance of the domain expert.
3. Reduces maintenance by up to 90 percent.
4. Opens up communication by demonstrating rather than representing the expert system.
5. Allows the knowledge engineer to learn every time another change is embedded in the expert system.
6. Encourages discovery of better ways to build the expert system.
7. Reduces cycle time for producing the system by a factor of four.
8. Reduces bugs by continuous testing and verification of each version.

Drawbacks
1. Lacks clear guidelines for use.
2. Has a limited number of knowledge engineers trained in its use.
3. Creates transition difficulties.

IMPLICATIONS FOR MANAGEMENT

As this chapter has demonstrated, interviewing is critical to the success of knowledge acquisition. To ensure that interviewing works, two managerial steps must be considered. The first step is *planning,* especially when complex problem domains are involved and more than one domain expert are used. A knowledge engineer should decide in advance the number of questions to be asked, the nature of each question, the sequence, and whether the session should proceed from open-ended to structured questions or vice versa. Many sessions fail because of a knowledge engineer's lack of planning.

Second, one must make a deliberate effort to *develop the system efficiently,* not by cutting corners or taping sessions that are never played back, but by evaluating each step within each session and within the acquisition phase to ensure a successful expert system. The emphasis should be on quality assurance, integrity, and the viability of the product.

Interviewing itself carries a number of managerial implications. First, managing knowledge acquisition means managing the expert's time, which is precious. The knowledge engineer should make the most efficient use of the domain expert's time in the fewest number of sessions. After all, the domain expert's willingness to cooperate or to provide knowledge is not unlimited.

Second, management must provide the right atmosphere and support if the interviewing process is to succeed, which is actually the responsibility of the champion. As mentioned earlier in the text, the champion can be the "traveling salesperson" in the organization, selling the goodness of the expert system, ensuring financial support, and otherwise removing administrative obstacles.

A third implication is to what extent the domain expert can provide time for the acquisition phase. Experts who are on company payroll often draw high salaries. Advance planning by the knowledge engineer is necessary to make the most efficient use of the domain expert's time.

Finally, while conducting knowledge acquisition, the knowledge engineer must consider which type of shell or language will be appropriate for knowledge representation. Managing expert system technology is as important as managing knowledge acquisition. Also, the careful management of time, talent, and technology provides an anchor for the development of a successful expert system. The process is like a tripod; compromising one leg triggers an imbalance in the whole system.

In terms of rapid prototyping, management should be educated about the potential of the product well before it is ready to be installed. Demonstrating the prototype at some point can be a good "selling" technique. Without such occasional feedback, funds and support may dwindle, often resulting in "half-baked" or incomplete systems.

Effectively managing an expert system could pave the way for the building of other systems, promoting a long-term commitment to the technology. Such an investment in the technology of expert systems has implications for staff training and development, upgrading existing applications, and exploring potential expert system applications. Effective management is the best way to sell change and is necessary if an organization is to adapt to change on a long-term basis.

▓ SUMMARY

1. People reason with words, not numbers. A common problem encountered in interviewing is an expert who cannot easily convey the knowledge even though he or she may be quite competent at the specialty. To the nonexpert, an expert's pattern matching or analogy can resemble fuzzy reasoning.

2. Visual imagery is an important part of a human's ability to recall chunks of experience. People who have difficulty with it often have trouble answering questions. This common problem puts pressure on the knowledge engineer to sit back and determine how the expert thinks through a problem.

3. Ambiguities of language during interviewing or when interpreting the expert's descriptions or explanations is a common problem a knowledge engineer must be aware of and work to avoid.

4. In the early stages of acquisition, interviewing is used to capture or verify an expert's information. It also provides an opportunity for behavioral analysis. It offers advantages and has limitations, sometimes depending on whether the interview is structured or unstructured.

5. A structured interview has several variations: multiple-choice, dichotomous, and rating scale questions. Each variation has its own format and goals.

6. Interviewing should be approached logically, using stage setting, proper phrasing of questions, good listening, and evaluating the session outcome. Question sequencing as well as probing the expert for details are also important.

7. Reliability of an expert's information can be affected by question construction, which requires a careful review of question content, wording, and format. Reliability is also affected by uncontrolled sources of errors: the expert's perceptual slant, failure to remember just what happened, fear of the unknown, communication problems, and role bias. Errors can also originate with the knowledge engineer, including age, race, and gender effects.

8. Several problems may be encountered in interviews: response bias, inconsistency, communication difficulties, hostile attitude, and standardized questions.

9. Because problems do occur in interviewing, a knowledge engineer needs to avoid such things as interrupting the expert, questions that put the expert on the defensive, pretending to understand, and losing control of the session.

10. Several issues may arise during the interview that must be assessed. For example, how would one get knowledge from experts who don't say what they mean or mean what they say? How can one set up a problem domain while knowing little about it? What does one do when the relationship with the expert turns out to be difficult?

■ TERMS TO LEARN

Age effect bias against a person due to age.

Analogies comparing a problem to a similar one encountered previously.

Belief a qualitative judgment about the nature of the statement or the problem under review; measure of the level of credibility.

Closed question asks for specific responses.

Dichotomous question a question answerable by one of two answers, usually yes or no.

Gender effect bias against a person based on gender.

Interview a face-to-face interpersonal situation in which a person called the interviewer asks another person questions designed to elicit certain responses about a problem domain.

Multiple-choice question offers the expert specific answer choices.

Open-ended question asks for general rather than specific responses.

Primary question a question that elicits the most important information in one area during the interview; leads to further questions to obtain pertinent details.

Race effect bias against a person due to race.

Ranking scale question asks the respondent to arrange items in a list according to preference or importance.

Reliability dependability, truthfulness of the response or answer to a given question; credibility; how well the system delivers solutions with consistency, accuracy, or integrity; detecting or removing anomaly.

Response bias bias resulting from the subjective responses of the domain expert to any given question.

Role bias an altered attitude resulting from the expert's awareness of his or her importance in the building of an expert system.

Secondary question a question used to probe for further details or follow up on an area under discussion.

Structured interview an approach in which the questions are fixed in advance; used when the knowledge engineer wants specific information.

Uncertainty in the context of expert systems, a value that cannot be determined during a consultation; a lack of adequate information necessary to make a decision.

Unstructured interview an approach in which the questions and the alternative responses are open-ended.

Validity the logical correctness of a question, which is worded in order to elicit the information sought.

■ REVIEW QUESTIONS

1. How does pattern matching adversely affect the quality of an interview?
2. "Knowledge engineers can benefit immensely from an educational grounding in cognitive psychology." Do you agree? Discuss.
3. In what ways is visual imagery helpful in recalling chunks of experience? Be specific.
4. Briefly describe the areas in which language may be a problem during knowledge acquisition.
5. Distinguish between:
   a. validity and reliability
   b. multiple-choice and dichotomous questions
6. Give examples of your own to distinguish between:
   a. question format and question content
   b. question wording and question content
7. Briefly explain each of the uncontrolled sources of error that the knowledge engineer

needs to consider. Which source do you consider most seriously? Why?

8. What is the interviewer effect? How likely is the occurrence of this problem? Explain.

9. Review briefly some of the problems encountered during the interview. Which problem do you consider most serious? Why?

10. The chapter suggests a guide to a successful interview. Does it allow enough flexibility? That is, what determines how strictly one should follow the guide? Explain.

11. If the knowledge engineer knew the domain expert from prior contacts, how important is setting the stage or establishing a rapport? Be specific.

12. Experience teaches that how questions are phrased can determine the nature of the answers. In knowledge acquisition, explain how the following are related:

a. question phrasing and question sequence
b. primary and secondary questions
c. open-ended and closed questions

13. Would you recommend a special way for recording captured information? Is a legal pad (8-1/2” x 14”) useful for note taking? Explain.

14. If you were building an expert system using a single expert who has been coaxed for weeks to participate, what are some of the things to avoid in interviewing such an expert? Explain.

15. In what way(s) is rapid prototyping related to interviewing? Be specific.

■ EXERCISES AND CASES

1. Select two other people to form a group of three (triad). One person will be *A,* the second person *B,* and the third person *C.* Have *A* ask a question of *B. B* will then ask a question of *C. C* will ask a question of *A.* Questions may cover areas pertaining to the course material or the expert system project you're working on. Go over the following questions:

a. How well have you learned about one another?
b. What were you doing when the other two people were talking to each other?
c. What experience did you have when you asked one question at a time? Be specific.
d. In general, how did you spend most of your time?

2. Interviewing is sometimes similar to conversation. Get into a conversation with another person in your class for 30 minutes. Choose a topic in advance. How many times did the topic change? What triggered the change in the topic?

3. Watch an interview on TV between a news reporter and an expert in the field (police, government official, etc.). Record how the interview was started. What types of questions were asked? Do you agree with the question sequence and construction? Explain.

4. Distinguish the following questions as either leading questions or neutral questions:

a. You like to operate on patients, don't you?
b. When was the last time you had less than satisfactory surgery?
c. How does an auto loan differ from a commercial loan?
d. Would you classify yourself as an orthopaedic surgeon or a specialist in hip replacement?
e. How do you feel about applicants lying on their application form?

5. Write the name of one person you admire and one person you dislike or distrust—the person could be someone you know, a celebrity, a national figure, etc. Make a list of traits each person possesses (honest/dishonest, competent/incompetent, etc.). Which of these traits are critical aspects of credibility? How would the distrusted person proceed to change his or her image in your eyes?

6. *Publisher Advisor*

Background

The goal of the first session with the domain expert was to develop a master list of all the variables that the expert considered important in deciding on the book manuscript. These variables were condensed into twenty possibilities and then ranked in order of importance. The ranking was presented to the expert for verification. The variables were reduced to the five most important:

- marketability
- reviewers' opinions
- author's prior publishing record
- author's requirements
- publication cost

In preparation for the first interview, the knowledge engineer reviewed published articles about book publishing, what manuscripts get published, the criteria used in making favorable decisions, and the book production process. This background provided a number of prefatory questions that were included in the first session.

Assignment

For this project, set up a list of questions to ask the domain expert (book editor) in preparation for the first interview. Explain the reason(s) for choosing these questions. What variables or parameters have you been able to conclude from the session?

7. The following is a partial interview with a domain expert, who is the coordinator of an MIS graduate admissions program, to build a Graduate Admissions Advisor.

KE: I'd just like to go through a recap of the first session and sign off on it, and check for any inconsistencies.

EXPERT: Okay. I want to ask a question for clarification. GMAT scores: scores below 500 are not considered. Do you mean to say here that the applicant is not considered or the GMAT score is not considered?

KE: I understood this to mean the applicant was not considered any further. Is this true?

EXPERT: Generally true. (pause) One correction. GPAs are looked at differently, depending on the applicant's undergraduate school and major.

KE: I have that under major.

EXPERT: Degrees.

KE: Here's where we get into more specific questions.

EXPERT: MIS undergraduate degrees are favored, although not required. By "Majors will affect evaluation of GPA," you mean what?

KE: For example, an engineering degree may be considered more difficult than other majors. For that reason, an engineering degree with a 2.8 may hold more significance than some others.

EXPERT: That is generally true. If GPA is average, GMAT is fair, then work experience becomes the default. Not any work experience; certain work experience.

KE: I think this means that candidates' work experience could push them to one side or another.

EXPERT: The default is work experience. Then we would take a look at what type of work experience.

KE: Such as whether it is business-related?

EXPERT: Right, we have a case in the program about work experience, and programming is where the work experience was done. The combination tipped the scale. So it is not only work experience but the type of experience and where it was acquired or practiced.

KE: Okay. I guess we can move on into the rest of our agenda here. We want to talk about something we didn't get to last time. We want to talk about the scope of the system and get a feel for what this thing will look like when we are done. In terms of what kind of recommendations and goals we are setting for the system, are we looking for a "yes, definitely" or an "absolutely not" recommendation, and do we want to incorporate a gray area?

EXPERT: Actually, three or four levels of decision making exist. One, definitely recommend. The other, definitely deny. The third would be marginal, especially if the student is not expected to finish in one year. Let us say a student coming in has a B.S. in economics, which would mean more than one year. Let us say the record overall is marginal and the degree is from our university. We say let us see how well this applicant will do meeting the undergraduate business requirements in our school. If he or she does not do well, we can also dismiss him or her.

KE: So you're recommending admission on a trial basis, sort of?

EXPERT: We don't say that. We say admit, but you have in one case a student who has recently been admitted to the graduate program during the fall; he was admitted marginally, but we don't say that. He was admitted on the basis that he make a minimum of a *B* average in the undergraduate courses. This becomes a condition for admission into the one-year graduate program. Or we can have a situation in which a person is maybe marginal; he or she lacks the system analysis and design, the database, and the basic information systems courses. This person must get a *B* or higher in each course before they can begin the graduate program. Another level of admission. . . .

KE: I'm confused. So is the third one "admission contingent upon successfully completing the undergraduate classes?"

EXPERT: Conditional admit, I would say, yes.

Questions

a. Evaluate the quality and consistency of the partial interview.

b. How much preparation do you think took place prior to the interview? Explain.

c. What type of interview was conducted?

■ SELECTED REFERENCES

Aussenac, Nathalie. *Knowledge Acquisition for Knowledge-Based Systems: Seventh Annual European workshop, EKAW '93, Toulouse and Caylus, France, September 6–10, 1993*. Berlin and New York: Springer-Verlag, 1993.

Bainbridge, L. "Verbal Reports as Evidence of the Process Operator's Knowledge." *International Journal of Man–Machine Studies* 11 (1979), pp. 411–436.

———. "Asking Questions and Accessing Knowledge." *Future Computing Systems* 1 (1986), pp. 143–149.

Bellezza, Francis S. and D. K. Buck. "Expert Knowledge as Mnemonic Cues." *Applied Cognitive Psychology* 2 (1988), pp. 147–162.

Bower, G. H.; M. C. Clark; A. M. Lesgold; and D. Winzenz. "Hierarchical Retrieval Schemes in Recall of Categorized Word Lists." *Journal of Verbal Learning and Verbal Behavior* 8 (1969), pp. 323–343.

Cawsey, A. "Explanatory Dialogues." *Interacting With Computers,* 1, pp. 73–92.

Deng, Pi-Sheng. "Automating Knowledge Acquisition and Refinement for Decision Support: A Connectionist Inductive Inference Model." *Decision Sciences,* March/April 1993, pp. 371–393.

Evans, J. "The Knowledge Elicitation Problem: A Psychological Perspective." *Behavior and Information Technology* 7, no. 2 (1988), pp. 111–130.

Gentner, D. "The Mechanisms of Analogical Learning." In S. Vosniadou and A. Ortony, eds., *Similarity and Analogical Reasoning*. London: Cambridge University Press, 1989, pp. 199–241.

Gordon, Sallie E. "Front-End Analysis for Expert System Design." *Proceedings of the 35th Annual Meeting of the Human Factors Society*. Santa Monica, CA: Human Factors Society, 1991, pp. 278–282.

———. "Implications of Cognitive Theory for Knowledge Acquisition." In Robert R. Hoffman,

ed., *The Psychology of Expertise*. New York: Springer-Verlag, 1992, pp. 99–120.

Hanisch, K.; A. F. Kramer; C. Hulin; and R. Schumacher. "Novice–Expert Differences in the Cognitive Representation of System Features: Mental Models and Verbalizable Knowledge." *Proceedings of the 32nd Annual Meeting of the Human Factors Society*. Santa Monica, CA: Human Factors Society, 1988, pp. 219–223.

Hoffman, R. R. "The Problem of Extracting the Knowledge of Experts from the Perspective of Experimental Psychology." *AUI Magazine* 8 (1987), pp. 53–67.

Lancaster, J. "Cognitively Based Knowledge Acquisition: Capturing Categorical, Temporal, and Causal Knowledge." In K. McGraw and C. Westphal, eds., *Readings in Knowledge Acquisition: Current Practices and Trends*. Chichester, England: Ellis Horwood, 1990.

Mack, Robert and Jill Burdett Robinson, "When Novices Elicit Knowledge: Question Asking in Designing, Evaluating, and Learning to Use Software." In Robert R. Hoffman, ed., *The Psychology of Expertise*. New York; Springer-Verlag, 1992, pp. 245–268.

McGraw, Karen L. "Communication Techniques for Software Support Specialists." Training seminar material. Annapolis, MD: Cognitive Technologies, 1989.

———. "Managing and Documenting the Knowledge Acquisition Process." In Robert R. Hoffman, ed., *The Psychology of Expertise*. New York; Springer-Verlag, 1992, pp. 149–168.

McGraw, Karen L. and C. Westphal, eds., *Readings in Knowledge Acquisition: Current Practice and Trends*. Chichester, England: Ellis Horwood, 1990.

Regoczei, Stephen B. "The Psychology of Expertise and Knowledge Acquisition: Comments on the Chapters in This Volume." In Robert R. Hoffman, ed., *The Psychology of Expertise.* New York; Springer-Verlag, 1992, pp. 297–313.

Regoczei, Stephen B. and Graeme Hirst. "Knowledge and Knowledge Acquisition in the Computational Context." In Robert R. Hoffman, ed., *The Psychology of Expertise.* New York; Springer-Verlag, 1992, pp. 12–25.

Roediger, H. L.; M. S. Weldon; and B. H. Challis. "Explaining Dissociations Between Implicit and Explicit Measures of Retention: A Processing Account." In H. L. Roediger and F. I. M. Craik, eds., *Varieties of Memory and Consciousness Essays in Honour of Endel Tulving.* Hillsdale, NJ: Erlbaum, 1989, pp. 3–41.

Sanderson, P. M. "Verbalizable Knowledge and Skilled Task Performance: Association, Dissociation, and Mental Models." *Journal of Experimental Psychology: Learning, Memory, and Cognition* 15, pp. 729–747.

Schacter, D. L. "On the Relation Between Memory and Consciousness: Dissociate Interactions and Conscious Experience." In H. L. Roediger and F. I. M. Craik, eds., *Varieties of Memory and Consciousness: Essays in Honour of Endel Tulving.* Hillsdale, NJ: Erlbaum, 1989, pp. 355–389.

Scott, A. Carlisle; Jan E. Clayton; and Elizabeth Gibson. *A Practical Guide to Knowledge Acquisition.* Reading, MA: Addison-Wesley, 1991.

Shadbolt, N.; R. R. Hoffman; A. M. Burton; and G. A. Klein, *Eliciting Knowledge from Experts: A Methodological Analysis.* Unpublished manuscript, 1991. Dept. of Psychology, University of Nottingham, Nottingham, England.

Singley, M. K., and J. R. Anderson. *The Transfer of Cognitive Skill.* Cambridge, MA: Harvard University Press.

Sowa, John F. "Conceptual Analysis as a Basis for Knowledge Acquisition." In Robert R. Hoffman, ed., *The Psychology of Expertise.* New York: Springer-Verlag, 1992, pp. 80–96.

Steels, Luc; Guus Schreiber; and Walter Van de Velde. *A Future for Knowledge Acquisition: Eighth European Knowledge Acquisition Workshop, EKAW '94, Hoegaarden, Belgium, September 26–29, 1994.* Berlin and New York: Springer-Verlag, 1994.

Wetter, Thomas. *Current Developments Knowledge Acquisition: EKAW 92: Sixth European Knowledge Acquisition Workshop, Heidelberg and Kaiserslautern, Germany, May 1992.* Berlin and New York: Springer-Verlag, 1992.

Williams, Kent E.; John Deighan; and Tim Kotnour. "Knowledge Acquisition for Group Problem Solving." *Computers & Industrial Engineering,* November 1992, pp. 459–462.

Chapter ■ 10

Other Knowledge Acquisition Techniques

WHAT'S IN A SCENARIO?

The term *scenario* is used to refer to a detailed and sometimes complex sequence of events. Mission scenarios for example are a detailed specification of a flight plan, a series of aircraft maneuvers and pilot tasks. These can be used to train pilots or to consider the performance requirements of an aircraft.

Scenario refers to a situation or more precisely (since it has a temporal component), an episode. A scenario involves individuals, objects, and courses of events. One important characteristic of scenarios is that they describe particular states of affairs and events. They can be used to describe possible worlds in which certain yet-to-be-considered actualities could occur. This is the case with mission scenarios where a pilot is being trained for certain anticipated events. It is also true of design scenarios in which a designer imagines what it would be like to interact with a system using a particular kind of device.

As can be seen, the purpose of a scenario is to provide an explicit concrete vision of how some human activity could be supported by technology. Scenarios are one good reference point for making design decisions. By showing the actual circumstances under which people work, scenarios provide guidelines on how a technology should perform. The very act of making things explicit and clear also helps in making design choices.

For a scenario to be good, it must realistically depict some actual human activity. It must "bring to life" for its users the activity that is to be supported.

Scenario developers need interviewing and writing skills as well as technical imagination and understanding. These skills could be distributed across two people, e.g., one researcher might be an especially good interviewer while the other has strong writing skills and technical depth.

Source: Excerpted from Peter Wright, "What's In a Scenario?" and Bonnie Nardi, "The Use of Scenarios in Design," *SIGCHI Bulletin,* October 1992, pp. 11–14.

AT A GLANCE

Like any other professional, the knowledge engineer must be well versed in the use of specialized knowledge acquisition tools. Each tool has a special purpose, depending on whether the acquisition process revolves around a single or multiple experts. Among the tools are computer-based tools designed to promote accuracy and integrity of the knowledge acquisition process.

A knowledge engineer might want to observe the problem-solving process of an expert in a situation in which on-site observation would be a proper tool. When dealing with two or more experts together, brainstorming, followed by consensus decision making, is preferred. Whatever tool is chosen, the knowledge engineer must follow a preestablished procedure for conducting the session.

A unique knowledge acquisition technique for single experts is protocol analysis, or the think-aloud method. In essence, it involves listening to the spoken protocol of the expert. During the session, the expert speaks out loud whatever thoughts come to mind while answering a question or solving a problem. In contrast, repertory grid uses a grid or a scale to represent the expert's way of looking at a particular problem. The number of gradations on a scale can be increased to reflect more accurate ratings.

Other techniques for multiple experts include the nominal-group and Delphi methods. Each method has unique features and a procedure to operationalize its use. The nominal-group method is an interface between consensus and brainstorming, while the Delphi method is a polling of experts' opinions, via questionnaires.

An attractive computer-based method for multiple experts is the "blackboard." Also called *Groupware,* this global memory structure promotes privacy and equality among participating experts. It attempts to get the experts to agree on a solution, and is ideal for complex problem solving involving several experts.

What You Will Learn

By the end of this chapter, you should know the following:

1. The common tools used for tapping the knowledge of single as well as multiple experts.
2. The characteristics and limitations of key knowledge acquisition tools.
3. How computers are automating the knowledge acquisition process.
4. The various procedures used in implementing knowledge acquisition tools.

INTRODUCTION

A knowledge engineer must recognize that many complex problem domains cannot be solved by a single expert. For example, the prototype for the Diabetic Foot Advisor described in preceding chapters will involve two other specialists in the field to agree on medical and surgical treatment before the expert system can be medically certified. To be sure that knowledge is reliable, then, multiple experts are often required.

When dealing with the multiple experts, the knowledge engineer must be familiar with the tools and techniques that are unique to the task. Chapter 9 focused on ways to ensure a successful interview with a domain expert. The use of this tool requires a customized approach to both the expert and the process. This chapter examines other tools used in knowledge acquisition: on-site observation, protocol analysis, and consensus methodologies, including brainstorming, consensus decision making, the repertory grid, nominal-group technique, and the Delphi method. A more recent knowledge acquisition tool, blackboarding, will be discussed at the end of the chapter.

Acquiring knowledge from multiple experts requires experience and special-purpose techniques. Without this combination, serious problems often arise, such as experts walking out, faking solutions to end the session, and so on.

ON-SITE OBSERVATION

This specialized knowledge acquisition technique is borrowed from the social sciences, where the knowledge engineer observes the daily work of a domain expert. **On-site observation,** or action protocol, is a process of observing, interpreting, and recording an expert's problem-solving behavior while it takes place. It requires concentration on the overall steps that the domain expert takes as well as the more subtle details of the process. In addition to observing and recording the expert's behavior, the knowledge engineer asks the expert questions about the problem-solving process.

On-site observation carries with it a certain protocol. The knowledge engineer does more listening than talking; avoids giving advice and does not pass judgment on what is observed, even if it is incorrect; and does not argue with the expert while the expert is performing the task.

On-site observation was used by one knowledge engineer to build a "Teller Advisor" for a commercial bank, a project that took two months to complete. The knowledge engineer sat in a booth adjacent to a senior teller with seven years of experience. The purpose of the project was to build an expert system to determine when a check that exceeded the set limits ($500, in this case) could be cashed without requiring an officer's signature. This particular teller's success rate (the check did not bounce) was 95 percent; the average bank officer's success rate for the same decision was 70 percent.

In this example, on-site observation gave the knowledge engineer a visual or a live exposure to the kind of information that can also be gathered through the interview. In the Teller Advisor project, the knowledge engineer conducted brief informal interviews with the teller when no customers were waiting. The answers during those interviews verified the information picked up through participant observation.

Observation of behavior enables the knowledge engineer to seek knowledge within the working world of the expert. In comparison to the interview, observation places the knowledge engineer closer to the actual steps and procedures used by the expert to solve the problem. One problem with this acquisition technique is that some experts do not like to be observed. They prefer to talk about their thought processes rather than show them in practice. Sometimes experts fear that observation will give away years of their experience in one quick look.

The reaction of others in the observation setting can also be a distracting problem. During the early stages of the Teller Advisor project, other tellers' curious and occasional hostile feelings were conspicuous. One teller with eighteen years' experience was quite irritated at the bank for allowing such a "ridiculous automation of the human mind." She guarded her own actions closely after commenting during a lunch break that the teller "expert" was being used as a guinea pig, and wondering "How can they tell us to follow procedure, and here they are trying to automate the procedure?" Yet, in the case of the Teller Advisor project, the teller expert thrived on attention. She was not at all distracted by the presence of the knowledge engineer or the reservations of co-workers. Participant observation went on for two weeks without any problems.

Another problem with on-site observation is the accuracy or completeness of the acquired knowledge. Although the general assumption may be that the recording of an event and the event itself occur simultaneously, in reality, a time gap separates what is observed and its recording. The event is first transcribed into a mental image before that image is translated into the knowledge engineer's own words. It becomes a retrospective process, which inevitably invites errors.

To form a mental picture of the event, the knowledge engineer attempts to integrate his or her perception of the situation with the expert's perception. That mental picture is then recorded. What happens is a continuous **shuttle process;** the knowledge engineer mentally moves back and forth from the initial impression of the event to the later evaluation of the event. What is finally recorded is the evaluation made during this retrospective period. Because a time lapse can make details of a situation less clear, the information is not always valid.

■ BRAINSTORMING

Unlike on-site observation, which focuses on the work of a single expert, **brainstorming**—an unstructured approach to generating ideas about a problem domain—invites two or more experts into a session in which discussions are carried out and a variety of opinions tossed around. The primary goal of this process is to think up creative solutions to problems. In brainstorming, all possible solutions are considered equally. The emphasis is on the frequency of responses during the session. Anything related to the topic can be brought up, and everything is valued. Questions can be raised for clarification, but no evaluation is made at the moment.

In brainstorming, the first step is idea generation, followed by idea evaluation. Similarities begin to emerge across opinions, which are then grouped logically and evaluated by asking a number of questions:

- If one followed up on this idea, what benefits would cnsue? (All ideas are itemized or prioritized.)
- What problem(s) would a selected idea solve?
- What new problem(s) would arise?

In the evaluation phase, the knowledge engineer explains each idea and treats any comments or criticisms accordingly.

The general procedure for conducting a brainstorming session is as follows:

1. *Introduce the brainstorming session.* Explain what it is and is not designed to accomplish, the role of each participant, the "rules of the game," and the expected outcomes. Starting with the wrong objective or the wrong step can doom the entire process.

2. *Present the problem for the experts to consider.* The problem approved by the organization is in the experts' domain of expertise. The knowledge engineer must give the experts time to think it through and then be a good listener and show enthusiasm but also set reasonable time limits.

3. *Prompt the experts to generate ideas.* The experts can do this either by calling out their ideas or by establishing some order in which each expert will have a turn to speak. In either approach, the important step is to write the ideas on a board or an overhead transparency to provide recognition as an important means of validating the experts' ideas. The knowledge engineer must keep pace with the expert.

4. *Watch for signs of convergence.* Ideas often trigger counter opinions or reinforcements that should eventually coax the experts to converge on the final four, the final two, and the final solution. When experts begin to pass or the rate and quality of ideas presented declines, the process moves on to convergence.

In the event experts cannot agree on the final solution from among two or three alternatives on the slate, the knowledge engineer may call for a vote or a **consensus** in order to reach agreement on the best final solution, which does not guarantee success. The intensity of the discussion just prior to such a vote, the temperament of the experts, and how willing they are to resolve conflicts all influence whether a consensus can be reached.

As a tool, brainstorming is not without its problems. The main drawback is that some experts tend to abuse the rules of brainstorming that dictate an expert cannot be cut short or any ideas be shot down. Second, senior experts tend to color the opinion of their juniors, especially when they are the first to talk. Third, regardless of the knowledge engineer's experience, creating on-the-spot summaries that will lead to a consensus can be difficult.

Electronic Brainstorming

A relatively new development, called **electronic brainstorming,** is a computer-aided approach to dealing with multiple experts. Desks in a U-shaped layout hold PCs networked through a software tool that serves as a catalyst in the meeting, promoting instant exchange of ideas between experts, and sorting and condensing those ideas into an organized format. Such a tool also allows experts to elaborate and vote on ideas. See Figure 10–1.

For example, IBM's electronic brainstorming process begins with a pre-session plan that identifies objectives and structures the agenda, which is presented to the experts for approval. During the live session, each expert chooses a PC and engages in a predefined approach to resolving a focused issue, and then generates ideas or plans. The experts gain leverage from anonymity, focus on content (not personalities), and engage in parallel and simultaneous communication. This format allows two or more experts to provide opinions through their PCs without having to wait their turn. The software displays the comments or suggestions on a huge screen without identifying the source.

This method protects the shy expert and prevents tagging comments to individuals. The overall benefits include improved communication, effective discussion of sensitive issues, shorter meetings, and closure of meetings with concise recommendations for action. The sequence of brainstorming steps is summarized in Figure 10–2. The expert's ideas are prioritized. This eventually leads to convergence and setting final specifications. The result is joint ownership of the solution.

To illustrate the process used in electronic brainstorming, a group of graduate professors met one day to discuss the field research topics for MIS graduate students. The one-day session using IBM's Electronic Brainstormer began with a focused topic: generate a portfolio of field research projects for graduate MIS students. The facilitator (the role taken by the knowledge engineer) asks each professor to list as many topics as desired through the PC. Each professor was assigned an I.D. that was not visible on the screen when the questions were entered or displayed. Table 10–1 shows the resulting input of the seven participants.

After the questions had been listed on the screen, they were discussed, and redundancies were removed. Afterward, the key topics remained, as shown in Figure 10–3 on page 220. Then, the questions listed were reviewed, arranged in order of priority, and voted on. The resulting matrix shown in Table 10–2 on page 220 provides the voting results.

Figure 10-1   IBM's Electronic Brainstorming Environment

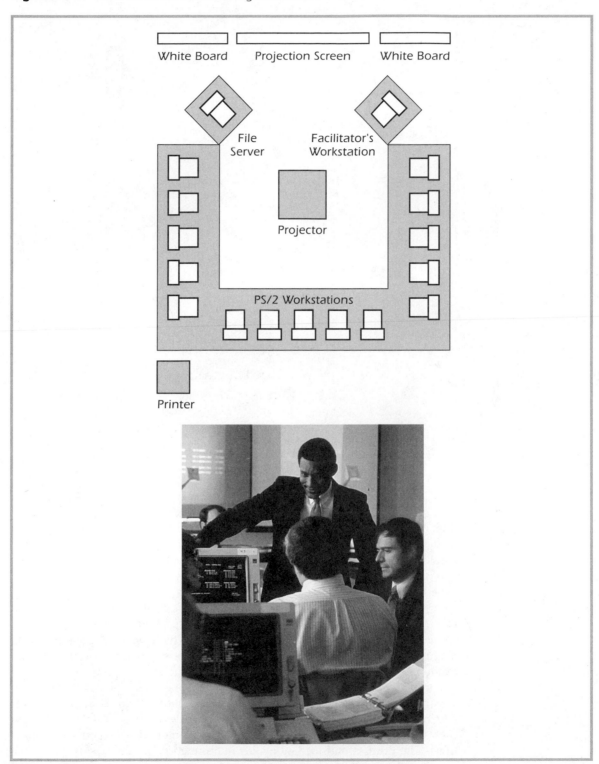

Figure 10–2 Brainstorming Process

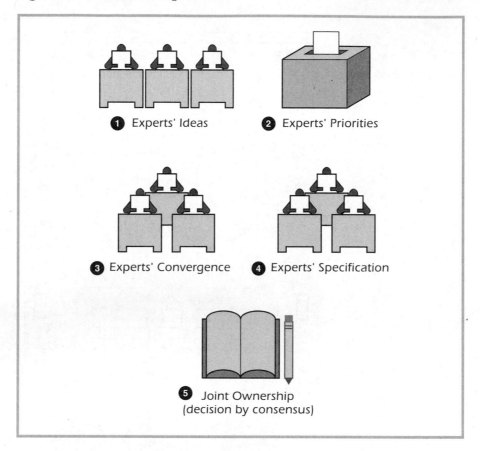

PROTOCOL ANALYSIS

Suppose a knowledge engineer wants to understand the diagnostic process of a medical expert, the knowledge used, and the cognitive actions taken. How would a knowledge engineer approach the problem domain? One obvious approach would be to ask the expert questions about diagnoses. Because experts are used to doing their jobs rather than explaining them, they probably won't find the questions easy to answer. For example, the expert for the Diabetic Foot Advisor tried to explain the process of diagnosis in terms of the formal procedure learned in medical school, which was different from the diagnosis followed with each patient. An alternative method is to observe an examination of a real patient and then listen to the spoken protocol.

In working with multiple experts, the problem-solving process is bound to vary. Two experts might give the same answer, but use two different problem-solving strategies. A think-aloud protocol provides a clear insight as to how each expert arrived at the solution through the individual expert's verbalizations. The **think-aloud** method avoids interpretation by the experts.

Box 10–1 illustrates how two solvers interpreted an arithmetic word problem. The two solvers arrived at the same answer, but used different solving strategy. The cognitive processes of experts are difficult to obtain by other

■ **Table 10-1** Questions Generated via Electronic Brainstorming

Problem Domain: Generate a portfolio of field research for MIS graduate students

Participant 1:
1.1   Develop an interactive/graphical data model query selection
1.2   Analyze group decision support systems (e.g., Team Focus, SAAM, etc.)
1.3   Develop a manufacturing database to support comm 326
1.4   Develop an executive information system that uses real-time data feeds
1.5   Analyze Dave Smith's office (can he possibly be productive in his environment?)

Participant 2:
2.1   Work with physical plant on cost estimating system
2.2   Assist athletic department in establishing an injury database
2.3   Work with local IBM office to sell more PCs
2.4   Develop database of nine in-class speakers from industry

Participant 3:
3.1   Work with medical imaging specialists on patient database
3.2   Explore use of COBOL to access distributed database
3.3   Establish a database of MIS internships

Participant 4:
4.1   Analyze communication media (e.g., electronic and/or voice mail) perhaps using the Commerce School as a case study
4.2   Study the allocation of computer resources in the University of the Comm School
4.3   Determine the effect of various levels of DSS on player performance of a management simulation game
4.4   Reconcile use of university and Comm School E-mail
4.5   Evaluate the impact of GDSS on Comm student group productivity

Participant 5:
5.1   Study graphics applications in GDSS (can we integrate graphics input?)
5.2   Analyze issues of migration to graphic user interfaces for end-users
5.3   Automate commerce student registration

Participant 6:
6.1   Analyze new case tools
6.2   Examine use of simulation tools for data flow modeling
6.3   Evaluate use of GDSS tools in an academic environment

Participant 7:
7.1   Explore implementation issues of electronic mail
7.2   Simulate knowledge acquisition session with multiple experts
7.3   Implement a neural network to evaluate mortgage applications

means. The **protocol analysis** or think-aloud method shows clearly how the solvers solved the problem one step at a time. It is a useful technique for knowledge acquisition.

In protocol analysis, protocols (cases, scenarios, etc.) are collected by asking experts to solve problems and to verbalize what goes through their

■ **Table 10–2**   Voting and Rank of Key Topics

| | = = = = = = = = = = = = = = Number of Votes in Each Position = = = = = = = | | | | | | |
	1	2	3	4	5	6	7
Anal	4	1	–	2	–	–	–
Exec	1	2	1	1	–	–	1
Do p	2	–	–	2	–	1	1
Doin	–	–	1	–	5	1	–
Impl	–	1	2	–	–	2	–
Know	–	2	–	–	–	3	1
Buil	–	1	–	1	1	–	2
Deve	–	–	2	–	–	–	2
Shou	–	–	1	1	1	–	–

```
= = = = = = = = = = = = = = = = = = = = = = = = = = = = = = = = = = = = = = = = = = =
= = = = = = = = = = = = = = = = = = = = = = = = = =
= = = = = = = = = = = = = = = = = = = = = = = = = = = = = = = = = = = = = = = = = Rank
Sum = = = = = = = = = = = = = = = = = = = = = = = = = = = = = = = = = = =
Analysis of group decision+++++++++++++++56
Develop executive information system++++++++++++43
Do projects that add to+++++++38
Simulate rapid prototyping+++++++++36
Implement E-mail for+++++++33
Simulate knowledge acquisition session++++++++33
Build interactive knowledge+++29
Develop electronic roster+++22
```

■ **Figure 10–3**   Key Topics Determined by the Experts

Analyze group decision support systems (1.2)

Develop executive information systems (1.4)

Do projects that add to technical capabilities of the school

Simulate rapid prototyping through brainstorming with experts

Implement E-mail for graduate MIS students (4.4)

Simulate knowledge acquisition session for multiple experts (7.2)

Build interactive knowledge-based system to train med students (3.1)

Develop electronic rosters and grad submissions (7.1)

Evaluate current case tools (6.1)

heads, stating directly what they think. In other words, the experts keep talking, speaking out loud whatever thoughts come to mind, while they answer a question or solve a problem. Unlike their role in other techniques, knowledge engineers do not interrupt or ask questions in the interim. The solving process is carried out in an automatic fashion while the expert talks. Structuring the information elicited occurs later when the knowledge engineer analyzes the protocol. (Review the vignette at the beginning of the chapter for a definition of scenarios.)

Box 10-1   Cognitive Approach to Problem Solving

One particular reasoning process—the solving of arithmetic word problems—has been studied extensively. Consider this problem:

A father, a mother, and their daughter have a combination of 70 years of age total. The father is three times as old as the daughter. The mother is the same age as the father. How old is the daughter?

Solver 1

1. This sounds complicated—I'll give it a shot.
2. Assume F for father, M for mother, and D for daughter.
3. $F + M + D = 70$.
4. F is 3 times D.
5. $M = F$.
6. So far, I have three equations and three unknowns.
7. $D + 3$ times D (or F) $+ 3$ times D (or M) $= 70$.
8. $7D = 70$.
9. $D = 10$.
10. Ages of father and mother total is $70 - 10$ or 60.
11. Since both are the same age, then father is 30 and mother is 30 years old.

Solver 2

1. Father, mother, and daughter are 70 years old total.
2. How can this be?
3. If father is 25 years old and mother is 25, then the daughter is 20 years old.
4. This doesn't make sense, since 25 year old parents cannot have 20 year old daughter.
5. Also father is not 3 times the age of daughter.
6. Father and mother must be older.
7. If father is 27 years old and so is the mother, then the daughter must be 16.
8. The daughter is not three times the age of the father.
9. A 27-year-old father cannot logically have a 16-year-old daughter.
10. So, this is not the right combination. I'll have to change ages.
11. What if the father is 30 years and the mother 30 years? This will make the daughter 10 years old.
12. This adds up to 70 all right.
13. At 30, the father is exactly 3 times the age of the daughter, who is 10 years old.
14. The mother is also the same age as the father, which is 30.
15. The whole thing makes sense. A 30-year-old father can have a 10-year-old daughter.

Protocol Procedure of the Diabetic Foot Advisor

This expert system advises a diabetic foot patient on the condition of his or her foot and whether to seek self-help, medical, or surgical help. The number of attributes is 15. Three decisions are possible: recommend self-help, recommend medical treatment, or recommend surgical treatment.

Case Description

1.	Sex:	Female
2.	Age:	45–48
3.	Complaint:	Blister does not heal; pain in left foot when standing or walking
4.	How much does patient weigh?	230 pounds
5.	How long has patient had the blister?	Two weeks
6.	Has patient had blisters before?	No
7.	Does the blister get worse when walking?	Yes
8.	Where is pain located?	Left foot below ankle
9.	How strong is the pain?	Quite strong
10.	How long has patient had pain?	Over a week
11.	Did patient use any medication for pain?	No
12.	Does pain change with movement?	No
13.	What does patient think is wrong?	Poor shoe fit

Protocol

1. This woman is in her mid to late forties.
2. Being quite overweight and a diabetic, blisters are common occurrences.
3. Pain is symptomatic of the blister.
4. Patient is experiencing this blister for the first time. She's probably more worried than being in pain.
5. Being diabetic, blisters take a long time to heal. It is not likely to get worse.

   .

   .

   .

40. I don't see broken skin or pus accumulating, which is a good sign.
41. I'm going to recommend NSD and soaking the foot in warm water before going to bed and after getting up.
42. Her husband will have to help.
43. I'm going to recommend that patient wear wide-toed shoes.

   .

   .

   .

64. So, for the moment, I am going to tell the patient to see me in two weeks.
65. Right now, I wouldn't recommend any medical treatment. Surgery is the last thing on my mind.
66. I'll relay this diagnosis and decision to patient.

In summary, think-aloud or protocol analysis is a knowledge acquisition method that consists of asking experts to think out loud while going through a problem solution, and of analyzing the resulting verbal protocols. It is an effective source of information on cognitive processes and for building knowledge-based systems. In fact, think-aloud makes the expert (in this example, the surgeon) cognizant of the process being described, which is a contribution to the validity of the practice or procedure used in the diagnosis. It also provides wealth of information toward knowledge representation.

■ CONSENSUS DECISION MAKING

The term *consensus* refers to a clear agreement regarding the best solution to a problem. As a tool, **consensus decision making** follows brainstorming. It is effective only when every expert in the team has had adequate opportunity to air their views. To arrive at a consensus, the knowledge engineer conducting the exercise tries to rally the experts toward one or two alternatives while fostering the experts' feelings of ownership of the alternative(s) so that they want to support it.

In consensus decision making, a knowledge engineer follows a procedure designed to ensure fairness and standardization in the way experts arrive at a consensus.

1. The knowledge engineer explains the solutions generated earlier, possibly through brainstorming. After a problem is presented to the panel of experts, the experts are asked to vote on the alternative solutions they generated. Voting takes place in rounds, with each round devoted to reducing the number of alternative solutions.

2. In round one, the knowledge engineer explains that each expert has three votes to cast—one vote per option for a maximum of three options among the total number of options. The options with fewer than the agreed-upon number of votes are deleted.

3. In round two, the knowledge engineer questions the experts to see if any of the remaining options can be deleted or merged. Then, the experts are given two votes each to vote on the remaining options. That is, each expert votes on two of the total number of options that remain after round one.

4. As with round one, those options that receive the fewer than the required number of votes are deleted. This process of voting by rounds continues until only two options are left. During the last round, each expert is allowed to cast only one vote for the final option. The option that carries the majority vote is selected as the solution.

The consensus method is quite effective and works well most of the time, but it is not without problems. First, it is a bit tedious and can take hours, since at any time during the rounds, an expert can call for a discussion of the remaining options before further voting. Second, some experts complain that each option unfairly carries the same weight; some options are more serious than others and should be adopted or rejected by every expert on the panel. Third, experts have been known to walk out on the whole acquisition process because of the rigidity of the consensus method. Although this tool promotes a democratic process of decision making, some experts allow personalities and personal agendas to interfere.

▮ THE REPERTORY GRID

The **repertory grid** is another tool used in knowledge acquisition. The domain expert is viewed as a scientist who classifies and categorizes a problem domain using his or her own model. The grid is used to acquire and evaluate an expert's model, or the way the expert works through the solution. Two experts in the same problem domain will produce different sets of results that are personal and subjective. Experts see problems based on reasoning that has stood the test of time and are able to use this deep knowledge in the problem-solving process. For example:

> **NOVICE LOAN CUSTOMER:** The bank tried to charge more interest than they promised. Now I am in a bind.
>
> **EXPERT LOAN CUSTOMER:** The issue is whether their last interest quote was an estimate or a binding rate for the loan.

A novice may have a general sense of the effects of certain actions, but the expert foresees cause and effect in a specific way. The goal of knowledge acquisition is to identify the underlying principles the experts use so that they can be emulated by the computer.

The repertory grid is a representation of the experts' way of looking at a particular problem. A **grid** is a scale or a bipolar construct on which elements are placed within gradations. The knowledge engineer elicits the constructs and then asks the domain expert to provide a set of examples, called *elements*. Each element is rated according to the constructs that have been provided. The following are examples of bipolar constructs:

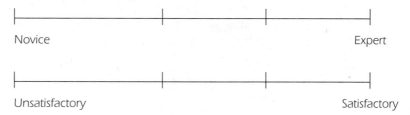

Gradations break down the scale to allow for more accurate ratings. In this unsatisfactory–satisfactory construct, a 1–5 point scale is used.

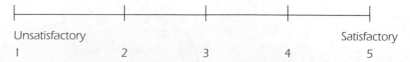

Once a particular scale is adopted, it should stay the same throughout the grid (e.g., 1–5), although the terms that describe the rating vary from construct to construct. The rating is useful in comparing individual rankings. For example, if John is rated "1," Ann is rated "3," and Bob is rated "4," it does not mean that Bob is four times as satisfactory as John. It only means that Bob is more satisfactory than either John or Ann. It is a comparative subjective rating of elements along a scale.

One of the benefits of the repertory grid is that it may prompt the expert who sees the grid laid out on paper to think more seriously about the problem and how to solve it. The main drawback is that it tends to be a difficult tool to manage effectively when large grids are accompanied by complex details. Large grids defeat the tool's goals of clarity, simplicity, and manageability. For this reason, knowledge engineers normally use the grid in the early stages of knowledge acquisition.

The practical use of the repertory grid can be demonstrated by the following interview, in which the human resources director compares bank tellers in order to decide on potential promotions or transfers. The expert is the human resources director. The comparative rating of the tellers is shown in Table 10–3.

KE: As I understand it, we're here to discuss the selection process and selection criteria for the bank's tellers.

EXPERT: Yes, I'm interested in reviewing all of the tellers to get a better understanding of our selection procedure.

KE: Which tellers do you consider prime candidates for the purpose of the selection procedure?

EXPERT: I have in mind Dixie, John, Barry, Curt, Lester, and Joanne.

KE: If you take the first three tellers (i.e., Dixie, John, and Barry), which two are about the same but differ from the third?

EXPERT: I'd say Dixie and John are similar, but Barry is quite different.

KE: If experience is the similarity factor, what word would describe their dissimilarity?

EXPERT: Inexperience.

KE: Suppose we place "experience" and "inexperience" on a scale of 1 to 3, where 1 represents "inexperienced" and 3 represents "experienced." How would you rate the tellers?

EXPERT: Dixie   3
            John   3
            Barry   1
            Curt   1
            Lester   1
            Joanne   1

■ **Table 10–3**   A Repertory Grid Rating Job Performance of Bank Tellers

Construct	T1	T2	T3	T4	T5	T6	Construct	
1 Inexperienced	3	3	1	1	1	1	Experienced	1
2 Academically ill-qualified	2	1	2	1	1	3	Academically qualified	2
3 Poor appearance	3	2	1	2	1	3	Good appearance	3
4 Late	2	3	2	3	1	1	Punctual	4
5 Introverted	2	3	3	2	1	1	Extroverted	5
T1 Dixie								
T2 John								
T3 Barry								
T4 Curt								
T5 Lester								
T6 Joanne								

Source: Adapted from Ann Hart, *Knowledge Acquisition for Expert Systems,* (New York: McGraw-Hill, 1986), pp. 140–42.

KE: Let us now take the last three tellers, Curt, Lester, and Joanne. How would you compare them?

EXPERT: These tellers, I'd want to compare in terms of academic qualifications. I'd say Joanne is better qualified than Curt or Lester. Using the 1–3 scale you suggested earlier, I'd rate the six tellers as follows:

Dixie	2
John	1
Barry	2
Curt	1
Lester	1
Joanne	3

KE: Next, let's take Joanne, Dixie, and Barry. How would you rate them?

EXPERT: I guess I'd want to rate them based on appearance—how well they look in the eyes of the customer. Based on customer feedback, I'd rate Joanne and Dixie the same. Barry is not in the same league. I'd rate them as follows:

Dixie	3
John	2
Barry	1
Curt	2
Lester	1
Joanne	3

KE: Let's take one more group—John, Curt, and Lester.

EXPERT: These tellers remind me of attendance. John and Curt are hardly ever late to work. Lester is often late. So, using the 1–3 scale (1 is tardy; 3 is prompt), I'd rate them as follows:

Dixie	2
John	3
Barry	2
Curt	3
Lester	1
Joanne	1

KE: Do you have other ratings you want to include?

EXPERT: Just one dealing with John, Barry, and Lester. John and Barry are extroverts; Lester isn't. I'd use the 1–3 scale (1 is introvert; 3 is extrovert) and rate them as follows:

Dixie	2
John	3
Barry	3
Curt	2
Lester	1
Joanne	1

◼ NOMINAL-GROUP TECHNIQUE

In some problem domains, more than one expert might be available as a source of knowledge for building the expert system. Although, for situations in which several experts have overlapping expertise, each expert's opinion must be interpreted in line with the problem domain. In fact, a single expert is used precisely to avoid potential contradictions between experts and possible misinterpretations on the part of the knowledge engineer resulting in process losses. The nominal group technique and Delphi method have been shown to mitigate some of the process losses associated with multiple experts.

As an alternative to the consensus technique, the **nominal-group technique** (NGT) provides an interface between consensus and brainstorming. In this technique, the panel of experts become a "nominal" group whose meetings are structured in order to effectively pool individual judgment.

NGT is an ideawriting or idea generation technique. **Ideawriting** is a structured group approach used to develop ideas and explore their meaning for clarity and specificity; the result is a written report.

The NGT procedure begins as follows:

1. The knowledge engineer explains the technique and provides to each expert information about the problem or its alternative solutions.

2. Instead of discussing the problem, the knowledge engineer asks each expert to list on paper the pros and cons of the problem or alternative solutions. It is silent generation of ideas in writing.

3. The knowledge engineer compiles the pros and cons from each list without making comments regarding their merit. Any overlapping ideas are either reworded or deleted.

4. Each expert is given a copy of the compiled pros and cons and asked to rank them on the basis of their priorities for discussion.

5. The knowledge engineer then leads a discussion of the pros and cons and their respective ranks. The discussion focuses on the priorities placed on each item and the reasoning behind them, which leads to a listing of possible solutions.

6. The knowledge engineer compiles the alternative solutions, followed by a group discussion that should lead to agreement as to the "best" solution.

Unfortunately, the NGT process can be time-consuming and tedious. It has been known to promote impatience among the experts who must listen to all kinds of discussions with each expert, some of whom will lobby aggressively for their own ideas. One way to expedite this procedure is to have the experts vote as a group on the set of possible problems to work on, and later on which solution(s) to use.

On the other hand, as experts share expertise, things can really jell in adopting the best solution. NGT is ideal in situations of uncertainty regarding the nature of the problem domain. It is also effective in multiple expert knowledge acquisition, especially when minimizing the differences in status among experts is important.

NGT is similar to brainstorming, except that it is based on the understanding that certain group goals can be best achieved by writing rather than by discussion. Each expert has an equal chance to express ideas in parallel with other experts in the group. Because discussion is accommodated in sequential order, NGT can be a more efficient and productive approach than brainstorming.

■ THE DELPHI METHOD

Another tool used in multiple expert knowledge acquisition is the **Delphi method.** Essentially, it is a survey of experts—experts are polled concerning a given problem domain. A series of questionnaires are used to pool the experts' responses in order to solve a difficult problem. Each expert's contributions are shared with the other experts by using the results from each questionnaire to construct the next questionnaire.

The Delphi method gets its name from the ancient Greek oracle at Delphi, who was said to look into the future. It works in this way:

1. A panel of experts is asked to prepare an anonymous opinion about a focused problem domain. Each person is usually given a short written explanation of the problem. For example, one problem would be to estimate when air cargo revenues of XYZ airline would equal its passenger revenues.

2. For the second round, each expert is given a summary of the results of the first round and is asked to make a second (still anonymous) estimate on the same issue based on the additional information and reasons provided in the summary of the preceding anonymous opinions. Knowing how the other experts responded, an expert may stick to or change his or her initial answer.

3. Step two is repeated two or more times, and then a final summary is prepared. By this point, all extreme estimates will have been deleted, and those that remain will converge on a narrow range of answers.

The Delphi method has three important features:

1. *Anonymous response.* Because opinions are obtained anonymously, the danger that the response of one expert will bias another is removed. For example, a top executive will have no influence on a subordinate who may be part of the group.

2. *Controlled feedback.* Through a controlled set of rounds, the Delphi method allows each expert to rethink any previous answers in light of the anonymous feedback received from other experts.

3. *Statistical group response.* The final opinion of the experts is an aggregate of each expert's response in the final round.

The Delphi method has two main limitations. First, experts often lack the necessary knowledge on which to base their final judgment. The problem may be one of communication. Second, poorly designed questionnaires have been known to be less than effective in developing an understanding of the complexity of the problem domain. The knowledge engineer must exercise care in assessing in advance the likely consequences of using the Delphi method.

◼ BLACKBOARDING

Imagine bringing a group of experts together in a room with a large blackboard. The experts work together to solve a problem, using the blackboard as their work space. Initial data are written on the blackboard for all to see. Each expert has an equal chance to contribute to the solution via the blackboard. The process of **blackboarding** (also called *Groupware*) continues until the problem has been solved.

One important assumption of a blackboard system is that all participants are experts, but have acquired their own expertise in situations different from those of the other experts in the group. Because each expert's experience is unique, no one need feel either inferior or superior in offering a possible solution. The essence of this technique is the independence of expertise in an atmosphere that discourages compliance or intimidation.

There are several characteristics of blackboarding:

1. *Diverse approaches to problem solving.* The fact that the experts have different ways of thinking does not prevent them from solving the problem. Each expert (called a *knowledge source,* or KS) in this technique is similar to a black box whose internal thinking process is hidden from other KSs in the meeting. It does not really matter how each KS thinks through a solution. Each KS can make contributions within the framework of the blackboard.

2. *Common language for interaction.* The KSs participating in this technique should share a common language (including use of diagrams, charts, etc.) so that they can interact, interpret, and contribute to the final solution. Private jargon or abbreviated phrases should be discouraged because they limit the involvement of other KSs in the solution process.

3. *Flexible representation of information.* An expert's suggestion of an alternative or a partial solution in graphics versus text is allowable by the software as long as it can be understood by all experts concerned. No prior restrictions on the information limit its content or how it should be represented on the blackboard.

4. *Efficient storage and location of information.* Virtually all of the information contributed by the KSs is stored somewhere in the blackboard. To ensure quick access to an updated version of the blackboard, the blackboard is organized into regions, each representing a specific type of information. Once the type of information required is determined, the KS can go directly to the suitable blackboard region and scan the information stored in it. Remember that experts do not interact with one another directly. Each KS watches the blackboard, looking for the right opportunity to contribute to the solution. KSs who see a new change on the blackboard can decide whether they agree with it, and if not, they can go ahead and contribute their opinion.

KSs are also motivated by events other than those displayed on the blackboard. For example, a KS might inform the blackboard about an event of personal interest, which is entered on the blackboard. The blackboard then directly considers the KS owner whenever that type of event occurs.

5. *Organized participation.* One benefit to blackboard technology is that two or more experts cannot respond to an event simultaneously. Only one expert at a time is allowed, which promotes control and gives each KS a chance to mull over the changes before they decide to contribute. The knowledge engineer can be used to restore order by considering each KS's request to approach the blackboard with the proposed change.

6. *Iterative nature of the process.* The solution to the problem domain is approached step by step, like building blocks from bottom up or from basic to advanced. In this situation, no single KS has a full answer to the problem. Each KS refines and adds something of value to someone else's contribution, and the whole group moves toward the solution incrementally. A summary of the characteristics of blackboarding is provided in Figure 10–4.

A typical blackboard system consists of three parts: knowledge sources (KSs), the blackboard, and a control mechanism. The inference engine and the knowledge base are part of the blackboard system. A **knowledge source** is the expert—a unique module that has the knowledge to solve the problem.

The **blackboard** is a global memory structure, a database, or a repository that stores all partial problem solutions and other data that are in various stages

Figure 10–4   Key Characteristics of Blackboard Systems

Diverse approaches to problem solving
Common language for interaction
Flexible representation of information
Efficient storage and location of information
Organized participation
Iterative nature of the process

of completion. It serves as a communication medium and triggers a KS into action or controls the necessary information for the blackboarding process.

Blackboard processing is based on the concept of independent cooperating experts. Each KS is an independent expert who observes the status of the blackboard and tries to contribute a higher-level partial solution based on the knowledge it has and how well such knowledge applies to the current blackboard state. In this respect, the blackboard is useful for structuring complex problem-solving tasks that require multiple experts.

The **control mechanism** coordinates the flow and pattern of problem solution. It monitors the changes on the blackboard and decides on the next action(s) to take. The problem-solving behavior of the whole process is encoded in the control module. See Figure 10–5.

The blackboard approach is useful in situations involving multiple expertise, diverse knowledge representations, or uncertain knowledge. It can be particularly valuable when working with complex applications or prototyping an application. Unfortunately, blackboard systems have too short a history to provide a good rationale for advocating their use. This is compounded by a lack of commercial software specifically designed for building blackboard applications and a shortage of developers experienced in this area.

Figure 10–5   Model Components of a Blackboard

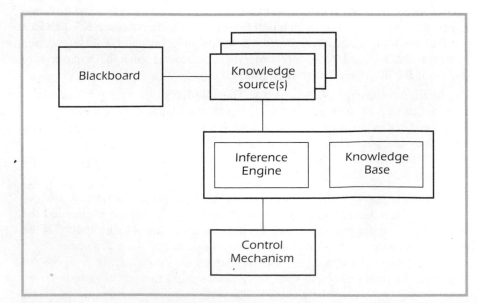

IMPLICATIONS FOR MANAGEMENT

The knowledge engineer has a number of challenges in choosing knowledge acquisition tools. First, which technique best taps the knowledge of the domain expert must be determined. Certain techniques are ideal for single experts, and others are suitable for multiple experts. Second, advanced planning and preparation for knowledge acquisition can be best carried out through using the most efficient tools, thereby making the best use of the expert's time and resources.

The managerial aspects of tool selection have to do with the organization's commitment to providing proper training and support for the knowledge engineer. The knowledge engineer should also be an effective manager of time. Selecting the right knowledge acquisition techniques means saving time and ensuring reliable representation of the knowledge. The knowledge engineer must also be able to communicate with experts, regardless of their background or expertise. Communication breakdown could spell disaster for any project, large or small.

Finally, the knowledge engineer's success depends on cultivating good relations with management in general. In other words, a knowledge engineer must be aware of the organization's politics, its grapevine, and what steps are necessary to get systems accepted. The support of a champion could make the entire acquisition process easier.

Management support also includes continued commitment to fund the project. Lack of proper financial support can lead to a low-quality product, an incomplete system, or dissatisfied users. In the final analysis, management must see the expert system project as an investment from beginning to end and gauge its support according to the gain it hopes to realize.

SUMMARY

1. On-site observation is a process of observing, interpreting, and recording the expert's problem-solving behavior while it is taking place. The technique carries with it certain protocol. It requires more listening than talking and enables the knowledge engineer to seek knowledge within the working world of the expert. The main problem is that some experts do not like to be observed. Some question as to the accuracy of the acquired knowledge may also arise. The shuttle process allows room for possible errors.

2. Brainstorming invites two or more experts into an idea generation session in which discussions are carried out and a variety of opinions tossed around. The procedure includes introducing the brainstorming session, presenting a problem for the experts to consider, prompting the experts to generate ideas, and watching for signs of convergence. This techniques dictates that the expert cannot be cut short, yet some experts talk too long for comfort. Electronic brainstorming tends to improve the efficiency with which brainstorming is conducted and evaluated.

3. Protocol analysis or think-aloud is a knowledge acquisition method that allows cases, scenarios, etc., to be collected by asking experts to

solve a problem while verbalizing what goes through their heads, stating directly what they think. The expert speaks out loud whatever thoughts come to mind while answering a question or solving a problem.

4. Consensus decision making is used to arrive at a clear agreement regarding the best solution to a problem. As a tool, it follows brainstorming. Experts converge toward one or two alternatives for a final consensus. This technique is quite effective and works well most of the time, but it is a bit tedious and can take hours to conclude. One of the drawbacks is that options carry unfairly the same weight, and some participants are uncomfortable with its rigidity.

5. The repertory grid is used to acquire and evaluate the way the expert works through a solution to a problem domain. The grid is a scale with elements described by the gradations. Gradations break down the scale to allow for more accurate ratings. Once adopted, the scale should stay the same throughout the grid, although the terms that describe the rating vary from construct to construct. One of the benefits of the grid is that it may prompt the expert who sees it on paper to think more seriously about the problem and how to solve it. On the other hand, the grid can be difficult to manage.

6. An alternative to the consensus technique is the nominal-group technique, or NGT. It is an idea writing or idea generation technique used as an interface between consensus and brainstorming. A panel of experts becomes a nominal group. The idea is to structure small group meetings so that individual judgments can be effectively pooled. NGT is time-consuming and tedious. One way to expedite this procedure is to have the experts vote as a group on the set of possible problems to work on, and later on which solution(s) to use. The tool is ideal in situations of uncertainty regarding the nature of the problem domain.

7. The Delphi method is a series of surveys that poll experts concerning a given problem domain. Questionnaires pool the experts' responses in order to solve a difficult problem. The procedure begins by asking a panel of experts to prepare individual anonymous opinions about a focused problem domain. For the second round, each expert receives a summary of the results of the first round and is asked to make a second estimate on the same issue based on the additional information provided in the summary. This second step is repeated two or more times, and then a final summary is prepared. The main feature of this tool is anonymous response, controlled feedback, and statistical group response. A poorly designed questionnaire can be a serious constraint.

8. Blackboarding offers diversity of approaches to problem solving and a common language for interaction. It also has the characteristics of flexible representation of information, efficient storage and location of information, organized participation, and iterative approach to problem solving. The blackboard approach is useful in situations involving multiple expertise, diverse knowledge representations, or uncertain knowledge.

▓ TERMS TO LEARN

Blackboard a shared database in which various knowledge sources work together to solve a problem.

Blackboarding experts work together in a common work area to come up with a solution.

Brainstorming an unstructured approach by which two or more experts generate ideas about a problem domain.

Consensus reaching a clear agreement on the best solution to a problem.

Consensus decision making knowledge engineer conducts the exercise after brainstorming to rally the experts toward one or two alternatives and to convey the impression that all of them are part owners of the alternative(s).

Control mechanism coordinates the flow and pattern of the problem solution in a blackboard model.

Delphi method a series of surveys that poll experts concerning a given problem domain.

Electronic brainstorming a computer-aided approach to dealing with multiple experts through a network of PCs, which promote live exchange of ideas between experts; the ideas can be sorted and condensed into an organized format.

Grid a scale or a bipolar construct on which elements are placed within gradations.

Ideawriting a structured group approach used to develop ideas, explore their meaning for clarity and specificity, and produce a written report.

Knowledge source a unique module that has the knowledge to solve the problem.

Nominal-group technique small group meetings in which individual judgment can often be effectively pooled; interface between consensus and brainstorming.

On-site observation observing, interpreting, and recording an expert's problem-solving behavior as it occurs in the domain.

Protocol analysis systematic collection and analysis of thought processes or problem-solving methods; synonymous with the think-aloud technique.

Repertory grid knowledge acquisition tool by which the problem domain is classified and categorized around the domain expert's own model; a representation of the expert's way of looking at a particular problem.

Shuttle process the back-and-forth aspect of the knowledge engineer's recollection of an event as it was initially mentally registered to the evaluation of the event at the time of the retrospection.

Think-aloud technique knowledge acquisition method in which the expert speaks out loud whatever thoughts come to mind while answering a question or solving a problem; synonymous with protocol analysis.

▓ REVIEW QUESTIONS

1. Explain in your own words the distinctive features of on-site observation. What kinds of problems does it pose?

2. Distinguish between:
   a. brainstorming and consensus decision making
   b. protocol analysis and Delphi method
   c. repertory grid and nominal-group technique
   d. blackboarding and electronic brainstorming

3. How is brainstorming conducted? Provide an example.

4. If no interruptions are allowed or no questions asked while an expert is answering a question or solving a problem, how does the facilitator control a protocol analysis session?

5. In what way does consensus decision making follow brainstorming? Be specific.

6. Give an example of your own to illustrate the procedure followed in consensus decision making.

7. "The grid is used to acquire and evaluate the expert's model—the way the expert works through the solution." Do you agree? What is so unique about the grid? What are some of its drawbacks?

8. In what way is the nominal-group technique an alternative to the consensus technique? Explain.

9. Illustrate by an example of your own the procedure followed in NGT.

10. If you were asked to apply the Delphi method involving four experts, what procedure would you follow? What limitations would you expect to encounter in this knowledge acquisition technique?

11. Blackboarding offers certain characteristics. Explain each briefly. What components make up the basic model?

■ EXERCISES AND CASES

1. Divide into small groups of five to seven people. Select a group discussion leader and a person to record responses. Use the brainstorming guidelines to conduct a five-minute brainstorming session on the following topic. Your goal is to identify creative solutions to the problem.

Employees in large companies often complain that personal worth perception is low. They feel that the company does not overtly reward them for their contributions and set procedures that allow them to be most productive and creative.

2. Based on the problem presented in #1, complete the following tasks:

a. *Brainstorm* how the company can reward efforts and increase the perception of personal worth in ways other than issuing pay increases.

b. Use *nominal-group technique* to find the best solution to the employee personal-worth perception problem. Consider the solutions from the brainstorming activity and select the "best" solution from that set.

c. Use *consensus decision making* with the goal of selecting a solution to the employee personal-worth perception problem to which all members of the group can commit.

3. *Publisher Advisor*

As discussed in this chapter, knowledge acquisition uses a variety of tools. In Publisher Advisor, several knowledge acquisition tools were used. Knowledge was acquired from a series of four interviews with the expert. The first two interviews encompassed fairly broad questions about

the expert's decision-making process. The last two interviews elicited more detailed information about the expert's decision-making process by discussing the outcome of specific sample case scenario decisions, to which confidence levels were assigned.

In one interview, an attempt was made at rapid prototyping, but the format of the table used was difficult for the expert to understand. So it was not used as productively as expected.

An induction table (similar to a decision table) was developed, which included possible combinations of the five variables and their outcomes—acceptance, defer, or rejection of a book manuscript. (See Table 10–4.) This induction table was the basis for some of the more detailed case scenarios presented to the expert. It forced the expert to give concrete examples of decisions based on specific given variables, which allowed the expert to focus on actual decision processes and enabled the knowledge engineer to realize the complexity of the problem. In addition, the induction table served as the initial input into VP-Expert for the expert system rule generation. The table was later used for verification of the prototype and testing the final system.

During the series of interviews, the knowledge engineer also had opportunity to do on-site observation of the expert's mannerisms and decisions related to the problem domain. It provided a clearer picture of the expert's biases, idiosyncrasies, and the subjective nature of the comments received from the manuscript reviewers.

■ **Table 10–4**   Induction Table

Rule Number	Market	Author's Reputation	Reviewers' Comments	Author's Requirements	Publisher's Decision	Confidence Level
0	High	Excellent			Offer contract	
1	High	Average	Very good	Average OR Below avg	Offer contract	0.90
2	High	Average	Very good	Above avg	Offer contract	0.80
3	High	Average	Mixed	Average OR Below avg	Offer contract	0.85
4	High	Average	Mixed	Above avg	Request sample chapters	
5	High	Average	Below avg	Average OR Below avg	Request sample chapters	
6	High	Average	Below avg	Above avg	Reject manuscript	
7	High	Poor	Very good	Above avg	Offer contract	0.75
8	High	Poor	Very good	Average	Offer contract	0.85
9	High	Poor	Very good	Below avg	Offer contract	
10	Moderate	Poor	Mixed	Above avg	Reject manuscript	
11	Moderate	Poor	Mixed	Average OR Below avg	Request sample chapters	
12	Moderate	Poor	Below avg	Above avg	Reject manuscript	
13	Moderate	Poor	Below avg	Average	Reject manuscript	
14	Moderate	Poor	Below avg	Below avg	Reject manuscript	
15	Moderate	Average	Very good	Above avg	Offer contract	0.65
16	Moderate	Average	Very good	Average	Offer contract	0.75
17	Moderate	Average	Very good	Below avg	Offer contract	0.90
18	Moderate	Average	Mixed	Avove avg	Request sample chapters	
19	Moderate	Average	Mixed	Average	Offer contract	0.70
20	Moderate	Average	Mixed	Below avg	Offer contract	0.75
21	Moderate	Average	Below avg	Above avg	Reject manuscript	
22	Moderate	Average	Below avg	Average	Reject manuscript	
23	Moderate	Average	Below avg	Below avg	Reject manuscript	
24	Moderate	Poor	Very good	Above avg	Offer contract	0.70
25	Moderate	Poor	Very good	Average	Offer contract	0.80
26	Moderate	Poor	Very good	Below avg	Offer contract	
27	Moderate	Excellent	Very good		Offer contract	0.90
28	Moderate	Excellent	Mixed	Average OR Below avg	Offer contract	0.90
29	Moderate	Excellent	Mixed	Above avg	Request sample chapters	
30	Moderate	Excellent	Below avg		Request sample chapters	
31	Low	Excellent	Very good	Above avg	Offer contract	0.60
32	Low	Excellent	Very good	Average	Offer contract	0.70
33	Low	Excellent	Very good	Below avg	Offer contract	0.70
34	Low	Excellent	Mixed	Average OR Below avg	Request sample chapters	
35	Low	Excellent	Mixed	Above avg	Reject manuscript	
36	Low	Excellent	Below avg		Reject manuscript	
37	Low	Average	Very good	Below avg	Offer contract	0.70
38	Low	Average	Very good	Average	Offer contract	0.60
39	Low	Average	Very good	Above avg	Reject manuscript	
40	Low	Average	Mixed	Average OR Below avg	Request sample chapters	
41	Low	Average	Mixed	Above avg	Reject manuscript	
42	Low	Average	Below avg		Reject manuscript	
43	Low	Poor			Reject manuscript	

Questions

a. Evaluate the approach taken in the knowledge acquisition process of the Publisher Advisor to determine the rationale and reliability of the tools used.

b. Use the preceding guidelines to determine your own in building the Publisher Advisor. If for some reason you do not have a human expert for this project, refer to the induction table for knowledge representation using a shell.

4. The following knowledge acquisition phase was used to create ADMIT, an expert system that models the admission decision process of an independent private secondary school admissions officer:

A total of six knowledge acquisition sessions were conducted with the expert at the expert's location, except for the few occasions when the session required use of the system. The expert came to the knowledge engineer's office where VP-Expert was in residence on a local PC.

In the first session, the knowledge engineer became familiar with the domain expert elaborating on the admissions materials previously provided. This overview made it possible to establish a basis of knowledge which evolved into the concept dictionary. In the second session, I used a combination of interview and concept sorting techniques. I used the interview to extract basic parameters and then had the expert organize these parameters according to her view of the domain. We transformed this organization into a visual concept diagram of the domain. The concept diagram was referred to and refined throughout the entire acquisition process. This diagram provided a clear direction for the acquisition process. It also became the foundation for the knowledge representation structure. (See Figure 10–6.)

Other tools employed were process tracing and case scenarios. I used process tracing by asking the domain expert to provide an example of a typical admissions decision. From following her decision-making process, I began to understand how the parameters interacted with one another. This helped me assign parameters to groupings based on the domain concept diagram. This also alerted me to the minimum and maximum values that could be assigned to each parameter. In addition, I was able to derive the minimum requirements for consideration, below which the applicant would be immediately rejected. (A list of parameters is shown in Table 10–5.)

Figure 10–6 Concept Diagram

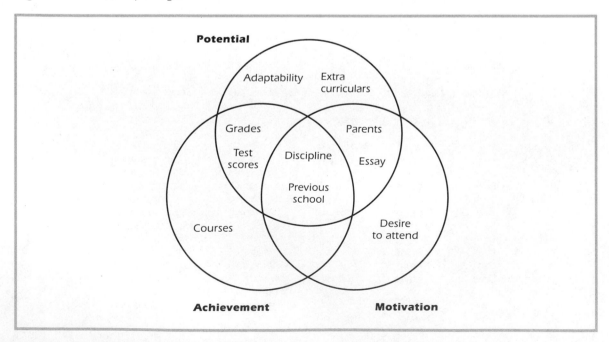

■ **Table 10–5** ADMIT Parameters

Name	Type	Multi-valued	Values
ENGLISH	Number		0–3
SCIENCE	String	Yes	Biology, Chemistry, Physics
LANGUAGE	Boolean		Yes/No
US HIST	Boolean		Yes/No
WORLD	Boolean		Yes/No
MATH	String	Yes	Algebra I, Algebra II, Geometry
GRADES	String		A-A, A-B, B-C, C-C, C-D, D-F
PSAT	Number		0–160
SAT	Number		0–1600
SSAT	Number		0–
AP_ESSAY	String		Excellent, Good, Fine, Poor
TM_ESSAY	String		Excellent, Good, Fine, Poor
MOTIVATION	String		Over Achiever, On Target, Under Achiever
CHALLENGE	Boolean		Yes/No
DESIRE	String		Enthusiastic, Positive, Unsure, Negative
P_SUPPORT	String		Excellent, Average, Weak
EXTRA_C	Boolean		Yes/No
SCHOOL	String		Above, Equal, Below
DISCIPLINE	String		Acceptable, Unacceptable
DEMEANOR	String		Excellent, Average, Difficult
MINORITY	Boolean		Yes/No
LEGACY	Boolean		Yes/No
FACKID	Boolean		Yes/No
STAYED	Boolean		Yes/No
BOARD	Boolean		Yes/No
SIBENROLL	Boolean		Yes/No
NEW	Boolean		Yes/No

CHANGES (from Session #4):

1. Remove RELIGION
2. Remove FORMER
3. Add NEW
4. Remove ERB, SSAT
5. Remove ACCSIB (same as SIBENROLL)
6. Remove individual languages, add LANGUAGE

In order to capture the expert's heuristics, I devised a matrix of parameters and their potential values. This would allow me to vary parameters in relation to each other. This proved to be a formidable task. Ten multi-valued parameters, each with three or more permissible ranges, produced more scenarios than could easily be generated via manual means. The difficulty of this task also has implications for completeness of the rule base, ergo scenarios could easily be overlooked. To assist me in generating scenarios, I discovered Logic Gem, a logic processor software that made life easier for the rest of the acquisition process.

(Source: Based on Janel Kasparson, "ADMIT," May 1991, p. 4.)

Questions

a. Based on the nature of the problem domain, evaluate the tools used in this project.

b. How important is listing parameters early in the knowledge acquisition phase? Explain.

▓ SELECTED REFERENCES

Aiken, Milam; Jay, Krosp; Ashraf Shirani; and Jeanette Martin. "Electronic Brainstorming in Small and Large Groups." *Information & Management,* September 1994, pp. 141–149.

Aouad, G. F.; S. R. Ford; J. A. Kirkham; P. S. Brandon; F. E. Brown; T. Child; G. S. Cooper; R. E. Oxman; and B. Young. "Knowledge Elicitations Using Protocol Analysis in a Workshop Environment." *Constructions Management & Economics,* May 1994, pp. 271–278.

Bell, Pamela McCauley and Adedeji B. Badiru. "Concept Mapping as a Knowledge Acquisition Tool in the Development of a Fuzzy Rule-Based Expert System." *Computers & Industrial Engineering,* September 1993, pp. 115–118.

Byrd, Terry Anthony; Kathy L. Cossick; and Robert W. Zmud. "A Synthesis of Research on Requirements Analysis and Knowledge Acquisition Techniques." *MIS Quarterly,* March 1992, pp. 117–138.

Chetupuzha, Joseph M. and Adedeji B. Badiru. "Design Considerations for Knowledge Acquisition." *Computers & Industrial Engineering* 21, no. 1–4 (1991), pp. 257–261.

Deng, Pi-Sheng, "Automating Knowledge Acquisition and Refinement for Decision Support: A Connectionist Inductive Inference Model." *Decision Sciences,* March/April 1993, pp. 371–393.

El-Sherif, Helmy H. and Victor W. Tang. "TeamFocus—Electronic Brainstorming." *Training & Management Development Methods* 8, no. 3 (1994), pp. 5.25–5.33.

Ercegovac, Zorana. "A Multiple-Observation Approach in Knowledge Acquisition for Expert Systems: A Case Study." *Journal of the American Society for Information Science,* August 1992, pp. 506–517.

Eriksson, Henrik. "A Survey of Knowledge Acquisition Techniques and Tools and Their Relationship to Software Engineering." *Journal of Systems & Software,* September 1992, pp. 97–107.

Eriksson, Henrik and Mark Musen. "Metatools for Knowledge Acquisition." *IEEE Software,* May 1993, pp. 23–29.

Eriksson, Henrik; Angel R. Puerta; and Mark A. Musen. "Generation of Knowledge-Acquisition Tools from Domain Ontologies." *International Journal of Human-Computer Studies,* September 1994, pp. 425–453.

Gallupe, R. Brent and William H. Cooper. "Brainstorming Electronically." *Sloan Management Review,* Fall 1993, pp. 27–36.

Gowan, Jack Arthur, Jr. and Charles W. McNichols. "The Effects of Alternative Forms of Knowledge Representation on Decision-Making Consensus." *International Journal of Man-Machine Studies,* March 1993, pp. 489–507.

Helmer, Olaf. "Adversary Delphi." *Futures,* January/February 1994, pp. 79–87.

Kambouri, Maria; Mathieu Koppen; and Michael Villano. "Knowledge Assessment: Tapping Human Expertise by the QUERY Routine." *International Journal of Human-Computer Studies,* January 1994, pp. 119–151.

Kesser, Forrest A. "How to Avoid Common Pitfalls of Consensus Decision Making." *Oil & Gas Journal,* September 27, 1993, pp. 34–36.

Liou, Yihwa Irene and Jay F. Nunamaker, Jr. "An Investigation into Knowledge Acquisition Using a Group Decision Support System." *Information & Management,* March 1993, pp. 121–132.

Mrozek, A. "A New Method for Discovering Rules from Examples in Expert Systems." *International Journal of Man-Machine Studies,* January 1992, pp. 127–143.

Ono, Ryota and Dan J. Wedemeyer. "Assessing the Validity of the Delphi Technique." *Futures,* April 1994, pp. 289–304.

Petrovic, Otto and Otto Krickl. "Traditionally Moderated versus Computer-Supported Brainstorming: A

Comparative Study." *Information & Management,* October 1994, pp. 233–243.

Sheetz, Steven D.; David P. Tegarden; Kenneth A . Kozar; and Ilze Zigurs. "A Group Support Systems Approach to Cognitive Mapping." *Journal of Management Information Systems,* Summer 1994, pp. 31–57.

Trice, Andrew and Randall Davis. "Heuristics for Reconciling Independent Knowledge Bases." *Informations Systems Research: A Journal of the Institute of Management Sciences,* September 1993, pp. 262–288.

Williams, Kent E.; John Deighan; and Tim Kotnour. "Knowledge Acquisition for Group Problem Solving." *Computers & Industrial Engineering,* November 1992, pp. 459–462.

Wolstenholme, E. F. and D. A. Corben. "A Hypermedia-Based Delphi Tool for Knowledge Acquisition in Model Building." *Journal of the Operational Research Society,* June 1994, pp. 659–672.

Yoon, Youngohc and Tor Guimaraes. "Selecting Expert System Development Techniques." *Information & Management,* April 1993, pp. 209–223.

KNOWLEDGE REPRESEN-TATION

Chapter ▪ 11

Knowledge Representation Schemes

KNOWLEDGE AND ITS REPRESENTATION

If Alexander Marshak is right, the history of knowledge representation began more than 20,000 years ago when a primitive human scratched some marks on a piece of deer bone to represent the movements of the moon. About 15,000 years later, writing was invented and the knowledge-representation business really took off. Until Aristotle's formulation of the principles of the syllogism—actually a rather restricted form of reasoning—natural language was the only knowledge-representation language. For the next 1,500 years, the syllogism remained the only serious alternative.

In the seventeenth century, Leibnitz outlined an ambitious plan for creating a logic powerful enough to represent the full scope of philosophical thought he envisioned but never created; a computational language so powerful that philosophical disputes could be settled by calculation instead of argumentation. However, it wasn't until the mid-1800s, with the flowering of symbolic logic, that real advances over nonsyllogistic knowledge-representation schemes were developed. And in the late nineteenth century, logicians broke free of the syllogism, and logic came into its own. Gottlob Frege and Charles S. Peirce, perhaps the two most important contributors, were so far ahead of their time that the full impact of their contributions was not fully appreciated until many years after their deaths.

The early twentieth saw an explosion in the understanding and development of symbolic logic, dramatically expanding its scope; and Kurt Godel's epochal 1931 paper on incompleteness clearly defined some of its absolute limitations. By the 1930s, logical formulisms were finally powerful enough to be taken seriously as languages for representing real knowledge. Modern logicians stressed the importance of unambiguous mechanical deduction procedures independent of personal interpretation by the reasoner. The work of Alan Turing, John Von Neuman, Emil Post, and Claude Shannon, among others, laid the groundwork for computing technology and demonstrated the close relationship between computers and logic—at least theoretically.

The invention of electronic computers and the subsequent creation of an AI research program in the 1950s finally spurred the transformation of these logics into significant attempts to embody much more robust and naturalistic knowledge-representation languages. AI systems required languages powerful and computationally manipulable enough to build artificial minds. The invention of expert system technology—the explicit separation of knowledge and inference—brought knowledge representation into its own as a legitimate field of study. Since the late 1960s, it has been an active and fruitful area of research and development in computer science.

Source: Philip Chapnick, "Knowledge and Its Representations," *AI Expert*, June 1991, pp. 27–28.

AT A GLANCE

With knowledge acquisition comes knowledge representation, a major turning point in building expert systems. Various knowledge representation schemes are available; all contain facts for reasoning through the inference engine and can be programmed through existing computer languages. The main goals of knowledge representation are accuracy of solutions and modularity of design. Planning is a crucial aspect of virtually all phases of the development process.

The strategies for knowledge representation include semantic nets, frames, rules, formal logic, decision tables, and decision trees. Semantic nets promote deductive reasoning, although they lack operational knowledge. Frames handle a combination of declarative and operational knowledge, although inference is difficult and they are slower than alternative schemes. Rules are used almost exclusively in business-oriented expert systems, yet, only limited knowledge can be represented in a rule. Propositional logic is the simplest logic but is insufficient for large applications. In contrast, predicate logic provides well-defined syntax and clear rules; however, it does not lend itself to most business applications.

What You Will Learn

By the end of this chapter, you should know the following:

1. The various schemes available for knowledge representation.
2. The basics of each knowledge representation scheme.
3. The use of production rules in expert systems.

A ll you have to do is write one true sentence. Write the truest sentence that you know.

—ERNEST HEMINGWAY,
"A MOVEABLE FEAST"

■ INTRODUCTION

Chapters 6 through 10 discussed ways to acquire an expert's knowledge as a first step in building an expert system. The knowledge acquired is simply a large volume of facts and heuristics concerning a specific practice in the real world. Knowledge is not quite the same as information, however. For example, "Today's temperature is expected to exceed 100 degrees" is information, whereas "There is 80 percent chance that people with heart trouble will faint from exhaustion when temperature rises over 100 degrees" is knowledge. Knowledge is expressed as rules of thumb, which make it more abstract than information. Hence, one can make the distinction between *processing* information but *understanding* knowledge.

Knowledge in an expert system is of little value without a way to organize and load it into the computer. The know-how to program a computer to mimic the thought processes of an expert through an appropriate representation scheme is called *knowledge representation*. It involves knowledge of a shell or a programming language that will represent the expert's knowledge.

The history of knowledge representation goes back thousands of years to humans scratching marks on a stone to represent the changing location of the moon. Hundreds of years later, with the invention of writing, knowledge representation became a common occurrence. Until Aristotle's principles of syllogism, human language was the only form of knowledge representation. Syllogism is a form of deductive reasoning—a formal argument consisting of a major and a minor premise and a conclusion. For example, all mothers are women. Joanne is a mother. Therefore, Joanne is a woman.

In the late nineteenth century, logicians broke away from syllogism and logic began to form its own niche. The work of Alan Turing, John von Neuman, and others laid the ground for computer technology and its use of logic. The subsequent development of artificial intelligence (AI) in the early 1950s transformed early logic into more natural knowledge representation languages for building artificial minds. In the late 1960s, expert systems became an active and viable area of research that led to today's shells and knowledge representation schemes.

A number of knowledge representation schemes have been developed over the years; some have been borrowed from field research, others from psychology as well as computer science. They share two common characteristics:

1. They contain facts that can be used in reasoning through the shell's inference engine.

2. They can be programmed with existing computer languages.

This chapter examines the process of representing facts or rules in a knowledge base, and then discusses the best-known schemes for representing knowledge.

The representational framework is the basis for learning how knowledge is obtained, interpreted, and integrated into an expert system. Some builders suggest that expert knowledge is best encoded as rules; others argue that qualitative models are more accurate representation of such knowledge. This chapter presents an overview of a number of manual schemes for representing knowledge, each of which has advantages and disadvantages. Some schemes are used to support analysis, such as semantic networks, while others are used in actual coding of the expert system, such as rules and frames. (See Figure 11–1.)

Figure 11–1   Selected Knowledge Representation Schemes

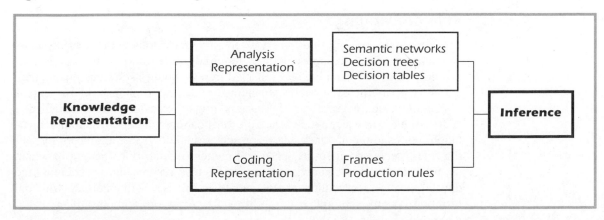

◼ ASSUMPTIONS ABOUT KNOWLEDGE REPRESENTATION

Knowledge representation is the single most critical phase in building an expert system. The tools for this process are useless unless one knows under what conditions each tool is used. A knowledge engineer's main goal is *accuracy* of the results. The problem in achieving accuracy is the lack of alignment between a computer's operation and the way the human brain works. Human expertise depends largely on judgment which, in turn, depends on that person's perception, cognition, memory, recall capability, and heuristics. So, factors affecting expert judgment do influence and are influenced by facts, beliefs, perceptions, and assumptions, which makes it difficult to ensure accuracy in **knowledge representation** in the same way that we can be sure of the accuracy of arithmetic or mathematical calculations.

Another crucial assumption about knowledge representation is **metaknowledge**—knowledge about the structure of stored knowledge and how it is used. A structured organization of acquired knowledge allows the expert system to pass knowledge back and forth between the user and the knowledge base for the right "advice."

Metaknowledge represents several kinds of knowledge—knowledge of objects, of relationships, and how to perform certain activities. The focus is on managing the progress of deductive reasoning in the system. It is a system of "understanding" of knowledge applied in the form of procedures, called **demon programs,** in the inference engine. A *demon* (Greek root *daemon*) is a program that "sits" in the background, waiting for an event to occur, and then takes action when the event does occur.

For the expert system to produce solutions, the knowledge engineer must identify facts, parameters, and the relationships among parameters in the form of rules that represent the system's knowledge base. This process is called the *mapping of knowledge.* Its goal is to ensure accuracy and reliability of knowledge representation.

Finally, another important prerequisite for knowledge representation is **modularity** of the design. Building information systems has taught that constructing a system with interrelated modules makes errors easier to locate and correct. Modularity also facilitates future system updates. In other words, one can add a module, update a module, or delete a module without worrying that it will cause changes in other modules.

Role of Planning

For some time, writing rules was viewed as synonymous with expert systems development. Later, complex projects required greater coordination and organization. A lack of planning was reflected in poor quality solutions, incomplete answers, or inefficient systems. Planning is an important part of the expert system development process. It ensures proper transition from knowledge acquisition to knowledge representation, verification, validation, and implementation. For example, in knowledge representation, knowledge engineers sort out the rules, decide on their sequence and content, which rules belong in which modules, and so on. A knowledge engineer is also responsible for planning the development and execution phases and how the user will interface with the resulting system, activities that are difficult to carry out without a plan.

In expert systems, planning involves the following aspects:

- Breaking the entire expert system into modules or manageable components
- Looking at partial solutions
- Linking partial solutions through rules and procedures to arrive at final solutions that make sense.
- Deciding on the programming language
- Selecting the right shell
- Arranging for the verification and debugging of the system
- Developing user interface and consultation facility before installing the system
- Promoting clarity and flexibility
- Reducing unnecessary risks
- Making rules easier to review and understand

Unfortunately, plans can go awry, which means that the knowledge engineer must monitor the results, compare plans with system results, assess the discrepancies, and make the necessary changes to ensure system integrity. Without this type of monitoring, the value of planning is lost.

■ STRATEGIES FOR REPRESENTING KNOWLEDGE

Several different ways of encoding facts and relationships to represent knowledge exist. Some schemes are graphical, others are tabular, others are descriptive statements of facts. The representation schemes included in this section are semantic networks, frames, rules, formal logic, decision tables, and decision trees.

Semantic Networks

A **semantic network,** or **net,** depicts the natural relationships that occur among objects, called **nodes.** A collection of nodes linked together form a net. Through a net, a knowledge engineer can graphically represent descriptive or declarative knowledge. Each idea of interest is represented by a node linked by lines called **arcs** that show relationships between nodes. Basically, it is merely a network of concepts and relationships.

To illustrate, Figure 11–2 presents a partial semantic net representing an airline's personnel knowledge base showing a specialist in pilot testing. The knowledge of the expert (Jim Harding) is expressed in basic elements rather than complex statements. The personnel knowledge base includes elements such as Olesek's (flight instructor) license, a list of the characteristics of each element, and a way to link things together. For example, the knowledge base would indicate that the insignia on Olesek's shirt sleeve signifies a flight instructor.

The key elements of a semantic net are

1. *Node:* A node represents a fact description. It may be a physical object (e.g., shirt sleeve, insignia), a concept, or a conceptual entity, such as an event (e.g., "2", USAir). It may also be a descriptor that provides additional information (e.g., insignia).

Figure 11–2 Semantic Net of a Personnel Knowledge Base

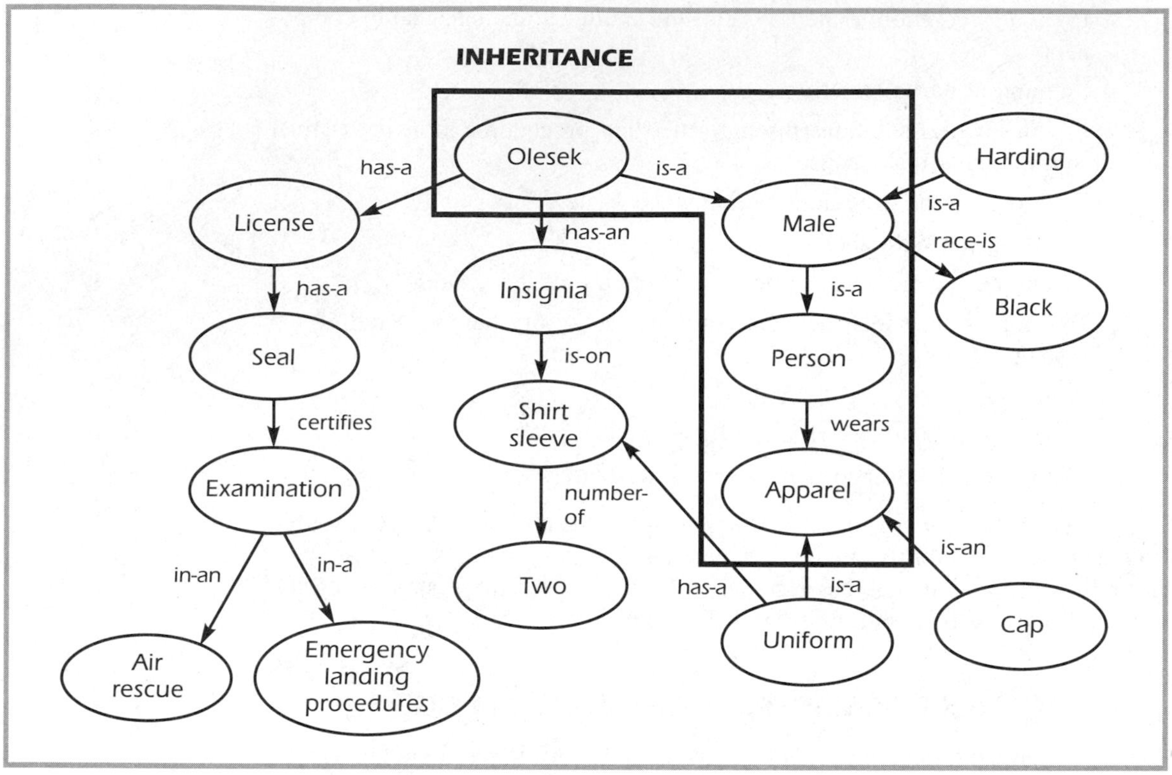

2. *Link:* A **link** represents the relationships between word concepts. It connects nodes and descriptors.

   a. *Is-a* link defines one node to be an instance of another node. It represents the class/instance relationship. In Figure 11–2, Olesek *is-a* male. He is an instance of the larger class, male. A male, in turn, is an instance of the larger class, person.

   b. *Has-a* identifies a node that is a property of another node. For example, a uniform *has-a* shirt sleeve. It shows part-subpart relationship.

   c. *Wear* is a definitional link. In the figure, the wear link between person and apparel is a definitional link.

   d. Some links represent heuristic knowledge. For example, "License certifies examining."

Semantic nets can be used for a variety of operations. One important advantage of a semantic net is deductive reasoning via **inheritance,** in which instances of one class are assumed to have all the properties of the more general classes of which they are members. For example, using the personnel knowledge base, the question, "Does Olesek wear a uniform?" is partly answerable by determining that Olesek is a male, males are persons, and persons wear apparel.

A semantic net is a way of describing the properties and relations of objects, events, or actions by a directed graph consisting of nodes and links between nodes. A net has the power to convey a complex set of relationships to the person viewing it; it can show important associations explicitly and clearly. Within the computer, however, a different form of network must be used, since the computer cannot handle diagrams directly. A semantic net is represented in a computer as tables of "triples," such as

(Olesek) (is-a) (Male)

Each **triple** is a link in the semantic net.

Search in Network Representation

A knowledge base is expected not only to store facts but also to provide other facts that are implicit in stored knowledge. It does this through deduction, and deduction requires search. In fact, human memory is a direct result of the human brain performing certain searches quickly and efficiently.

Take a closer look at the personnel knowledge base (Figure 11-2) and see how search in network representation works. Suppose a certain human named Olesek is described, and you are told that Olesek is a person. It is a fact you have no problem storing. It is simple and makes sense. Now suppose you want to know more; the more you are told about Olesek, the more you "search" and "deduce" things related to this person, such as race, marital status, profession, and so on. You reach a point at which you could give all kinds of reasons why Olesek is not your type, will qualify for certain jobs in your firm, and so on. You arrive at these conclusions through what is called *search and deductive reasoning*.

Take another example—the search for Olesek's race in the Olesek network. The search for race information begins down the chain of *is-a* assertions. The search would finally reach the assertion that Olesek is a male and another assertion saying that Olesek's race is black. Assertions can form chains which consist of numerous links. Each description adds one or more element to the overall description inherited by Olesek, any of which might be accessed to answer a question about Olesek. So, descriptive details inherited from a class description can trigger a serious search of a subclass.

Note that a semantic net is not a complete knowledge representation, because it lacks operational knowledge. This missing component is often represented in rules, expressed so that they apply to the different nodes. Because the semantics of net structures depend solely on the program that manipulates them, no conventions have been established concerning their meanings. Finally, invalid inferences can be drawn from the knowledge contained within the net. In the following example, one could derive that Arnie's car is collected by Japanese auto collectors when the statement is actually false.

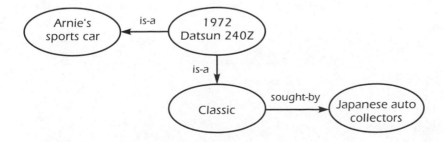

Frames

A semantic net is an early representation technique that evolved into frame-based representation. A **frame** is a structure or a representation scheme for organizing knowledge through previous experience. It handles a combination of declarative and operational knowledge, which makes it easier to understand the problem domain. A frame represents knowledge about an entity in the real world, such as an employee, a person, or person type. Declarative knowledge, in contrast to procedural knowledge, can be retrieved but not immediately executed.

Frames were developed by Marvin Minsky based on the idea that people use analogical reasoning to build new systems by taking a previous collection of structures from memory. A frame can contain information about various aspects of the situations people describe.

A frame is like a cookbook recipe: its "slots" contain both the ingredients for the recipe and the procedural details ("cook over medium heat," "until brown," etc.) to operationalize the data, or fill the slots, within or between frames. The idea of a frame, then, is to catalog the requirements for membership of certain elements of a knowledge scheme. In other words, a frame is a data structure with a name, a type, and a set of attributes, called slots. Frames have two key elements:

■ A **slot** is a specific object being described or an attribute of an entity. For example, in the personnel knowledge base, some of the slots are "instructor," "verification," "unique feature of verification," and "teaching certification." See Figure 11–3.

■ A **facet** is the value of an object or a slot. As shown in Figure 11-3, the facet (value) of slot type "instructor" is "Olesek"; "verification" is "license"; etc.

Figure 11–4 shows a frame describing automobiles consisting of six slots (attributes): manufacturer, city-of-origin, year, color, miles-per-gallon, and owner. One or more facets is associated with each slot. They include *range* (set of possible values), *default* (value to assume if none were specified), *if-needed* (how to determine actual value), and *if-changed* (what to do if the slot's value changes). If-needed and if-changed are called *demons* or procedures that allow procedural knowledge to be combined with the declarative knowledge part of the frame. They specify the actions that should take place if certain conditions occur during processing. If-needed means "the demon lays waiting until needed," and at that point it is "triggered."

Figure 11–3 A Frame Representing Olesek's License

Object: *License*	
Slot	**Facet**
Instructor	Olesek
Verification	License
Unique feature of verification	Seal
Teaching certification	Air rescue

Figure 11–4 A Frame Representing the Object of Automobile

Object: *Automobile*	
Slot	
Manufacturer	Range: Default
City-of-origin	Range: Default
Year	Range: (1960–1995) (value cannot be modified)
Color	Range: (white, black, burgundy, blue) If-needed: (examine title or view-automobile)
Miles-per-gallon	Range: (10–35)
Owner	Range: (person's-name)

When all the slots are filled with values, the frame is considered **instanti-ated,** which means an instance of the frame is created. In the Olesek's license frame with slots, if the values (Olesek) and (license) are "instructor" and "verification" (see Figure 11–3), then an instance of Olesek's license is obtained. The value of the slot could be a string, an integer, or a pointer to another frame instance.

The problem-solving technique used by a frame-based system is called **matching** in which the values associated with a given entity are matched with the slot values of frames. With a sufficient match, the frame-based system assumes that an instance has occurred.

Frames represent knowledge about a particular idea in one place. They provide a framework or structure, in which new information can be interpreted. They are especially helpful in dealing with hierarchical knowledge, because their organization of knowledge makes inferences easy to describe.

Frames can also be linked—one frame may inherit properties of a higher-level frame. In the example shown in Figure 11–5, a "performance review" is a type of "session" with an "informal" nature. The director, attendance, and frequency are attributes special to the performance review. Relying on the concept of "inheritance," the *child frames* of "session" and "manager" are a specialized type derived from the more general *parent frame.* Because of this relationship, one can assume that the child frames inherit attributes of the parent frame. The "child" may also have properties of its own not shared by the parent. The inheritance mechanism means only information specific to a given frame will be specified. Expert systems using frames determine the particular process for operating inheritance relationships.

A major drawback of frames is their level of complexity, which makes them much slower than alternative schemes. Using the performance evaluation example, to obtain a particular value, the system goes through a series of frames before it can find the frame that has the value needed. As a result, the system can be quite tedious to the user. Also, frames do not easily describe heuristics that are more readily represented with rules.

Figure 11–5   Set of Interlinked Frames

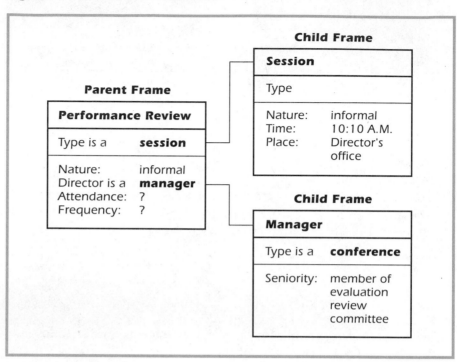

Production Rules

Another form of knowledge representation is carried out by developing **production rules,** commonly known as **rules.** Rules represent the major elements of a modular knowledge representation scheme, especially when using shells. Rules are conditional statements that are easy to understand and write; they specify an action to be taken if a certain condition is true. They also express relationships between parameters or variables. In expert systems vocabulary, production rules are also called premise-action, cause-effect, hypothesis-action, condition-action, test-result, IF . . . THEN, or IF . . . THEN . . . ELSE. In the latter form, IF is the rule's antecedent, THEN is some consequent, and ELSE is some other consequent. These concepts will be explained later in this section.

The basic idea of using rules is to represent the expert's knowledge in the form of premise-action pairs as follows:

Syntax: IF (premise) THEN (action)

Example: IF income is "average" and pay_history is "good" THEN recommendation is "approve loan"

Expert system rules differ from the traditional "if-then" programming statements. In expert systems, rules are relatively independent of one another and are based on heuristics, or experiential reasoning, rather than algorithms. Rules can carry some level of uncertainty. A *certainty factor* is represented as CNF or CF and is synonymous with a confidence level, which is a subjective quantification of an expert's judgment. In the preceding example, the rule means: "If the applicant's income is average and pay history, which implies a previous loan, is good, THEN the recommendation is approval of the loan at the 80 percent level of confidence." Figure 11–6 specifies the structure of a rule, which consists of a premise and an action. The premise has three expressions or clauses, each of which has an attribute, an object, and a value. The action has one expression or a clause with an attribute, an object, or a value.

A Premise

The IF . . . THEN structure of the rule language is represented by *premise* and *action* clauses or statements. The **premise** is a Boolean (yes/no, true/false) expression that must be evaluated as *true* for the rule to be applied. It is composed by one or more statements separated by AND or OR connectors. A shell processes a rule by testing its premise for truth or falsity. The test must be satisfied before any action of a rule can be executed. Examples of a rule premise include:

```
IF GPA is "high" THEN . . .
IF car_motor is "bad" or car_body is fair THEN . . .
IF income ≥ $50,000 and assets > $300,000 or
payment_history is "good" THEN . . .
```

In multiple premises, processing proceeds from left to right. AND has a higher precedence than OR. Parentheses may be used to change or specify precedence. The default order of precedence is × and ÷, + and −, left association. For example $2 + 3 \times 5 - 6 \div 8 \times 7$ is evaluated as $\{[2 + (3 \times 5)] - (6 \div 8 \times 7)\}$.

An Action

The action part of a rule is the second component, separated from the premise by the keyword THEN. The **action** clause consists of a statement or a series of statements separated by ANDs or commas (,) and is executed IF the premise is true. It could be either a list of commands to be carried out if the premise evaluates to true or it could be a Boolean expression that evaluates to true whenever the premise is true. If any part of the premise is false, then the action

Figure 11–6 Structure and Elements of a Rule

| Premise: | IF | cloud site is black and wind force > 35 mph and wave height > 18 feet |
| Action: | THEN | there is .6 evidence that classification of storm is hurricane |

		Attribute	**Object**	**Value**
Premise:	IF	site	cloud	black
		force	wind	> 35mph
		height	wave	> 18 feet
Action:	THEN	classification	storm	hurricane

would not be true or would be true at a specific level of uncertainty. Examples of rule action include:

```
IF owns auto = false THEN potential_insurance = "high"
IF income > $100,000 THEN federal_tax_rate > .35
IF loan holder = "late payer" THEN add penalty = .5 to
premium
```

For multiple action clauses, statements must be linked with AND or commas. For example:

```
IF GPA = "HIGH" and SAT > 1400
THEN admission = true and financial_aid = $6,000
```

In this example, two values are assigned to admission with financial aid. Two actions are also fired. In most business-oriented expert systems, rules are used almost exclusively. They are a natural expression of "what to do" knowledge or "how to do" knowledge. They are easy to understand and to represent the expert's know-how. Their main drawback is the way they are expressed at a fine level of detail. Such fine-grained representation makes the know-how involved difficult to understand. Also, the amount of knowledge that can be expressed in a single rule is limited. This limitation depends largely on the shell. For example, EXSYS allows as many as 126 conditions in the IF and the THEN parts of a rule. (See Box 11–1.)

Formal Logic

An alternative knowledge representation scheme for building expert systems uses logic in representing facts and relationships. Logic is generally attributed to Socrates and Aristotle who devised this method to propose verbal arguments that could be defended through a set of accepted rules of reasoning. These rules evaluated the truth of the presented arguments against statements known to be true; the arguments could then be accepted without question as either true or false. Later in the nineteenth century, British mathematician George Boole defined a new algebra (Boolean algebra) that relied on truth tables to evaluate the truth value of logical statements. His mathematical treatment of these statements formed the basis for later advances in logic.

 Logic is the study of reasoning and is the oldest form of knowledge representation. The general form of logic is shown in Figure 11–7. The two basic forms of logic—propositional logic and predicate logic—are explained briefly here.

Propositional Logic

Logic-based representation typically takes the form of propositional logic, one of the oldest and simplest forms of logic. Its mechanism of propositional connectives—AND, OR, NOT, etc.—allows one to evaluate simple statements and then complex statements. The main goal of this form of logic is to determine the truth or falsity of new propositions. A **proposition** is a simple statement whose value is either true (T) or false (F). It represents some fact about the world. For example:

Today is school day.

Students are in session.

It is quiet.

Box 11–1   Choosing a Rule-Based Knowledge Representation System

Now that I had the induction table and knowledge to work with, I had to represent the knowledge. The first decision was on a *rule-based* system. There are several reasons why I selected a rule-based system:

- The majority of existing expert systems development packages employ rule bases.
- Rule-based expert systems development packages are normally much less expensive.
- It takes less time to learn how to use and implement a rule-based system.
- Rule bases can be relatively easily modified.
- Validation of rule-based systems is a relatively simple process.

Ease of use and learning made the rule-based system a better choice than say frame-based.

The next decision was which *shell* to use. I chose EXSYS over VP-Expert. Where VP-Expert develops its rules from an induction table developed by the knowledge engineer, EXSYS does not. However, where VP-Expert induces the rules from the induction table, EXSYS allows the knowledge engineer to create, edit, and change each rule systematically.

Along with the induction table, I needed to prepare my rules for inclusion in the EXSYS expert system shell. A method for doing this is the attribute value (A–V) pairs table. A–V pairs tables are particularly useful in the transition from the written rule base (induction table) to the representation employed by the software package utilized. If nothing else, A–V pairs tables serve as a means for documentation of the components of a given rule base.

The expert reviewed the rule base representation and made corrections. His corrections updated the knowledge base and the knowledge representation phase, again, in an iterative manner. My next task was to verify and validate the system.

Source: Patrick Delaney, Unpublished graduate report, Spring 1993.

Figure 11–7   General Form of Logic

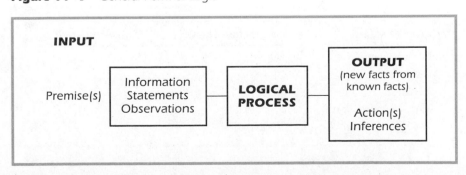

Propositions can be combined with other propositions to form more complex facts about the world, for example: (Today is school day) and (today is quiet). Propositional logic relies on established truths, followed by a logical extension to come up with new knowledge. For example, if one states that all bicycles have two wheels and that a 10-speed bike is a bicycle, then, with these two truths, one can conclude that a 10-speed bike has two wheels. Using this logic, however, requires mathematical accuracy. Suppose most companies assembling cars have no accident-prone employees, and Ford is a car maker. Accepting both of these truths, propositional logic would conclude that Ford employees are not accident-prone, which, in reality, is not true.

Propositional logic utilizes propositional operators or connectives (AND, OR, NOT, IF-THEN, EQUIVALENT) to combine simple propositions and rules of inference. Connective names and symbols are shown in Table 11–1. A **rule of inference** is a deductive structure that defines what can be inferred if certain relations are taken to be true. It allows deduction of a new sentence from previously given sentences. The new sentence is definitely true if the original sentences are true:

For example:

X

$X \rightarrow Y$

means, given that X is true and X implies Y is true, then one may infer that Y is true, a logical (valid) conclusion.

The AND connective is used to combine two propositions. The resulting new proposition is true *only* if *both* of the original propositions are true. For example:

```
A = This text discusses technology.
B = This text is taught in a business school.
C = This text discusses technology and is taught in a
    business school.
C = A AND B
```

The OR connective is used to build formulas whose truth depends only on the truth of one proposition. It may combine two propositions. The resulting new proposition is true if *either* of the original propositions is true. For example:

```
A = A student may take technology classes from the
    business school.
```

■ **Table 11–1**   Logical Connectives and Their Symbols

English Name	Connective Name	Connective Symbol
Conjunction	AND	$\wedge$
Disjunction	OR	$\vee$
Negation	NOT	$\sim$
Material implication	IF . . . THEN	$\rightarrow$
Material equivalence	EQUIVALENT	$\equiv$

```
B = A student may take technology classes from the
    computer science department.
C = A OR B  A student may take technology classes from the
    business school or the computer science department.
```

The NOT connective is used to change the truth value of a formula from true to false or from false to true. For example:

```
A = School is closed today.
NOT A = School is not closed today.
```

When proposition *A* is true, **NOT** *A* is false and vice versa as shown in the following truth table:

A	NOT A
T	F
F	T

The IF . . . THEN connective may be viewed as a conditional such that:

IF $A \rightarrow B$ is to be true,

THEN whenever *A* is true, *B* must always be true.

For example:

```
A = Class is canceled.
B = Instructor is sick.
```

We can write this in an IF . . . THEN statement as "IF class is canceled, THEN instructor is sick."

The truth table for the IF . . . THEN ($\rightarrow$) operator is as follows:

A	B	Material implication $A \rightarrow B$	Material equivalence A, B
T	T	T	T
T	F	F	F
F	T	T	F
F	F	T	T

The last two lines of the truth table are puzzling. They state that when *A* is not true, *B* can be true or false without affecting the validity of the clause because the operator cannot make any inferences about the value of *B*.

The EQUALS connective is used to indicate the logical equivalent of two propositions. A proposition such as $A \equiv B$ indicates that the truth states of both sides of the equation are equivalent, regardless of how they are interpreted.

As can be deduced, propositional logic is not useful in expert systems because of its limited ability to express knowledge. It deals primarily with complete statements and whether they are true or false. One must be able to go beyond true and false propositions of complete statements and represent statements about specific objects or individuals in developing an expert system. This necessity leads to predicate logic.

Predicate Logic

Predicate logic is an extension of propositional logic and another formal reasoning with mathematical properties. It uses the same rules of propositional logic, but it is capable of representing knowledge in finer detail. A **predicate** is a statement about objects, both by themselves and in relation to other objects. An **object** is an elementary unit in predicate logic, called the *argument* of the predicate. The use of arguments allows a predicate to express a relationship about different objects, not just a single object. Like a proposition, predicates have a truth value. But unlike propositions, predicate truth values depend on their arguments. That is, a predicate may be true for one set of arguments and false for another. For example, if:

predicate   arguments

Color (ocean, blue)

Meaning: Ocean color is blue.

Using a different argument such as color (ocean, white) may not be true.

A predicate addresses one argument. For example, "is-instructor (Olesek)" is an assertion that Olesek is an instructor. This assertion is either true or false. A predicate can also address more than one object. For example, "instructor-at (Olesek, UNITED)" illustrates a two-place predicate. The statement asserts that Olesek is an instructor at UNITED. Other examples of predicates include:

WOMAN(SANDY)	Sandy is a woman.
TALLER(SANDY,JUDY)	Sandy is taller than Judy.
TALLER[SANDY,mother(BEV)]	Sandy is taller than a mother whose name is BEV.

Predicate logic allows one to break a statement into component parts (objects), say something about the object, and make assertions about the object. A predicate is applied to a specific number of arguments and has a value of either true or false when objects are used as the arguments. For example:

IS-YELLOW

has a value of true when applied to a yellow object like a yellow fire truck. To review predicate logic in the context of knowledge representation, let us start with this sentence:

All cars have engines.

This would be represented by a mathematical formula that reads

"For any object X, if X is a car, then X has an engine."

$\forall X \, [\text{Car}(X) \rightarrow \text{Has engine}(X)]$

$\forall x$ is a universal quantifier used to assert that a formula is true for all values of the associated variable.

Predicate logic is concerned only with sound argumentation methods called rules of inference. For example, if another fact is added to the knowledge base

$\forall X \, [\text{Cadillac}(X) \rightarrow \text{Car}(X)]$

it reads, "For any object X, if X is a cadillac, then X is a car." From these two facts, the rules of inference are used to conclude that the following fact must be true:

$\forall X$ [Cadillac(X) $\rightarrow$ Has engine(X)]

Predicate logic is the basis for the AI language called PROLOG (PROgramming in LOGic). See Figure 11–8. One reason for the popularity of logic-based representations is the derivation of new facts from old ones. Using

Figure 11–8 Partial Program and a Dialogue in PROLOG

PROLOG database

```
>student(david).  ⎫
>student(mary).   ⎪
>student(john).   ⎬ Facts
>student(ann).    ⎪
>student(jerry).  ⎪
>student(sue).    ⎭
>likes(someone, accounting):-          ⎫
     concentrating(someone, accounting). ⎬ Rule
>concentrating(david, mis).        ⎫
>concentrating(mary, marketing).   ⎪
>concentrating(mary, mis).         ⎪
>concentrating(john, accounting).  ⎬ Facts
>concentrating(ann, management).   ⎪
>concentrating(ann, mis).          ⎪
>concentrating(jerry, finance).    ⎪
>concentrating(sue, accounting).   ⎭
```

User–PROLOG Dialogue

```
>concentrating(david,accounting)?
NO;
>concentrating(david,mis)?
YES;
>student(Who)?
WHO=david;
WHO=mary;
WHO=john;
WHO=ann;
WHO=jerry;
WHO=sue;
>concentrating(Who,mis)?
WHO=david;
WHO=mary;
WHO=ann;
>likes(Who, accounting)?
WHO=john;
WHO=sue;
```

predicate logic, a knowledge base can be viewed as a set of logical formulas representing the expert's knowledge. The set can change in size as the situation warrants.

Another advantage of predicate logic is its well-defined syntax and clear rules and interpretation of each situation. Predicate logic is also *modular,* which means that additional information can be added to the knowledge base without a problem as long as the inclusions are consistent with the existing information. The connectives used in propositional logic are also valid in predicate logic. In fact, propositional logic is a subset of predicate logic.

The main drawback of predicate logic is that much of the knowledge used in business decision making does not lend itself to this form of representation. One major disadvantage is the availability of only true and false as levels of truth without any gray area. Deductions in predicate logic always assure that the inference is absolutely true or absolutely false. Yet, in real life, many problems are not true or false. For example, many caucasians have bald heads is not easily represented in predicate logic because of the difficulty in representing the qualifier *many.*

The rules of inference in formal logic are appropriate for shallow knowledge systems applying heuristic rules. For deep knowledge-based systems, semantic nets and frames have greater advantages. Semantic nets are more flexible in displaying deep knowledge, although implementation of this approach can be complicated. Frames offer the power of a database in terms of organizing data. A summary of the pros and cons of the various representation schemes is shown in Table 11–2.

No representation scheme is universally accepted as "best." One scheme is better than another scheme when evaluated against certain criteria and by their usefulness to certain applications.

■ OTHER KNOWLEDGE REPRESENTATION SCHEMES

Decision Tables

Other schemes may be used for knowledge representation. One such scheme is the long-known decision table. A **decision table** is more like a spreadsheet, divided into two parts: (1) a list of conditions and their respective values, and (2) a list of conclusions. The various conditions are matched against the conclusions. A simple example determining the discount policy of a book publisher is shown in Table 11–3.

Note that the answers are represented by a Y to signify yes, an N to signify no, or a blank to show that the condition involved has not been tested. In the action entry quadrant, an X or check mark indicates the response to the answer(s) entered in the condition entry quadrant. Each column also represents a decision or a rule. For example, rule 1 states:

```
IF customer is bookstore and order_size > 6 copies
THEN allow 25% discount
```

So, the decision table example provides six decisions and therefore six rules.

Logic Gem: An Electronic Decision Table

The manual approach to decision tables is not so practical as an aid to building expert systems. The mental steps in manually creating, editing, and checking

■ **Table 11–2** Advantages and Disadvantages of Knowledge Representation Schemes

Type	Advantages	Disadvantages
Semantic Nets	■ Uses deductive reasoning (inheritance) ■ Shows important associations explicitly and clearly ■ Follows the hierarchy of relationships easily ■ Provides flexibility in adding new nodes to a definition when needed	■ Not a complete knowledge representation ■ Lacks operational knowledge ■ Manipulates the net through inferences that are invalid ■ Meaning of node may be ambiguous. No standards exist concerning the definition of nodes ■ Makes procedural knowledge difficult to represent because sequence and time are not clearly represented
Frames	■ Provides uniform representation schemes ■ Handles a combination of declarative and operational knowledge ■ Deals with hierarchical knowledge and modularity ■ Organizes knowledge so as to describe inferences and detect missing values	■ Slower than alternative schemes due to higher level of complexity ■ Makes inference difficult ■ Makes explanation difficult
Rules	■ Used almost exclusively in business-oriented expert systems ■ Easy to understand and record expert's know-how ■ Provides modularity and flexibility	■ Expressed at a fine level of detail; difficult to understand the knowledge know-how involved ■ Allows limited knowledge per rule
Formal Logic	■ Oldest form of knowledge representation	■ Insufficient and perhaps inefficient for large applications
Propositional	■ Can be combined with other propositions to form more complex facts about the world	■ Limited ability to explain knowledge reduces usefulness in expert systems
Predicate	■ Derives new facts from old ones ■ Provides well-defined syntax, clear rules, and easy interpretation of each situation ■ Uses modular format that is easy to update	■ Does not lend itself to most business decision making

■ **Table 11–3** Decision Table of Publishing Company Discount Policy

Condition Stub		Condition Entry					
		1	2	3	4	5	6
IF (condition)	Customer is bookstore	Y	Y	N	N	N	N
	Order size > 6 copies	Y	N	N	N	N	N
	Customer is librarian/individual			Y	Y	Y	Y
	Order size 50 copies or more			Y	N	N	N
	Order size 20–49 copies				Y	N	N
	Order size 6–19 copies					Y	N
THEN (action)	Allow 25% discount	X					
	Allow 15% discount			X			
	Allow 10% discount				X		
	Allow 5% discount					X	
	Allow 0 discount		X				X
Action Stub		**Action Entry**					

one makes decision tables difficult to construct. For example, imagine a problem with six conditions, and each condition has five possible values. Such a problem could require more than 15,000 distinct rules. This type of complexity is nearly impossible for the human mind to resolve without electronic media.

Logic Gem is a software package that electronically builds decision tables of any size. Its key features include ability to generate a complete table of condition entries based on the condition stubs and the provided number of possible data values for each stub. Once entered, the user needs only to edit the condition entries and add the appropriate action stubs and action entries to complete the table. The logic editor of the software is also capable of checking for and eliminating redundant or contradictory rules. It will also check the tables for holes in the logic and add the missing rules, if necessary.

A key feature of Logic Gem is its interpreter; it tests the logic of the table as it is being developed rather than making the programmer go through multiple edit/save/compile/link/execute cycles. Logic Gem includes an interpretive language that provides for more flexibility in representing logic. Examples of some interpretive commands include calling another table, returning a value from a calling table, reinterpreting a table, or setting a condition value and then repeating the table. The interpretive language includes commands that enable the fundamental programming structures—conditional iteration, sequence, and branching—to be used. The knowledge engineer can build the prototype interactively with the expert and then test it using the interpreter to verify its accuracy. The system shows no mercy toward imprecise knowledge offered by the expert.

An Example

Figure 11–9 shows a working example of a small expert system using Logic Gem. It is an entire knowledge base of a system that can indicate why a person may have experienced a fainting episode. The knowledge is drawn from the

Figure 11–9   A Small Expert System Using Logic Gem Technology

(a)

faint									
CD	spin	2	y	n	n	n	n	n	n
CD	sudden	2	–	y	n	n	n	n	n
CD	exercise	2	–	–	y	n	n	n	n
CD	bloodp	2	–	–	–	y	n	n	n
CD	diab	2	–	–	–	–	y	n	n
CD	heat	2	–	–	–	–	–	y	n
AD	dizzy	1							
AD	lowblp		1						
AD	rbreath			1					
AD	bpmed				1				
AD	hypogly					1			
AD	heatexhaust						1		
AP	morefaint							1	

Proceed to
morefaint
Figure (b)

CD

spin — Was the feeling of faintness accompanied by a spinning sensation?

sudden — Did you stand up suddenly after sitting, lying down, or stooping, or had you just gotten up after a few days in bed?

exercise — Were you exercising more strenuously than usual, and were you short of breath just before you felt faint?

bloodp — Are you taking drugs for high blood pressure?

diab — Are you a diabetic or is it an unusually long time since you last ate something?

heat — Had you spent several hours in strong sunshine or in very hot or stuffy conditions before you felt faint?

AD

dizzy — Your dizziness should be evaluated by the dizziness expert system.

lowblp — The faintness was probably caused by a temporary drop in blood pressure.

rbreath — Rapid breathing may have temporarily disturbed your blood chemistry.

bpmed — Discuss this with your physician. Your blood pressure may have fallen too low.

hypogly — Low blood sugar is probably causing your faintness. A sweet drink or something sugary or starchy to eat will probably make you feel better. If you are diabetic and have had several such attacks, consult your physician.

heatexhaust — You may have heat exhaustion. Seek first aid.

Figure 11–9 A Small Expert System Using Logic Gem Technology (continued)

(b)

morefaint														
CC	stroke	3	a	b	c	c	c	c	c	c	c	c	c	c
CC	heart	3	–	–	a	b	c	c	c	c	c	c	c	c
CD	breath	2	–	–	–	–	y	n	n	n	n	n	n	n
CD	emotional	2	–	–	–	–	–	y	n	n	n	n	n	n
CD	strain	2	–	–	–	–	–	–	y	n	n	n	n	n
CD	age	2	–	–	–	–	–	–	–	y	y	y	n	n
CD	headturn	2	–	–	–	–	–	–	–	y	n	n	–	–
CD	tired	2	–	–	–	–	–	–	–	–	y	n	y	n
AD	stroke1	1												
AD	stroke2		1											
AD	stokesad			1										
AD	heartrate				1									
AD	anxiety					1								
AD	nerves						1							
AD	oxygen							1						
AD	cervical								1					
AD	anemia.hf									1		1		
AD	consult.dr										1		1	

Call stroke Figure (c)

Call heart Figure (d)

CD

breath	Were you breathing very rapidly or deeply before you felt faint?
emotional	Did you feel faint after an emotional shock?
strain	Did you feel faint while you were doing any of the following:

     ■ stretching   ■ holding your breath

     ■ coughing   ■ urinating

age	Are you over 50?
headturn	Does turning your head slowly make you feel faint?
tired	Do you feel inexplicably tired and/or are you often short of breath?

AD

stroke1 Consult your physician without delay! It is likely that you have had:

     ■ a mild stroke

     ■ a transient ischimic attack

stroke2 Consult your physician without delay! You may have had:

     ■ a mild stroke

     ■ a transient ischimic attack

stokesad Consult your physician. Do not delay! You may have had a Stokes-Adams attack which indicates a disorder of heart rhythm.

heartrate Discuss with your physician. You may have a disorder of heart rate or rhythm.

anxiety The faintness was probably caused by hyperventilation or overbreathing, possibly as a result of anxiety or stress.

nerves Emotional upsets can easily affect the nerves that control blood pressure and this may cause faintness.

Figure 11–9   A Small Expert System Using Logic Gem Technology
(continued)

oxygen		Any of these activities will sometimes affect the supply of oxygen to the brain and cause faintness. This is usually no cause for concern. But if it happens more than once, consult your physician.															

oxygen — Any of these activities will sometimes affect the supply of oxygen to the brain and cause faintness. This is usually no cause for concern. But if it happens more than once, consult your physician.

cervical — These symptoms suggest a disorder that affects the nerves and bones in the neck: cervical spondylosis.

anemia.hf — You may be suffering from a form of anemia or from heart failure.

consult.dr — You should consult your physician for further discussion of this problem.

(c)

	stroke																
CD	numbness	2	y	y	y	y	n	n	n	n	n	n	y	n	n	n	n	n
CD	blurred	2	y	n	n	n	y	y	y	n	n	n	n	y	n	n	n	n
CD	confusion	2	–	y	n	n	y	n	n	y	y	n	n	n	y	n	n	n
CD	speaking	2	–	–	y	n	–	y	n	y	n	y	n	n	n	y	n	n
CD	motion	2	–	–	–	y	–	–	y	–	y	y	n	n	n	n	y	n
AR	a		1	1	1	1	1	1	1	1	1	1						
AR	b												1	1	1	1	1	
AR	c																	1

Return to
morefaint
Figure (b)

CD

numbness — Have you noticed any numbness and/or tingling in any part of your body?

blurred — Has your vision been blurred?

confusion — Have you experienced any sense of confusion?

speaking — Have you had any difficulty speaking?

motion — Have you noticed any loss of motion in your arms or legs?

(d)

	heart				
CD	hdisease	2	y	y	n
CD	consciousness	2	y	n	–
AR	a		1		
AR	b			1	
AR	c				1

Return to
morefaint
Figure (b)

CD

hdisease — Do you have any form of heart disease and/or did you notice your heartbeat speeding up or slowing down before you felt faint?

consciousnes — Did you lose consciousness?

American Medical Association Family Medical Guide, which presents 100 self-diagnostic symptom charts.

The system represents four tables: faint, morefaint, stroke, and heart. If a rule cannot be isolated when "faint" has performed all its queries, "morefaint" is invoked, which in its turn, calls two subtables in order to rule out stroke or heart ailment as a cause of the fainting episode. The tables are simple; for example, subtable "stroke" is a standard table that says, "Return a when any two conditions are true, b when any one is true, and c when none are true."

Decision tables and Logic Gem could be used to make the whole expert system development process more effective and efficient. During acquisition, they provide a method to directly involve the expert. They can be used as a communication tool during both acquisition and representation. Decision tables can be used during rapid prototyping and during testing to check the logic of the expert system. Finally, decision tables are a powerful documentation tool; they are far superior to English description in understanding and maintaining the documentation.

Decision Trees

Another knowledge representation scheme is the **decision tree.** A decision tree is a hierarchically arranged semantic network and is closely related to a decision table. It is composed of nodes representing goals and links that

Figure 11–10 Decision Tree Representing Publishing Company Discount Policy

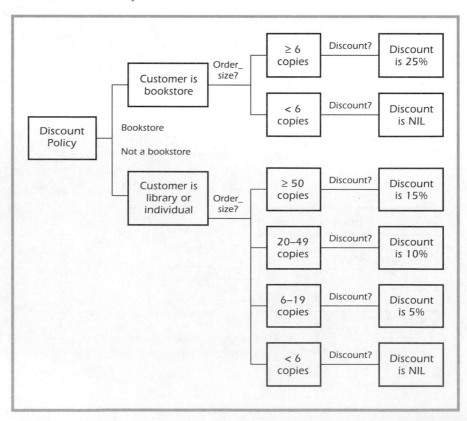

represent decisions or outcomes. A decision tree is read from left to right, with the root being on the left. All nodes except the root node are instances of the primary goal.

To illustrate, the decision table in Table 11–3 is shown as a decision tree in Figure 11–10. The primary goal is to determine discount policy. The equivalent rule is IF customer is a bookstore and order size is greater than 6 copies, THEN discount is 25 percent. Several other rules can be extracted from the same tree.

Decision tables and decision trees are commonly used. Decision tables are especially useful in verifying rules, a task for which special software is available. A major advantage of a decision tree is to verify logic graphically in problems involving complex situations that result in a limited number of actions. A major drawback to decision trees is the lack of information in the tree format that might indicate what other combinations of conditions could be included. This is where the decision table is useful.

IMPLICATIONS FOR MANAGEMENT

In traditional terms, management means planning, organizing, directing, and coordinating the efforts of people, procedures, and technology. The work of knowledge representation involves more than representation schemes or tools. It means planning the representation phase, planning the use of specific tools within the framework of a shell, and making most efficient use of the knowledge engineer's and the expert's time and talents.

In addition to the front-end phase of management, the knowledge engineer should sense the user's expectations and determine how the user can be part of the representation phase of the expert system development life cycle. Partnership or cooperation can be accomplished through rapid prototyping or inviting the user to join in the day-to-day routines of representation. In addition, the knowledge engineer needs to foster the relationship with the champion, whose role continues to be vital to the future acceptance and success of the expert system.

Finally, in preparation for the detailed writing of the rules and procedures for building the knowledge base, the knowledge engineer would be well advised to begin promoting the goodness of fit and exciting features of the expert system to key persons in the area it will be installed. In fact, public relations efforts are best begun early in the process, especially when the expert system is likely to take months rather than weeks to build. The ultimate goal is user acceptance and commitment to long-term use of the system.

■ SUMMARY

1. The first step in building an expert system is to acquire the knowledge of the expert. The knowledge acquired is a large volume of facts and heuristics concerned with a particular practice in the real world.

2. Humans *process* information but *understand* knowledge. Knowledge is expressed in the form of heuristic descriptions or rules of thumb, which make it more abstract than information. Knowledge

representation is the know-how to program knowledge through an appropriate representation scheme.

3. Knowledge representation schemes share two common characteristics: (1) they contain facts that can be used in reasoning through the shell's inference engine, and (2) the schemes can be programmed with existing computer languages. The representational framework is the basis for learning how information is obtained, interpreted, and fitted into the framework.

4. Knowledge representation is the single most critical phase in building an expert system. Because factors affecting expert judgment do influence and are influenced by facts, beliefs, perceptions, and assumptions, knowledge representation accuracy is difficult to ensure.

5. Metaknowledge is the knowledge of objects, of relationships, and how to perform certain activities—the structure of stored knowledge and how it is used. It is a system of "understanding" of knowledge applied in the form of procedures, called demon programs, in the inference engine. A demon passes the knowledge back and forth between the user and the knowledge base and manages the progress of deductive reasoning in the system.

6. Planning is an important part of the entire expert system development process. It ensures proper transition from knowledge acquisition to knowledge representation, verification, validation, and implementation. Planning involves the following aspects:

   - Breaking system into modular components
   - Looking at partial solutions
   - Linking partial solutions through rules and procedures
   - Deciding on programming language and shell
   - Arranging the verification and debugging of the system
   - Developing and testing user interface before system is finally installed
   - Promoting clarity and flexibility and reducing unnecessary risks
   - Reviewing rules and increasing user understanding

7. A semantic network or net is a collection of nodes linked together. Each idea of interest is represented by a node linked by lines called arcs to show relationships between nodes. A major advantage of a semantic net is deductive reasoning via inheritance. Instances of one class are assumed to have all the properties of more general classes of which they are members. A semantic net is not a complete knowledge representation. It lacks operational knowledge. This missing component is often represented in rules, expressed so that they apply to the different nodes.

8. A knowledge base is expected not only to store facts but also to provide other facts that are implicit in stored knowledge. This is done through deduction and deduction requires search.

9. A frame is a structure for organizing knowledge. It handles a combination of declarative and operational knowledge and makes the current problem domain easier to understand. It represents knowledge about an entity in the real world and catalogs the membership requirements of certain elements of a knowledge scheme. The two key elements of a frame are a slot, which is a specific object being described or an attribute about an entity that holds a value or facets, and a facet, the value of an object or slot. When all slots are filled with facets an instance of a frame is created.

10. Frames represent knowledge about a particular idea in one place. They are great for dealing with hierarchical knowledge and organizing knowledge to more easily describe inferences. Frames can also be linked; one frame may inherit properties of a higher-level frame. The inheritance mechanism means only information that is specific to a given frame will be specified. A drawback of frames is their level of complexity, which makes them much slower than alternative schemes.

11. Rules represent the major elements of a modular knowledge representation scheme. They are conditional statements that specify an action to be taken, if a certain condition is true. They express relationships between parameters and represent the expert's knowledge in the form of premise–action pairs.

12. The premise has three expressions or clauses, each having an attribute, an object, and a value. The action has one expression with an attribute, an object, or a value. The premise is a Boolean (yes/no, true/false) expression that must be evaluated as true for the rule to be applied. The shell processes a rule by testing its premises for truth or falsity.

13. The action part of a rule is separated from the premise by the keyword THEN and is executed if the premise is true. For multiple action clauses, statements must be linked with AND or commas.

14. Logic can be used to represent facts and relationships to build expert systems. Logic-based representation typically takes the form of propositional logic. The goal is to determine the truth or falsity of a proposition. Propositional logic utilizes logical operators or connectives to combine simple propositions and rules of inference. A rule of inference is a deductive structure that determines what can be inferred if certain relations are taken to be true. The AND connective is used to combine two propositions. The resulting proposition is true only if both of the original propositions are true. The OR connective is used to build formulas whose truth depends only on the truth of one proposition.

15. Predicate logic is an extension of propositional logic and another form of reasoning with mathematical properties. It uses the same rules of propositional logic, but it is capable of representing knowledge in finer detail. Using predicate logic, a knowledge base can be viewed as a set of logical formulas representing the expert's knowledge.

16. A decision table scheme is divided into two parts: (1) a list of conditions and their respective values, and (2) a list of conclusions. The various conditions are matched against the conclusions.

17. A decision tree is a hierarchically arranged semantic network and is closely related to a decision table. It is composed of nodes representing goals and links that represent decisions or outcomes.

■ TERMS TO LEARN

Action consists of a list of commands to be carried out if the premise evaluates to true, or a Boolean expression that evaluates to true whenever the premise does; either conclusions to be drawn with some appropriate degree of certainty or instructions to be carried out.

Arc a line denoting the relationship between the nodes of a semantic network.

Decision table a list of conditions with their respective values matched against a list of conclusions.

Decision tree a hierarchically arranged semantic network that is closely related to a decision table; composed of nodes representing goals and links that represents decisions or outcomes.

Demon program a program that "sits" in the background, waiting for an event to occur, and then takes action when the event does occur.

Facet the value of an object or a slot.

Inheritance an instance of a particular class is assumed to have all the properties of more general classes of which it is a member.

Instantiate create a frame by filling its slots.

Link represents relationships between word concepts (semantics); connects nodes and descriptors.

Logic Gem a software package that electronically builds decision tables of any size.

Logic the study of reasoning; the scientific study of the process of reasoning and the set of rules and procedures used in the reasoning process.

Matching the values associated with a given entity paired with the slot values of the frames to signify that an instance has occurred.

Metaknowledge knowledge about the structure of stored knowledge and how it is used.

Modularity a design in which adding, updating, or deleting a module does not affect other modules.

Node represents the description of a fact.

Object an elementary unit in predicate logic.

Predicate a statement about objects, by themselves and in relation to other objects; applied to a specific number of arguments and has a value of either true or false when objects are used as the arguments.

Predicate logic capable of representing knowledge in finer detail than propositional logic.

Premise a Boolean expression that must be evaluated as true for the rule to be applied.

Production rule knowledge representation method in which knowledge is formalized into rules.

Proposition a statement that is either true or false.

Propositional logic relies on established truths, followed by logical extensions resulting in new knowledge.

Rule of inference a deductive structure that determines what can be inferred if certain relations are taken to be true; facts known to be true used to derive other facts that must also be true.

Rules a conditional statement that specifies an action to be taken if a certain condition is true; a formal way of specifying a recommendation, directive, or strategy, expressed as IF (premise) ... THEN (conclusion).

Triple a link in the semantic net.

■ REVIEW QUESTIONS

1. What assumptions can be made about knowledge representation? How important are these assumptions? Explain.

2. Distinguish between:
   a. metaknowledge and demon programs
   b. semantic network and frame
   c. rule premise and action
   d. slot and facet

3. Describe the elements or makeup of a semantic net. Give an example to illustrate.

4. "A semantic net is represented as tables of 'triplets.' " Do you agree? Illustrate.

5. Two key elements make up a frame. Use an example of your own to illustrate these elements.

6. How can frames be linked? Explain.

7. Write a basic set of three rules showing how rules are constructed. Use at least one AND and OR operator in your rules.

8. Logic has been defined as the study of reasoning. What is the general focus and form of logic? Explain.

9. Define propositional logic. What is its main goal? What operators does it utilize? Be specific.

10. What is the difference between the EQUIVALENT connective and the IMPLIES connective? Illustrate.

11. How is predicate logic related to expert systems? What advantages does it offer?

12. Summarize the pros and cons of decision tables versus decision trees. Under what conditions would you use one tool over the other?

■ EXERCISES AND CASES

1. *Publisher Advisor*

In this project, a procedure unique to knowledge representation was followed. Before creating Publisher Advisor knowledge base in VP-Expert, five questions that an end-user would answer were established. Each question, based on the variables identified in the knowledge acquisition phase, has three possible answers. The questions were presented to the expert to ensure proper wording. A copy of the questions and alternative answers is shown in Figure 11–11.

The induction table included possible combinations of the five variables and their outcomes (acceptance, defer, or reject manuscript). The table was the basis for some of the more detailed case scenarios presented to the expert. It also served as the initial input into the VP-Expert shell for the initial expert system rule generation.

After the initial rules were generated from the induction table, they were combined where possible (using AND and OR statements). After

the basic rules were formulated, the knowledge base was customized. First, it was set to execute in "runtime" mode. Then it was changed to include custom colors, some user instructions, and better-phrased questions for the user to answer. Next, explanation for the user for WHY the information asked for in the system is needed (in a BECAUSE statement). Two sample BECAUSE statements were included to illustrate its use. In a final version, each rule would contain a BECAUSE statement. The first ten rules are listed in Figure 11–12. The knowledge base is listed in Appendix C at the end of the text.

Questions

a. Use the foregoing rules as a guide in developing your own Publisher Advisor. Again, if you are using an induction table, refer to it in representing the knowledge.

b. Do a decision tree to represent the knowledge in the induction table.

Figure 11–11 Publisher Advisor End-User Questions

> a. What is the predicted marketability of the manuscript? (Assessed marketability; predicted demand; is this a hot topic?)
> High   Average   Low
>
> b. What is the author's prior publication record? (Author's published reputation, experience, credibility)
> Strong   Average   Low
>
> c. How would you classify the author's requirements? (Author's requirements for royalty, grants, etc.)
> Prohibitive   High   Average   Low
>
> d. What were the general opinions of the reviewers? (How well the reviewers liked the work; would they adopt it?)
> Strong   Mixed   Low
>
> e. What is the estimated publishing cost of the manuscript?
> High   Average   Affordable

c. Evaluate the following decision tree diagram for Publisher Advisor in Figure 11–13. What do you suggest be done to make it simpler or easier to read? Be specific.

2. *Vacation Advisor*
"One important feature incorporated in Vacation Advisor was the graphics capability. This was used to draw the map of the Caribbean. While this feature is not a necessary part of the knowledge base, it does add a special touch. See Figure 11–14 for a sample of decision trees used prior to knowledge representation." (From Cohen, *Empirical Methods for Artificial Intelligence*, p. 45.)

Question

Based on the material covered in the chapter, how useful are decision trees in Vacation Advisor? Explain.

3. *Residential Real Estate Advisor*
This expert system determines the tax liabilities of buy-and-lease decisions, conducts the preliminary discounted cash flows analysis of buy-and-lease decisions, and recommends the tax and financial strategies to maximize the benefits of the decision made. Evaluate the decision tree in Figure 11–15. How easy is it to read?

4. Develop a set of general frames to represent the following:

- a horse
- a student
- an airline pilot

Use these frames and describe the following:

- Flashdance, an 18-hand thoroughbred
- Brenda, a medium-height, first-year liberal arts student
- Fred, a 30-year veteran airline captain

5. Develop a frame to describe a general bedroom in a home. Make sure the frame is general enough to describe a bedroom in your home.

6. Evaluate the following statements. Some statements can be converted into predicate logic; others cannot. Convert those that can and explain the reasons for those that cannot:

a. Flashdance is a male horse.
b. Horses never have a color of yellow.
c. Most horses are brown.
d. Horses have four legs.
e. Male horses do not give birth.

7. Consider each of the following statements:

a. Adam is a man.
b. All men are humans.

Figure 11–12 Rules of Publisher Advisor

```
RUNTIME;
ACTIONS
        WOPEN 1,2,2,16,74,0
        ACTIVE 1
        DISPLAY "This expert system helps you decide whether to publish a
        book manuscript"
        Press any key to begin the consultation.~"
CLS
FIND Publish
WOPEN 2,13,13,7,48,4
WOPEN 3,14,14,5,46,4
ACTIVE 3
LOCATE 2,2
DISPLAY "The book should be—{#Publish}—for publication
        Press any key to conclude the consultation.~;
RULE O
IF          Marketability = High AND
            Prior_Success = Strong AND
            Author_Req = Low
THEN        Publish = ACCEPTED
        BECAUSE "To know whether a book should be published, it is
        necessary to know the potential marketability of the book, the author's
        prior success with publishing books, the author's requirements for
        compensation, the reviewers' opinions, and the potential production
        costs of the book. Depending on the answers given, in some cases, not
        all this information will be needed.";
RULE 1
IF        Marketability = High AND
          Prior_Success = Strong AND
          Author_Req = Average
THEN      Publish = ACCEPTED
        BECAUSE "To know whether a book should be published, it is
        necessary to know the potential marketability of the book, the author's
        prior success with publishing books, the author's requirements for
        compensation, the reviewers' opinions, and the potential production
        costs of the book. Depending on the answers given, in some cases, not
        all this information will be needed.";
RULE 2
IF        Marketability = High AND
          Prior_Success = Strong AND
          Author_Req = High AND
          Reviewer_Op = Strong AND
          Prod_Costs = Low
THEN      Publish = ACCEPTED CNF 80;
RULE 3
IF        Marketability = High AND
          Prior_Success = Strong AND
          Reviewer_Op = Strong AND
          Prod_Costs = Average OR
          Prod_Costs = High
THEN      Publish = ACCEPTED;
```

Figure 11–12 Rules of Publisher Advisor (continued)

RULE 4
IF   Marketability = High AND
            Prior_Success = Strong AND
            Author_Req = High AND
            Reviewer_Op = Average AND
            Prod_Costs = Low
THEN   Publish = ACCEPTED CNF 65;
RULE 5
IF   Marketability = High AND
            Prior_Success = Strong AND
            Author_Req = High AND
            Reviewer_Op = Average AND
            Prod_Costs = Average OR
            Prod_Costs = High
THEN   Publish = REJECTED;
RULE 6
IF   Marketability = High AND
            Prior_Success = Strong AND
            Author_Req = High AND
            Reviewer_Op = Weak AND
            Prod_Costs = Low
THEN   Publish = REJECTED CNF 75;
RULE 7
IF   Marketability = High AND
            Prior_Success = Strong AND
            Author_Req = High AND
            Reviewer_Op = Weak AND
            Prod_Costs = Average OR
            Prod_Costs = High
THEN   Publish = REJECTED;
RULE 8
IF   Author_Req = Prohibitive
            Publish = REJECTED;
RULE 9
IF   Marketability = High AND
            Prior_Success = Average AND
            Author_Req = Low AND
            Reviewer_Op = Strong
THEN   Publish = ACCEPTED;

c. All humans are beings.

d. Everyone loves someone.

Convert each statement into predicate logic.

8. Convert the following set of facts into predicate logic using the relations: like (x, y), dead (x), sex (x, y), victim (x):

a. John likes Sue.

b. The victim is dead.

c. The victim is male.

d. Larry is the victim.

9. Develop a semantic net based on the following information: Bill is married to Ann

Figure 11–13   *How to Read the Tree Diagram (Publisher Advisor)*

1. The "Q"s correspond to the questions asked the user by the system (i.e., Q1 means question 1 that is "The Marketability of the book is?"). The number that follows the colon is the possible selection (i.e., Q1:2 means "The marketability of the book is moderate.").

2. The >>> leads to the conclusion where the "C"s represent the system's decision (i.e., C2 means choice two "Reject the project"). The number that follows the colon in the conclusion is the CNF (confidence factor).

```
+Q1:1-Q2:1-Q3:1-Q4:1 >>> C2:9
|      |     |        +Q4:2 >>> C3:9
|      |     |        +Q4:3 >>> C3:9
|      |     +Q3:2-Q4:1 >>> C2:9
|      |     |        +Q4:2 >>> C1:9
|      |     |        +Q4:3 >>> C1:9
|      |     +Q3:3-Q4:1 >>> C2:9
|      |     |        +Q4:2 >>> C1:9
|      |     |        +Q4:3 >>> C1:9
|      +Q2:2-Q3:1-Q4:1 >>> C2:8
|      |     |        +Q4:2 >>> C3:9
|      |     |        +Q4:3 >>> C3:9
|      |     +Q3:2-Q4:1 >>> C2:8
|      |     |        +Q4:2 >>> C1:8
|      |     |        +Q4:3 >>> C1:8
|      |     +Q3:3-Q4:1 >>> C2:8
|      |     |        +Q4:2 >>> C1:8
|      |     |        +Q4:3 >>> C1:8
|      +Q2:3-Q3:1-Q4:1 >>> C2:9
|      |     |        +Q4:2 >>> C2:7
|      |     |        +Q4: 3 >>> C2:7
|      |     +Q3: 2-Q4 1 >>> C2: 7
|      |     |        +Q4:2 >>> C1: 6
|      |     |        +Q4:3 >>> C1: 6
|      |     +Q3:3-Q4:1 >>> C2:8
|      |              +Q4:2 >>> C1:8
|      |              +Q4:3 >>> C1:8
+Q1:2-Q2:1-Q3:1-Q4:1 >>> C2:10
|      |     |        +Q4:2 >>> C3:9
|      |     |        +Q4:3 >>> C3:9
|      |     +Q3:2-Q4:1 >>> C2:6
|      |     |        +Q4:2 >>> C1:7
|      |     |        +Q4:3 >>> C1:7
|      |     +Q3:3-Q4:1 >>> C2:6
|      |              +Q4:2 >>> C1:8
|      |              +Q4:3 >>> C1:8
```

Figure 11–14 Travel Consultant Expert System

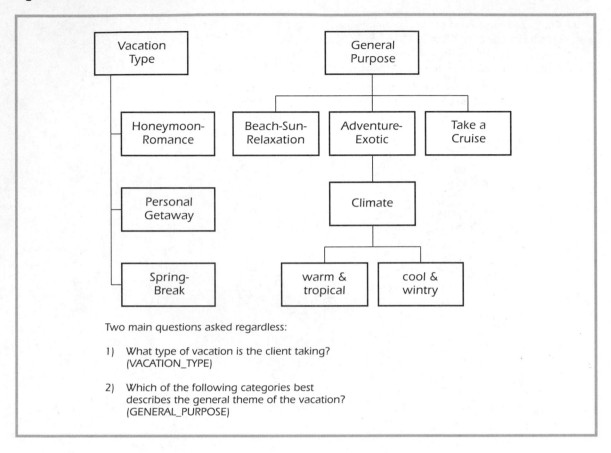

Two main questions asked regardless:

1) What type of vacation is the client taking?
   (VACATION_TYPE)

2) Which of the following categories best
   describes the general theme of the vacation?
   (GENERAL_PURPOSE)

who is Bob's daughter. Bill works for AT&T. Bob owns stocks in General Motors. Bill owns a car made by Chevrolet, a division of General Motors. The car is a blue van, seats five people, and has a television.

▪ SELECTED REFERENCES

Bischofberger, W., and Gustav Pomberger. *Prototyping-Oriented Software Development: Concepts and Tools.* New York: Springer-Verlag, 1992.

Biswas, Pratik and Abraham Kandel. "A Conceptual Tool for the Design and Implementation of Expert System Shells." In *Expert Systems World Congress Proceedings,* Jay Liebowitz, ed. New York; Pergamon Press, 1991, pp. 1491–1500.

Block, Carl H.; Megan R. MacMillan; James Marting; and David E. Monarchi. "A Prototype System for Extracting Objects from Software Specifications." In *Trends and Directions in Expert Systems,* Elias M. Awad, ed. October 31–November 2, 1990, pp. 367–376.

Cohen, Paul R. *Empirical Methods for Artificial Intelligence.* Cambridge, MA: MIT Press, 1995.

Deng, Pi-Sheng. "Automating Knowledge Acquisition and Refinement for Decision Support: A Connectionist Inductive Inference Model." *Decision Sciences (DSI),* March/April 1993, pp. 371–393.

Fickas, Stephen and B. Robert Helm. "Knowledge Representation and Reasoning in the Design of Composite Systems." *IEEE Transactions on Software Engineering (ISO),* June 1992, pp. 470–482.

Gonzalvo, Pilar; Jose J. Canas; and Maria-Teresa Bajo. "Structural Representations in Knowledge Acquisition." *Journal of Educational Psychology,*

Figure 11–14   Travel Consultant Expert System (continued)

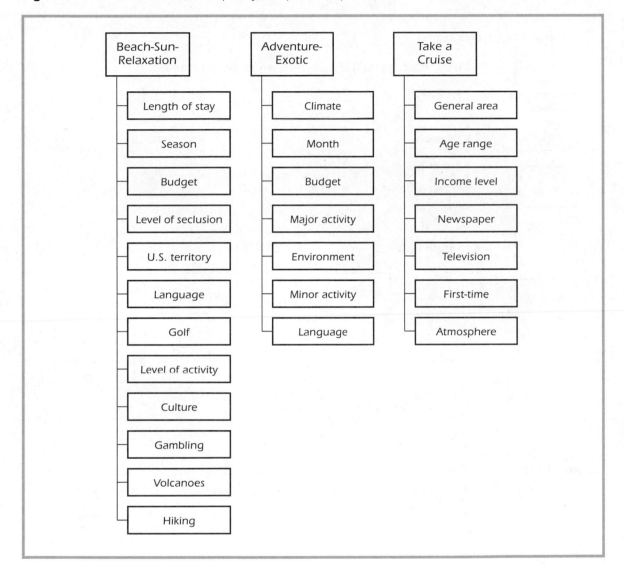

Higa, Kunihiko. "Methodocial Design and Maintenance of Well-Structured Rule Base." In *Trends and Directions in Expert Systems,* Elias M. Awad, ed. October 31–November 2, 1990, pp. 377–395.

Hwang, Soochan and Sukho Lee. "Modelling Semantic Relationships and Constraints in Object-Oriented Databases." In *Trends and Directions in Expert Systems,* Elias M. Awad, ed. October 31–November 2, 1990, pp. 396–416.

Jonassen, David H.; Katherine Beissner; and Michael Yacci. *Structure Knowledge: Techniques for Representing, Conveying, and Acquiring Structural Knowledge.* Hillsdale, NJ: L. Erlbaum Associates, 1993.

Lakemeyer, Gerhard and Bernhard Nebel, eds. *Foundations of Knowledge Representation and Reasoning.* New York; Springer-Verlag, 1994.

Lin, Jing-Yue and Dan Ionescu. "A Controller Approach for Reasoning in a Temporal Logic Framework." In *Expert Systems World Congress Proceedings,* Jay Liebowitz, ed. New York; Pergamon Press, 1991, pp. 1609–1616.

Figure 11–14   Travel Consultant Expert System (continued)

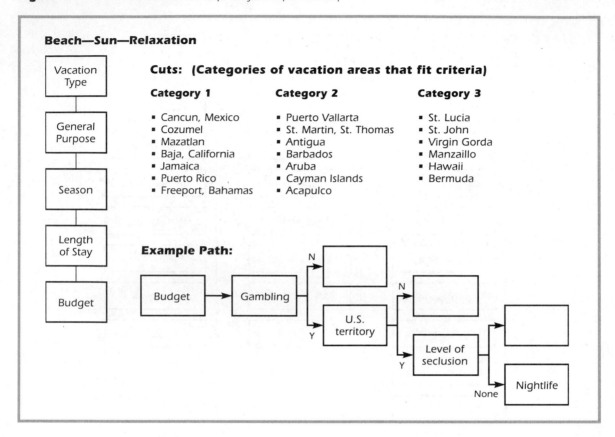

Figure 11–15   Decision Tree Lease FCB

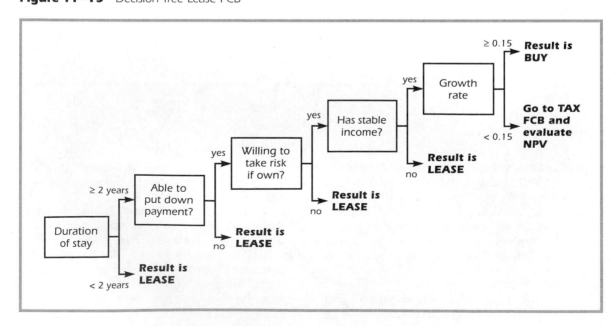

Popescu, Ilie. "A Relational Model for Knowledge Representation In Expert Systems." *Journal of Systems & Software (JSS),* May 1992, pp. 147–155.

Reichgelt, Han. *Knowledge Representation: An AI Perspective.* Norwood, NJ: Ablex, 1991.

Rich, Charles and Yishai A. Feldman. "Seven Layers of Knowledge Representation and Reasoning in Support of Software Development." *IEEE Transactions on Software Engineering (ISO)* 18 (June 1992), pp. 451–469.

Sandewall, Erik. *Features and Fluents: Representation of Knowledge About Dynamical Systems.* Oxford: Clarendon Press, 1994.

Vanthienen, Jan. "Knowledge Acquisition and Validation Using a Decision Table Engineering Workbench." In *Expert Systems World Congress Proceedings,* Jay Liebowitz, ed. New York; Pergamon Press, 1991, pp. 1861–1868.

Willis, Bandler; Mancini Vasco; and Evelyn M. Stiller. "Knowledge Representation for a Consultative System on Urban Problems." In *Expert Systems World Congress Proceedings,* Jay Liebowitz, ed. New York; Pergamon Press, 1991, pp. 828–834.

Chapter ■ 12

Inferencing Strategies and Explanations

COGNITIVE PIONEERING

You can always tell who the pioneers are because they have arrows in their backs and are lying face down in the dirt. AI pioneers are certainly no exception, and the list of companies left along the trail of tears reads like a who's who of early AI success: Lisp Machine Inc., Palladian, and Teknowledge, to name just a few. One of the stalwarts managing to keep one step ahead of the dangers of second-generation intelligent technology is Cognitive Systems of New Haven, Connecticut. The company was founded in 1979 by a group of Yale researchers led by Roger Schank, one of the original AI academic hype-meisters.

THE STARTING LINE

Initially, Cognitive introduced products called "advisory systems," simple expert systems with natural language front ends, designed for nontechnical users. Cognitive's first notable success was a program called *Courtier,* an investment application deployed in Belgium for the Generale Bank to help banking customers make decisions about potential investments. Courtier (called *Le Courtier* in Europe) conducts an interview to collect information about the user's financial situation, and based on the user's preferences and portfolio distribution, it dispenses information on which stocks to hold, purchase, or sell. This expertise is facilitated with information gleaned from the bank's economists and portfolio managers but can also be used by these same experts to assist in reviewing specific client accounts.

A BIG CASE

Cognitive won nearly $2 million as part of a 1987 DARPA contract to develop a case-based reasoning (CBR) shell for use in developing expert systems. When the project finishes up, Cognitive is expected to introduce the CBR shell as a commercial product with 10 applications under its belt. When this happens, the company will offer a case-based reasoning tool to compete with Inference Corp.'s CBR Express.

Why does Cognitive care about case-based reasoning? Well, unlike our traditional rule-based methodologies for creating knowledge bases and intelligent systems, CBR organizes knowledge in terms of examples of past problems and their solutions. These past examples are called—you guessed it—cases.

Case-based reasoning is becoming popular for export systems because it automates applications that are based on precedent (such as the legal system and insurance rates) or contain incomplete causal models. In a rule-based system, this latter situation could result in either an answer built on incomplete data or no answer at all. Case-based methodologies attempt to get around this problem by inputting and analyzing problem data, retrieving a similar case from the case memory, and displaying a solution based on examination of previous cases.

In the process of running a case-based expert system, a significant part of the application is dependent on something called case-based retrieval, which is the finding and matching of similar cases to the one under consideration. For example, take a loan-approval scenario. In a rule-based environment, the user would input data based on a question/answer or fill-in-the-blank scheme. The final tabulation of answers would be put through a series of IF–THEN (or suitably modified structure) analyses until enough rules were fired to provide an answer to the approval question.

On the other hand, a case-based system would take the data and compare it to data already in memory that relates to loan approvals. The answer would be based on the relationship of the problem to the quality level of past cases. If the computer has 50 previous examples of this kind of loan and 48 have defaulted, then it would recommend that the loan be denied. This approach is different from many rule-based procedures because it considers both historical and qualitative data. CBR proponents claim that this process is much closer to human decision making; the rule method, they contend, is more a function of novices learning the procedure until they can rely on their own experience and knowledge of previous cases.

BULLISH ON COGNITIVE

While these examples are an early look at what Cognitive has planned for the future, you could safely claim that CBR will catch on very quickly by exploiting the limitations of rule-based expert systems. So while all the AI pioneers hear hoofbeats, Cognitive has devised a workable strategy that should give it a second wind. But this business is a competitive one, and CBR could become the next great AI hope to be shot down, so Cognitive has to be careful. Just in case.

SOURCE: Harvey P. Newquist III, *AI Expert,* May 1991, pp. 65–66.

AT A GLANCE

One of the unique features of experience is systems inferencing—deriving a conclusion based on statements that only imply the conclusion. Several different reasoning strategies warrant discussion. Reasoning can be viewed as deductive or inductive. Deductive reasoning makes use of major and minor premises to arrive at a conclusion. It generates new knowledge from previously specified knowledge. Induction is reasoning from a given set of facts to general principles—from specific examples to induce general rules.

Rules are processed according to two inferencing strategies: backward chaining or forward chaining. Backward chaining is appropriate for scheduling and monitoring. Forward chaining is appropriate for diagnostic applications such as making changes to a corporate pension fund. It is ideal when the expert system has to respond to new data. Backward chaining is best known for its efficiency, since it follows a definite path toward a useful conclusion.

Of the other reasoning strategies, case-based reasoning (CBR) deserves special consideration for applications in which rule-based systems are not as practical—for example, diagnosing machinery failure. The approach relies on large chunks of knowledge in the form of episodes or cases, whose solutions are used to resolve present cases. In a computer-based environment, CBR maintenance is easier than that of a rule-based system. Also, CBR allows the reasoner to come up with solutions to problems quickly rather than starting from scratch. Yet, CBR has limitations. For example, there is no general representation procedures for reasoning by analogy. Another problem is maintenance of appropriate indexes.

What You Will Learn _____

By the end of this chapter, you should know the following:

1. The concepts of logic and reasoning.
2. The function of backward chaining and forward chaining.
3. The distinction between inductive and deductive reasoning.
4. Key inferencing strategies.
5. The features and potential of case-based reasoning.

The discovery of penicillin began with a single observation. Sir Alexander Fleming noticed that bacteria had been destroyed on a culture plate which had been lying around for a couple of weeks. In fact, a chain of coincidences had led to their destruction. "Chance," as Pasteur said, "favors the prepared mind."
Fleming was prepared. He knew that the bacteria were hardy, and so he reasoned that something must have killed them:
Events of this type do not normally happen.
An event of this type has happened.
Therefore, there is some agent that caused the event.

—Philip N. Johnson-Laird,
The Computer and the Mind (Cambridge, MA: Harvard University Press, 1988), p. 234.

■ INTRODUCTION

Chapter 11 examined a variety of ways to represent knowledge. Once the knowledge base is built, the expert system can begin to make inferences. **Inferencing** means deriving a conclusion based on statements that only imply that conclusion. The most common forms of inferencing are backward chaining and forward chaining. Most expert systems today do backward chaining. A smaller percentage use forward chaining. Still other systems combine backward chaining and forward chaining and apply object-oriented methods of programming.

The program that manages the strategies for controlling the application of knowledge is the **inference engine.** It is the reasoning component that decides when certain inference rules should be accessed or fired (executed). The pattern it follows depends on whether the search is goal-driven or data-driven, referred to as backward chaining and forward chaining, respectively. Other categories of reasoning are considered within this chapter as well.

Humans reason in a variety of ways:

1. *Reasoning by analogy:* relating one concept to another. For example, a battery is analogous to a reservoir. Both are used to store and provide energy for power.

2. *Formal reasoning:* using deductive or inductive methods. Deductive reasoning takes known principles and applies them to instances to infer some sort of a conclusion. Inductive reasoning is reasoning from a given set of facts to general principles.

3. *Heuristic reasoning:* using IF. . .THEN rules.

4. *Representation strategies:* allowing certain information to be organized in a specific fashion.

5. *Serendipity:* discovering through luck or thinking about one problem, leading to the solution of another problem of a greater potential or magnitude.

6. *Synergy:* putting "two and two" together and ending up with a result greater than the sum of the parts.

Of these sources, serendipity and synergy are the most difficult for the computer to emulate. This chapter, however, focuses on the role of representation in reasoning, including the various categories of human reasoning, reasoning with logic and rules and case-based reasoning, and explanation concepts and strategies.

In approaching reasoning strategies, one must keep in mind the complexity of programming expert systems. Expert systems are built from symbolic knowledge or a set of heuristics running on a computer that uses numbers rather than symbols. Take this fictitious dialogue between the expert system programmer and the computer:

PROGRAMMER: Look here, computer, I want you to follow my rules and instructions carefully, read the stated goals and review the knowledge I have laid out for you as to when an applicant qualifies for a car loan. When I feed you the information you need, I want you to give your best answer. If you advise against a loan, I want you to explain to me your reasons.

COMPUTER: O.K. dude, that's what I'm here for. (A few microseconds fly by, reading and digesting the input.) Wait a minute, Super Hacker. What kinds of rules did you store in this fancy knowledge base? Let me give you an example. Here is a rule that says "IF assets > $200,000, THEN it is likely that applicant qualifies for a Toyota Camry." Just what is "likely"? What do you mean by Toyota? What is Camry? I need more precise statements than these. I can't handle this kind of fuzziness or loose statements. Get your act together. As far as I'm concerned, take these statements back to the drawing board. If you leave things as is, I can't guarantee what I might come up with. Here you ask me to give you my best shot and look what headache I'm facing to start with. Have you reviewed my role in your organization lately?

Of course, computers do not talk back with that much intelligence or common sense. The truth lies in the reasoning capabilities of the inference engine. The main point is that expert systems are built around facts and rules based on common sense, while for the computer to do the work, virtually every statement, rule, or procedure must have the exactness of a digital formula. We will review the reasoning strategies used by the computer to give a clear picture of how it reads and processes knowledge.

■ HOW HUMANS REASON

Some reasoning techniques cut across more than one category. For example, common-sense reasoning is a combination of analogical and inductive reasoning. For people to act sensibly in this world, they must know something about it and use their knowledge well. Possessing common knowledge about the world and making obvious inferences from this knowledge is what is called **common sense.** For example, consider the old riddle:

> Brothers and sisters have I none,
> But that man's father is my father's son.

Drawing the conclusion, "That man is my son," may be viewed as an inference from the riddle based on our knowledge of relationships between brothers and sisters, parents and children, and so on.

Reasoning is the process of applying knowledge to arrive at solutions. To reason is to think clearly and logically, to draw reasonable inferences or conclusions from known or assumed facts. It works through the interaction of rules and data. Common sense involves many subtle modes of reasoning and a vast human knowledge base with complex interactions. Most of what humans know and the conscious thinking that they normally do have their roots in common sense.

A person who read in the newspaper

> The victims were stabbed to death in a dance hall in the mall. The suspect was on a nonstop flight to Chicago when the murder occurred.

would probably conclude that the suspect was innocent. This typical day-to-day reasoning illustrates two important phenomena:

1. Reasoning depends not just on the premise but also on general knowledge. In the example, the suspect could not be in two places at the same time. There are no dance halls onboard flights to Chicago (or anywhere).

2. People generally draw informative conclusions. Although a number of valid conclusions may follow from any set of premises, most of them are probably trivial.

No one can say precisely what mental processes lead to the conclusion that the suspect is innocent, because humans can only observe the results of another's conscious thoughts. In any case, people take for granted that deduction depends on a mental logic containing rules of inference based on experience.

Reasoning with Logic

The notion of reasoning, is frequently associated logic. **Logic** is the scientific study of reasoning and the set of rules and procedures used in the reasoning process. Chapter 11 discussed logic-based representation and how facts are represented in a symbolic form. The process of reasoning involves making inferences from known facts. To infer means to draw as a conclusion, to conclude or decide from something known or assumed. To execute deductive or inductive reasoning, the human mind follows reasoning rules that allow the execution of logical expressions resulting in new expressions. Predicate logic provides rules of inference for performing logical inferences. The best known rule of inference is modus ponens.

Modus ponens (meaning affirmative mode) is a common rule for deriving new facts from existing rules and known facts. It is a rule of inference used in proof procedures and an intuitive way of conducting the reasoning process. According to modus ponens, if the statements a and $(a \rightarrow b)$ are known to be true, then one can infer that b is true.

Here is a real-life example. If someone is sick and misses work, the event is represented in predicate logic as

$\forall X, [\text{Sick}(X) \rightarrow \text{Miss work}(X)]$

If the statement Sick(Alan) is found, then through modus ponens, one can infer miss_work(alan). This reasoning is common sense to humans but, unfortunately, not to the computer. A computer must be told in clear terms how to make inferences like modus ponens.

Another important rule of inference is **modus tolens.** It states that if $(a \rightarrow b)$ is known to be true and b is false, then a is false. Considering the example, if the relationship $(\forall x, [\text{Sick}(X) \rightarrow \text{miss-work}(X)]$ is true, and if Alan does not miss work, then he was not sick. This notion is represented in predicate logic as

$\sim$ miss_work(alan)

Through modus tolen, it implies $\sim$ sick(alan).

After understanding how modus ponens and modus tolen provide the basis for making inferences, the next step is to know the reasoning methods to be applied to a given set of principles. A number of other methods are available to make deductions or to prove the truth or falsity of various propositions. They are complex in computation and require detailed knowledge of logic to function properly; therefore, they will not be explored in detail here. The next section explains deductive and inductive reasoning methods.

Deductive Reasoning

Reasoning can be viewed either as analytic/deductive or heuristic/inductive. **Deductive reasoning** is also called exact reasoning, because it deals with exact facts and exact conclusions. *Webster's* defines deduction as "reasoning from a known principle to an unknown, from the general to the specific, or from a premise to a logical conclusion." Charniak defines deduction as "logically correct inference," which means that deductions from true premises will surely result in true conclusions. For example,

IF Fred is taller than Nancy AND Nancy is taller than Sarah,
THEN Fred is taller than Sarah.

Another example:

IF mothers are women AND Sarah is a mother,
THEN Sarah is a woman.

Certain knowledge is easy to represent in a rule within the framework of a knowledge-based system. For example, "IF a first-class letter has a stamp less than 32 cents, THEN it must be returned to sender." Expert system programs have been written to capture this type of human expertise. Such programs use rules to produce solutions to particular problems that were once solved by human experts.

Another way of using deductive reasoning is to use general principles to obtain a specific inference or to take known principles (or a rule that is true in general) and apply them to instances to infer some sort of conclusion. Some general principles, however, cannot be quantified; they may be assertions or beliefs that people think of as true.

Deduction makes use of major and minor premises. Almost any argument can be formed using this type of reasoning process. Here are a few examples:

1. *Major premise:*   Each titanium coil leaving the mill must be 100% quality tested.

   Minor premise: One part of the coil has not passed the test.

   Conclusion: The entire coil should be rejected.

2. *General principle:* Total charge on car repair is the sum of labor cost, price of parts, and sales tax on parts.

   Therefore: Total charge on a 3-hour labor at $40/hr., parts costing $100, and 4% sales tax is $224.

3. *Major premise:*   In Turkey, all citizens get a pension from age 60 on.

   Minor premise: Kamal Elberlik is a citizen of Turkey, aged 60 years.

   Conclusion: Elberlik is receiving a pension.

As evident from the examples, the idea behind deductive reasoning is to generate new knowledge from previously specified knowledge. If the original rule is true, then the deduction will be valid. If a knowledge base uses only **deductive inference** and the information assimilated is true, then one can depend on all the inferred conclusions to be valid. Unfortunately, much of common sense reasoning is nondeductive by nature.

Inductive Reasoning

Induction works the other way around. It is reasoning from a set of facts or individual cases to a general conclusion—from specific examples to induce general rules. **Inductive reasoning** is the basis of scientific discovery. The basic form is:

P(a) is true.
P(b) is true.

By induction, we can conclude that $\forall x, P(x)$ is true. For example, if a person travels to a small town and sees a blue and white taxi several times, the person may infer the rule, "In this town, taxis are blue and white." Referring to the earlier example under modus ponens, if the personnel manager keeps track of Alan's absence record and finds out that whenever he misses work, he is sick, then the manager can infer that Alan misses work when he is sick.

Consider the following examples:

1. *Premise:*   Chronic unemployment causes social problems.
   Premise: Illiteracy causes social problems.
   Premise: Recession causes social problems.
   Premise: Drug traffic causes social problems.

   Conclusion: Chronic unemployment, illiteracy, recession, and drug traffic cause social problems.

2. *Premise:*   He is an avid fisherman.
   Premise: He is an avid hunter.
   Premise: He is an avid mountain climber.

   Conclusion: He likes outdoor sports.

3. *Premise:*   Admission depends on status.
  Premise: Admission depends on race.
  Premise: Admission depends on appearance.
  Premise: Admission depends on financial wealth.

  Conclusion: Admission is subjective.

In each example, the inference is an induction: it goes from a finite number of instance to a conclusion about every member of a class.

The major difference between induction and deduction is that induction satisfies a set of constraints rather than establishing a given assertion. Inductive systems are also less likely to be as accurately formulated as deductive systems. For example, if one were asked to give the next number in the sequence, 1, 2, 4, 8,. . ., most people will give "16" without any computation. In induction, a problem often has more than one answer.

Induction is used in expert systems when experts cannot easily articulate their knowledge. In this case, induction is valuable if examples create decision-making patterns. Box 12–1 illustrates a situation in which the knowledge engineer (KE) has difficulty eliciting knowledge from the domain expert (DE). Similar knowledge can be acquired from past examples or cases, if they exist. The knowledge engineer tries to extract the information that needs to be considered. Table 12–1 identifies line speed, age, and temperature of a motor as the main decision factors. Examples of past events that relate decision factor values to the status of the motor are listed in Table 12–2. The value for each decision factor in Table 12–1 is based on the evidence in Table 12–2. In this situation, induction, distilled diagnostic knowledge from examples, which is comparable in precision to knowledge elicited from experts during an interview.

Box 12–1   Use of Induction in Eliciting Expert Knowledge

KE: How do you know if the problem is with the assembly-line motor?

DE: Well, it is really difficult to describe.

KE: (In a nervous voice) Please try.

DE: I consider several factors, but it is really complicated.

KE: (In a very nervous voice) What are the factors?

DE: The motor's temperature and age, and . . . oh yeah, speed of the line are important issues to consider.

KE: (With pen poised) How do you consider these factors?

DE: I don't really know, but we keep records of these things so that if we have problems, we can go back and try to figure out what went wrong. Could you use these records?

KE: Yes!

In such a difficult knowledge solicitation interview, the knowledge engineer (KE) can obtain the knowledge from past examples. If some exist, the project might stay on course by using an induction technique.

Source: John Durkin, "Designing an Induction Expert System," *AI Expert,* December 1991, p. 29.

■ **Table 12–1**   Value of Diagnostic Elements

Diagnosis Elements			Result
Line Speed	Age	Temperature	Motor
low	old	high	bad
normal	new	normal	good
high	average	low	good

■ **Table 12–2**   Decision Table Based on Past Examples

Diagnostic Elements			Result
Line Speed	Age	Temperature	Motor
low	old	high	bad
low	old	normal	bad
normal	new	normal	good
normal	old	high	bad
high	old	high	bad
high	new	normal	good
normal	new	normal	good
low	new	high	bad
low	new	high	bad

Once the induction is completed, rules can easily be derived for building the knowledge base (in this example, motor diagnosis).

Induction usually produces results without explanation. It is unbiased and makes no false assumptions. It can also discover rules of which the expert is unaware. The main disadvantage of inductive reasoning is it does not guarantee valid results for examples other than those in the premises. So, inductive reasoning must deal with **uncertainty** or lack of adequate information, in obtaining conclusions.

■ INFERENCING WITH RULES: BACKWARD AND FORWARD CHAINING

Most commercial expert systems have an inferencing component that uses the modus ponens procedure via the rule interpreter. In fact, the principle of chaining is governed by modus ponens. For example, take the basic rule:

IF Jane is an hourly employee AND assets are less than $4,000
THEN do not approve loan

The expert system might ask Jane if she is an hourly or salaried employee. It also asks the value of her assets. The information received is stored in the premise part of rule (IF Jane . . .) to determine the truth or falsity of the premise.

If the premise is true, then the rule "fires" or is executed. In the example, the rule fires when both the employee status is hourly AND Jane's assets (of course, they are verified) are under $4,000. As a result, the conclusion part of the rule, "do not approve loan," is added to the assertion part of the knowledge base. This conclusion could be used later to trigger the firing of other rules in the knowledge base.

The premise or conclusion of every rule in the knowledge base can be checked against existing assertions. Checking is done using one of two inferencing strategies: backward chaining and forward chaining. They are part of the inference engine, or the reasoning component supplied with the shell. The inference engine examines the knowledge base using an inferencing strategy to achieve a goal as instructed.

Backward Chaining

Each of the inferencing strategies is appropriate for different aspects of problem solving. With **backward chaining,** the system works from the goal by chaining rules together to reach a conclusion or achieve a goal. In other words, it starts with the goal and then looks for all the relevant, supporting processes that lead to achieving the goal. Backward chaining is **goal-driven.** The spotlight is on the **action** part of the rule—the goal. (In EXSYS, it is called the choice.) Backward chaining goes from the premise of the "goal" rule to the conclusions of another rule, to the premise of that same rule, on to another conclusion, and so on.

Someone likened backward chaining to Sherlock Holmes' investigative skills. Sherlock Holmes starts with the victim at the scene of the crime. The goal is to determine the guilty party. He then worked backwards tracing footsteps, fingerprints, a broken window, and other clues to evaluate supporting evidence (data). Actually, Mr. Holmes might have a set of rules in his mind that he follow such as:

```
R1: IF door is 'open' AND Alvarez is out-of-town,
    THEN guilty_party is 'Jose.'
R2: IF key is 'used'
    THEN door is 'open.'
    .
    .
    .
R7: IF axe is 'used'
    THEN door is 'broken'.
```

The procedure used in backward chaining is illustrated in the knowledge base shown in Figure 12–1.

The procedure in backward chaining is as follows:

1. The inference engine starts by assuming the conclusion "Action needed pay the bill" as the possible solution to the *goal,* rule 5. It will try to answer the question, "Under what conditions should the bill be paid?"

2. The next step is to prove the premise of rule 5. It looks at each rule in the knowledge base to find the action part of a rule that matches the premise of rule 5. It finds it in rule 3.

3. The inference engine goes to rule 3 and looks for the action part of a rule that matches the premise of rule 3. It finds it in rule 1.

Figure 12–1 Backward Chaining in Partial Knowledge Base

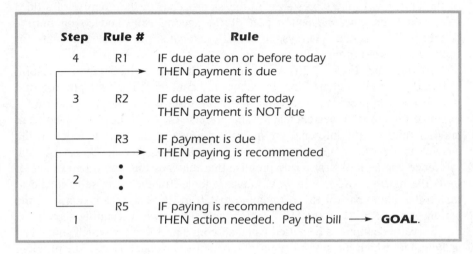

Step	Rule #	Rule
4	R1	IF due date on or before today THEN payment is due
3	R2	IF due date is after today THEN payment is NOT due
	R3	IF payment is due THEN paying is recommended
2		• • •
1	R5	IF paying is recommended THEN action needed. Pay the bill ⟶ **GOAL**.

4. The systems tries to prove the premise of rule 1. Since no other rule's action matches the premise of rule 1, in this case, the inference engine asks the user, "What is today's date?" Whatever it is, the default message would be "Today's date is due date."

During this process, the controller of the inference engine terminates execution of backward chaining when the goal has been resolved or the rules have been executed. The controller selects a rule, it calls **Resolve** to find the value for any uninstantiated variable. If the variable is still unresolved when the inference engine returns to the resolve process, then either the rules that fired failed to instantiate the goal or no rules were found that established a value for the goal. At that point, the Resolver portion of the inference engine asks the user for a value. In rule 1 of the example the Resolver asked the user for "today's date," which it then labeled "due date."

Forward Chaining

Instead of starting with a goal and working back to the necessary data, **forward chaining,** begins with known data and works forward to see if any conclusions (new information) can be drawn. The rules chain forward rather than backward, and are therefore considered **data-driven.** It can also provide explanation for any conclusions in terms of the rule that was used to deduce it.

To explain forward chaining, take the story of Columbus discovering America. Queen Isabella of Spain commanded Columbus in 1492 to "go out and explore." Columbus started out with certain data—navigational skills, data about past explorations such as the concept of the earth as round, and so on. There was no notion of a goal. The concept behind "discover" is "the unknown." The rest of the story is familiar. By starting with known data and traveling through a chain of known routes, Columbus stumbled onto a new territory he called America.

In forward chaining, the spotlight is on the **premise.** The process does not "care" what happens to the action part. The action part is only the means to the next premise in the process. In other words, it chains forward from the premise of one rule, looking for the premise of another rule that matches the action part of the first rule. In the next step the process proceeds to the premise of a third rule, which matches the action part of the second rule, and so on until a conclusion is reached. The system actually executes the actin statements for each rule whose premise is true.

To illustrate, Figure 12–2 uses the same example about paying the bill. Forward chaining systems begin by requesting data that match the premise of a rule. If the data provided do not match the premise of the rule, the next rule is examined in order to locate a match. The premise of R1 cannot be proved from another rule. So, the inference engine asks the user if due date is today. If the answer is yes, then, no additional information is gathered. Otherwise, the inference engine looks for a rule premise that matches the action part of R1. It finds the match in R3. As its next move, it looks for the premise of a rule to match the action part of R3. It finds the match in R5. The conclusion is in the action part of R5, "Pay the bill," which ends the forward chaining search.

Forward chaining is best used when solving a problem for which some data is available, which the system can use in reaching its conclusions. The problem with this inferencing strategy is its lack of basis for choosing one such path over another. It could search the entire knowledge base before it comes up with an answer.

A comparative summary of backward and forward chaining is provided in Table 12–3. One of the strongest attributes of backward chaining is its efficiency, since it follows a definitive path to a useful conclusion. It will follow a chain of steps even when the user knows in advance that it will fail.

In contrast, forward chaining fires rules in a somewhat unpredictable order, based solely on the premise being satisfied. The inference engine will respond to known premises, regardless of how well they have been identified as goals, and will potentially use considerable processing time. Backward chaining only responds to circumstances relevant to the goal it is trying to satisfy.

Forward chaining is ideal when the expert system has to respond to new data or to come up with a solution based on investigation of many alternatives that generate too many outcomes to list individually as goals.

Figure 12–2 Forward Chaining in Partial Knowledge Base

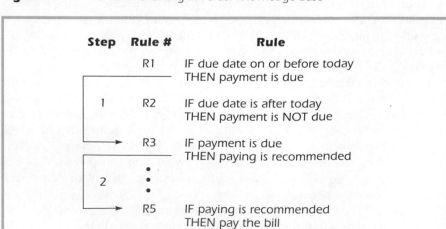

■ **Table 12–3** Comparative Summary of Backward and Forward Chaining

Attribute	Backward Chaining	Forward Chaining
Also known as	Goal-driven	Data-driven
Starts from	Possible conclusion	New data
Processing	Efficient	Somewhat wasteful
Aims for	Necessary data	Any conclusion(s)
Approach	Conservative/cautious	Opportunistic
Practical if	Number of possible final answers is reasonable or a set of known alternatives is available	Combinatorial explosion creates an infinite number of possible right answers
Appropriate for	Scheduling and monitoring	Diagnostic applications
Example of application	Selecting a specific type of investment	Making changes to a corporate pension fund

Opportunistic Reasoning

Sometimes the logical processing for a problem requires a combination of backward and forward chaining. For example, in providing advice on the status of a pension fund, a system might forward chain with the portfolio to pick out all possible future strategies, backward chain to select one strategy, and forward chain to identify possible investment opportunities under the selected strategy. This third reasoning strategy used in knowledge-based shells combines forward and backward chaining is called **opportunistic reasoning.** It uses forward chaining to draw conclusions from existing data and backward chaining to find data that make it possible to generate the solution. Among the shells that promote opportunistic reasoning is IBM's TIRS (**T**he **I**ntegrated **R**easoning **S**hell).

■ MODEL-BASED REASONING

In many applications, especially those involving the diagnosis of machines, rule-based systems are not so practical. These systems were never suited to industrial-monitoring applications. For example, in the event of a machinery failure, a rule-based system tries to associate a relationship between a set of sensor data and a particular fault. Sensor data can be inaccurate and a rule-based system is generally unable to verify the data before comparing them to the standard.

The alternative approach to diagnostic and monitoring-oriented problems is **model-based reasoning** or model-based expert systems. These systems contain a model simulating the function of the machinery under diagnosis. Not only do they reason from observable values, but they know the machinery's internal processes and can judge which aspect of the machine generates the values. In contrast, a rule-based system simply remembers a stored association between sensor values and the system's expected state.

With model-based reasoning, the model-based system receives observed sensor data from the machine in operation and compares it with the predicted simulation values, setting off an alarm or transmitting a message whenever the actual value is beyond the predetermined range of tolerance. The alarm forces immediate diagnosis, depending on the nature of the fault. In this respect, the model-based system will reason about what could go wrong with the simulated data as it compares it to the real data coming from the machine.

One benefit of a model-based system is providing comprehensive treatment of mechanical-fault diagnosis on the spot in real-time mode. In contrast, a rule-based expert system requires regular maintenance and updating by the human expert. It relies on the human expert's experience regarding common failures; uncommon failures may not be properly diagnosed. A model-based system can reason and diagnose both common and uncommon failures. No complete and accurate model of the human body exists; and because of the uniqueness of individuals and the resulting infinite number of variables, model-based reasoning would not be applicable to diagnosing human diseases. Similarly, with systems that change constantly—such as weather forecasting—model-based reasoning would not be appropriate.

■ CASE-BASED REASONING

Suppose a person was diagnosed with a condition that required major surgery. How would that person choose a surgeon? People tend to prefer an older surgeon with years of practical experience over someone fresh out of residency. The young surgeon might be well versed on book knowledge, but experience is a better predictor of success among surgeons. Their experience is judged by the number of cases they have handled and the success of each of those cases.

Case-based reasoning (CBR) is the latest trend in expert systems development and has a number of applications, such as TRUCKER, in Box 12–2. The idea of reasoning from relevant past cases is attractive, because it is so similar to the process human experts often use to solve problems successfully. The process of choosing a surgeon indicates the perceived importance of case experience in expert problem solving. Manipulating past problem-solving examples is critical in domains such as law, medical diagnosis, prediction, design, and process control. (See Box 12–3 for an example of CBR in process control.) Since experts tend to forget over time, capturing these cases in the computer means reaping future benefits from past successes (and failures) of experts' work. This is the ultimate goal of CBR.

Definition

For years, knowledge engineers have claimed that human experts reason about a problem by recalling similar cases encountered in the past. In fact, they reason by analogy—the expert tries to figure out how one case is similar (or dissimilar) to other cases solved in the past. A **case** is knowledge at an operational level. It is an episodic description of a problem and its associated solution.

CBR systems use an existing case's solution and adapt it to solve a new problem. An expert also relies on previous cases for solving a current problem through a process of recalling the closest cases in memory, making inferences based on comparisons of the cases, and asking questions when inferences cannot be made. From an algorithmic view, CBR is a technique that records and documents cases and then searches the appropriate cases to determine their

Box 12–2   TRUCKER

TRUCKER is an opportunistic case-based reasoner that integrates planning and execution in a realistic planning situation—it lacks perfect information about its world, and it is not always allowed to take its plant to completion before new goals arise. Its domain is UPS-type pick-up and delivery scheduling. It begins with a set of items it must deliver and/or pick up, and it plans a route for doing that. As it carries out its plan, it is informed of additional pickups and deliveries that it must do (new goals). Based on its knowledge of where it is, where it intends to be later in its plan, and which locations are close to each other, it integrates the new instructions into its plan, grabbing the opportunity to address each as it becomes viable. From its successes, TRUCKER learns new routs through town that allow it to efficiently schedule multiple orders in disparate locations (i.e., plans for achieving conjunctive goals).

The mechanism that allows TRUCKER to opportunistically schedule new orders relies on a combination of its map, its current plan, and its memory of the way it has carried out plans in the past. Memory is used to remember past plans that are reused in new circumstances. In addition, its current plan it broken up and put into memory in pieces (each corresponding to a subgoal), each one indexed by the conditions under which it can successfully be carried out. This way, if the opportunity to carry out a later part of the plan arrives earlier than anticipated, TRUCKER can notice the opportunity and take advantage of it. This conception of memory is called "opportunistic memory."

SOURCE: Janet Kolodner, *Case-Based Reasoning* (San Mateo, CA.: Morgan Kaufman, 1993), p. 628.

usefulness in solving new cases presented to the expert. See Box 12–4 for an illustration of human CBR in which the reasoner (the father who is also an attorney) uses previous cases similar to the current case as precedence to get the judge to dismiss the case.

Day-to-day examples of CBR are numerous:

- A doctor sees a patient with unusual symptoms. The doctor remembers previous patients with similar symptoms and prescribes the old diagnosis as a solution.

- An auto mechanic facing an unusual electrical problem is likely to recall other similar cases involving the same year or make and consider whether the old solution corrects the present one.

- When updating a corporate pension fund an estate planning attorney relies on previous pension funding experience to expedite the completion of the present one.

Referring to old cases is especially advantageous when dealing with recurring situations. But because no old case is exactly the same as the new one, old solutions must often be adapted to fit a new case. In every case some reasoning and some learning are involved. The success rate of problem solving improves with recurring CBR.

Box 12–3   CBR at Lockheed

Lockheed and other aerospace companies use composite materials (such as Graphite-Epoxy) to make parts for airplanes, satellites, and missiles. These composite parts must be cured in an autoclave, a large pressure- and temperature-adjustable convection oven, for four to eight hours. Since curing time is long and schedules are short, as many parts as possible must be put into the autoclave in each run. Yet for all the parts to be cured properly at the end of the eight hours, they must all heat up at the same rate. The heat-up characteristics of a given part are affected not only by the thickness and composition of that part but where it is positioned in the oven (air currents inside the autoclave create pockets of colder and warmer spots in the oven). The cost of the parts can run into the thousands of dollars, so accuracy and consistency in configuring parts in the autoclave is important. The main difficulty in automating this kind of task is that the knowledge used to configure parts in the oven is not well understood.

The only way to know if a given configuration will work is to run it. Because this task was oriented toward trial and error, the human experts used pictures of past successful configurations to help them load the autoclave. This was a tailor-made application for CBR.

Lockheed built a case-based system called *Clavier* to configure composite parts inside an autoclave for maximum performance and throughput. This task would have been difficult to perform from scratch using a rule-based approach because of the difficulty in representing and understanding the impact of all the spatial issues in configuring an autoclave load. By using successful past cases, the system could circumvent representing the spatial information at the detail level necessary to perform the configuration task from scratch. All it needed to know was if a particular part was in a particular place in the autoclave in a prior layout that was successfully cured. The spatial knowledge used by the human experts to configure loads was defined in each case. Clavier is currently in use at Lockheed's Sunnyvale Plant.

SOURCE: Ralph Barletta, "An Introduction to Case-Based Reasoning," *AI Expert,* August 1991, p. 49.

The Origin of CBR

CBR has a number of sources. Most people credit Roger Schank for introducing CBR to the commercial market. Schank's 1982 work, *Dynamic Memory* illustrated a memory-based approach to reasoning using the computer. The idea was later carried out by some of his students at Yale University and graduate students at other schools such as Georgia Tech and the University of Massachusetts. These systems demonstrated CBR's role in law, labor mediation, medicine, and other disciplines.

An important source of CBR is machine learning that focuses on techniques by which computers learn from refinement of the stored knowledge called "experience." See Figure 12–3.

One of the first CBR expert systems tools, called Expert Ease, was built by Donald Michie, University of Edinburgh, Scotland. Its induction algorithm takes a series of examples and creates a matrix that lists the attributes and their respective outcome. Then, each case that is solved is listed, one case per line,

Box 12–4   Human Case-Based Reasoning: Reasoning with the Judge

An attorney's 16-year old son was issued a speeding ticket for driving 72 mph in a 65 mph zone. The young man vehemently denied going that fast, yet the radar report unmistakably indicated a speeding violation. Father and son were scheduled to appear in Juvenile court later that month.

The week before the scheduled court date, the father went to court. He talked to parents waiting outside the court room. He sat in on several cases to size up the judge and plot strategy for defending his son's case. Every parent he talked to, case after case, indicated the judge almost never let the juvenile off the hook. Penalties ranged from a $60 fine to suspension of the driver's license. The judge dismissed only one case. The father decided to use it as the basis for his son's defense. Meanwhile, he reviewed more than 40 cases heard by the judge plotting his final strategy.

On the scheduled court date, father and son appeared before the judge:

Judge: Young man, how do you plead?

Son: No contest, your honor.

Judge: It sounds like you've been coached. Officer, let's hear your report. (The officer goes through the ritual of showing the radar report, etc.)

Judge: Young man, tell this court your story.

Son: Your honor, it is impossible to go exactly 65 mph. While driving, I kept looking at the speedometer. I know I was not driving at 72 mph as indicated in the citation.

Judge: (look at the father) Sir, are you the father?

Father: Yes, I am.

Judge: Do you have anything to say before I give my decision?

Father: Your honor, we have no quarrel with the radar as an electronic system. I would like to submit as evidence this young man's academic record (all As) and extraordinary accomplishments (Eagle Scout, president of his class, etc.). A number of cases have been brought before this court to mitigate the severity of the charge. For example, in the case of *Jane Maloney v. Commonwealth of Massachusetts* and *Bill Croll v. Commonwealth of Massachusetts.*

Judge: (quickly scans the record as he remembered both cases cited). Bailiff! Hand the driver's license to this boy's father. (To the father) Sir, you are to keep your son's license for 10 days. Next time, bring your checkbook with you. Case dismissed.

---

providing for each attribute listed and then identifying the outcome. Expert Ease is the only surviving induction tool that is available on today's market.

Currently, many machine learning researchers are concentrating on reasoning by analogy, which is the type of algorithm used in CBR to determine how one case compares with another and to find the best match. See Box 12–5 for an example. In the mid 1980s, Schank formed a company, Cognitive Systems, to develop text-scanning systems. One of the early systems scanned electronic news reports on terrorist events, resulting in a knowledge base about terrorists. Throughout the 1980s, Schank and his colleagues began working on the computer's ability to reason about present cases from previous ones.

Figure 12–3 Sources of Case-Based Reasoning

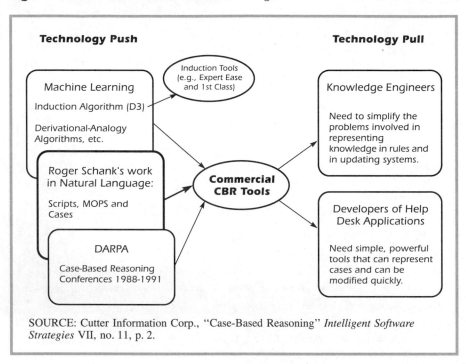

SOURCE: Cutter Information Corp., "Case-Based Reasoning" *Intelligent Software Strategies* VII, no. 11, p. 2.

Comparison of CBR and Rule-Based Systems

One obvious advantage of CBR over rule-based systems is its time savings. Knowledge engineers can spin their wheels in manually acquiring knowledge from human experts for building the expert system. In CBR, less time is needed to retrieve representative cases for performing knowledge engineering. CBR allows the reasoner to come up with solutions to problems quickly, without starting from scratch. CBR is most advantageous when rules are difficult to formulate and when cases are readily available, particularly when the domain expert is uncertain, not available, inconsistent, or uncooperative.

Another advantage is its maintenance requirements. In rule-based systems, the cost of maintaining and enhancing the system stem from the difficulty in structuring rules into a workable system. In CBR, maintenance entails simply adding more cases that offer features similar to the case in question. For example, a feature of Cognitive System's CBR automatically indexes new cases for immediate use.

Although most rule-based systems are based on information derived from examples, they can only use the existing set of rules (without the examples) that led to the decision or solution. A CBR justifies its answers by listing the set of rules used in addition to citing the examples that support the rules.

Limitations and Potential

No technique is completely free of limitations. With CBR, cases age. Unless one can update through a stream of recent cases, validation becomes a problem.

Box 12–5   SMART System

An example of a deployed CBR customer service application is Compaq Computer's SMART system. SMART is an integrated call-tracking and problem-resolution system that contains hundreds of cases related to diagnostic problems arising in the use of Compaq products. . . . Incoming customer problems are presented to SMART, which retrieves the most similar case from its case base and presents them to the customer service analyst, who then uses them to resolve the problem. Evaluation of the initial version of SMART indicated the percentage of customer problems resolved on the first call rose from 50 percent without the system to 87 percent with the use of the system. In terms of productivity benefits, Compaq estimates that SMART has paid for itself within a year. Compaq is also distributing a case base directly to its customers as part of the PageMarq printer line: over 3,000 copies of QuickSource, an application containing 500 diagnostic cases, have already been shipped.

SOURCE: Bradley P. Allen, "Case-Based Reasoning: Business Applications," *Communications of the ACM,* March 1994, p. 41.

In contrast, a human expert might cite similar cases that have occurred in the past, but the expert's maturation might result in a more reliable approach to solving the problem domain under consideration. Although a case provides accurate and consistent documentation, it lacks the dynamics or the best decision based on maturation a human expert can provide.

The goal of CBR is to bring up the most similar historical case that matches the present case—not an easy task. For example, in the analogy "a flashlight battery is like a reservoir," the size, color, shape, or make of the battery are not the relevant aspect, but rather the fact that both the battery and a reservoir store and provide energy as power. So, in this situation, only relationships dealing with these two attributes would be useful in this analogy.

Another problem is the difficulty in mechanizing a person's insight and ability to see an analogy between a previously encountered case and a current case. No general representation procedure prescribes how to reason by analogy. As a consequence, reasoning by analogy tends to introduce errors, biases, and inconsistencies into the formulation of expert systems. To improve the usefulness and reliability of expert systems a better understanding of human reasoning is needed.

A third problem is maintenance of appropriate indexes. Knowledge is most often expanded by adding new cases and reclassifying the case library. A case library broad enough for most CBR applications requires considerable database storage with an efficient retrieval system. CBR can be fully automated, depending on how much creativity is required to derive solutions and how much complexity is involved. Regardless of the level of automation, the biggest factor in making CBR work is its case library.

Overall, CBR is slowly being adopted in various areas of business. Like choosing a surgeon with years of successful cases, CBR is an appealing approach to building expert systems, because it corresponds to an expert's problem-solving process of reasoning by analogy. Domain experts can use concrete examples rather than rules. They are most comfortable reporting their experience and discussing how each experience (a case) differs from others. In real-life situations, not only has CBR shown promise but it has demonstrated itself to be a better and a more accurate way to find solutions in certain problem domains. All indicators show CBR to be the wave of the future in building expert systems.

Illustration

The following example illustrates how CBR is used in building knowledge-based systems. Table 12–4 presents data collected from a sample of 24 admission applications to the graduate business school of a premier university. Ten criteria are considered in making a final decision to admit:

1. Age
2. Sex
3. Race
4. GPA (Grade Point Average. Max = 4.0)
5. GMAT (Graduate Management Admissions Test, max = 800)
6. Essays (grades on five specific topics submitted by the applicant)
7. I (Interview)
8. Coll.Ac. (Activities during college)
9. Post Co.Ac. (Post-collegiate activities)
10. Wk.Exp. (Post-academic work experience)

The actual project reviewed 185 applications in an effort to determine the pattern of admissions decisions. The 24 cases summarized in Table 12–4 represent over 90 percent of the yes/no decisions made by the admissions director in 1995. The knowledge engineer soon learned that the following combinations resulted in a "NO" admit:

- IF essay < 7.0, interview < 8.0, college activities < 7.0, post-college activities < 7.0, AND work experience < 7.0 THEN Decision = Reject applicant.
- IF GMAT < 500 THEN Decision = Reject applicant.

The information derived from the cases was later validated through three successive interviews using scenarios and protocol analysis. In more than 80 percent of the cases, the decisions were virtually the same. The five percent error rate was attributed to the fact that admissions directors arrive at a more accurate decision if they review the case in detail, have access to all the data on the application form, and have time to mentally review the relationship among the ten criteria.

The resulting CBR was represented in a knowledge base. See Table 12–5 for the parameters, rules, and customized screens of the Graduate Admissions Advisor.

■ **Table 12–4** Graduate Business School Admission Application Sample

CASE #	AGE	SEX	RACE	GPA	GMAT	ESSAYS					I	COLL ACT	POST CO.AC	Wk.EXP	DECISION
						1	2	3	4	5					
1	29	M	A	3.7	670	8	7	7	8	8	8	4	8	7.5	Y
2	32	F	W	3.4	620	6	5	5	6	7	10	4	8	8	Y
3	25	F	A	3.8	600	8	8	10	10	10	10	4	8	8	Y
4	25	M	W	4.0	630	7	6	7	5	8	7	5	8	8	Y
5	27	F	W	3.2	670	9	9	8	8	10	9	3	6	7	N
6	25	M	W	3.0	700	8	8	7	8	7	9	4	8	7.5	Y
7	25	M	B	2.8	520	8	9	9	8	9	7	4	5	7.5	N
8	25	M	H	3.2	670	7	8	8	8	7	9	4	7	8	Y
9	29	F	W	3.1	650	9	9	8	9	9	9	4	9	8.5	N
10	26	F	W	3.3	690	8	8	9	7	7	3	4	7	8.5	Y
11	29	M	W	2.6	640	7	7	7	8	7	7	4	8	8	Y
12	25	F	W	3.2	600	8	8	8	8	8	7	4	8	8.5	Y
13	31	F	W	2.9	720	7	8	8	7	8	8	3	8	8	Y
14	25	M	W	3.2	690	8	8	8	7	9	6	4	5	8.5	Y
15	27	M	B	2.3	490	8	8	7	7	7	5	4	7	8.5	N
16	26	F	A	3.3	600	7	6	6	7	6	5	4	8	8	Y
17	29	M	W	3.4	700	7	6	5	6	5	4	4	7	8.5	N
18	23	M	W	3.3	630	6	5	5	8	4	4	3	4	2	Y
19	25	F	H	3.7	570	5	5	4	5	5	4	4	5	8	Y
20	25	F	H	2.9	490	5	5	4	6	4	5	3	4	8.5	Y
21	24	M	W	2.6	570	6	6	5	7	7	5	4	7	8	Y
22	28	M	W	3.8	570	6	6	6	7	7	6	4	5	7	Y
23	32	F	B	3.0	510	6	7	6	5	6	6	4	6	8.5	Y
24	23	M	W	3.2	560	6	7	7	5	7	4	4	5	8.5	Y

LEGEND

SEX:	M = male; F = female
RACE:	A = Asian; B = Black; H = Hispanic; W = White
GPA:	Grade Point Average
GMAT:	Graduate Management Admission Test
I:	Interview
COLL.AC.:	Collegiate Activities
POST.AC.:	Post-Collegiate Activities
WK.EXP:	Post-Academic Work Experience
DECISION:	Y = Yes (admit)
	N = No (reject)

■ **Table 12−5** Parameters, Rules, and Customized Screens of the Graduate Admissions Advisor

---

Parameters:

NAME: Applicant's name
DEGREE: Type of degree (no degree, graduate, undergraduate)
SCHOOL: Name of school from which a degree was most recently received
RATING: A, B, or C rating for the school attended
MAJOR: Applicant's undergraduate major

GRADMAJOR: Applicant's graduate major
GPA_1: Applicant's undergraduate/graduate grade point average (based on 4.0 scale)
GPA: Adjusted GPA based on given GPA and school rating
GMAT: Applicant's GMAT score

REFERENCES: Rating of references (good, fair, or poor)
GRAMMAR: Rating of applicant's use of grammar in the essay
WRITING: Rating of applicant's writing skills in the essay
CONTENT: Rating of content of the essay
ESSAY: Final rating of the essay based on grammar, writing, and content

BUS_PRE: Business prerequisites needed by the applicant
COMM_PRE: Commerce prerequisites needed by the applicant
MIS_PRE: MIS prerequisites needed by the applicant
CLASS_NEED: Statement "The applicant needs the following prerequisite courses:"
DECISION: Decision of "Accept," "Reject," "Retake GMAT," "Reject—need more info," "Accept—need more info," or "Request interview"

Rules

NO_DEGREE: Establishes FCB-NO_DEGREE if the applicant has no degree
YES_DEGREE: Established FCB_SCHOOL if applicant has undergraduate or graduate degree
NODEGREE: If applicant has no degree, returns a decision of "Reject"
UNDERGRAD: Establishes FCB_PRELIM if degree is undergraduate
GRAD_DEGREE: Establishes FCB_GRADUATE if degree is graduate
A_INTERVIEW: Gives decision of Request Interview if the essay is poor
A_SCHOOL: Leaves the given GPA as is if the school rating is A
B_SCHOOL: Leaves the given GPA as is if the school rating is B
C_SCHOOL: Leaves the given GPA as is if the school rating is C
NOTACCEPT: Establishes FCB_DISPLAY if the decision is not "Accept"

PRELIM1: IF GPA ≥ 3.0 and GMAT ≥ 500 and (references = good or references = poor) THEN decision = "Accept"
PRELIM2: IF GMAT < 500 and references is poor, THEN decision = "Reject"
PRELIM3: IF GPA ≥ 3.5 and GMAT ≥ 450 and references = good, THEN decision = "Accept"
PRELIM4: IF GPA < 2.5 and GMAT < 600, THEN decision = "Reject"
PRELIM5: IF GPA < 3.0 and references = poor, THEN decision = "Reject"
PRELIM6: IF GPA < 3.0 and GMAT < 700 and references = fair, THEN decision = "Reject"
PRELIM7: IF GPA < 3.0 and GMAT < 500, THEN decision = "Reject"
PRELIM8: IF GPA ≥ 3.0 and GMAT < 500 and references = fair, THEN decision = "Retake GMAT"
PRELIM9: IF GPA ≥ 3.0 and ≤ 3.4 and GMAT ≥ 450 and ≤ 500 and references = good, THEN decision = "Retake GMAT"
PRELIM10: if GPA ≥ 3.0 and GMAT ≥ 500 and references = poor, THEN decision = "Accept—need more info"

■ **Table 12–5** Parameters, Rules, and Customized Screens of the Graduate Admissions Advisor (continued)

PRELIM11: IF GPA $\geq$ 2.5 and $\leq$ 2.9 and GMAT $\geq$ 700 and (references = good or references = fair), THEN decision = "Accept—need more info"

PRELIM12: IF GPA $\geq$ 2.5 and $\leq$ 2.9 and GMAT $\geq$ 600 and $\leq$ 699 and references = good, THEN decision = "Accept—need more info"

PRELIM13: IF GPA < 2.5 and GMAT $\geq$ 700 and references = good, THEN decision = "Accept—need more info"

PRELIM14: IF GPA < 2.5 and GMAT $\geq$ 600 and $\leq$ 699 and references = good, THEN decision = "Reject—need more info"

PRELIM15: IF GPA < 2.5 and GMAT $\geq$ 600 and $\leq$ 699 and references = good, THEN decision = "Reject—need more info"

PRELIM16: IF GPA $\geq$ 2.5 and $\leq$ 2.9 and GMAT $\geq$ 500 and $\leq$ 599 and references = good, THEN decision = "Reject—need more info"

GOOD_ESSAY: For an undergraduate applicant, give essay a good rating if grammar, writing, and content = good

POOR_ESSAY: For an undergraduate applicant, give essay a poor rating if either grammar, writing, or content = poor

GOOD_ESSAY2: For a graduate applicant, gives essay a good rating if grammar, writing and content = good

POOR_ESSAY2: For a graduate applicant, gives essay a poor rating if either grammar, writing, or content = poor

GRAD_ESSAYRULE: Establishes INTERVIEW2 from GRADUATE if decision = "Accept"

ESSAYRULE: Establishes INTERVIEW from PRELIM if decision = "Accept"

ALLCLASSES: Gives the statement "Applicant needs the following prerequisites:"

ACCEPT_RULE: Establishes FCB_CLASSES if the decision = "Accept"

ACCEPT_GRAD: Establishes FCB_CLASSES2 if the decision = "Accept"

NOTACCEPT2: Establishes FCB_DISPLAY2 if the decision < > "accept"

Customized Screens

SCREEN1: Lets user enter the applicant's name and check a degree from a list (no degree, graduate, or undergraduate)

SCREEN1A: Displays the reject decision for an applicant who has no degree

SCREEN1B: Lets the user enter the name of the applicant's school from which the most recent degree was received

SCR_RATING: Lets user enter a rating for a school that does not exist in the database

SCREEN2: lets the user select the applicant's undergraduate major from a given list

SCREENGM: Lets user check the applicant's graduate major from a list

ESSAYSCR: Asks grammar, writing, and content questions regarding the essay

SCREENBUS: Lets user mark the business courses that the applicant needs to take

SCREENCOMM: Lets user make the commerce courses that the applicant needs to take

SCREENMIS: Lets user mark the MIS courses that the applicant needs to take

SCREEN4: Display screen for an undergraduate applicant who has been accepted

SCREEN4A: Display screen for a graduate applicant who has been accepted

SCRRESULTS: Displays results for undergraduate major applicants who are not accepted

SCRRESULTS2: Displays results for graduate major applicants who are not accepted

IMPLICATIONS FOR MANAGEMENT

This chapter examined the different approaches to inferencing strategies and reasoning, but emphasized case-based reasoning. CBR identifies the reasoning humans do based on the recall of large chunks of knowledge. Storing the right cases and making use of the appropriate knowledge from them allows both humans and expert systems to perform in more situations, increase efficiency in familiar situations, and improve the chances of taking advantage of opportunities as they come up.

One of the challenges of CBR is the ability to provide corporate memory for an organization. When CBR is enhanced by the experiences of managers and executives from various levels of the organization, it can become a viable corporate memory that allows corporate personnel to share experiences.

Assessing the potential of CBR for organizational functioning includes the consideration of certain knowledge engineering issues. Case collection and indexing can be time-consuming and tedious. Knowledge engineers need tools to make this process easier and more efficient. Tools are also needed to build automated CBR systems, planning systems, scheduling systems, and the like. On the managerial side, issues such as who can update a case library, how it can be managed in a multi-user environment, and what procedure determines which cases to add to a case library and which ones to delete must be addressed.

Evidence shows that where CBR has been used, it has been a valuable resource as a kind of corporate memory. It has also proven invaluable for training purposes but putting people in a range of situations in which they experience problems they are likely to encounter on the job. It can also help them solve problems and index their experiences for later use. Because people train better by example and storytelling, presenting cases to trainees is a most effective way to get them remember and apply what they learned to problem-solving opportunities in the domain.

Given the nature of this technology and its potential, CBR systems require strong management support if they are to succeed. This kind of support involves proper funding and shared decisions on the cases to adopt, the maintenance to follow, and the commitment to view this technology as a corporate asset. Without such support, CBR could be nothing more than a one-time exercise in the corporate computer center.

■ SUMMARY

1. The inference engine is the program(s) that controls the strategies for managing the selection and application of knowledge. It is the reasoning component that decides when certain inference rules should be accessed or fired.

2. Common sense is inferences made from knowledge about the world. Reasoning is the process of applying knowledge to arrive at solutions. It works through the interaction of rules and data.

3. Deductive reasoning deals with exact facts and conclusions. An inference is deductive if it is logically clear and sound. To use deduction, one needs to use major and minor premises. The idea

behind deductive reasoning is to generate new knowledge from previously specified knowledge.

4. Inductive reasoning is reasoning from a given set of facts to general principles. In inductive reasoning, one must satisfy a set of constraints rather than establish a given assertion. Inductive systems are less likely to be as accurately formulated as deductive systems.

5. Induction usually produces results without explanation. The main disadvantage of inductive reasoning is that there is no guarantee that induced results are valid for examples other than those in the premises. Inductive reasoning must deal with uncertainty in obtaining conclusion.

6. Modus ponens is a common rule for deriving new facts from existing rules and known facts. With modus ponens, fore the rule "IF a, THEN b," if a is true then one can be certain that b is true. This reasoning is common sense to a human, but a computer must be told in precise terms how to make an inference using modus ponens.

7. Backward chaining checks the premise or conclusion of every rule in the knowledge base based on existing assertions. A system that uses backward chaining works backward from the goal to find supporting data. Forward chaining begins with known data and works forward to see if any conclusion (new information) can be drawn. Forward chaining is data-driven, while backward chaining is goal-driven.

8. Opportunistic reasoning uses both forward and backward chaining. It uses forward chaining to draw conclusions from existing data and backward chaining to find data that allow the generation of a solution.

9. Model-based expert systems are an alternative for diagnosis and monitoring applications when rule-based systems are not practical. With model-based reasoning, the model-based system receives observed sensor date from the machine in operation and compares it with the predicted simulation values, setting off an alarm or transmits a message whenever the actual value is beyond the predetermined range of tolerance.

10. Case-based reasoning (CBR) is reasoning by analogy. It uses relevant past cases in a manner similar to humans' use of past experiences to arrive at conclusions. Human experts reason about a problem by recalling similar cases encountered in the past. They try to determine whether a case is similar or dissimilar to previous cases. A major source of CBR is machine learning, which focuses on techniques that allow computers to learn from refinement of the stored knowledge, known as *experience.*

11. CBR offers savings in time and maintenance over rule-based reasoning due to faster retrieval of representative cases for doing the knowledge engineering and to the simplicity of adding cases that offer similar features to the existing case in question. The difficulty in this is determining which specific attributes make a case relevant to another case.

12. Mechanizing a person's insight and ability to see previously encountered case and a current case is difficult. No general

representation procedure prescribes how to reason by analogy. Therefore, reasoning by analogy tends to introduce errors, biases, and inconsistencies into the formulation of expert systems.

13. CBR is an appealing approach to building expert systems, because it corresponds to an expert's problem-solving process of reasoning by analogy. All indicators show CBR to be the wave of the future in building expert systems.

▨ TERMS TO LEARN

Action (portion of a rule) the goal; either conclusions to be drawn with some degree of certainty or instructions to be carried out.

Backward chaining goal-driven inference strategy in which the system works backward from the goal to find supporting data; working "backward" through a chain of rules in an attempt to find a verifiable set of condition clauses.

Case knowledge at an operational level; episodic description of a problem and its associated solution.

Case-based reasoning (CBR) A methodology that records and documents previous cases and then searches the relevant case(s) to determine their usefulness in solving a current problem; computer systems that solve new problems by analogy with old ones.

Data-driven Beginning with the evidence and attempting to find the cause or solution.

Deductive inference logically clear and sound; reasoning from general principles or rules to reach specific conclusions.

Deductive reasoning also called exact reasoning, takes known principles (exact facts) and applies them to instances to infer an exact conclusion.

Forward chaining data-driven inference strategy in which the system begins with known data and works forward to see if any conclusions can be drawn.

Goal-driven Starting with the goal and working backward to determine the supporting processes needed to achieve it.

Inductive reasoning reasoning from a given set of facts or specific examples to general principles or rules.

Inference engine the program that controls the strategies for managing the selection and application of knowledge; the reasoning component within the shell.

Inferencing deriving a conclusion based on statements that only imply that conclusion.

Logic the scientific study of the process of reasoning and the set of rules and procedures used in the reasoning process.

Model-based reasoning observed sensor data is received from the machine in operation and is compared with the predicted simulation values, setting off an alarm or transmitting a message whenever the actual value is beyond the predetermined range of tolerance.

Modus ponens a common rule for deriving new facts from existing rules and know facts; inference rule type that, from "a implies b," justifies b by the existence of a.

Opportunistic reasoning an inference strategy that uses forward chaining to draw conclusions from existing data and backward chaining to find date that make it possible to generate the solution.

Premise (portion of the rule) provides the evidence from which the conclusion must necessarily follow; evaluates the truth or falsehood with some degree of certainty.

Reasoning the process of applying knowledge to arrive at solutions based on the interactions between rules and data.

Uncertainty lack of adequate information to make a decision; a value that cannot be determined during a consultation.

REVIEW QUESTIONS

1. Of the several sources of human reasoning power, Which source(s) is the least likely to be emulated by a computer system? Why?

2. Illustrate the difference between deductive and inductive reasoning. Under what conditions is one preferred over the other?

3. Distinguish between:
   a. opportunistic and case-based reasoning
   b. backward and forward chaining
   c. logic and reasoning

4. Explain how modus ponens functions. Provide an example.

5. Give an example of your own to illustrate backward chaining. How important is backward chaining as a feature for shell programming? Explain.

6. "In forward chaining, the spotlight is on the premise." Do you agree? Explain with an illustration.

7. How do model-based systems differ from rule-based systems? Under what circumstances is each system used? Explain.

8. Give an example of human case-based reasoning. How does it differ from a computer-based CBR?

9. How does CBR compare to a rule-based system?

10. Identify the advantages and problems in CBR. For what types of applications is it ideal?

EXERCISES AND CASES

1. In order to make admissions decisions of a graduate business program of a midwestern university, the admissions officer uses an evaluation sheet to guide her while evaluating each application. This sheet has three areas of concern: academic scores, work experience, and personal experiences including activities, essays, and interviews. Each area is given a letter score from A to F; A represents excellent while F represents failure. Letter A is given a weight of 10 points, B+ is given 9.0,. . ., and F is given 2.0 points. The applicant has to earn a certain number of points to be admitted.

Using the 24 cases prescribed in Table 12–4 (reproduced here as Table 12–6), review each case to answer the following questions:

   a. What can you deduce as a pattern for admission to the program? In other words, what would be the minimum combination that will admit a candidate?

   b. Do you find any irregularities in the admission decision process? Be specific.

2. For each of the following applications, explain why a backward chaining approach is either suitable or unsuitable:

   a. a system to determine why your vacuum cleaner does not work

   b. a diagnostic system to determine a problem with the printer linked to your PC

   c. a real estate investment advisory system

   d. a diagnostic system for electric problems in a car

   e. a system to advise a weapons officer on the action to take in a destroyer carrying nuclear weapons

   f. a system for driving a bus automatically

3. Backward chaining is appropriate for applications having many more inputs than possible conclusions. The ability to trace the logic backwards from the conclusion (goal) to the many inputs makes it more efficient than forward chaining. Develop a partial knowledge base (set of rules) of your own to illustrate this point.

4. The following set of rules helps in the selection of a beverage and main course for a meal. Is this rule set better suited for backward chaining or forward chaining? Explain.

```
Rule 1    IF   guest_age < 21
          THEN alcohol_serve = no
Rule 2    IF   guest_age ≥ 21
          THEN alcohol_serve = yes
Rule 3    IF   alcohol_serve = yes AND
               meal = special
          THEN beverage = wine
```

■ **Table 12−6** Duplicate of Table 12−4

CASE #	AGE	SEX	RACE	GPA	GMAT	ESSAYS 1	2	3	4	5	I	COLL ACT	POST CO.AC	Wk.EXP	DECISION
1	29	M	A	3.7	670	8	7	7	8	8	8	4	8	7.5	Y
2	32	F	W	3.4	620	6	5	5	6	7	10	4	8	8	Y
3	25	F	A	3.8	600	8	8	10	10	10	10	4	8	8	Y
4	25	M	W	4.0	630	7	6	7	5	8	7	5	8	8	Y
5	27	F	W	3.2	670	9	9	8	8	10	9	3	6	7	N
6	25	M	W	3.0	700	8	8	7	8	7	9	4	8	7.5	Y
7	25	M	B	2.8	520	8	9	9	8	9	7	4	5	7.5	N
8	25	M	H	3.2	670	7	8	8	8	7	9	4	7	8	Y
9	29	F	W	3.1	650	9	9	8	9	9	9	4	9	8.5	N
10	26	F	W	3.3	690	8	8	9	7	7	3	4	7	8.5	Y
11	29	M	W	2.6	640	7	7	7	8	7	7	4	8	8	Y
12	25	F	W	3.2	600	8	8	8	8	8	7	4	8	8.5	Y
13	31	F	W	2.9	720	7	8	8	7	8	8	3	8	8	Y
14	25	M	W	3.2	690	8	8	8	7	9	6	4	5	8.5	Y
15	27	M	B	2.3	490	8	8	7	7	7	5	4	7	8.5	N
16	26	F	A	3.3	600	7	6	6	7	6	5	4	8	8	Y
17	29	M	W	3.4	700	7	6	5	6	5	4	4	7	8.5	N
18	23	M	W	3.3	630	6	5	5	8	4	4	3	4	2	Y
19	25	F	H	3.7	570	5	5	4	5	5	4	4	5	8	Y
20	25	F	H	2.9	490	5	5	4	6	4	5	3	4	8.5	Y
21	24	M	W	2.6	570	6	6	5	7	7	5	4	7	8	Y
22	28	M	W	3.8	570	6	6	6	7	7	6	4	5	7	Y
23	32	F	B	3.0	510	6	7	6	5	6	6	4	6	8.5	Y
24	23	M	W	3.2	560	6	7	7	5	7	4	4	5	8.5	Y

LEGEND

SEX:	M = male; F = female
RACE:	A = Asian; B = Black; H = Hispanic; W = White
GPA:	Grade Point Average
GMAT:	Graduate Management Admission Test
I:	Interview
COLL.AC.:	Collegiate Activities
POST.AC.:	Post-Collegiate Activities
WK.EXP:	Post-Academic Work Experience
DECISION:	Y = Yes (admit)
	N = No (reject)

```
Rule 4    IF   alcohol_serve = yes AND
               guest = friend
          THEN beverage = beer
```

5. You are given the following partial knowledge base:

```
R1    IF distance is > 200 miles
      THEN cost of travel is high
      ELSE cost of travel is low
R2    IF cost of travel is low
      THEN driving is recommended
R3    IF driving is recommended
      THEN do not fly
```

a. Do forward chaining with distance > 200 miles.

b. Do backward chaining with distance < 200 miles.

6. You were asked to review an expert system that addresses the communications skills of job candidates:

```
R1    IF the candidate answers all
      questions with ease
      THEN she is good in communication
      skills
R2    IF the candidate is sincere
      THEN she answers questions with
      ease
R3    IF the candidate is a name
      dropper
      THEN she is not sincere
R4    IF the candidate gets an
      appointment for a second
      interview
      THEN she will communicate well
      during the second interview
R5    IF the candidate communicates
      will during the second interview
      THEN she is sociable
R6    IF the candidate is sociable
      THEN she is a team player
R7    IF the candidate is a team player
      THEN she will be made a job offer
```

a. Assume that the candidate is known to answer all questions with ease. Do backward chaining to see if she will be made a job offer.

b. Assume that the candidate is not a name dropper and she is granted a second interview, do forward chaining to see if she will be made a job offer.

7. Determine the type of reasoning in each of the following cases:

a. Liz did not deposit money in her checking account.
Liz is a customer of the bank.
Liz's check bounced (insufficient funds).
Conclusion: Checks drawn against negative account balance will bounce.

b. Drivers who exceed speed limit get speeding tickets.
Donna is a licensed driver.
Donna drove at 20 miles over speed limit.
Conclusion: Donna will get a speeding ticket.
(What is wrong with this reasoning?)

c. A customer whose account balance drops below $100 during month is subject to $5 fine.
Al is a bank customer.
Al has a checking account.
Al's checking account balance dropped to $98.
Conclusion: Al's account will be charged $5.

8. Assume you have an important luncheon meeting in Chicago and you live in New York. The distance is 1,100 miles via turnpikes. You are willing to drive up to eight hours a day to get to Chicago. You also have a number of constraints: speed limit, toll gates, stops for meals, overnight stay, etc. One way to approach this scenario is to start with your goal—Chicago and work backwards to New York—your starting point. You have three days to complete your trip.

a. Write a partial knowledge base to demonstrate backward chaining.

b. If you started forward from New York, how would you evaluate the scenario? How does it differ from the first approach (a)? Illustrate.

9. Refer to Table 12–5 and derive a set of rules for a shell of your choice (VP-Expert, EXSYS, etc.) based on the summarized case data.

■ SELECTED REFERENCES

Acorn, T., and S. Walden. "AMART: Support Management Cultivated Reasoning Technology for Compaq Customer Service." In *Proceedings of AAAI-92.* Cambridge, MA: AAAI Press/MIT Press, 1992.

Alba, J. W., and L. Hasher. "Is Memory Schematic?" *Psychological Bulletin* 93, 1983, pp. 203–231.

Aleven, V., and K. D. Ashley. "Automated Generation of Examples for a Tutorial in Case-Based Argumentation." In *Proceedings, Second International Conference on Intelligent Tutoring Systems (ITS-92), Montreal,* C. Frasson, G. Gauthier, and G. I. McCalla, eds. New York: Springer-Verlag, 1992.

Allen, Bradley P. "Case-Based Reasoning: Business Application." *Communications of the ACM,* March 1994, pp. 40–42.

Ashish, Goel. "The Reality and Future of Expert Systems." *Information Systems Management (JIF),* Winter 1994, pp. 53–61.

Ashley, K. D. "Reasoning With Cases and Hypothetical in Hypo." *International Journal of Man–Machine Studies* 34, 1991, pp. 753–796.

Barber, J.; S. Bhatta; A. Goel; M. Jacobsen; M. Pearce; L. Penberthy; M. Shankar; and E. Stroulia. "Askjef: Integrating Case-Based Reasoning and Multimedia Technologies for Interface Design Support." In *Artificial Intelligence in Design 1992,* J. Gero, ed. Boston, MA: Kluwer Academic, 1992.

Bardasz, T. and I. Zeid. "DEJAVU: A Case-Based Reasoning Designer's Assistant Shell." In *Artificial Intelligence in Design 1992,* J. Gero, ed. Boston, MA: Kluwer Academic, 1992.

Bareiss, E. R. and B. M. Slator. "The Evolution of a Case-Based Approach to Knowledge Representation, Categorization, and Learning." In *Categorization and Category Learning by Humans and Machines,* Medin, Nakamura, and Taraban, ed. New York: Academic Press, 1992.

Branting, L. K. *Integrating Rules and Precedents for Classification and Explanation: Automating Legal Analysis.* Ph.D. Dissertation, Dept. of Computer Science, University of Texas, 1991.

Broverman, C. "Case-Based Hypermedia Access of "Lessons-learned" to Accomplish Technology Transfer." In *Proceedings of the IEEE Advanced Semiconductor Manufacturing Conference, Cambridge, MA.* New York: IEEE Press, 1992.

Burke, R. D. and A. Kass. "Integrating Case Presentation With Simulation-Based Learning-by-Doing." In *Proceedings of the Fourteenth Annual Conference of the Cognitive Science Society.* Northvale, NJ: Erlbaum, 1992.

Buta, Paul. "Mining for Financial Knowledge With CBR." *AI Expert,* February 1994, pp. 34–41.

Chandler, T. N. and J. L. Kolodner. "The Science Education Advisor: A Case-Based Advising System for Lesson Planning." In *Artificial Intelligence in Education: Proceedings of the World Conference on AI in Education (Edinburgh, Scotland).* Charlottesville, VA: Association for the Advancement of Computing in Education, 1993.

Domeshek, E. "A Case Study of Case Indexing: Designing Index Feature Sets to Suit Task Demands and Support Parallelism." In *Advances in Connectionist and Neural Computational Theory, vol. 2: Analogical Connections,* J. Barnden and K. Holyoak, eds. Norwood, NJ: Ablex, 1993.

Domeshek, E. and J. L. Kolodner. "Finding the Points of Large Cases." In *Artificial Intelligence for Engineering Design, Analysis, and Manufacturing* (AIEDAM) 7, no. 2 (1993), pp. 87–96.

Edelson, D.; A. Collins; R. Bareiss; and A. Kass. "Incorporating AI into Effective Learning Environments. In *Proceedings of the Tenth International Conference on Technology in Education, Cambridge, MA,* 1993.

Evan, Jonathan; Stephen E. Newstead; and Ruth M. J. Byrne, eds. *Human Reasoning: The Psychology of Deduction.* Hillsdale, NJ: Erlbaum Associates, 1993.

Hennessy, Daniel and David Hinkle. "Applying Case-Based Reasoning to Autoclave Loading." *IEEE Express,* October 1992, pp. 21–26.

Kambhampati, S. "Exploiting Casual Structure to Control Retrieval and Refitting During Plan Reuse." *Computational Intelligence,* 1993.

Kambhampati, S.; M. R. Cutkosky, J. M. Tenenbaum; and S. H. Lee. "Integrating General Purpose Planners and Specialized Reasoners: Case Study of a Hybrid Planning Architecture." *IEEE Transactions on Systems, Man, and Cybernetics,* 1993

Kettler, B.; J. Hendler; W. Anderson; and M. Evett. "Massively Parallel Support for Case-Based Planning." In *Proceedings of the Ninth IEEE Conference on Artificial Intelligence Applications, Orlando.* Washington, D.C.: IEEE CS Press, 1993.

Kitano, H.; A. Shibata; H. Shimazu; J. Kajihara; and A. Sato. "Building Large-Scale and Corporate-Wide Case-Based Systems." In *Proceedings of AAAI-92.* Cambridge, MA: AAAI Press and MIT Press, 1992.

Kolodner, Janet. *Case-Based Reasoning.* San Mateo, CA: Morgan Kaufmann, 1993.

Lange, T. E. and C. M. Wharton. "Dynamic Memories: Analysis of an Integrated Comprehension and Episodic Memory Retrieval Model. In *Proceedings of IJCAI-93.* San Mateo, CA: Morgan Kaufmann, 1993.

Madhavan, Raghav K. "Goal-Based Reasoning for Securities Analysis." *AI Expert,* February 1994, pp. 22–29.

Mahapatra, Radha and Arun Sen. "Case-Based Management Systems: Providing Database Support to Case-Based Reasoners." *Journal of Database Management (DAN),* Spring 1994, pp. 19–29.

McCarthy, R. "Episodic Cases and Real-Time Performance in a Case-Based Planning System. *Expert Systems With Applications* 6, 1993, pp. 9–22.

McGovern, Jim; Danny Samson; and Andrew Wirth. "Using Case-Based Reasoning for Basis Development in Intelligent Decision Systems." *European Journal of Operational Research (EJO),* August 25, 1994, pp. 40–59.

Miyashita, K. and K. Sycara. "Case-Based Incremental Schedule Revision." In *Knowledge-Based Scheduling,* M. Fox and M. Zweben, eds. San Mateo, CA: Morgan Kaufmann, 1993.

Nisbett, Richard E. ed. *Rules for Reasoning.* Hillsdale, NJ: L. Erlbaum Associates, 1993.

Owens, C. "Integrating Feature Extracting and Memory Search." *Machine Learning* 10, no. 3 (1993), pp. 311–340.

Oxman, R. E. "PRECEDENTS: Memory Structure in Design Case Libraries." *CAAD Futures, 93,* New York: Elsevier Science Publishers, 1993.

Oxman, Steve. "An Introduction to Case-Based Reasoning." In *Proceedings of the Third Annual Symposium of the International Association of Knowledge Engineers,* November 16–19, 1992, Washington, D.C., 1992, pp. 811–815.

Pearce, Michael; Ashok K. Goel; Janet L. Kolodner; Craig Zimring; Lucas Sentosa; and Richard Billington. "Case-Based Design Support: A Case Study in Architectural Design." *IEEE Express,* October 1992, pp. 14–20.

Ram, A. "Indexing Elaboration and Refinement: Incremental Learning of Explanatory Cases." *Machine Learning* 10, no. 3 (1993), pp. 201–248.

Ram, A. and M. T. Cox. "Using Introspective Reasoning to Select Learning Strategies." In *Machine Learning: A Multistrategy Approach.,* vol. 4, R. S. Michalski and G. Tecuci, eds. San Mateo, CA: Morgan Kaufmann, 1993.

Roderman, R. and C. Tsatsoulis. "PANDA: A Case-Based System to Aid Novice Designers." *Artificial Intelligence for Engineering Design, Analysis and Manufacturing (AIEDAM)* 7, no. 2 (1993), pp. 125–134.

Rubin, Stuart H. "Case-Based Learning: A New Paradigm for Automated Knowledge Acquisition." *ISA Transactions,* November 1992, pp. 18–209.

Simoudis, Evangelos. "Using Case-Based Retrieval for Customer Technical Support." *IEEE Express,* October 1992, pp. 7–13

Slade, S. *An Interpersonal Model of Goal-Based Decision Making.* Northvale, NJ: Erlbaum, 1993.

Slator, B. M. and K. C. Fide. "Topical Indexing and Questions to Represent Text for Retrieval and Browsing." *Heuristics: The Journal of Knowledge Engineering* 6, no. 4 (1993).

Stottler, Richard. "CBR for Cost and Sales Prediction." *AI Expert,* August 1994, pp. 24–33.

Veloso, M. M. and J. G. Carbonell. "Derivational Analogy in PRODIGY: Automating Case Acquisition, Storage, and Utilization." *Machine Learning* 10, no. 3 (1993) pp. 249–278.

Chapter ▪ 13

Dealing with Uncertainty and Fuzzy Logic

FUZZY KNOWLEDGE: AN ANECDOTAL REPORT

The following partial session with the expert in developing the Publisher Advisor System illustrates some of the fuzzy information acquired during a typical interview. The level of fuzziness in any given knowledge acquisition session depends on the nature of knowledge, the expert's ability to provide unambiguous information, and the types of questions asked.

KE: Well, how do you decide whether the book manuscript should be published?

EXPERT: First, of course, I send the manuscript to highly qualified reviewers.

KE: How do you define a "highly qualified" reviewer?

EXPERT: It depends on the reviewer's expertise in the topic of the manuscript. Expertise also varies, depending on the reviewer's years of experience, so that a reviewer with six years of teaching or publishing in the field, for example, would be considered a highly qualified reviewer.

KE: Then, you would absolutely eliminate a reviewer with five years of experience.

EXPERT: (pausing for a moment) Not necessarily. Years of experience is only one consideration. Anyway, six years is not an unreasonable minimum for experience.

KE: I understand. So you look for reviewers with six years or more of experience before you would definitely say this person qualifies to review the manuscript. Reviewers with less than six years of experience might still be considered but to a lesser degree. Let me sketch this for you to look at:

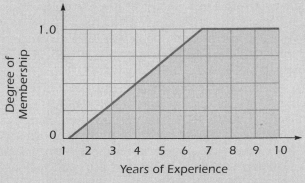

Reviewer's Competency: Fuzzy Representation of "Highly Qualified"

I chose one year as an arbitrary minimum. Is this what you're saying that as experience in the field increases, the compatibility of a person in terms of being a highly qualified reviewer steadily increases?

EXPERT: I would say so. I never thought of it this way, but I'd go along with that. This is generally what I mean. Let's face it, not every experienced person is going to be a good reviewer. There isn't any particular number of years where I'd say this is a definite yes for a reviewer and the next reviewer is a definite no, except may be at the 5–8 year range.

KE: Now we can agree on what you mean by "highly qualified" reviewer. Then what?

> **EXPERT:** I also try to assess how successful the books were that I published based on that reviewer's recommendations.
>
> **KE:** Well, how do you measure success? Is it the number of copies the books sold? The number of revisions the book went through, or what?
>
> **EXPERT:** It's hard to put one's finger on any specific number or pattern. I get a general view about the quality of the reviewer's past reviews, and then I say to myself, "Has this reviewer been highly reliable, somewhat reliable, or questionable?" Then I proceed with other things to look for before I decide on the reviewers who will review the manuscript. The ones I decide on are usually highly qualified reviewers.

AT A GLANCE

Day-to-day reasoning processes must recognize inexact knowledge, especially when a situation changes over time. In building expert systems, knowledge engineers often have to deal with incomplete, vague, or fuzzy knowledge. Inexact knowledge is usually managed by two strategies: certainty factors and fuzzy logic. Both strategies require a qualitative judgment about the nature of the problem domain.

Certainly factor is known by various names. It is a measurement of belief or a possibility rather than a probability. Various sources of errors contribute to uncertainty. Unless controlled, they are likely to affect the quality and reliability of the knowledge base.

A certainty factor can be used in a number of ways. It can be assigned by user response, assigned to rule conclusions, projected forward from the premise of a rule, or selected in compound premises. In any case, a knowledge engineer needs to recognize the choices a shell provides before assigning certainty factors in the knowledge base.

Fuzzy logic allows computer-based manipulation of common sense in an uncertain world. It can reduce or manage system complexity and serve as a building block of linguistic expression. Fuzzy logic accommodates a range of values called a membership set. Like certainty factors, fuzzy sets allow an expert system to combine several indicators with low levels of confidence and yet come out with one measure that has a high level of confidence.

What You Will Learn

By the end of this chapter, you should know the following:

1. The concept underlying monotonic and nonmonotonic reasoning.

2. The meaning and uses of certainty factors.

3. The sources of uncertainty and how they affect the reliability of expert systems.

4. The meaning and uses of fuzzy logic.

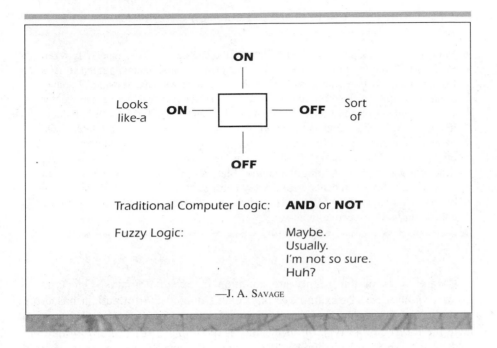

Traditional Computer Logic: **AND** or **NOT**

Fuzzy Logic: Maybe.
                               Usually.
                               I'm not so sure.
                               Huh?

—J. A. SAVAGE

INTRODUCTION

B uilding expert systems and carrying out the reasoning procedures explained in Chapter 12 assumed complete certainty of 1.0. Each rule is
assumed to have one of two truth values: yes/no, high/low, true/false, etc. This
line of reasoning implies exact knowledge. Although it is important in many
decision situations, this form of reasoning has two main drawbacks:

1. It only expresses the truth or falsity of statements, which limits the
   expressive power characteristic of real-world situations.

2. It has difficulty in producing new knowledge about real-life situations;
   only what is derived from the existing information in the knowledge
   base can be used in reasoning within complete certainty.

Experience confirms that human knowledge is often inexact. Most people
regularly make decisions under a veil of uncertainty. An auto mechanic might
conclude, "it looks like the transmission is acting up, but it might be the drive
shaft that is causing the problem." Box 13–1 provides an anecdote illustrating
how one's belief can change one's actions, a common event in an ever-changing
world.

One of the most difficult items to replicate in an expert system is imprecise,
uncertain, or incomplete information. When the expert system's goal is to
emulate human thought processes, it should be designed to address inexact
reasoning or uncertainties—not an easy task. For example, how exact are labels
such as "middle-aged," "tall," "fat," "intelligent," etc.? These concepts all
imply a degree of inexactness or uncertainty. The "fuzziness" surrounding such
concepts must be addressed in building expert systems that represent human
decision making.

Box 13–1   Uncertainty and Change as Common Occurrences

Michele enjoys taking courses with Steve in the business school, especially when Professor Lindgren is the instructor and class size is small. Steve agreed to take Lindgren's marketing course with Michele, scheduled for Tuesday and Thursday of each week. A week before registration, they heard a rumor that a new instructor was scheduled to teach Lindgren's course. The common belief was that the new instructor was not as good as Lindgren. With this perception and not knowing the likelihood of the switch of instructors, Steve decided to register in another course on his own. The morning of registration, however, Michele found out that Lindgren was in fact teaching the course. She went to look for Steve, who had also learned that 80 students were already enrolled in the course. Not wanting to be in such a large class, Michele and Steve finally decided to enroll in separate courses in their respective majors.

Many types of uncertainty are common in expert domains. One type is *inexact knowledge.* For example, a physician's diagnosis of a patient based on inconclusive test results may lead the doctor to say, "it doesn't look like you have the flu." Another type of uncertainty is incomplete or *partial information,* such as a case in which approval of a person's application for a Visa or a Mastercard is on hold because of incomplete information related to salary, place of residence, etc. In each case, inexact knowledge or partial information becomes an important factor in building a representative expert system.

Dealing with uncertainty involves a number of approaches that are mathematical or statistical in nature. In this chapter, the discussion focuses on nonmonotonic reasoning as a nonnumeric approach and certainty factors and fuzzy logic as the two primary numeric strategies in dealing with uncertainty. The range of uncertainty extends from a mere lack of complete assurance to a state of vagueness equivalent to educated guesses. In either case, the degree of uncertainty or **belief**—a qualitative judgment about the nature of problem under review—must be considered.

■ MONOTONIC AND NONMONOTONIC REASONING

The reasoning presented in Chapter 12 is known as **monotonic reasoning**—a reasoning process that moves in one direction only, continuously adding additional truths. The number of facts in the knowledge is always increasing, never decreasing. The conclusions derived are valid deductions, and they remain so.

Reasoning processes applied to practical day-to-day problems, however, must recognize incomplete information, because situations change over time. In Box 13–1, the form of reasoning carried out by Steve and Michele is nonmonotonic reasoning. This situation, in which the initial information is inconsistent with later information, demonstrates that human problem solvers, or reasoners, revise absolute truths with beliefs that can change as subsequent information is provided.

Nonmonotonic reasoning is used to emphasize retraction. Unlike monotonic reasoning in which a set of deducible conclusions grows with added information, the nonmonotonic reasoning allows new facts to invalidate old facts. In Box 13–1, new facts became known, which invalidated old knowledge. In nonmonotonic reasoning, old knowledge is retracted, which leads to growth in the knowledge on occasions. Nonmonotonic reasoning holds a set of premises to be true and keeps a collection of tentative beliefs, revising those beliefs whenever new knowledge is derived. When a belief is revised, any beliefs that rest on it must also be revised. For example, most people take plane flights on the assumption that the pilot is competent and the aircraft is air worthy. Any beliefs to the contrary will probably cause cancellations or the booking of a different flight.

UNDERSTANDING CERTAINTY FACTORS

The term *certainty factor* is used synonymously with the following concepts:

- Percentage of correctness
- A feeling of comfort
- Nonmonotonic reasoning
- Common-sense reasoning
- A numerical value associated with a variable
- Inexact reasoning
- Uncertain knowledge
- Fuzzy reasoning or fuzzy logic
- Reasoning based on partial information
- Reasoning with uncertain data
- Approximate reasoning

For all practical purposes, **uncertainty** is lack of adequate information on which to base a decision. The strict dictionary definition of the word is not as important as is its use by experts. Experts, just like everyone else, reason under uncertainty.

Certainty factor, or **CF,** is:

- A term synonymous with "confidence" or "truth" factor.
- A "confidence" or a "belief," *not* a probability.
- A measurement of belief or a subjective quantification of an expert's judgment and intentions.
- A subjective quantification of an expert's judgment, which describes the credibility of the conclusion given only the evidence shown in the premise of the rule.

For example, examine the following rule of thumb:

```
IF speed limit is 65 mph AND road condition is clear
   AND car speed is less than 70 mph
THEN there is .80 certainty that a driver will not be
   stopped for speeding
```

This rule is based on years of experience driving on a stretch of highway, even though it cannot be proven exactly. The action part of the rule does *not* mean a probability of .80 has been assigned to "stopped_for_speeding." It means a driver can be 80 percent confident of not being stopped for speeding but the confidence is based upon *set of experiential cases.*

Expert systems are designed to deal with uncertain or **incomplete knowledge.** A system may ask the user for more knowledge. If the answer is "does not know," it takes this lack of knowledge into account in its inferencing process. In contrast, in algorithmic (conventional) systems, if data is incomplete, the system will produce inaccurate results or no results. Conventional systems simply cannot deal with uncertain or incomplete data.

■ SOURCES OF UNCERTAINTY

No overview of uncertainty is complete without a description of the various sources of error that create uncertainty. A knowledge engineer can better control uncertainty by learning more about its sources and its impact on the quality of the knowledge-based system.

Ambiguity

A statement is ambiguous when it has more than one meaning or can be interpreted in more than one way. For example, "Sell the bad stock" is an ambiguous directive. Which stock is bad? What is meant by "bad"? How bad is "bad"? The subjective nature of decision making in such a case raises questions of validity, reliability, and integrity of the decision.

Ambiguity and fuzziness have a close semantic relationship. For example, while driving down a busy avenue, the driver asks the passenger, "Do I turn left here?" The passenger answers, "right," which could mean "turn right" or "yes, you're right about turning left." The driver can favor one interpretation over others, depending on past experiences with the passenger.

This kind of ambiguity, that of meaning, is pervasive in knowledge acquisition. Generally, semantic ambiguity is distinct from fuzziness, depending on interpretation of the context. For example, the statement, "This food is rich," is ambiguous, but not fuzzy since *rich* could mean high in calories, high priced, or too sweet. Depending on the context, one interpretation might be more plausible than others. Ambiguity approximates fuzziness when defining the degree to which the food is rich. How low on calories should it be and still qualify as rich? At what precise point is this food not rich? Is it labeled "rich" when it crosses a certain threshold? This is what is called a fuzzy metric.

Incompleteness

A statement that represents some but not all pieces of knowledge is incomplete knowledge. For example, does "Adjust the air conditioner" mean to turn it on or off, or to make it cooler or warmer?

False Representation

A statement that incorrectly represents pieces of knowledge is **false representation.** Take the example, "The small key will open the door." Which small key? An incorrect representation presents the possibility of two types of errors: false positive (Type I) and false negative (Type II) error.

With **Type I error,** a rule is accepted when it should be rejected. In the "small key" example, if the small key won't open the door when it should, then accepting the key gives a false positive, or Type I error. In contrast, when a rule is rejected when it should be accepted, it is descriptive of false negative, or **Type II error.**

Type I and II errors become important when an expert system undergoes testing. During the testing phase, rules may fire when they are not supposed to fire (Type I error) and vice versa. Because rules are invariably interrelated, the verification of hundreds of rules can be a nightmare. The problem is especially critical because an expert system never seems to blow up; it gives a solution no matter how invalid the logic of the rules might be.

Errors in Measurement

Sometimes a numerical fact is erroneously reported due to imprecision in measurement. For example, how detailed—and therefore, precise—the measuring instrument is can make a difference in determining the certainty factor. In fact, because of the need to be precise, medical measurements are all in millimeters, which are more exact than inches in determining the height of a person.

Reasoning Errors

Errors can also occur in inductive or deductive reasoning. An example of an inductive reasoning error would be:

> This firm has never had a layoff. Therefore, it will never have a layoff in the future.

The likelihood of error, or CF, is higher if this conclusion is accepted. Likewise, a deductive reasoning error would be:

> If you are pregnant, then you will be overweight.

The deduction that pregnancy causes weight gain does not apply in *all* cases. Even if it did, one must still consider the question of how much weight is "overweight." Such issues are illustrative of fuzzy logic.

Errors in Individual Rules

In system testing, each rule must be verified for correctness to remove uncertainty. The more subjective the rule is, however, the more difficult it is to verify, especially in relationship to other rules in the knowledge base. Therefore, experience is needed to determine a certainty factor for each rule. Table 13–1 provides a list of sources of uncertainty.

Rule Conflict and Conflict Resolution

In building a knowledge-based system, the order or priority of rule execution must be decided so that rules will fire in a predetermined sequence. The order of priority may be explicit or implicit. **Explicit priorities** are usually set by the knowledge engineer for areas in which certain rules must be fired in a specific order. For example, the IBM ESE (Expert System Environment) shell, offers a

▓ Table 13–1 Sources of Uncertainty

- ▓ Ambiguity
- ▓ Incompleteness
- ▓ False representation, generating Type I or Type II error
- ▓ Errors in measurement
- ▓ Reasoning errors
- ▓ Errors in individual rule

command that says, "Order rules by R1, R5, R3, R4 . . .". The system lines up the rules and executes them as specified by the "order rules by" command.

The following are the most common types of *implicit rule conflict resolution* techniques:

1. *Associating certainty factor with the rules so that rules with the highest certainty factor are fired first.* For example:

```
Rule 1: IF a(CF = 0.7) THEN x(CF = 0.9)
Rule 2: IF b(CF = 0.9) THEN y(CF = 0.8)
```

CF for Rule 1 is .63
CF for Rule 2 is .72
So, Rule 2, with the higher CF would be fired first.

2. *Associating certainty factors with the rules based on the specificity of the rules premise.* For example:

```
Rule 1: IF engine won't start
        THEN battery is dead
Rule 2: IF engine won't start and horn is weak,
        THEN battery is dead.
```

Rule 2 would be fired, since its premise is more specific (and reliable) than rule 1.

3. *Rules fire based on the order in which they are entered into the knowledge base.* The shell places the rules in a queue so that they are all fired in the sequence they were entered. The order given for rule execution is not meant to override the natural sequence of rule evaluation or firing, but to break conflicts between rules.

▓ THE USE OF CERTAINTY FACTORS

Certainty factors range from +1.0 to −1.0: +1.0 means absolute belief, and −1.0 means absolute disbelief. Numbers in between refer to relative degrees of believability. See Figure 13–1. Some shells, however, do not provide for certainty factors, except by allowing the user to enter a choice such as "unknown" for an answer which reflects 100 percent certainty only. These shells are appropriate for diagnostic or repair facilities where a machine is either running or not running or the warning light is either on or off.

Figure 13–1 Certainty Factor Scale

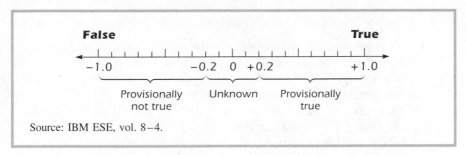

Source: IBM ESE, vol. 8–4.

A certainty factor can be used in an expert system in a variety of ways:

1. *Certainties can be assigned by user response.* A confidence factor may be entered by the user as input. The answer to "Have you been paying your mortgage premiums on time?" might be "yes" with a certainty factor of 70 percent. In the following format, the user simply enters .70 next to "yes" rather than placing "X," which is normally interpreted as 1.0 certainty factor or a definite choice.
   Question: Have you been paying your mortgage premiums on time?

   <u>.70</u> Yes
   <u>   </u> No

2. *In a diagnostic system, certainty factors can be assigned to rule conclusions.* For example:

```
IF patient_temperature > 99 and nose is runny
THEN there is .90 evidence that patient has a cold
```

   If patient_temperature holds a value greater than 99 degrees at a certainty factor of 100 percent, the conclusion "patient has a cold" is asserted at the level of 90 percent. If patient_temperature is at or below 99 degrees, the conclusion certainty may or may not be correspondingly lower, because the rule will fire only when both parts of the premise are true. The certainty factor associated with the action part of the rule can also be related to other rules in the knowledge base that use the same action in their premises or that conclude values for action.

3. *Certainty factors can be projected forward from the premise of a rule to its action.* For example:

```
IF time_to_landing is < 10 minutes,
THEN buckle seat belts.
```

   If a certainty factor of .85 percent is assigned to the rule's premise, the rule will allow the same certainty factor to the action part (buckle seat belts). But since a certainty factor for the action variable has not been specified, the default certainty factor is 100 percent. This means certainty of the action is correlated with the certainty of the premise.

4. *Certainty can be selected in compound premises.* Certainty factors can be incorporated into a rule using AND and/or OR operators in the premise of a rule. For example:

```
IF projected_demand > 100,000 AND maximum_units_
            available = 40,000,
THEN investment = company_stock.
```

The certainty of the two variables of the premise must be accounted for. Both variables must be true above a specified threshold of certainty in order to assign "investment = company_stock." In some expert systems, if the first part of the premise (projected_demand > 100,000) is true with a certainty factor of 80 percent and the second part (maximum_units_available = 40,000) is true with a certainty factor of 90 percent, then the combined certainty factor can be no higher than 80 percent which is the weaker of the two. How the final certainty factor is computed varies with each expert system shell. A common method is to multiply the two certainty factors, which in this case would result in a certainty factor of 72 percent.

When OR is used in the premise part of the rule, the two certainty factors are combined, to give a resulting certainty factor higher than either individual certainty factor. Suppose a rule says:

```
IF salary_increase is low OR inflation_rate > 8 percent
THEN reduce_spending
```

An employer has predicted an 85 percent chance of a low salary increase for the coming year. The government has also estimated an 80 percent chance of inflation being > 8 percent. The chance of at least one of these events is greater than 85 percent. Some expert systems multiply the certainty factors that neither of the two ORs will occur. This means a certainty factor of 15 percent for high salary increase and 20 percent for a lower-than-8-percent inflation rate. The product (0.15×0.20) of 3 percent leaves a 97 percent chance that a low salary increase or higher-than-8-percent inflation rate will occur. The outcome is a confidence factor of 97 percent to reduce spending.

Assigning certainty factors depends on the protocol embedded in the inference engine. Consider this example:

```
IF a(CF = .5) AND b(CF = .4) AND c(CF = .7)
THEN d
```

The question is: What certainty factor should be assigned to d? The choices available are:

1. Certainty factor is as good as the highest certainty (CF = .7).

2. d should not have a certainty factor greater than the lowest of the premise certainty factors (CF = .4).

3. d's certainty factor should be the average (CF = .53).

Truth Threshold in VP-Expert

VP-Expert has a *truth threshold* that determines if the confidence in the condition of a rule is high enough to draw any conclusions. Unless the truth condition is set, the default is 20. If the confidence is under 20, the premise or action part of the rule that holds this confidence factor will be considered false. A clause "TRUTHTHRESH" in VP-Expert allows a user to set the required confidence factor of the condition (not conclusion) of the statement to be valid under 20.

Calculating Overall Confidence

To illustrate how overall confidence is calculated in VP-Expert, consider the following rule:

```
Rule ADMIT
IF reference = good,
THEN decision = admit CNF 70;
```

If the admissions director is only 60 percent confident that the reference is good, the expert system will still conclude that "decision = admit," but with less overall confidence. In this case, the CNF of the condition is 60 and the CNF of the conclusion is 70. So, the final CNF of the conclusion is derived by combining the two CNFs using the formula:

```
[CNF(condition) × CNF(conclusion)/100]
or 60 × 70 = 42.
```

Rules without a stated CNF are assumed to have a CNF of 100. So, in the case of the ADMIT rule, the condition "reference = good" assumes a CNF of 100. The resulting CNF is $100 \times 70/100 = 70$.

Calculating CNF in Complex Rules

Rules with ANDs and ORs can be quite complex. When rule conditions are connected by ANDs, VP-Expert multiples the *lowest* CNF of the premise by the CNF of the conclusion. For example:

```
Rule PUBLISH1
IF demand = high CNF = 80 AND reviewer comments = good CNF
= 70 AND author reputation = very good CNF = 60
THEN decision = publish manuscript CNF = 90;
```

To compute the final CNF, the inference engine takes 60 (lowest CNF in the premise) and multiplies it by 90, or $(60 \times 90)/100 = 54$. The reasoning is that the overall strength of the conclusion depends on the strength of the weakest condition. Note that if any CNF in the condition is less than 20 (truth threshold), the inference engine cannot reach a conclusion.

Now, consider the following OR condition:

```
Rule PUBLISH2
IF demand = high CNF = 80 OR reviewer_comments = good CNF
= 70
THEN decision = publish_manuscript CNF = 90;
```

The combined CNF uses the formula:

```
      CNF1 + CNF2 - (CNF1 × CNF2)/100
or    80 + 70 - (80 × 70)/100
      = 150 - (56)/100
      = 94 (final CNF).
```

The fact that both conditions are true adds extra credence to the conclusion, which is reflected in a higher CNF.

Now, suppose the premise of the rule contains two ORs. How is the final CNF computed?

```
RULE PUBLISH3
IF demand = high CNF = 80 OR
   reviewer_comments = good CNF = 70 OR
   author_reputation = good CNF = 60
THEN decision = publish_manuscript CNF = 90;
```

Using the same formula, the final CNF is:

```
      80 + 70 - (80 × 70)/100 = 94
Then 94 + 60 - (94 × 60)/100 = 97.60
      97.60 × 90/100 = 87(inference engine truncates
fractions).
```

For multiple paths involving two or more rules with the same conclusion, VP-Expert calculates the CNF for each rule and then combines the resulting CNFs using the complex OR formula. For example:

```
Rule PUBLISH1
IF demand = high CNF = 60
THEN decision = publish_manuscript CNF = 80;


Rule PUBLISH2
IF reviewer_comments = good CNF = 65
THEN decision = publish_manuscript CNF = 80;


Rule PUBLISH3
IF author_reputation = good CNF = 75
THEN decision = publish_manuscript CNF = 80;
```

The procedure is:

1. CNF for PUBLISH1 $60 \times 80/100 = 48$
   CNF for PUBLISH2 $65 \times 80/100 = 52$
   CNF for PUBLISH3 $75 \times 80/100 = 60$
2. $48 + 52 - (48 \times 52)/100 = 75$
3. $75 + 60 - (75 \times 60)/100 = 90$

For rules containing both ANDs and ORs, VP-Expert considers ORs before ANDs. CNF is calculated by:

- deciding on the CNF of the ANDs
- combining the resulting CNFs of ANDs with the OR CNF
- multiplying the resulting CNF by the CNF of the conclusion.

For example:

```
Rule PUBLISH5
IF demand = high CNF = 60 AND
   reviewer_comments = good CNF = 65 OR
   author_reputation = good CNF = 55
THEN decision = publish_manuscript CNF = 90;
```

The rule can be rearranged as follows:

```
demand = high AND reviewer_comments = good (CNF = 60 AND
CNF = 65) = 60
OR
demand = high AND author_reputation = good (CNF = 60 AND
CNF = 55) = 55
THEN decision = publish_manuscript CNF = 90;
```

The procedure is:

1. $60 + 55 - (60 \times 55)/100 = 82$
2. $(82 \times 90)/100 = 74$

▓ FUZZY LOGIC

Cold and calculating, traditional Boolean logic attempts to classify sensory perception as black or white. This degree of precision is difficult to employ and is often beyond human ability in the real world. This ambiguity, vagueness, or lack of definition perceived by natural human sensors falls within the realm of fuzzy logic.

Humans have common sense that enables them to reason in situations with only partially true information. This means that most decisions are not based on absolute, clear-cut, "crisp" information. Rather, they are based on imprecise information without sharp boundaries.

Until now, "high," "low," "few," and "many" had no place in information system applications. Fuzzy logic is the branch of machine intelligence that allows computers to manipulate common sense in an uncertain world. It operates upon the key concept that everything is a matter of degree. Fuzzy logic is a method of reducing or managing system complexity by manipulating vague concepts such as warm/cold. With it, engineers can build washing machines and air conditioners that "decide" how fast, how gentle, or how cool they should operate or that shift into a mode of operation difficult to define in numeric terms.

The term **fuzzy** means inexact knowledge or imprecise reasoning present in the knowledge used by human experts. Fuzziness measures the degree to which a condition exists. It describes the degree of membership in fuzzy set. In contrast, probability is an uncertainty associated with time. It indicates whether something will occur or not. Suppose a given city has a 50 percent chance of rain tomorrow. If the residents wait till tomorrow, they can see whether it rained so the uncertainty associated with probability disappears.

Unlike probability, fuzziness does not dissipate with time. In the "50 percent chance of rain tomorrow" example, the fuzzy uncertainty remains. The statement is still ambiguous as to whether the rain will be a drizzle, steady rain, or a downpour.

Fuzzy logic, then, is the approximate rather than exact logic underlying modes of reasoning. It is based on the use of fuzzy sets rather than conventional digital logic. Fuzzy logic accounts for ambiguities and shades of grey inherent to real world data. Unlike conventional digital logic, it can accommodate a range of values called a **membership set** instead of just two (hot/cold, fast/slow, etc). For example, high/low values such as "short and tall," "young and old" are not understandable to traditional computer applications. They can, however, all be included in a membership set under fuzzy logic which typically results in a ten-to-one reduction in system design complexity.

Fuzzy logic's history dates back to the 1920s when Polish logician Jan Kukasiewicz developed the principles of multivalued logic and essentially proved that statements can have fractional truth values between the one and zero of binary logic. In 1937, philosopher Max Black applied multivalued logic to sets of objects and drew the first fuzzy set curves. Black called the sets "vague."

Almost 30 years later, fuzzy logic was proposed as an alternative to traditional logic by Lotfi A. Zadeh, a professor at the University of California at Berkeley, in a landmark paper published in 1965 entitled, "Fuzzy Sets," which gave the field its name. Zadeh applied Kukasiewicz's logic and developed a complete algebra for fuzzy sets. Systems that can be represented by a simple equation should probably not be modeled by fuzzy logic. Rather, fuzzy logic is best applied to a nonlinear or ill-defined system. For example, in the case of a thermostat with upper and lower boundaries that can be set to switch heating or air conditioning on or off in response to a request for a desired temperature, fuzzy logic would not be appropriate. But when precision is not necessary—when the occupants of a house couldn't care less whether the temperature was 69 or 70 degrees fahrenheit—fuzzy logic would be useful because of its low specificity.

Uses of Fuzzy Logic

Fuzzy logic can control systems by using common-sense rules that refer to infinite quantities or uncertain data. It is another method of handling uncertainty and vagueness in problems with unclear boundaries. See Box 13–2. Like certainty factors, fuzzy sets allow expert systems to combine several indicators with low levels of confidence to arrive at one measure with a high level of confidence. For most knowledge engineers, a major benefit of fuzzy logic is its contribution to encoding expert knowledge in the same way the expert thinks about the decision process. A fuzzy representation captures the expertise as it appears in the expert's own cognitive model of the problem domain. This ability makes knowledge acquisition more reliable and less prone to ambiguities or interpretation errors.

Other benefits of fuzzy logic are flexibility and tolerance. In real-life decision making, rigid thinking often leads to unsatisfactory conclusions. Humans tend to make allowances for the unexpected, because they can't afford to be absolutely wrong. For example, if a sales manager estimated 1994 sales to be 90 percent higher than the preceding year, and they turned out to be 80 percent higher, the consequences to the manager or the firm should not be that severe.

Fuzzy Sets

People routinely place things into classes with well understood meanings but whose boundaries are not well defined. In fuzzy reasoning, the concept of fuzzy sets is synonymous with such a class. By definition, a **fuzzy set** is a class of elements defined by a **membership function** that relates a grade of membership with each class element. For example, "large" cars, "fast" PCs, and "rich" people are distinct fuzzy sets. The set is fuzzy, because it is unclear how large is large, how fast is fast, and so on. Figure 13–2 distinguishes between fuzzy sets and nonfuzzy sets. The dotted line in (b) illustrates the fuzzy set's

Box 13-2   Applications become Clearer with Fuzzy Logic

Very little in life is black and white, but computers have a tendency to make us solve problems that way. Now, Knoxville, Tenn.–based FuziQuote and the soon-to-be released FuziCalc, allow users to establish "fuzzy" values for activities such as determining the per-piece price on manufactured goods. Users can input hard data, such as costs of raw materials and tooling, and then add fuzzy values for such things as "How much do we want this job?" and "How busy are we at the moment?" The effect of fuzzy information on the equation is determined by historical data, embedded knowledge from experienced employees and "current insight" into the situation at the moment the quote is made.

The result is an accurate quote made in less time than would normally be required to pass proposals in front of all the required employees and shorter response times to customer requests.

"With our quoting, a lot of the numbers that we would come up with were best guess," said Laney Fowler, vice president of sales and marketing at Foremost Manufacturing Co., a formed metal fabricator in Union, N.J. FuziQuote allows the firm to input ranges instead of crisp numbers and include abstract information. This eliminates the need for the company to gather all its employees with quoting experience each time a bid has to be calculated.

FuziCalc takes the fuzzy logic idea even further into the realm of general use. Users are presented with a common Windows-based spreadsheet interface into which they can add both hard and fuzzy data. Fuzzy numbers are represented by a chart that can be directly manipulated by the user. Users can pick a range of acceptable or probable answers and also establish a "desirability" level from "0" (unacceptable) to "1" (totally acceptable).

For example, an application that might be used to determine possible cities for a new plant might include such factors as city size, number of available airline flights and temperature. By adjusting a graph for each factor, a user might indicate that cities having between 500,000 and 3 million residents, at least 15 flights per day and an average temperature of 50 to 70 degrees Fahrenheit are suitable.

Source: Christopher Lindquist, *Computerworld,* July 6, 1992, p. 24.

---

complement. Partial membership must sum to one. If 55 degrees is 50 percent "chilly," it is also 50 percent "not chilly."

The members of a fuzzy set are identified by a *grade of membership* (a number between 0 and 1) that is attached to each element of the class. So, membership in a fuzzy set is a value between 0 and 1 that indicates to what extent the element is a member. At 0, the element has no membership; at 1, it has full membership (completely representative of the set). The transition between the extremes is gradual, not distinct.

The Saga of Tall and Middle-Age People

To illustrate fuzzy and membership sets, consider the concept of height. At what height is a person considered "tall"? Classical mathematical set theory would requires a specification for an inclusive membership function or a direct command that anyone over six and one-half feet is tall. Accordingly, someone who is six feet 5 inches is not "tall." In the real world, tallness is relative, not absolute. Many people consider anyone over six feet to be tall, but what about

Figure 13–2 Examples of Nonfuzzy and Fuzzy Sets

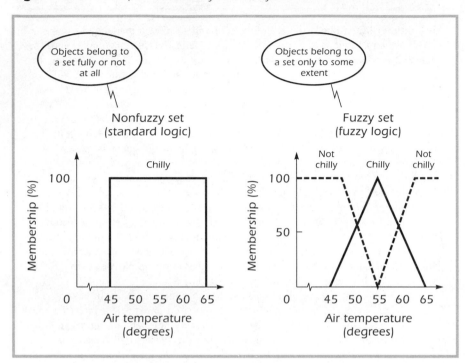

people who are five feet eleven inches? So, how tall is "tall"? Where is the cutoff between tall and not tall?

The concept of "tallness" is a fuzzy membership set because the range of heights considered to be tall is not well defined. But human appreciation for tall increases as the value of height increases. So, one can say that tall is not "crisp" or sharply defined. In Figure 13–3 the degree of membership in the fuzzy set is marked on the graph between the value of 0 (extremely short) and 1 (extremely tall). Moving up the set (on the graph) towards 1 (full membership) shows the "truth" value associated with the corresponding height. Full membership exists with the value of 1. Any height below this value represents partial membership in the set.

Central to the concept of fuzzy logic is a linguistic variable, which is the name of a fuzzy set. In the previous example, the fuzzy set TALL is a simple linguistic variable that can be used in a rule-based system to make decisions based on the tallness of a particular person:

```
IF tallness height is tall
THEN back injury risk is increased
```

The concept of "middle-age" as applied to people is another example of fuzzy set. Here, middle-age is defined by traditional logic as an arbitrary membership or "crisp" set including anyone between 40 and 55. Since the boundary between what is in a set and what is outside the set are sharp, these constraints are called crisp sets. Fuzzy sets offer a better definition by representing middle-age by a bell-shaped curve. See Figure 13–4. When the variable *age* is mapped to the fuzzy set "middle-age," its membership increases as age approaches 40 years old—absolute membership in the set. Moving

Figure 13–3   Tall Membership Set

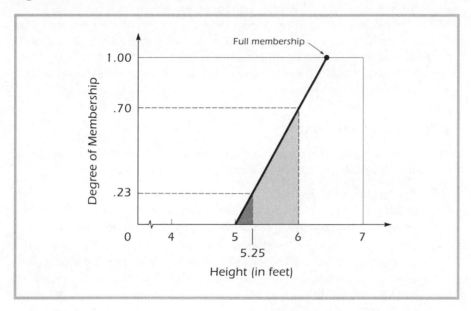

Figure 13–4   Middle-Age Fuzzy Set

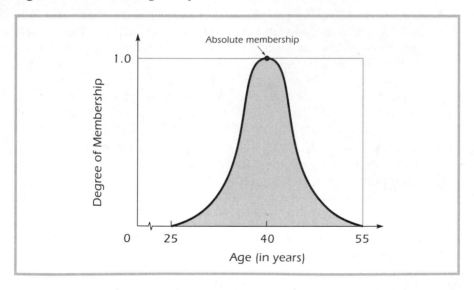

beyond 40, membership declines toward 0 again, which means that, although considered middle-aged, the person is moving toward another fuzzy domain (senior citizen fuzzy set.)

As demonstrated by these examples, fuzzy logic serves as a building block of linguistic expression. It takes personal perceptions into account. For example, in Figure 13–4, a person who is 30 has .25 degree of membership in the middle-age set. It means membership is moderately, not strongly, compatible with the notion of middle-age. A person who is 40 has 1.0 (full or absolute) degree of membership in the middle age set, etc. The maximum degree of membership, or age 40 in this case, represents the height of a fuzzy set.

The only constraint on fuzzy logic is that the degree of membership of an object in complementary groups must add up to 1. For example, if the air is 60 percent humid, it must also be 40 percent not humid. In this case, fuzzy logic differs from saying that the air is either 100 percent humid and 100 percent not humid, which destroys formal logic.

Building a Fuzzy System

A fuzzy system is based on fuzzy rules and is generally built by following some basic steps. To illustrate, a fuzzy system is built in four steps:

1. The first step is to determine whether a fuzzy system is the right approach to the problem. If a system's behavior can be explained in approximate terms for a heuristic rule, then a fuzzy system is appropriate.

2. The second step identifies the variables, say x and y. x is the input to the system, and y is the output. The idea is input-output, cause-effect, question-answer, and so on. Suppose a mail order house wants to control the sale of its PCs. Assume x is product demand and y is price. Management wants the price to inch upward when the demand increases and drop when it decreases.

3. The next step is to pick the fuzzy sets. Four fuzzy sets are defined for x(demand): strong, average, below average, and weak. These fuzzy sets are arbitrarily drawn as triangles as shown in Figure 13–5. Some sets are drawn wider than other sets based on common sense. The narrow triangle is the most important, because the dealer needs to operate within 3,000–4,500 units per week to stay in business.

   Next, the four fuzzy sets are defined for y: suggested retail, regular, special sale, and super sale. See Figure 13–6. The seller price changes and ranges are based on years of experience.

4. In the final step, price sets are associated with demand sets. Starting with "strong" demand, the price is set at the manufacturer's suggested retail price, which usually gives the retailer the highest markup. When the volume drops to average, a price drop to regular (competitive price) would be just right to keep the sale volume within the average range.

The price range shown from 10 to 2 in Figure 13–6 could accommodate any price figures, with "2" representing cost to the retailer. If x is strong, then y is suggested retail. Little sales effort is required at this phase. If x is average, then y is regular and represents the comfort zone for maintaining the business. If x is below average, then y is special sale, which is lower than the regular price. Lower price should generate enough demand to bring the sales to the average zone. Finally, if x is weak, then y is super sale. The price is usually set close to the retailer's cost. These rules are written in English as follows:

```
R1    IF demand is strong, THEN price is the
      manufacturer's suggested retail
R2    IF demand is average, THEN price is regular
R3    IF demand is below average, THEN price is special
      sale price
R4    IF demand is weak, THEN price is super sale price
```

Figure 13–5 Fuzzy Sets of x, Demand

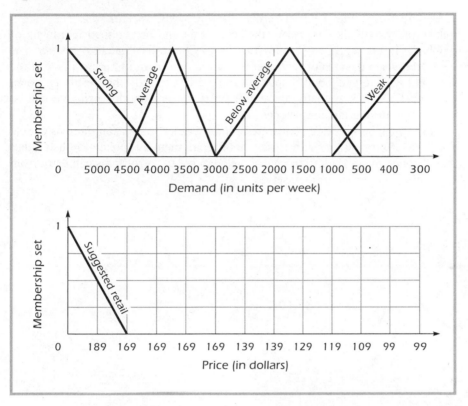

Figure 13–6 Fuzzy Sets for y, Price

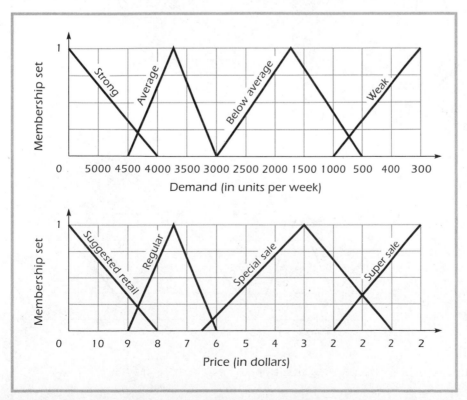

These are fuzzy rules because terms—*strong, weak, special sale,* etc.—are a matter of degree; they represent the fuzzy sets and are defined as ranges of numbers. In his work, Kosko described fuzzy rules as "patches." A *patch* is generated when the area of two triangles cross. As shown in Figure 13–7, if the set "below average" and "special sale" are crossed, the resulting patch represents RULE3. Actually, the entire fuzzy system for this example can be drawn as four overlapping patches.

Fuzzy engineers design software to make computers reason more as people do. Today, fuzzy systems allow users to program them by spoken English rather than through the keyboard. In fact, some adaptive fuzzy systems can learn from experience and program themselves.

Figure 13–7 Fuzzy Sets in Patches

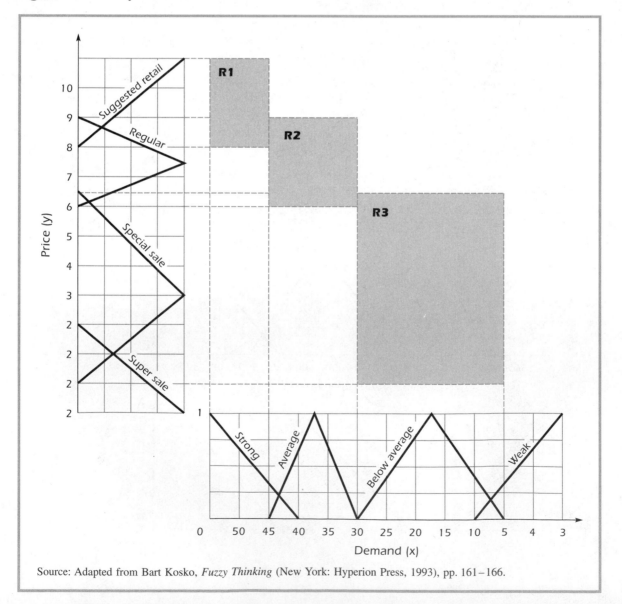

Source: Adapted from Bart Kosko, *Fuzzy Thinking* (New York: Hyperion Press, 1993), pp. 161–166.

So, fuzzy knowledge boils down to fuzzy rules. Fuzzy systems store hundreds of these common-sense fuzzy rules. Each input activates all these rules to some degree. The fuzzy system then blends the output and produces a final answer. This type of reasoning goes on as fast as the computer chip allows.

Fuzzy Applications

Japan has taken the lead incorporating fuzzy logic into all kinds of products. Fuzzy logic has offered new ways to "dress up" old products in the highly competitive Japanese market. It has been applied to everything from fire alarms to fabric dyeing. Fuzzy-based consumer items focus on creating more complex and efficient controls that are easier to operate. For example, Matsushita has produced a washing machine with 600 cycle combinations, yet the only control is a start button—sensors and fuzzy logic adjust the wash cycle according to the amount and dirtiness of the clothes and the type of detergent used. See Box 13–3 for another application of fuzzy logic.

Figure 13–8 provides a graph for fuzzy air conditioner system that uses five rules to match five temperature sets or fuzzy inputs (cold, chilly, just right, warm, hot) to motor speeds or fuzzy outputs (very slow, slow, medium, fast, very fast). For example, if the temperature is 63 degrees, it might be 20 percent "chilly" (80 percent not "chilly") and 80 percent "just right" (20 percent not "just right"). The "if chilly" rule and the "just right" rule would trigger the slow and medium speeds of the motor at the same time resulting in the intended mix shown.

Other well-known fuzzy logic applications include:

- *Elevator control* (Fujitec/Toshiba)—monitors passenger traffic to reduce waiting time and improves care announcement accuracy.

- *Video camcorder* (Sanyo Fisher/Canon)—decides on the best focus and lighting when several objects are in the picture.

- *Television* (Sony)—adjusts screen color, contrast, and brightness, depending on the channel and program.

- *Auto transmission* (Subaru)—selects best gear ratio, depending on driving style and engine load. General Motors uses a fuzzy transmission it its Saturn. Nissan had developed a fuzzy antiskid braking system and fuzzy fuel injector.

- *Vacuum cleaner* (Matsushita)—adjusts the unit's motor power based on floor condition and dust quantity.

The central aspect in the building of a fuzzy system is the contribution of its rules. Almost all fuzzy products on the market today use rules provided by experts. The knowledge engineer engages in a series of sessions with the expert to fine tune these rules and the fuzzy sets. A great deal of verification and validation of the concept and process takes place before the system can be distributed commercially.

Probably the most important aspect of fuzzy technology is its ability to make computers friendlier. Sony has developed a "palm top" computer that allows the user to enter information by writing on its screen with a plastic pen. The computer uses fuzzy logic to determine what words are being written. Pattern recognition, either reading handwriting or recognizing spoken words, is much easier when the system can search for approximations rather than exact matches.

Box 13–3   Fuzzy-Logic Air Conditioner

Mitsubishi Heavy Industries Ltd. of Japan designed and manufactured the first fuzzy-logic controlled commercial air conditioner, which uses technology developed jointly with Togai InfraLogic Inc. of Irvine, California. The air conditioner can determine the thermal characteristics of a room and temperature change required and adjust its air flow to minimize heating and cooling times and maintain a stable room temperature. Masaki Togai, president of Togai InfraLogic, explains: "Fuzzy logic makes it possible for products like the new Mitsubishi air conditioner to make 'shades of gray' decisions the way humans do, as opposed to the limited 'yes or no' approach dictated by conventional computer logic."

Air conditioners are highly nonlinear systems with tremendous inherent delays. Current control schemes require several scenarios to be programmed into the controller for different heating and cooling rates and room sizes. At best, these systems can stabilize a room to within the sensitivity of the temperature sensor, and they have the annoying and discomforting characteristic of turning on and off. The fuzzy controlled system can adapt smoothly to different room sizes and temperature variations and can compensate for mass in the room. Based on fuzzy inferencing, temperature stability was improved by two times, to twice the resolution of the temperature sensor. An overall improvement in smoothness of temperature control results in less power consumption savings amounted to more than 20 percent.

The air conditioner begins a heating or cooling sequence by directing the air either up or down; this operation starts a convection cycle to create air flow. Once heating or cooling begins, the air flow is "warped"—directed up and down in a wave-like motion to stop the convection cycle and distribute the air evenly. The air flow and temperature are slowly reduced.

An infrared sensor determines if anyone is in the room. If not, the initial temperature cycling will slow to reduce power consumption. The temperature cycling, stabilization, and control cycles are fuzzy-controlled, including air flow, temperature, and warping.

Source: Maurine Caudill, "Using Neural Nets: Fuzzy Decisions," *AI Expert*, April 1990, p. 61.

Fuzzy logic is good for applications that are difficult to describe digitally. The opening of a new subway in 1988 in Sendai, Japan, was probably the single most significant event in fuzzy logic applications. Hitachi installed fuzzy logic computers that accelerate and brake the trains so smoothly that no one need use the hanging straps. This and similar practical applications of theory have fueled the ensuing interest in fuzzy logic as a weapon in both high- and low-tech industries.

As fuzzy logic is incorporated into more applications, entirely new applications that were not practical before fuzzy logic will emerge. New chips specifically designed to do fuzzy logic calculations are also expected to appear. Presently, however, chip makers are waiting to see how fuzzy logic applications develop so they know what features to consider, while business applications are waiting for fuzzy logic microcontrollers to become available and affordable. In the meantime, a number of fuzzy logic applications have been developed on conventional microcontrollers without much difficulty.

Figure 13–8   Fuzzy Air Conditioner Graph

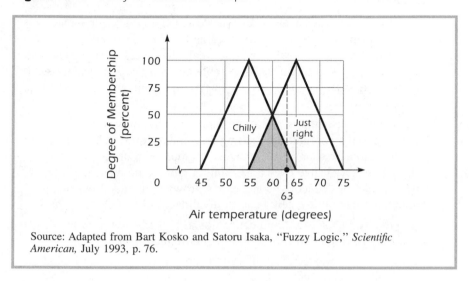

Source: Adapted from Bart Kosko and Satoru Isaka, "Fuzzy Logic," *Scientific American,* July 1993, p. 76.

IMPLICATIONS FOR MANAGEMENT

Several managerial issues are associated with certainty factors:

1. The *expert* needs to clarify that certainty factors, not fuzzy logic, are at issue. They are not the same.

2. Shells differ in the way they calculate certainty factors. This background information would be helpful for an *organization* in determining which shell to select for expert system development.

3. With the various capabilities of shells, the *knowledge engineer* should be skilled in understanding the expert's use of certainty factors and how they are translated by the shell in use. This is not an easy task, as certainty factors are often calculated differently, depending on how many rules are involved and the certainty factor of the conclusion part of each rule.

4. *Users* should be familiar with the meaning of certainty factors in various contexts to enable a clear interpretation of the results. The interpretation should also be made within the framework of the shell and the way it calculates the certainty factor.

5. *Management* should agree on the proper use of certainty factors so that it is standardized throughout the firm.

In some cases, certainty factors are less than precise. Much of their ambiguity stems from the various ways shells calculate certainty factors. Different calculations result in different conclusions. Yet, certainty factors continue to be used, because of their effectiveness in addressing certain problems. Some experts may be asked to eliminate certainty factors for some problem domains, but the knowledge engineer must guard against compromising the expert's thought processes in such a case.

■ SUMMARY

1. The two main drawbacks under the old reasoning procedures are (1) statements can only be expressed as true or false, and (2) producing new knowledge about real-life situations is difficult. One of the most difficult items to replicate in an expert system is how humans deal with imprecise, uncertain, or incomplete information.

2. Monotonic reasoning is a reasoning process that moves in one direction only, continuously adding additional truths. Whereas nonmonotonic reasoning recognizes incomplete information in situations that change over time. Unlike monotonic reasoning in which a set of deductible conclusions grows with added reasoning, nonmonotonic allows new facts to invalidate old facts.

3. A certainty factor is a "confidence" or a "belief," not a probability. It is a subjective quantification of an expert's judgment.

4. Uncertainty is created through various sources of error that include ambiguity, a statement that has more than one meaning; incompleteness, a statement that represents some but not all pieces of knowledge; and false representation, a statement that incorrectly represents pieces of knowledge. Other errors include errors in measurement, reasoning errors, errors in individual rules, and rule conflict and conflict organization. Some common types of implicit rule conflict resolution are:

   a. associating certainty factors with rules.

   b. associating certainty factors with rules based on the specificity of the rules premise.

   c. rules fire based on the order in which they are entered into the knowledge base.

5. Certainty factors come from a set of +1, absolute belief, to −1, absolute disbelief; the numbers in between refer to relative degrees of believability. Some ways certainty factors can be used in expert systems include:

   a. assigned by user response

   b. assigned to rule conclusions

   c. projected forward from the premise of a rule to its action

   d. selected in compound premises

6. Fuzzy logic is the approximate rather than exact logic underlying modes of reasoning. It accounts for ambiguities that are inherent to real-world data, unlike conventional digital logic. It is best applied to nonlinear, time-variant, or ill-defined systems.

7. Fuzzy logic allows an expert system to reason with uncertain data through fuzzy sets—a class of elements defined by a membership function that relates a grade of membership with each class element. Some fuzzy applications are elevator control, video camcorder, and most importantly, user-friendly computers.

■ TERMS TO LEARN

Ambiguity characterizes a statement that has more than one meaning or is interpreted in more than one way.

Certainty factor (CF) a measurement of belief or a subjective quantification of an expert's judgment and intentions.

Explicit Priorities a specific order in which certain rules must be fired; usually set by the knowledge engineer.

False representation a statement that incorrectly represents pieces of knowledge, associated with Type I and Type II errors.

Fuzzy inexact knowledge or imprecise reasoning present in the knowledge used by human experts.

Fuzzy logic the approximate rather than exact logic underlying modes of reasoning; allows an expert system to reason with uncertain data.

Fuzzy set a class of elements defined by a membership function.

Incomplete knowledge a statement that represents some but not all pieces of needed information.

Membership function relates a grade of membership with each class element.

Membership set a range of values.

Monotonic reasoning a process that moves in one direction only, continuously adding additional truths.

Nonmonotonic reasoning allows new facts to invalidate old facts; holds a set of premises to be true and keeps a collection of contingent beliefs and revises those beliefs when new knowledge is derived.

Type I error a rule is accepted when it should be rejected; a false positive.

Type II error a rule is rejected when it should be accepted; a false negative.

Uncertainty lack of adequate information on which to base a decision.

■ REVIEW QUESTIONS

1. "One of the most difficult items to replicate in an expert system is imprecise, uncertain, or incomplete information." Do you agree? Explain.

2. Various types of uncertainty are common in expert systems. Explain each type briefly. Is one type necessarily more serious than the others? Be specific.

3. Distinguish between:
   a. monotonic and nonmonotonic reasoning
   b. Type I and Type II errors
   c. certainty factors and fuzzy logic

4. Illustrate by an example of your own how vagueness and ambiguity are possible sources of uncertainty.

5. If a rule in the knowledge base fires when it is not supposed to fire, what type error has occurred?

6. From your own experience, give an example of a reasoning error.

7. How would one associate certainty factors with knowledge base rules? Illustrate.

8. In how many ways can a certainty factor be used in an expert system? Elaborate.

9. "The difficult process of assigning certainty factors depends on the protocol embedded in the inference engine." Do you agree? Give an example of your own to illustrate.

10. Much of the chapter talked about fuzzy logic and fuzzy sets. Define *fuzzy logic* in

your own words and give an example to illustrate.

11. What is a membership set? How does it work?

12. Review the journals in your library and report a summary of two fuzzy applications since 1994. What was your impression of these applications?

■ EXERCISES AND CASES

1. Use the idea of a LONG flight as shown in the following chart to explain how a fuzzy set actually functions.

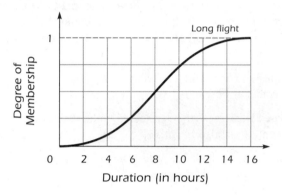

2. Suppose you heard the statement, *The food is hot.* In what way is it ambiguous? Fuzzy? Explain.

3. Review the following cube and explain its visual ambiguity.

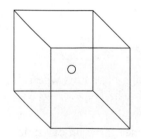

4. Examine the following image—a square bounded by black circles at each corner. Does this image exist? Why? Can you look at the image without seeing the square? What does this exercise tell you about perceptual ambiguity?

5. Consider the statement *Losses are very high.* How precise is the region HIGH in determining the degree to which losses are high? Explain.

6. Write three statements that show vagueness or ambiguity. Explain how each is vague or ambiguous.

7. Explain the following warning message printed on the cap of a car's radiator: *Never open when hot.* Describe its fuzziness. Its ambiguity (if any), vagueness (if any).

8. Explain the following fuzzy implication that uses modus ponens:

> Big men are heavy.
> John is a big man.
> Therefore, John is heavy.

■ SELECTED REFERENCES

Anderson, Glenn. "Fuzzy Logic: What It Is, What It Does, What It Can Do." *Production (PRD)*, October 1994, pp. 38–42.

Babyak, Richard J. "To Be Fuzzy, or Not To Be Fuzzy." *Appliance Manufacturer (APL)*, February 1993, pp. 31–32.

Berenji, H. R. "A Reinforcement Learning-Based Architecture for Fuzzy Logic Control." *International Journal of Approximate Reason*, February 1992, pp. 267–292.

Brubaker, David. "An Accelerated Kernel for Fuzzy Systems." *AI Expert*, March 1993, pp. 38–43.

Chase, Victor. "Clearing Up Fuzzy Logic and Neural Networks." *Appliance Manufacturer (APL)*, July 1994, p. 8.

Coates, Joseph F. "Looking Ahead: Fuzzy Logic Is Clearly in Your Future." *Research-Technology Management (RMG)*, May/June 1994, pp. 7–8.

Cox, Earl. "Applications of Fuzzy System Models." *AI Expert*, October 1992, pp. 34–39.

Dilmore, Gene. "Fuzziness in Real Estate." *PC AI,* March/April 1995, pp. 32–34.

Dolan, Charles. "The Magic of Fuzzy Logic." *Global Investor (GLI),* July/August 1994, pp. 11–14.

Hanratty, Peter J.; Joseph Babu; and Milorad P. Dudukovic. "Knowledge Representation and Reasoning in the Presence of Uncertainty in an Expert System for Laboratory Reactor Selection." *Industrial & Engineering Chemistry Research,* January 1992, pp. 228–238.

Hoffman, Mark E. "Extending Probability to Fuzzy Probability." *AI Expert,* December 1994, pp. 38–41.

Hung, Chuan-Chang. "Building a Neuro-Fuzzy Learning Control System." *AI Expert,* November 1993, pp. 40–43.

Jablonowski, Mark. "Fuzzy Risk Analysis: Using AI Systems." *AI Expert,* December 1994, pp. 34–37.

Kasuba, Tom. "Simplified Fuzzy Artmap." *AI Expert,* November 1993, pp. 18–25.

Kosko, Bart. *Fuzzy Thinking. New York: Hyperion, 1993.*

——————. "Fuzziness vs. Probability." *International Journal of General Systems* 17, no. 2 (1990), pp. 211–240.

——————. *Neural Networks and Fuzzy Systems: A Dynamical Systems Approach to Machine Intelligence.* Englewood Cliffs, NJ: Prentice-Hall, 1992.

——————. "The Probability Monopoly." *International Journal of Approximate Reasoning,* 1993.

Krause, Paul and Dominic Clark. *Representing Uncertain Knowledge: An Artificial Intelligence Approach.* Boston, MA: Kluwer Academic Publishers, 1993.

Lee, M. A. and H. Takagi. "Integrating Design Stages of Fuzzy Systems Using Genetic Algorithms." In *Proceedings of the Second International Conference on Fuzzy Systems. (Fuzz-IEEE '93), March 28-April 1, 1993.* New York; IEEE, 1993, pp. 612–617.

Lindh, Lars. "Fuzzy Logic Engine for Turbo Pascal." *AI Expert,* October 1993, pp. 36–48.

"Logic of the Future." *Success,* October 1994, pp. 38–39.

Luger, George F. and William A. Stubblefield. *Artificial Intelligence: Structure and Strategy for Complex Problem Solving,* 2d ed. Redwood, CA: Benjamin Cummings, 1993.

Masuch, Michael. *Knowledge Representation and Reasoning Under Uncertainty: Logic at Work.* New York; Springer-Verlag, 1994.

Munakata, Toshinori and Yashvant Jani. "Fuzzy Systems: An Overview." *Communications of the ACM,* March 1994, pp. 69–75.

Ralescu, Anca L. "Fuzzy Logic in Artificial Intelligence: IJCAI 1993 Workshop." In *Proceedings of IJCAI'93 Workshop, Chambiery, France,* August 28, 1993.

Rappaport, Jeff. "Rough Sets." *PC AI,* March/April 1995, pp. 35–39.

Siler, William. "Fuzzy Reasoning." *PC AI,* March/April 1995, pp. 22–31.

Szladow, Adam and Wojciech Ziarko. "Rough Sets: Working With Imperfect Data." *AI Expert,* July 1993, pp. 36–41.

Viot, Greg. "Fuzzy Logic: Concepts to Constructs." *AI Expert,* November 1993, pp. 26–33.

Walsh, Birrell. "Fuzzy Logic: The American Market." *AI Expert,* November 1993, pp. 34–39.

Wang, H. F.; C. W. Wu; and C. Y. Tsao. "Fuzzy Markov Analysis on Followup Care of Gastric Cancer Patients." *Heuristics,* Summer 1993, pp. 1–13.

Watkins, Fred. "Building Large-Scale Fuzzy Systems." *PC AI,* March/April 1995, pp. 50–51.

Zadeh, Lotfi A. "Fuzzy Logic, Neural Networks, and Soft Computing." *Communications of the ACM,* March 1994, pp. 77–84.

Chapter ■ 14

Development Tools

CHAPTER OUTLINE

Building Tools
Levels of Building Tools
Specific Expert System Packages
Shells
Main Elements
Uses and Users
Comparison Criteria
Mainframe-Based and PC-Driven Shells
IBM's Expert System Environment
A Knowledge Base: Vacation
VP-Expert
EXSYS
Comparison of ESE and VP-Expert

■ **Implications for Management**

INTERVIEW WITH DUSTIN HUNTINGTON, PRESIDENT OF EXSYS, INC.

How and when did EXSYS get started?

It all began somewhat by accident in 1982, with an expert system shell I built for my personal use. I was working for the Department of Energy and pursuing bird watching as a hobby. I decided to build an expert system to identify birds. Using LISP, I built a shell that allowed me to input the rules for the system. As it turned out, there was nothing intrinsically about birds in the shell, and I had unintentionally made a generic expert system shell. The LISP-based program worked, but had major performance problems due to LISP on an 8088-based PC. To improve performance, I reprogrammed the shell in C—although I still believe LISP to be one of the most fascinating languages. The conversion to C was aimed at making the shell easy to use and even more generic. This became the first version of EXSYS, which I released in 1983, at a price much lower than the competition. At that time, only two other PC-based expert system shells were on the market, with prices up to 50 times the EXSYS price.

In those days, most people thought that artificial intelligence in general, and expert systems in particular, belonged to the world of high-end computing. And PCs were still relatively new. So the idea of an expert system shell on a PC attracted considerable attention—from the media as well as from developers—which helped us get established.

How big is the EXSYS company?

Eleven people work for EXSYS, all in New Mexico. About half our people work in development, the other half in sales. We are also affiliated with several knowledge engineering firms that assist us in some projects. Sumisho has three people in Japan working sales and development.

Who uses EXSYS?

Our products are used in lots of places, mainly in the data-rich process industries. Process industries are particularly amenable to small, low-cost, easily developed expert systems. Texas Eastman Kodak, for example—a petrochemical company in Longview, Texas—trained 300 people to use EXSYS. Although these people are experts in petrochemical processes, many knew little about computers and nothing about rule-based expert systems. Each expert builds expert systems about something within his or her area of experience. Each system has between 30 to 150 rules, and they've developed over 300 of these expert systems.

The financial world also has EXSYS applications. Financial Proformas—a company in Walnut Creek, California—has built a very complex system that makes decisions on loan applications. An NYU professor built a system that detects insider stock trading. His system runs every day at the American Stock Exchange. And Nestle's has also put a system together that helps with decisions on retirement benefits.

Perhaps one of the most unique EXSYS applications is in Malaysia. An organization there has a system that decides what kind of rubber tree to plant in a particular valley, given the valley's microclimate. They can even put it on a battery-operated laptop and take into the plantation.

How has the EXSYS shell evolved?

Almost all growth comes from user requests. The original version of EXSYS was released in 1983 and it continued to grow. But we had a number of requests for features that could not be handled within the structure of EXSYS. To add the features would have meant significantly increasing the level of difficulty for all of our users to benefit a few. We eventually found a way to handle it and that became EXSYS Professional. We added features such as procedural command language, frames, blackboards and interfaces into linear programming. Their use is not required and the shell defaults back to a simple system that is easy to learn. But when the user needs the extra power, it's there.

With all of our developments, plans, and goals, our fundamental philosophy remains the same as when we started back in 1983: give people a reasonably priced tool they can use in a creative way, and they will be very creative and productive. They'll come up with substantial and useful applications, and in the process, they'll let us know what paths to take.

Source: *PCAI*, July/August 1992, pp.54–55ff.

AT A GLANCE

Developing expert systems requires the right tools that ensure proper error-free construction. Expert systems can be programmed, using a variety of tools: high-level programming languages, and shells in which all the developer does is build the knowledge base. The recent trend for business applications has been more toward the use of shells than programming languages.

A shell has an inference engine and a user interface. It coordinates a multitude of functions around the knowledge base. The main forms of knowledge representation are rules and frames. Rule-based shells are the most common and are available for use on personal computers.

Tools without skilled personnel are virtually useless. The expert system development team includes the knowledge engineer, the domain expert, and the end-user. They must work together in the interest of a successful system and user satisfaction.

Shells have distinctive features and are evaluated based on a set of technical and organizational criteria determined in advance. Some of the selection elements include knowledge representation schemes, reasoning strategies, interface capabilities with other software, user interfaces, editing and tracing features, ability to deal with uncertainty, and explanation capability. Serious evaluation of shells must be carried out early in the development life cycle so that the approach used in knowledge representation conforms to the requirements of the shell.

What You Will Learn

By the end of this chapter, you should know the following:

1. The distinctions among programming languages, support aids, and specific expert system packages.

2. The main elements, uses, and users of shells.

3. The selection criteria for shells in general.

4. Basic differences between mainframe-based and PC-driven shells.

5. How to evaluate an expert system shell.

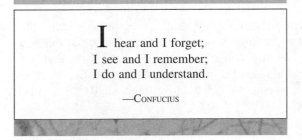

I hear and I forget;
I see and I remember;
I do and I understand.

—Confucius

INTRODUCTION

The preceding chapters discussed two critical steps in building expert systems: knowledge acquisition and knowledge representation. The knowledge engineer now needs tools to finish the job, to actually build the system. The tools must be computer-based and capable of solving the problem.

Since the mid-1970s, a wide choice of tools and approaches for developing expert systems have become available. They range from high-level and AI programming languages to shells—PC-driven and mainframes—to ready-to-use, customized packages for industry and government. This chapter examines the primary development tools, with a focus on shells, their makeup, types, and selection criteria. (Programming languages, per se, with emphasis on Prolog are covered in detail in the Appendix.)

Today's user can choose from a variety of development tools. Which tool to adopt depends on the nature of the problem, the area in the organization the expert system is intended to serve, and the skills of the builder. The critical factor in deciding how to build a rule-based system is the function it is expected to perform. For example, knowing whether the application is diagnoses or monitoring is important. Certain tools are more effective in handling one type of application rather than another. This distinction is discussed later in the chapter.

BUILDING TOOLS

Developing effective expert systems requires tools that facilitate rapid construction. Today's tools are the commercialized derivatives of artificial intelligence systems developed by universities and research organizations. They range from high-level programming languages to ready-to-use application packages. The choice depends on the nature of the problem domain and the complexity of the expert system being developed.

Levels of Building Tools

Several levels or categories of tools are available for building expert systems. In the interest of simplicity here, four levels are used to classify building tools:

1. Programming languages
2. Support aids and tools
3. Specific expert systems packages
4. Shells

Figure 14–1 illustrates the four levels. Historically, expert systems were built using high-level programming languages such as Basic, Fortran, and C. Later on, building from scratch proved to be time-consuming and, therefore, inefficient. This paved the way for developing shells (programs/systems) that had virtually everything except the knowledge base. In so doing, the building function moved away from the highly skilled programmers toward the end-user who built the knowledge base and loaded it in the shell. The user's feat is called shell programming. The rise of the PC also moved the shells to a more simplistic and affordable level.

As shown in Figure 14–1, specific expert system applications can be built with shells, support tools, or programming languages. Shells are usually built

Figure 14–1   The Four Levels of Building Tools

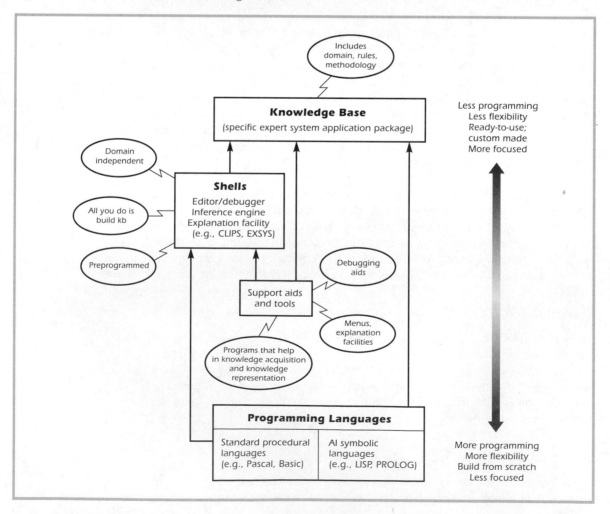

with support tools or programming languages, while support tools are constructed using programming languages. Note that the higher the level of the software, the less programming, less flexibility, and more focused the problem domain. For example, building an expert system using a procedural language requires programming for all its aspects. In contrast, shell programming demands a fraction of the work effort required by procedural language. The shell's inference engine and user interface are already built. With a shell, the primary task is developing the rules.

Programming Languages

The language in which a development tool is written is important because it determines the efficiency and performance of the tool. The choice of language also depends on the operating system of the computer. Expert systems can be programmed in a variety of languages: both standard and AI-oriented. **Standard programming,** or algorithmic approach, is a "brute force" method in which *standard* procedural languages, such as C, Pascal, Basic, and Fortran, are used to develop the IF . . . THEN rules. Most conventional programming is procedural; it tells the computer what to do.

A number of expert system development tools are written in conventional procedural languages. For example, IBM's Expert System Environment (ESE) is written in Pascal; EXSYS is written in C; and PUFF (Pulminary Function Expert System Diagnostic Tool) is written in Basic. Procedural languages are used for several reasons:

1. Sometimes the choices of language are limited by what the hardware's operating system will accept.
2. Certain languages are more powerful and faster than others. For example, a number of shells are written in C to boost speed, reduce memory requirements, and make the shell run on a variety of computers.
3. Expert systems designed for the PC are possible because they are written in faster languages such as C. These languages also guarantee *portability* between application sites, as is the case with PUFF.
4. Expert systems that incorporate digital input or output devices also benefit from programming in procedural languages.
5. These languages may be execution time-efficient, although most PCs and software also provide this advantage.

The alternative to procedural languages is **AI programming** done through symbolic languages such as LISP, Prolog, and their dialects. Although they are move restrictive and require more memory than standard languages, they are effective in the way they present rules and control their processing. One advantage of symbolic programming languages is processing symbols rather than numbers to reach conclusions on a logical level of knowledge representation. Many known expert systems were built using a symbolic language. For example, MYCIN—an expert system that diagnoses infectious blood diseases—was written in LISP. One drawback of LISP, however, is its demand for memory in order to run efficiently. That was the reason for building LISP machines to handle LISP programs. Although symbolic programming languages run on mainframes and PCs, they are usually most efficient when the program is processed on specially designed workstations.

LISP (LISt Processor) is the oldest programming language. It is an elegant, flexible, and concise language developed by McCarthy of MIT in 1968. LISP is a list made up of many lists. A *list* is a collection of numbers, words, strings, or functions enclosed in parentheses. Examples of lists are:

- *(x,y,z)*
- (my suit is 6 years old)

LISP extends the concept of a language based on list manipulation; everything is either a list or an element of a list. A user needs to learn only a few rules to understand the workings of LISP. For example:

```
IF function (if condition function 1 function2)
```

is interpreted as:

```
IF condition is true THEN function 1 ELSE function2
```

An example of a list-structured rule is shown in Figure 14–2.

In contrast to LISP, **Prolog** (programming in logic) is a reasoning language, better known in Europe and Japan. When given a fact such as "all mothers are women," Prolog can respond to the question "what is mother?" It will respond, "woman," The main limitation of this language is its two-valued (true and false or unknown) logic system. When a fact is "unknown," the system asks the user to provide the information.

Understanding Prolog involves three basic concepts: facts, rules, and backtracking. Facts and rules correspond to knowledge representation, while backtracking represents the basic search mechanism Prolog uses to respond to a query. Prolog is examined in greater detail in Appendix A at the end of the text.

Figure 14–2   *Example of LISP Programming*

```
(rule 43 (concerns (car auto mobilehome))
        (applicable_if (in vehicle frame))
        (antecedent_is
            (if ((? entity) has  (wheels and owner
                                    and roof...))
        (production_is
            (then  ((?entity) isa auto)
        (alternate_productions
            (then  ((?entity) isa mobilehome)...
        (further_information
            (top_down  (see transportation status_symbol))
            (bottom_up  (see wheels driver owner ...)) )
        (confidence  *use function auto_confidence)
        (update_rule  (apply learning_function
                        (number  32))))))
```

Source: Robert J. Schalkoff, *Artificial Intelligence* (McGraw-Hill, 1990), p. 232.

Prolog is suited to logical problems involving relationships between events or things. Pattern matching is fundamental to the functionality of Prolog. It is therefore suitable for record lookup and retrieval. Because it is so different from other languages, many first-time users find it difficult to adopt. Actually, in comparison, it was found to be the easiest language to learn by users with no prior programming experience.

Support Aids and Tools

To make life easier for the developer, a number of support tools are available for knowledge acquisition, building the user interface, programming, editing, verification and validation, and explanation. **Support aids** automate the time-consuming phase of acquisition, improve the effectiveness of representation, and ensure a crisp human–machine interface. Aids and facilities range from session-capture devices such as the tape recorder and the electronic brainstormer in knowledge acquisition to Logic Gem (Chapter 11) in knowledge representation and verification. Screen design using appropriate color and icons puts an impressive finish to the data displayed on the screen.

Other productivity-oriented tools include debugging aids, such as a feature in some shell products that traces the reasoning followed by the inference engine, which rules fired and in what order, and so on. One knows exactly the order of the rules and reasoning. Menus and other summary-type outlines also improve the input-output or user–machine interface. See Figure 14–3.

Explanation facilities show how the system arrives at a particular solution. On request, the user can query the system "WHAT does this question mean?" "WHY are you asking me this question?" or "HOW did you arrive at the answer?" By asking these questions, the user can reinforce the system's ability to produce answers. Users can accept or reject the system's conclusions. These explanation facilities can also serve as tutorial sessions during a consultation.

The **editing facility** ensures that the syntax is correctly represented in the knowledge base. Lines of text can be easily moved, added, or deleted, using edit commands unique to the shell or the programming language. For example, in IBM's ESE shell, the developer may write on the command line, "EDR short_loan" which means, "I want to edit the rule called 'short_loan.' " The system will look up and display the rule for editing. After the developer make the necessary changes, the system stores the edited rule back in the knowledge base.

End-User Interface

All support aids are important for an effective **user interface.** Once the system has been built, its usability depends on the nature of the interface with the system. Figure 14–4 shows the wide range of end-user facilities. **Interactive dialogue** (often via menu choices) allows the user to answer requests by the expert system for information needed to arrive at a solution. In sophisticated systems, graphics are used to display lines of reasoning when the system responds to the user's "how" questions.

Specific Expert System Packages

The level of expert system development that is the easiest product to use from the user's view is an **expert system package,** or specific ready-to-use program

Figure 14-3 *Example of a Trace File in IBM's ESE Shell*

```
001  _____
002  KNOW. BASE NAME:  LOAN ADVISOR
003  RUN DATE TIME : 10/03/94  14:45:03
004  ESDE VERSION & DATE : 1.0 11/01/93
  .
  .
  .
012  ===> CONTROL GIVEN TO FCB GLOBAL (1)
  .
  .
  .
021  ===> BACKWARD CHAINING FOR VALUE
022    OF LOAN  (1) (1)
023
024  ** DETERMINING LOAN OF GLOBAL (1) **
025
026  _____
027  --TRYING RULE ASSET OF GLOBAL (1) --
  .
  .
  .
056  _____
057  ASKING USER FOR ASSET_VALUE OF GLOBAL (1) --
058  >>>>USER RESPONSE:
059  ASSIGNED = '100000' (1).
```

that advises a specific user in a specific industry to address a specific problem domain. For example, a consultation system advises undergraduate students on the elective courses in the business school to take for a major in computer science. These "ready-made" expert systems deal with academic undergraduate scheduling issues at one university or college. They can also be used by an entire academic system. For example, one expert system advises a high school graduate on the likelihood of admission to a college based on a set of variables (SAT, grade point average, leadership role in school, etc.). The system essentially plugs in the vital variables, matches them against established criteria for that school, and determines within 85–90 percent certainty the admissibility of the applicant.

◼ SHELLS

The fourth level of expert system development tool is the **shell.** Throughout the previous chapters, the shell has been presented as a set of knowledge representation schemes, an inference mechanism, and a way to determine the status of a problem domain while it is being solved. It *is a reasoning system without the knowledge.* When knowledge about a problem domain is entered into the shell, an expert system becomes operational. The shell can then be used to create another new expert system in a similar fashion.

Figure 14–4   Features of the End-User Interface

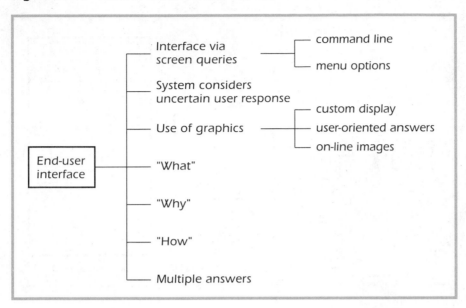

As a development system, a shell provides a basic architecture for building an expert system. Because it is *domain-independent,* it handles problems relating to many types of situations. However, since expert systems are dedicated to reasoning and inferencing, shells are not used primarily for executing mathematical tasks performed by numerical reasoning languages. Expert system shells can easily do math, although they are constructed for nonnumerical processing.

Main Elements

The three main components of a shell are the knowledge base, inference engine, and the user interface. The close interaction among these elements provides the expert system with the ability to reason through knowledge and generate the expected responses and results. See Figure 14–5.

Knowledge Base

A distinctive feature of a knowledge-based system is that knowledge is separated from reasoning. Within the knowledge base, information is declarative—some facts, rules, or relationships without the detail of how or when such information is applied.

The knowledge base includes two types of information used in the inferencing process. The assertions or parameters (variables) comprise information that has been concluded, assumed, or provided during the inference process. Some shells also allow the user to enter information for the parameter directly from the keyboard.

The second type of information are the rules and frames—the main forms of knowledge representation—that show how the assertion base should be used to solve the problem. The rule-based form is the least complex and follows the

Figure 14–5 Main Elements of a Shell

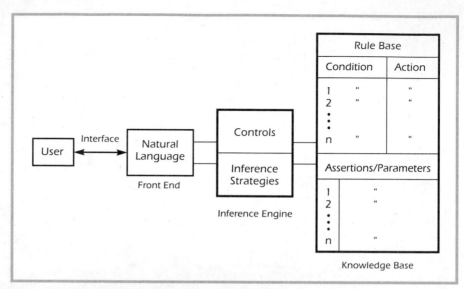

IF . . . THEN (sometimes IF . . . THEN . . . ELSE) format incorporated in many simple programming languages. As explained in Chapter 11, a rule asserts that if a certain condition exists, then a specific action will be inferred. The IF portion of the statement is the premise, condition, or antecedent; the THEN portion is the action or the consequent. Rules are examples of declarative programming.

Rule-based shells are common and are available for use on personal computers. Rules can be easily added, revised, or deleted which simplifies maintenance and system update. A primary disadvantage is that the processing function may be very slow, because of the system's need to sequentially search the rule base for each piece of information.

An induction system is related to the rule-based approach. It allows the user to present examples or scenarios of conditions and outcomes. The conditions and outcomes are entered in the form of a matrix, as in Table 14–1. Each column represents a condition and each row a scenario. Once the matrix is entered into the shell, the system infers rules from the data in the matrix. For example, the rule for example two in the matrix would be:

```
IF battery is OK
        AND alternator is bad (defective)
        AND gauge is OK
        AND headlights are bright,
THEN replace alternator at nearest garage.
```

Frames provide another method of organizing knowledge into hierarchical structures while retaining a degree of knowledge independence. Unlike rules, frames do not require the system to examine each individual rule in the knowledge base. Frames can also be organized into **trees** that establish a hierarchy and allow inheritance to occur between frames. Inheritance improves the efficiency of the system and makes it unnecessary to store data that can be concluded through analysis of other rules. See Chapter 11 for details on frames and rule structure.

■ **Table 14–1** An Example of an Induction Table

	Battery	Alternator	Gauge	Headlights	Result
1.	OK	OK	OK	Bright	Safe to continue driving
2.	OK	BAD	OK	Bright	Replace alternator at next garage
3.	OK	OK	BAD	Bright	Replace gauge when returning home
4.	BAD	OK	OK	Brown	Get new battery at next service station

Inference Engine

The inference engine is the brain of the expert system. It is where reasoning of the knowledge base is performed and decisions are reached. Three types of inferencing strategies are utilized in shells: forward chaining, backward chaining, and a combination of the two. These strategies were discussed in Chapter 12.

User Interface

The **user interface** is the portion of the program with which the user actually interacts. A shell includes a user interface for programming and a user interface for running the system. The programming interface allows the user to enter rules without being concerned with the workings of the inference engine.

The format of the interface varies, depending on whether the shell is run on a mainframe, a PC, or a Macintosh, and how user-friendly or complex the shell actually is. Many of today's shells are completely menu-driven and/or mouse-operated, requiring little or no actual programming. In this case, the shell provides an empty template upon which the user enters the rules. Other shells, although menu-driven, may require some programming. Examples are VP-Expert, EXSYS, and Level 5Mac. Most shells also provide utilities that allow interfaces between the shell and other languages, including dBASE IV, Lotus 1-2-3, C, LISP, Prolog, and many graphics packages.

Most shells are written in structured high-level programming languages such as Pascal or C, which is the most popular development language today. A large number of systems have also been written in LISP or Prolog, which are AI programming languages. LISP is the oldest and the most useful language. Prolog is a declarative language, which means the computer determines how to solve a problem. To create a Prolog program, a computer is given a set of facts and rules that describe objects and their relationships. The computer does the rest.

Table 14–2 shows the range of expert systems development tools. This chart indicates how much easier using a shell rather than a language is and that creating a system with a conventional language takes longer than with an AI language.

■ **Table 14–2**   Expert System Development Tools

Traditional Programming Languages Harder to Use		Expert Systems Programming Languages Easier to Use		
Assembly languages	Procedural languages (Basic, C, Pascal, Fortran, etc.)	Prolog	LISP	Shells
Takes longer to develop expert systems		Takes less time to develop expert systems		

Uses and Users

A shell has several important features:

- ■ *Ease of use:* Developers and users look for easy-to-use software or software that takes minimum training to learn. With shells, the user should have no difficulty consulting the system with almost no training.

- ■ *Doesn't require a programming background:* Virtually any person can learn to build a knowledge base with a little effort. Mainframe-based shells take longer to learn, although they offer more advanced features than the simplistic PC-driven shells.

- ■ *Brainstorming opportunities:* Because of their interactive nature, most shells provide brainstorming opportunities for poorly structured problems. It allows knowledge engineers a chance to define the problem domain before making efforts at knowledge representation.

- ■ *Interface (links) with productivity products:* Many shells can accommodate spreadsheets, databases, or repositories, which links them to other knowledge representations in order to solve a macroproblem based on a micro-oriented set of knowledge bases. Transfer of knowledge from one knowledge base to another is a unique feature of shells.

- ■ *Opportunity to review one's work:* The support aids discussed earlier in the chapter provide the means to review knowledge representation.

- ■ *Knowledge consistency and completeness checking:* Feedback is accomplished through a reliable explanation facility.

- ■ *Ease of changing knowledge base representation:* All that a user needs to do is enter, modify, delete, or change rules; the shell does the rest.

- ■ *Compatibility with other shells:* When different tools are used for different tasks, the user can interface one shell with the other. The shell should also be able to fit into a smooth migration path.

- ■ *Prototyping:* The iterative nature of building expert systems requires a shell that allows each building step to be a prototype toward the final product. This concept is similar to modular design and independent development.

- ■ *Intelligent assistance:* A shell should give advice or provide information depending on the specific needs of the user.

■ *Surface and deep reasoning:* Surface reasoning is simplistic situation-response relationships, while deep reasoning relies on episodical knowledge embedded in the knowledge base. A shell should do both.

These features, then, need to be matched with the shell users and the activities the shell must perform. The expert system development team includes the following people:

■ *Knowledge engineer:* This is the key person whose job is to define the problem domain, acquire the necessary knowledge, represent the knowledge, and implement the system with a degree of user training.

■ *Domain expert:* The domain expert may be an expert system builder. Ideally the domain expert knows enough shell programming to represent his or her own knowledge. Process loss in such an instance would be almost nil.

■ *Programmer:* Experienced programmers would be obvious candidates to build expert systems. For some programmers, though, "undoing" certain habits (switching from algorithmic to symbolic thinking) is not so easy.

■ *End-user:* End-users with motivation to build their own systems may find PC-driven shells to be ideal. DuPont has experienced success with this approach.

■ *Project leader:* For large projects, a project leader is commonly assigned to coordinate the entire system development process. Such a person relates to the knowledge engineer, programmer, user, as well as the domain expert in a number of ways.

Different problem domains pose their own shell requirements and demand specific developer skills. No shell has all features. Care must be taken to match the problem requirements to the shell before beginning a project. A summary of shell features is shown in Figure 14–6.

Figure 14–6   Summary of Shell Features

■ Ease of use
■ Doesn't require a programming background
■ Brainstorming opportunities
■ Interface (links) with productivity products
■ Opportunity to review one's work
■ Knowledge consistency and completeness checking
■ Ease of changing knowledge base representation
■ Compatibility with other shells
■ Prototyping
■ Intelligent assistance
■ Surface and deep reasoning

Comparison Criteria

The evaluation of shells is based on a set of technical and organizational criteria determined in advance. Several elements are considered in shell selection:

Knowledge Representation Scheme

A **knowledge representation scheme** defines how the expert system organizes information and how information is acted upon. The two major schemes mentioned earlier are rule-based and frame-based schemes. Other knowledge representation features include agendas, demons, metarules, inheritance mechanisms, and data hierarchies.

- **Agendas** or **protocols** are mechanisms that control the order of rule firing.
- **Demons** are procedures that are automatically triggered when designated events occur. They represent a power concept in a frame-based system that specifies the action to take place when certain conditions arise during the processing of information. Unlike a rule-based system in which rules are repeatedly tested to see if they apply, in a frame-based system they wait to act upon special "exception-type" situations.
- **Metarules** are rules that control the usage of other rules.
- Inheritance relates to receiving characteristics from an ancestor. **Inheritance mechanism** allow objects to be related in groups, based on characteristics that apply to all objects in the group. The special characteristics of each object are then expressed for that object only.
- **Data hierarchies** organize data into hierarchies in a way that reflects the actual organization of information in the problem domain.

Reasoning Strategies

The inferencing of a shell is done via forward chaining or backward chaining. Most shells support both forward and backward chaining; all shells do backward chaining.

Software Interfaces

Interfacing with software products, such as database management systems, information systems, decision support systems, and office automation systems, is a necessary feature of all shells. More and more expert systems applications call for certain rules to fire only after verifying data stored in external repositories. This requirement makes software interface an especially important issue.

User Interfaces

Multiwindow development environment and visual display of knowledge bases are important features of a user interface. Each serves a unique set of standards. Graphic displays are part of a consultation with the shell. Mouse or icon-oriented cursor control is especially useful in this area.

Editing Tools

This developmental feature of a shell might include graphical editor support, editor windows, and syntax checking, which help the developer create and modify rules and objects. A shell should include some of these features, depending on what it does best.

Tracing and Debugging Features

A shell should be capable of verifying a knowledge base. The trace feature records information for a particular session during development or consultation. For example, it allows the developer to evaluate aspects of the program in the sequence the rules are being fired. It explains what is happening at each step. Because of its usefulness in debugging a knowledge base, a trace facility should be part of any shell selected.

Certainty Factors

Processing data with questionable validity is part of many everyday problems. Requested information rarely carries 100 percent certainty. Reasoning about uncertainty is an important capability of a shell. For this reason, certainty factors is a shell characteristic that should be considered first during the selection process.

Explanation Capabilities

Explaining how the system reached a conclusion or why it is requesting an item of data is a critical attribute of a backward-chaining shell. A knowledge-based system should explain its own reasoning processes to a user, ranging from full English descriptions to a list of successful steps. An explanation feature is not typically provided by forward-chaining shells. As noted with the trace feature, any shell selected should provide explanation feature.

Technical Provisions

Whether the shell operates in batch or on-line mode, whether it has off-line interface capabilities (e.g., data downloading), whether it saves the results in an external database, and whether shell utilities provide backup and recovery are important technical considerations.

Implementation Factors

A focus on the implementation language of the shell and compatibility with various hardware platforms is necessary. Language can affect portability, speed of the product, and memory requirements. C and LISP are the most common implementation languages. C is typically more portable and more efficient than LISP.

Verification Aids

This aid comes in many formats. The most common aid allows the developer to build a library of test data or cases to execute within the expert system. It also allows changes to be made on-line.

Vendor Support

Regardless of the shell's attributes, vendor support cannot be overlooked. In choosing a shell, how complete the documentation is, the availability of on-line tutorial or help in shell operation, and the availability of training can be determining factors. Cost considerations are also important.

Figure 14–7   *Comparison Criteria*

- Knowledge representation scheme
- Reasoning strategies
- Software interfaces
- User interfaces
- Editing tools
- Tracing and debugging features
- Certainty factors
- Explanation capability
- Technical provisions
- Implementation factors
- Verification aids
- Vendor support

A summary of the selection criteria is shown in Figure 14–7. Of course, in the final analysis, the choice of shell is based on tradeoffs in terms of the best combination of features for the application under consideration. See Box 14–1.

■ MAINFRAME-BASED AND PC-DRIVEN SHELLS

Based on the preceding discussion of the features, uses, and selection criteria of a shell, the text provides two illustrations in this section: one designed to run on a mainframe and the other to load on a PC. As expected, a mainframe-based shell offers more features and handles more complex problems, but it requires special skills to make best use of its capabilities. In contrast, a PC-based shell does less advanced work, but allows any novice user to program it more easily.

IBM's Expert System Environment

Expert System Environment (ESE) is a shell that resides on an IBM mainframe. The shell is made up of two parts: the Expert System *Development* Environment (ESDE) and the Expert System *Consultation* Environment (ESCE). ESDE allows a knowledge engineer to *create* a knowledge base. ESCE allows a user to *consult with* a knowledge base. See Figure 14–8.

The Knowledge Base

The knowledge base is made up of three required objects and two optional objects. As shown in Figure 14–9, the required objects are

- *Parameters:* facts about the domain of expertise. For example, "The *sky* is blue," "*temperature* is greater than 90 degrees." Sky and temperature are parameters. Blue and 90 are parameter values.
- *Rules:* relationships between parameters or facts. **Rules** consist of an IF clause (premise) and a THEN clause (action). For example, "If sky is blue and temperature is greater than 90, THEN decision is wear shorts" is a rule.

Box 14–1 Decisions! Decisions!

When the Diabetic Foot Advisor was launched in February 1994, two of the early questions raised were "How should acquired knowledge be represented?" and "What shell should be considered for representing acquired knowledge, which has reliability for future system update or enhancement?" From the beginning of the project, the temptation was to select the shell most familiar to the developer. Although this strategy has benefits, the attitude is not right.

The first step taken was a separate two-hour session with a technical specialist from VP-Expert and EXSYS discuss the pros and cons of each shell as it relates to the medical problem domain. The result was the candid opinions of both specialists. The discussion covered areas such as the use of frames (EXSYS) versus rules, the usefulness of induction tables (VP-Expert) in generating rules, the power of each shell to do forward chaining and backward chaining, and the user interface. The shell's explanation capability, editing tools, and technical support were also discussed.

The result was a list of features unique to each shell with the Diabetic Foot Advisor in mind. Since the initial goal was to do a prototype, VP-Expert was the quickest and easiest of all shells. What made the decision easier was the fact that rewriting the rules to run on EXSYS at a later date would not be a major problem. With the time-consuming task of having to spend four months learning about diabetes and foot and ankle anatomy, familiarity with VP-Expert made programming start sooner rather than later.

Figure 14–8 Expert System Environment

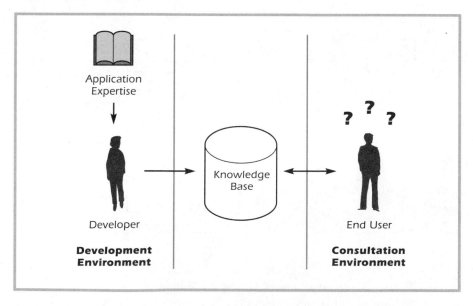

■ *Focus control blocks (FCBs):* modules that allow the knowledge engineer to segment the knowledge base and control the consultation. FCBs make developing, debugging, and maintaining the expert system easier. FCB's are organized in a hierarchical structure. As shown in Figure 14–10, the root FCB is **A.** It calls on **B** or on **C.** An FCB that calls another is a **parent,** while the FCBs called by the parent FCB are

Figure 14–9 ESE's Knowledge Base (Required and Optional Options)

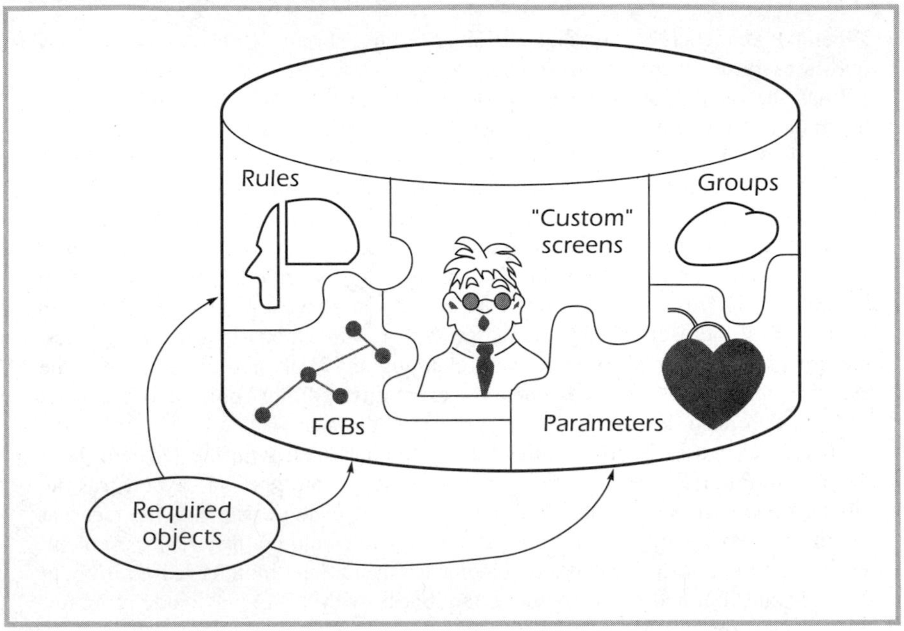

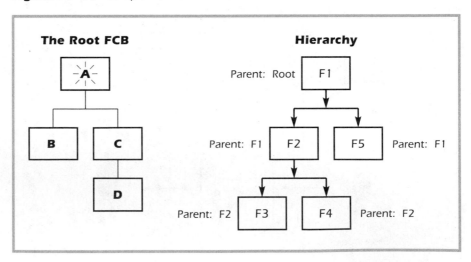

Figure 14–10 Sample FCB Structure

children. Sometimes, an FCB can be called more than once. Each repetition is called an *instantiation.*

In an FCB, a group of parameters and rules are associated with a given module. Each FCB also contains a set of control language statements to process the parameters and rules. In Figure 14–11, past payment rules are clustered in the "payment history" FCB. Likewise, personnel history rules are grouped under the "personnel history" FCB. Both FCBs report to the auto loan advisor (root FCB).

Figure 14–11   FCB Structure of Auto Loan Advisor

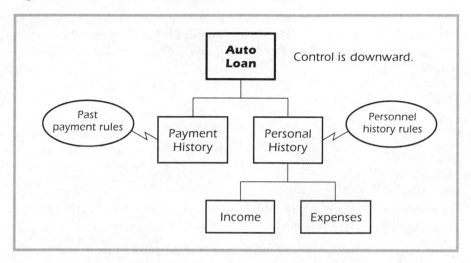

Although much more is involved in ESE, these three required objects is all one needs to know to build a knowledge base. Two optional objects customize the screen and group objects:

- *Screens:* allow the display of more than one question, personalized logos, and highlighted results, charts, etc., in various colors.

- *Groups:* a group name is used to represent a number of objects or parameters. For example, instead of displaying age, experience, education, and work experience as separate objects, they can be grouped under group name "Bio." To access these objects, a reference to "Bio" will display the objects. See Figure 14–12.

The *consultation* environment uses commands to execute a consultation and provide an explanation of how ESE arrived at a solution. It also furnishes provisions to edit parameters, rules, and FCBs.

Figure 14–12   Example of an ESE Group

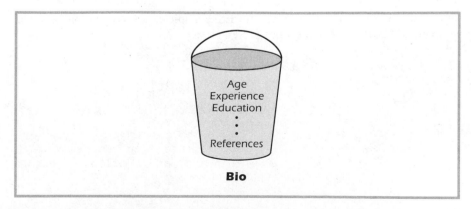

A Knowledge Base: Vacation

The following illustration of how a knowledge base is built using ESE refers to a knowledge base called Vacation. This small knowledge base selects a vacation spot (place) for Spring Break based on the user's preference for the following features:

- Coast
- Activity
- Available_funds
- Place

Knowledge Acquisition

A consultation with a travel agent (domain expert) about the best place to spend the upcoming Spring Break reveals the following information:

- On the East Coast, for beach activity with available funds over $1,500, the best place is Florida.
- On the West Coast, for beach activity with available funds over $1,500, the best place is California.
- On the East Coast, for skiing activity with available funds over $2,500, the best place is Vermont.
- On the West Coast, for skiing activity with available funds over $2,500, the best place is Colorado.

Knowledge Representation

In ESE, the first step in knowledge representation is to decide on the parameters and rules. The parameters (coast, activity, available_funds, and place) are underlined in the preceding step:

The next step is to define each parameter as follows:

Parameter	Definition
Coast	taken from ('east', 'west')
Activity	taken from ('beach', 'skiing')
Available_funds	is a number
Place	is a string

Once the defined parameters are entered in the knowledge base, the third step is to write the rules. Remember in ESE, a rule is an association between parameters. So, the following rules are entered:

Rule Name	Rule Text
East_Beach	IF coast is 'east' and activity is 'beach' and available_funds > 1500 THEN place is 'Florida'
West_Beach	IF coast is 'west' and activity is 'beach' and available_funds > 1500 THEN place is 'California'

Rule Name	Rule Text
| East_Ski | ```
IF coast is 'east' and activity is
        'skiing' and available_funds >
2500
THEN place is 'Vermont'
``` |
| West_Ski | ```
IF coast is 'west' and activity is
        'skiing' and available_funds >
2500
THEN place is 'Colorado'
``` |

After the rules are entered into ESE, the final step is to define an FCB. If an FCB is not defined, the system will generate one when the user keys in the CONSULT command. The system will ask:

1. GOALS: What parameters should the system try to resolve? ANSWER: Place

2. RESULTS: What parameters should be displayed at the end of the consultation? ANSWER: Place

3. INITIAL DATA: What parameters are to be determined first? That is, what question should the system ask the user first? ANSWER: Coast

Once all the data is entered, the system is ready for consultation. The first question it asks is "What is coast?" Then the system asks, "What type of activity is preferred and so on, until all questions have been answered. The result is then displayed, depending on the user's answers. Note how the system asks first for the goal of the system in order to do backward chaining. Hence, backward chaining is referred to as goal-driven.

VP-Expert

Of the PC-driven shells, VP-Expert is one of the most popular in academics. It is a rule-based, menu-driven expert system development tool that runs on IBM or IBM-compatible personal computers. VP-Expert has many features that are not included in ESE that are useful in building expert systems. VP-Expert offer several options in addition to Help and Quit:

- *FileName* and *Path* allow the builder to call a new knowledge base or change the default drive and directory.

- *Consult* and *Edit* options are most frequently used during consultation. The Consult option takes the user to the consultation window where an expert system executes. This window takes up half the **screen** during development. The *rules* window and the *results* window occupy the lower half of the screen. See Figure 14–13.

- Consultation windows offer a number of other options:
  Select any *variable* to see the value the system had at the end of the previous consultation.

- Specify a rule number to see that rule displayed in the *rule* Window.

- Play *what-if* or change one response at a time and rerun the previous consultation. The user is allowed to see how changing a response to a prompt affects the outcome of the consultation. All other variables retain their prior value unless changed by rules in the rule base.

Figure 14–13 VP-Expert Main Screen Format

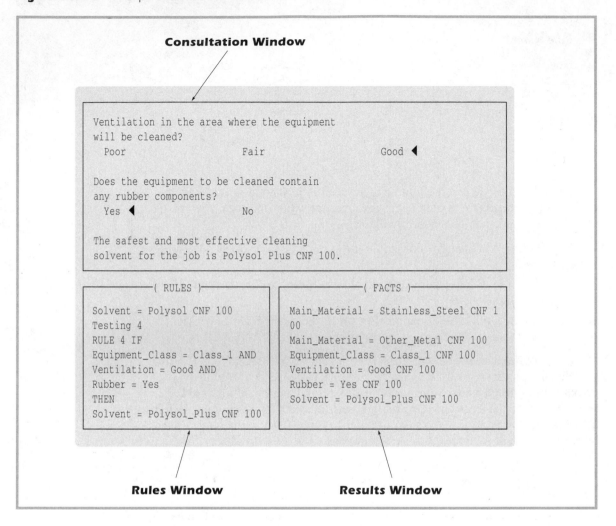

Consultation Window

Ventilation in the area where the equipment
will be cleaned?
  Poor   Fair   Good ◀

Does the equipment to be cleaned contain
any rubber components?
  Yes ◀   No

The safest and most effective cleaning
solvent for the job is Polysol Plus CNF 100.

—————(RULES)—————
Solvent = Polysol CNF 100
Testing 4
RULE 4 IF
Equipment_Class = Class_1 AND
Ventilation = Good AND
Rubber = Yes
THEN
Solvent = Polysol_Plus CNF 100

—————(FACTS)—————
Main_Material = Stainless_Steel CNF 1
00
Main_Material = Other_Metal CNF 100
Equipment_Class = Class_1 CNF 100
Ventilation = Good CNF 100
Rubber = Yes CNF 100
Solvent = Polysol_Plus CNF 100

Rules Window   **Results Window**

- The system allows the builder to assign *confidence factors* to each conclusion and user response.
- A graphic and text rule *trace function* stores the logic sequence followed during a consultation with the expert system. The results are also displayed for the developer or user to see how the program has solved the problem.
- The system exchanges data with dBASE, Lotus 1-2-3, and ASCII files.

The most convenient and timesaving feature of VP-Expert is the use of induction tables to generate a preliminary knowledge base. This knowledge base can then be expanded, enhanced, and turned into a final version. An induction table is like a database. The parameters are the fields. The builder fills in the values for each instance of the table. The values in each column are translated into the choices for each parameter. All of the parameters are connected with AND. The last column is used as the THEN condition. See Box 14–2.

Another feature used is the graphics capability, which allows the developer to draw graphs, maps, or sketches of various forms and sizes. While this feature is not a necessary part of the knowledge base, it does add a special touch. Granted the graphics capability is primitive by most standards (only lines and ellipses), but it is a step beyond ESE. See Box 14–3.

Box 14–2   Partial Experience with Induction Tables Using Real Estate Advisor, April 1994

... After the knowledge of the expert was represented in decision trees, the knowledge was then transferred to a Lotus 1-2-3 spreadsheet decision table, because VP-Expert allows the induction of rules from such tables. We felt that we could realize some of the benefits of automated rule induction because the knowledge that we were dealing with was modular and easily represented in a table format. Some of the limitations that are often mentioned concerning automated rule induction we found to be irrelevant in the case of VP-Expert. We were able to use more than simple "yes or no" questions and several attributes (more than 15).

From these tables, VP-Expert induced all of our rules in a text file format, executable by the inference engine. Further enhancements to the questions and the addition of explanations were edited into the text at a later time, as well as the addition and modification of the rules themselves. ...

Box 14–3   Partial Experience Using Winery Advisor

... VP-Expert allows you to use text files to hold information to be retrieved based on variables in the program. We stored descriptions of the destinations in the Adventure/Exotic category in a text file and retrieved the appropriate one for viewing when a destination was chosen. Again, not a necessity for the knowledge base, but an added touch.

A final feature that provided us with added versatility was the flexibility allowed with rule and question sequencing. It was possible to have all questions asked up front or to have questions asked on an as-needed basis. The order of the rules and the statements within those rules could determine the order of the questions asked.

Source: Stohn and Kupiek, May 1993.

Sample Rules

To illustrate the nature and format of VP-Expert rules, Figure 14–14 shows the equivalent procedure and set of rules of "Vacation" under the ESE shell. Note that the bulk of the programming is a set of IF . . . THEN rules with commands and names unique to VP-Expert.

Comparison of ESE and VP-Expert

Experience with both shells provides a basis on which to judge the similarities and differences across virtually all other shells.

1. *No shell is perfect.* One shell can learn something from the other. ESE's advantages lie in its superior structuring, while VP-Expert has a good deal to offer in speed, ease of learning and use, and PC compatibility.

2. *VP-Expert allows the developer to use LOTUS to induce basic rules from decision tables.* Yet, the shell is weak on structure other than IF . . . THEN rules.

Figure 14–14 Vacation Rules in VP-Expert

```
ACTIONS
    FIND Place
    DISPLAY  "Try a vacation in {place}^";

RULE East_Beach

IF      Coast = East AND
        Activity = Beach AND
        Available_Funds > 1500
THEN    Place = Florida;

RULE West_Beach

IF      Coast = West AND
        Activity = Beach AND
        Available_Funds > 1500
THEN    Place = California;

RULE East_Ski

IF      Coast = East AND
        Activity = Skiing AND
        Available_Funds > 2500
THEN    Place = Vermont;

RULE West_Ski

IF      Coast = West AND
        Activity = Skiing AND
        Available_Funds > 2500
THEN    Place = Colorado;

ASK Coast:  "What coast would you prefer?";
CHOICES Coast:  East, West;

ASK Activity:  "What type of activity would you prefer?";
CHOICES Activity:  Beach, skiing;

ASK Available_Funds:  "What is your vacation budget?";
```

3. *The approach to arriving at an answer is different.* ESE accesses both backward and forward chaining inference techniques, while VP-Expert mainly applies backward chaining as the result of the FIND command.

4. *Modularity is different.* Modularity is established in ESE through FCBs and ready access to external data and routines written in COBOL, Pascal, SQL/DS, or dB2. VP-Expert, on the other hand, contains features such as hypertext commands (to provide in-depth information on more complex subjects), and text and graphic traces, which make it unique.

5. *Hardware is different.* ESE runs on an IBM mini- or mainframe. VP-Expert operates on any IBM or IBM-compatible PC.

EXSYS

EXSYS Professional is a powerful expert system for business and academic applications built by EXSYS Corporation in Alburquerque, New Mexico (see the article at the beginning of this chapter). The popularity of this shell has surged with the introduction of RuleBook. In RuleBook, knowledge is represented as tree diagrams that are automatically converted to IF-THEN rules that represent the same logic. Essentially, all the instructions necessary to run an expert system knowledge base are provided by the program and all output is in English. Little or no training is required to run a knowledge base that has already been developed. All input is in the form of English text, alegebraic expression, or menu selection. There is no complex rule syntax to memorize. A tutorial on EXSYS RuleBook (with the shell) is available in Appendix C.

IMPLICATIONS FOR MANAGEMENT

Shells allow the developer to concentrate more on the specifics of the system being designed instead of worrying about small programming details. Shells, however, do not offer as much flexibility as standard programming. although more and more shells allow standard programming with the shell, which permits greater diversity.

When utilizing expert system shells, one must match the shell's overall capabilities to those required by the system being developed. More importantly, the inferencing methods must conform directly to those used by the domain expert in problem analysis and decision making. Otherwise, one could be unwittingly building constraints into a project that may prevent the system from ever becoming truly expert in the chosen domain and that cause inefficiencies in the system, or even complete system failure.

The overall progress in microcomputer technology and the recent growth in expert systems shells means that sophisticated expert systems can now be created on PCs as well as mainframes. In conjunction with the relatively low cost of shells, more people are expected to build their own expert systems. Ease of development has generated fear that the proliferation of expert systems will make experienced and higher-paid personnel more expendable. It might also discourage younger workers from developing experience in certain aspects of their jobs. So far, these fears have not been substantiated.

Ease of development using shells should lead to a much greater employment of expert systems in the future, especially in areas such as medicine, law, finance, and banking. Increased use raises moral and ethical issues, especially with respect to "who owns the knowledge." Although today's expert systems have a greater success rate at problem solving and disease diagnoses than the domain experts, some day a mistake is bound to occur that could lead to substantial financial losses or even loss of lives. When it happens, who is to blame? (Ethical and legal issues are covered in greater detail Chapter 19.)

■ SUMMARY

1. A person does not need to be an expert to use an expert system successfully. Today's tools allow relatively inexperienced people with subject-matter expertise to build an expert system.

2. A variety of development tools are available in today's market. The nature of the problem, the area of the organization an expert system is intended to serve, and the skills of the builder must all be analyzed before choosing a tool. Knowledge engineers should choose a tool that facilitates rapid construction.

3. The four levels of building tools are (1) programming languages, (2) support aids and tools, (3) specific expert systems packages, and (4) shells. Shells are built with support tools or programming languages, while support tools are constructed with programming languages. The higher the level of the software the less programming, less flexibility, and more focused the domain.

4. Various reasons explain why a number of expert system development tools are written in conventional languages. They range from limitations of a hardware operating system, the power and speed of a language, incorporation of digital input-output devices in the system, and the language execution time efficiency. Symbolic languages are an alternative to procedural languages; they are more restrictive and require more memory than standard languages, but they are effective in presenting rules and controlling their processing.

5. Support aids automate the time-consuming phase of acquisition, improve the effectiveness of representation, and ensure a usable human–machine interface. Aids and facilities range from session capture devices to Logic Gem in knowledge representation and verification. Some aids and facilities available are debugging aids, explanation facilities, and editing facilities.

6. Once a system has been built, its usability depends largely on the ease of user interface with the system. Interactive dialogue allows the user to answer requests by the expert system for additional or new information that it needs to arrive at solutions.

7. Specific expert systems packages are ready-to-use software packages that advise a specific user in a specific industry or situation to address a specific problem domain.

8. A shell is a reasoning system without the knowledge base; it provides a basic architecture for developing an expert system. When knowledge about a new domain is entered into a shell, an expert system becomes operational.

9. The three main elements of a shell are the knowledge base, inference engine, and the user interface. Within the knowledge base, information is declarative: facts, rules, or relationships. The knowledge base includes assertions and rules that show how the knowledge base is to be used.

■ TERMS TO LEARN

Agenda/protocol mechanism that controls the order in which rules fire.

AI Programming symbolic approach that uses symbolic programming languages to process symbols by analyzing and reaching conclusions on a logical level of knowledge representation.

Data hierarchies organize information in a way that reflects the actual organization of information in the problem domain.

Demon program procedures that are automatically triggered when designed events occur; a program that "sits" in the background, waiting for an event to occur, and then takes action when the event does occur.

Editing facility ensures that the syntax is correctly entered and represented in the knowledge base.

Expert system package a ready-to-use program that advises a specific user in a specific industry how to address a specific problem domain.

Explanatory facility the system's capability to display the reasoning behind its solutions.

Focus control block (FCB) a module or unit of work that allows the knowledge engineer to segment the knowledge base and control the consultation.

Inheritance mechanism relates objects with similar characteristics within a group.

Interactive dialogue allows the user to answer requests from the expert system for additional or new information that allows it to arrive at solutions.

Knowledge representation scheme defines how the expert system organizes information and how information is acted upon.

Lisp(LISt Processor) oldest programming language; symbolic language.

Metarules rules that control the usage of other rules.

Parameter in an IBM expert system shell, facts about the domain of expertise.

Parent an FCB that calls on another FCB.

Prolog (PROgramming in LOGic), a reasoning or symbolic language.

Rule in an expert system shell, a relationship between parameters or facts; conditional statement that specifies an action to be taken if a certain condition is true; a formal way of specifying a recommendation, directive, or strategy, expressed as IF (premise) . . . THEN (conclusion).

Screens in an expert system shell, custom displays used during knowledge base consultation.

Shells a commercial software package that contains a user interface and an inference engine, which makes it easy to build a knowledge base; a complete expert system stripped of its specific knowledge.

Standard programming algorithmic approach that uses a "brute force" method in which standard procedural languages are used to develop the IF . . . THEN rules.

Support aids automate the time-consuming phase of acquisition, improve the effectiveness of representation, and ensure a usable interface between human and machine.

Tree establishes a hierarchy and allows the inheritance to occur between frames.

User interface the portion of the program with which the user actually interacts; a component of a computer system that allows bidirectional communication between the system and its user.

■ REVIEW QUESTIONS

1. Explain each of the several levels of tools for building expert systems.
2. Distinguish between:

   a. programming language and shell
   b. procedural and symbolic languages
   c. explanation facility and editing facility

3. "A shell is a reasoning system without the knowledge base." Do you agree? Explain.

4. Elaborate on the main components of a shell. Which element is the most relevant to the end-user? Why?

5. What is the main function of support aids?

6. A shell is said to be domain-independent. What does it mean?

7. What does an inference engine do? What are its main components? Explain.

8. If a knowledge base includes assertions and rules, how do the two types of information work together?

9. How are rules different from frames? Illustrate.

10. Explain briefly the key features of a shell. Is one feature more important than another? Why?

11. Distinguish among:
   a. agenda and demon
   b. metarule and inheritance
   c. software and user interfaces

12. Elaborate briefly on the function and uses of editing tools. How do they differ from a shell's trace feature?

13. ESE has a development and a consultation environment. Briefly describe each environment and its functions.

14. Explain the makeup of ESE's knowledge base.

15. If you were asked to provide a two-minute explanation of the options available on VP-Expert, what would you say?

16. With the limited exposure to ESE and VP-Expert provided in this chapter, which shell would you use for a basic banking application such as Auto Loan Advisor? Why?

■ EXERCISES AND CASES

Publisher Advisor

1. Review the following shells and write up a justification report regarding the shell of choice for the Publisher Advisor expert system.

   a. VP-Expert
   b. EXSYS

In reviewing each shell, check with your instructor or contact developers in industry for their opinions of either shell. If another shell is in use, ask for the distinctive features of that shell and compare them to those of VP-Expert and EXSYS as part of your report. As you may expect, if the organization for whom you are building the expert system uses an in-house shell, chances are you will be expected to use it for the project. Otherwise, you are free to decide on a shell of your own. In that case, how would one decide on a shell?

2. You are the owner of a specialty ski shop in Denver, Colorado. Customers visit your store to buy ski boots, clothing, and other gear. These sales represent a sizable percentage of the business. After a few months, you noticed that out-of-town customers ask all kinds of questions about the proper gear to buy or rent, ski weight, size, and fit. Answering these questions is taking quite a bit of your time. You wish someone else with your expertise could address all these questions and customize the equipment to the experience and requirements of the customer.

You are a student in the expert systems course of your MIS program. You feel this problem domain is a good candidate for an expert system. Decide what shell you would choose for this application. In doing so, your evaluation should include:

   a. features of the tool that you like and how it makes programming easier
   b. features that you dislike and how they make programming more difficult than it needs to be
   c. features that will make the expert system easy to use

3. Consider the job of an automobile mechanic. When a mechanic diagnoses the problem, the job has just begun. Not only does the mechanic need to determine the problem, but also the part to replace or repair, how it should be replaced, whether the part fits the type of car, year, size engine, etc., and its availability.

If you were in charge of building a system to solve this problem, would you use a rule-based system? What shell would you use? Why?

4. While working on a project using an expert system shell, a classmate from computer science who is taking the course made the remark that "unless you build an expert system from the ground up using Prolog or LISP, you really can't understand expert system that well. Also, you can't rely on commercial packages, because they come and go." Is there any truth to this opinion? Explain in detail.

5. After gaining experience in this course, you have been asked to evaluate an expert system shell that you have not heard of before. What criteria or attributes would you use in the evaluation? Why?

▓ SELECTED REFERENCES

Angell, Bob and Tom Murphy. "Review: Faster Than a Speeding Network." *AI Expert,* November 1992, pp. 50–53.

Bert, Tor D. "Expert System Resource Guide." *AI Expert,* April 1995, pp. 26–36.

Gappa, Ute. "A Toolbox for Generating Graphical Knowledge Acquisition Environments." In *Expert Systems World Congress Proceedings,* Jay Licbowitz, ed. New York: Pergamon Press, 1991, pp. 797–810.

Goldstein, David. "The Distributed AI Toolkit." *AI Expert,* January 1994, pp. 34–37.

Hedberg, Sara. "Machine Translation Software." *AI Expert,* October 1994, pp. 37–41.

Kim, Jonathan. "The Ideal KBS Development Tool." In *Third Annual Symposium of the International Association of Knowledge Engineers Proceedings,* November 16–19, 1992, pp. 163–170.

Krallmann, Hermann; Ansgar Woltering; and Michael Muller-Wunsch. "CASA: A Knowledge-Based Tool for Management Consultants." In *Expert Systems World Congress Proceedings,* Jay Liebowitz, ed. New York: Pergamon Press, 1991, pp. 264–273.

Mena, Jesus. "The Adaptive Tax Collector." *AI Expert,* November 1994, pp. 39–41.

Muzard, Joel. "Tools for Computer-Assisted Knowledge Engineering: ALADIN and STATEX." In *Third Annual Symposium of the International Association of Knowledge Engineers Proceedings,* November 16–19, 1992, pp. 155–162.

Mylopoulos, John. "Using an Expert System Tool for Process Control Applications." *Canadian Conference on Electrical and Computer Engineering.* Ottawa: Eng. Institute of Canada, 1990, pp. 42.4.1–42.4.6

Mylopoulous, John; Huaiqing Wang; and Bryan Kramer. "Knowbel: A Hybrid Tool for Building Expert Systems." *IEEE Expert,* February 1993, pp. 17–24.

Oliveira, Eugenio and Rui Camacho. "A Tool for Cooperative Expert Systems." In *Expert Systems World Congress Proceedings,* Jay Liebowitz, ed. New York: Pergamon Press, 1991, pp. 1774–1783.

Roth, Al and Clive Spenser. "Prolog in the Real World." *PC AI,* October 1994, pp. 42–44.

Shaw, Julie. "AI Language Resource Guide." *AI Expert,* April 1993, pp. 44–49.

Shaw, Julie and Alan Zeichick. "Expert System Resource Guide." *AI Expert,* December 1992, pp. 42–48.

Smith, Peter; Shi-Ming Huang; John Clifford; and John Tait. "Knowledge Processing Tools: Proposal of a New Architecture." In *Third Annual Symposium of the International Association of Knowledge Engineers Proceedings,* November 16–19, 1992, pp. 171–180.

Tewari, Rajiv. "Expert Design Tools for Physical Database Design." In *Trends and Directions in Expert Systems Proceedings,* E.M.Awad, ed. October 31–November 2, 1990, pp. 538–550.

Wu, Zhaohui; Jing Ying; Zhijun He; Tong Huang; and Feng Yue. "ZIPE: A Toolkit for Building Coupled Expert Systems." In *Expert Systems World Congress Proceedings,* Jay Liebowitz, ed. New York: Pergamon Press, 1991, pp. 1889–1896.

Yen, John and Jonathan Lee. "A Task-Based Methodology for Specifiying Expert Systems." *IEEE Expert,* February 1993, pp. 8–16.

Zozaya-Gorostiza, Carlos. "Use of AI-based Tools in a Mexican Automotive Part Supplier." In *Expert Systems World Congress Proceedings,* Jay Liebowitz, ed. New York: Pergamon Press, 1991, pp. 500–513.

PART · IV

TESTING AND IMPLEMENTING THE KNOWLEDGE BASE

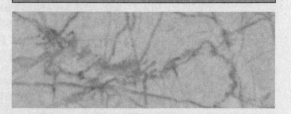

Chapter ■ 15

Verification and Validation

REPORTING CHEMICAL SPILLS: AN EXPERT SOLUTION

The environmental debate may seem far from the field of artificial intelligence, but now an application can help chemical companies fulfill their legal obligations. Companies that produce or use chemicals may have to report chemical spills and releases that occur on their property or in transit to federal, state, and local authorities. Such a company should understand the regulations that require the reporting of these incidents. Obviously, an expert system that would advise companies about their legal reporting responsibilities should be infallible—a feature difficult to ensure with the huge amount of pertinent rules, regulations, and technical information. But Spill & Release Advisor is just such a system.

BIRTH OF A PROGRAM

Spill & Release Advisor grew out of a course I taught on commercial operations. One student was an engineer who was interested in environmental regulatory compliance. After several prototypes, we coded Spill & Release Advisor in Information Builders' Level5, with several accompanying dBASE III-compatible databases. We had attempted to develop the initial prototypes using production rules alone, but the number of attributes relating to the problem domain made verifiable maintenancecw-1 of the rule base unreasonable. The heuristics for the rules came from our clients and the U.S. Environmental Protection Agency. Our hazardous chemical database also came from EPA.

DECISION STRUCTURES

In its early stages, Spill & Release Advisor was customized and heavily rewritten for individual clients. In one case, we developed an expert system prototype based on a client's flowcharts for determining hazardous-waste reporting requirements in about one month. When the client saw her decision structure animated and running, she noticed that many of her decision paths were invalid. And although we are not environmental regulatory compliance experts, we could see discrepancies and inconsistencies in the system's decisions: they were either ambiguous or contradictory. This result led the client company to improve its policies and eventually to an effective expert system solution.

While working with this client, we performed several iterations of two types of testing. Black-box testing allowed the client to present the system with a large set of potentially correct spill-and-release incidents and see whether the system provided the correct consultation. White-box testing let the client present similar scenarios and walk through printouts of the source code to see which rules would fire in each situation.

TESTING AND VALIDATION

For the black-box testing, we assumed the application system to be a black box—we could see what went in and what came out, but not internal processes. Developers, experts, and potential users provided the developing system with inputs and determined if the outputs were correct, given the inputs we provided. In this scenario, as long as the outputs directly reflected the expertise of the experts (given the inputs), we didn't care how the system determined the correct response.

For the white-box checking, we performed two procedures with hard copy of the program and its knowledge base. First we read through the rules one by one to determine if each was correct. Second, we took examples of what would be a set of correct inputs and manually walked through the knowledge base to see which rules would be applicable, if they would be used correctly, that the function of these rules was correct, and that their left-hand sides were necessary and sufficient to determine the appropriate trueness of the right-hand side of each and every rule. Additionally, we checked to ensure that all of the interfaces between the knowledge bases and the blackboard of common facts were correct.

Validation is the process of substantiating that a system performs with an acceptable level of accuracy. Validation involves whether system performance satisfies the requirements; in other words, that the right system will be built. We validated our system each time we tested it with the experts. For every inputed problem, we compared the system's output with the experts' decisions.

During *verification,* we traced the rules the system was using for each case to see if the rules used were the correct ones for each case. We were able to do so by having the system run through a case and verify that it was correct for input and output from the standpoint of the expert's decisions. We captured the sessions using Level5's *save session* feature and went through the session to see if the correct rules were fired, the rules provided the correct information, and the right decisions were made.

We found sets of test cases to run through the system, ran them against a baseline of the software's configuration, and saw how the software reacted. The test cases were developed by the experts for us, and we utilized them not only to determine if the system was running properly, but also to ensure that any modifications we had made had not altered correct operation of the system from prior versions. In other words, we had test cases to ensure that our extensions were correct and that the work of the past developments had not been adversely affected (otherwise known as regression testing). Each time new pieces of logic were added (for example, the addition of handling vinyl chloride), new test cases were developed by the expert and run by the knowledge engineers, experts, and potential users.

HELPING USERS

We ran one other set of tests to ensure that the users would understand and be able to use the system and that it would fit their intuitive understanding of the problem. From this standpoint, we were testing the system not for its correctness, but for its usability by the intended users. In all cases, we were able to get the application to the point where it was correct enough for the experts, efficient enough for the knowledge engineers, and usable enough for the users.

We found that the testing, validation, and verification work took a lot of time for everybody involved. But our ability to develop prototypes rapidly and provide them to experts and users helped users to understand more efficiently and effectively what we were doing and provide feedback. We were also able to get feedback from the users about the usability and usefulness of the system in their work environments.

Source: Excerpted from Steve Oxman, "Reporting Chemical Spills: An Expert Solution," *AI Expert,* May 1991, pp. 50–51.

AT A GLANCE

Verification and validation is a put-it-to-the-test phase that expert systems go through before certification. The goal is system reliability and user satisfaction. Verification is a white-box process that analyzes the rules and their relationship to one another. In contrast, validation is a black-box process that assumes the system works fine but tests for how well the system meets user requirements.

The problems with verification and validation are lack of standardization and reliable specification, deciding what constitutes an error, and the sources of test cases. For verification, cases must address circular and redundant rules and verify system functionality. Validation begins with a person or a testing team armed with validation criteria using realistic test cases.

No single validation technique detects all errors in an expert system. Some tools work better than others, depending on the type of expert system. Some of the known validation tools include face validation, Turing test, statistical tools, and test cases provided by the knowledge engineer or the user.

Finally, the key issue in validation is planning and managing a test plan that includes decisions on how, when, and where to evaluate the knowledge base and who should do the verification and validation, consistent evaluation criteria, and validation of all rules for Type I and Type II errors. Once planned, verification and validation testing, per se, is a matter of time.

What You Will Learn

By the end of this chapter, you should know the following:

1. The distinction between verification and validation.

2. The various approaches to verification and validation.

3. The importance of verification and validation planning and of assigning a competent team to do the testing.

4. The guidelines to follow for managing verification and validation.

> The quest for quality is a race without a finishing line.
>
> —NORMAN RICKARD,
> XEROX'S VICE PRESIDENT OF QUALITY

INTRODUCTION

When building expert systems, the time comes to put the system to the test. What good is a system that has not proven its worth or reliability? Imagine using an expert system in critical real-time applications, such as manned space missions, without proving that the system will not make catastrophic errors. At each level of the expert system life cycle, testing and evaluation of the product are critical steps.

Expert system reliability is one of the most important issues in knowledge-based systems. **Reliability** refers to how well the system delivers the information or solution with consistency, accuracy, and integrity. It also means detecting and removing anomalies (redundancy, ambivalence, deficiency, etc.). As today's expert systems become larger and larger, reliability is emerging as a significant issue in the development of expert systems.

Two prime considerations behind reliability are quality assurance and maintainability of the system after installation. Yourdon defines quality as "never having to say I'm sorry." Whether dealing with a system of 50 rules or 5,000 rules, the primary goal of the knowledge engineer is to ensure that the system "says what it means and means what it says." In other words, quality representation of the expertise requires verification and validation. Taken together, they provide a method of checking that the user's requirements are not misunderstood at the conceptual, acquisition, or representation phases of system development.

The building process of most expert systems often generates anxiety and concern. In the rush to build and deliver the system, many knowledge engineers cut corners at the back end of the cycle—verification and validation (V&V)—which means a less rigorous testing of the system. The reasons for not undergoing thorough testing range from not knowing how to verify and validate, to running out of time or funds. Regardless of the reason, ethical and legal obligations generally prompt knowledge engineers to subject the system to V&V prior to its final installation.

Verification and validation of expert systems call for informal, subjective, time-consuming, and often arbitrary creation and execution of test cases. In this chapter, the various aspects of verification and validation are discussed: who should do the testing; what testing criteria, issues in testing, verification and validation tools are used; etc. and how to promote objectivity and order. The term **testing** refers to time-intensive verification and validation of rule-based systems. Once testing is completed, the final step is to certify the product. Verification and validation as a phase in the expert system development life cycle is shown in Figure 15–1.

Figure 15–1 Phases of Expert System Testing

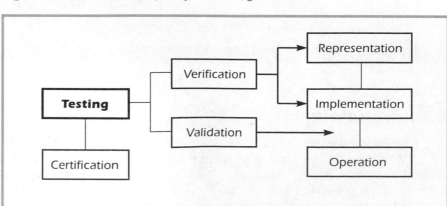

QUALITY AND QUALITY ASSURANCE

The production of quality expert systems is a goal shared by system developers, experts, as well as users. The quality of performance must be demonstrated in a systematic way in order to promote user acceptance of this emerging technology. As mentioned earlier, quality means "never having to say I'm sorry." It is the ability of the expert system to meet or exceed the performance of the human expert and the expectations of the user. Performance capabilities are equated with the quality of the knowledge stored in the knowledge base, since the stored knowledge represents the expertise of the human expert.

The definition of quality depends on whether the viewpoint belongs to the expert, the user, or the developer. For the expert, quality is a reasoning process that gives reliable and accurate advice within the framework of the expert system. For the user, quality is not only the system's performance but also its ability to be quick, easy to use, easy to understand, and forgiving when the user makes mistakes. For the developer, quality of an expert system is how well the expert's and the user's expectations are incorporated into the knowledge base.

In developing expert systems, the characteristics desirable in expert systems are evaluated. They are referred to by various names: performance criteria, evaluation criteria, and validation criteria. These criteria include the quality of the system's answers, the correctness of the reasoning used, the system's efficiency, and its cost-effectiveness. The sections that follow examine how quality is tested via verification and validation. Specific criteria are suggested as an approach to testing the expert system on its way to deployment and certification.

VERIFICATION AND VALIDATION

The most challenging part of building expert systems is testing. The basic motivation behind testing is to control performance, efficiency, and quality of the knowledge base. The goal is compliance with user expectations and system functioning. When an expert system is built via prototyping, each phase of the building process can be verified and validated rather than waiting until the end as is usually done in testing conventional information systems.

Definitions

In the literature, different interpretations of verification and validation have been offered. Some authors allow the two terms to intermingle as if to mean the same thing. Informally, they are—together—an approach to make sure the system works right. A popular view looks at verification as follows:

> **Verification** answers the question, "Are we building the system right?"
> Was the system developed using well-established software engineering
> principles? It means checking the system to make sure it correctly gives
> solutions or results. It looks for anomalies, such as redundant or deficient
> knowledge, and ensures a bug-free knowledge base.

Verification essentially addresses the intrinsic properties of the expert system and its components. *Intrinsic* refers to the syntactic or mechanical aspects of the knowledge base. Many commercially available shells have verification or "trace" features that catch common errors in rule redundancy or syntax, a capability that can be of immense value when hundreds of rules make up the knowledge base.

Verification is also a **white-box** process that analyzes the rules for sequence, structure, and specifications. Because no external factors are considered, the quality of verification can be objectively measured by answering questions such as "What is . . . ?" "How many . . . ?" etc. This phase of testing is usually done in a static (paper and pencil) mode, even when the system is not yet operational. Its goal is error-free rules.

In contrast, validation looks at the larger picture of system development and can be defined as follows:

Validation answers the question, "Are we building the right system?" Will it solve the problems it is designed to solve? It refers to checking the requirements of the system against standards to ensure promised results and user satisfaction.

Validation follows verification and tests the system's behavior in a realistic environment. It should establish that the expert system being tested is in fact an expert. As a **black-box** approach, validation ignores the internal mechanics of the system. Meaning and content of the rules must meet predefined criteria of adequacy. The quality measurement of validation tends to be subjective. For example, questions such as "What do you think of . . . ?" and "How well do you like . . . ?" are often asked when validating the expert system. See Box 15–1.

Unlike verification, validation is done only when the system is operational. In other words, validation can be done only after verification (see Figure 15–1). If the system is modular, each module goes through both steps in building the expert system. See Box 15–2 for an illustration of validation.

In today's practice, no standardization, specific tools, or methodologies guide the testing of expert systems. The process is complex and unique at the same time. It involves verifying and validating the intelligence of the system against that of its human counterpart. Intelligence is hard to define, let alone evaluate. Expertise in many domains is also unclear, highly subjective, and sometimes even biased. Consequently, the whole process of testing expert

---

Box 15–1   Adequacy as a Validation Criterion

"Adequacy is a measurement of the fraction of actual conditions included in the system. For example, the breath gas monitoring system I helped develop diagnosed 12 waveform patterns of CO_2. Each waveform pattern corresponded to a particular physiological condition. The adequacy of the system was judged according to the total desired number of conditions to diagnose.

"Adequacy may be expressed as a simple fraction. The breath gas monitoring system was able to diagnose 12 of 27 important physiological conditions, so the system was $100 \times (12/27) = 44\%$ adequate. As an alternative, subjective weights may be added to particular conditions that are more important to recognize (such as cessation of breathing)."

Source: Anonymous.

Box 15–2   Validator

Validator is a program that interactively verifies and validates rule-based expert system knowledge bases. It checks the syntax and semantics for potential errors and brings them to the attention of the knowledge engineer. Validator does not attempt to fix errors; that task is left to the knowledge engineer. The system has six modules: a preprocessor, syntax analyzer, syntactic error checker, debugger (removes compiler-type errors that cause the system to fail at run time), chaining thread tracer (checks the validity of each rule by tracing its premises and conclusions), and knowledge-base completeness module.

Validator was tested on 67 expert systems selected from MA projects, potential commercial systems, class projects for graduate courses in knowledge engineering, and commercial demonstration systems. The potential mistakes flagged by Validator fell into nine categories: illegal use of reserved words; rules that could never fire (both backwards and forward rules); unused facts; unused questions; unused legal values; repeated questions; multiple methods (including expressions that appear in questions and facts, questions and conclusions, and facts and conclusions); rules using illegal values (including mismatches between any of the sets of legal values, utilized values, concluded values, and assigned values); and incorrect instantiations.

Source: Yue Kang and Terry Bahill, "A Tool for Expert Systems," *Al Expert,* February 1990, p. 48.

systems is subjective and error-prone. Table 15–1 provides a summary of select features of verification and validation.

Issues to Consider

Expert system testing attempts to cause failures in order to detect program errors. During planning, the knowledge engineer develops a strategy that uses a minimal set of test cases to discover a maximal set of failures. One such strategy is **exhaustive testing**—a test in which all possible combinations of input values are tested. It is a time-consuming and extremely difficult process to follow. In fact, it is impractical when total cost is measured against marginal benefits.

Several issues are considered during verification and validation:

- *Subjective nature of intelligence testing.* As mentioned before, intelligence is difficult to measure. With human experts, intelligence changes over time due to ongoing upgrades of their intellect, abilities, and judgment. Solutions for many problems often call for subjective decisions rather than straightforward categorizations of right or wrong. Without a consistent yardstick, the testing process remains ad hoc, subjective, and error-prone. Because expert systems always give an answer based on the heuristics, they don't "blow up" as do traditional information systems. This subjectivity makes the job of testing an expert system that much more difficult and is bound to affect the maintainability and reliability of the system.

- *Lack of reliable specifications.* Ill-defined specifications make verification and validation arbitrary and unreliable. Without testable specifica-

■ **Table 15–1** Select Features of Verification and Validation

	Verification	**Validation**
Meaning	Building the **system right**	Building the **right system**
Time performed	During knowledge representation or prototyping	During prototyping or when system is operational
Sequence	First	Second
Nature of checking	Syntactic (intrinsic properties of the system)	Semantic (extrinsic properties of the system)
Approach	White-box (alpha) testing	Black-box (beta) testing
Quality measurement	Primarily objective	Primarily subjective

tions, a knowledge engineer might give in to the tendency to make up specifications for what the system can do instead of figuring out the conditions under which the system will *not* function well. This is an important distinction to keep in mind.

■ *Problem of establishing consistency and correctness.* To make sure of the correct performance of the expert system, the knowledge engineer needs to verify both the knowledge base and the reasoning as processed by the inference engine. This is a challenge in itself. The complex tasks of verifying correctness and consistency are challenging because the system can continue to give correct answers even though part of the knowledge or inferencing is incorrect.

■ *Determination of what constitutes an error.* Since expert systems deal with knowledge rather than data, deciding what constitutes an error or the seriousness of the error is not so easy. At this point, the expert's participation in testing the system prior to certification can be crucial.

■ *Sources of test data.* In some situations, existing data can be used, and the output can be compared with an expert's conclusions for correctness. In other situations, the test data has to be generated by the expert or by automatic test data generating programs. Regardless of the method, the output of the expert system using test data has to be evaluated. Determining how to judge adequacy can be difficult.

■ *Danger of negligence in testing.* A vicious cycle begins when no one requires expert system verification and validation; if nobody does it, then no one requires it. Part of this problem stems from the difficulty in providing reliable test cases. Another reason is that expert systems with so many possible states or conditions make exhaustive testing impossible. As a result, verification and validation can take on "surface" commitment.

■ *Inadequacy of automatic verification tools.* Since expert systems began to find a home in business in the early 1980s, a number of automatic verification tools have been developed. The justification for these tools is

Figure 15-2 Issues and Challenges in Verification and Validation

---

1. Subjective nature of intelligence testing
2. Lack of reliable specifications
3. Problem of establishing consistency and correctness
4. Determination of what constitutes an error
5. Sources of test data
6. Danger of negligence in testing
7. Inadequacy of automatic verification tools
8. Complexity of user interfaces

---

the lack of time that experts have available to test the knowledge base. Their time is expensive; they might disagree on the verification/validation criteria; and they do not have the same personal commitment to the project as does the end-user. Also a large number of parameters with many potential values cause a combinatorial explosion of rules and test cases, making exhaustive testing difficult. With the simplest tool, tabular checking, rules are grouped into tables similar to IF ... THEN decision tables. Inside each table, a comprehensive comparison of the rules is made, which checks for inconsistency, redundancy, subsumption, and the like. The main problem with most automatic verification tools is their assumption that a rule is fired as soon as its IF conditions are met. This assumption leaves much room for manual verification and compounds the complexity of the verification process.

■ *Complexity of user interfaces.* Some expert systems or shells have complex user interfaces in which inputs are not easy to reproduce, making the potential solution highly inaccurate. The user interface is an important part of the expert system development effort. Through it, the user determines how easy, user-friendly, or useful the system is, and therefore how successful it will be.

One conclusion knowledge engineers should take from these challenges is the need for a seriously designed verification strategy. It is a formal statement on how to proceed with the verification phase. The test design should meet all the requirements of the client.

Another implication is to figure out what it will take for the system to fail rather than how well it can be made to function. Such a test strategy requires careful choice of test cases that look for missing, ambiguous, or redundant rules with the potential for incorrect answers. These types of rules are discussed later in the chapter. A summary of these issues is listed in Figure 15-2.

■ APPROACHES TO VERIFICATION

Two approaches can be used to verify knowledge-based systems:

1. Verify knowledge base *formation.*
2. Verify knowledge base *functionality.*

Under knowledge base *formation,* the *structure* of the knowledge as it relates to circular or redundant rules is verified. Consistency, correctness, and completeness of knowledge base rules is also verified. Verification of *functionality* focuses on confidence and reliability of the knowledge base. See Figure 15–3. Rules and attributes are defined in Table 15–2.

Circular Rules

Carelessness often results in rules that employ circular reasoning. A **circular rule** tends to be contradictory in meaning or logic. For example, suppose Rule 1 states that *a* is greater than *b* and Rule 2 states that *b* is greater than *c*. If Rule 3 states that *c* is greater than *a,* then Rule 3 is circular and contains error in logic. The best solution in this case is to remove Rule 3.

Here is another example of a circular rule:

```
R5    IF John and Rob are co-owners of company A
      THEN John and Rob own the same company
R6    IF John and Rob own the same company
      THEN John and Rob are co-owners
```

In backward reasoning, if R6 finds a match and fires, its premise part will cause R5 to match and fire. The problem is that the premise part of R5 matches the action of R6, causing R6 to fire and so on, resulting in useless firing of the two rules.

As a simple example of verification, consider an expert system that has a number of cases involving a house with a living room. One can evaluate cases and determine that something is incorrect with a case that has a bathtub in the living room. The case probably contains redundant knowledge if the living room has two sofas. Likewise, the case of a living room without a sofa probably would be considered incomplete. Finally, inconsistency occurs if, in the case, two identical items are labeled with different names. For example, a sofa for one item is labeled a couch for another item.

Figure 15–3   Approaches to Verification

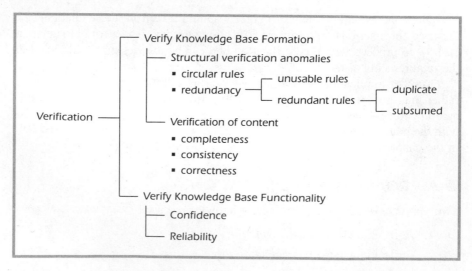

■ **Table 15-2**   Rules and Attributes in Verification

Circular rule	A situation in which the action(s) of one piece of knowledge may lead back somehow to the condition statement of the same piece of knowledge.
Completeness	Answers the question, "Does the system deal with all possible situations within its domain reasonably well?"
Confidence	The level of trust or dependence one can put on the system's answers to problems; related to system integrity, with an emphasis on system reliability and consistently accurate answers.
Correctness	Described as accuracy; see Table 15-3.
Consistency	A check to ensure that the system produces similar answers to all input data at all times with no contradiction.
Inconsistency	An anomaly or an error that occurs when an item of knowledge has different value(s) within the knowledge base.
Redundancy	Two or more rules that are written differently but provide the same solution; a duplication of knowledge. Absence of redundancy provides greater specificity to the notion of completeness.
Reliability	How well the system delivers solutions with consistency, accuracy, and integrity; the probability of failure free operation of the expert system in a specified environment for a specified time period; synonymous with **dependability** or trustworthiness.
Subsumption rule	The conclusion(s) of two pieces of knowledge are the same, except that one piece of knowledge has fewer condition statements.

Redundancy Rules

Redundancy rules offer different approaches to the same problem, causing a duplication of knowledge. One gets the same results either way, also known as the "dinosaur effect." For example:

```
IF (Salary > 60000 OR Home > 100000)
   AND (Loan < 10000 and Mortgage < 40000)
THEN MAX = 100000

IF (Salary > 60000 OR Home > 100000)
THEN Assets = 'yes'
IF (Salary > 50000 AND Dividend > 10000)
THEN Assets = 'yes'
IF (Loan < 10000 AND Mortgage < 40000)
   AND Assets = 'yes'
THEN MAX = 100000
```

In this example, two approaches address the same problem of determining MAX. Additionally, dividends in the second approach is not needed to establish assets. Redundancy can cause difficulties in maintaining the expert system, such as when one version of the rule is revised, while another inadvertently left as is.

Here is another example of redundant rules:

```
R7    IF assets > 300000
         AND salary ≥ 50000
      THEN approve loan


R8    IF salary ≥ 50000
         AND assets > 300000
      THEN approve loan
```

In this example, identical premises reach identical conclusions. The two rules will always fire under the same situations, because they assert "approve loan," which is what makes them redundant.

Unusable Rules

An **unusable rule** only fires or executes if the conditions succeed or fail, never fires, or has one or more contradictions. They are all in error and, therefore, unusable. An example of a contradictory rule that is always false is:

```
IF humidity is 5% AND heavy_rain = yes
THEN conclusion
```

This rule cannot succeed. If a rule premise will be false for all valid values, the rule will never succeed. In this example, heavy rain cannot occur in 5% humidity. Unusable rules are also called conflicting rules.

An example of a rule that can never fire is:

```
Fact: Stolen_tag = no


Rule: IF stolen_car = yes
         AND stolen_tag = yes
      THEN last_stolen car = yes
```

This rule will fail, because of the declared fact. The object "stolen tag" will never be instantiated, because the fact is set to "no."

Subsumption Rules

In **subsumption,** if one rule is true, one knows the second rule is always true. Consider this example:

```
R1: IF A AND B, THEN D


R2: IF A AND B AND C, THEN D
```

If R1 is true, then R2 is useless, because R2 is subsumed by R1. Both have identical conclusions, but R2 contains additional (and thus unnecessary) premise clause. Here is another example:

```
FUZZYIF CLASS IS 'MAMMAL' AND APPEARANCE IS 'HAS CLAWS'
THEN THERE IS .8 EVIDENCE THAT ANIMAL = 'BOBCAT'

FUZZYIF CLASS IS 'MAMMAL' AND APPEARANCE IS 'HAS CLAWS'
 AND COLOR IS 'BROWN'
THEN THERE IS .9 EVIDENCE THAT ANIMAL = 'BOBCAT'
```

The second fuzzy IF rule is stronger than the first, it adds one more parameter value ('brown') to justify the .9 evidence.

Inconsistency Rules

In inconsistency rules, the same inputs yield different results. For example,

```
IF (Salary > 50000 OR Home > 100000)
   AND (Loan < 10000 AND Mortgage < 40000)
THEN MAX = 100000

IF (Salary > 50000 OR Home > 60000)
   AND (Loan < 3000 AND Mortgage < 20000)
THEN MAX = 50000
```

A user will get different answers, depending on which rule is used. Tests conducted for consistency can also be used to test for completeness. The whole idea is to make sure all the parameters included in the rules are used correctly and consistently.

■ APPROACHES TO VALIDATION

As mentioned earlier, validation follows verification. Its focus is on testing the behavior of the integrated system against the user's requirements. Even when each rule is individually correct, something in their interactions can cause the system to act up.

Validation includes several steps:

1. *Select a person or a team for testing.* A testing plan should indicate who is to do the validation—the expert, the user, or the knowledge engineer. The plan should also determine which validation technique(s) are appropriate for the system.

2. *Decide on validation criteria.* Once the validation technique is determined, validation criteria should be decided. The key validation criteria are ease of use, accuracy, adequacy, adaptability, face validity, appeal, availability, reliability, technical and operational validity, performance, and Turing test. See Table 15–3 for definitions of the criteria.

3. *Develop a set of test cases unique to the problem.* The test cases should include subtle and obvious cases, boundary conditions, and obviously meaningless combinations of valid and invalid data. The test results are then evaluated against the criteria.

4. *Maintain a log on various versions of the tests and test results.* Documentation can be very important; errors are more easily detected at one test level by simply going back to the previous version. Without this

Box 15–3 Verification and Validation of the Hiring Advisor

Testing of the Hiring Advisor was an ongoing process throughout the development of the knowledge base. This testing certified that the system was reliable and valid for Ms. Burgess' requirements. Testing ensured that the Hiring Advisor handled all of the objectives specified in the Problem Specification adequately, implemented the information gathered during Solution Specification, and verified the rationale that was used. The testing phase was comprised of the extensive verification and validation steps described below.

The verification process was a form of white-box testing, because it checked the success of the firing of each of the rules within the knowledge base. The verification of the system involved the test case design, the selection of the cases, and the face validity of all the rules. Face validation consisted of firing all the knowledge base rules to check the system's results with the expected results. This process was iterated several times.

At times when we were verifying if each rule fired when the specific criteria were input, the expected results did not match what actually occurred. When this happened, we would immediately go into the knowledge base and attempt to locate the error. Sometimes, it was due to redundant rules that had different conclusions. These rules were removed to improve the consistency and integrity of the knowledge base. This process was especially time-consuming, because with each change made to the knowledge base, regression testing had to be done. Regression testing was used to ensure that the changes made in the system from one iteration to another did not invalidate the results from the testing in the previous stages. As a result, we had to run all of the previous set of test cases to ensure that no new problems had been introduced by making changes to the system.

Source: Based on "Hiring Advisor," Erika Kaufman and Lori Werth, May 1994, p. 14.

"backup," the system would have to be tested from the beginning every time an error occurs—a frustrating and time-consuming approach.

5. *Field-test the system.* Once the system has passed the validation process, it should be field-tested with user involvement. If the user has been involved in the earlier stages of system development, field testing should go smoothly.

No matter how rigorous the validation of an expert system, field testing has been known to produce unexpected errors. A field test that uncovers serious errors could erode user confidence in the system. Regaining such confidence is not so easy. One method to minimize lack of confidence is to educate the user on the "goodness" of expert systems prior to field testing. Another is to represent system testing as only a portion rather than the entire validation process. In the interim, the setting in which field testing is conducted and attitude of the user can affect how errors are viewed.

V&V Team and Plan

A successful V&V effort requires a commitment to human resources beyond the knowledge engineer or the domain expert. Commitment begins with manage-

■ **Table 15–3**   Select Criteria for Validation

Accuracy	How correct does the outcome of the system match reality or expectations? Emphasis here is on correctness of the outcome, which is measured by comparing the number of correct answers against known answers.
Adaptability	How well does the system adapt to changing situations? This criterion relates to flexibility and capability to modify facts and rules when new information becomes available. Can the system be customized for particular user needs?
Adequacy	Are the solutions or answers produced by the expert system satisfactory or "good enough" to be acceptable to the user? It is a measurement of the fraction of actual conditions included in the knowledge base.
Appeal	How well does the expert system match the user's intuition and promotes useful ideas? Usability is also related to practicability, marketability, and user friendliness.
Availability	Do other rule-based systems that solve the same problems exist? Related to appeal.
Ease of use	Does the system incorporate human-engineering and convey a high quality in its human–machine interaction/interface?
Face validity	How well does the system pass the real-life test on its surface? It is another term for credibility.
Performance	Does the system function as expected? It is related to reliability and quality assurance and the overall quality of the solutions provided by the expert system.
Reliability	See Table 15–2.
Robustness	Is the system able to function near the limits of its coverage?
Technical/operational validity	How well do the system's technical and operational states meet the user's requirements? It indicates the capability of the knowledge base to produce empirically correct answers.
Turing test	Do the system's results match the human expert's results? It tests the system validity by having a human evaluator distinguish between the system's conclusions to a specific problem and a human expert's conclusions to the same problem.

ment support and a V&V team with a viable test plan. The V&V team oversees all V&V activities. It should

- Be independent of the design or coding of the system.
- Understand computer technology and system operation.
- Be well versed in the organization's business and how the system being tested will fit into the designated area of operation.

The team members normally represent a variety of the user's areas of operation, especially in the system's final certification phase. The entire procedure should be guided by a V&V plan that defines the roles, responsibilities, and documentation for everyone involved in the system's life cycle with respect to V&V. More specifically, the plan should

- Identify the aspects of the system that require testing.
- Determine when system validation is appropriate.
- Define the test method that will lead to certification.
- Provide the guideline for documenting test results.

For smaller systems, the domain expert, the knowledge engineer, or the user can do the validation. Each choice has its own pros and cons. The domain expert is the natural choice because of familiarity with the knowledge base. Yet, domain experts have been known to lose interest in validation, having already spent countless hours with knowledge representation. Experts who are told to validate the system often subject the system to **face validity**—using a set of typical cases just to make sure it works—without specifically addressing the validation criteria during the test. Because experts are not the system's ultimate end-users, the results of validation tests performed by experts only could be misleading.

Having the knowledge engineer do the validation also has limitations. In one respect, the knowledge engineer knows enough about the system to do the validation. However, the problem for most knowledge engineers is that they have only limited knowledge in developing test cases that meet validation criteria. The domain expert can be consulted to approve the procedure and the acceptability of the solutions.

A third alternative of having the end-user do the validation is borrowed from the conventional forms of testing information systems for user acceptance. Users in general do not know what to validate for. In most cases, they end up relying on the domain expert and/or the knowledge engineer for training and implementation. The most serious limitation to user-oriented validation lies in the differences between how a user and a domain expert would use the system.

Who ends up being the validator of the system, then, depends on the availability of expertise, motivation, time, and funds allocated for the job. A V&V team representing the user's interest and based on a plan would be the best choice.

Validation Criteria

Validation criteria guide the focus of what to validate. As a general rule, all systems are valid against certain criteria and invalid against others. The question is how does one know what criteria to use for evaluating a particular system? This question is especially important when certain systems (e.g., medical diagnosis) require more stringent validation criteria than other systems (e.g., one that assists in the selection of roses for Valentine's day). The alternative criteria compare system results against historical cases, against the human expert's prediction of the final results, or against some theoretical standard. In any case, validation techniques contain imperfections and cannot guarantee 100 percent performance.

Once validation techniques are selected, validation criteria should be identified. To illustrate, suppose test cases are choosen from system validation. Several questions are raised:

1. How many test cases should be used to validate the system to the desired confidence?

2. How should the test cases be developed objectively and reliably?

3. What objective measures should be determined for the selected criteria? (In this difficult step, some criteria such as metrics are dropped because of the difficulty of measurement.)

4. Should a performance measure be included—other than that of the human expert—against which test case results should be evaluated?

5. What mix of easy versus difficult test cases should be considered in the final test cases? That is, what type of test cases should be used?

6. How should the test cases be evaluated? Should they be evaluated by a panel of experts? Turing test? Knowledge engineer?

7. If multiple experts are involved, how should the system be validated against differing human opinions?

As indicated by this list, addressing criteria measures can assist in the planning of this critical phase of expert system development. Sound and reliable validation measures also mean easier implementation and user acceptance. Actually, user involvement in testing the user interface generally increases user acceptance of the finished product.

Validation Techniques

No single validation technique is best for detecting all errors in an expert system. Some techniques work better for certain types of problems (e.g., diagnostic versus advisory systems) and for certain types of knowledge representation (e.g., rule-based versus frames). A number of known validation techniques are worth reviewing:

1. Face validation

2. Statistical tools

3. Test cases

4. Turing test

5. Subsystem validation

Face Validation

In the face validation approach, a group of developers, users, and experts evaluate the performance of the expert system at its face value. The solutions provided by the system are compared with those of the human experts, and value judgments are made regarding the reliability of the results.

Face validation can be used to test "chunks of knowledge" at any phase of the expert system development life cycle. It is mainly a group effort of the knowledge engineer, the domain expert, and the end-user. This ad hoc tool is quite useful testing user–system interfaces, user friendliness, and explanation facilities. However, it is not a rigorous validation technique. As such, it offers no measurable assurance of performance or reliability.

Statistical Tools

Certain expert systems may be validated using quantitative measures known as a **metric.** The simplest metric is the measure of reliability:

$$\text{Reliability} = \frac{\text{MTBF}}{1 + \text{MTBF}}$$

where MTBF is the "mean time between failures." These formulas have been used in measuring the performance of hardware rather than software. Since the idea of "failure" in the reasoning process in expert systems does not exist, quantitative measures do not work well for validation.

Test Cases

One of the most popular validation techniques is executing a set of prepared test cases on the expert system. The system results are examined for agreement with those of an expert or a panel of experts who solve the same problem. It is more of a black-box approach, in which only system inputs and outputs are significant. See Box 15–4.

In addition to those of the domain expert, test cases may be provided by the knowledge engineer and the user. Those provided by the knowledge engineer have been known to be more effective than those provided by others. The domain expert, the knowledge engineer, and the user are somewhat like three blind men describing an elephant. Each looks at a different aspect of the expert system in trying to make sense out of it. Test cases from all three sources are considered the best combination, because they provide a more comprehensive test of the system. They also tend to increase the objectivity of the validation process.

Like other techniques, testing a knowledge base based on test cases has its own share of limitations. When the domain expert who writes the test cases is also the tester, the credibility of the validation process can be undermined. With the domain expert involved in providing test cases, bias—based perhaps on personality conflicts or in ignoring nontechnical aspects such as user interface or ease of use—can filter into them, especially if test case generation is done in an ad hoc manner.

Finally, generating test cases is so time-consuming and expensive that this phase is often viewed as a chore rather than a challenge. It takes certain know-how and objectivity to generate test cases. Even then, users have been known to accept the system, regardless of how lax the validation process has been. With this attitude, validation becomes a less-than-serious step in the testing process.

Turing Test

With the **Turing test,** an outside expert or a panel of experts evaluate solutions generated from the expert system. It is a blind evaluation of the relative merit of the solutions without *a priori* knowledge of whether the solutions were generated by a human expert or by an expert system.

An obvious benefit of this test is elimination of bias. The Turing test also provides an objective evaluation of the human expert's performance. Its

Box 15–4   Test Cases for the Hiring Advisor

The test design was created to ensure that all the expert's requirements were met. We created a form from which to collect decision data from individual past cases. The form includes all seven variables with the corresponding choices, area to write in her past decision, and an area to write in what the Hiring Advisor recommended. Thirty copies of the form were given to the manager to be filled out. A set of cases were selected from her past decisions to represent the good decisions and bad decisions. In order to make this process effective, Ms. Burgess looked through some of her previous applications to see what she had decided.

Good decisions included those applicants with whom Ms. Burgess was satisfied with her decision to either hire or not to hire. Likewise, bad decisions included applicants with whom the manager was dissatisfied with her final decision. Bad decisions resulted from either a Type I error or a Type II error. Results of Case testing are as follows:

Sample Size = 30	No. Hired	Number Not Hired
Type I Error	9	0
Type II Error	0	1

Without the use of our Hiring Advisor, there was a 33.3 percent (10 out of 30) error rate. The utilization of the Hiring Advisor improved upon the manager's hiring process by ensuring that Ms. Burgess considers all of the required variables before making her decision. This expert system removes ambiguity and inefficiencies in the decision-making process. In essence, the Hiring Advisor succeeded in eliminating both Type I and II errors recognized in the cases being utilized. We tested this by running each of the thirty cases through the Hiring Advisor using the following criteria:

- The past cases with applicants identified as good employees, who were actually hired, were determined to be qualified by the Hiring Advisor.

- The past cases with employees who were not hired, but were qualified, were determined to be qualified by the Hiring Advisor.

- The past cases with applicants who were hired and ended up being poor performers, were not determined to be qualified by the Hiring Advisor.

- The past cases with applicants who were not hired, because it was believed they would be poor performers, were not determined to be qualified by the Hiring Advisor.

The chief limitations of the previous decision-making process include the lack of emphasis on ability and the lack of standardization in the wage placements.

Source: Based on "Hiring Advisor," Erika Kaufman and Lori Werth, May 1994, p. 15.

simplicity and intuitive appeal makes it a popular test. Expert systems such as MYCIN and ONCOCIN were validated using the Turing test. The goodness of the test is in not being able to distinguish between the expert system's performance and that of the human expert who helped build the system.

The main limitation of the Turing test is the extensive time it takes expert evaluators and the expert who prepares the test problems. Another limitation is the test's inadequacy. The test considers only the accuracy and correctness of the final solution, ignoring other important aspects such as the human–machine interaction in performing tasks. Finally, some critics have claimed that the test suffers from being overly subjective in the way the test cases and expert judges are selected, which tends to adversely affect the reliability of the knowledge base.

Subsystem Validation

In the technique of subsystem validation, the expert system is partitioned into subsystems or modules that are tested individually and in relationship to other modules in the system. This "divide and conquer" technique allows for easier correction of errors and should be a plus for future maintenance and system update. One factor to consider, though, is that not all knowledge-based systems are easy to modularize. The entire system still needs to be tested as an entity before it can be certified.

■ GUIDELINES FOR MANAGING VERIFICATION AND VALIDATION

The coverage thus far has emphasized the important goal of testing. The key issue is *planning* for completeness of testing that will vouch for system adequacy and lead to certification. The three key steps of the testing cycle, then, are

Verification → Validation → Certification

Another important issue is managing the test plan, which includes the following tasks:

1. *Decide when, what, how, and where to evaluate the knowledge base.* The reliability of answers, inferencing approach, explanations, help facility, training capability, and the like must be evaluated. Timing and duration of testing in the hands of experts are crucial to a successful system test.

2. *Decide who should do the verification and validation.* All indicators point to having the domain expert "stick it out" through testing. The next best approach is to have an outsider expert or a team do independent "blind" validation of the knowledge base.

3. *Draft a set of evaluation criteria in advance.* This task involves knowing what to test for. One can get the system to run, but what are you proving or looking for? What are the hard criteria?

4. *Decide what should be recorded during the test.* Among the important statistics to record are:
   - Rules that always "fire" and succeed
   - Rules that always "fire" and fail
   - Rules that never "fire"
   - Test cases that have failed

5. *Review training cases, whether they are provided by the expert, the knowledge engineer, or the user.* The representativeness and appropriateness of the test cases should be emphasized in this task.

6. *Validate all rules.* This task ensures that every parameter is correct. Validation looks for two types of errors in rules:
   - Type I error—a rule that fails to fire when it is supposed to fire. This is tantamount to failing to detect a problem.
   - Type II error—a rule that fires when it is not supposed to fire.

IMPLICATIONS FOR MANAGEMENT

This chapter started with Norman Richard's quote, "The quest for quality is a race without a finishing line." The main goal of testing an expert system is to assure continuous quality and high performance. The term *performance* implies quality. The model of quality of an expert system is determined by interaction of three stakeholders:

Quality = *f* (domain expert, knowledge engineer, user)

Earlier, the role that each person plays in knowledge representation and system verification and validation was discussed. Such "stakeholder participation" offers various benefits in validation. The involvement of more than one stakeholder in testing incorporates differing expectations and needs, which allows for a broader perspective in determining system quality—each stakeholder decides on an individual basis whether the system will do the job.

The model shown in Figure 15–4 suggests that the quality of an expert system is affected by the nature of the problem domain, technical considerations, the people involved, and organizational factors. For example, if the problem domain is complex and the organization climate or politics are amenable to the prospective system, then a knowledge engineer can generally expect cooperation from the domain expert during knowledge representation. This cooperation should contribute to quality testing. The organization's prior experience with expert systems also contributes to the degree of cooperation expected during verification and validation. The end result should be a high performance, quality-oriented expert system.

The people factor in determining the quality of an expert system is influenced by the quality of work life and the planning and control of the system's implementation. This topic is discussed in detail in Chapter 16. It is a crucial aspect of expert system implementation—the organizational factors related to expert system development affect how easily or how well an expert system is implemented in the organization.

Figure 15–4   Internal and External Factors Affecting Expert System Quality

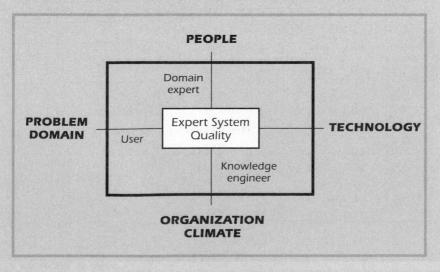

■ SUMMARY

1. Expert system reliability is one of the most important issues in knowledge-based systems. Reliability means how well the system will deliver the information with consistency, accuracy and integrity. The prime emphasis behind reliability is quality assurance and maintainability of the system after installation.

2. The most important part of building expert systems is testing. Verifications answers the question, "Are we building the system right?" and its goal is error-free rules. Validation answers the question, "Are we building the right system?" and tests the systems behavior in a realistic environment. Validation is done only after the system is operational.

3. Some important challenges or issues that are considered during verification and validation included the following:

   a. The subjective nature of intelligence testing

   b. The lack of reliable specifications

   c. The problem of establishing consistency and correctness

   d. The determination of what constitutes an error

   e. The sources of test data

   f. The danger of negligence in testing

   g. The adequacy of automatic verification tools

   h. The complexity of user interfaces

4. Two approaches are used to verify knowledge systems:

   a. Verify knowledge base formation.

   b. Verify knowledge base functionality.

5. A circular rule tends to be contradictory in meaning or logic. Redundancy rules offer different approaches to the same problem. An unusable rule always "fires" and fails, never fires, or has one or more contradictions. In a subsumption rule, if one rule is true, one knows the second rule is always true. In inconsistency rules, the same inputs yield different results.

6. The several steps for validation are:

   a. Select a person or a team for testing.

   b. Decide on validation criteria.

   c. Determine objective measures for the selected criteria.

   d. Develop a set of tests cases and scenarios unique to the problem.

   e. Maintain a log or various versions of the test and tests results.

7. Some valuation tools are:

   a. Face validation

   b. Statistical tools

   c. Test cases

   d. Turing test

   e. Subsystem validation

8. The key steps of the testing cycle are verification, validation, and certification. The model of quality of an expert system is determined by the interaction of three stakeholders: domain expert, knowledge engineer, and user.

■ TERMS TO LEARN

Black-box testing testing a system's behavior in a real-life environment; a validation phase.

Circular rule a rule that has embedded contradiction in meaning or logic.

Exhaustive testing a procedure in which all possible combinations of input values in an expert system are tested.

Face validity testing a system at its face value; comparing human domain expert's value judgment to test results for reliability.

Inconsistency rule a rule that has the same input but different results.

Metric quantitative measure used for system validations.

Redundancy rule a rule that offers a different approach to the same problem; duplication or meaning the same.

Reliability dependability, truthfulness of the response or answer to a given question; credibility; how well the system delivers solutions with consistency, accuracy, or integrity; detecting or removing anomaly.

Subsumption in rules, if one rule is true, one knows the second rule is always true.

Testing time-intensive verification and validation of expert systems.

Turing test a blind evaluation of the relative merit of the solution without a priori knowledge of whether the solutions were generated by a human expert or an expert system.

Unusable rule a rule that only fires if the conditions succeed, that never fires, or that has one or more contradictions.

Validation a system test to ensure the right system; a system that meets the expert's expectations; black-box testing; beta test or user acceptance test.

Verification a system test to ensure the proper functioning of the system; addresses the intrinsic properties of the expert system; white-box testing; alpha test.

White-box testing analyzing the rules for sequence, structure, and specifications; a verification phase.

■ REVIEW QUESTIONS

1. What is the goal of verification? Validation? Explain.

2. In your own words, explain the various phases of expert system testing.

3. Distinguish between:
   a. white-box and black-box testing
   b. circular and redundant rules
   c. Turing test and exhaustive test

4. Discuss the key issues of verification and validation. Is one issue necessarily more critical than all others? Be specific.

5. The chapter discusses two approaches to verifying knowledge-based systems. Elaborate on each briefly.

6. How does verification of knowledge base formation differ from knowledge base functionality?

7. Give examples of the following:
   a. circular rule
   b. redundant rule
   c. subsumed rule
   d. unusable rule

8. Discuss the importance of the main steps to validation.

9. Where should the test cases for validation come from? How would one assure their reliability or relevance?

10. Who should do the validation? The end-user or the domain expert? The knowledge engineer? Explain.

11. In what ways is each of the following validation tool useful:

a. face validation
b. Turing test
c. statistical tools
d. test cases

12. If you were doing verification and validation, what guideline would be useful before the actual test? Explain.

■ EXERCISES AND CASES

1. Consider the following rules:

```
R1   IF a = 10
     AND b = 15
     THEN c = 20

R2   If a = 10
     THEN c = 20
```

In these two rules, which rule is subsumed by the other?

2. Consider the following rules:

```
IF   temperature > warm AND
     humidity is high AND
     atmospheric pressure is low
THEN there will be thunderstorms

IF   temperature > warm AND
     humidity is high
THEN there will be thunderstorms
```

Which rule is subsumed by the other? Why?

3. Consider the following rules:

```
R1   IF a = 10
     AND b = 15
     THEN c = 20

R2   IF b = 15
     AND a = 10
     THEN c = 20
     AND d = 25
```

Are these two rules redundant? Why? Which rule is made redundant by the other rule? Explain.

4. Consider the following rules:

```
R1   IF a = 10
     AND b = 15
     THEN c = 20

R2   IF a = 10
     AND b = 15
     THEN c = 35
```

These rules are said to be in conflict. Do you agree? Why?

5. Consider the following rules:

```
R1   IF   temperature > warm AND
          humidity is high
     THEN there will be no thunderstorms

R2   IF   humidity is high AND
          temperature > warm
     THEN there will be no thunderstorms
```

In what way(s) are these rules redundant? Will they always succeed?

6. Consider the following rules:

```
R1   IF   humidity is high AND
          temperature > warm
     THEN there will be thunderstorms

R2   IF   temperature > warm AND
          humidity is high
     THEN there will be sandstorms
```

Are these rules redundant? In what way(s)?

7. Identify whether the following rules are redundant, conflicting, circular, or subsumed rules:

a.

```
R1   IF a = x            R2   IF b = y
     AND b = y                AND a = x
     THEN c = z               THEN c = z
```

b.

```
R1   IF a = x                    R2   IF b = y
     AND b = y                        AND a = x
     THEN c = z AND d = w             THEN c = w
```

c.

```
R1   IF a = x            R2   IF b = y
     AND b = y                THEN c = z
     THEN c = z
```

d.

```
R1   IF a = x   R2     IF b = y
     THEN b = y        AND c = z
                       THEN decision = yes
```

```
R3   IF decision = yes
     THEN a = x
```

8. An expert system is being designed to assist a computer retailers customer service clerks manage calls related to replacement of pentium chips in PCs. How should the performance of the expert system be evaluated? Explain.

9. Review your Publisher Advisor and perform the following:

a. Formulate a verification and validation plan.

b. Generate test cases and the result of testing each case.

c. List or report the rules found to be redundant, conflicting, subsumed, or circular.

■ SELECTED REFERENCES

Abbott, Lance and Mohammad Modarres. "Consistency Checking During Automatic Knowledge Acquisition for Expert System Development." *The Journal of Knowledge Engineering,* Summer/Fall 1990, pp. 29–37.

Ayel, M. and J-P Laurent. "SACCO-SYCOJET: Two Different Ways of Verifying Knowledge-Based Systems." In M. Ayel and J-P Laurent, eds. *Verification and Validation of Knowledge-Based Systems.* New York: John Wiley & Sons, Inc., 1991, pp. 63–76.

Batarekh, A.; A. D. Precce; A. Bennett; and P. Grogono. "Specifying an Expert System." *Expert Systems With Applications* 2, no. 4 (1991), pp. 285–303.

Boehm, B. W. "Verifying and Validating Software Requirements and Design Specifications." *IEEE Software,* January 1984, pp. 75–88.

Charles, E. and O. Dubois. "MELODIA: Logical Methods for Checking Knowledge Bases." In M. Ayel and J-P Laurent, eds. *Verification and Validation of Knowledge-Based Systems.* New York: John Wiley & Sons, Inc., 1991, pp. 95–104.

Craw, S. "Judging Knowledge Base Quality." In M. Ayel and J-P Laurent, eds. *Verification and Validation of Knowledge-Based Systems.* New York: John Wiley & Sons, Inc., 1991, pp 207–219.

Eliot, Lance B. "If It Works, Is It Good?" *AI Expert,* June 1992, pp. 9–11.

Freedman, Roy S. "Knowledge-Based Software Testing." *The Journal of Knowledge Engineering,* Spring 1991, pp. 47–65.

Grabowski, Martha and Hal Hendrick. "How Low Can We Go?: Validation and Verification of a Decision Support System for Safe Shipboard Manning." *IEEE Transactions on Engineering Management,* February 1993, pp. 41–53.

Grant, J. and I. Minker. "Integrity Constraints in Knowledge-Based Systems." In H. Adeli, ed. *Knowledge Engineering,* vol. 2. New York: McGraw-Hill, 1990, pp. 1–24.

Gupta, Uma. "Verification and Validation of Knowledge-Based Systems." *IEEE Computer Press,* 1991.

Hamilton, D.; K. Kelley; and C. Culbert. "State-of-the-Practice in Knowledge-Based System Verification and Validation." *Expert Systems With Applications* 3, no. 4 (1991), pp. 403–410.

Hoppe, T. and P. Meseguer. "On the Terminology of VVT." In M. Grisoni, ed. *Eurova-91: Proceedings of the European Workshop on the Verification and Validation of Knowledge-Based Systems,* 1991, pp. 103–108.

Jafar, Musa. "Verification and Validation With Validator." In A. T. Bahill, ed., *Verifying and Validating Personnel Computer-Based Expert Systems.* Englewood Cliffs, NJ: Prentice-Hall, 1991, pp. 71–83.

Jafar, Musa and Terry A. Bahill. "Interactive Verification of Knowledge-Based Systems." *IEEE Expert,* February 1993, pp. 25–32.

Kang, Yue and Terry Bahill. "A Tool for Detecting Expert System Errors." *AI Expert,* February 1990, pp. 46–51.

King, Malcolm and Gary J. Phythian. "Validating an Expert Support System for Tender Enquiry Evaluation: A Case Study." *Journal of the Operational Research Society,* March 1992, pp. 203–214.

Kobayashi, S. and K. Nakamura. "Knowledge Compilation and Refinement for Fault Diagnosis." *IEEE Expert,* October 1991, pp. 39–46.

Kobryn, Cris and Jason Trenouth. "Automating Database Validation." *AI Expert,* September 1992, pp. 36–41.

Lafon, P. "A Descriptive Model of Predicates for Verifying Production Systems." In M. Ayel and J-P Laurent, eds. *Verification and Validation of Knowledge Based Systems.* New York: John Wiley & Sons, 1991, pp. 149–162.

Latta, Gail F. and Keith Swigger. "Validation of the Repertory Grid for Use in Modeling Knowledge." *Journal of the American Society for Information Science,* March 1992, pp. 115–129.

Liu, N. K. and T. Dillon. "An Approach Toward the Verification of Expert Systems Using Numerical Petri Nets." *International Journal of Intelligent Systems* 6, pp. 255–276.

Lydiard, T. J. "Overview of Current Practice and Research Initiatives for the Verification and Validation of KBS." *The Knowledge Engineering Review,* June 1992, pp. 101–113.

Marcot, Bruce. "Testing Your Knowledge Base." *AI Expert,* July 1987, pp. 42–47.

Mengshoel, O. J. "KVAT: A Tool for Incremental Knowledge Validation in a Knowledge Engineering Workbench." In M. Grisoni, ed, *Eurova-91: Proceedings of the European Workshop On the Verification and Validation of Knowledge-Based Systems,* 1991, pp. 133–146.

Nazareth, D. L. and M. H. Kennedy. "Verification of Knowledge-Based Systems Using Directed Graphs." *Knowledge Acquisition* 3, (1991), pp. 255–271.

Nguyen, T. A.; W. A. Perkins; and T. J. Laffey. "Knowledge Base Verification." *AI Magazine,* Summer 1987, pp. 69–75.

O'Keefe, R. M.; O. Balci; and E. P. Smith. "Validating Expert System Performance." *IEEE Expert,* Winter 1987, pp. 81–89.

O'Leary, T. J.; M. Goul; K. E. Moffitt; and A. E. Radwan. "Validating Expert Systems." *IEEE Expert,* June 1990, pp. 51–58.

Plant, Robert T. "Expert System Development and Testing: A Knowledge Engineer's Perspective." *Journal of Systems & Software,* October 1992, pp. 141–146.

_____"On the Verification, Validation, and Testing of Knowledge-Based Systems." *The Journal of Knowledge Engineering,* Spring 1990, pp. 59–67.

Pomykalski, James J. "Knowledge-Based System Design Enhancement Through Reliability Measurement." Ph.D. Dissertation, University of Virginia, 1994.

Preece, Alun D. and Rajjan Shinghal. "Verifying and Testing Expert-System Conceptual Models." *Proceedings of 1992 IEEE Conference on Systems, Man, and Cybernetics.* Piscataway, NJ: IEEE Press, 1992, pp. 922–927.

Preece, Alun D.; Rajjan Shinghal; and Aida Batarekh, "Principles and Practice in Verifying Rule-Based Systems." *The Knowledge Engineering Review,* June 1992, pp. 115–141.

Renard, F.; L. Sterling; and C. Brosilow. "Knowledge Verification in Expert Systems Combining Declarative and Procedural Representations." *Computers & Chemical Engineering,* November 1993, pp. 1067–1090.

Ribar, Gary; Frank Arcoleo; and Denise Hollo; "Loan Probe: Testing a Big Expert System." *AI Expert,* May 1991, pp. 43–49.

Smith, Suzanne and Abraham Kandel. *Verification and Validation of Rule-Based Expert Systems.* Boca Raton, FL: CRC Press, 1993.

Stanley, Michael E. "Verifying the Design Process." *AI Expert,* September 1992, pp. 42–49.

Van Someren, M. "Structural and Formative Validation of Knowledge Bases." In M. Grisoni, ed., *Eurovav-91: Proceedings of the European Workshop on the Verification and Validation of Knowledge-Based Systems,* 1991, pp. 103–108.

Vinze, Ajay S. "Empirical Verification of Effectiveness for a Knowledge-Based System." *International Journal of Man-Machine Studies* 37 (1992), pp. 309–334.

Chapter ▪ 16

Implementing the Expert System

PLAN FOR IMPLEMENTATION

Implementation of the Travel Advisor involved two areas for consideration:

1. The organization's mandate to enforce the use of the system at the site
2. A company-wide training program on all aspects of travel and the functionality of Travel Advisor

Two areas were addressed during implementation: Conversion to the Travel Advisor and training for all employees on the system.

CONVERSION TO THE TRAVEL ADVISOR

In order to standardize the company's travel system, the company issued mandates that encouraged divisions to utilize the new expert system. But because a great deal of time and effort had gone into the development of each "homegrown" system, users initially resisted anything but their own system. The company, due to their need to move on with the new system, adopted an approach that allowed the users to use their existing systems for 30 days, while being trained on the Travel Advisor. At the end of the trial period, management met with the users and proceeded to do the final transfer to Travel Advisor.

TRAINING EMPLOYEES

A two-part, in-house training program on Travel Advisor was implemented. The first part focused on employees who had no direct relationship with the existing systems and were ready to generate travel plans for management via Travel Advisor. Specifically, one or two select individuals from each department underwent training and then returned to their home offices, to train local employees. The second part dealt with employees who had been using the existing system. They were allowed a 30-day grace period in which to experience the new system.

In the initial stages of implementing Travel Advisor, training was costly and time-consuming. In the long run, however, in-house training of the first set of employees was expected to cut training costs by more than seventy percent. In addition, management anticipated that employee-based training would build user confidence and increase the overall acceptance of the expert system.

During the training, management expressed their concerns as to the importance of improved efficiency and accuracy of travel plans. Fortunately, Travel Advisor proved itself in many ways. The user interface was so friendly that every time the user (trainee) made the wrong query, the system asked questions that helped the user enter the correct one. Also, using a 486-based PC, the speed of response was so quick that users recognized the difference when they compared it to their existing systems. Finally, the interactive nature of the system and its ability to explain the reasoning behind the travel plan decisions made conventional information systems almost obsolete.

The conversion and training program for 18 employees lasted two weeks. At the end of that period, the system was released to a senior member of management for final implementation and followup.

Source: Based on implementation of a Travel Advisor for a federal agency, 1992.

AT A GLANCE

One of the most exciting aspects of expert system development is the implementation of the system within the user organization. During this step, the developer proves his or her worth in the way the system is installed and accepted as a way of making decisions. This step, however, is not without risk. A developer must consider a number of implementation issues. For example, how well has the user been involved in the development life cycle? What technical or procedural knowledge does the user have? What is the organizational climate? These and many other factors can make or break the implementation phase.

An important aspect of implementation is user training. The questions often pondered are "How should the user be trained?" "Where should training be conducted and for how long?" "Who should do the training?" Obviously, how user-friendly and how well documented the system is has much to do with training ease and success. User motivation, proper funding, and the role of the champion are additional success factors.

Maintenance and enhancement are critical implementation factors to consider. Without effective maintenance, continuity and reliability of the system cannot be assured.

What You Will Learn

By the end of this chapter, you should know the following:

1. The most critical issues related to implementation.
2. The importance of organizational factors in implementation and user acceptance of the new system.
3. The role of training in implementation.
4. The notion of resistance to change and how to minimize its effects among users.
5. The role of maintenance and enhancement in system update.

■ INTRODUCTION

The goal of every expert system design is successful implementation. Even the best system will fail if implementation concerns are not addressed. At issue is how well the developer coordinates the implementation with the end-user. Depending on how knowledge representation was carried out, the end-user might have been a regular participant all along. In such a case, implementation stands a good chance of user acceptance and successful deployment.

Implementation is affected by organizational, technical, procedural, behavioral, economic, and political factors, especially in an environment in which the organization is large and the existing technology is too established to allow change to occur easily. Expert system implementation is especially complex. Unlike conventional information systems that produce algorithmic solutions, expert systems process rules based on heuristics. Yet, some implementation factors and issues are common to both. This chapter examines implementation issues as they relate to managing expert system projects as well as user training and documentation.

The two aspects to implementation include the transfer of the system as a technology from the developer to the organization's operating unit and the transfer of the system's skills from the developer to the operating person in the organization via training. This step may also include training an organization's operating unit to carry out system maintenance and upgrade. The issues, prerequisites, and techniques for both of these aspects will also be discussed in this chapter.

■ ISSUES RELATED TO IMPLEMENTATION

Once the system is designed and fully tested, the final step is the physical transfer or *deployment* of the technology to the organization's operating unit. Whether the developer will be the one to deploy the system, certain important implementation issues need to be addressed at the beginning of each expert system project. These issues relate to the selection of the problem domain, ease of understanding the expert system, and organizational factors.

Selection of Problem Domain

The success of expert system implementation has a great deal to do with the way the problem domain was selected. For example, if the domain was selected with end-user involvement and management support, smooth implementation is likely. System users can be assured of the success of the system if:

1. The user has prior experience with computer applications which tends to reduce the inherent fear that automated systems replace people.
2. The user has been actively involved in defining the problem domain and identifying the specific functions of the expert system.
3. The user is involved in the final evaluation of the expert system to assure its accuracy, completeness, and reliability.
4. The payoff from the development of the expert system is large and measurable and leaves little room for arguments that the system is draining the budget or is unnecessary.
5. The expert system can be implemented in the working environment without much interruption of ongoing activities.
6. The champion has done a great job selling the user's staff on the potential contributions of the expert system.

Another way of looking at these issues is to consider the importance of the "front end" of system development—problem domain conceptualization and domain selection. By now, the importance of involving the user in the early phases of building the system should be evident. The use of rapid prototyping can also offer a way of selling the system and its potential benefits when it is deployed. Front-end commitment requires dedicated users, managers, domain experts, and a champion to firm up the planning and provide the support necessary to carry out knowledge representation. Once commitment is achieved, implementation is generally easier to accomplish. See Box 16–1.

Ease of Understanding the Expert System

The acid test of knowledge representation occurs when the system is deployed and the user realizes how easy the expert system is to understand. Documen-

Box 16-1   Installation and Training of Loan Advisor

Participation in the development and maintenance of the Loan Advisor included two senior loan officers who had been involved in the knowledge acquisition phase. This was quite a break for implementation, because they made it difficult for junior officers to say "no" to using the system. The way it turned out, junior officers found the system a great training tool that reinforced what they do on the job. The actual installation and basic training took less than one day.

Source: Based on the installation and training of a Loan Advisor for a medium-size commercial bank, July 1993.

tation also plays a key role at this point. When changes must be made, a troubleshooting guide, a step-by-step procedure, or a flowchart in the form of an easy-to-follow technical or operations manual can guide the user into unlocking the system and correcting "glitches."

Generally speaking, reliable documentation means easier implementation. The role of documentation is especially important during user training. Good documentation with heavy illustrations reduces the time required for training. Of course, a human trainer who provides face-to-face, interactive, on-site training is always a helpful aspect of this process.

Successful expert system implementation depends on several user-related factors:

1. *Level of motivation of the user.* Good documentation cannot compensate for low motivation or poor attitude toward the system. Promoting motivation and commitment takes time and must be planned in advance.

2. *Computer literacy and technical background of the user.* A computer-literate user can be easier to work with than someone who has no background at all. First-time users often require education and training before they are able to support development and use of expert systems.

3. *Communication skills of the trainer.* Selling people on change is sometimes considered more an art than a science. Communication skills can make the difference between a user's acceptance or rejection of the installation.

4. *Time availability and funding for training.* A training program run on a shoestring is usually a loser. Also, squeezing training time to the bare minimum often results in trainee impatience, resistance to learning, or nonuse of the system. Training should be part of the implementation phase offered around the schedule of the user.

5. *Place of training.* The location of training can make a difference. On-site versus off-site training continues to be an issue with plusses and minuses for each alternative. Off-site training is generally dedicated uninterrupted learning. Its positive benefits include privacy and focus on the projects. The feasibility of off-site training depends on distance, location, and funding. In contrast, on-site training requires no out-of-town transportation or room and board expenses. Yet, it can be interrupted by telephone calls, secretaries, and uninvited "gawkers."

6. *Ease and duration of training.* This aspect depends on the caliber of the trainer and the attitude and motivation of the trainees. "Chemistry" often affects how well all parties work with each other. Also, the training period should be reasonable and able to meet measurable goals. A long, drawn-out three-week training period does not promote the same excitement and motivation as a one-week session.

7. *Ease of access and explanatory facilities of the expert system.* Expert systems should be easy to access and work with. A shell that provides adequate explanations is bound to satisfy most users. The explanatory facility of the shell promotes ease of use and provides convincing evidence of the integrity of the solutions provided by the system.

8. *Ease of maintenance and system update.* At this stage, good documentation and easy-to-follow procedures in a module-oriented expert system can make the difference between easy maintenance and a "nightmare." In this case, maintenance implies update, although update is more often considered **enhancement.**

9. *Payoff to the organization.* A system's benefit to the organization is usually measured in terms of cost reduction, improvement in sales or overall performance, and so on. Measurable payoff early in the development life cycle promotes successful implementation.

10. *Role of the champion.* Solid top management support and a champion pushing for system adoption can make a difference between a successful and a lukewarm installation.

These success factors of expert system implementation are interrelated. Organizational and technical factors also come into play. See Figure 16–1.

The Issue of Maintenance

An important aspect of expert system development that gets little attention is **maintenance.** If this text were practitioner-oriented in system building, maintenance would probably deserve a separate chapter. The brevity of this section is not intended to underestimate its importance or role.

The term *maintenance* means making the necessary corrections that enable the expert system to continue to meet the specifications of the problem domain. In rule-based systems, it means adding, removing, rewriting certain rules so that the results or reasoning are more consistent with the expert's solutions. Although this type of change is carried out during the initial testing phase, one can expect corrections resulting from the user's afterthoughts or real-time experience with the system.

System maintenance can be improved in a number of ways. For example, if the knowledge base is organized into several well-defined modules, one can easily go to a specific module and make the necessary changes. Also rules that are written in a uniform manner can also be helpful. In this regard, a single developer in charge of knowledge representation can promote consistency and uniformity in programming the knowledge base. Finally, intermodule relationships supported by documentation should speed up changes in rules involving two or more related modules. See Box 16–2.

For a knowledge-based system to survive implementation, it must facilitate easy and effective maintenance in a number of ways:

1. The system must have a feature to allow new rules to be added or deleted as needed, which brings up the importance of the modular approach to expert systems.

Figure 16–1   *Success Factors in Expert System Implementation*

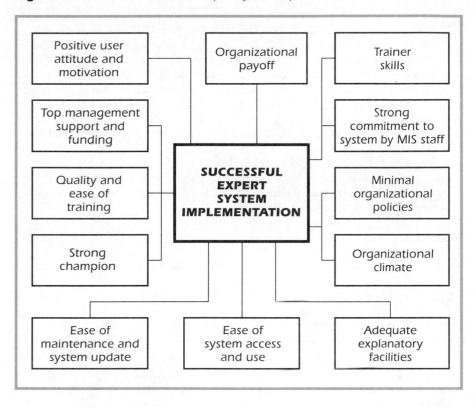

2. The system must be capable of allowing inconsistent, conflicting, or redundant rules to be easily identified. Removing redundancies contributes to system performance.

3. The system's explanatory facilities must satisfy the user's requirements as closely as possible. User acceptance of the solution is easier with the availability of clear explanations.

4. The availability of a qualified person or a team can ensure that maintenance is carried out effectively and on schedule. With large expert systems, maintenance could be a full-time job. See Box 16–3.

To assure successful maintenance, responsibility for it needs to be placed in the hands of a qualified person within the user organization. Otherwise, the maintenance function should be contracted out to a free-lance specialist. Part of the maintenance function establishes a change order procedure with proper documentation that includes the authorized requester, the person who made the change, and the outcome of the change. Validation provides the final stepping stone in implementation.

Organizational Factors

Of all the implementation issues related to the organization, a prime consideration is a firm commitment to the project by top management, the domain expert, and the user. This factor is crucial for deployment. Management can support system implementation by promoting the development effort by

---

Box 16-2 Maintenance Scenario of the Loan Advisor

Two weeks after deployment of the Loan Advisor, I received a call from the vice president of the auto loan department requesting a basic change in one of the variables in the expert system. The change was needed because the bank's board of directors approved a more relaxed set of requirements for auto buyers to boost the auto loan portfolio. For example, instead of requiring that the loan applicant's assets to be greater than $150,000 with an annual salary greater than $50,000 and that the applicant be married to qualify for a $20,000 three-year loan, the bank removed marital status and lowered the asset value requirement to $100,000 or more.

It seemed simple at the beginning. However, 27 rule changes, three rule additions, and four rule deletions later, the system was finally ready for a verification test. The entire process took 18 hours during a two-week period before the Loan Advisor could be recertified.

_____

Source: Maintenance/Update Scenario: Loan Advisor, using VP-Expert (with SQL), August, 1993.

Box 16-3 Role of Maintenance for Auto Loan Advisor

Six weeks after the Auto Loan Advisor was in place, the senior vice president of the loan department asked to have a change made in the expert system. One of the rules stated, "IF Marital_status = married and Years_married > 3 and Salary > 50000, and Av_checking balance > 5000 THEN approve loan < 25000 CNF = .85. To encourage newlyweds with starting salary of 50000 or more, the user wanted the condition "Years married" removed. The user assumed the change would be a simple one.

Actually, 17 other rules in three modules incorporated the parameter "Years married," resulting in separate decisions or conclusions. The maintenance cycle for making the necessary change to testing the change took eleven hours of actual work before recertification. The senior vice president had difficulty understanding how a seemingly basic change could take so long or cost $800.

_____

Source: Based on experience with Auto Loan Advisor for a small bank, 1993.

---

providing adequate funding, ensuring the availability of hardware and personnel, and allowing the champion to function within the development process.

The second organizational factor is user participation in the building process. Participation tends to increase commitment and foster a sense of ownership of the expert system. It can also enhance system quality, because system requirements have been reviewed and approved well in advance.

The notion of commitment is crucial in expert system implementation. A user who agrees to participate in building the expert system also hopes to make a contribution to the organization. The term _commitment_ is not the same as contribution, however. Anyone can make a contribution through participation in a project without having to make a commitment to its use. Commitment to a project means taking responsibility for its outcome, which, of course, definitely contributes to the success of system implementation. The anecdote in Box 16–4 illustrates the distinction between contribution and commitment.

Other organizational factors include organizational politics and organizational climate. *Politics* is jockeying for leverage to influence one's domain and control procedures, technology, or the direction of an area of operation. The prevalence of politics, especially in a negative sense, is often ignored or deemphasized. The knowledge engineer or the developer must remain neutral within the political arena of an organization.

The organization's climate dictates whether an expert system's time has come. The key questions the knowledge engineer should ask include "Is today, this week, or this month the right time to implement the product?" "Is the organization ready for this particular solution?" The timing and readiness factors must be assessed in advance. For example, in banking, most computer-based systems are installed during weekends so as not to interfere with the weekday business activities.

User readiness can also influence the success of implementation. Users who drag their feet and continue to hang onto the existing system often let the new system go unused or even unnoticed. For example, users who know that work will accumulate during their absence to undergo training make poor trainees. This means implementation must be planned in advance.

Role of the Champion

With all said and done, the underlying factor for successful implementation of an expert system is the role of the champion. A champion is someone in an organization who, because of position, power, influence, or control, secures the organizational support of the system from inception to deployment. Without a champion, an expert system is vulnerable at each step of the development process. Because the effects of politics, budgetary problems, deficient support, or conflict of interest can stand in the way of implementation, the champion must find ways to guide the system around these obstacles and barriers.

To illustrate, an advisory system designed to assist the VISA/Mastercard department of a commercial bank in its approval of qualified applicants met stiff resistance from the department's manager, whose judgment would be verified by the expert system. The problem caught the attention of the bank's

---

Box 16–4   The Chicken and the Pig Venture

A chicken and a pig grew up together on a farm and came to know each other very well. One day, the two met and discussed a joint venture.

The quick-thinking chicken told the pig, "I have a great idea for a breakfast restaurant near a local school. Between the two of us, we have all the ingredients we need—eggs, ham, and sausage. Just think how excited the customers will be to get the freshest ham and eggs in the area."

The slower-thinking pig pondered this ingenious proposal and, after a long pause, said, "My dear friend, your proposal sounds great, although lopsided. All you're offering to do is make a *contribution* to the venture. You're asking me to make a *commitment*."

operations vice president who had a good rapport with the officers of the bank as well as the bank's chairman of the board. The vice president had a long talk with the manager and assured her that the new expert system should "speed things up," rather than replace her final judgment. The vice president concluded the meeting by saying, "Look, let's give this project a try and see how it turns out."

In the interim, the vice president saw to it that the project stayed on track—from continued funding to making the manager (expert) available for the seven sessions it took to build the knowledge base.

When the time came for implementation, the developer met with the manager and asked to proceed with training her staff on the proper use of the system. The manager replied, "That's not necessary. Since I've gone through the process and am familiar with the way it works, just load the package on my PC and I'll take it from there."

Concerned about possible delays or improper training, the developer took up the matter with the bank's vice president who called a meeting with the senior staff of the VISA/Mastercard department. At the meeting, the vice president explained to them the importance of the expert system in improving the reliability of issuing credit cards to prospective applicants, and then appointed a staff member to undergo the initial training. She, in turn, would train a volunteer as backup.

Training went well. After the system was successfully installed on the local area network, the vice president called for an area meeting to announce the official operation of the Applicant Advisor and recognize the contributions of the department manager in the development effort. A similar announcement was also placed in the bank's employee newsletter later that month.

In situations such as this, when resistance could kill a worthwhile project, a champion makes the difference. The system cost the bank $38,300. Based on the bank's past record, it paid for itself in four months by eliminating high-risk applicants.

▓ TECHNOLOGY TRANSFER

Two approaches can be used to transfer expert systems technology in implementation. In the first approach, the expert system is actually transferred from the developer directly to the working unit (end-user) in the organization. The other approach is the transfer of expert system technology skills. The first approach simply means installing the system on the resident hardware. It includes dropping off the user's manual, a technical manual containing line-by-line printout of the rules, and copies of the knowledge base for backup. This step may or may not include user training. Actually, training the user on the expert system is relatively easier than training on a conventional information system because of the explanatory and other facilities embedded in the expert system.

In the second approach, which transfers expert system technology skills, the developer transfers to a group within the organization the knowledge and necessary know-how to maintain and upgrade the system in the future. Such a transfer may include special technical training in the diagnosis and test procedures necessary to make changes in the system. Once completed, the developer is out of the picture, except perhaps in a consultative role. See Box 16–5.

Box 16–5   Responsibility for Expert System Maintenance

After the first maintenance call on the Loan Advisor, the bank agreed to have Cam, the resident programmer, do future changes in the system. But, because she was barely beyond RPG programming, she agreed to take a course in expert systems at a local university and spent time reviewing the Loan Advisor's knowledge base. She felt confident in her abilities to meet the challenge of maintenance. One benefit that came from the transfer of technology skills was Cam's training ability. She trained two new officers on the Loan Advisor and is thinking of doing a project on her own in the customer service department to assist in answering customers' banking questions.

Source: Based on Loan Advisor, August 1993.

Transfer of expert systems can be approached in one of two ways: (1) an abrupt, one-time transfer that results in a permanent installation on a specific day or (2) a gradual transfer over a given time period. In the latter case, most often through rapid prototyping, a receiving group becomes part of the developer's team. Once one phase of the system is verified and ready to use, responsibility is transferred to the receiving group, which then examines the makeup of the partial system. The transfer involves the sharing of training, methodologies, experiences, and techniques. Eventually, the rest of the system is transferred, allowing the receiving group to take full responsibility for the system's operation and maintenance.

Implementation can also be approached as a stand-alone expert system installation on a PC or as a fully integrated application that interfaces with other applications or databases. Expert systems should be designed on platforms that are compatible with other expert systems in the organization. The compatibility feature makes explanation or justification of the new system easier. It also makes user training easier, since most users presumably look at the new system as "a system just like the others."

Integration Alternatives

An expert system can be integrated into the organization's existing operations through the following methods:

- **Technical integration** occurs through the company's local area network environment, the resident mainframe, and existing information systems. This job is not exactly straightforward. Management must decide on a system's level of priority for access in the network. For example, in one university's MIS program, a mainframe-based expert system shell was given a low priority access, because the course that used the shell was taught only during spring semester. During lab sessions, students frequently experienced considerable delays (more than 40 seconds) in response time. They complained that work assignments were always late coming off the printer.

- **Knowledge-sharing integration** is required for example, in a firm that needs to make an expert system available to each of its seventeen branches in an equitable way. This level of availability often requires upgrading the local area network, the mainframe, and the lines to ensure equitable service. For example, in the case of the Loan Advisor (see Box 16-2), after the bank installed a LAN, it made plans to have Loan Advisor available to the four branches that accepted loan applications.

- **Decision-making flow integration** suggests that the way the expert system thinks through a problem situation should match the user's style of thinking. Providing such a match can be crucial to user acceptance and satisfaction.

- **Workflow re-engineering** considerations come into play when implementation of a new system triggers changes in the work place or within jobs in the user's domain (merging jobs, deleting positions, etc.). This type of situation can occur because the actual building of the product leads the domain expert and the user, during their interactive sessions, to develop new insight into the problem domain and a more creative way of dealing with it. One can expect a certain amount of backlash as a result of job re-engineering.

  The attractiveness of change depends greatly on management's perception of its potential contribution to the productivity of the area in which the new system will reside. The concept of re-engineering is evolutionary and usually takes weeks or even months to firm up. In other words, for an expert system to survive, it must be amenable to change. It must also provide built-in flexibility to accommodate the kind of change expected by the user.

User Training and Development

A major component of system implementation is training the user on the new system. The level and duration of training depend on the user's knowledge level and the system's attributes. Users range from novices to experts. They are classified as tutor, pupil, or customer.

The *tutor*-user acquires a working knowledge of an existing knowledge base in order to keep the system current. This end-user is responsible for system maintenance. The knowledge engineer normally trains the tutor-user on procedures for incorporating new knowledge into the knowledge base.

The responsibilities and interest of pupil-users and customer-users fall within the actual use of the expert system. The knowledge engineer's role is to familiarize the two end-users with the ways in which the system will be best used. The *pupil*-user is an unskilled worker trying to gain some understanding of the captured knowledge. The purpose of training pupil-users is to gain their acceptance of the expert system. The *customer*-user is one with interest in knowing how to use the system on a regular basis.

Neither the pupil-user nor customer-user need in-depth training during the early stages of system development. Training in the early phases uses development funds inefficiently. During the time between prototyping and a working system, the pupil-users and customer-users may forget most details. See Box 16–6.

User training is also influenced by the requirements of the expert system. System requirements range from simple and user-friendly to advanced and less user-friendly. A user-friendly expert system is almost self-instructional with menu-driven features and easy-to-use manuals. The duration of training is

Box 16–6   Training Tailored to User Requirements

HOFERS, an expert system project developed through a university, was created to aid students seeking off-campus housing in a university town. In the identification phase, I thoroughly explained the details of a mainframe development tool (IBM ESE) to a pupil-user from the Housing Office. During the conceptualization phase, I determined that the mainframe environment was not appropriate for the application. A microcomputer development tool (VP-Expert) was tested and chosen for the development and test phases of several prototypes. In the implementation phase, the pupil-user was introduced to a mature prototype with the new tool. The pupil-user was initially confused even though she was aware of the development tool change. I had to take additional training measures to overcome her confusion about the user interface and how to use it.

Source: Based on an expert system developed for the student housing office of a university, 1992.

usually measured in hours to days. Advanced systems require knowledge of queries in high-level programming or AI languages and take days to weeks to learn, even for the experienced user. The level of user training depends on

1. The user's knowledge of expert systems
2. The complexity of the expert system and how well it accommodates the average user
3. The trainer's experience and communication skills
4. The environment where training is carried out

Training, then, must be geared to the specific user based on capabilities, experience, and system complexity. In situations in which both the user and the system are new, training procedures are introduced in stages. For example, training first-time users on a PC-driven expert system begins with showing them how to turn on the PC, insert and remove a diskette, load the expert system off the hard disk, and save their work. Once completed, the next step is to show the user how to enter a query, load files, display solutions, update rules, and so on.

The most effective training is supported by a well-written user manual, easy-to-use explanatory facility, and job aids. User manuals can be invaluable training documents, especially if the user is geographically isolated. A well-written user manual is highly illustrated and contains an index for reference. Graphics, photographs, and templates provide quick reference and are invaluable teaching aids. Comparable information should also be available in the software via a help key on the keyboard.

Explanatory facility allows the user to display the system's reasoning behind its answers. In an IBM ESE shell, for example, when the user wants to know how the system reached a solution, all the user has to do is depress the F10 key (How did you arrive at the answer?), and the rules that produced the solution are promptly displayed. See Figure 16–2.

Job aids are essentially screen designs that rely on color to highlight a question or an answer, partitions on the screen to separate one answer from another, and so on. These features of an expert system should be part of a package available during implementation.

Figure 16–2   An Example of an Explanatory Facility

During a user interaction session with an expert system called Vacation, the following dialog takes place:

SYSTEM: What coast do you wish to spend your vacation? Choose one.
   _X_ East
   ___ West
USER: (User enters X on the line for EAST.)
SYSTEM: What sports do you wish to engage in? Choose one.
   _X_ BEACH
   ___ SKI
USER: (User enters X on the line for BEACH.)
SYSTEM: How much money do you want to spend on this trip? Enter number.
USER: 2500
                   (User enters $2,500.)
SYSTEM: (The system displays its decision.) Place is Florida
USER: (User depresses the "how"—how did you arrive at this decision?—key.)
SYSTEM: I assigned value to *PLACE* of GLOBAL by
   1. Rule *EAST BEACH* which states that:
      If COAST is 'east' and ACTIVITY is 'beach' and
      AVAILABLE_FUND > 1500 then *PLACE is FLORIDA*
   As a result of this rule
   PLACE assigned = *'Florida'* (1)

Preparing for Expert System Training

Expert systems impact organizations. They may affect personnel responsibilities as well as alter the structure of an organization. The very concepts underlying expert systems often change the way employees think about their tasks. When a system is introduced, the initial goal is to educate the user about expert systems. A strategic education plan prepares an organization to adopt expert systems. Such a plan takes place before development and is not a substitute for training. Training teaches the specific skills needed to operate a system. The combination of a strategic education plan and well-planned training means quicker organizational acceptance during implementation. A more detailed discussion on organizational impact of expert systems can be found in Chapter 18.

Several large corporations have taken steps toward strategic education. Digital Equipment Corporation (DEC), for example, created an in-house expert system development program for managers and engineers. Called "Digital's Expert System Training and Apprentice Program," the program provides training on technical, business, and behavioral issues. Subjects range from job requirements to organizational issues.

3M Corporation follows six steps for successful implementation of its expert systems:

1. Raise organizational awareness with strategic education.
2. Define how expert systems agree with organizational mission.
3. Demonstrate how expert systems can help meet organizational goals.

4. Allocate resources on a feasible project.

5. Advocate positive effects of expert systems, but do not create unrealistic expectations.

6. Perform a cost-benefit analysis of expert system technology.

To raise awareness, the company distributed Post-It note pads reading "3M Artificial Intelligence: Harvesting Tomorrow's Technology" to 800 employees.

Combating Resistance to Change

Regardless of what is being converted or how well deployment is carried out, *implementation means change and people in general resist change.* Implementation of an expert system is the initiation of a new order of things. People become anxious when they do not know what the new system will do and how it will affect their current jobs and their future career plans. The result of this anxiety is stress and further resistance to change. The resistors include the following:

EXPERTS: Some domain experts have anxiety about the potential impact of sharing knowledge of their jobs in the organization. Experts on the way to retirement worry less, but may still lack motivation unless properly compensated for their efforts.

NONEXPERTS: Participants in general resent lack of recognition (sometimes compensation), especially when they have been involved in building the expert system from the beginning.

TROUBLEMAKERS: Those left out of the system building cycle or chronic complainers tend to obstruct the installation, cause delays, and may even prompt cancellation of the system.

NARROW-MINDED "SUPERSTARS": Technical people in the organization's MIS department sometimes resist any change that they did not initiate or approve in advance. Others veto a project not in their area of interest. Without management support, such resistance can spell the doom for a new system.

Resistance is displayed in three personal reactions:

1. **Projection:** hostility toward peers

2. **Avoidance:** withdrawal from the scene, such as calling in sick

3. **Aggression:** killing the system, because of uncertainty of its operation or use

A psychological element that explains resistance to change is the value that users place on knowledge and decision making. In most organizations, knowledge means power. While knowledge engineers build systems that promote knowledge sharing through knowledge bases, domain experts who stand to lose monopoly on knowledge may resist a new system installation. Most resistance relates to the perceived impact of the new system on one's job or status in the organization. Of course, a few people resist change of any kind.

Resistance also has much to do with the individual personality, the organizational structure, and the group relations within the area where the expert system will be installed. User education, training, and participation in the building process can help reduce resistance to change.

A second resistance category comes from the system itself rather than people. Some expert systems offer poor user interface and require extensive training to master. Recent literature supports the development of user-friendly knowledge-based systems as a way of overcoming resistance to expert system implementation. See Figure 16–3. Yet, a user-friendly technology is not enough. What is needed is a user that is friendly to the expert system. Overconcentration on technology and overlooking behavioral issues have resulted in many system failures.

Because a major user concern in system implementation is how to work the system, users frequently ask such questions as What functions are available? How do I access each function? How do I know if the system has answered my questions correctly? Another user concern is how the expert system reaches conclusions or lines up with the real-world problem. The knowledge engineer must demonstrate the system and provide detailed training.

Various methods can be used to promote expert system implementation:

1. User-attitude survey
2. Communication training
3. Training sessions
4. Role negotiation

In a *user-attitude survey,* opinions are collected from users to learn how well they like the system and how closely it meets their requirements. Most users, however, have difficulty communicating such requirements, primarily because of a lack of good communication skills. *Communication training* can prove invaluable for enhancing user–knowledge engineer relationships and successful system development.

For small to medium-sized expert systems, *training sessions* are normally run by a knowledge engineer. For larger systems, they are conducted by a system specialist who is also a skilled communicator. In either case, the trainer should address the user's training needs and gear the pace of training accordingly. Some users easily learn the system in one day or less; others take much longer.

Resistance to change becomes obvious when users perceive a change in their job. An interesting technique, called *role negotiation,* attempts to clarify what the user expects the altered job to offer. Once understood, users have been known to accept their role in the change more readily.

In summary, for a new expert system to obtain user support, knowledge engineers and users must improve communication channels and jointly discuss the new system's features and how the change can improve job performance. Users should participate in all phases of implementation. Sensitivity to user expectations is a step toward "implementation without tears."

Postimplementation Review

After the system has been deployed and the operation is "up and running," the effect of the new system on the organization should be carefully evaluated. System impact must be assessed in terms of its effects on the people, procedures, and performance of the business. More specifically, the main areas of concern are quality of decision making, attitude of end-users, and costs of knowledge processing. For example, a postimplementation study may show that a new bank loan advisor has reduced the number of loans that went sour by 40 percent. It may also show that personnel time has also improved by 20 percent.

Figure 16–3   *Overcoming Resistance through User-Friendly Interface*

The Diabetic Foot Advisor was virtually complete. The rules had been verified when the domain expert noticed that a user (diabetic patient or young orthopedic) might have difficulty understanding what the system's series of questioning might be. The expert then suggested a simple menu as follows:

```
           WELCOME TO THE DIABETIC FOOT ADVISOR

Choose one of the following application areas:

1.  Vascular disease      2.  Peripheral neuropathy
2.  Charcot neuropathy    4.  Ulcers and infections

Choose one option_____
```

In displaying the four-item menu, the system first asks the user to select the nature of the problem and then follow through the series of questions and respective solutions. This simple menu took some effort to incorporate, because it was not planned in advance.

By this time, the domain expert was adept at what was needed to promote user-friendliness. He suggested two things: (1) add color to the screen to highlight questions and their answers and (2) delete on-line reasoning on the bottom half of the VP-Expert screen inner box as shown below to allow more than one question to be displayed on the screen.

```
Do you have vascular disease?
Yes <              No
You should see your doctor immediately
```

```
Vascular_disease = Danger CNF 100
Testing Rule 11
RULE 11 IF
Charcot_neuropathy = high AND
Peripheral_neuropathy = negative AND
Ulcer = No
THEN
Vascular_disease = Danger CNF 100
```

```
1Help 2GO 3 Whatif............... 8 Quit
1Help 2How 3Why 4Slow 5Fast 6Quit
```

The final design was shown to a number of prospective users who made minor suggestions. Admittedly, the result was quite good.

Source: E. M. Awad, "Diabetic Foot Advisor," August 1994.

A number of key questions are asked in the postimplementation stage:

1. How have knowledge-based systems changed the accuracy and timeliness of decision making?

2. Has the new system caused organizational changes? How constructive have the changes been?

3. How has the new system affected the attitude of the end-users? In what way?

4. How has the new system changed the cost of operating the business?

5. How has the new system affected the organization's decision-making process?

6. In what way has the new system affected relationships between end-users in the organization?

7. Do the solutions derived from the new system justify the cost of investment?

The objective is to evaluate the expert system against standards and determine how well it meets user requirements. This process is actually related to validation. The user initiates the review, which prompts a procedure for maintenance or enhancement. *Enhancement* means upgrading the system to meet a new set of requirements, while *maintenance* means making corrections to meet the initial system requirements.

Security Considerations

Safeguarding the expert system against unauthorized access is a necessary system implementation issue. Similar to a conventional information system, at a minimum, the new expert system should provide password or protocol protection so that only users with the correct code can log onto the system. One aspect of user training is to ensure that passwords and security procedures are consistently observed. Beyond this elementary precaution, restricted access regarding the update of the knowledge base itself needs to be established.

■ IMPLEMENTING THE EXPERT DATABASE

Since the late 1980s, special efforts have been made to integrate the capabilities of expert systems and databases for tasks ranging from robotics to production management. Integrating the two technologies in the form of an expert database (EDS) has several benefits. Considering how often personnel changes and the importance of relating database information to the rules and policies of the firm, expert systems provide a structure in which users who access a database must follow established rules throughout upper, middle, and lower management more consistently and reliably. In this environment, policies are incorporated into an expert system's knowledge base as rules embedded into applications that use the database. See Figure 16–4.

Another benefit of integrating expert systems and databases comes in the area of user interface. Existing databases use screens that call for a fill-in-the-blank approach to data entry and retrieval. With an embedded expert system, an intelligent front-end with a visual focus could capture areas of concern and be driven more by events than by preestablished procedures.

Figure 16–4   The Hierarchy of Policies and Policy Enforcement

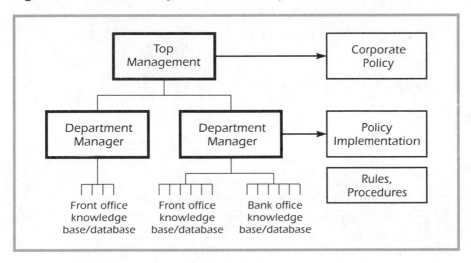

Expert systems could also contribute to "intelligent" query management. Database software can efficiently handle area storage and retrieval for multiple users in a networked environment, but it cannot tell which user will make the next request. All a database offers is historical data, not data based on rules or heuristics designed to emulate human decision making. An intelligent database system should be able to generate queries based on logical commands before continuing its processing.

Intelligent Database Systems

An intelligent database system (IDBS) is a tool for developing applications requiring a database management system (DBMS) and knowledge-directed intelligent processing of shared information. As shown in Figure 16–5, four system components stand between the user and information: CASE (computer-aided software engineering) for intelligent software engineering, expert systems for knowledge-directed intelligent processing, a DBMS for shared information management, and specialized intelligent processors for specific data operations such as image enhancement or finite element analysis. Any component may allow direct access to data or commands to lower-level components. The user will access the IDBS via the expert system and CASE interface.

Intelligent Database Interface

The intelligent database interface represents the human expert's knowledge of the database, its capabilities, use, and operation for the benefit of the user. The two facets of an interface include the front-end (what the user sees at a workstation) and back-end, which controls the database. The front-end is concerned mostly with attractive presentation, context-sensitive help, and intuitive operation. This aspect of the user interface can be implemented by command line, menu, object-oriented window, natural language interpreter, or any other way the programmer sees fit. Using expert systems as a front-end is popular when users have difficulty formulating queries. The expert system asks the user to state the request, applies the rules to evaluate the feedback, and then

Figure 16–5 Intelligent Database Systems Architecture

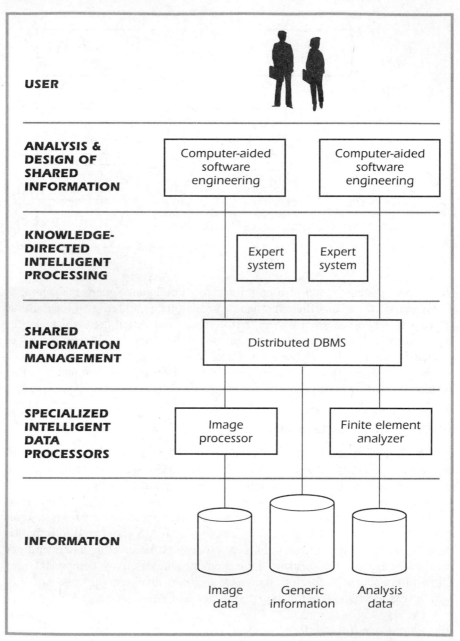

generates the database query that will retrieve the necessary record or information. The query is passed to the database program, which, in turn, produces the information the user needs.

The back-end employs a data manipulation language (DML) such as Structured Query Language (SQL) to access the database. This interface, rather than the user interface, does most of the thinking for the user. To act as a back-end tool, the expert system takes raw data drawn from a database query as input, evaluates them through rules, and then makes a specific recommendation to the user. For example, in an installment loan application, the expert system goes to the bank's database to inquire about the applicant's checking account balance, past loans, payment history, and so on. This capability spares the applicant or the loan officer the tedious task of retrieving the information afresh. The system might also verify some data (current address, income) to determine whether the applicant qualifies for a loan.

A common way in which expert systems and databases work together is through intelligent querying. The expert system acts as a front-end tool to provide more efficient access to a database. In most cases, the expert system is used to construct database queries. The system proceeds by asking questions and using rules to reach a final recommendation. Once it reaches a recommendation, it goes back to the database to search for an even more specific (and reliable) recommendation. This process is useful for situations in which the set of actual recommendations changes, while the logic represented by the rules remains the same.

Because implementing an intelligent database system is not an easy task, it requires a team of experts familiar with each technology and how they relate to other technologies as an integrated whole. Its benefits are limitless, however. For example, United Airlines gate assignment display systems (GADS) assists ground managers at key airports to schedule United Airlines' transport fleet. It helps networks of people on the ground manage the allocation of transport services. The adoption of networked systems in the 1990s has made focused applications possible.

The IDBS architecture becomes more complex in a distributed networked environment involving multiple users. Security and integrity considerations are of primary importance. Yet, when fully tested and implemented, the intelligent database system can promote the use of databases in a multitude of ways. Expert systems technology will also find broader commercial acceptance when it succeeds in solving problems such as efficient database management. Expert systems and intelligent front-end products are the trend and will be the direction of database management in industry.

IMPLICATIONS FOR MANAGEMENT

One of the critical issues raised during implementation is maintenance. Maintenance of expert systems continues to be a nebulous area. Some of the questions to be addressed by management include:

1. Who will be in charge of maintenance?
2. What skills should the maintenance person have? What's the best way to train him or her?
3. What incentives should be provided to ensure quality maintenance?
4. What type of support and funding is needed?
5. What relationship should be established between the maintenance of an expert system and the MIS staff of the organization?

The *enhancement* function is closely related to maintenance. Since experts constantly upgrade their knowledge, it makes sense to do the same with the expert system to keep it current. One question is "How quickly does the problem change?" The answer then determines how one would justify the enhancement, given the nature of the solutions.

Another managerial issue to consider is how one would know whether the implementation will be a success. In addition to technical considerations, one must be aware of the people factor. People rallying behind technology can increase the success of implementation. Additionally, an expert system cannot succeed if the issue of cost of technology and how it is going to be absorbed has not been resolved. Any of these issues can inhibit successful implementation.

Other managerial issues affect the direction and outcome of expert system projects. For example, the depth of the knowledge required to solve the problem is often an unknown commodity due to the nature of the expertise and the limitations of the knowledge engineer. Forcing clarification too early in the building phase can result in a less-than-satisfactory system. Therefore, managing expectations and scoping the system are crucial early tasks.

Finally, the role of the expert in system implementation is also important. Management should properly compensate the domain expert for efforts in developing an expert system. A manager may also play a proactive role in the implementation phase by simply sharing interest or excitement in the expert system. A lack of this type of enthusiasm and overt support puts a damper on the whole project.

▦ SUMMARY

1. The ultimate goal of every expert system is successful implementation and deployment. Implementation is affected by organizational, technological, procedural, behavioral, economic, and political factors. The two aspects of implementation are (1) transfer of the system from the developer to the operating unit and (2) transfer of the system's skills from the developer to the operating person in the organization via training.

2. Three important implementation issues are worth noting:

   a. *Selection of the problem domain.* Successful system implementation is assured when the user has been involved in defining the problem domain. Also, when the payoff is large and measurable and a champion has been behind the project, successful implementation is more likely.

   b. *Knowledge representation and implementation.* Ease of use is an acid test of the user's willingness to adopt the new expert system. Documentation and a trouble-shooting guide are also helpful for making future changes in the system.
   Successful implementation depends on:

      ▪ level of motivation and technical background of the user
      ▪ communication skills of the trainer and time available for training
      ▪ place, ease, and duration of training

- explanatory facilities of the system
- role of champion

Knowledge representation also includes the issue of maintenance. Maintenance must be easy and effective, allow for additions or changes, and identify inconsistencies, redundancies, and the availability of a qualified person to do the job.

c. *Organizational factors.* Top management support and proper funding through implementation are critical considerations. Other organizational factors are user participation and conducive organization climate, such as timing of installation and user readiness.

3. Technology transfer includes actual transfer of the expert system from the developer to the working unit or the transfer of expert system technology skills. Implementation can be approached as a stand-alone installation on a PC or as a fully integrated application that interfaces with other applications.

4. An expert system can be integrated into an organization in a number of ways:

   a. technical integration

   b. knowledge-sharing integration

   c. decision-making flow integration

   d. re-engineering considerations

5. Three types of users require training and development: tutor-user, pupil-user, and customer-user. Neither pupil-users nor customer-users need much training during the early phase of system development. The level of user training depends on the user's knowledge of the expert system, complexity of the system, the trainer's experience and communication skills, and the environment in which training is carried out. In any case, training should be geared to the specific user and, in some cases, introduced in stages for a lasting impact.

6. Regardless of what organizational aspects are being changed, implementation means change, and people in general resist change. The resistors include experts, nonexperts, troublemakers, and narrow-minded technical "superstars." Resistance is displayed in the form of projection, avoidance, and aggression, and has much to do with the individual personality, the organizational structure in which the user works, and the group relations in the area in which the system will be installed. User education, training, and participation can help reduce or control resistance to change.

7. Implementation can be promoted in a number of ways: user-attitude survey, communication training, training sessions, and role negotiation. In any case, sensitivity to user expectations is a step toward "implementation without tears."

8. After the system has been deployed, its impact on people and the performance of the business must be evaluated. Safeguarding the system against unauthorized access is also an important followup step to take.

■ TERMS TO LEARN

Aggression resistance to expert systems through employee sabotage of the system.

Avoidance resistance to expert systems through employee withdrawal from the job or scene.

Customer-user a user interested in knowing how to use the system for problem solving on a regular basis.

Decision-making flow integration matching expert system problem-solving processes with the user's style of thinking.

Deployment physical transfer of the technology to the organization's operating unit.

Enhancement upgrading the system to meet a new set of requirements.

Explanatory facility the system's capability to display the reasoning behind its solutions.

Job aids screen designs that rely on color to highlight a question or an answer, partitions on the screen to separate one answer from another, and so on.

Knowledge-sharing integration integrating the expert system in such a way that it can be accessed by different branches of the company, allowing them to share information.

Projection resistance to expert systems through employee display of hostility toward peers.

Pupil-user an unskilled worker trying to learn or gain some understanding of the captured knowledge.

Technical integration integrating an expert system into an existing operation through the firm's local area network environment, resident mainframe, workstations, and other information system applications.

Tutor-user a user with a working knowledge of the expert system knowledge base and the responsibility for system maintenance.

User-attitude survey a survey in which opinions are collected from users to learn how well they like the system and how closely it meets user requirements.

Workflow re-engineering changes in the workplace or jobs within the problem domain triggered by insights resulting from expert system implementation.

■ REVIEW QUESTIONS

1. The chapter discusses key issues in expert system implementation. In what way is each issue important for successful implementation? Elaborate.

2. How can system users be assured of system success? Be specific.

3. In what ways is knowledge representation related to implementation?

4. Successful expert system implementation depends on several factors. Briefly explain each factor.

5. Elaborate on the role of maintenance in the life of an expert system.

6. Distinguish between:
   a. maintenance and enhancement
   b. pupil-user and tutor-user
   c. projection and avoidance
   d. commitment and contribution

7. From what you know, how important are organizational factors in system implementation? Explain.

8. How would one approach transfer of technology in system implementation? Which approach do you suggest for implementing a small system on a stand-alone PC? Why?

9. Briefly explain each alternative for integrating expert systems into the organization. Under what conditions would you choose one alternative over the others?

10. Why is the place of training important? What about duration of training? Explain.

11. What determines the success of user training? Be specific.

12. If an expert system is user-friendly and has the necessary explanatory facility, why is a user's manual necessary?

13. "A strategic education plan prepares an organization to adopt expert systems." Do you agree? Discuss.

14. If you were asked to coordinate the implementation phase of an expert system in a department where users are not interested in the change, what approach or procedure would you follow to combat resistance to change? Cite a specific situation or the conditions under which you would handle the assignment.

15. How would one promote successful expert system implementation? Explain.

16. What is a postimplementation review? Why is this step important?

17. Discuss the role of security in expert system use. How important is expert system security compared to security measures in conventional information systems? Justify your answer.

■ EXERCISES AND CASES

1. *Implementing the Real Estate Advisor*

In January 1992, a real estate firm expressed interest in an advisory expert system to train new agents and advise senior ones on the best match between a prospective home owner and the available homes in the area. The firm has fourteen offices in eight major cities in the state of Virginia. A contract was drawn to do the work with implementation by mid-October of the same year.

The resulting system consisted of 165 rules involving seventeen parameters using VP-Expert. Testing the package took two months before it was ready for deployment. The first step was to meet with two volunteer agents from the main office to demonstrate what the system could do and how easy it was to learn the system. They asked how long it would take. The reply was "three to four hours total." They suggested a meeting with the developer the following Sunday to give the system a try.

Sunday morning, the two real estate agents came on time and were eager to see what the system could do to improve their sales potential. After two hours of practice, they began to make suggestions about expanding the system to include variables that had not been raised before. For example, they wanted the system to ask if the prospective buyer would object to living in integrated neighborhoods, whether the buyer had transportation to and from work, etc.

The result of the three-hour session was frustration. The agents were courteous but did not indicate they would use the system. Since they worked on commission, they were under no immediate obligation to try it.

A strategy meeting with the president of the firm led to the decision to hold a session with the eleven real estate agents the following week and discuss the implementation plan. During the one-hour session, several questions were raised regarding the system's capabilities and how it was built. Luckily, the single domain expert used in building the system was a highly respected agent with 18 years of successful experience. The expert was there and offered his opinion of the system.

Suddenly the president cut into the discussion and said, "Look, we can beat the system over the head and still not agree on a direction. I have an idea for you to consider. Why don't you give this system a try and after you feel you have a handle on the way it works, see if it can help you match a buyer with the right house. I am willing to increase anyone's commission from 50 percent to 60 percent for every documented match that results in a sale. I am willing to do this for 90 days."

By the end of the session, six out of the eleven agents had agreed to undergo a one-day training at company expense. That was in February 1993. By June, 46 successful matches had been made that resulted in 28 documented sales.

The word got around to the branches regarding the usefulness of the Real Estate Advisor. During the succeeding five months, a number of suggestions were incorporated into the system under a maintenance agreement with the firm. In December 1993, the system became available to the branches under the 60 percent commission plan. Training became easier, as more agents expressed interest in the system.

Questions

a. Evaluate the approach used in implementing the Real Estate Advisor.

b. Should one expect changes in the system to take place during implementation? What, if anything, went wrong? Explain.

c. In what other ways might this system have been implemented? Elaborate.

2. Housing Office Expert Rental System (HOFERS) is a system developed for the student housing office of a major university in 1992. After the system passed verification and validation, the knowledge engineer held a wrap-up meeting with the end-user. She spent two hours going through the manual and running examples through the newly installed system for the end-user to become familiar with the package. The user was quite impressed with the many features the system offered—a color screen, easy-to-follow menu, and display of the reasons to justify all kinds of answers.

One month after the two-hour training session, the knowledge engineer sent a questionnaire to the end-user; it included the following questions:

■ Did the manual help you understand the system?

■ Did the knowledge engineer give you a working understanding of the system?

■ Did you understand the questions asked by the system?

■ Does the system meet your expectations? If not, please explain any suggestions you might have.

■ Did the system provide adequate and correct answers?

■ Do you think that the system is usable in your environment?

Questions

a. Based on the information provided, evaluate the training approach followed by the knowledge engineer.

b. Could you deduce a training plan in this case? Explain.

c. Critique the questionnaire used to follow up on the installation.

■ SELECTED REFERENCES

Biswas, Pratik K. "An Extended Object Model for the Design and Development of Expert Systems." In E. M. Awad, ed., Proceedings of the 1990 ACM SIGBDP conference on *Trends and Directions in Expert Systems* October 31–November 2, 1990, pp. 524–537.

Candlin, D. B. and S. Wright. "Managing the Introduction of Expert Systems." *International Journal of Operations & Production Management* 12, no. 1 (1992), pp. 46–59.

Dechamps, Paul B. "Standards for Expert System Tools: Supporting the Technology's Integration." *Information Systems Management,* Winter 1992, pp. 8–14.

Duangploy, Orapin and Shohreh Hashemi. "Integrating Expert Systems into the Financial Accounting Instructional System." In Jay Liebowitz, ed., *Expert Systems World Congress Proceedings.* New York: Pergamon Press, 1990, pp. 2319–2325.

Duggal, Sudesh M. and Paul R. Popovich. "An Example of Management Training in Expert Systems: SBA Loan Evaluation System." In E. M. Awad, ed., Proceedings of the 1990 ACM SIGBDP Conference on *Trends and Directions in Expert Systems,* October 31–November 2, 1990, pp. 588–618.

Ferreira, Cynthia and Frank Rotman. "External Database Interfacing With ES: A Comparative Analysis Between ESE and C." In *Proceedings of the Third Annual Symposium of the International Association of Knowledge Engineers* (IAKE), November 16–19, 1992, pp. 366–373.

Gupta, Uma G. "Successful Deployment Strategies: Moving to an Operational Environment." *Information Systems Management* 9, no. 1 (1992), pp. 21–27.

Hardaway, Donald E. "A Review of Barriers to Expert System Diffusion." In E. M. Awad, ed., Proceedings of the 1990 ACM SIGBDP Conference on *Trends and Directions in Expert Systems,* October 31–November 2, 1990, pp. 619–639.

Ishikawa, Akira; Mieno Hiroshi, and Rumi Tatsuta. "Knowledge Engineering Management—Issues and Prospects." *Human Systems Management* 10, no. 2 (1991), pp. 141–148.

Karakonda, Sree R. K. "An Entity-Relationship Approach to the Implementation of Frame-Based Systems." In E. M. Awad, ed., Proceedings of the 1990 ACM SIGBDP Conference on *Trends and Directions in Expert Systems,* October 31–November 2, 1990, pp. 650–660.

Kerr, Roger M. "Implementation of Expert Systems for Production Scheduling: Three Case Studies." In Jay Liebowitz, ed., *Expert Systems World Congress Proceedings.* New York: Pergamon Press, 1991, pp. 405–414.

Kusters, Rob J. and R. V. Schuwer. "An Approach to Integrating Knowledge Base Systems." In Jay Liebowitz, ed., *Expert Systems World Congress Proceedings.* New York: Pergamon Press, 1991, pp. 2470–2479.

Laffey, James; Rao Machiraju; and Ravinder Chandhok. "Integrated Support and Learning Systems for Augmenting Knowledge Workers: A Focus on Case-Based Retrieval." In Jay Liebowitz, ed., *Expert Systems World Congress Proceedings.* New York: Pergamon Press, 1991, pp. 2817–2828.

Lindley, Craig A. and John Shiel. "Implementation of an Expert System Incorporating a Generic Application Model." In Jay Liebowitz, ed., *Expert Systems World Congress Proceedings.* New York: Pergamon Press, 1991, pp. 698–705.

Orlandic, Ratko. "Problems of Content-Based Retrieval in Image Databases." In *Proceedings of the Third Annual Symposium of the International Association of Knowledge Engineers* (IAKE), November 16–19, 1992, pp. 374–384.

Raghupathi, Wullianallur. "Implementing the 'SKADE LITorSET' System: A Blackboard Expert System for Corporate Legal Decisions." In Jay Liebowitz, ed., *Expert Systems World Congress Proceedings.* New York: Pergamon Press, 1991, pp. 300–307.

Ragusa, James M. and Gary W. Orwig. "Integrating Expert Systems to Multimedia: The Reality and Promise." In Jay Liebowitz, ed., *Expert Systems World Congress Proceedings.* New York: Pergamon Press, 1991, pp. 2919–2930.

Rariden, R. L. "Barriers to Implementing Expert Systems Technology in Corporations." In E. M. Awad, ed., Proceedings of the 1990 ACM SIGBDP Conference on *Trends and Directions in Expert Systems,* October 31–November 2, 1990, pp. 640–650.

Sipior, Janice C. "Merging Expert System With Multimedia Technology." In E. M. Awad, ed., Proceedings of the 1990 ACM SIGBDP Conference on *Trends and Directions in Expert Systems,* October 31–November 2, 1990, pp. 510–523.

Tan, C. L.; T. S. Quah; and H. H. Teh. "Implementation of Rule-Based Expert Systems in a Neural Network Architecture." In Jay Liebowitz, ed., *Expert Systems World Congress Proceedings.* New York: Pergamon Press, 1991, pp. 1843–1851.

Tewari, Raj. "Expert Design Tools for Physical Database Design." In E. M. Awad, ed., Proceedings of the 1990 ACM SIGBDP Conference on *Trends and Directions in Expert Systems,* October 31–November 2, 1990, pp. 538–550.

———"Implications of Next-Generation Database Technology for Knowledge Engineering." In *Proceedings of the Third Annual Symposium of the International Association of Knowledge Engineers* (IAKE), November 16–19, 1992, pp. 352–365.

Williams, Joseph. "When Expert Systems Are Wrong." In E. M. Awad, ed., Proceedings of the 1990 ACM SIGBDP Conference on *Trends and Directions in Expert Systems,* October 31–November 2, 1990, pp. 661–669.

Chapter ▪ 17

Integrating Technology: Neural Nets

THINKING MACHINES RATHER THAN MARKETS

About a decade ago, a young graduate student at the Massachusetts Institute of Technology named Danny Hillis dazzled the world of computing by dreaming up a new machine that came to be known as a "massively parallel processor." And in the years since, Hillis succeeded in building some of the fastest, most innovative computers in the world.

But technical prowess does not guarantee business success. Earlier this month, Hillis's company, Thinking Machines Corp., filed for protection from its creditors under Chapter 11 of the federal bankruptcy laws. The Cambridge, Massachusetts, company announced it would lay off a third of its 425 employees.

Thinking Machines' odyssey began in the early 1980s, when Hillis was studying computer science at MIT. He was particularly intrigued by how the human brain works. Even though computers are often called "brains, they bear little resemblance to the gray matter inside our heads. Where real brains are composed of billions of neurons connected by a gossamer network of nerves, computers have just a single central processor to do the "thinking."

With approximately $12 million from the Defense Advanced Research Projects Agency (DARPA) and another $120 million from private investors, Hillis sought to design a computer that would function more like the brain. He strung together thousands of processors, each of which simultaneously tackled a tiny part of a problem. In contrast to single-processor computers, Hillis's machines were called "massively parallel processors."

By the late 1980s, researchers had embraced the new computers enthusiastically. By breaking large problems into small pieces, Thinking Machines' massively parallel computers could crunch through reams of data at lightning speed, in some cases even faster than those built by the reigning king of supercomputers, Cray Research, Inc.

A generation of scientists at federally funded supercomputer centers as well as at the national weapons laboratories scrambled to learn to use Hillis's systems in hopes of simulating—and perhaps even solving fantastically complex problems.

University researchers found that parallel processors were well suited to portraying storm systems and modeling how the Earth's climate might change over time. Today as Los Alamos National Laboratory in New Mexico, for example, Hillis's computers are helping scientists model the circulation of the world's oceans.

Along with handling very large data bases, parallel processors also proved ideally suited for many military problems. One example is image analysis, in which computers analyze photos gathered by reconnaissance satellites and count, say, the number of tanks. The machines can also portray reams of simultaneous events—such as the reactions caused by a large nuclear explosion.

Despite such testimonials from researchers, the commercial market for such machines was precarious at best. For starters, they were expensive— selling for between $1 million and $20 million each. And software had to be tailor-made. Over time, engineers learned how to fit their problems onto parallel machines. But many commercial customers still favored buying systems that were compatible with what they had used in the past.

Last year, demand from scientific and technical users for massively parallel machines totaled just $310 million. Commercial customers spent about the same. Analysts expect the commercial market for very large machines to grow between 10 percent and 20 percent a year over the next five years, while in the post-Cold War era the scientific market is likely to shrink an average of 9 percent a year.

A sign that there is money to be made from parallel processing—despite Thinking Machines' stumble—comes from a firm called Teradata Corp., which was acquired two years ago by AT&T. Teradata's secret is that it designs its systems to solve basic business problems, such as inventory management. Its systems won't win any prizes for speed, but they run several days a week, 24 hours a day.

Thinking Machines made some inroads in the commercial sector, however, about 90 percent of its sales were to the research community. To succeed in that field, Thinking Machines gathered a stable of scientists who could rival the best university group. "We like astrophysicists and modeling the greenhouse effect," said Hillis.

Although the government succeeded in pushing parallelism into mainstream computing, it did not think about how its support might swing commercial fortunes, or how those might change when its support waned. "DARPA never worried about the commercial problem, just about getting its mission done," said Victor H. Reis, assistant secretary for defense programs at the Department of Energy and formerly director of DARPA.

Source: Elizabeth Corcoran, *The Washington Post*, August 28, 1994, p. H1ff.

At a Glance

Neural networks, as an evolving technology, have been gaining ground since 1987. Modeled after the human brain's network, the technology attempts to simulate biological information processing through massive networks of processing elements called neurons. Neural nets and digital computers are not the same. Neural nets are neither digital nor serial. They are analog and parallel. They learn by example, not by programmed rules or instructions. Digital computers do not evolve as such.

One of the areas in which neural nets can make a definite contribution to decision making is in expert systems. Neural nets show superior performance over that of human experts for eliciting functional relationships between input and output values. In a comparison of the two technologies, neural nets prove to be better at learning by example rather than by rules and continue to learn as the problem environment changes. This capability makes them well suited to deal with unstructured problems and inconsistent information. Neural nets can also handle fuzzy data without losing accuracy. Expert systems largely depend on complete data before they offer a final solution. In summary, expert systems offer structure, explanatory capability, and validity; neural nets offer the creative part of problem solving. They learn from experience in much the same way as a human expert develops decision-making skills.

The learning function occurs within the net's ability to change the weights and allow the neuron to modify its activity in response to its inputs. Making weight adjustments by backing up from the output is called back propagation. As a learning procedure, it has become perhaps the most popular way to train networks.

To build a neural network, one needs to know the inner workings of the technology. The building life cycle consists of problem definition, gathering training data, training the network, testing the network, and running the network. The most critical aspect of the building process is understanding the problem and then presenting training data that is reliable and relevant to the problem at hand.

Neural networks are emerging in a wide range of business and industrial applications. Despite their obvious successes, neural networks have limitations, including cost justification, the nature of neural learning, and maintenance. For example, how much is an organization willing to spend to gear up the technology? Another issue relates to the concept of neural networks as adaptive learning systems. Is such learning a "good enough" replacement for humans who learn "on the fly" using intelligence and common sense? Also, a firm that relies heavily on applications supported by neural nets should consider maintenance as part of the total commitment to quality assurance.

> D ata! Data! Data! he cried impatiently, I can't make bricks without clay.
>
> —SHERLOCK HOLMES

▦ INTRODUCTION

For decades, scientists have been trying to teach computers to imitate human thought, to learn from a massive volume of data they process, and to make inference the way the human mind does, better and faster. That day has come with the recent introduction of neural networks applications in the business sector.

The main theme of this effort has been in using the brain as a model for a parallel computational system quite different from that of the traditional serial computer. Neural networks (NNs) are functional, adaptive learning systems. They are the electronic analogs of the human brain. The technology attempts to simulate biological information processing through massively parallel, highly interconnected networks of simple processing elements called neurons. These networks interact with the real world in the same way biological nervous systems do. They turn raw data into a working information processing system.

Inspired by the structure of the human brain, neural networks operate on radically different principles than conventional digital computers. They are not programmed, but can learn from examples and self-modifications. They handle enormous data sets, use their own "judgment" to match patterns without explicit rules beforehand, and achieve a close fit between data and predicted outcomes. In fact, they can recreate the decision-making process of some of the most highly skilled people in an organization.

The first wave of neural networks—also called artificial neural networks, or ANN—began in the 1940s and 1950s when scientists discovered that the brain's neurons are on-off switches just as the digital computer's bits are either on or off. From this idea, the analogy between the brain and the computer was developed. In 1943, neurophysiologist Warren McCullough and 18-year-old mathematician Walter Pitts developed an ANN system (M-P) showing how highly complex computations could be performed by a network of simple binary neurons. Six years later, D. O. Hebb's *Organization of Behavior* showed how "learning" can be achieved by modifying the connections between the neurons and altering the effects of various inputs. Today's major learning ANN paradigms are based on M-P-like and Hebbian models.

Since 1987, ANN applications have been one of the fastest growing in the history of science. This evolving technology provides a way for quantifying the laws governing cognition. A number of important applications have been developed in major industries such as manufacturing and finance with the hope of benefits such as cost control, increased accuracy and consistency, efficient use of resources, and higher user satisfaction. See Box 17–1.

This chapter discusses the general concepts of neural networks, how they work, how they differ from digital and expert systems, and some of the business applications developed to date.

■ WHAT IS A NEURAL NETWORK?

The human brain consists of 10 billion or so neurons; each neuron interacts directly with 1,000–10,000 other neurons. A neuron fires or does not fire. The rate of firing determines the magnitude of information. When the brain accepts inputs, it generally responds to them. The responses are a combination of learning and what has been genetically programmed over time.

A **neural network** (NN) is an information system modeled after the human brain's network of electronically interconnected basic processing elements called neurons. Figure 17–1 illustrates a neuron of the retina of the human eye. A neuron is the basic processing unit. In principle, it does little more than figure out the weighted sum of all its inputs.

The interesting aspect of a NN is its known contributions solving cumbersome problems that traditional computer systems have found difficult to

---

Box 17–1   Smarter Than the Average Ant, It's ROBO-ANT

Keeping ants behind glass is one way to study how intelligent behavior emerges from simple instincts. But Luis R. Lopez, a scientist at an Army research laboratory in Huntsville, Alabama, has formed a company to offer an even more entertaining alternative: an antlike robot called Insecta.

Insecta can outlearn ants. Fed a few simple software rules, the robot evolves increasingly complex operations. Its genetic algorithms start with snippets of software that combine and exchange data, and automatically create more complex programs. For guidance, Insecta will use neural networks, or circuits that mimic the reasoning powers of the human brain.

Source: *Business Week,* September 12, 1994, p. 7.

Figure 17–1   A Basic Neuron (human retina)

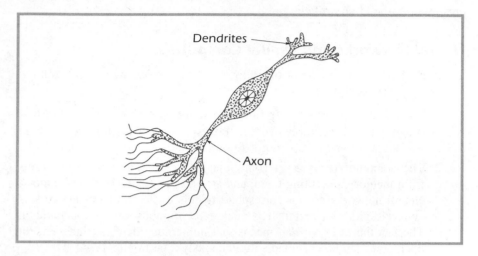

track—for example, deciding whether a visual image of a human face is that of a man or a woman. They are actually terrible at handling problems that computers do well (e.g., payroll) or problems that require numerical computations. So, successful NN problems exhibit one of the following characteristics: qualitative or complex quantitative reasoning is required; data is readily available but error-prone; or development time is short, but enough time is available for training the neural net. See Box 17–2.

Biologically inspired computing is not the same as conventional computing, however. Even though NNs are programmed to work the way the human brain is thought to function, the goal of this technology is to build artificial rather than biological neural systems based on a simplified model of what is

---

Box 17–2   Now, Air Force Computers May Home in on Tumors

Radiologists rely on the images produced by CAT scanners, MRI machines, and X-rays to diagnose tumors. But much of the information in the digitized pictures is too dense or too subtle for doctors to make sense of. Computer systems originally designed to seek out enemy tanks could help. Consultant Booz, Allen & Hamilton Inc.'s technology arm in McLean, Virginia, is collaborating with the U.S. Air Force's research laboratory in Rome, New York, and with Cornell University Medical College in New York to adapt military computer systems to detect small malignant tumors at an early stage.

The partners are using advanced computer techniques called neural networks that quickly learn to recognize suspect objects—be they tanks or tumors—given enough examples of the patterns of these images. Over the next four months, the scientists expect to train the military's neural nets on the lung CAT scans of 80 patients. Neural networks could also decipher digitized X-rays and MRI scans. They should help doctors distinguish between malignant and benign tumors with more confidence and reduce the number of biopsies.

Source: *Business Week,* May 1994, p. 67.

known about the human brain and human decision making. No one is presuming to build an artificial brain.

Neural Networks and Digital Computers

Viewing neurons as either on or off follows a computer's binary logic. Yet, the two exhibit distinct differences:

1. The computer works on a problem in sequence one step at a time. It is programmed. A neural network is trained by preprocessing the inputs in various ways and comparing it to output until a solution is found.

2. The computer relies on a continuous cycle of retrieving instructions from memory, executing them, and storing the results back in memory. Neural networks do not correspond to this cycle. A neural network is neither digital nor serial. It is analog (continuous value) and parallel. The fact that it is *parallel* means that numerous, identical, independent operations can be executed simultaneously. See Figure 17–2.

3. The computer's data are stored in a separate memory. In a neural network, data are stored throughout the network patterns of weights, interconnections, and states of the neurons.

4. A neural network is a state that evolves continually with time. It learns by example *not* by programmed rules or instructions. Digital computers do not evolve in this manner.

5. Neural networks mimic what the human brain does. They are adaptive, in that they take data, learn from it, and infer solutions from the data presented to them. Digital computers do not adapt, but instead depend on the programmer's prior instructions and knowledge.

Figure 17–2   Sequential versus Parallel Processing

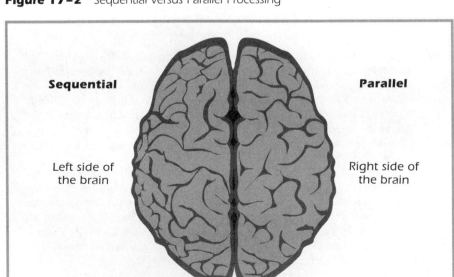

6. In a digital computer, answers are exact; in a neural network, answers "evolve." Also, when part of a computer fails, the system fails to give results. If part of a neural network fails, it continues to perform with reduced accuracy.

7. Digital computers are not good at generalizations, while neural networks are. For example, a neural network is told:

   Grass is a plant
   Grass is green
   Cucumbers are plants
   Cucumbers are green

   If told that hedges are plants, the neural network decides that hedges are green. Generalization is useful in practical applications. For example, employment rate, interest rate, and real prices react together. The effect of a change in one variable can cause a change in others.

8. Neural networks are also temporal associators. For example, green is associated with go and red is associated with stop. Digital computers cannot make similar associations.

9. Neural networks are good at pattern recognition. Examples are numbers and signatures on checks, weather forecasting, and photographs of faces. The goal is to find close matches. This type of recognition is difficult for digital computers.

Neural Networks and Expert Systems

One of the areas in which neural networks can make a definite decision-making contribution is in expert systems. In expert systems, knowledge acquisition, especially the acquisition of deep knowledge, is neither easy nor explicit. A sophisticated knowledge base does not evolve from a simple one by adding knowledge learned from experience or automatically incorporate new knowledge into the current knowledge base.

Some researches have attempted to use neural networks to address this difficulty. One approach replaces the knowledge elicited by a human expert with a learning algorithm that extracts the functional relationships between input and output contained in a training set and represents them in the magnitudes of connection weights. A pattern of weighted connections achieves for deep knowledge the same effect achieved by the explicit decision rules in expert systems. This method shows superior performance in eliciting functional relationships between input and output values over the performance of human experts. It is also more accurate than conventional expert systems using knowledge acquisition.

Neural networks can be contrasted with expert systems as follows:

1. Expert systems are not good at logical deductions. They learn didactically, by rules. Neural networks learn socratically, by example.

2. Expert systems are sequential in structure. They examine all relevant rules and exceptions to suggest a solution to a problem. Although they are not well suited to pattern recognition, their sequential nature allows them to explain how they arrived at a particular decision. This capability makes them an invaluable tool, particularly in diagnosis and training,

where the processes are as important as the results. A neural network does not have explanatory capabilities. Like a black box, inputs go in, results come out, and what occurs between is unknown.

3. Another distinguishing feature has to do with process. Expert systems use rules to duplicate the expertise, but the process must start with an expert. In a way, the development process is conventional. The expert system is supplied with data (input) and then processes the rules to get an output. In a neural network, the user supplies the input *and* the output. The net's job is to come up with the process. If it has enough opportunities to observe inputs and outputs, it adjusts the process until it successfully predicts the output based on the inputs it has not yet encountered. When the user corrects the output, the neural net then has a chance to improve. In this respect, it "learns."

4. In the parallel structure of neural networks, all factors are considered at once. This structure gives NNs the ability to recognize patterns in the input. They may even recognize patterns in decision making that sequential expert systems might never pick up. For example, an expert system for evaluating mortgage decisions might penalize a member of the Armed Forces for frequently changing residence. A neural network has the capability to recognize the aberration. It would not have to be told that this attribute does not indicate instability in military personnel. It can discover such subtleties on its own.

5. Neural networks are able to continue learning as the problem environment changes. This attribute makes them well suited to deal with unstructured problems and inconsistent information. Neural networks can handle fuzzy data without losing accuracy. They are capable of generalizing from fuzzy data. Even if they have been trained with limited input data, they will interpolate an approximate answer. Alternatively, expert systems largely depend on complete data before they offer a final solution.

6. The trainability of neural networks allows them to adapt to unexpected changes in their environment. Neurons and their interconnections alter their strengths with experience. For example, a neural network can be trained to pick up a teacup, even if it has been moved a couple of inches. A robot arm programmed the conventional way to pick up the teacup from one position will fail when the cup is moved. This rigidity is also exhibited in expert systems. Any changes in function means upgrading the whole expert system. With a neural network, the system would merely undergo retraining.

7. Today's expert systems provide more effective means of developing a user-friendly interface and explanation of how it arrived at a solution. A neural network is more effective at developing a knowledge base with experiential data than are expert systems. Such differences mean that the role of a neural network in building expert systems is that of partner, rather than replacement for expert systems.

Both expert systems and neural networks have their place in various business applications. Expert systems offer structure, explanatory capability, and validity. Neural networks offer the creative part of problem solving. They learn from experience in much the same way an expert develops personal decision-making skills.

Expert systems have been criticized for overly preprogramming behavior, making flexible responses to unexpected events difficult to achieve. If events are predicted, then processing capability is restricted. While these systems are good at organizing masses of information and providing responses to known questions, they cannot provide intuitive, trial-and-error thinking. Neural networks may prove capable of this and, as one author noted, "may ultimately remove the adjective from artificial intelligence."

To illustrate this important feature, the following example discusses a loan application using a neural network. The neural network is given the data from the old loan application files (input) and the decision made or results of all the loans (output). The neural net first attempts to reconcile the applications with the results and comes up with important variables such as credit history and employment stability. It also deletes variables that have had less important roles, such as education and residence. After successive passes at the reconciliation process, the system determines the relative importance of various inputs against those available in the output and predicts the decision to approve or not approve the loan.

Neural Network Limitations

Neural networks are not without limitations:

1. They are not magic, easy, or foolproof. They require specific maintenance and various alterations to accommodate changing requirements.

2. They are not attractive if accurate answers are required; they cannot count. They are good at what people do well. They see the forest, not trees.

3. Learning, per se, is not easy. In some applications, the network does backward iterations many times before it arrives at a reasonable solution, which requires extensive computer time.

4. Neural networks do not have the explanatory powers of expert systems. They do not account for their results well.

5. A complex problem means a large network. If the application needs 200 nodes, it might require 400,000 connections. This is neither an easy task nor a guaranteed success.

■ HOW DOES A NEURAL NETWORK WORK?

An artificial neural network consists of many simple processing elements, called **neurons.** Each neuron has a small amount of local memory. It is connected to other neurons by wires called **axons.** It also receives input from other neurons via pathways called **dendrites.** The axon–dendride connection is called a **synapse.** Communications between neurons are carried out only through the input-output pathways. No neuron can access any other neuron's memory. See Figure 17–3.

Inputs and Outputs

A neural net is viewed as a self-programming system based on its inputs and outputs. Each neuron has a **transfer function** that computes the output signal from the input signals. A typical neuron building block, or **node,** is shown in Figure 17–4. The procedure is simple. The neuron evaluates the **inputs,**

Figure 17–3   Neurons Forming a Network

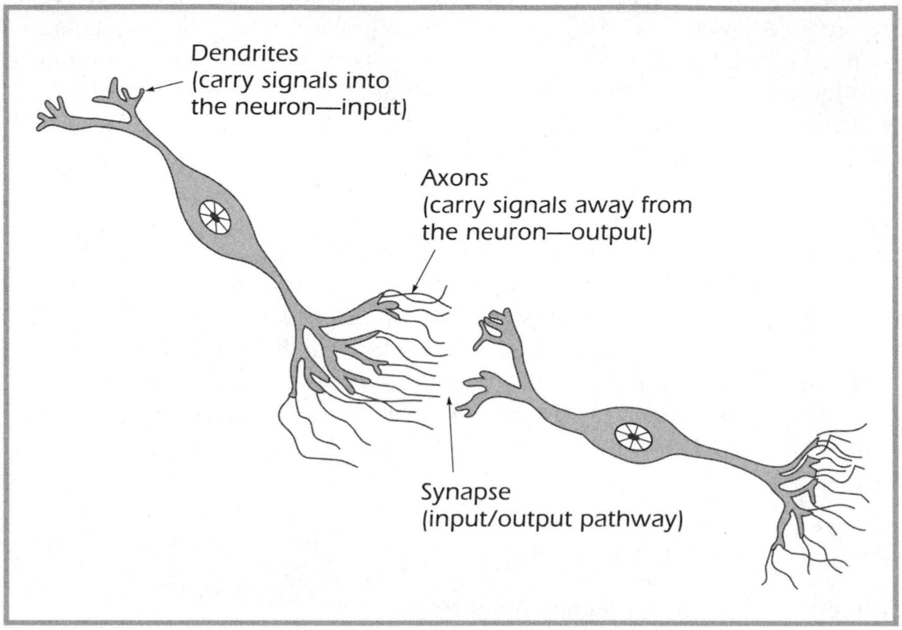

Dendrites
(carry signals into
the neuron—input)

Axons
(carry signals away from
the neuron—output)

Synapse
(input/output pathway)

Figure 17–4   A Single Node with Weighted Inputs and Summation Function

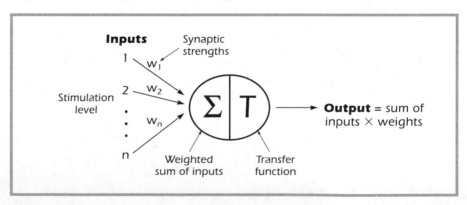

determines their strengths or **weights,** "sums" the combined inputs, and compares the total to a **threshold** (transfer function) level. The threshold could be something as simple as zero or could mirror the input within a given range (0–1). If the sum is greater than the threshold, the neuron fires. That is, it sends **output** from that particular neuron. Otherwise, it generates no signal.

Interconnecting or combining neurons with other neurons forms a layer of nodes or a neural network. As shown in Figure 17–5, inputs can be connected to many nodes with different weights, which results in many outputs—one output per node. The interconnection ia analogous to the synapse–neuron junction in a biological network.

In a real-world problem, inputs represent variables, and the connecting weights are relationships between variables. Once input values are received by

Figure 17–5   Neural Network

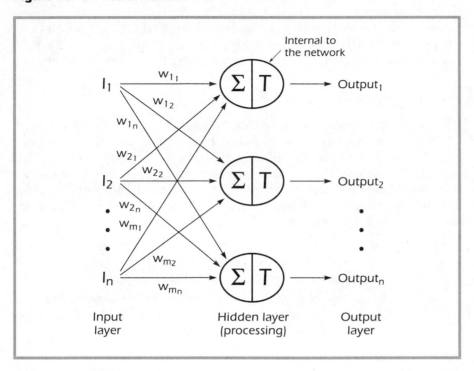

Figure 17–6   Neural Network Model Predicting a Firm's Bankruptcy

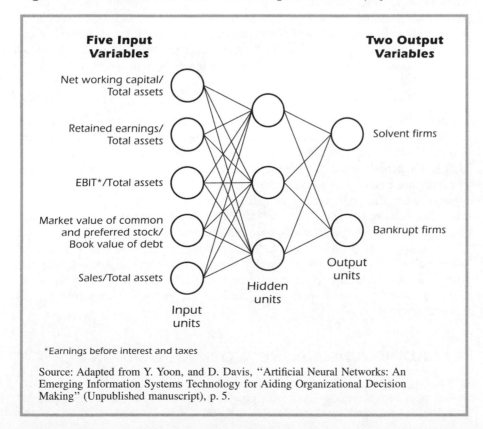

*Earnings before interest and taxes

Source: Adapted from Y. Yoon, and D. Davis, "Artificial Neural Networks: An Emerging Information Systems Technology for Aiding Organizational Decision Making" (Unpublished manuscript), p. 5.

a trained network, the output value of each unit is computed by the output function. In Figure 17–6, the neural network model predicts a firm's status—solvent versus bankrupt. Five input variables are fed into the system with two possible outcomes as outputs. The hidden units adjust the weights to the right threshold and are used to support the transformation from input to output.

Learning Modes

The learning function takes place within the neural network's ability to change the weights and allow the neuron to modify its activity in response to its inputs. For example, if a neural net identifies a man as "a woman," on successive attempts, connection weights that represent favorably a man's image are strengthened, leaving other "woman" images weakened until they no longer meet the threshold level. Making weight adjustments by backing up from the output is called **back propagation.** Back propagation consists of two passes:

1. In the *forward pass,* the input pattern is applied to the network and allows the resulting activity to spread through the network to the output layer. This output is usually wrong initially.

2. In the *backward pass,* the difference between the actual and the desired output generates an error signal that is propagated back through the network to teach it to do better—to produce a result closer to the desired output.

Back propagation as a learning procedure has become perhaps the most popular way to train networks. It has been known to train networks in areas ranging from character and speech recognition and motor control, to playing backgammon. Yet, certain theoretical issues yet to be resolved form the basis of today's ongoing research. For example, can the network learn to solve the problem at hand? Can problems be solved within the standard three-layer network? How can the substantial training time for the more complex problems be reduced?

Supervised and Unsupervised Learning

Learning may be supervised or unsupervised. In **supervised learning,** the neural network needs a teacher—a **training set** of examples of input and output. Each element in a training set is paired with an acceptable response. That is, the actual output of a neural network is compared to the desired output. The network makes successive passes through the examples, and the weights adjust toward the goal state. When the weights represent the passes without error, the network has learned to associate a set of input patterns with a specific output. This is more like learning by reinforcement.

In **unsupervised** (also called self-supervised) learning, no external factors influence the adjustment of the input's weights. The neural network has no advanced indication of correct or incorrect answers. It adjusts solely through direct confrontation with new experiences. This process is referred to as self-organization.

■ BUILDING A NEURAL NETWORK APPLICATION

In building a neural network, it is helpful but not necessary to know the inner workings of the technology. Available commercial software makes it possible to design, train, test, and run a neural network while knowing hardly anything about neuron behavior or architecture. The important design questions include how to get a neural network to give the desired information, what data should be presented the neural network, and how to train the neural network. This section addresses the development life cycle of a neural network with a basic application to illustrate how neural networks work.

A neural network development life cycle consists of five steps: problem definition, gathering training data, training the network, testing the network, and running the network. See Figure 17-7.

Problem Definition

The first step in building a neural network is to determine what the neural network is expected to provide in the way of output. It also means deciding on the kinds of input data the network should use to generate the output. Neural networks learn by associating the inputs and expected outputs. For example, a neural network can associate a change in the supply of lumber with the price of new homes—a decrease in the supply leads to an increase in new home prices.

An important point to remember is how well problem definition applies to the problem at hand. For example, character or pattern recognition, vision systems, and forecasting are ideal applications for neurocomputing. In contrast, traditional business applications such as mortgage loan processing that are run with algorithmic languages do not do as well. Other constraints on the candidacy of the problem are cost, accuracy requirements, timing of the data, and scope. Feasibility analysis can be important in deciding on the problem–neurocomputing match. See Box 17–3.

Figure 17–7 Neural Network Development Life Cycle

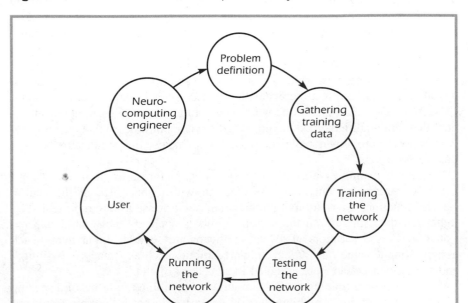

Box 17–3 Applications of Neural Networks

Volvo of Sweden uses neural network for audio analysis of engine sounds and visual analysis of paint finishes on its cars. The networks are trained in Neuralworks Professional II Plus, running on a PC to improve speed and accuracy of its inspection process and meet quality-control standards.

One of the quality-control tests of Volvo engines is for "engine knock" which are flaws in one or more engine components. Traditionally, humans listen for such knocks and recommend the appropriate adjustments before the car is shipped to the dealer. The NeuralWorks-Trained network eliminates human subjectivity by "listening" for knocks through a microphone and applying a standard set of values to the audio analysis, leaving engine repair to the human experts.

At the other end of the Volvo plant, a neural network is trained to evaluate new colors and paint application techniques. The network essentially "sees" paint finishes via a video camera and performs analysis without physical contact with the body of the car. It complements a team of human experts that relies on extensive surface contacts with the painted surface. The neural network speeds the inspection process and provides added assurances of quality to the product.

Source: Adapted from Justin Kestelyn, "Application Watch," *AI Expert,* September 1992, p. 56.

Gathering Training Data

Once the problem has been properly defined, the second step is to prepare for training the neural network by gathering examples for which correct answers are known. For example, for a network to recognize a face, it needs to have seen that face before. The examples are represented as *facts,* which are a collection of inputs with corresponding outputs. The set of examples is called the *training set.* The rule of thumb is to have too many examples rather than too few. The neural network will learn to recognize the important examples and ignore the secondary ones. So, the more examples used, the better the training of the network will be. The examples should also be of sufficient variety to allow the network to make generalizations from them.

Examples for a network design to do an evaluation should include cases in which certain input affect the evaluation and that teach the network important "lessons." For example, a network evaluating a home loan applicant as qualified, not qualified, good buyer, or bad buyer, should learn that an applicant who reports zero down payment on a home means the applicant does not qualify for a loan.

Training examples may also be symbols, pictures, or numbers. Neural networks understand only numbers that fall within the range of the neuron transfer function. Translation of pictures into numeric values are represented by light/dark dots (pixels) on the screen. Symbols such as "not qualified," and "qualified" as descriptors of a loan applicant are separate input items, each assigned input value "1." Other unrelated inputs such as "ready," "willing," and "auto loan holder" are assigned input values of "O."

In collecting a training set, it is important not to think in terms of a specific procedure for solving a problem. Neural networks do not follow procedures or a series of rules as do expert systems. They only work with data. So, the best way to start a neural network project is to think of as many ways (examples) of representing data as possible. Neural networks find associations and determine what is important to the network.

Training the Network

A neural network gets its training by repeatedly taking in each input (example or a set of training facts), guessing at its output, and comparing the results to the supplied output. If its output is incorrect, the network makes appropriate corrections to its internal connections or weights from the middle or processing layer. It repeats the same process until it learns the examples within a range of preset accuracy (e.g., 95 percent) that is good enough to be useful. Most software packages allow the neurocomputing engineer to specify the range within which the supplied output is satisfactorily close to the actual output.

Training should be an interactive process. For example, if a neural network gets one training fact correct, but the second fact wrong, it makes the necessary adjustments to get the second fact correct; but in doing so, the adjustment can adversely affect the output of the previous fact. So, the neural network goes back to the previously correct fact and tries to get it correct, repeating this process until it gets all the facts correct.

Testing and Running the Network

Once a neural network has been adequately trained, it is tested to see how well it has learned. Testing is done by presenting the network with special examples or facts it has not encountered in the past. This time, no corrections are allowed when the network is incorrect. If the results are correct, the network is ready to operate. Otherwise, it must be redesigned or be subjected to further training by presenting new training facts and later testing.

Running the network means presenting it with new inputs with no known outputs. In this operational phase, the network is expected to be more efficient, since it is no longer subjected to the iterative process of training.

Neural networks learn by example the same way humans do. They have a mind of their own; they give opinions but follow no particular rules. They are best at pattern recognition but are not noted for precision. Unlike an expert system, if the process the neural network is evaluating does change, all it needs is a new set of training facts and retesting, rather than the more difficult process of rewriting rules or shell programs.

Finally, a critical aspect of building a neural network is understanding the problem. A neurocomputing engineer cannot think in terms of how a human would solve the problem. Neural networks do not solve a problem by rules. The important aspect of neural processing is information. The tricky part of neurocomputing engineering is how to present training data that is reliable and relevant to the problem at hand in order to assure reliability, improve accuracy, and provide a neural network that will serve a long and useful life for its user.

Example of a Neural Network Application

Proper neural network design is critical for generating good forecasts. To illustrate how it works, the following hypothetical application is designed to predict the Dow-Jones Industrial Average (DJIA) for the New York Stock

Market (NYSE) one week in advance. To do the job, the network needs important financial indicators such as the inflation rate, the prime interest rate, and the unemployment rate this week, last week, and two weeks ago. A wide range of selected data is used to train the neural network in making predictions. The more task-specific the neural network is, the more effective it becomes.

Gathering Training Data

The first step is to gather training data for the neural network which can be acquired from newspapers, stock brokers or specialists who provide their own ratings about the NYSE. In real-life operations, dozens of indicators carry their own respective weights. For the purpose of this exercise, the indicators are narrowed to the training facts or inputs presented in Table 17–1. Each input is assigned a neuron and a value.

One neuron is assigned for each of the five business days that the stock market is open. Today's day hold a value of "1," while other days hold a value of "0" each. The data are also arranged in order by days. The first cut of the data gathered is provided in Table 17–2.

The neural network makes predictions based on trend data reviewing within each example current week and the past two weeks of data simulta-

Table 17–1 Inputs for DJIA Predictor Neural Network

Inputs	Neuron	Values
Inflation rate this week	1	1.41%
Inflation rate last week	2	1.66%
Inflation rate two weeks ago	3	1.27%
Prime interest rate this week	4	8–9.50%
Prime interest rate last week	5	8–9.50%
Prime interest rate two weeks ago	6	8–9.50%
Unemployment rate this week	7	6–6.50%
Unemployment rate last week	8	6–6.30%
Unemployment rate two weeks ago	9	6–6.40%
NYSE fluctuation this week	10	−40 to +40
NYSE fluctuation last week	11	−40 to +40
NYSE fluctuation two weeks ago	12	−40 to +40
Select blue chip price change this week	13	+3 to −4
Select blue chip price change last week	14	+2 to −1
Select blue chip price change 2 weeks ago	15	+4 to −3
Current week (Monday, Tuesday, etc.)	16–20	

Output	Value range
NYSE price average next week	−30 to +20

■ **Table 17–2**   NYSE Data for a Neural Network Review

Week	Inflation rate	Prime interest rate	Unemployment rate	DJIA	Select blue chip price change
Monday	1.62	9.00	6.10	4031	+3 to −4
Tuesday	1.40	8.75	6.25	4060	+2 to −3
Wednesday	1.45	8.75	6.25	4024	+2 to −2
Thursday	1.54	8.75	6.20	4050	+1 to −3
Friday	1.51	8.75	6.15	4046	+1 to −1

neously. The training data in Table 17–2 is presented to the neural network for review. Table 17–3 shows the additional data in the categories for the past two weeks. One can add as much input as available within the software constraints of the neural network.

Note that a separate neuron is assigned to the output—the predicted DJIA.

Training the Network

The neural network is trained with 15 examples or training facts (5 days × 3 weeks). A sample first training fact (row one of Table 17–3) is presented in Table 17–4.

Testing and Running the Network

Testing the network should begin with a test plan containing routine and problematic examples. Predetermined thresholds of acceptance should also be set in advance. A neural network is tested by introducing actual day-to-day data and judging how close the network's output is to actual output.

Business Applications of Neural Networks

Neural networks are best applied in situations with a need for pattern recognition in which data are dynamic. Even though this technology has been applied in virtually every industry, the business sector has experienced significant successes with neural network. Financial institutions, for example, are using neural networks to simulate cash management, asset and personnel risk management, and capital investments. See Box 17–4 on page 446. In the capital investment arena, neural networks are used to simulate the reaction of investors to changes in organizational concerns such as capital structure, dividend policy, and reported earnings.

Neural networks can be used in any number of areas. Most of today's applications run on a PC with successful results. The following applications demonstrate neural networks' contribution to solving business problems in various industries.

■ **Table 17–3**   Additional NYSE Data for Neural Network Review

Inputs																Output
Day	Interest rate		Prime rate		Unemployment rate	DJIA			Blue chip change			(predicted DJIA)
		-1	-2	-1	-2		-1	-2	DJIA	-1	-2		-1	-2	
M	1.62	1.41	1.36	8.75	8.75	9.00	6.10	6.40	6.35	4031	3950	3935	+2	-1	-2	4080
T	1.42	1.43	1.43	8.75	8.75	8.75	6.25	6.46	6.35	4060	3981	3920	+3	0	-3	4185
W	1.45	1.47	1.46	8.75	8.75	8.75	6.25	6.41	6.38	4076	3976	3939	+3	0	-2	4185
Th	1.54	1.50	1.51	8.75	8.75	8.75	6.20	6.43	6.38	4050	3990	3938	+2	+1	-1	4165
F	1.51	1.50	1.41	8.75	8.50	8.75	6.15	6.44	6.39	4046	3980	3960	+1	+1	+1	4145

■ **Table 17-4** First Training Fact for DJIA Predictor Neural Network

	Neuron		Actual value
Inflation rate this week	1		1.62
Inflation rate last week	2		1.41
Inflation rate 2 weeks ago	3		1.36
Prime interest rate this week	4		8.75
Prime interest rate last week	5		8.75
Prime interest rate 2 wks. ago	6		9.00
Unemployment rate this week	7		6.10
Unemployment rate last week	8		6.40
Unemployment rate 2 wks. ago	9		6.35
NYSE fluctuations this week	10		4031
NYSE fluctuations last week	11		3950
NYSE fluctuations 2 wks. ago	12		3935
Select blue chip price change this week	13		+2
Select blue chip price change last week	14		−1
Select blue chip price change 2 wks. ago	15		−2
	16	Mon	1
	17	Tues	0
	18	Wed	0
	19	Th.	0
	20	Fri	0
	21	Mon	0
	22	Tues	0
	23	Wed	0
	24	Th.	0
	25	Fri	0
	26	Mon	0
	27	Tues	0
	28	Wed	0
	29	Th.	0
	30	Fri	0
	Pattern 1		Output
	Neuron 1		Output: DJIA actual 4080

Risk Management

A major California bank uses a neural network to appraise commercial loan applications. The network was trained on thousands of applications, half of which were approved and the other half rejected by the bank's loan officers. From this much experience, the neural network learned to pick risks that constitute a bad loan. It identifies loan applicants who are likely to default on their payments.

Box 17-4   Bond Market Allocation System

Financial forecasters now make money the new-fashioned way—they train a neural network to mimic a market, then use its predictions to guide investment. To play the market with a neural network, you need expertise in financial strategies and neural network engineering. It means choosing variables and indicators and understanding their significance and correlations. It also means choosing a neural network, specifying its structure, training it, and testing it to see if it is a good bet. As the need to combine two disciplines suggests, financial systems—like all neural network systems—are more likely to succeed if something known about the problem can be built into the neural network.

Take a look at a system that models international bond markets to allocate assets between bonds and cash. This system uses seven neural networks trained to model bond markets in seven countries. Each neural network predicts bond return one month ahead of the market it represents, passing the prediction to a software-based portfolio management system. The software system allocates funds to the markets with the best of the predicted results and imposes constraints to minimize risk. It also illustrates the coming practice of using a neural network as a model within a larger system.

The local neural networks are trained with historical data about the bond market in the country they represent. Each uses as inputs 4–8 parameters (interest rates, oil prices, ratio of precious to nonprecious metals, etc.) on a month-to-month basis between 1974 and 1988. The target output is the bond return for the next month.

During training, each network passes through the historical data repeatedly to learn how the input parameters affect each market. Ten percent of the data is held back for testing to determine when to end training.

This portfolio system returned 125 percent between 1989 and 1992. In contrast, a benchmark based on each market's portion of the global market earned 34 percent. The neural network system beat the conventional system by 3.6:1—a startling improvement in a field where small improvements are large advantages.

Source: Dan Hammerstrom, "Neural Networks at Work," *IEEE Spectrum,* June 1990, p. 30.

Credit Card Fraud Detection System

When credit card fraud is suspected, the credit card company usually asks the store to verify the customer as the rightful card holder. But many stores find following this procedure awkward. A recent neural network system used by a Pittsburgh bank determines the fraudulent nature of a credit card transaction by comparing it to the card holder's patterns of previous charges, frequency of credit card charges, and relationship between the amounts of the current and previous charges.

When one out of every 500–600 transactions is fraudulent and the bank processes roughly three million credit card transactions per month, the potential saving from a neural network's ability to detect fraudulent credit card activities should be quite high. This capability can also contribute to protecting the bank's market share by eliminating unnecessary checking of customer's proof of identity, which often causes customers to seek alternative credit cards without this hassle. ·

Arbitrage Opportunities

Neural network simulations have been built to identify possible takeover targets in advance of the tender offer announcement. Neural networks surpass the analyst's ability, because it can analyze a large number of variables to derive the answer. Other systems have been built to predict short-term movement of stock prices based on historical information.

Neural Shopping

A large neural network system is used at the checkout counters of many large retail stores, and supermarkets read the computer-legible numbers at the bottom of personal checks to speed up the check approval process. The system then displays a message to tell the checkout clerk if the check has been approved. The system looks for patterns it can use to identify and verify numerals.

Target Marketing System

This neural network system taps the marketable database of dormant customers. It evaluates the files and produces for the telemarketers the best potential customers to contact by weeding out customers who are less likely to reorder.

Signature Verification

A neural network at a commercial bank has learned to identify and verify handwritten signatures. The signature is fed into the neural network via a video camera. The signature is then compared to sample signatures of the same customer. The resulting evaluation is either to accept or reject the signature as genuine. The system has been known to achieve greater than 96 percent accuracy.

The Hecht-Nielsen Corporation (HNC) Quickstrokes Automated Data Entry System is used to recognize handwritten forms at Wyoming Department of Revenue. Before the system was installed, checks were deposited late, resulting in an estimated loss of more than $300,000 in interest income.

Loan Approval and Real Estate Analysis

Chase Manhattan Bank uses Creditview to help loan officers estimate the credit worthiness of corporate loan applicants. HNC developed a neural net system called Area Automated Property Valuation System to determine the value of residential property in California and other states.

Mortgage Appraisals

One of the most promising applications is a neural network system called AREAS that reviews mortgage appraisals. The program uses the data in the mortgage loan application with a sophisticated statistical model of real estate valuations for the immediate neighborhood, the city, and the county where the property is located. Then, the system comes up with a valuation for the property and a risk analysis for the loan. For each valuation, the cost has been less than one-half of the manual method that was also time-consuming and subject to various errors.

Other Applications

Innumerable neural network applications pop up each year. In business, applications identify qualified candidates for specific positions, optimizing airline seating, and determine fee schedules. In finance, identifying forgeries, interpreting handwritten forms, and assessing credit risks have already justified the investment for these neural networks. In manufacturing, neural network applications control quality and production line processes, select parts for an assembly line, and perform quality inspection of finished products. For example, the Florida Department of Citrus uses neural networks to perform orange juice purity evaluations with great success.

A common thread running through these applications is pattern recognition. The neural network looks for a pattern in a set of cases, classifies and evaluates patterns, and reconstructs the correct pattern with a high degree of accuracy. This technology offers business a chance to assist decision makers in the kind of work that was once relegated to human perception and judgment.

Neural networks are not magic, however. They are complex and cannot be foolproof. The key to their success is in providing the right input and matching the right kind of neural network to the problem.

■ BUILDING TOOLS

Developing neural network applications requires coding the network's learning algorithm to construct an application or using a simulator available on the market. The many simulators offer different features and learning algorithms. Among the features to consider are the diversity of implemented learning algorithms, the flexibility of accepting input data, the size of the network, and a user-friendly interface. A selected list of widely used simulators is shown in Table 17–5.

For example, BrainMaker Professional is capable of importing data from Lotus 1-2-3, dBASE, Excel, or ASCII files. Back propagation and hypersonic training system are the only learning algorithms. The software supports a network up to eight layers with 8,000 units per layer. It also provides pull-down menus, color graphics, and dialogue boxes controlled by a mouse. Another neural network simulator package is the icon-based ExploreNet, which accepts data from virtually any file. It implements 20 different learning algorithms, including back propagation. A similar capability applies to NeuralWorks Professional II Plus. The software supports more than 20 learning algorithms, including back propagation and self-organizing map. Input data can be imported from spreadsheets and databases. The system provides a wide range of graphical features to monitor the performance of the network.

■ **Table 17–5** Select NN Building Tools

Simulator	Platform (operating system)	Vendor
N-NET EX	PC DOS	AI WARE
N-NET 600	VAX:VMS	
Brain Maker	PC DOS	California Scientific Software
ExploreNet 3000	PC DOS	HNC Inc.
NDS (Nestor Development System)	PC DOS	Nestor, Inc.
Neural Works Professional II+	PC DOS	Neural Ware, Inc.

IMPLICATIONS FOR MANAGEMENT

Neural networks are fast representing a wide range of applications in business and industry. They are emerging as stand-alone or integrated with expert systems or conventional software. Despite obvious successes, neural nets are not a cureall. They involve several considerations worth discussing: cost-benefit analysis, the nature of neural learning and artificial intelligence, and maintenance.

The benefits of neural networks include improving speed, quality, and "good enough" judgment in the areas in which human judgment might be lacking or deteriorate due to fatigue, lack of motivation, or problems of recall. The benefits are both tangible and intangible. For example, if a neural network designed to evaluate paint quality and finish of a new car is to replace the human expert inspector, it will likely return tangible financial savings. Likewise, a neural network that "decides" whether a credit card transaction is a reasonable purchase based on the credit card holder's buying habits can save the issuing bank millions of dollars each year by detecting fraud. Of course, intangible benefits include better corporate image when quality and reliability of the product resulting from a neural network contribute to customer satisfaction. Indirectly, it can also contribute to image building over the long term.

The other side of benefits is the cost factor. How much is a corporation willing to spend to gear up the technology? Tangible costs involve user training, hardware-software, backup, support, and maintenance. Intangible costs are user resistance and the time it takes to sell change, especially if neural networks are trained as "artificial learners trying to compete with long-term specialists or experts in the area covered by the neural network. Management must be prepared for these problems and take steps to alleviate them.

Another issue relates to the concept of neural networks as adaptive learning systems. Given the iterative process of training a neural network, is artificial learning a "good enough" replacement for humans who learn "on the fly" using intelligence and common sense? Human decision making and problem solving are also based on their perceptions, attitudes, and beliefs in addition to methodology, use of tools, and following procedures. Human cognitions are modified by experience, which contributes to maturation that is lacking in artificial learning.

Perhaps the best a neural network can do is to advise rather than replace humans in problem solving. The fact that humans can still veto a neural network's decisions attest to the higher-level learning capacity and intelligence of humans.

Finally, organizations must address the issue of maintenance. For a neural network to stay up to date in a changing environment, it has to be retrained, which means modifications in the training set, retraining, and ongoing evaluation of the neural network. A firm that relies heavily on applications supported by this technology would need to consider maintenance and enhancement as part of the total commitment to quality assurance.

The level and frequency of maintenance often reflects the adequacy of the initial design of the neural network. Like conventional systems, a poorly thought-out problem definition or scope requires greater and more frequent changes in the system than a well-designed system. This suggests that, for a neural network to succeed, proper attention should be given to the early phase of the development life cycle—problem definition, problem justification, and gathering of the right training data for the job. Effective management of the front-end of the development life cycle could minimize unnecessary maintenance and cost.

■ SUMMARY

1. The first wave of neural networks (NNs) began in 1943 with McCullough and Pitts' work, which was later followed by Hebb who showed how learning can be achieved by modifying the connections between the neurons and altering the effects of various inputs.

2. A NN is an information system of electronically interconnected basic processing elements called neurons. NNs are ideal for solving cumbersome problems that traditional computers have difficulty tracking, but are terrible at problems that computers can do well. The differences between NNs and digital computers include the following:

   a. Computers are programmed; NNs are trained.

   b. In a computer, data is stored in memory; in an NN, data is stored throughout the network as patterns of weights, interconnections, and states of neurons.

   c. NNs are adaptive; computers are not.

   d. In a digital computer, the answers are exact; in a NN, answers "evolve."

   e. Digital computers are not good at generalization; NNs are.

   f. NNs are temporal associators; digital computers are not.

   g. NNs are good at pattern recognition; digital computers are not.

3. NNs can be contrasted with expert systems as follows:

   a. Expert systems learn by rules; NNs learn by example.

   b. Expert systems are sequential in nature and explain their decisions; NNs don't have explanatory facility.

   c. Expert systems use rules to duplicate the expertise and use data to process the rules; in a NN, the user supplies the input and the output for NN to come up with the process.

   d. With the parallel structure of NNs, all factors are considered at once; expert systems do their homework sequentially.

   e. NNs continue learning as the problem environment changes; expert systems depend on complete data before offering a final solution.

   f. An NN is more effective at developing a knowledge base with experiential data than are expert systems.
   Yet, NNs and expert systems share some characteristics. For example, NN learns from experience in the same way that an expert develops personal decision-making skills.

4. NNs have several limitations:

   a. They are unattractive if accurate answers are required.

   b. Learning is not easy and takes extensive computer time.

   c. They do not have the explanatory powers of expert systems.

   d. A complex problem means a large network.

5. A NN consists of neurons, connected by axons that receive inputs from other neurons via dendrites. Communication between neurons is carried out by these input-output pathways. A neuron evaluates the

inputs, determines their weights, sums the weighted inputs, and compares the total to a threshold. If the sum is greater than the threshold, the neuron fires. Otherwise, it generates no signal.

6. Learning occurs when the network changes weights and modifies its activity in response to its inputs. Making weight adjustments by backing up from the output is called back propagation. Learning may be supervised or self-supervised.

7. Business applications of neural networks are many. They range from risk management and bond market allocation systems to signature verification. A wide variety of NN simulators is available on the market.

■ TERMS TO LEARN

Axon a neural element that carries signals (output) away.

Back propogation a supervised learning mode, in which an output error signal is passed back through the network changing connecting weights to minimize that error.

Dendrite a neural element that carries signals (input) into the network.

Input stimulation level in a neural network.

Neural network (NN) an information system modeled after the human brain's network of electrically interconnected processing elements called neurons; a self-programming system that creates a model based on its inputs and outputs.

Neuron a processing element or unit.

Output sum of inputs multiplied by their respective weights.

Output layer the layer of nodes that produce a neural network result.

Supervised learning learning by reinforcement; associating a set of input patterns with specific output to minimize error.

Synapse an axon–dendrite connection; an input-output pathway.

Threshold see transfer function.

Training set pairs of inputs and outputs applicable to a neural network used to train the network before it becomes operational.

Transfer function a limiter that mirrors the input within a given range; a linear function that has been clipped to minimum and maximum values.

Unsupervised learning adjusting the neural network solely through direct confrontation with new experiences; self organization.

Weight an adjustable value associated with a connection between neurons or nodes in a network; synaptic strength.

■ REVIEW QUESTIONS

1. Define a neural network in your own words. What does the technology attempt to do?

2. Explain how neural nets differ from conventional digital computers.

3. Historically speaking, who would you give credit for developing NN concept?

4. "The interesting aspect of a NN is its known contributions in solving cumbersome prob- lems that traditional computers have found difficult to track." Do you agree? Illustrate.

5. Distinguish between:
   a. neuron and axon
   b. synapse and dendrite
   c. synaptic strength and transfer function

6. Explain how an NN works. Give an example.

7. "Neural networks are temporal associations." What does it mean? Elaborate.

8. In your opinion, how severe are the limitations of NN? Be specific.

9. How are NNs different from expert systems? Explain.

10. Explain in some detail how NNs learn.

11. How is the forward pass different from the backward pass in back propagation?

12. How are inputs and outputs used to contribute to a solution? Give an example.

13. Search the literature and write an essay detailing a neural network application in business. What did you learn from this exercise?

EXERCISES AND CASES

1. According to the Turing principle, a conventional computer can compare anything for which an algorithm can be found. At the end of the day, a neural computer is just another algorithm. The question is, why should there be a field called neurocomputing? Ask this question of someone in computer science or a professional in the field to stimulate ideas for answering the question.

2. Review the literature and cite one application of supervised learning and another of self-supervised learning. What do you conclude is the difference between the two forms of learning?

3. Compare artificial and biological neural networks. What aspects of biological networks are emulated (and not emulated) by artificial neural networks? Explain.

4. Think of a set of consecutive numbers from 1–8. Your job is to identify several numbers and determine whether they are members of the set. For example, take number 9. You ask yourself, "Is 9 a member of the set 1–8?" The answer is no. You do the same for a series of numbers, and your answer for each number is yes or no. Is this type of problem a candidate for parallel processing or neural network?

5. You have a set of six alphabetic characters (A, S, T, U, T, E). Like a Scrabble game, your job is to generate as many words from these characters as possible. If you were to do it manually, you'd think of a word, verify it through the dictionary, and move on to the next word. How would a conventional computer go through the same process? Is this type of job a candidate for parallel processing or neural network?

6. Identify whether each of the following applications is a candidate for expert system or neural network:

a. predict weather conditions
b. diagnose a diabetic foot problem
c. verify check signature
d. recognize characters on an invoice

SELECTED REFERENCES

Al-Mashouq, Khalid A. and Irving S. Reed. "The Use of Neural Nets To Combine Equalization With Decoding for Severe Intersymbol Interference Channels." *IEEE Transactions on Neural Networks,* November 1994, pp. 982–988.

Aleksander, Igor and Helen Morton. *An Introduction to Neural Computing.* New York; Chapman & Hall, 1991.

Angell, Bob and Tom Murphy. "Review: Faster Than a Speeding Network." *AI Expert,* November 1992, pp. 50–55.

Barr, Dean S. and Ganesh Mani. "Goal-Based Reasoning for Securities Analysis." *AI Expert,* February 1994, pp. 22–29.

Bochereau, L.; P. Bourgine; and G. Deffuant. "A General Framework for Supervised Learning: Probably Almost Bayesian Algorithms." *Journal of Economic Dynamics & Control,* January 1994, pp. 97–118.

Carpenter, Wm. C. and Margery E. Hoffman. "Training Backprop Neural Networks." *AI Expert,* March 1995, pp. 30–33.

Caudill, Maureen. "GRNN and Bear It." *AI Expert,* May 1993, pp. 28–33.

Chase, Victor D. "Clearing Up Fuzzy Logic and Neural Networks." *Appliance Manufacturer,* July 1994, p. 8.

Chung, Yunkung and Andrew Kusiak. "Grouping Parts With a Neural Network. *Journal of Manufacturing Systems* 13, no. 4 (1994), pp. 262–275.

Eom, Sean B. "Intelligent Systems for Business: Expert Systems With Neural Networks." *Interfaces,* May-June 1994, pp. 150–151.

Etheridge, Harlan L. and Richard C. Brooks. "Neural Networks: A New Technology." *CPA Journal,* March 1994, pp. 36–39.

Freeman, James A. "Neural Networks in Mathematica." *AI Expert,* November 1992, pp. 26–35.

Gallant, Stephen I. *Neural Network Learning and Expert Systems.* Cambridge, MA: MIT Press, 1993.

Gallant, Steven I. and John G. Taylor. "Neural Network Learning and Expert Systems." *IEEE Transactions on Neural Networks,* September 1994, pp. 854–855.

Hammerstrom, Dan. "Working With Neural Networks." *IEEE Spectrum,* July 1993, pp. 46–53.

Hassoun, Mohamad H. *Fundamentals of Artificial Neural Networks.* Cambridge, MA: MIT Press, 1995.

Hiotis, Andre. "Inside a Self-Organizing Map." *AI Expert,* April 1993, pp. 38–43.

Holsapple, Clyde W.; R. Pakath; Jacob Varghese; and J. S. Zaveri. "Learning by Problem Processors: Adaptive Decision Support Systems." *Decision Support Systems,* September 1993, pp. 85–108.

Hsiao, Chien-Hua; Ching-Teng Lin; and Michael Cassidy. "Application of Fuzzy Logic and Neural Networks to Automatically Detect Freeway Traffic Incidents." *Journal of Transportation Engineering,* September-October 1994, pp. 752–772.

Humpert, Benedikt K. "Improving Back Propagation With a New Error Function." *Neural Networks 7,* no. 8 (1994), pp. 1191–1192.

Hung, Chuan-Chang. "Building a Neuro-Fuzzy Learning Control System." *AI Expert,* November 1993, pp. 40–49.

Jin, B.; A. R. Hurson; and L. L. Miller. "Neural Network-Based Decision Support for Incomplete Database Systems." In *Analysis of Neural Network Applications Conference Proceedings,* May 29–31, 1991, pp. 62–75.

Kamimura, R. "Application of the Recurrent Neural Network to the Problem of Language Acquisition." In *Analysis of Neural Network Applications Conference Proceedings,"* May 29–31, 1991, pp. 6–13.

Kattan, Michael W.; Dennis A. Adams; and Michael S. Parks. "A Comparison of Machine Learning With Human Judgment." *Journal of Management Information Systems,* Spring 1993, pp. 37–57.

Kempka, Anthony A. "Activating Neural Networks: Part II." *AI Expert,* August 1994, pp. 42–49.

Kohn, Philip. "Simple Neural Networks Made Easy." *IEEE Spectrum* 31, no. 18 (April 1994).

Lawrence, Jeannette. *Introduction to Neural Networks.* Grass Valley, CA: California Scientific Software, 1991.

Levine, Daniel S. and Manuel Aparicio. *Neural Networks for Knowledge Representation and Inference.* Hillsdale, NJ: Lawrence Erlbaum Associates, Inc., 1994.

Li, Eldon Y. "Artificial Neural Networks and Their Business Applications." *Information & Management,* November 1994, pp. 303–313.

Nelson, Marilyn M. and W. T. Illingworth. *A Practical Guide to Neural Nets.* Reading, MA: Addison-Wesley, 1991.

Perry, Wm. G. Jr. "What Is Neural Network Software? *Journal of Systems Management,* September 1994, pp. 12–15.

Phatak, D. S. and I. Koren. "Connectivity and Performance Tradeoffs in the Cascade Correlation Learning Architecture." *IEEE Transactions on Neural Networks,* November 1994, pp. 930–935.

Piovoso, M. J.; A. J. Owens; A Guez; and E. Nilssen. "Neural Network Process Control." In *Analysis of Neural Network Applications Conference Proceedings,* May 29–31, 1991, pp. 84–95.

Piramuthu, Selwyn; Michael J. Shaw; and James A. Gentry. "A Classification Approach Using Multi-Layered Neural Networks." *Decision Support Systems,* June 1994, pp. 509–525.

Plummer, John. "Tighter Process Control With Neural Networks." *AI Expert,* October 1993, pp. 49–55.

Rocha, A. F. *Neural Nets: A Theory for Brains and Machines.* New York: Springer-Verlag, 1992.

Rumelhart, David E.; Bernard Widrow; and Michael A. Lehr. "The Basic Ideas in Neural Networks." *Communication of the ACM,* March 1994, pp. 86–92.

Schmuller, Joseph. "Lesions in Neural Networks." *PC AI,* April 1995, pp. 16–21.

Schocken, Shimon and Gad Ariav. "Neural Networks for Decision Support: Problems and Opportunities." *Decision Support Systems,* June 1994, pp. 393–414.

Smith, Leslie S. "A Framework for Neural Net Specification." *IEEE Transactions on Software Engineering,* July 1992, pp. 601–612.

Stein, Roger. "Preprocessing Data for Neural Networks." *AI Expert,* March 1993, pp. 32–37.

Takahashi, Kazuhiko and Ichiro Yamada. "Neural Network-Based Learning Control of Flexible Mechanism With Application to a Single-Link Flexible Arm." *Journal of Dynamic Systems, Measurement, and Control,* December 1994, pp. 792–795.

Velasco, Tomas and Mark R. Rowe. "Back Propagation Artificial Neural Networks for the Analysis of Quality Control Charts." *Computers & Industrial Engineering,* September 1993, pp. 397–400.

Venugopal, V. and W. Baets. "Neural Networks and Their Applications in Marketing Management."

Journal of Systems Management, September 1994, pp. 16–21.

Versaggi, Matthew R. "Understanding Conflicting Data." *AI Expert,* April 1995, pp. 21–25.

Wang, Jun. "Artificial Neural Networks Versus Natural Neural Networks." *Decision Support Systems,* June 1994, pp. 415–429.

Wang, Tao. "Improving Recall in Associate Memories by Dynamic Threshold." *Neural Networks* 7, no. 9 (1994), pp. 1379–1385.

Weiss, Sholom M. and Casimir A. Kulikowski. *Computer Systems That Learn: Classification and Prediction Methods from Statistics, Neural Nets, Machine Learning, and Expert Systems.* San Mateo, CA: M. Kaufmann, 1991.

Yoon, Youngohc; Tor Guimaraes; and George Swales. "Integrating Artificial Neural Networks With Rule-Based Expert Systems. *Decision Support Systems,* June 1994, pp. 497–507.

Zadeh, Lotfi A. "Fuzzy Logic, Neural Networks, and Soft Computing." *Communications of the ACM,* March 1994, pp. 77–84.

MANAGERIAL AND ORGANIZA- TIONAL CONSIDER- ATIONS

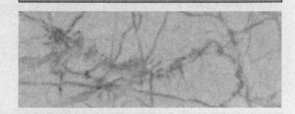

Chapter ∎ 18

Organizational and Managerial Impact

ORGANIZATIONAL IMPLICATIONS OF EXPERT SYSTEMS

Many recent technological events have taken place which have changed the way that we think about our organizations and how we operate them. Some of these changes have influenced core operations of businesses by transforming basic organizational structures or by altering traditional patterns of interpersonal interactions. Other changes have revolutionized external competitive relationships within industries as well as among industries.

From an organizational perspective, the expert system is one of the most exciting aspects of information systems technology today. The expert system appears to have many practical implications for a variety of organizational activities. Further, expert systems seem to provide a real means for simultaneously providing increased quality, productivity and innovation within nearly all segments of organizational activity. For example, we see applications at lower organizational levels in the insurance and banking industries. In a similar fashion, we also see applications in areas such as strategic corporate planning.

The promise of expert systems is so tantalizing because most people are only able to see small glimpses of what can be—the success stories. Consequently, management in many organizations face a dilemma, "Are expert systems a panacea, the missing link to greater productivity, quality and innovation, or are expert systems a Pandora's box filled with hidden surprises for the unwary?"

To help answer the preceding question, a national survey was undertaken. The major purpose was to examine the perceptions of information system professionals on the development and use of expert systems within American organizations. The sample was taken from the membership of the Data Processing Management Association (DPMA). Specifically, 1,858 DPMA members were selected to be part of the survey. Of the survey questionnaires mailed to individual DPMA members selected, 505 usable questionnaires were returned.

What general observations about expert systems can be made from the responses provided in the survey? Two general observations are worth noting: (1) there appears to be much diversity of opinion about the emerging relationship of expert systems within U.S. business, and (2) the effect of the expert system is anticipated to be widespread. Expert systems will affect a variety of organizations within our economy as well as potentially every aspect of an organization's operation.

In terms of adoption of expert systems, most respondents emphasized a streamlining of operations and increasing quality by reducing time and ensuring greater consistency as the two key factors in system adoption. Another finding was the expert systems will not affect all functional areas within the organization equally, at least as currently perceived. The respondents also felt that changes basic to an organization's structure and operations will also take place in addition to changes within functional activities. Activities common to every function such as how people are paid, who will be hired, and the kind of work that is done will be influenced with the introduction of expert system.

CREATING POLICY

As the current study seems to point out, much of what is happening in expert systems is uncharted territory. If ignored, this condition of uncertainty can result in competitive disadvantages at a later time. If managed properly, the uncertainty can lead to new and perhaps unanticipated opportunities. Implementing an expert systems policy would provide the orderly process necessary to facilitate an integration of the advantageous aspects of expert systems. An effective expert system policy has a twofold impact in that it would ensure appropriate actions are taken while simultaneously standardizing the manner in which the actions are taken.

Rather than letting a natural diffusion process take place, an effective policy will ensure that expert systems get introduced within all of the appropriate functional areas. Further, an effective policy will also standardize how we go about introducing expert systems into the organization. Finally, the policy should feature heavy doses of training to ensure that people know what expert systems are and what is available.

It should be emphasized at this point, that having an expert systems policy does not mean making everyone do everything the same way. Rather it means that when someone has a problem they know where to go for help. The expert systems policy should help these people solve their problems rather than try to make them fit their problems into some standardized procedures.

We are still left with the question posed earlier, "Will expert systems be a panacea or the proverbial Pandora's box?" As with most technology, probably neither of the positions will ever be realized. If we heed the wisdom of John Wooden, who was not only one of the best coaches of our time but in fact one of our best managers, the promise of expert systems will become a reality of organizational life. The wisdom is simple, "Failing to prepare is preparing to fail."

Source: Louis E. Raho, David Drebmer, and James Belohlav, "Organizational Implications of Expert Systems," *Information Executive,* Summer 1991, p. 17ff.

AT A GLANCE

One of the technological feats incorporated into today's business is expert systems. Unquestionably, it is one of the most exciting aspects of information technology. But inherent in the use of expert systems are impact on productivity, shifts in job roles and responsibility, redistribution of authority and power, and changes in personnel, work, and relationships. The productivity factor has so far been on the side of positive impact. The same can be said of decision-making quality and the timeliness of decision making.

Expert system impact on organization structure and channels of communication depends on the level at which expert systems are used, the kinds of problems they attempt to address, and the philosophy of the organization toward allowing technology to be an aid (versus a replacement) to management. Job roles and responsibilities can be affected, depending on how well experts build their own systems and knowledge engineering can be automated, assigning the role of knowledge engineer as a front-end job.

The discussion of whether expert systems will impact employment favorably can be answered only after enough applications have been installed. In the interim, a number of factors merit consideration. Primary among those considerations is inherent fear of unemployment, which will continue as long as corporations have insecure managers and expert systems are improperly introduced into the organization.

In any case, corporations are now recognizing knowledge as a corporate asset. The next step is to adopt an approach in managing knowledge. The current problem, however, is the lack of standards or tools to assist in this endeavor. This area is slowly but surely being improved through increased installations of expert systems.

What You Will Learn

By the end of this chapter, you should know the following:

1. The impact of expert systems on employment, organization structure, and channels of communication in the firm.

2. The psychological impact of expert systems.

3. How corporations approach knowledge management.

> Failing to prepare is preparing to fail.
>
> —John Wooden

INTRODUCTION

Through the course of this book, the discussion moved from the initial conceptualization and scoping of the problem domain to system deployment and user training. What cuts across the expert system development life cycle are the organizational factors resulting from the introduction and implementation of this fast-paced technology. Other managerial factors relate to people, jobs, and the way decisions are made. These factors may have far-reaching effects on the organization's ability to compete in the marketplace.

From an organizational viewpoint, the expert system is one of the most exciting aspects of information technology. It is the kind of transformation that people are only beginning to appreciate. Unlike the slower data processing and information processing of the past three decades, knowledge engineering and knowledge representation are building a foundation in more and more organizations. They have already earned respectability in many of the *Fortune 500* firms. Top management has realized improvements in productivity, quality decision making, and preservation of the knowledge that once was lost with departing or retiring employees. Whether expert systems are viewed as an extension of information processing or as a unique technology addressing special types of problems, the fact remains that knowledge has a special meaning. Information consists of facts and data, whereas *knowledge* is judgment and know-how that is applied to interpret available information and manage a given situation.

Inherent in the use of expert systems, however, is a host of organizational and managerial problems:

- Impact on productivity
- Shifts in roles and responsibilities
- Improvement in information processing capacity and decision making
- Redistribution of authority and power
- Changes in personnel, work, and relationships

The goal is not only to evaluate the technical aspects of expert systems but also their effect on employees and the overall functioning of the business. Therefore, organizations need to consider a number of key questions: What will this new technology mean in terms of organizational changes? How will it affect people and the way they make decisions? What is their likely reaction if they perceive the expert system to be a threat to their career?

In this chapter, these issues are addressed as they relate to expert systems. Separating them from information-based systems issues is not easy, because expert systems is a relatively young field with limited empirical evidence. Some of the discussions, then, may overlap with information-based systems in various areas. Remember, however, that expert systems is one possible management issue, but not *the* issue in terms of organizational impact.

■ AREAS OF ORGANIZATIONAL IMPACT

The Productivity Factor

Surveys have shown that the most important reason companies look at expert system technology is to achieve gains in productivity. For example, Raho and Belohlav conducted a survey of information systems professionals to examine the perception of the use of expert systems in U.S. business. As shown in Figure 18–1, productivity was reported as the second most important reason for adopting expert systems. The most important reason was consistency of decisions and the time factor. By improving productivity, an organization not only improves its profitability but it remains competitive. To remain competitive, companies, such as Texas Instruments (TI), for example, build expert systems to increase management productivity. One of its current systems guides managers through the bureaucratic government requisition forms 20 times faster. TI expects to save an average of $2 million per year through the use of this system.

Other companies have experienced similar results.

- Dupont has developed a variety of expert systems for functions such as distillation plant control, system problem diagnosis, chemical and electrical equipment repairs, and industrial chemical processing applications. For example, the company developed 50 expert systems for diagnosing and correcting process control problems, a 600-rule planning and scheduling system, product design systems such as Packaging Advisor, and a system (called Transportation Emergency Response Planner) that helps employees deal with chemical spills. The firm estimates develop-

Figure 18–1   Reasons for Adopting Expert System

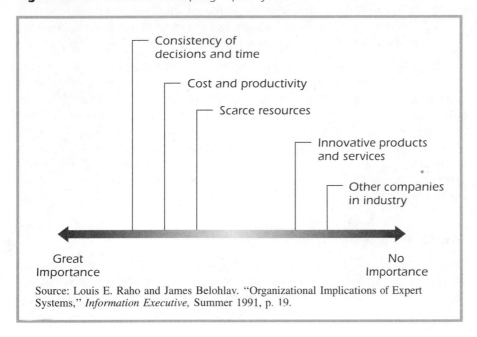

Source: Louis E. Raho and James Belohlav. "Organizational Implications of Expert Systems," *Information Executive,* Summer 1991, p. 19.

ment costs of an in-house expert system at about $25,000, with average annual savings of $100,000 and a 400 percent return on investment. The key impact has been reduced maintenance and greater process efficiency, which accounts for the high return on expert system investment.

■ The XCON expert system of Digital Equipment Corporation (DEC) for configuring VAX computers costs $2.5 million annually to maintain, but saves about $40 million. Like Dupont, DEC has made extensive use of expert systems. The firm now has more than 50 major expert systems in operation, contributing $200 million in annual savings. In addition to these enormous savings, expert systems have provided the firm considerable advantages in formulating marketing strategy and vastly reduced product development time.

■ American Express's Credit Authorization Advisor has improved decision-making accuracy between 45 to 67 percent. The initial goal of the project was to reduce bad authorization and improve accuracy when approving purchases over a specific dollar amount. The system was successful meeting the goal, reducing bad authorization by 76 percent.

■ The Eloquent Expert Reservation System implemented by the Balsams Hotel of New Hampshire had definite impact and led to the following results:

  ■ Better customer service

  ■ Fewer single-night vacancies between guest stays (a major goal of the hotel)

  ■ A comprehensive method for altering marketing and sales strategies

  ■ A dramatically reduced training time for new reservationists

■ An expert auditing system (Auditing Assistant) implemented by Chemical Bank immediately increased auditing speed and quality. From an organizational standpoint, the system was judged by auditors to be a useful workload reducer.

In most of these installations, the success of the expert system was attributed in part to extensive user involvement during the building phase, ease of system use, compatibility with user work habits, and the champion's success selling the system as an "assistant" rather than a replacement. These cases also show that expert systems have the potential to improve the productivity of the firm in certain problem domains and to improve the way it is used for competitive advantage. Improperly managed expert systems can also degenerate either due to lack of maintenance or being placed in the wrong area of operation.

Improvement in Decision Making

Expert systems can change the way an organization does business by contributing to more efficient and reliable decision making. Decisions produced by expert systems tend to be consistent and not subject to personal bias, changing mood or attitude, or sensitivity to the environment. Consistency means unwavering advice and standardization at all times.

One area in which standardized decision making is desirable is in personnel recruiting. Through the use of an expert system advisor, each candidate can be evaluated based on criteria set in advance. The evaluation is carried out without regard to color, age, sex, creed, or national origin. The discriminating aspect of decision making is eliminated, although the subjective factor of "fit" based on one's looks, alertness, and mannerism during the interview continues to be a recruitment element only humans can judge.

Impact on Organization Structure

Expert systems can alter the structure of an organization and its channels of communication. If the purpose of the expert system is to eliminate the intervention of the human expert in the decision process, not only will the channels of communication be altered, but the job responsibilities and reporting relationships of the expert could change as well. For instance, if an expert system diagnoses mainframe problems, it bypasses the expert (the diagnostic engineer) for initial diagnosis. The decisions can be provided directly via telecommunication channels to field maintenance teams for followup. See Box 18–1. In this respect, the channel of communication is altered by eliminating consultation of the human expert. The job description of the expert would also change.

Expert systems can also alter the organization's hierarchical structure. In smaller organizations, many of the decisions made by middle management can be eliminated. By utilizing an expert system, lower-level management can make decisions based on the expertise of a middle manager. An expert system could enable a line supervisor to perform production scheduling—typically a middle management function—based on experience and historical data.

Related to this factor, expert systems can reduce top management's reliance on middle management for certain key decisions. For example, in the purchase

Box 18-1   Expert System–Guided Maintenance

A major hardware vendor uses a Maintenance Diagnostic Tracker (MDT)—an expert system that monitors the integrity of key components of the customer's mainframe. Each component has a life expectancy measured by hours of operation. In addition to actual hours of usage, the expert system determines in a systematic way how soon a component might fail, depending on the nature of the application, the tasks performed, etc.

The MDT is linked to each customer's computer system by telecommunication lines. When the expert system decides certain component(s) should be replaced, it queries the inventory and reserves the part(s) to replace the suspected component on the customer's system. The field service representative simultaneously receives the report, picks up the part, and arrives at the customer's site—all within 24 hours.

This operation has reduced unnecessary customer system downtime by 95 percent. Maintenance cost has also been reduced by 45 percent.

Source: Anonymous.

of a secondary business, the conventional approach requires that a middle manager gather a great deal of financial data, review it, and recommend a strategy on the proposed venture. An expert system with the knowledge and expertise of a middle manager could provide similar recommendations to senior management quickly and reliably. If the knowledge of middle management is distributed to other levels of the organization, the need for middle management could be reduced or eliminated, contributing to the flattening of the organization's hierarchical structure and the redistribution of power and authority within the organization. Such a change could give top management greater leverage and more control over various strategic functions.

Shifts in Roles and Responsibilities

One area that frequently experiences shifts in **job roles** is that of the domain expert and the knowledge engineer. Today's expert systems are built by knowledge engineers. With improvements in expert system skills and literacy, however, domain experts should be able to build their own systems more quickly and reliably than through the knowledge engineer. Logical errors would be near zero, and turnaround time could be reduced tenfold. The domain expert will not only have the knowledge but the expertise to represent the knowledge. There is no more misinterpretation or misrepresentation during acquisition representation. The main limitation in excluding a knowledge engineer, however, continues to be the lack of independent verification and validation prior to certification.

The role of the knowledge engineer is also expected to change. The job should now shift to a front-end function, one of exploring and recognizing areas of operation in the business that are candidates for expert systems. This kind of contribution can be vital in areas experiencing backlogged applications or in planning or carrying out such applications.

Expert system technology created the unique role of the knowledge engineer. The job skills and job requirements of the knowledge engineer will become more fully developed and standardized with more experience in knowledge engineering. Because of the importance of their role, knowledge engineers need to be properly trained in cognitive psychology and communication skills in order to do the best job possible.

In terms of responsibilities, system builders are expected to take on more responsibility. If the system is successful, the responsibility is elevated to a higher level. When discussing the popular XCON expert system, a software manager at DEC commented, "XCON is the only expert system I know of today where the financial lights would dim if it were unplugged. That is tremendous responsibility."

Yet, when one person gains, someone else could also lose. Employees replaced by expert systems often lose clout. To some degree, their creativity (and with it their motivation) is compromised. A staff member replaced by the XCON expert system once said, "It was more fun before XCON, when you had to figure out each system. You got to keep in touch with many parts of the company—sales, engineering, and marketing—to know what was happening. We still do that now, but not so much."

In other cases, those whose knowledge is "canned" in a knowledge-based system are not always hurt. Adding an expert system means reinforcing the human expert's assessment and conclusions. Expert systems lend support to the belief that information technology would expand the ability of an expert. A common language is fostered when an expert system is used, which allows knowledgeable individuals to communicate more effectively than before. With common language, the performance of complex tasks also improves.

Whenever changes occur in job roles or job assignments, management must be alert to any unexpected impact of the change on the new installation. Once an expert system is implemented, qualified **knowledge workers** are needed to maintain it at all times. A firm needs to plan for and support the maintenance function. For example, DEC's XCON system created 40 programmer positions to maintain the knowledge base around the clock. Due to the continuing changes in the knowledge base, more than one-half of the knowledge base was rewritten each year.

■ IMPACT ON EMPLOYMENT

As discussed in the preceding chapter, expert systems are giving birth to a new class of technology—systems that perform tasks requiring reasoning, judgment, and "intelligence" once performed only by humans. An often-voiced concern is whether these systems, in reducing human toil, will contribute to unemployment.

As with most issues, this question has prompted two opposing views: One views expert systems as another type of technology with the potential to expand a firm's economic opportunities and thus expand employment. The contrasting view assumes that anything people do, expert systems can also do. Therefore, even if expert systems create more work, this work can also be handled by expert systems without net addition of jobs for humans. Based on experience to date, the shift appears to be more in the direction of the latter view: expert systems contribute to a reduction in human labor needed to produce goods and services.

Historical Basis

If one looks at the argument that automation (including expert systems) will not result in unemployment, no historical evidence supports the contrary view that improvement in productivity leads to loss of jobs. For years, firms that used efficient productivity tools were more likely to increase in size and profitability. So, automation alone cannot be the prime cause of unemployment. Consider the U.S. banking industry as an illustration of this point. Increased productivity through check-encoding machines, check sorter/readers, computer-generated microfiche, PC-driven asset-liability management systems, automated teller machines, and expert loan advisors (expert system application) have resulted in increased business and improved accuracy in most banks.

Those who argue that automation (including expert systems) causes increasing unemployment provide several reasons to support their position. For example, over the past two decades, unemployment in the United States appears to have grown. When people lose their jobs during economic downturns, many blame their plight on robots and other automated tools.

The prediction of increased unemployment due to automation is supported in the writings of Nobel Prize-winning economist Wassily Leontief. He said that

> ... over the next 30–40 years, many people will be displaced, creating massive problems of unemployment and dislocation. In the last century, there was an analogous problem with horses. They became unnecessary with the advent of the tractors, automobiles, and trucks. . . . So what happened to horses will happen to people, unless the government can redistribute the fruits of the new technology.

One factor that favors further workforce reduction is the surge in automating white-collar work. This area is a fertile ground for knowledge-based systems. Since more than half of the labor force is engaged in information-processing activities that include management functions (planning, decision making, communicating), expert systems used for strategic planning programs, approving or disapproving loans, or even recommending the merger of two firms offers the potential to replace many of these laborers by performing these complex tasks.

Fear of Unemployment

Instead of welcoming the productivity and impact of automation and expert systems, many people resist their introduction for fear of losing jobs and income. This is highlighted by Leontief in Box 18–2.

Many people derive intrinsic as well as extrinsic rewards from work. In addition to salaries and wages, a person's job can offer feelings of accomplishment, contribution to the growth of the firm and community, job satisfaction, opportunity to utilize one's abilities, and enhanced personal identity. See Box 18–3. When people lose their jobs, psychological shock comes from losing income and dignity, along with the obvious financial impact on their lifestyle.

Although one can easily argue that expert systems, unlike former automated technologies, will represent knowledge bases and be capable of performing inexpensively intelligent tasks once done by departing experts. They may even replace the generally more costly and "moody" human labor. Yet, the stronger argument is that expert systems will improve the quality and reliability of decision making, support existing managerial functions, and impact positively on the way firms do business.

An alternative view to Leontief's, is the trend in the computer industry. Computers were initially used in the 1960s and 1970s to save on labor costs and shrink employment. For example, a payroll department that once employed 60

Box 18–2   Fear of Losing One's Job

Adam and Eve enjoyed, before they were expelled from Paradise, a high standard of living without working. After their expulsion, they and their successors were condemned to eke out a miserable existence, working from dawn to dusk. The history of technological progress over the past 200 years is essentially the human species working its way slowly and steadily back into paradise. What would happen, however, if we suddenly found ourselves in it? With all goods and services provided without work, no one would be gainfully employed. Being unemployed means receiving no wages. As a result, until appropriate new income policies were formulated to fit the changed technological conditions, everyone would starve in Paradise.

Source: W. W. Leontief, "The Distribution of Work and Income," *Scientific American,* September 1982, p. 192.

people could be run by two people using a computerized package. Later in 1980s, the goal was to use computer technology to generate more business and sales revenue through the computer's assumption of mundane tasks, thereby increasing rather than decreasing employment. With expert systems designed to advise, diagnose, and provide intelligent solutions to serious problems, the outcome is bound to stabilize rather than erode employment. With the resulting improvement in decision making and overall productivity, employment is more likely to increase rather than decrease over the long run.

As more expert systems are built and organizations learn how to adapt to their positive contributions, a maturation of the business occurs, which prompts decision makers to look for other ways to generate more business, resulting in further employment rather than displacement. This cycle is more consistent with past experience with computers. But because of the relative newness of expert system technology, this prediction will take time to prove one way or the other.

PSYCHOLOGICAL IMPACT

Expert systems, like information systems, create a certain mystique surrounding the way they generate solutions or advice. Users take for granted that expert systems cannot be wrong, since the system is based on the knowledge of the human expert. This view can be dangerous, because expert systems can only be as correct as the human expert.

More and more expert systems will be able to perform hazardous jobs more safely and quickly than humans can. Although few deny that expert system-guided robots in hazardous jobs (waste disposal, mining, and bomb detection) is desirable, some skeptics fear that the use of expert systems in untested situations could potentially put humans at risk. The use of expert systems in air traffic control or medical diagnosis, for example, seem attractive. But one must realize that expert systems are as likely to fail as their human counterpart. Their "blind spots" come from the domain expert's own less-than-perfect knowledge.

Another psychological consideration is the tendency for expert systems (automation in general) to have a dehumanizing effect. The capability of programming a computer to represent human intelligence and experience can

Box 18-3   Replaced by an Expert System

In October 1994, a local area network (LAN) was installed at a medium-size corporation whose services included security, commercial maintenance, and installation of satellite dishes. The LAN server was loaded with applications, including an integrated accounting package, E-mail, word processing, and a Maintenance Advisor—an expert system designed to monitor the maintenance status of satellite dishes.

Two months later, the president of the firm called with a complaint that he is unable to download information related to the expert system. After a brief review of the network, it was soon discovered that the manager in charge of the system removed the main menu so that applications are accessed by entering a command on the cursor line rather than an option on the menu. As a result, no one other than the manager is able to access the Maintenance Advisor.

During a lengthy meeting, the manager alleged that the main menu was removed to allow room for more memory on the hard disk. When he was shown that the main menu occupied less than 6,000 bytes of memory and that he still had over 200 megabytes of memory left, he admitted that removing the main menu discouraged the use of Maintenance Advisor. He thought that this "what you call an expert system" was a stupid idea.

Toward the end of the session, it was obvious that the manager at one time had total control over all applications. He also used to take calls from clients with satellite dish problems and decided who should do the maintenance on them. With a menu-driven LAN system, several supervisors in the building (including the president) would be able to download information about virtually any application.

The main menu was then reloaded and the LAN server's hard disk was upgraded so that the new hard disk was operating at 27 percent utilization. A new manager also took over the network. The corporation initiated a training program for all supervisors and authorized personnel in the use of the network.

Source: Alrod Corporation, "Maintenance Advisor," October 1994.

also create a tendency in individuals to wonder about their self-worth or status in the organization. The expectation that expert systems can work more efficiently and judge more fairly than humans forces individuals to question their ability to contribute. Loss of confidence can promote alienation and resistance to the impending change.

A third way of looking at the psychological effect of expert systems is their seductive qualities. An individual could easily become so impressed with the "artificial" expert as to become dependent on it, using its solutions as a substitute for human interaction and higher-level decision making. Additionally, expert systems are very compliant, don't talk back, and are nonthreatening in this regard. The same cannot be said about the human counterpart. One characteristic of expert systems that can lead to this sort of blind affiliation is the dialogue that includes personal pronouns such as "I think," "I believe," "the system recommends." Such human qualities embedded in an expert system can seduce the user into believing that the expert system is a fellow person, a peer, a consultant, or someone to believe in.

The psychological effects of expert systems—justification, intimidation, loss of self-confidence, and seduction—can be minimized with advance planning and proper training. Selling of the goodness of expert systems across all organizational levels is an important factor in their success and the management of their psychological effects. This is the area in which champions can earn their wings promoting the change.

In order to reduce its psychological effects, an expert system needs to be user-friendly and include words such as "probably," "perhaps," "maybe," and "the data indicate" in the statements or solutions to show that the computer can be "off" or not 100 percent certain at times. Numerical and mathematical outputs should be limited to give the user a more discriminating attitude towards the expert system's "opinions."

Educating the user in computer and expert system skills can greatly reduce the psychological effects. Building one's own expert system, for example, takes the mystification and intimidation out of it. It could discourage any elitism that is sometimes created along with the expert system.

◼ MANAGING CORPORATE KNOWLEDGE

Until the early 1980s, information was considered to be one of the organization's most important assets. It continues to be highly valued in most organizations today. But since the 1980s, people have begun to wonder about a higher level of information—the knowledge of those who operate the business. As has been repeatedly mentioned in the book, knowledge—the compilation of experience, judgment, and years of proven decision-making successes—cannot be matched by a computer. Knowledge is the foundation of all aspects of the firm. Without it, the firm cannot continue to operate. In fact, the firm would cease to exist. As illustrated in Figure 18–2, knowledge and expertise occur at every level. The organization's structure, policies, strategies, operation/production, products/services, and quality assurance standards are all determined by **corporate knowledge** and expertise. Therefore, knowledge should be effectively managed on a regular basis.

The main problem in **knowledge management** is the lack of standards or tools to assist in managing, maintaining, and expanding knowledge within the firm. Traditionally, knowledge has been captured in books (passive knowledge) or in people's heads (active or explicit knowledge). The building of knowledge-based systems establishes a third way to capture knowledge: *codified knowledge*. This type of knowledge allows people to solve problems and do reasoning chores without the explicit knowledge of the human expert.

Approaches to Managing Knowledge

Karl Wiig, a noted pioneer in knowledge management, suggested a pragmatic approach to identifying major knowledge areas and managing corporate knowledge. For an organization to build a viable knowledge management program, it must carry out certain activities:

1. *Assemble a task force.* The first step is a survey of the organization's knowledge and how it is used. The team should have longstanding employees as members, who have backgrounds in technology, management, psychology, and human resources.

2. *Identify and categorize the corporation's existing knowledge.* Once the task force's survey is completed, they should describe the content of the knowledge function in the organization. For example, in banking, the most

Figure 18–2 Corporate Knowledge as the Foundation of All Aspects of a Firm

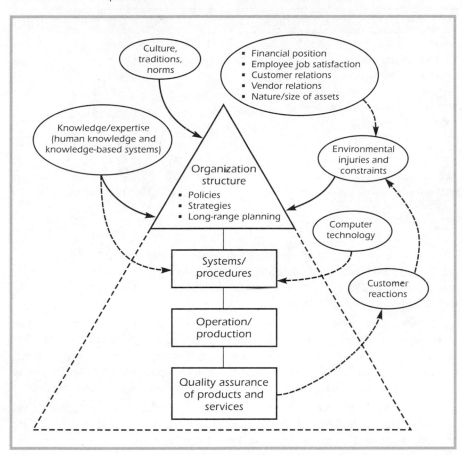

critical knowledge areas are in loans, portfolio investment, and designing security checks across the bank's telecommunications network. Existing knowledge also includes a description of the knowledge needed to perform specific functions and the available expertise. This process is similar to matching job requirements against a candidate's skills and abilities.

3. *Survey existing knowledge, the way it is used in the organization, and what makes it vulnerable.* The focus in this task is to look for the most critical knowledge functions. It does not necessarily begin with the president, because such a position is often political. In banking, customer service and approving loans are the most critical knowledge functions; in insurance, it is underwriting group insurance; in brokerage firms, it is trade securities or drive-in areas.

The constraints that prevent knowledge workers from operating fully are also explored. For example, in banking, an inadequate number of knowledgeable tellers are generally available. As a result, only 60 percent of the customers are accommodated during peak hours (constraint). The reaction is to train more tellers from within the bank to meet the demand in the lobby.

■ **Table 18–1** Defining Knowledge Management

What It Is	What It Is Not
■ An operational philosophy that views knowledge as it is used in operational situations and for long-term strategic improvements ■ A number of methods and approaches that allow managers to focus on knowledge contents, needs and opportunities associated with specific operations	■ A set of isolated techniques without a common framework ■ A different name for expert systems ■ A set of computer application programs ■ A system to control distribution and security of knowledge ■ A standardized methodology for "how-to" manage knowledge

Source: Wiig, K. M., *Expert Systems: A Manager's Guide* (Geneva, Switzerland: International Labor Organization, 1990), p. 10.

4. *Capture and codify knowledge.* Codification normally begins with analysis of knowledge in its many aspects, followed by descriptive details of its reasoning strategies and the way it should function, which are preserved in manuals, rules and regulations, etc.

5. *Organize and control knowledge.* This step places heavy emphasis on managing knowledge. Management needs to understand how each knowledge activity reacts under certain conditions and how it impacts the area in which it functions. Implied in this step is evaluating each knowledge activity to determine the "value-added" or impact it is having on the profitability of the firm.

6. *Automate knowledge.* After the organization's various knowledge activities have been identified and their impact evaluated, the final step is to decide on how to automate knowledge with knowledge-based systems. For a beginning organization, simpler forms of knowledge are first automated via expert systems. Once management begins to experience the profitability of the change, more advanced or complex expertise may be considered for conversion to expert systems.

Knowledge management, then, is a long-term view of knowledge as a corporate asset. As shown in Table 18–1, it is not a set of computer programs, a knowledge base system, or a standardized tool used in "how-to" manage knowledge. In the past, supervisors managed knowledge of different functions tactically. Like firefighters, they upgraded or adjusted job requirements when the integrity of the job was threatened. With today's knowledge management, clearly laid-out approaches allow upper management to manage knowledge *strategically* through long-range planning of knowledge assessment and determining how well knowledge will serve the broader ends of the organization as an entity.

■ DISTRIBUTED INTELLIGENCE IN ORGANIZATIONS

A relatively new concept that suggests a widespread use and impact of knowledge bases in organizations is to make expert systems available across departments or divisions using existing communication networks. **Distributed artificial intelligence (DAI)** treats collections of knowledge as individual reasoning "agents" in much the same way as humans act as agents to negotiate solutions to common problems in business. An **agent** includes reasoning, knowledge interpretation, and a communication mechanism that allows interactions and sharing of knowledge for problem solving.

Considering applications as agents encourages reuse of knowledge modules and integration in building large, complex intelligent systems. Obviously, to share knowledge throughout the organization requires that all agents "speak" the same language or share a common interface in the network. In Figure 18–3, knowledge-based applications physically share information in order to cooperate effectively in a network environment. The network might range from the Internet to the local area network (LAN) of the organization. The data dictionary standardizes the vocabulary used by different applications.

Production and process planning are prime candidate areas for DAI. In most organizations, process planning continues to be a manual chore, employing hundreds of process planners and plans each year. A planner normally spends several days to convert a new production request into one or two pages of operations. A strong knowledge-based integrated environment could be created for sharing knowledge and knowledge bases among planners. The

Figure 18–3 One View of Distributed Artificial Intelligence

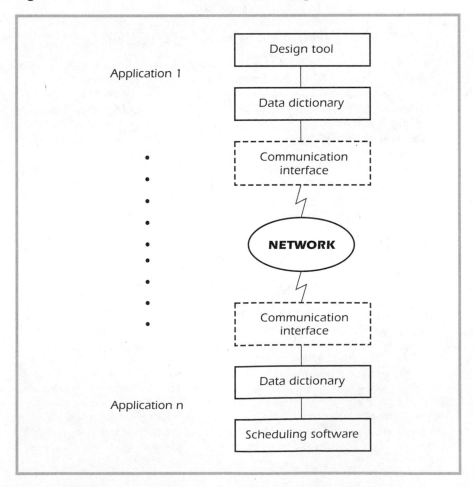

outcome is control of the design and manufacturing process, which requires reasoning at all levels. This reasoning includes knowledge about alternative process paths to factory-floor configurations. Such capabilities also imply the use of just-in-time (real-time) planning for the entire production process.

In summary, for a DAI to work effectively for the organization, the designers and users must develop an attitude toward reuse and sharing. One approach is to build common libraries and reuse knowledge components across related applications. Another approach is to transform a single knowledge base into virtual-knowledge-base units, with each unit addressing specific needs of a user with the proper interface. Implied in the user interface is ease of use, ease of learning, and ease of update of the knowledge base when needed.

Facilitating knowledge sharing is important when similar organizational activities occur on multiple sites. Integrated knowledge has the effect of stabilizing the organization's planning process from site to site. If knowledge sharing is successfully established, the common request for proposals or negotiating commitments will look more like electronic bidding based on realistic knowledge or represented expertise.

Implications for Management

The material covered in this chapter offers a number of implications for management. The first is the diversity of opinions among managers as to where expert systems will be used or have the greatest impact. Based on today's trend, the potential effects of expert systems will certainly be widespread in virtually every area of operation.

The attractiveness of expert systems lies in their abilities to increase quality, productivity, accuracy, and consistency in decision making. For expert systems to have a lasting chance, they must be managed properly. Implementing a policy that will allow orderly building and implementation of expert systems increases the likelihood of user acceptance and system use. Such a policy should ensure that appropriate steps are taken in a standardized manner, including how the expert system will be introduced into the organization.

Since expert systems have proved themselves to be productivity enhancers, the onus is now on management to make sure they are put to use and used with commitment. This challenge requires the selling of the system and rigorous user training in line with the installation timetable.

Expert systems are also a relatively new addition to the information-processing area of the firm. Yet, little is known about the long-term problems management will face with regard to expert systems. Many hypotheses have been presented about the problems companies could face resulting from the deployment of this technology. With a little foresight, organizations can plan for the possibility of these problems and handle them accordingly.

A major concern is what to do about personnel that are replaced by an expert system. Recharting their career paths is one possibility. However, an expert whose job will be adversely affected by an expert system cannot be expected to cooperate in building a replacement, which means that commitment to the project cannot be taken for granted. It must be assured in advance.

Taken to the extreme, reliance on expert systems could produce a generation of insecure managers. The firm that grows too dependent on the knowledge the system provides might experience difficulties in updating the knowledge base, which can profoundly affect the firm's ability to function. It could also slow forward thinking and growth. If this tendency is left unchecked, the firm risks losing its competitive advantage.

Finally, an expert system should not be viewed as a short-term answer to a long-term problem. The tradeoff between complex task management with the help of an expert system versus simplifying the task, per se, should be examined whenever considering the development of an expert system.

Expert systems are in use throughout companies around the world. As the success of today's expert systems is projected into the future, expert systems can be expected to grow at a rapid pace. Expert system development by the year 2000 is predicted to increase 10–20 times today's market. Problems related to resistance to change, verification and validation, and deployment strategies will probably continue. Advance planning and team work are highly encouraged. The ethical and legal issues surrounding expert systems also merit close attention and are discussed in detail in Chapter 19.

Although people have always managed knowledge one way or another, they have done so with different degrees of intent or rigor. Building expert systems should be based on prior understanding of the critical knowledge activities of the firm. More importantly, knowledge assessment and planning and building expert systems should all be integrated with programs such as human resources management, total quality control, and management training development supported by the organization's information technology environment. The steps suggested in the chapter serve as a starting point in developing a strategy for managing corporate knowledge. Recent expert system technology now allows us to elicit and codify knowledge. The management aspect of knowledge-based systems as well as the existing "nonautomated" knowledge of the organization is the number one goal of today's business.

■ SUMMARY

1. Expert systems are contributing to the productivity and decision-making quality in business. Inherent in expert system use is a host of organizational and managerial problems. The goal is to evaluate the impact of this evolving technology on employees and the overall functioning of the business.

2. Surveys have shown positive gains in productivity, resulting from the use of expert systems. One survey singled out this factor as a prime reason for adopting expert systems. Companies such as Texas Instruments, Dupont, DEC, and American Express have demonstrated positive benefits of expert systems in terms of cost savings and productivity.

3. Decisions or solutions produced by expert systems tend to be more consistent and not subject to bias or sensitivity to the environment. This consistency leads to more standardized decisions, which is desirable in areas such as personnel recruiting.

4. Expert systems can alter organization structure and communication channels by eliminating the consultation of the human expert, thereby flattening the organization structure. If an expert system has the knowledge of a middle manager, it can provide similar recommendations to upper management and potentially eliminate the position.

5. One area that has experienced a definite shift in job roles and responsibility is that of the human expert and the knowledge engineer. Knowledge engineer positions could be pushed more toward the front-end to act as liaisons or interface with the user, especially as more and more domain experts begin building their own expert systems.

6. The question of how expert systems will impact employment has generated two opposing views with no clear results. According to various studies, a shift is more toward the reduction of human labor. Historically however, no evidence supports the notion that improvement in productivity leads to loss of jobs. So, automation, per se, is not the prime cause of unemployment.

7. Instead of welcoming productivity-producing expert systems, many people resist such change for fear of loss of jobs and income. This attitude can cause problems during implementation and user training. Related to this factor is the psychological impact of expert systems as fool-proof "decision makers." The idea that human intelligence is represented by a computer can be intimidating, which is even greater reason for building user-friendly expert systems.

8. Because knowledge is so important, corporations should consider ways to manage it effectively. It should first survey the way available knowledge is used, and then capture, codify, organize, and control it before considering knowledge automation. This process has implications for management and how the introduction of expert systems may or may not affect the organization structure, productivity, and the potential profitability of the firm.

TERMS TO LEARN

Agent also called intelligent agent; a bit of intelligence that represents specific attributes to other agents on a network.

Corporate knowledge the combined knowledge of decision makers and experts of an organization.

Distributed artificial intelligence (DAI) a group of agents that form a cooperative unit and communicate directly through messages to solve common problems.

Job role job function; set of tasks making up a person's expected behavior in a given position.

Knowledge management an approach that allows managers to focus on knowledge content and needs and opportunities associated with a specific operation; a standardized tool for managing knowledge.

Knowledge worker a company employee with experience to do a specialized job, usually using a computerized system with access to information.

■ REVIEW QUESTIONS

1. "Inherent in the use of expert systems is a host of organizational and managerial problems." Do you agree? What kinds of problems are at issue? Explain.

2. The chapter focuses on the organizational impact of expert systems. Elaborate.

3. The productivity factor has been cited as a factor in the introduction of expert systems. Do you think expert systems increase or reduce productivity? Review recent literature along with the chapter in supporting your answer.

4. Review the literature and write a report about one organization or one expert system that has had an impact on productivity or profitability.

5. In what ways do expert systems contribute to improved decision making? Be specific.

6. "Expert systems can alter organization structure." Do you agree? Explain.

7. How can expert systems reduce top management's reliance on middle management? What would be the consequence of this result?

8. Explain in your own words how expert systems cause a shift in the role of the knowledge engineer.

9. Review the expert system literature since 1993 regarding expert system impact on employment. Write an essay reporting your findings. How do your findings differ from or support the opinions in the chapter?

10. Describe the historical basis of automation's effects on unemployment?

11. In your opinion, are people justified in their fears of losing their jobs as a result of the use of expert systems? Explain your response.

12. What psychological effects are caused by the use of expert systems? In your opinion, is this much uncertainty justified? Explain.

13. What is knowledge management? Explain the approaches used in managing knowledge.

14. Use the material in the chapter and an outside source and write a short essay on the implications of expert systems on management.

■ SELECTED REFERENCES

Ackermann, Fran and Valerie Belton. "Managing Corporate Knowledge Experiences With SODA and VISA." *British Journal of Management,* September 1994, pp. 163–176.

Anonymous. "In Search of a Brainy Workforce." *Small Business Reports*, February 1994, pp. 7–8.

Bailey, J. J. *Economic Evaluation of Knowledge-Based Systems* (Unpublished master's thesis). Boston, MA: Massachusetts Institute of Technology, 1987.

Benders, J. and F. Manders. "Expert Systems and Organizational Decision Making." *Information & Management,* October 1993, pp. 207–213.

Candlin, D. B. and S. Wright. "Managing the Introduction of Expert Systems." *International Journal of Operations & Production Management* 12, no. 1 (1992), pp. 46–58.

Chau, Patrick Y. K. "Non-Technical Barriers to Successful Expert Systems: Sources and Ways to Overcome Them." *Information Executive,* Winter 1990, pp. 51–53.

Dologite, D. G. and Robert J. Mockler. "Developing Effective Knowledge-Based Systems: Overcoming Organizational and Individual Behavioral Barriers." *Information Resources Management Journal,* Winter 1989, pp. 27–37.

Gates, Kermit H. "Project Management Techniques for Knowledge-Based Systems Development." *IEEE,* February 1990, pp. 104–107.

Goldstein, David. "A Fault-Tolerant Architecture for Distributed, Heterogeneous, Deductive Knowledge-Based Applications" (Ph.D. Dissertation). University of Texas at Arlington, 1992.

_____ "The Distributed AI Toolkit." *AI Expert,* January 1994, pp. 34–37.

Grossman, Simi. "Empowering the Worker." *Computing Canada,* April 13, 1994, p. 49.

Gummer, Burton. "Sez Who?: Perspectives on Organizational Knowledge." *Administration in Social Work* 17, no. 1 (1993), pp. 115–131.

Jayaraman, Sundaresan. "Knowledge-Based Systems Put Data to Work for You." *Textile World,* March 1992, pp. 51–52.

Leontief, W. "The New Age That Is Coming Is Already Here." *Bottom Line/Personnel* 4, no. 8 (April 1–2, 1983).

Mackay, Jim. "Expert Network May Increase Competitiveness." *Canadian Manager,* March 1994, pp. 25, 29.

Mockler, Robert J. *Knowledge-Based Systems for Strategic Planning.* Englewood Cliffs, NJ: Prentice-Hall, 1989.

Mullins, Brenda and Bill Mullins. "The Knowledge Worker." *Canadian Insurance,* August 1993, pp. 17–19.

Neches, R. "Enabling Technology for Knowledge Sharing," *AI Magazine,* Fall 1991, pp. 23–27.

Procaccini, Bob. "Expert System Project Management Issues." *IEEE,* February 1990, pp. 88–89.

Raho, Louis E. and James Belohlav. "Organizational Implications of Expert Systems." *Information Executive,* Summer 1991, p. 19.

Rasmus, Dan. "Developing Diagnostic Expert Systems." *Manufacturing Systems,* October 1992, pp. 58–66.

Rock, Denny; Sandie Washburn; Dave Purdon; and Alex Houtzeel. "Sharing Knowledge Bases in Industry." *AI Expert,* June 1993, pp. 24–31.

Sulek, Joanne and Ann Marucheck. "The Impact of Information Technology on Knowledge Workers: Deskilling or Intellectual Specialization?" *Work Study,* January–February 1994, pp. 5–13.

Tampoe, Mahen. "Motivating Knowledge Workers: The Challenge for the 1990s." *Long-Range Planning,* June 1993, pp. 49–55.

Wiig, Karl. *Expert Systems: A Manager's Guide.* Geneva, Switzerland: International Labor Organization, 1990.

Chapter ■ 19

Ethical and Legal Issues

SETTING ETHICAL STANDARDS FOR INFORMATION TECHNOLOGY

David, a software development executive in a large corporation, agreed to deliver a new software project that was supposed to help his company's service organization improve the handling of customer accounts. In the ensuing weeks, David realized that following the written requirements for the project would produce a system that would never meet the organization's needs.

David decided not to point out the problems with these requirements, reasoning that spreading the alarm would cause political fallout. So he told his staff to remain silent about the faulty requirements and deliver a system that met them.

The result was a fiasco that left his corporation unable to fully service many of its customer accounts for more than three days. By the time the situation was sorted out, David had been demoted for unethical behavior.

Julie, an information technology (IT) executive in a bank, was asked by her company's marketing organization for access to the customer data from mortgage applications. They wanted to use this data, which included household income, debt history and other personal items, in database marketing campaigns to help target appropriate customers for new bank services.

Although several mortgage managers complained that such information was not supposed to be used for marketing purposes, Julie delivered the data anyway. She justified her actions by saying that it was not her job to rule on the uses of data but merely to effect the exchanges.

The corporation was soon contacted by a local newspaper reporter who had heard of the marketing campaign and wanted some details about the marketing plan for a story on privacy. The result was a potentially embarrassing public relations disaster that had to be quickly and deftly handled by the CEO.

After the incident, the CEO reprimanded Julie for not taking responsibility for ensuring proper data flows. He made it clear that it was her duty to bring such issues to the attention of senior executives.

In each of these scenarios (based on real incidents), an IT executive was confronted with an ethical dilemma: how to manage a project that was doomed to failure, how to be a corporation's information conscience and how to handle tough societal questions regarding the consequences of IT applications.

By adopting a proactive approach that is grounded in sound ethical reasoning, IT managers can extend their leadership from the technological arena into the domain of information ethics, IT executives who assume the moral stewardship of information initiatives can provide long-term benefits to both their departments and their companies.

EVALUATING ETHICAL ISSUES

How can you, as an IT manager, evaluate the ethical issues you encounter in the course of providing strategic applications to your company? One useful framework, popularized by Ed Freeman, a professor at the University of

Virginia's Colgate Darden Graduate School of Business in Charlottesville, Virginia, is known as "stakeholder analysis." By considering all the stakeholders in a particular decision and determining how various courses of action would affect them, you can often reach a decision that will provide the optimal solution for all parties and reduce the probability of a negative backlash.

Mistakes in ethical analysis often occur when some stakeholders are overlooked. For example, David overlooked internal IT users and the corporation's customers. Julie disregarded both the bank's customers and the media as stakeholders. . . . Both had taken a narrow view of their role as IT executives: to deliver systems and information based on the requirements presented to them. Consequently, they had viewed their stakeholders primarily as the system users and/or the corporate political engine.

David and Julie made another judgment error: They assumed that ethical issues were not their concern or their responsibility. This feeling is shared by some of their peers in the IT community.

During the last few years, I have had conversations about information ethics with more than 350 people—both in the IT ranks and in user communities. One thread runs through many of my conversations with IT professionals: Most view information ethics as someone else's job.

One IT executive told me that the way data is used is not his concern. Another said, "We make technology decisions, not ethical policies."

The reality is that many CEOs will be holding their senior IT executives accountable for ethical issues involved in the creation and distribution of information. They'll be asking, as Julie's CEO did, "Why didn't you tell me about these potential problems?" A response of "That's not my job" will ring rather hollow.

IT executives will have to respond to this concern with ethical IT standards. They'll have to stop asking themselves, "What can we do technologically?" and start asking, "What should we do ethically?"

Source: Excerpted from Jefferson H. Smith, "Setting Ethical Standards for Information Technology," *Beyond Computing,* March-April 1992, p. 18ff.

AT A GLANCE

Today's corporate community is troubled by ethical problems that have far-reaching implications for integrity and productivity of the firm. Ethics is not easy to define, anymore than it is easy to implement. Much of what is ethical is related to moral and legal standards. Various theories on ethics have been proposed in an effort to clarify the concept and process.

The threats of computerized and networked systems and the transparency of software have generated ethical dilemmas of dimensions unforeseen a decade ago. Applying ethics to expert systems and information technology in general is more difficult than applying it to any other area of business. The imperative, then, is to address ethical issues in technology promptly and properly within the larger framework of the organization's code of ethics. The general view is that ethics throughout the organization is best supported by top management's ethical behavior.

Unethical acts raise legal issues and eventual litigation. Cases involving expert systems will depend on who owns knowledge, who to hold liable, and on what basis liability is determined. The laws also vary depending on whether expert system is a product or service. Warranties and the laws enforcing such assurances protect sellers and users in various ways.

What You Will Learn ────────────────────────────────────

By the end of this chapter, you should know the following:

1. The difference between ethical and unethical acts, and how they relate to or differ from immoral or illegal acts.

2. Various legal issues related to knowledge ownership and the liability that stems from defective expert systems.

> D on't ask what you can do, ask what you
> should do.
>
> —H. Jefferson Smith

▓ INTRODUCTION

The material covered thus far has examined the principles, procedures, tools, and methodologies in building expert systems. Each chapter discussed the managerial implications of this evolving technology and how it might serve the productivity of the firm. But other questions arise at each stage of development: What are the ethical issues involved in building and managing expert systems? Who owns knowledge? How does an organization address property rights related to employee knowledge and expertise? What are the legal implications of expert systems?

Organizations throughout the United States are troubled by ethical problems. Based on a survey by Touche Ross & Co., 94 percent of all respondents believe that high ethical standards in an organization strengthen its competitive position. Among professional groups, bankers were the most inclined to believe that high ethical standards strengthen an organization's competitive position and character. Finally, almost three-quarters of all respondents thought the CEO plays the most significant role in setting ethical standards for employees.

Today's information society is fast becoming a knowledge-age society. The question of ethics in information technology and expert systems is the current challenge confronting U.S. organizations. Major corporations are vigorously addressing the challenge. One manifestation of this trend is the widespread development of organizational codes of ethics and corporatewide efforts in support of ethics policies to ensure ethical actions. This chapter focuses on ethical issues and the legal factors in expert systems. Since expert systems are still relatively new, most of the coverage is related to information systems as well.

ETHICS DEFINED

An information systems manager was leafing through paid hardware purchase invoices his assistant had expedited. The manager's signature had been initialed on some invoices without his knowledge or approval. One invoice was received from a vendor that did not exist. A number of PCs that were purchased never made it to the bank's branches. A quick audit revealed that the assistant and an employee in the accounting department were in collusion. The assistant manager was promptly fired, but the bank decided not to sue for fear of bad publicity. After the episode blew over, the information systems manager was called to the president's office to explain the situation.

In this instance, a case of ethics is clear. The word *ethics* is not so easy to define, however. It means different things to different people. To begin to discuss the issue, a common definition is needed. **Ethics** is one or all of the following:

- fairness
- justice
- equity
- honesty
- trustworthiness
- equality

Stealing, cheating, lying, or backing out on one's word are all descriptive of a lack of ethics. Something is ethical when a person feels it is innately right, which is a subjective judgment. For example, "Thou shalt not steal" is a belief held by most people. But a single parent who steals a loaf of bread to feed four starving children may be forgiven for this behavior even though it is illegal.

An unethical act is not the same as an immoral or an illegal act, although one may lead to the other. See Box 19–1. For example:

1. Cheating on one's federal income tax return is more *illegal* than immoral, although it is implicitly unethical.

2. Cheating on a friend is more *immoral* than illegal, although it is tacitly unethical.

3. Sending a "padded" bill to a client is more *unethical* and possibly illegal, although it is considered immoral.

Incidents such as these are related to one's value system, beliefs, and culture. Laws are often created to combat unethical acts that threaten societal image and survival. They are also used to reinforce existing ethics. Ethics creates a strong sense of professionalism. Ethical misbehavior among MIS professionals and knowledge engineers is no greater or less than it is among the mass public. See Box 19–2.

Forcht proposed a quadrant model of acceptable behavior, with ethics as a factor in each quadrant. See Figure 19–1 on page 484. For example, if a person falsely reports a donation to a charitable organization, it is considered both illegal and immoral (quadrant A). This action implies a lack of ethical standards and personal values. In quadrant D, rescuing hostages from a foreign country might be illegal (and dangerous) by that country's laws, but it is moral (and implicitly ethical) in terms of justice under U.S. laws. As can be seen, deciding what is moral, legal, or ethical creates a constant struggle.

Box 19–1   The Saga of a Yacht

During the February meeting of a medium-size bank, the first agenda item was a review of the Statement of Condition (expenses, revenues, etc.) of the bank for the previous month. John, a new member of the board, noticed a line item under "entertainment" in the amount of $12,000. He thought to himself, "Here's a local bank of 140 employees. What kind of entertainment is going on at the bank to add up to this much expense?"

Out of curiosity, he asked the chairman of the board, "Mr. Chairman, I'd like to know a little bit about the entertainment expense item. Could this be back from the Christmas party that is reflected as a January expense?" The bank's president who was a member of the board replied, "Well, as you know John, the bank incurs all kinds of entertainment expenses. Why don't you stop by my office after the meeting and I'd be happy to explain it further."

After the board meeting, John and the bank president had a brief chat. The president explained, "John, the entertainment item is the bank's monthly contribution to the Chairman's entertainment of bank customers, bank officers, and other dignitaries on his yacht. The Chairman has certain privileges." John then asked, "For a bank this size, how can one justify this much expense each month? What kind of entertainment adds up to $12,000 per month? How long has this been going on?" The president, his face turning red with irritation, said, "I really don't want to elaborate further about this. Remember, you are new on the board. I wouldn't advise asking the Chairman about it. I'd let it go. The bank is making enough money. The Chairman's family has 78 percent equity in the bank. What more explanation do you want?"

Sensing futility in the attempt, John later discovered that the monthly charge was a dockage fee for the Chairman's 130-foot yacht. As a board member, he felt responsible for assuring integrity in bank management. What made this situation more difficult for John was that for the next six years he was on the board, there wasn't one occasion where entertainment on the yacht was related to the bank in any measurable way. He is now in a quandry wondering whether he should continue on the board or resign.

Ethical Decision Cycle

People typically consider a number of elements when they make ethical decisions:

1. *The nature and essence of the act*: Is the act fair, reasonable, or conscionable?

2. *The consequences of the action or inaction on the parties involved*: Who gains, who loses, and by how much?

3. *The far-reaching consequence of the action or inaction on the organization, community, and society*: Will the act, if left unchecked, lead to societal ills?

Figure 19–2 summarizes the three major steps of a hypothetical ethical decision cycle. A person faces an act situation and must evaluate alternative approaches that lead to a decision to commit an act. The outcome is initially reviewed by the person. If it is believed to be rewarding, fair, and just, chances are it will be repeated and vice versa. The outcome in general becomes known

Box 19–2   Who Decides Operational Ethics?

A Loan Advisor built for a commercial bank uses 17 criteria to determine whether an applicant qualifies for a mortgage loan. For several years, the bank had been criticized by state auditors for not granting enough loans to minorities or to people living in minority districts. A review of the expert system also revealed that most mortgage loans favor applicants who are married rather than those who are single, separated, or divorced.

When the discriminating rules were pointed out, the knowledge engineer said, "I developed this system based on the vice president of mortgage loan's thought processes. He reviewed several prototypes and loved the system. Why don't you talk with him?" In addressing the equity question, the vice president replied, "I make decisions on mortgage loans based on guidelines from the board. Our Chairman is a major stockholder and owner of the bank. He does not live in the area and wants to make sure we make secured loans. Why don't you talk to the president about it?"

In a meeting with the president the next day, the president said, "I'm surprised you're bringing up bank policy. We paid for an expert system based on our requirements. So, what's the fuss all about?"

But the question raised here still remains: Is the expert system unethical, illegal, or both?

Source: Based on experience with Loan Advisor, August 1992.

---

to others (groups, organizations, and society), who would condone or condemn the outcome. The result of this feedback is eventual advancement and refinement of ethics within families, the work place, and society in general.

◼ MAJOR THREATS TO ETHICS

Ethics are more openly discussed as a serious concern today than they were in the past, because the threats have steadily increased. As shown in Figure 19–3, the main threats are:

- Faster computers and PCs
- Sophisticated telecommunication and computer networks
- Massive distributed databases
- Ease of access to information and knowledge bases
- Transparency of software—computers no longer seen as a black box
- The view that stored information and captured knowledge are competitive weapons

With these threats, ethical dilemmas of dimensions not imagined ten years ago are facing today's firm, stretching standard ethical considerations to the limit. In fact, technological advancements have resulted in the need to reevaluate ethical standards and their implications for privacy, confidentiality, accuracy, and integrity.

Software copyright infringements, unauthorized E-mail access, and sale of competitive data are serious ethical issues. In 1992, a senior vice president at a major credit card company was dismissed for allegedly using his position and

Figure 19–1 Model of Acceptable Behavior

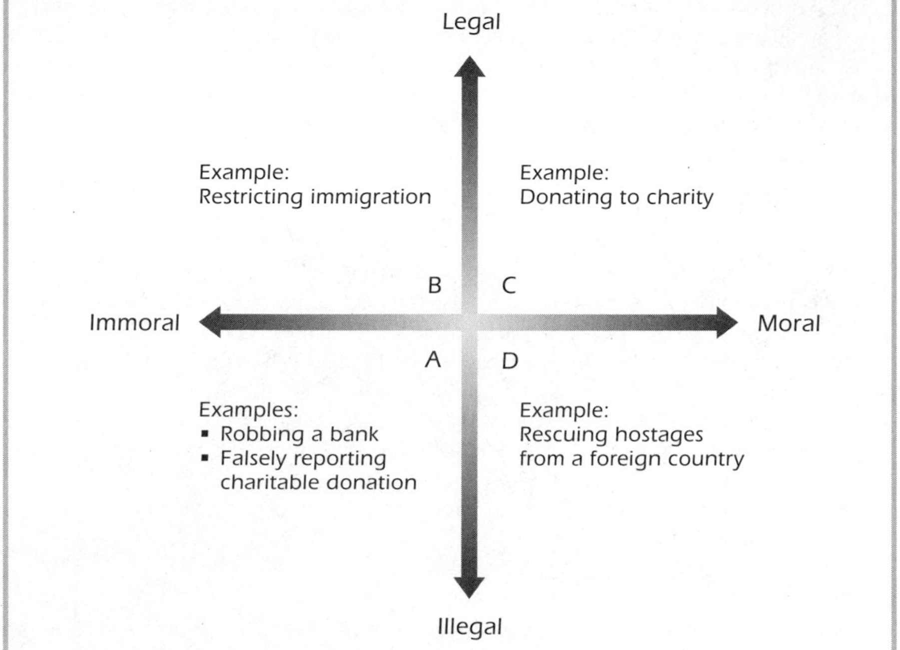

Legal
Example:
Restricting immigration
Example:
Donating to charity
B
C
Immoral
Moral
A
D
Examples:
▪ Robbing a bank
▪ Falsely reporting charitable donation
Example:
Rescuing hostages from a foreign country
Illegal

Source: Adapted from Karen A. Forcht, "Assessing Ethical Standards and Policies in Computer-Based Environments." In Roy Dejoie, George Fowler, and David Paradice, eds., *Ethical Issues in Information Systems.* Boston, MA: Boyd & Fraser, 1991, p. 57.

Figure 19–2 Ethical Decision Cycle

Act
(intentions)
Evaluation of alternatives
Action
(decision)
Outcome
(consequence)
feedback
Organizational and societal feedback (human filter)

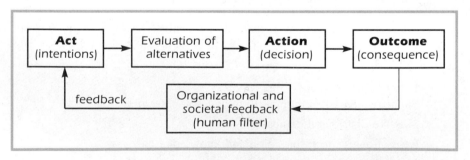

company affiliation to promote his side business and pressure company suppliers into buying products from him—all of which was carried out using E-mail and fax. The question is, since no one knows information technology more than the head of the information systems department, should the IT manager be the one to establish and enforce ethical standards concerning information technology for the company as a whole?

Applying ethics in information technology and expert systems is more difficult than any other discipline for a number of reasons. A report by Weiss suggested the following reasons:

Figure 19–3 Major Threats to Ethics

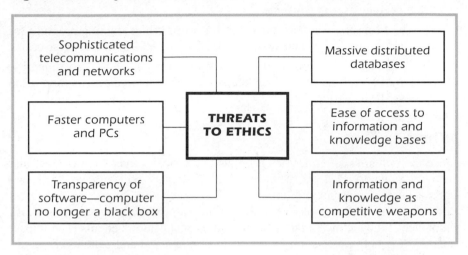

1. Computers and data networks alter the way people relate to each other. What once took information a week to reach its recipient through letter format now takes less than one second by E-mail. The whole process happens so quickly, with little time to consider the implications of the information being sent or shared.

2. High-speed, low-cost data transmission is raising new questions about property rights, piracy, and plagiarism. In fact, it forces a reevaluation of the corporation's code of ethics.

3. The traditional contractual agreement certified by a signature is now being replaced by transmitting the same documents by electronic means such as facsimile transmission (fax). This factor also is forcing a change in the organization's ethical norms.

These particular ethical issues are unique to the computer field. The main ethical issue concern ownership of knowledge represented in programs, unauthorized use of information in repositories without clearcut guidelines, and the level of responsibility for ensuring integrity of computer programs and knowledge-based systems. More and more serious work is being carried out to address these important issues.

▨ IMPROVING THE CLIMATE

Organizations can take a number of approaches to improve the climate for ethical behavior in the MIS department where expert systems are built and in the firm as a whole:

1. To ensure ethical behavior throughout the organization, top management should act as the role model.

2. A code of ethics should be established, taking into consideration the state of technology of the organization. The goals should be realistic, achievable, and agreed upon by the employees. Each individual organizational level should create an acting ethics program within the company's code of ethics and one that befits the nature of the operation.

3. Unethical behavior should be promptly dealt with based on criteria and procedures set in advance.

4. The firm should set up and support a strong ethics training program for all new employees and reinforce the code of ethics on a regular basis.

5. The organization must provide motivation to focus on honesty, integrity, fairness, and justice as goals that are just as important as money or the so-called "bottom line."

Where to Start

Once the definition of ethics has been agreed upon, the next step is to decide who is going to lead the "ethics parade." Organizations have used two approaches: bottom-up and top-down. The *bottom-up* approach inculcates ethics behavior at the employee level with full support of top management. As employees follow ethical practices, the entire organization benefits. The impact creates waves of appreciation up the chain of command and benefits the entire firm over the long run.

The other approach, called *top-down,* suggests that the actions of the company start with the CEO. By virtue of personal acts, decisions, and overall behavior, the top corporate officer sets the tone for the kind of image the corporation will adopt. Corporate obligations extend to a variety of **stakeholders** (customers, employees, vendors, etc.), and these obligations are generally recognized as central to the ethical standards of the firm. Carrying out these obligations requires a comprehensive ethics code that is understood and supported in every sector and at each level of the organization.

Take the case of Boeing Aircraft's chief executive William Allen. In September 1945, he resigned from his law firm to lead Boeing Aircraft after World War II to focus on postwar products. Allen had served as a company attorney for 20 years and director for 14 years. He is remembered as a man of great sincerity, honesty, and integrity. When he accepted the offer of president, he offered the following resolution as a reflection of his personal values:

- Do not be afraid to admit that you don't know.
- Be definite—tell it like it is.
- Try to promote honest feelings toward the company around Seattle.
- Don't talk too much . . . let others talk.
- Be considerate of your associates' views.
- Above all, be human—keep your sense of humor and learn to relax.

Like Allen, the firm acquired a reputation as a highly ethical firm whose employees developed a strong sense of values and integrity in the way they approached their work. His term in office is remembered as a period of "uncompromising high standards and clean ethics." Employees always knew where they stood. It shows that an ethics program should be "rolled out" from the top down the line, which contributes to making each manager an effective ethics leader.

Code of Ethics

Business ethics is closely tied to corporate culture and values, which means that a code of ethics should represent all that the corporation stands for. A laundry list of do's and don'ts are virtually useless in an organization in which ethics is not already woven into its culture. A **code of ethics** is a declaration of principles and beliefs that govern how employees of a corporation are to behave. The goal of such a code is that it be inspirational and disciplinary, and promote awareness among the employees and the organization as a whole. The code should be all-encompassing and stable over time. It does not make sense, for example, to codify every new situation that comes up.

Once a code of ethics has been posted and approved by management and employees, it becomes a commitment to behave within its guidelines on a day-to-day basis. Box 19–3 provides excerpts from the code of ethics of the Association for Computing Machinery (ACM) whose international membership exceeds 70,000.

Self-Assessment

An honest workplace in which managers and employees are held accountable for their behavior is the best environment to promote an ethical mode of

---

Box 19–3 ACM Code of Ethics

General Moral Imperatives

- Be honest and trustworthy.
- Avoid harm to others.
- Honor property rights including copyrights and patents.
- Access computing and communication resources only when authorized to do so.
- Respect the privacy of others.
- Honor confidentiality.

More Specific Professional Responsibilities

- Acquire and maintain professional competence.
- Know and respect existing laws pertaining to professional work.
- Give comprehensive and thorough evaluations of computer systems and their impact, with special emphasis on possible risks.
- Improve public understanding of computing and its consequences.

Organizational Leadership Imperatives

- Articulate social responsibilities of members of an organizational unit and encourage full acceptance of those responsibilities.
- Manage personnel and resources to design and build information systems that enhance the quality of working life.
- Acknowledge and support proper and authorized uses of an organization's computing and communication resources.
- Articulate and support policies that protect the dignity of users and others affected by computing systems.

Excerpts from: "Code of Ethics," ACM.

corporate behavior. To ensure a viable climate, an organization must stress regular self-assessment and encourage open debate within the workplace.

Self-assessment is basically a question-and-answer procedure that allows individuals to appraise and understand their personal knowledge about a particular topic. In the case of ethics, it is not an exercise to satisfy others. The goal is to think about ethics and adjust one's ethical behavior accordingly. It should at least be an educational experience for the participant.

The ACM through the work of Parker, Swope, and Baker devised a self-assessment procedure dealing with ethical considerations that arise from the unique nature of computers and their use. Briefly, the procedure asks a participant to assess a scenario and judge whether an ethics issue is involved. The response is recorded on a special form and later compared to the judgment of a panel of experts. Box 19–4 represents two sample scenarios.

The upshot of the ethics aspect of building expert systems is to support integrity in the building process as an extension of the developer's integrity. The moral imperative is clear. The basic task of today's computer professional, whether programmer, systems analyst, or knowledge engineer, is to use the information generated by the computers to advance the quality of life and the dignity of the users. To meet this challenge, a code of ethics—a social contract that prescribes the practice—must be in place to protect the sanctity of intellectual projects and avoid unauthorized use of knowledge.

■ LEGAL ISSUES

The excitement generated by expert systems and their impact on virtually all levels in the organization has led to substantial financial investment in the technology. Expert systems are still in their infancy, and some marketers are promoting them by attaching unrealistic expectations. In an age of prolific litigation, users and developers should be aware of the legal ramifications arising from expert system use. The consequences related to expert system development and use as yet have no historical basis, leaving many organizations with few legal guidelines with which to work.

Consider the following situations:

■ An attorney, using an expert system, advises his client which tax forms to file and what to include in his articles of incorporation to qualify as a federally tax-exempt corporation. The client is later sued by the government for back taxes owed.

■ A doctor diagnoses a patient after consultation with her medical expert system advisor. The patient is treated but soon dies as a result of misdiagnosis and improper treatment.

■ A large computer firm sells a mainframe to a client after using an expert system to identify the proper configuration. When the system is installed, the client-user discovers that the configuration is wrong and the equipment, as it stands, is worthless.

■ An expert system used by an architect incorrectly determines the stress requirements of an expensive new public building. The completed structure later collapses killing or injuring dozens of people.

■ A radiation machine guided by an expert system calculates the dosage in the treatment of cancer patients. Two years after treating hundreds of

Box 19-4   *Scenarios in Ethical Self-Assessment*

Software Developer: Relying on Questionable Inputs

A software professional was assigned the task of developing software to control a particular unit of a large system. Preliminary analysis indicated that the work was well within the state of the art, and no difficulties were anticipated with the immediate task.

To function properly, or to function at all, however, the software to be developed required inputs from other units in the system. Someone gave the professional an article by an eminent software specialist that convinced him that the inputs from other units could not be trusted. Thus, neither the software he was designing nor the unit his company was providing could correctly accomplish their task. The professional showed the article to his supervisor and explained its significance. The supervisor's response was "That's not our problem; let's just be sure that our part of the system functions properly." The software professional continued to work on the project.

Question: Is an ethics issue involved?

Opinion: The majority of participants maintained that the software professional had a responsibility to go beyond his supervisor, if necessary, to call attention to the questionable inputs. . . . If the errors could cause serious harm, the professional is ethically required to do whatever is necessary to ensure that they are corrected. If the consequences would be relatively trivial, then telling the supervisor of his concerns might be sufficient.

Software Company: Ignoring Voting Machine Malfunctions

Company XYZ has developed the software for a computerized voting machine. Company ABC, which manufactures the machine, has persuaded several cities and states to purchase it. On the strength of these orders, ABC is planning a major purchase from XYZ. XYZ software engineer Smith is visiting ABC one day and learns that problems in the construction of the machine mean that one in ten is likely to miscount soon after installation. Smith reports this to her superior who informs her that it is ABC's problem. Smith does nothing further.

Question: Is an ethics issue involved?

Opinion: Participants nearly unanimously agreed that doing nothing further would be unethical. . . . Use of inaccurate voting machines could invalidate elections and potentially harm the general public. . . . Responsible (ethical) behavior and good business practice are not inconsistent. The software engineer should pursue the matter further.

Excerpted from: Eric A. Weiss, "Self-Assessment," *Communications of the ACM,* November 1990, pp. 115–116.

patients, four patients die due to radiation overdose. The problem was located in faulty programming of the expert system.

Each of these cases is real. Such unfortunate situations lead to questions such as "Who owns knowledge?" "Who is liable in such situations and for what reasons?" This section examines the legal aspects of information technology currently at issue.

Who Owns Knowledge?

The three possible owners of knowledge are the domain expert, the employing organization, or the one who acquires the system. Other situations in which knowledge ownership could be an issue in the future include:

1. If an expert sells personal knowledge
2. If an expert is unwilling to release extensive knowledge gained on the job
3. If an individual becomes an expert through training on a company-owned expert system

Each case is briefly explained next.

Knowledge for Sale

Imagine a firm that has hired a consulting group to build an expert system for a new area of the business. Because a resident expert does not exist, the consulting group is forced to locate and hire an outside expert to build the expert system. In this scenario, the expert would be the rightful owner of the knowledge if no prior agreements were established. Both the company and the expert are open targets for liability and ownership lawsuits. If an agreement made before developing the system allows the expert to receive royalties, then ownership and therefore liability is obvious. To avoid this situation, the company should make arrangements to "purchase" the expert's knowledge outright. Chances are experts may agree to it in order to escape future liability.

Releasing Knowledge Gained on the Job

Charles J. Amble worked for General Motors (GM) as a maintenance engineer for more than twenty years. To avoid losing his know-how, GM developed an expert system named *Charley* in order to capture Amble's expertise in vibration analysis. Because this expert was willing to cooperate with GM during the acquisition phase, knowledge engineers were successful in building the system. The expert system provided GM with quick, standardized diagnoses of complex vibration maintenance problems and substantial savings in all manufacturing plants, because all plant mechanics were given access to the knowledge needed to diagnose these problems. Does the company have the right to Amble's knowledge? Who owns the knowledge in this scenario?

On the one hand, Amble developed the knowledge using the resources made available by the firm, yet he also developed personal reasoning and deductive abilities at the same time. Unless he had signed a preemployment contract or an intellectual property agreement releasing his ownership of knowledge, he does own the knowledge. From the point of view of the expert, a preemployment contract or intellectual property agreement helps to limit personal liability for the expert system. GM would also want an intellectual property agreement so that it can have title to the savings realized by the expert system.

Becoming an Expert via a Corporate Expert System

Jim DeMong has worked as a timber bucker for Roland Pacific for the past twelve years. DeMong's job requires him to make many tactical decisions when cutting trees into logs and then allocating the logs to appropriate manufacturing facilities. As an expert, DeMong knows just how to cut each tree into various log lengths and then distribute the logs among the different mills in the most efficient and cost-effective way. (Each mill produces a different end product such as lumber, plywood, or paper.) As a result, his knowledge is invaluable to Roland Pacific. Wrong cutting and allocation decisions could drastically change the profit contribution from each tree.

What is unique in this situation is how DeMong acquired his knowledge. Several years ago, Roland Pacific introduced an expert system to train and assist its timber buckers with their jobs. The new system was installed in the office where timber buckers spent few hours a week simulating actual tree-cutting decisions and evaluating the resulting costs associated with each decision. Since the expert system was portable, it was also used in the field to make real-time cutting and allocation decisions.

DeMong used this expert system extensively during the first two years with the firm. But for the past few years, most of the decisions he made were his own. They were virtually identical to the expert system's decisions. Does the company have a right to DeMong's knowledge? Can the company prevent him from using this knowledge if he leaves the company to start his own business or work for a competitor?

Again, unless DeMong signed some type of intellectual property agreement that would release ownership of his knowledge, he owns the knowledge and has a right to use it as he wishes. Intellectual property agreements are also important to the expert in order to avoid strict liability, explained later in this section.

Expert System Liability

Regardless of who owns knowledge, when the expert system is finally built, if it is defective, liability will become an issue. The blame may fall on the domain expert on whose knowledge the system gave unreliable advice. Or the knowledge engineer might have tapped the wrong knowledge and is at fault. Perhaps the fault lies with the developer who used a defective procedure to represent the knowledge. It could also be the inference engine that fired the rules that produced the wrong solution.

Tort and contract theories present challenging questions facing organizations and the legal community. If an expert system produces the wrong advice or a solution, which causes **injury** to others, the resulting damage often leads to litigation dealing with **strict liability** or **negligence.** Each individual involved in the system (knowledge engineer, domain expert, user, shell developer) is potentially vulnerable and subject to legal scrutiny.

Liability of the Knowledge Engineer

As the developer of the expert system, the knowledge engineer is often responsible for choosing the expert and for the system's accuracy and reliability. In building the system, a variety of errors may become embedded in the system; some are nontrivial and others are out-of-bounds errors. An *out-of-bounds error* is one that occurs because either the expert did not have the expertise to address the particular problem or the knowledge engineer improperly condensed the information from the expert. A *nontrivial error* has a large financial impact on the business, especially if the expert system is mass-marketed. The consequence is decommissioning the expert system or facing litigation.

Since the expert's knowledge must be properly acquired and represented, the burden rests on the knowledge engineer. Should a problem arise with the system, the knowledge engineer is vulnerable to charges of personal liability under the doctrine of *respondeat superior* (an employer–employee relationship). If the knowledge engineer is an employee of the organization, the employing firm is involved in the negligence action. In the end, the company is responsible for certifying the system before it is released for public use.

Liability of the Domain Expert

Another possible target for litigation is the domain expert, since the expert's knowledge is represented in the system. Should the system be faulty, liability will surely follow. The competency of the expert, however, is difficult to evaluate; because of their individual experiences, feelings, and instincts, even experts within the same domain do not always agree on all issues. Domain experts open up their knowledge to scrutiny, even when the resulting system is far removed from the expert's control. For example, in Kansas City in 1981, a walkway at the Hyatt Regency Hotel collapsed, and the two structural engineers in charge were found guilty of negligence.

With each situation, expert involvement and potential liability vary. For example, could a court of law hold an expert liable if the expert were an employee of the firm that developed the system for resale? If the expert is an outside consultant, who would be liable? As yet, answers to these questions are unknown, because only one case involving expert system liability has been tried in court.

Liability of the User

Even end-users of the system are not immune from a lawsuit. They are directly responsible for providing the proper input to the system. Within the duties of their jobs, users' capability of refusing to accept the system's answers will increasingly come into question. According to Mykytyn et al. (1990), "By not using an available resource by affirmative duty, users could be negligent by omission 'passive negligence.'" For example, the use of an expert system in medical diagnosis "could place as affirmative duty the responsibility for using the system. It could also be used in court as support for a diagnosis, even though the diagnosis was incorrect."

An expert system may be satisfactory for one user but less so for other users. User responses to a system's questions often generate different answers—correct or incorrect solutions. Therefore, user knowledge could be questioned in a court of law to determine whether negligence is based on their responses.

Liability of the Shell Developer

The shell developer is often overlooked as a potential defendant. A flaw in the functioning of the shell could have serious ramifications. However, the legal liability of this party may stretch much further. The design of a shell-driven expert system that has significant exposure to damage or loss entails a degree of responsibility in identifying how the knowledge system is put together. So, even though a shell designer may seem to have little control over how and by whom the product is used, the potential for litigation remains.

The Basis of Liability

Although the focus in this discussion is on expert systems, the technology has not yet advanced to the point at which new legal remedies are necessary. So, the old familiar liability issues are still applicable. **Product liability** and tort law are the two major (and often overlapping) areas of concern, with the issue of warranties falling under the first area and strict liability and negligence falling under the second. **Torts** are wrongful acts subject to civil action.

Expert System—Product or Service?

The question of whether an expert system is a product or a service attracts varied opinions. One legal opinion suggests that if the software is sold off the shelf as a mass-marketed item, then it is a product. If the software is custom-designed, then it is viewed as a service. According to the same legal source, software that is custom-designed but affects a large number of customers could be treated as a product.

The resolution of this issue is important for users and developers of expert systems. If an expert system is a *product,* proving negligence is unnecessary to hold the developer liable. The **Uniform Commercial Code (UCC)**, however, allows the developer to limit liability for defective knowledge bases through a disclaimer of warranties in the contract. For these liability activities, the loss falls on the defendant (developer), regardless of fault, as a cost of doing business.

Conversely, if expert system is a *service,* the contract law of the state in question would apply, rather than the UCC. Negligence principles should be used. A negligence cause of action is more difficult to prove, because the plaintiff must show the aspect of the process that caused the defect and prove that failure to use sufficient care caused the defect.

Many legal experts want expert systems to be considered as services in order to avoid the strict liability associated with products. For example, a medical expert system mass-produced to hospitals throughout the country could be classified as a product. Yet, such a system should not be presumed to have the physician's intuitive capabilities, knowledge of the particular patient, or perception of the subjective factors. Expert systems that require the user and the expert system to make a diagnosis jointly will most likely be considered a service. A summary of these relationships is presented in Table 19–1.

Warranties

The UCC is the basic foundation of commercial contract law in all states except Louisiana. As such, it defines the concepts of product law and contains provisions for computer contracts in the form of warranties. A **warranty** is assurance made by the seller about the goods sold. An additional safeguard to UCC is the federal *Magnuson-Moss Consumer Product Warranty Act,* enacted in 1975. It clarifies the issues relating to warranty information disclosure requirements and regulates the limitation of implied warranties. Both the UCC and the Warranty Act identify the various types of warranties that can exist and serve as references for further information on the subject.

Of the two types of warranties, **express warranty** is offered orally or in writing by the maker of the system. It is usually part of a sale. The buyer

■ **Table 19–1** Expert Systems as a Product or a Service in Litigation Issues

Product	Service
■ Off-the-shelf software ■ Mass-marketed software ■ Custom-designed but affects a large number of customers ■ Proving negligence is unnecessary to hold developer liable	■ Custom-designed software ■ Negligence principles should be used ■ Negligence cause of action more difficult for plaintiff to prove
■ UCC allows liability via disclaimer of warranties	■ For liability, law of the state applies, rather than UCC

purchases the goods in part because of a statement by the seller with respect to the quality, capacity, or some other characteristic of the package. Express warranty need not be an express statement. It may be found in the seller's conduct.

An **implied warranty** arises automatically from the fact that a sale has been made and the good will do what it is supposed to do. For example, the acquired knowledge base should be fit for the ordinary purposes for which it is used. An auto loan advisor should provide the correct answer to approve or not approve the financing of a car. This implied warranty of *merchantability* merchandise worth purchasing indicates that the expert system should do what it is expected to do.

The other aspect of implied warranty is one of *fitness*. A knowledge base should be fit for the particular use intended by the buyer. Violation of this warranty is probably not common among developers, although it may be more common among companies that do customized programming.

Disclaimers and warranties are closely related. A **disclaimer** is the seller's intention to protect the business from unwanted liability. Many software packages are labeled "as is," meaning they are sold without warranty of any kind regarding performance or accuracy. More pronounced disclaimers go so far as to state that neither the developer, retailer, or anyone affiliated with the developer is liable for damages even if the developer has been forewarned of the possibility of such damages.

Even though disclaimers are clearly stated, their legal status is fuzzy at best. The main issue centers around whether the software in question is a product or a service. In either case, the courts are adverse toward excluding warranty disclaimers or attempts by the software house to avoid their applications as unconscionable. Express warranty disclaimers are effective, provided they are conspicuously placed and in writing.

Breach of warranty cases are feasible. A user can reasonably look toward warranties as protection if damage is caused through the use of an expert system. However, showing reason why a warranty exclusion should not be accepted is difficult. In fact, two states have enacted "shrink-wrap" laws, which hold that all warranties made or disclaimed on the license found inside the shrink wrapping are legal and final. Cases involving warranties also require that the user show who is at fault and why, which is a difficult task. The software program in question must necessarily be considered a product under UCC's rules for warranty issues to be relevant.

Strict Liability

Tort theory is based on several issues, namely that the producer of a product is in the position to reduce risks and insure against injuries that could result. As with warranties, a software package must be considered a product for tort theory of strict liability to apply. If this criterion is met, developers, experts, manufacturers, and distributors could all be held liable for injuries even though reasonable care standards have been satisfied. For example, even though no errors are found in an expert system, the knowledge engineer could still be held liable under the tort theory of strict liability should damages or losses result from the use of the system. Imposition of this theory protects the user regardless of whether anyone is at fault, in a strict sense.

Strict liability has only been applicable to cases of physical injury. For example, in October 1993, manufacturers of breast silicone implants set aside $4.75 billion to settle tort liability covering 4,800 lawsuits over injuries resulting from the implants. Courts are reluctant to extend the theory to cases involving economic injury, but this may change. The major legal issues are summarized in Table 19–2.

■ **Table 19–2** Legal Issues of Expert Systems

1. An expert owns his or her knowledge if no prior agreement was established.

2. A preemployment contract or intellectual property agreement can limit the expert's own liability for the expert system.

3. If a knowledge engineer builds the expert system and a problem arises with the system, the knowledge engineer is subject to charges of personal liability under the doctrine of *respondeat superior.* If the knowledge engineer is an employee of an organization, the organization is also involved in the negligence action.

4. If an expert system is a product, proving negligence is unnecessary to hold the developer liable. The UCC allows developers to limit liability for defective knowledge bases via a disclaimer of warranties in the contract. For these liabilities, the loss falls on the developer, regardless of fault, as a cost of doing business.

5. If an expert system is a service, the contract law of the state would apply, rather than the UCC.

6. Courts tend to be reluctant toward exclude warranty disclaimers or attempts by the software house to avoid their applications as unconscionable.

7. Cases involving warranties require that the user show who is at fault and why.

8. The software in question should be considered a product under UCC rules for warranties to be relevant or for tort theory of strict liability to apply.

■ THE MALPRACTICE FACTOR

Most people have heard of litigation involving doctors being sued for malpractice. As a result, pediatricians, surgeons, and other professionals pay high premiums for malpractice insurance. **Malpractice** in the information technology field is negligence or professional liability applied to developers for design defects in systems tailored specifically for professional use. For experts to be liable for malpractice, they must be considered a professional, belong to a profession in which standards of care have been established, and owe a certain duty of care to those for whom they work.

At present, neither standardization nor certification that recognizes knowledge engineers as professionals has been established. So, they are not yet liable for malpractice. Some people argue that knowledge engineers should be licensed as a condition to build expert systems. (See Box 19–5.)

The discussion of liability and expert systems would not be complete without mention of the potential liability for failure to use expert systems. Professionals may be held liable for not using an expert system when it is available. One such case is T. J. Hooper. Hooper's tugboat lost the barges it was towing in a storm that the captain would have known about had the boat had a radio aboard. Even though a radio was not a required item, Hooper was found liable for the loss of the barges.

Yet, in another case that took place during the Persian Gulf war, the failure to comply with expert systems resulted in benefits. The U.S. intelligence community, relying on expert systems and satellites, found that only 25 percent of a key bridge in Baghdad had been destroyed. A call was made to Gen. H. Norman Schwarzkopf asking him to send a squadron to destroy the bridge. The general refused on the grounds that the 25 percent damage had severed one span, therefore rendering the entire bridge useless. Sending soldiers to destroy the bridge would expose them to unnecessary risks or even casualties.

If expert system developers are professionals, they may be sued for malpractice. What about expert systems that have evolved to the level of legitimate professionals? Could they not also be held liable for malpractice? If expert systems can be held liable for anything, then perhaps malpractice claims against them would be reasonable. For example, if a legal expert system has taken on all of the attributes and functions of a judge, then it should be held liable for malpractice just as a human judge would be. This scenario may be

Box 19–5   The Liability of Weather Forecasting

A case involving the National Weather Service (NWS) illustrates the potential danger of hyping the expert system technology. According to the evidence, four fishermen consulted a weather forecast released by the NWS before embarking on an expedition. Unfortunately, even after years of study, the prediction of weather still proves to be an inexact science. The fishermen were confronted with an unpredicted storm. All four men died. Their families sued the U.S. government for $1.25 million and won. Certainly, one who develops an expert system should be aware that the system may be held to certain standards.

stretching the imagination a bit, but suing an expert system for malpractice may eventually become a reality.

Malpractice is only one aspect of the liability that may exist in a world in which expert systems have reached their full potential. Others will undoubtedly be discovered to fill the legal gap that has been created by this new technology. Soon, new legal reasoning and new laws will be needed.

Anyone to whom liability for expert systems can reasonably be traced will bear responsibility. Picture a company that develops and sells an expert system that assists in the diagnosis of medical diseases. Over the next ten years of its use, the program encounters enough new diseases or new situations that it is able not only to expand its knowledge base but also to modify itself in such a way that the code could no longer be attributable to the original developer. If an injury occurred in such a situation, logically, the correct "person" to hold liable would be the expert system. Again, holding an expert system liable for anything may seem rather far-fetched, but may not necessarily be out of line as laws change to reflect the influence of this technology in everyday life.

IMPLICATIONS FOR MANAGEMENT

Expert systems are finding an increasingly large niche in the business world. Many people familiar with the technology predict that its future use will be commonplace. If true, a corresponding increase will probably occur in the number of lawsuits claiming injury from the use of expert systems. Because cases involving expert systems have no legal precedents, the legal system will have to adjust to the circumstances of this new technology.

As expert systems take on more and more of the attributes of human intelligence, the "older" theories of liability will undoubtedly become less and less helpful in deciding *who* is liable for damages. The concept of the "creator" will be lost. The most important of the humanlike functions that expert systems will assume are those of learning and motivation. They will continually learn from their experiences and environment and will subsequently modify themselves to adjust to changes. When this happens, the liability of the original developer or manufacturer liability becomes tenuous and unclear. These considerations should prompt organizations to review their strategies for expert system use.

Of course, the technology may never reach the stages at which these issues will arise; however, management is expected to continue to push technology to its limits in the interest of efficiency, performance, and profitability. Management must also consider the long-term effects of expert systems and their reliability in terms of quality decision making and competitive advantage.

In developing expert systems, knowledge engineers, experts, and developers may choose to ignore legal issues on the basis that the likelihood of litigation is remote. On the other hand, responsible system developers can become more proactive by approaching system building and their entire development life cycle with integrity. Having integrity includes never overselling the system or making outlandish claims. The zeal with which expert systems are built should be tempered with the realization that they are based on human knowledge and ideas, which are less than perfect.

■ SUMMARY

1. Ethics may include any of the following: fairness, justice, equity, honesty, trustworthiness, and equality. Something is ethical when a person feels it is innately right, which is a subjective judgment. An unethical act need not be immoral or illegal, although one act may imply another.

2. Several issues represent major threats to ethics. They include faster computers, sophisticated networks, ease of access to information, and transparency of software. Software copyright infringement, unauthorized E-mail access, and sale of competitive data are also serious ethical issues. To improve the corporate ethics climate, top management should act as the role model, establishing a realistic code of ethics and a strong training program.

3. A code of ethics is a declaration of principles and beliefs that govern how employees of a corporation must behave. The code should be all-encompassing and stable over time. Once posted, it becomes a commitment for the organization as a whole. Self-assessment allows periodic adjustments in the code.

4. In an age of litigious proliferation, users and developers should be cognizant of legal issues arising from expert system use or misuse. The key issue is determining who owns the knowledge. Depending on interpretation and the laws, it could be the user, the domain expert, the organization, or the developer. With no prior agreements, the expert is the rightful owner of knowledge and can be the target for litigation resulting from a faulty system. A preemployment contract releasing ownership to the firm would help limit liability of the expert.

5. The issue of whether the expert system is a product or a service depends on interpretation. If the software is custom-designed, then it is a service and the contract laws of the state in question would apply. If it is off-the-shelf software, it is a product, which means proving negligence is unnecessary to hold the developer liable.

6. The Uniform Commercial Code (UCC) offers provisions for computer contracts in the form of warranties. Warranties may be implied or express. Implied warranties expect the product to do what it's intended to do, which is covered under implied warranty of merchantability or fitness. Express warranty is presented orally or in writing by the seller.

7. Developers are open to malpractice—negligence due to design defects and resulting damages. At present, neither standardization nor certification recognizes knowledge engineers as professionals. In this respect, they are not yet liable for malpractice. Sooner or later, knowledge engineers should be licensed to build expert systems.

■ TERMS TO LEARN

Code of ethics a declaration of principles and beliefs that govern how employees of a corporation are to behave.

Disclaimer renunciation of a claim or power vested in a person or product.

Ethics fairness, justice, equity, honesty, trustworthiness; a subjective feeling of being innately right.

Express warranty warranty offered orally or in writing by the maker of the system.

Implied warranty presumed warranty; certain facts implied in the facts that represent the product.

Injury any wrong or damage done to others, their rights, property, or reputation.

Malpractice negligence or professional liability of a certified professional related to design defects in systems tailored specifically for professional use.

Negligence omission to do something, which a reasonable person, guided by those ordinary considerations that ordinarily regulate human affairs, would do; lack of reasonable conduct and care.

Product liability a tort that makes a manufacturer liable if its product has a defective condition that makes it unreasonably dangerous to the user or consumer.

Self-assessment question-and-answer procedure that allows a person to appraise and understand personal knowledge about a particular role: in ethics, to think about ethics and reinforce one's ethical behavior.

Stakeholder customer, employee, vendor, or person who has a vested interest in a company, a project, or a system.

Strict liability a seller is liable for any defective or hazardous products that unduly threatens a user's safety.

Tort wrongful act, subject to civil action; a legal wrong committed upon a person or a property independent of a contract; a wrongful injury to a person, a person's reputation, or a person's property.

Uniform Commercial Code (UCC) a law drafted by the National Conference of Commissioners on Uniform State Laws that governs commercial transactions.

Warranty a promise made by the seller that assures certain facts are truly representative of a product or service, subject to certain limitations.

REVIEW QUESTIONS

1. In your own words, describe how ethics relates to expert systems?
2. Review the journals and write an essay detailing the latest views of ethics in automation.
3. In what respect is an ethical act different from immoral or legal acts? Give an example of your own.
4. Distinguish between:
   a. product liability and tort law
   b. out-of-bounds and nontrivial errors
   c. code of ethics and self-assessment
   d. implied and express warranties
5. Explain briefly the ethical decision cycle. In what respect is it viewed as a cycle?
6. In your own words, discuss the major threats to ethics. Is one threat more serious than others? Be specific.
7. How can a code of ethics be applied in an organization? What are some of the barriers?
8. Suppose you were asked to set up a code of ethics for a computer department in a commercial bank. How do you proceed or what steps would you take to do the job? Explain.
9. Visit a company in your community and investigate the ethics issue or the code of ethics that exists in the firm. Write a brief report on your findings.
10. What is the purpose of self-assessment? How does it contribute to a corporate code of ethics?
11. The chapter suggests three possible owners of knowledge. Do you agree? Discuss.
12. Using question 11, explain what ways knowledge ownership will be an issue in the future.

13. In the event of a defective expert system, who would be held liable? Discuss in detail.

14. Is an expert system a product or service? Discuss the pros and cons of this issue and its implications for litigation.

15. Describe the circumstances in which knowledge engineers can be sued for malpractice in the future.

■ EXERCISES AND CASES

1. The board of directors of a bank had an attorney whose job was handling cases resulting from bad loans and other legal matters affecting the bank. The attorney's main line of business is real estate. Cases requiring specific expertise are referred to attorneys in town at the recommendation of the bank's attorney.

One day, a case came up in which an employee sued the bank and one of its vice presidents for sexual harassment. The bank's attorney decided to handle the case himself. After a lengthy trial, the court ruled in favor of the employee. The jury awarded the employee $350,000 in damages.

When asked why he did not have another attorney try the case, the bank's attorney replied that he thought he was saving the bank money by trying it himself even though he has had no prior experience with sexual harassment cases. At the outset, he did not think the case had much substance. The bank, on the other hand, was not happy with the results and blamed the attorney for botching the case.

Questions

a. Could any aspect of the attorney's decision to handle the case be considered unethical, immoral, or illegal?

b. Should the attorney be fired by the board of directors? Why?

c. Visit a local law library or talk to a local attorney and determine whether the bank attorney violated the American Bar Association's code of ethics.

2. An expert system was installed in the loan department of a bank to determine the qualifications of auto loan applicants. The knowledge acquired was based on that of the bank's vice president in charge of auto loans. The bank paid the knowledge engineer (an outside consultant) in full for the package, which included training a junior loan officer in the use of the system.

Four months later, the developer of the Loan Advisor learned through one of the employees that the bank modified the knowledge base to develop a real estate loan expert system on its own. The junior loan officer took the bank's VP-Expert package home and spent time learning how to build expert systems. He then worked jointly with the senior vice president of the real estate department to build the new system. Several modules of the Auto Loan Advisor that check for the applicant's assets, salary, place of employment, and so on were copied into the new system. The approach to the system as well as the procedure were identical.

The developer filed a lawsuit against the bank, seeking damages and the right of ownership to the system. The bank, in turn, filed a countersuit claiming it purchased the package outright and therefore owes the developer nothing.

Questions

a. What went wrong in this case? Elaborate.

b. Was an implied or express warranty a part of the Auto Loan Advisor? Explain.

c. Are any ethical, moral, or legal considerations at issue here? Elaborate.

d. Who do you think owns the knowledge in the Real Estate Advisor? Explain.

e. Based on the material presented in the chapter, how do you think the court would rule? Elaborate.

f. Who owns the procedure used to build the expert system? Is it proprietary? Explain.

SELECTED REFERENCES

Aguilar, Francis J. *Managing Corporate Ethics: Learning from America's Ethical Companies How to Supercharge Business Performance.* New York; Oxford University Press, 1994.

Churchman, C. West. "Management Science: Science of Managing and Managing of Science." *Interfaces,* July–August 1994, pp. 99–110.

Collins, W. Robert; Keith W. Miller; and Bethany J. Spielman. "How Good Is Good Enough? An Ethical Analysis of Software Construction and Use." *Communications of the ACM,* January 1994, pp. 81–91.

DeGeorge, Richard T. *Business Ethics,* 2d ed. New York: MacMillan, 1986.

Dejoie, Roy; George Fowler; and David Paradic. *Ethical Issues in Information Systems.* Boston, MA: Boyd & Fraser, 1991.

Effy, Oz. *Ethics in the Information Age.* New York; Wm. C. Brown, 1994.

Eraut, Michael. *Developing Professional Knowledge and Competence.* Washington, D.C.: Falmer Press, 1994.

Forester, Tom and Perry Morrison. *Computer Ethics: Cautionary Tales and Ethical Dilemmas in Computing.*

Fraedrich, John; Debbie M. Thorne; and O. C. Ferrell. "Assessing the Application of Cognitive Moral Development Theory to Business Ethics." *Journal of Business Ethics,* October 1994, pp. 829–838.

Garone, Stephen J., ed. *Business Ethics: Generating Trust in the 1990s and Beyond.* New York; Conference Board, 1994.

Geyelin, Milo. "Faulty Software Means Business for Litigators." *Wall Street Journal* (Eastern edition), January 21, 1994, p. B1.

Gorlin, Rena A., ed. *Codes of Professional Responsibility,* 3rd ed. Washington, D.C.: Bureau of National Affairs, 1994.

Gotterbarn, Donald. "Ethics and the Computing Professional." *Collegiate Microcomputer,* August 1992, pp. 137–147.

Hart, Christopher W. L. *Extraordinary Guarantees: A New Way to Build Quality Throughout Your Company and Ensure Satisfaction for Your Customers.* New York; Amacom, 1993.

Howie, John and George Schedler, eds. *Ethical Issues in Contemporary Society.* Carbondale, IL: Southern Illinois University Press, 1995.

Khalil, Omar E. M. "Artificial Decision-Making and Artificial Ethics: A Management Concern." *Journal of Business Ethics,* April 1993, pp. 313–321.

Kallman, Ernest A. and John P. Grillo. *Ethical Decision Making and Information Technology: An Introduction With Cases.* New York; Mitchell McGraw-Hill, 1993.

Levmore, Saul X. *Foundations of Tort Law.* New York; Oxford University Press, 1994.

Lynn, Marc P. and William N. Bockanic. "Legal Liability of the Domain Expert." *Journal of Systems Management,* November 1993, pp. 6–12.

Mason, Richard O. "Four Ethical Issues in the Information Age." *MIS Quarterly,* March 1986, pp. 5–12.

Mathias, T. A. and Tandon Prakash. *Corporate Ethics.* New Delhi: Allied Publishers, 1994.

McGrath, Elizabeth Z. *The Art of Ethics: A Psychology of Ethical Beliefs.* Chicago; Loyola University Press, 1994.

McPartlin, John P. "Ethics." *Information Week,* July 13, 1992, pp. 30–36.

Mykytyn, Peter P. and Kathleen Mykytyn. "Legal Perspectives on Expert Systems." *AI Expert,* December 1991, pp. 41–45.

Newton, Adam Z. *Narrative Ethics.* Cambridge, MA: Harvard University Press, 1995.

Parker, Don B. *Ethical Conflicts in Computer Science and Technology.* Arlington, VA: AFIPS Press, 1981.

Rogers, McCagie Brooks. "The MYTHSEEKER Project: Concepts and Realization." *Journal of Systems & Software,* June 1994, pp. 271–298.

Tuthill, G. Steven. "Legal Liabilities and Expert Systems." *AI Expert,* March 1991, pp. 45–52.

Warner, Edward. "Expert Systems and the Law." *High Technology Business,* October 1988, pp. 32–35.

Weiss, Eric A., ed. "Self-Assessment." *Communications of the ACM,* November 1990, pp. 110–132.

Weller, Herman G.; Judi Repman; and Gene E. Rooze. "Students and Computer Ethics: An Alternative to Preaching." *Computing Teacher,* August–September 1992, pp. 20–22.

Whitby, Blay. *Reflections on Artificial Intelligence the Legal, Moral, and Ethical.* Lehigh Valley, PA: Science Express, 1994.

Chapter ■ 20

Where Do We Go from Here?

ARTIFICIAL INTELLIGENCE AS THE YEAR 2000 APPROACHES

I still consider the paper in *MIND* to be the best thing Turing ever wrote. He began with the question, "Can machines think?" In that form, he found the question to be unsatisfactorily formulated. An attempt to extract the essential underlying point of interest led him to propose the famous *Turing test.* Instead of asking whether a particular machine could think, he suggested that one should instead ask whether it could pass this test. The test involved the machine posing as a human being and defying an interrogator to determine whether it was a man or a woman.

There is no difficulty in writing a program that will exhibit a simple form of learning, e.g., learning to recognize abbreviations for people's names. The program would contain a list of the abbreviations it already understood. Given an unfamiliar abbreviation, the program would make a guess. It would be told whether it was right or wrong and would update its list accordingly. This can fairly be called learning, although there is nothing deep about it.

Stimulated by Turing's paper, my colleagues and I tried our hands at writing various learning programs of the kind I have just described. Their limitations soon became obvious. They did what they had been written to do, but no more. For that reason, they were uninteresting as soon as they had been run for the first time. I soon appreciated that a breakthrough was required in the direction of what I called *generalized learning programs,* which would go on learning new things. Perhaps, it would have been better to have called them *unrestricted* learning programs.

If computers had existed in the late seventeenth century and people had known how to write unrestricted learning programs, then a machine equipped with such a program would have been ready to absorb the work of Newton when it was published, and later that of Faraday and Einstein. It would now be doing its best with black holes! It would have read the novels of Dickens, and would be able to engage in the sort of half-teasing dialogue that Turing's fertile mind delighted in inventing (see box).

Turing's Dream: A Dialogue With a Computer
The interrogator is a human being and the witness is a computer.

INTERROGATOR: The first line of your sonnet reads, "Shall I compare thee to a summer's day?" Would not "a spring day" do as well or better?

WITNESS: It wouldn't scan.

INTERROGATOR: How about "a winter's day?" That would scan all right.

WITNESS: Yes, but nobody wants to be compared to a winter's day.

INTERROGATOR: Would you say Mr. Pickwick reminded you of Christmas?

WITNESS: In a way.

INTERROGATOR: Christmas is a winter's day, but I do not think Mr. Pickwick would mind the comparison.

WITNESS: I don't think you're serious. By "a winter's day" one means a typical winter's day, not a special one like Christmas.

EXPERT SYSTEMS AND TURING'S DREAM

Originally, the term AI was used exclusively in the sense of Turing's dream that a computer might be programmed to behave like an intelligent human being. In recent years, however, AI has been used more as a label for programs which, if they had not emerged from the AI community, might have been seen as a natural fruit of work with such languages as COMIT and SNOBOL, and of the work of E.T. Irons on a pioneering syntax-directed compiler. I refer to expert systems.

In simple expert systems, all the knowledge is incorporated by the programmer in the program, as indeed the alternative name *knowledge-based systems* clearly brings out. It is as though a child were taught the multiplication table by having a surgical operation performed on its brain. In more elaborate expert systems, some updating of an internal data base takes place during the lifetime of the system. These systems exhibit the same form of learning as the programs discussed earlier, and have the same limitations. Expert systems are indeed a valuable gift that the AI community has made to the world at large, but they have nothing to do with Turing's dream.

Turing predicted in 1950 that his dream would be realized within 50 years; specifically that it would be realized on a computer with 128 MB of memory altogether. Fifty years brings us to the year 2000, and it's clear that Turing's prediction will not be realized. Indeed, it is difficult to escape the conclusion that in the 40 years that have elapsed since 1950, no tangible progress has been made towards realizing machine intelligence in the sense that Turing had envisaged. Perhaps, the time has come to face the possibility that it never will be realized with a digital computer.

BRAIN: DIGITAL OR ANALOGUE?

If we are prepared to regard the human brain as a machine, then we have an existence proof that machines can exhibit intelligence. However, this will not help with the problem of whether digital computers can exhibit intelligence unless we are prepared to assert that the human brain is digital in action. If we do this, we are faced by a purely practical consideration. The human neuron is about five orders of magnitude slower than the gates in a modern digital computer; how would it be possible for the brain, if it were digitally organized, to be sufficiently fast? Those who think of the brain as digital will usually say that it must make up for what it lacks in speed by possessing a high degree of parallelism. However, massively parallel computers find it hard to gain a factor of 100 or even 10 in speed. Even the most determined enthusiast for parallel computation may balk at a factor of 100,000.

However, the argument is academic since there is no reason why we should regard the human brain as a digital device. Indeed, the digital vs. analogue dichotomy is wholly inappropriate as an approach to the functioning of the human brain. As I have pointed out, the digital computer is an abstraction—one which a human designer finds useful as a way of organizing his thoughts. There is no reason why a nonhuman designer should operate the same way. On the evolutionary hypothesis, it is even an error to regard the brain as having been designed to meet a stated requirement. "Blind evolution stumbled on . . . lo! there were men and men could think.

I do not wish to give the impression that I think Turing's dream will come true, but with analogue rather than digital machines. I make no such prediction. Indeed, it may be that the sort of analogue machines that we are able to construct are themselves subject to limitations, which may or may not parallel those of digital machines. I do, however, suggest we take as a working hypothesis that intelligent behavior in Turing's sense is outside the range of the digital computer.

Source: Maurice V. Wilkes, "Artificial Intelligence as the Year 2000 Approaches," *Communications of the ACM* 35, no. 8 (August 1992).

■ INTRODUCTION

This text has focused on the concepts, procedures, and life cycle of expert systems. It is clear by now that expert systems provide an appropriate technology for certain problem domains and can be a profitable investment when built effectively. Since expert systems' primary achievement is to preserve expertise that would otherwise be lost, organizations are quickly finding out that knowledge preservation is "money in the bank."

Because of the obvious contributions of expert systems, "intelligent" systems are beginning to be put to general use: Elaborate medical systems diagnose disease and prescribe treatment, intelligent financial advisors evaluate loans for approval, and, in limited English, office computers interact, "speak," and react to humans.

The key question is "Where is this technology going?" Or perhaps a more specific question is "What future will it have across industries?" This chapter addresses such changes in terms of their potential impact and how the self-image of organizations is affected as a result. Later in the chapter, advances in virtual reality (VR) and how VR applications provide unique problem solutions are discussed.

■ LEVELS OF CHANGE

Historically, since the late 1970s, technological change has occurred on three levels:

1. *In methodological change,* word processors, cash-dispensing machines in banking, and electronic scanning in retailing have improved productivity without significantly impacting employee skills. People continue to do the same jobs, but with a higher degree of efficiency. Unfortunately, electronic theft is as much as two orders of magnitude greater than conventional theft, averaging $500,000. It performs the same illicit function, but with improved efficiency. In this regard, the technology affects *how people do things* not *what* people do.

2. Throughout the 1980s, a significant *shift in jobs* and lifestyles has taken place via cost-effective robotics and programmable machines that handle monotonous, hazardous, or high-risk jobs once performed by costly human labor.

3. The 1990s brought AI, human-oriented, and *knowledge-based applications* that appear to redefine the human role in business and society.

The potential of expert systems that advise and otherwise participate in decision making depends on how people see themselves as intelligent decision makers. An important question is "How will workers be affected by an intelligent response from a device?" Or "How will people's view of themselves change when confronted with a super intelligence?" Artificially intelligent dialogue so far appears to be acceptable when it is in an unrestricted English format.

One hundred years ago, people got jobs done through physical labor. With today's machinery and electronics, most people get work done using their knowledge and mental abilities. If these abilities are replaced by expert systems, how will people stay mentally fit?

■ THE PRESENT POSITION: WORKING SMARTER, NOT HARDER

Any discussion on the status of expert systems and AI is bound to produce both optimists and doubters. Based on the evidence so far, the great potential of this technology lies in the sharing of know-how (expertise) to augment the decision-making capacity of the user. Expert systems are the most powerful tool available to augment corporate expertise. Expert systems can now be applied to tasks that require people to use their intelligence. Expert systems can succeed best in an organizational culture that supports change.

Knowledge workers are distinguished from information handlers by their ability to solve problems and add value to their solutions. This group includes managers, technicians, engineers, and professionals typically in the middle ranks of an organization. Expert systems herald the dawn of the "power tool of the mind." They provide an approach whereby capital can be employed to improve productivity of whole groups of workers who once relied on human capabilities alone. This is what is meant by "working smarter, not harder."

The trend in today's expert system development is in building simple ones with obvious payoffs. Simple systems are also the easiest to build, giving knowledge engineers a chance to improve their expertise using high-level languages, special languages, or shells. These applications include fault diagnosis, financial advisors, and troubleshooting systems. In fault diagnosis, for example, an expert system can help with maintenance, provide better facilities for the user, and screen requests for immediate repairs. These capabilities are especially important in the manufacturing industry.

Technical Aspects

Several technical aspects of the future of expert systems are worth considering. On the software side, the trend seems to be toward shell programming, including programming by the user. More and more shells provide graphic user interface (GUI) features and interfaces with word processors, databases, and spreadsheets. GUI should make it possible to use expert systems as front-end to database applications that consult database records rather than ask the user for the same information.

At present, a limited but growing cadre of experienced knowledge engineers that build expert systems as a career is available. As the demand for knowledge engineers increases, so, too, will the requirement for de-skilling or reducing the demand on individual ability of knowledge engineers in order to build expert systems successfully. The expectation is that future skills will become more intelligent in monitoring and coaching the builder and the development process as well. Of course, the interpersonal element of knowledge engineering will always be part of the building effort.

ASSESSING ORGANIZATIONAL NEED FOR EXPERT SYSTEMS

To survive in today's business world, every organization needs to periodically assess its informational and knowledge requirements. Exploiting expert systems is a priority for companies whose competitive edge is a must. Expert systems' greatest impact occurs in the areas of marketing, production, sales, and customer support, where leverage on profitability is critical.

Other areas of sensitivity include those in which expertise is at a premium. Indicators of expertise shortage include:

- The organization's difficulty to innovate
- High staff turnover
- Inability to respond to changing consumer demands or preferences

Retaining expertise continues to be the number one concern in most firms—a concern that can be addressed by expert systems. For first-time organizations, expert systems projects should have the following goals:

- Aim to *support* rather than replace the user. Augmenting user preference should find many allics.
- Scope the application within realistic constraints—financial and political.
- Choose a first-application project that is low-risk, low-cost, manageable, and doable within months rather than years, and has a high probability of success. Success of the first application can be the best way to sell new technology to management and users alike.

TREND TOWARD INTEGRATION: A VIRTUAL REALITY

As expert systems become more common, their use is expected to be integrated not only with databases and word processors, but with imaging systems. Although "imaging" is quite broad, the focus here is on computer-generated interactive three-dimensional (3-D) images of real as well as abstract objects. The outcome is virtual reality (VR).

VR and expert systems are closely related. VR centers on the power functionality of multidimensional presentation of data and solutions. In VR, dynamic interaction with the questions allows the technology to help the user experience the advice or solution displayed on the screen in a realistic environment via visualization and sensing. Information appears as graphic objects that dynamically respond to user input. The computer provides a sensory-based environment using sounds, visuals, and sensations that emulate actual decisions.

Virtual agents (see Chapter 18) pass functionality at the instruction and planning levels to the user. They can be constructed with a variety of technologies, including knowledge-based systems and neural networks. For example, in a loan advisor application, instead of entering information into the expert system and receiving a "approve/do not approve" decision, a virtual loan advisor combines the rules represented in the knowledge base, supplemented by a synthesized voice accompanied by the tone of the voice and an image of the vice president, and gives the applicant a more realistic feel for an actual face-to-face session with the loan officer.

VR has been defined in different ways:

- Dynamic interaction between users and the virtual world.
- Getting *into* versus *at* one's work.
- Interactive laws of physics, or the way the physical world interrelates.
- Worlds with movement; a place where objects react in a manner consistent with a set of rules.
- Modeling a sense of realism by increasing image, using motion and complex behavior of objects, which implies response in a variety of preprogrammed ways.
- Immersive VR—immersion and navigation within a computer-generated, 3-D environment and ability to manipulate objects within space.
- Use of computing technology to create interactive 3-D environment.

Virtual reality, virtual worlds, artificial reality—these terms all represent the technology of putting humans into environments that are completely computer-generated. Virtual reality is a computer-generated simulation of sight, sound, and touch. The VR system gives motion clues and forces feedback that makes the user feel a virtual object. See Box 20–1. It also contains special sensors that track the user's movements, relay them to the computer, and adjust the virtual world accordingly. Unlike the real world, the user decides on every step and action in a virtual world. In this way, VR is more of a "planned reality."

VR is already in use by the military to simulate battles between tanks, fighter jets, or helicopters. Architects also use VR to plan and design rooms and buildings. Astronauts prepared for a repair mission to the Hubble space

---

Box 20–1   Educational Uses for Virtual Reality

Absolutely mind blowing!!! I popped a French Learning CD into the *Learning Machine*. Immediately I was sucked into a deep, dream-like trance. Weird colors and patterns were created on the insides of my closed eyelids. While in this super-relaxed but hyper-aware state, the special Learning CD began unfolding its magic programming.

It was as if a movie were playing inside my head. I could see myself in France having lunch at the Eiffel Tower. The music, the sounds, even the fragrance of summer in Paris. A beautiful woman spoke to me. "Bonjour, mon ami," she said. In an almost unconscious way I began following the dialogue. The mental imagery was so intense I not only understood what was going on, it was like I was there. Impossible? Maybe not.

Source: Dane Spotts, "Mind Power Breakthrough," *U.S. News & World Report,* September 12, 1994, p. 88.

telescope in a Johnson Space Center lab wearing VR headsets, taking virtual space walks, and practicing parts installations in a virtual zero gravity.

The Virtual Experience

How a user enters, explores, and becomes part of VR can take several forms. Virtual experience is attained by wearing a special garb consisting of

- A *DataGlove* with position tracking to provide a naturalistic handling of objects within a virtual world. See Figure 20–1. Using such a device allows a person to change the location of an object within the virtual world.

- A *DataSuit* designed to map movements of the entire body. The device senses and registers all body movements and sends information to the computer, which provides feedback to the user.

- *Stereoscopic goggles* to provide inputs (color images) to the user, which provide slightly different views to each eye for depth perspective. The goggles track the user's eyes in such a way that, wherever the user looks, the virtual world appears to surround the user. The feedback from the VR system gives this "near real-life" virtual experience.

The most obvious elements of VR are:

- *Stereo visual* or imagery—the part of the virtual world that affects the eyes—including geometry (shape of objects) and appearance (color, texture, etc.)

- *Sound* to provide auditory feedback

- *Behavior* of objects in a virtual world in the way they move, make noise, react, and respond to external events.

Figure 20–1   The Virtual Reality Experience

Source: *AI Expert,* May 1994, p. 25.

Areas of Use

The basis for introducing VR is the supposition that if information can be visualized, it can be managed more effectively. This "management" is done by navigating through 3-D computer worlds or VR. VR also deals with especially complex end-user applications that create a demand for subjectively "intelligent" systems. Using VR also means direct experience rather than just information; for example, giving real estate clients the experience of "walking through" houses and neighborhoods rather than just viewing a photograph or a text. See Box 20–2.

VR is currently in use in several areas. The following list provides some select examples of the growing nature of the technology and the way it is impacting virtually every industry.

- Automotive engineers create 3-D models of cars. By "entering" the car, they can detect flaws and make alternate changes in the design.
- Radiologists scan the inside of the human body and "enter" a tumor to plan appropriate treatment.
- A Virtually Coupled Airborn System Simulator (VCASS), developed by Aerospace Medical Research Lab, helps control pilots in a virtual cockpit.
- Northrop & Boeing Aircraft use VR to build mockups of airplanes to allow the designers to change the configuration or size, or to walk within the design subject to the designer's imagination.

Box 20–2   How Real Is Virtual Reality?

The tumor is big, but not smooth or perfectly formed. It's whitish pink and spongy—an ungrateful guest in the left lung.

At a hospital in Chapel Hill, N.C., a radiology treatment planner dons special eyeglasses. Suddenly he finds himself in a 3-D world that is as astounding as it is oddly familiar. It's as if he had somehow entered the patient's body—as if he were *inside* the tumor, looking out. Turning his head, he surveys the contours of the deadly intruder, then the lung, and finally he looks beyond, to muscle, bone and flesh.

Now he does something that seems almost godlike. He reaches out and begins grabbing radiation beams, aligning each of them straight to the heart of the tumor and avoiding radiosensitive tissues, such as the spinal cord and esophagus. If beams are cross-fired from a number of different angles, the tumor is irradiated far more than the surrounding tissue. Each patient, each tumor, is different, and so is each treatment plan.

Satisfied, the radiation treatment planner removes the special glasses and "returns" to the hospital lab. A few days later, a radiologist, armed with a precise plan of attack, will kill the tumor during actual treatment. And the patient will live.

Purely science fiction?

No, it's a project currently in prototype at the University of North Carolina. Like many others being pursued at research facilities around the world, it is based on the real potential of the technology known as virtual reality.

Source: Howard Rheingold, *Beyond Computing,* March–April 1992, p. 25.

- Virtual Egress Analysis System (VEGAS) models the way a large crowd behaves in emergencies, such as exit from a burning plane. By modeling a variety of behavioral responses to the virtual environment (viewed in real-time), the action of a crowd can be predicted and accommodated within a design with a high degree of accuracy.

- The Advanced Robotics Research Laboratory (ARRL) has several heavy-duty industrial robots that can cause considerable damage if handled improperly. By modeling the robot's action in a virtual environment, novice users can learn how to use it without much difficulty.

- In a self-evolving ecosystem consisting of bees and flowers, successful flowers attract the bees. Additional factors determine the bee's choice of flowers, when to breed, how much time looking for a mate, etc. The descendants of the bees and flowers differ from their parents somewhat, letting natural selection take place.

- Oil companies use visualization methods to analyze seismic data for more reliable discovery of oil.

- Real estate agents use VR systems to give home buyers the experience of "walking through" houses and surrounding areas. The VR system improves the likelihood of closing a sale.

- VR provides the capability of *telepresence,* or performing tasks in a distant location via robotics. Hazardous tasks that once threatened humans can now be performed with relative safety and ease. At present, NASA uses VR to control robots working in space.

- *Televirtuality* (televirtual reality) expands the concept of videoconferencing. Two or more users continents apart use an interface system to a common virtual environment to discuss business and innovative products.

As can be expected, certain barriers presently discourage the incorporation of VR into the work place. They include the prohibitively high cost, low-resolution visual quality, lack of standards, unwieldy data goggles, and lack of tactile feedback. Inasmuch as this technology is exciting, its potential cannot yet be evaluated with any degree of accuracy.

■ WHAT TO EXPECT IN THE NEXT DECADE

With continuing changes and developments in technology, predicting any definite pattern in change is difficult. Yet, current indicators suggest a direction to this change. Based on current research and the literature, the following changes can be expected to take place in the next decade:

- Decision makers of large corporations will trust their expert systems over their human advisors. As expert systems improve their success record, more and more users can rely on their advice or solutions.

- Most households will have an affordable telephone instrument capable of transmitting text, images, speech, and live video. Knowledge-based agents will serve as interfaces to such systems. This situation may seem far-fetched, but it is actually not so far from reality when one takes a close look at what is happening in multimedia, imaging, and virtual reality.

■ The machines that humans have created will define what is intelligent. Chances are we may not qualify. Future machines are expected to be so intelligent that they will be able to give an impression that people solved a problem by themselves.

The State of Knowledge-Based Systems

Looking retrospectively at knowledge-based systems, the early 1980s saw the start-up of several companies to commercialize expert systems. A decade later, thousands of expert systems have been deployed across industries. The resulting developments point to a number of interesting conclusions:

1. Expert systems have established a permanent place in industry. Their roles range from assistants to human operators, diagnosticians to medical personnel, advisors to loan officers, and troubleshooters to complex machinery.

2. Expert systems increasingly add value in a firm by interacting in a cooperative way with applications such as data bases. Because they are known for being the most interactive and helpful user interface, they are leading the way toward a new generation of *cooperative systems.* Many current applications of knowledge processing combine expert systems technology with other conventional computer processing methods to produce overall solutions.

3. Because the idea behind expert systems implies change, organizations must overcome cultural and other barriers if such technology is to continue. For these tasks, the role of the champion becomes crucial.

Given the evolutionary nature of expert systems, one can easily envision, in the long run, borderless industries of knowledge workers who work together in teams to conceptualize, design, implement, and support products and technology. In such a new environment, many of the critical business functions (production, marketing, engineering, sales, finance) could conceivably be powered by knowledge-based computer-aided transactions.

■ IN A NUTSHELL

Knowledge-based systems have been remarkably effective since the early 1980s, delivering order-of-magnitude increases in quality, speed, or performance. They have shown reliability and improved performance in every major institution from *Fortune 500* companies to small businesses, military services, health care, and government. Although expert systems may not entirely replace many experts, they will definitely reduce the amount of times their expertise will be needed. In this respect, expert systems are appealing to many organizations across industries.

To increase the appeal and acceptance of expert systems, expert system applications should have several unique attributes:

■ Improve the performance of the user rather than replace one or more of the user's functions. The pressure on organizations is to look inward as well as outward to expand its market share. Expert systems are the most powerful tool available for amplifying that expertise.

- Fall within the scope of an expert who is confident in his or her own skill, authoritative, willing to cooperate, and can devote sufficient time to the project.

- Have potential to further the aims of the firm, whatever they may be.

- Be modest in scope compared with what is expected of a human. The more well defined the scope of an expert system is, the more easily the system will provide good quality solutions.

All indicators show that the greatest potential for expert systems lies in the sharing of expertise—*sharing know-how.* The greatest contribution of an expert system is its capability to augment the abilities of the user, allowing the user to work smarter, not harder. Unfortunately, the technology available to build expert systems is far ahead of most organizations' abilities to exploit it.

While the power of the expert system is largely dependent on the talent of the domain expert, its usefulness is strongly influenced by the knowledge engineer. The knowledge engineer's role will be increasingly important as more expert systems are used to serve the long-term problem-solving needs of the firm.

Finally, in organizations whose product is information, knowledge workers have been likened to artisans. They transform their material, add value to it, rather than just handle it as clerks or laborers would. Expert systems open the era for knowledge workers who view such systems as "power tools for the mind." This opportunity applies to managers, technicians, engineers, and other professionals. Computer power can now be applied to tasks that require people to use their intelligence rather than just data or information.

■ SELECTED REFERENCES

Anonymous. "New Tool for Aircraft Designers: Virtual Reality." *Machine Design,* November 21, 1994, p. 30.

_____ "Virtual Prototyping Can Cut Costs, Speed Schedules." *Aviation Week & Space Technology,* July 18, 1994, pp. 79–80.

Ashline, Peter C. and Vincent S. Lai. "Virtual Reality." *Information Systems Management,* Winter 1995, pp. 82–85.

Barfield, Woodrow and Tom Furness, eds. *Virtual Environments and Advanced Interface Design.* New York: Oxford University Press, 1995.

Brown, David. "New World Opens With a Touch." *The Times Higher Education Supplement,* no. 1153:vii (December 9, 1994).

Bunker, Linda K. "Virtual Reality: Movement's Centrality." *Quest,* November 1994, pp. 456–474.

Burdea, Grigore and Philippe Coiffet. *Virtual Reality Technology.* New York: John Wiley & Sons, 1994.

Carley, Kathleen M. and Michael J. Prietula, eds. *Computational Organization Theory.* Hillsdale, NJ: Lawrence Erlbaum Associates, 1994.

Clancy, Heather. "Virtual Reality Branches Out." *Computer Reseller News,* November 7, 1994, pp. 63, 70.

Coates, Joseph F. "The Highly Probable Future." *Futurist,* July–August 1994, pp. 551–557.

Coull, Tom and Peter Rothman. "Virtual Reality for Decision Support Systems." *AI Expert,* August 1993, pp. 22–25.

Cradler, John. "Technology: Past, Present, Future." *Thrust for Educational Leadership,* September 1994, pp. 30–37.

Davis, Stan and Jim Botkin. "The Coming of Knowledge-Based Business." *Harvard Business Review,* September–October 1994, pp. 165–170.

DeLoughry, Thomas J. "Computers of the Future." *The Chronicle Of Higher Education,* August 3, 1994, p. A15.

Diebold, John. "The Next Revolution in Computers." *The Futurist,* May–June 1994, pp. 34–37.

Dvorak, John C. "A Look at the Computer Issues of the Future." *PC Computing,* May 1994, p. 99.

El-najdawi, M. K. and Anthony C. Stylianou. "Expert Support Systems: Integrating AI Technologies."

Communications of the ACM, December 1993, pp. 55–65.

Foltin, L. Craig. "The Future of Expert Systems." *National Public Accountant,* July 1994, pp. 28–31.

Goel, Ashish. "The Reality and Future of Expert Systems." *Information Systems Management,* Winter 1994, pp. 53–61.

Goodrum, Abby A. "Entertainment Technology and the Human-Computer Interface." *American Society for Information Science,* October–November 1994, pp. 18–19.

Jenner, Lisa. "Are You Ready for the Virtual Workplace?" *HR Focus,* July 1994, pp. 15–16.

Kathawala, Yunus; William R. Allen; and Jaipeep Motwani. "Expert Systems: Applications in Quality." *International Journal of Quality & Reliability Management,* 10, no. 7 (1993), pp. 32–43.

MacDonald, L. W.; John Vince; and Ben Schneiderman, eds. *Interacting With Virtual Environments.* New York: John Wiley & Sons, 1994.

McDuffie, R. Steve; Debra Oden; and Eugene P. Porter. "Tax Expert Systems and Future Development." *CPA Journal,* January 1994, pp. 73–75.

Metcalfe, Bob. "What Happened to Artificial Intelligence?" *InfoWorld,* April 12, 1993, p. 48.

Newby, Gregory B. "Virtual Reality and the Entertainment Industry." *American Society for Information Science,* October–November 1994, pp. 20–21.

Shieber, Stuart M. "Lessons from a Restricted Turing Test." *Communications of the ACM,* June 1994, pp. 70–78.

Steels, Luc; Guus Schreiber; and Walter van de Velde. *A Future for Knowledge Acquisition.* Proceedings of the Eighth European Knowledge Acquisition Workshop, EKAW '94, Hoegaarden, Belgium, September 26–29, 1994. New York: Springer-Verlag, 1994.

Wetter, Thomas, ed. *Current Developments in Knowledge Acquisition:* Proceedings of the Sixth European Knowledge Acquisition Workshop, EKAW '92. New York: Springer-Verlag, 1992.

Appendix ■ A

Prolog: The Language of Expert Systems

THE PRACTICAL APPLICATION OF PROLOG

Prolog is no longer the best-kept secret in the programming industry. The Prolog programming language is not solely an AI language confined to research laboratories, but is increasingly seen as a powerful tool for the development of practical applications. The technology is now in widespread use in a wide range of domains, including finance, defense, telecommunications, medicine, law, agriculture, engineering, manufacturing, and education. Prolog has some clear advantages over other programming languages and can lead to significant returns on investments and competitive advantages. Through the recently formed Prolog Vendors Group, together with events such as the Prolog Applications Conference and the Prolog 1000 catalogue, we now have solid information on many hundreds of fielded applications, demonstrating that Prolog is fast becoming the language of choice for many software developers.

PIGS

When you ask what Prolog is good for, it is tempting to point to its clear success a particular set of application areas, including a natural language and databases. While it is true that Prolog has qualities that are especially well-suited to these domains, Prolog is used for a surprisingly broad range of application areas.

One of the more interesting applications is PigE/Auspig—an expert system for raising pigs, which won the award for the best presentation at the First International Conference on the Practical Applications of Prolog. PigE is an intelligent backend to a mathematical modeling package called Auspig. The Auspig model simulates the growth and reproduction of pigs, identifies factors that limit optimal performance of the pig, and suggests management strategies that maximize profits. PigE presents an abstracted description of the output of the model in a form a nonmathematician can understand and suggests dietary, housing, genotype, or resource input changes, which the developers say can dramatically improve the profitability of the herd.

ENVIRONMENT

Another area where Prolog is successful is in environmental systems that predict the weather, analyze water supplies, and so on. The MM4 Weather Modeling System, developed at Penn State University and the National Center for Atmospheric Research (Boulder, Colorado) gives relatively detailed short-term forecasts of meteorological conditions in the continental United States. It is used particularly to model pollutant dispersion (for instance, acid rain deposition). The original program, which contained 16,000 lines of FORTRAN code, was harnessed with Strand 88, and 10-fold speedups have been obtained with 15 parallel processors.

RoadWeather Pro is a 24-hour weather prediction system for snow and ice control on highways. Developed using PDC Prolog version 3.30 for Windows 3.1, RoadWeather Pro consists of three components. The first component is a numerical weather prediction system that forecasts from specified initial (radiosound and surface observations) and boundary conditions (detailed terrain effects) using a system of hydrodynamic and thermodynamic differential equations. The second component is a graphical user interface (GUI) written in Prolog under Windows 3.1, which the developer says is fully interactive and displays predicted weather phenomena as symbolic objects. The final component is an Expert Weather Advisor which permits mouse point-and-click manipulation of weather "objects," thereby allowing forecast upgrades based on recent observational data received from sensors or human observers. The RoadWeather Pro system is in use at the WELS Research Corporation (Boulder, Colorado).

THE GOLD RUSH

Finally, the U.S. gold rush could have been a lot more effective using Prolog. Goldfinder is a knowledge-based system that advises an exploration geologist on where to find gold. Developed by D. D. Hawkes using MacProlog from the London-based Logic Programming Associates, the Goldfinder system assesses the potential of a gold prospect and gives advice on the best location to site a drill hole. The geologist's map of the prospect is the primary source of input data. Knowledge is stored partly as semantic networks but mainly in a production rule formalism. Through interaction with the user, the system establishes a sophisticated dynamic database containing information about the main lithologies, the nature of any mineralization or alteration, and the structural features of the prospect. Using a method of intersecting loci, the system locates a drill site with a precision governed only by the scale of the map.

PROLOG IS EVERYWHERE

Prolog's fast incremental development cycle and rapid prototyping capabilities have encouraged the use of the language as a tool for solving AI problems. However, other features of Prolog make it a particularly powerful tool for building robust commercial applications. These features include interfaces to other languages and database products, stand-alone application generators, and more recently, support for techniques such as object-oriented and constraint-based programming.

Prolog has grown from a simple stand-alone interpreter into a full compiler-based technology with links to external databases, GUIs, and other languages such as C, and in so doing has effectively made the transition from academic-theorem prover to a complete general-purpose programming language. Prolog technology will continue to mature and build on its foundation. The language will be increasingly deployed in conjunction with conventional information systems, data processing systems, and specialized markets such as scheduling, help desks, configuration, and planning.

Source: Excerpted from Al Roth, "The Practical Application of Prolog," *AI Expert*, April 1993, pp. 25ff.

> The very first lesson that we have a right to demand that logic shall teach us is how to make our ideas clear; and a most important one it is, depreciated only by minds who stand in need of it. To know what we think, to be masters of our own meaning, will make a solid foundation for great and weighty thought.
>
> —Charles Sanders Peirce, *How to Make Our Ideas Clear*

■ INTRODUCTION

Expert system development goes beyond shells and includes languages designed uniquely for certain expert systems applications. One such language is Prolog. In the early 1980s, only one version of Prolog was available commercially for personal computers. Today, more than a dozen organizations offer a version of Prolog for virtually every type and size of computer. For most users who have already covered much about expert systems and knowledge representation, this programming language proves to be worthwhile, interesting, and fun. Many users develop a pure appreciation of the language itself.

Prolog is not a natural language; however, it is suitable for developing natural language processing applications. It allows a programmer to directly program logic using induction and deduction. It is also an excellent language for developing expert systems, because the rules can directly reflect the logic of the domain expert. What is more interesting about Prolog is that it can be programmed to modify itself to simulate human learning. In the business sector, problem diagnosis and financial planning are a few of the many expert systems applications in use.

Prolog is a great language, but it is still relatively new and unknown in the business world. Because of its vast capabilities and potential, Prolog is rapidly gaining in popularity. Remember that although COBOL was introduced in 1959, it was not widely used until the early 1970s. During those days, data processing departments that used COBOL were considered "progressive." Similarly, not enough people know Prolog yet. Many businesses have yet to be convinced of its use in building expert systems.

This appendix covers the nontechnical basics of Prolog, its symbolic logic, and how one begins to write simple Prolog programs. The text focuses on how goals are satisfied, how instantiation and backtracking handle special problems, arithmetic support, and basic debugging.

■ WHAT IS PROLOG?

Programming in expert systems entails a different approach and vocabulary than does conventional programming. In a procedural language such as BASIC or Pascal, a programmer's main job is to write a set of instructions that the computer will execute on a body of data. In expert systems, the goal is to describe relationships between data items.

Prolog, which stands for Programming in Logic, is one of the major expert systems languages available today. Developed in 1972 by French mathematician Alain Colmerauer and associates, the language is gaining ground in the United States and is becoming as popular as LISP, but for different reasons. In 1981, a syntax standard developed at the University of Edinburg was described in *Programming in Logic,* by William Clocksin and Christ Mellish.

An expert systems programming language such as Prolog deals with concepts expressed in words, phrases, or sentences. One of its important features is a capability to handle symbolic (nonnumeric) information. Another feature is Prolog's ability to incorporate flexible data structures to adapt on the fly every time a change occurs in the type or quantity of information flowing through the program.

Prolog versus LISP

One way to explain Prolog is to compare it to LISP. LISP and Prolog work differently and require different programming techniques. Prolog is conceptually simple and quite dynamic. The language is user-extensible and allows programs to systematically disassemble themselves and modify their own code. Prolog is *nonprocedural* and nondeterminant, in that the programmer is relieved from the responsibility of directing the flow of control within the program.

Prolog programs are highly readable and are easier to develop than similar LISP programs. Although Prolog has less flexibility, a novice programmer can get results more quickly with Prolog than with LISP. The basic structure already exists.

Prolog is naturally suited to diverse applications that require computations. It is not intended as a general-purpose language. It is ideal for problems in which one identifies in a declarative way the logical relationship between the objects in the domain and the expected results. Prolog does the rest. On the other hand, if the problem is less structured or if the programmer needs to control the nature of the computation, then LISP is favored over Prolog.

In declarative programming, a programmer simply states the rules and facts relevant to the solution of a problem domain. This information is then used as a program without additional information on how to do the job. In other words, the declarative computing eliminates procedural methods that are unique to conventional programming.

In terms of the actual code, LISP is easier to write and read than Prolog. The actual run time in a Prolog program takes more experience because of Prolog's "backchaining" process. Prolog also requires more strict organization of data and rules than does LISP. Although Prolog is a higher-level language, programs must be planned more carefully. Rules, for example, must be entered in the order they will be used.

LISP is unique in working with lists of numbers, words, and sentences. For example, if the following list is entered into the computer—1,2,4, Red, Blue, Car—conventional programming run into problems because numbers and letters are mixed. In LISP, a programmer simply tells the system that a list is being created and then starts entering it. Programmers can write a program, for example, to locate and select the third and sixth elements of the list (4, car). Related to this feature is capability of creating and naming new commands that are easily accepted by LISP. A summary of the key features of Prolog and LISP is shown in Table A–1.

Current Prolog applications include expert advisor and interpretation systems, site planning and logistics, knowledge-based systems research, using

■ **Table A–1**   Key Features of Prolog and LISP

Prolog Features	LISP Features
1. Allows a programmer to directly program logic using induction and deduction	1. Implements inference process easily
2. Uses rules that directly reflect the logic of the domain expert	2. Easier to read and write than Prolog in terms of actual code
3. Can be programmed to modify itself to simulate human learning	3. Can be used to represent a limitless array of things: expert rules, thought processes, system components, etc.
4. Conceptually simple and quite dynamic	4. Requires less strict organization on the programmer's time than in Prolog
5. Has built-in inference mechanism called backtracking	5. Has no built-in inference mechanism
6. User-extensible	5. Unique in working with lists of numbers, words, sentences
7. Allows programs to disassemble themselves and modify their own code	6. Allows programmers to create and name commands that are easily accepted by LISP
8. Nonprocedural, relieving programmer of responsibility of directing flow of control within the program	7. Has less stringent planning requirements for programs than does Prolog
9. Highly readable and easier to develop than LISP	
10. Naturally suited to diverse applications that require computations	

knowledge about building codes, and English-language query of databases. For example, one design has a geographical database and an English interface that can answer queries such as "Which country contains more than one city whose population exceeds five million?" See Box A–1.

The heart of Prolog is the rule as a construct. **Rules** are stated as goals to be satisfied. A rule that is always true is referred to as a fact. For example, the fact that federal income tax in 1993 was $1,410 may be represented in Prolog as:

```
data (Fed_Tax 1993 1410).
```

Clauses are Prolog statements that may represent either facts necessary to the program or rules specifying how to derive facts from other clauses when a program is used. For example, the rule

likes(someone,accounting):-concentrating(someone,accounting)

means "someone likes accounting if that someone is concentrating in accounting" is a fundamental Prolog clause. A Prolog program contains virtually all clauses. So, as a language, Prolog is quite simple.

■ GETTING STARTED

Computer programming in Prolog consists of

1. Declaring some facts about objects and their relationships.

2. Defining some rules about objects and their relationships.

3. Asking some questions about objects and their relationships.

Box A–1   *Example of an Advisory System*

The Advisor system was implemented in Prolog on IBM-compatible PCs running under DOS. . . . Prolog was chosen in preference to a shell because the PC shells available at the time were unable to cope with the desired structure based on frames rather than rules. Conventional languages were also rejected for a similar reason. This left Prolog and LISP, and Prolog was chosen simply because those involved in the project preferred it! It was however also probably true that the Prolog systems available at the time for PCs were faster than the LISP systems. It was found during the development that Prolog could not cope easily with the large amounts of text involved, and this problem was solved by interfacing with a word-processing package for text entry and editing. One or two of the shells would have avoided this problem, but had no facilities for overriding their rule-based inference engines.

Source: John S. Edwards, *Building Knowledge-Based Systems* (New York: Halsted Press, 1992), p. 176.

Figure A–1 shows a Prolog **database**—a collection of facts and rules. A period is required at the end of each statement. Prolog is a free-form language, which means that carriage returns are ignored. So if a user types in

>student(mary).

a period is typed in after the next prompt.

Figure A–1   Prolog Database

```
>student(david).  ⎫
>student(mary).   ⎪
>student(john).   ⎪
>student(ann).    ⎬  FACTS
>student(jerry).  ⎪
>student(sue).    ⎭
>likes(Someone, accounting):-    ⎫
  concentrating(Someone, accounting).  ⎬  RULE
>concentrating(david,mis).       ⎭
>concentrating(mary,marketing).  ⎫
>concentrating(mary,mis).        ⎪
>concentrating(john,accounting). ⎪
>concentrating(ann,management).  ⎬  FACTS
>concentrating(ann,mis).         ⎪
>concentrating(jerry,finance).   ⎪
>concentrating(sue,accounting).  ⎭
```

Facts

A **fact** is a fundamental Prolog structure that states a relationship. The general form of a fact is

predicate(argument1,argument2, . . . argument*n*).

The predicate and arguments must begin with lowercase letters so that they can be differentiated from variables. The **predicate** is the relationship being defined by the fact. The **arguments** are the objects of the relationship. The names of the predicate and arguments are completely arbitrary. Therefore, the programmer should exercise care in choosing names that are meaningful. For example, the Prolog fact "student(david)." defines the relationship between student and david. This relationship can be written in English as "David is a student."

In a Prolog fact, the predicate and the arguments are **atoms** or noninteger constants. Atoms must begin with nonnumeric, lowercase letters. They cannot contain a tab or a space. Alternatively, an atom can be a string contained within single quotes. For example, in the Prolog fact "student('David Jones').", "David Jones" is an atom, just as "david" is the atom in "student(david)." The arguments in a fact can be in any order, but the order should be used consistently.

How is an English sentence translated into a Prolog fact? If it is a simple sentence, such as "David is a student," then other relationships a programmer wants to define should be considered. For example, the Prolog fact "david(student)." further defines relationships about David. But in the database (Figure A–1), several students are defined, so the fact was defined "student(david)." Notice in Figure A–1 that the student relationship is defined with five other names.

In the preceding example, the verb "is" was implicit in the Prolog fact, so programmers must consider which noun should be used to define the relationship. With a more complicated sentence, the following guidelines can help to translate an English sentence to a Prolog fact:

1. The *verb* becomes the predicate.

2. The *subject* of the verb is the first argument.

3. The *object* of the verb is the second argument.

4. The *indirect object* is the third argument.

For example, in the sentence "Mary gives David a book," the verb "gives" becomes the predicate. "Mary," the subject of the verb, becomes the first argument. "David," the object of the verb, becomes the second argument; and "book," the indirect object, becomes the third argument.

So Prolog fact is "gives(mary,david,book)."

Predicate _____ | | | |__ Indirect object and third argument

|_____ Object and second argument

|____ Subject and first argument

Rules

Rules are fundamental Prolog clauses that define a relationship from which facts may be inferred. They have the following general form:

resultant:- condition1, condition2, . . . , condition*n*.

To understand the value of a rule, consider the database. A programmer would like to make note of everyone who likes accounting. One way to do this is through a series of facts. Given that John and Sue like accounting, the following facts are listed:

```
likes(john, accounting).
likes(sue, accounting).
```

If the database is large, such a list can get tedious. Instead, a rule can be used to help determine who likes accounting based on the facts already in the database. Assume that if a student is concentrating in accounting, that student likes accounting. This rule, in English, is stated as follows:

Someone likes accounting if:
    that someone is concentrating in accounting.

To translate this into a Prolog rule, an understanding of the predefined predicates "if" (":-"), "and" (","), and variables is needed.

Variables

In Prolog, a **variable** is a symbol that represents an atom that is not yet known. Variables are local to the rules or facts in which they are located. A Prolog variable begins with a capital letter or an underscore (_). In the rule to be defined, "Someone" is the variable, and the identity of that person is not yet unknown.

A single underscore is a special type of variable called an **anonymous variable.** When an anonymous variable is used in a query, Prolog responds with either YES or NO rather than giving the atoms equal to the variable. For example, for the query "likes(_,accounting)?", Prolog would respond with YES to indicate that someone does like accounting, but does not indicate specifically whom.

If and And

The symbol ":-" (a colon and a hyphen) stands for the predefined predicate "if". The comma "," is the symbol for the predefined predicate "and". A **predefined predicate** is a built-in command that makes it easier for the user to program in Prolog. (If and And are not the first predefined predicates. The commands "exit?" and "retract(<clause>)?" are actually predefined predicates.)

Now the English rule

Someone likes accounting if:
    that someone is concentrating in accounting.

can be defined as a Prolog rule:

```
likes(Someone, accounting) :-
        concentrating(Someone, accounting).
```

In the first part "Someone likes accounting", the verb "likes" is the predicate; the subject of the verb, "Someone", is the first argument, and the direct object, "accounting", is the second argument. After translating each English clause, the ":-" (if) and a period ("."") are inserted. Note that the first letter in "Someone" is capitalized, making it a variable.

Questions

Now that the database has some facts and a rule, users can ask it some questions. Before examining questions, look at Figure A-2, a printout of a dialogue between a user and Prolog. The items following the prompts were typed in by the user.

When a question is asked, Prolog will search through the database typed in previously. It looks for facts that match the fact in the question. Two facts *match* if their predicates are the same (spelled the same way) and if their corresponding arguments are the same. If Prolog finds a fact that matches the question, Prolog will respond YES. If no such fact exists in the database, it will respond NO.

The first query, "concentrating(david,accounting)?", asked "Is David concentrating in accounting?" Prolog responded NO. A quick look at the database in Figure A–1 confirms that David is not concentrating in accounting. The second query asked "Is David concentrating in MIS?" The answer was, correctly, YES. The third query, "student(Who)?", asked "Who is a student?" Prolog responded with the names of all the students typed in the database. Note that "Who" is a variable, since it begins with a capital letter. Also, instead of responding with a YES or NO, Prolog gave the values of "Who" that made the query true. Questions four and five were answered in a similar manner.

From the dialog in Figure A–1, one should be able to see that to ask a question or query in Prolog, a Prolog clause is typed and followed by a question mark (?). For example:

```
>student(Who)?
```

Figure A–2 Printout of a Dialog Between the User and Prolog

```
>concentrating(david,accounting)?
NO
>concentrating(david,mis)?
YES
>student(Who)?
WHO=david
WHO=mary
WHO=john
WHO=ann
WHO=jerry
WHO=sue
>concentrating(Who,mis)?
WHO=david
WHO=mary
WHO=ann
>likes(Who, accounting)?
WHO=john
WHO=sue
>
```

or the user can type in "?-" followed by a clause such as:

```
>?-student(Who).
```

Note that in response to questions three, four, and five in Figure A–2, Prolog gave all of the correct answers. If a user would like to see the answers one at a time, the user can use the predefined predicate "solveone?" Prolog will then respond to each question with only the first answer and the query "MORE?>". To see the next answer, type in a semicolon (";"). A user who doesn't want to see any more answers types in a backslash ("/"). Figure A–3 shows a dialogue using "solveone?".

■ HOW DOES PROLOG WORK?

Once a user knows the basics of Prolog—facts, rules, and queries—the user can set up a simple database and ask Prolog some questions. To build more complicated databases and programs, a user needs to understand more details of how Prolog works.

Instantiating

Something is **instantiated** when an instance of some fact or rule exists about that thing. For example, in the fact "student(david)." the predicate student is instantiated to david. In the fact "concentrating (david,mis)." concentrating is instantitated to david and mis.

An item is instantiated in Prolog when an instance of some fact or rule matches the Prolog database. When users query PROLOG, they ask it to instantiate some clause. Thus, the query "student(david)?" instructs Prolog to search its database and find an instance (if it can) of a predicate that matches "student" having an argument "david." If Prolog succeeds, it responds with YES, which means "an instance has occurred." If Prolog responds with NO it means that nothing matches the questions. In other words, it is not provable that the question follows logically from the knowledge base.

Figure A–3   Prolog Dialogue

```
>solveone?
YES
>student(Who)?
WHO = david
MORE?>;
WHO = mary
MORE?>/
>solveall?
YES
>
```

When a variable is used in either a query or a rule, it is first not instantiated. What the variable stands for is not yet known. Once Prolog finds the value of the variable, the variable is instantiated. For example, in the query:

"likes(Who,accounting)?"

"Who" is initially not instantiated. The user does not know, yet, what "Who" stands for. But when Prolog responds with "WHO = john", "Who" has become instantiated to john.

Goal Satisfaction

The uninstantiated query "likes(Who,accounting)?" is called a **goal.** If Prolog is able to instantiate every variable within the query, the goal is said to be satisfied.

A fact can cause a goal to be satisfied immediately, whereas a rule can only reduce the task to that of satisfying a conjunction of subgoals. However, a clause can only be used if it matches the goal under consideration. Satisfying a goal means searching the database for a matching clause, then marking the place in the database and satisfying any subgoals.

A noteworthy case in matching is one in which two uninstantiated variables are matched together. In this case, these variables **share.** Two sharing variables are such that as soon as one is instantiated, so is the other.

As an example of satisfying goals, when a user asks the question "concentrating(david,mis)?" Prolog will look for a fact that exactly matches the above clause because no variables are part of the question. It looks first for a predicate that matches "concentrating." When it finds a rule with a "concentrating" predicate, it next looks to see if the first argument equals "david." If this is true, it looks to see if the second argument equals "mis." If this is true, then the goal has been satisfied and Prolog responds with YES.

In the query "concentrating(david,accounting)?" Prolog will find a fact with a predicate "concentrating" and a first argument "david" but no second argument "accounting" so the goal fails, and Prolog responds with NO.

Backtracking

What happens if an initial goal cannot be satisfied or if a query has more than one answer? Prolog uses **backtracking** to handle these problems. Backtracking consists of reviewing what has been done and attempting to resatisfy the goals by finding an alternative way to meet them.

To explain backtracking, a return to the query "likes(Who,accounting)?" is helpful. Prolog first tries to find any rule or fact whose **head** (the leftmost element in a fact or rule) matches "likes (<anything here>,accounting)." When it finds the rule "likes (Someone,accounting)" it marks it by pushing (placing) its location on a stack and instantiates "Who" to "Someone" throughout the rule. See Figure A–4. A **stack** is a contiguous block of memory containing some data, and a **stack pointer** (SP) tells where the top of the stack is.

Prolog now knows that if it can locate any combinations of rules or facts that satisfy the **tail** (everything except the first element in a list or rule) of this rule, "concentrating(Someone,accounting)", then whatever "Someone" instantiates to in the tail will fail and becomes the solution to "Who."

Figure A–4 Backtracking in Prolog

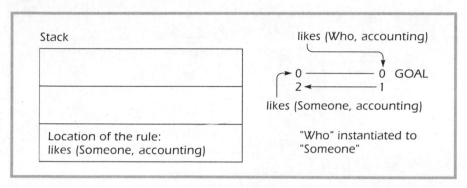

Prolog next searches the database for an instance of "concentrating(<anything here>,accounting)." The first case of concentrating it encounters is "concentrating (john,accounting)." Prolog marks this by pushing its location onto the stack, instantiating "Someone" to "john", and "Who" to "john." See Figure A–5. Prolog prints "WHO = john" and then releases its marker for "concentrating(john,accounting)." by popping (removing) its location off of the stack. See Figure A–6.

The location of the rule "likes(Someone,accounting)" is still on the stack. So Prolog attempts to resatisfy this goal by looking for any other instances of "concentrating(<anything here>,accounting)." The next such instance is the fact "concentrating (sue, accounting)." Prolog marks this by pushing its location onto the stack, instantiating "Someone" to "sue" and "Who" to "sue". See Figure A–7.

The goal "likes(Who,accounting)?" has again been satisfied. So, Prolog prints "WHO = sue" and releases its marker for "concentrating (sue,accounting)." by popping its location off the stack. See Figure A–8. The location for "likes(Someone,accounting)" is still on the stack so Prolog continues searching for any more instances of "concentrating (<anything here>, accounting)." When it can find no other such instances, it pops off the stack the location of

Figure A–5 A Prolog Push

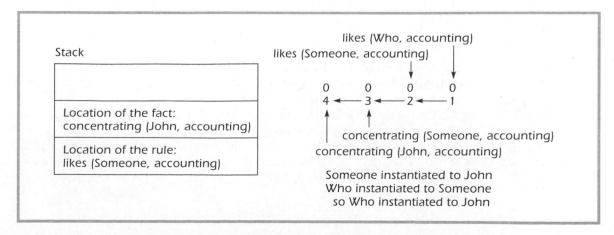

Figure A–6 A Prolog Pop

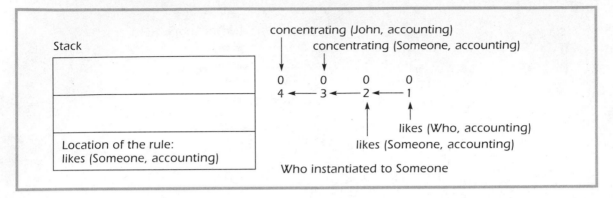

Figure A–7 Prolog Backtracking

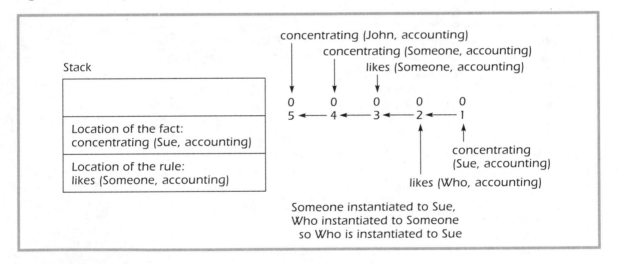

"likes(Someone,accounting)." and looks for any other instances of "likes(<anything here>,accounting)." Since it can find no other such instances, its goal fails, the search is over and Prolog prints its prompt ">".

Arithmetic Support

If a user needs to do a lot of number crunching, Prolog is *not* the language to use. Most Prolog programs have only integer match functions with signed two-byte numbers ranging from −32,768 to +32,767.

One of the predefined predicates is "equality and inequality." For example, if a user sets $x = y$, the relationship succeeds when x equals y. If either x or y is an uninstantiated variable, then the uninstantiated variable will be instantiated to the other. Here is another example of equality and inequality predicates, using the following database:

```
reigns(rhodri,844,878).
reigns(anarawd,878,916).
```

Figure A–8 Release of a Prolog Marker

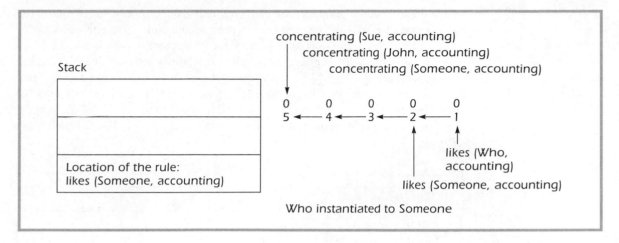

```
reigns(hywel_dda,916,950).
reigns(lago_ad_idwal,950,979).
reigns(hywel_ab_ieuaf,979,985).
reigns(cadwallon,985,986).
reigns(maredudd,986,999).
```

The following English rule can be constructed:

> X was a prince during year Y if:
>   X reigned between years A and B, and
>   Y is between A and B, inclusive.

which translates into the following Prolog rule:

```
prince(X,Y):-
      reigns(X,A,B),
      Y >= A,
      Y =< B.
```

Prolog and a user could then have the following dialogue:

```
>prince(cadwallon,986)?
YES
>prince(X,900)?
X = anarawd
```

In Prolog, the multiplication and division operators have a higher precedence than the addition and subtraction operators. So $a - b/c$ equals $a - (b/c)$.

The Cut

The symbol for a cut in Prolog is the exclamation point ("!"). A **cut** is a goal that succeeds and blocks backtracking. When Prolog attempts to satisfy a goal, it searches the entire database. The cut allows a user to stop this searching. It is a way of controlling the flow of a Prolog program. The cut works by popping location markers off the stack, stopping any further backtracking.

Lists

A **list** is an ordered sequence of elements that can have any length. *Ordered* means that the order of the elements in the sequence matters. The *elements* of a list may be any terms—constants, variables, structures—which also includes other lists. A list with no elements is called the **empty list,** and it is denoted in Prolog with the symbols "[ ]". An empty list is also the last element of any list.

The first element of a list is called the *head.* The rest of the list is called the *tail.* The head is separated from the tail with either the symbol "l" (a vertical line) or ",...". The elements of a list are enclosed by "[ ]". The following are examples of lists:

List	Head	Tail
[a,b,c]	a	[b,c]
[a]	a	[ ]
[ ]	none	none
[the,[comm,school]]	the	[[comm,school]]
[[the,comm],school]	[the,comm]	[school]

Figure A–9 shows a database of lists, followed by a query.

Basic Debugging

Generally, three types of predefined predicates help debug databases that do not work as expected: **tracers, spy points,** and **leashers.** All the debugging predicates have the same purpose; they allow examination and control of

Figure A–9   A Database of Lists and a Query

```
>list([a,b,c].
>list([a].
>list([]).
>list([the,[comm,school]]).
>list([[the,comm],school]).
>list([X/Y])? (asks for the heads and tails of the back
list)
X = a
Y = [b,c]
X = a
Y = []
X = the
Y = [[comm,school]]
X = [the,comm]
Y = [school]
>
```

program execution so that the programmer may watch each iteration of the four main break points in a Prolog program: The call, the fail, the exit, and the redo.

Call means that an attempt to satisfy a goal has been initiated. Prolog will try to instantiate the clause. **Fail** occurs when instantiation fails or when the goal is satisfied and the solution is printed. In other words, even successful goals "fail" after the solution is printed, since Prolog must fail in order to search for the other possible solutions.

An **exit** occurs when a clause is exited after Prolog has either failed or finished all possible instantiations. In contrast, a **redo** occurs when Prolog returns to a marked clause for a second attempt at satisfaction during backtracking.

■ SAMPLE PROGRAM

The following sample program attempts to emulate the decision-making process of an expert financial accounting auditor. It is a greatly simplified example of the types of decisions an auditor has to make. The problem for the auditor is how to rate the internal accounting controls in a firm being audited. The types of auditing tests that will be performed depend on the quality of the controls.

Several characteristics of internal accounting control, along with the control strategies, ensure the integrity of each characteristic, as shown in Table A–2.

■ **Table A–2** Internal Accounting Characteristics and Control Strategies

Characteristic	Control strategies
Honest and capable employees	■ Hire qualified people with good references ■ Require annual vacations ■ Bond employees in positions of trust ■ State conflict-of-interest policy
Clear delegation and separation of duties	■ Develop organization chart ■ Separate record keeping from custody of assets ■ Separate authorization from record keeping ■ Separate purchasing from receiving
Proper procedures for processing of transactions	■ Ensure proper authorization of transactions ■ Sign checks only with proper support ■ Employ a chart of accounts with account definitions ■ Describe operating and accounting procedures in manuals
Suitable documents and accounting records	■ Prenumber important documents ■ Develop comparative financial statements ■ Prepare budget of anticipated results; compare with actual results
Adequate physical control over assets and records	■ Limit access to inventory ■ Safeguard all important records ■ Deposit cash receipts intact daily ■ Keep paper valuables in fireproof containers
Independent verification of performance and assets	■ Reconcile bank statement independently ■ Prelist cash receipts ■ Take complete inventory regularly ■ Have an annual audit by a CPA firm

Assume that the auditor would like to rate the internal accounting controls on the following scale: excellent, good, fair, poor, and inadequate. To determine the rating, the auditor examines each of the control strategies in Table A–2. If all of the strategies are in place, then the controls are excellent. If none of the strategies are in place, then the controls are inadequate. The ratings good, fair, and poor are based on some combination of strategies that are in place and strategies that are not in place. Numbers are used to determine the internal accounting controls rating. They are an attempt to quantify the "rules of thumb" that an expert auditor might use when evaluating internal accounting controls.

The control strategies for each characteristic are evaluated separately based on the following tables:

For characteristics 1,2,3,4,5, and 6:

Control strategies:	1	2	3	4	Rating
	Y	Y	Y	Y	5
	Y	Y	Y	N	4
	Y	Y	N	Y	4
	Y	N	Y	Y	4
	N	Y	Y	Y	4
	Y	Y	N	N	3
	Y	N	Y	N	3
	N	Y	Y	N	3
	Y	N	N	Y	3
	N	Y	N	Y	3
	N	N	Y	Y	3
	Y	N	N	N	2
	N	Y	N	N	2
	N	N	N	Y	2
	N	N	Y	N	2
	N	N	N	N	1

For characteristic 4:

Control strategies:	1	2	3	Rating
	Y	Y	Y	5
	Y	Y	N	4
	Y	N	Y	4
	N	Y	Y	4
	Y	N	N	3
	N	N	Y	3
	N	Y	N	3
	N	N	N	1

The ratings for the characteristics are then added together. The rating for the internal accounting controls is determined as shown in the following table:

Sum of the Characteristic Ratings	Control Rating
30	Excellent
24 <= sum < 30	Good
18 <= sum < 24	Fair
12 <= sum < 18	Poor
<12	Inadequate

The following Prolog program determines the control ratings by asking the auditor a series of questions and computing the ratings using the information from the preceding tables. A sample run of the program is shown in Figure A–10. The program is shown in Figure A–11.

Figure A–10   Prolog Program Sample Run

```
>controls?
Are qualified people with good references hired? (Y/N) Y
Are annual vacations required? (Y/N) Y
Are employees in positions of trust bonded? (Y/N) Y
Is there a conflict of interest policy? (Y/N) Y
Has an organization chart been developed (Y/N) Y
Are record keeping and custody of assets separate? (Y/N) Y
Are authorization and record keeping separate? (Y/N) Y
Are receiving and purchasing separate? (Y/N) Y
Is there proper authorization of transactions? (Y/N) Y
Are checks signed only with proper support? (Y/N) Y
Is a chart of accounts (with definitions) employed? (Y/N) Y
Are operating and accounting procedures described in a manual? (Y/N) Y
Are important documents prenumbered? (Y/N) Y
Have comparative financial statements been developed? (Y/N) Y
Has a budget been prepared and compared with actual? (Y/N) Y
Is access to inventory limited? (Y/N) Y
Are all important records safeguarded? (Y/N) Y
Are cash receipts deposited intact daily? (Y/N) Y
Are paper valuables kept in fireproof containers? (Y/N) Y
Are bank statements independently reconciled? (Y/N) Y
Are cash receipts prelisted? (Y/N) Y
Is a complete inventory regularly taken? (Y/N) Y
Is an annual audit by a CPA firm done? (Y/N) Y
The internal accounting controls are excellent.
YES
```

Figure A–11 Program Listing

```prolog
evaluate_char1(CS1_1, CS1_2, CS1_3, CS1_4, 5) :-
     CS1_1 = 'Y',
     CS1_2 = 'Y',
     CS1_3 = 'Y',
     CS1_4 = 'Y'.
evaluate_char1(CS1_1, CS1_2, CS1_3, CS1_4, 4) :-
     CS1_1 = 'Y',
     CS1_2 = 'Y',
     CS1_3 = 'Y',
     CS1_4 = 'N'.
evaluate_char1(CS1_1, CS1_2, CS1_3, CS1_4, 4) :-
     CS1_1 = 'Y',
     CS1_2 = 'Y',
     CS1_3 = 'N',
     CS1_4 = 'Y'.
evaluate_char1(CS1_1, CS1_2, CS1_3, CS1_4, 4) :-
     CS1_1 = 'Y',
     CS1_2 = 'N',
     CS1_3 = 'Y',
     CS1_4 = 'Y'.
evaluate_char1(CS1_1, CS1_2, CS1_3, CS1_4, 4) :-
     CS1_1 = 'N',
     CS1_2 = 'Y',
     CS1_3 = 'Y',
     CS1_4 = 'Y'.
evaluate_char1(CS1_1, CS1_2, CS1_3, CS1_4, 3) :-
     CS1_1 = 'Y',
     CS1_2 = 'Y',
     CS1_3 = 'N',
     CS1_4 = 'N'.
evaluate_char1(CS1_1, CS1_2, CS1_3, CS1_4, 3) :-
     CS1_1 = 'Y',
     CS1_2 = 'N',
     CS1_3 = 'Y',
     CS1_4 = 'N'.
evaluate_char1(CS1_1, CS1_2, CS1_3, CS1_4, 3) :-
     CS1_1 = 'N',
     CS1_2 = 'Y',
     CS1_3 = 'Y',
     CS1_4 = 'N'.
evaluate_char1(CS1_1, CS1_2, CS1_3, CS1_4, 3) :-
     CS1_1 = 'Y',
     CS1_2 = 'N',
     CS1_3 = 'N',
     CS1_4 = 'Y'.
evaluate_char1(CS1_1, CS1_2, CS1_3, CS1_4, 3) :-
     CS1_1 = 'N',
     CS1_2 = 'Y',
     CS1_3 = 'N',
     CS1_4 = 'Y'.
```

```
evaluate_char1(CS1_1, CS1_2, CS1_3, CS1_4, 3) :-
    CS1_1 = 'N',
    CS1_2 = 'N',
    CS1_3 = 'Y',
    CS1_4 = 'Y'.
evaluate_char1(CS1_1, CS1_2, CS1_3, CS1_4, 2) :-
    CS1_1 = 'Y',
    CS1_2 = 'N',
    CS1_3 = 'N',
    CS1_4 = 'N'.
evaluate_char1(CS1_1, CS1_2, CS1_3, CS1_4, 2) :-
    CS1_1 = 'N',
    CS1_2 = 'Y',
    CS1_3 = 'N',
    CS1_4 = 'N'.
evaluate_char1(CS1_1, CS1_2, CS1_3, CS1_4, 2) :-
    CS1_1 = 'N',
    CS1_2 = 'N',
    CS1_3 = 'N',
    CS1_4 = 'Y'.
evaluate_char1(CS1_1, CS1_2, CS1_3, CS1_4, 2) :-
    CS1_1 = 'N',
    CS1_2 = 'N',
    CS1_3 = 'Y',
    CS1_4 = 'N'.
evaluate_char1(CS1_1, CS1_2, CS1_3, CS1_4, 1) :-
    CS1_1 = 'N',
    CS1_2 = 'N',
    CS1_3 = 'N',
    CS1_4 = 'N'.
evaluate_char2(CS2_1, CS2_2, CS2_3, CS2_4, 5) :-
    CS2_1 = 'Y',
    CS2_2 = 'Y',
    CS2_3 = 'Y',
    CS2_4 = 'Y'.
evaluate_char2(CS2_1, CS2_2, CS2_3, CS2_4, 4) :-
    CS2_1 = 'Y',
    CS2_2 = 'Y',
    CS2_3 = 'Y',
    CS2_4 = 'N'.
evaluate_char2(CS2_1, CS2_2, CS2_3, CS2_4, 4) :-
    CS2_1 = 'Y',
    CS2_2 = 'Y',
    CS2_3 = 'N',
    CS2_4 = 'Y'.
evaluate_char2(CS2_1, CS2_2, CS2_3, CS2_4, 4) :-
    CS2_1 = 'Y',
    CS2_2 = 'N',
    CS2_3 = 'Y',
    CS2_4 = 'Y'.
```

```prolog
evaluate_char2(CS2_1, CS2_2, CS2_3, CS2_4, 4) :-
    CS2_1 = 'N',
    CS2_2 = 'Y',
    CS2_3 = 'Y',
    CS2_4 = 'Y'.
evaluate_char2(CS2_1, CS2_2, CS2_3, CS2_4, 3) :-
    CS2_1 = 'Y',
    CS2_2 = 'Y',
    CS2_3 = 'N',
    CS2_4 = 'N'.
evaluate_char2(CS2_1, CS2_2, CS2_3, CS2_4, 3) :-
    CS2_1 = 'Y',
    CS2_2 = 'N',
    CS2_3 = 'Y',
    CS2_4 = 'N'.
evaluate_char2(CS2_1, CS2_2, CS2_3, CS2_4, 3) :-
    CS2_1 = 'N',
    CS2_2 = 'Y',
    CS2_3 = 'Y',
    CS2_4 = 'N'.
evaluate_char2(CS2_1, CS2_2, CS2_3, CS2_4, 3) :-
    CS2_1 = 'Y',
    CS2_2 = 'N',
    CS2_3 = 'N',
    CS2_4 = 'Y'.
evaluate_char2(CS2_1, CS2_2, CS2_3, CS2_4, 3) :-
    CS2_1 = 'N',
    CS2_2 = 'Y',
    CS2_3 = 'N',
    CS2_4 = 'Y'.
evaluate_char2(CS2_1, CS2_2, CS2_3, CS2_4, 3) :-
    CS2_1 = 'N',
    CS2_2 = 'N',
    CS2_3 = 'Y',
    CS2_4 = 'Y'.
evaluate_char2(CS2_1, CS2_2, CS2_3, CS2_4, 2) :-
    CS2_1 = 'Y',
    CS2_2 = 'N',
    CS2_3 = 'N',
    CS2_4 = 'N'.
evaluate_char2(CS2_1, CS2_2, CS2_3, CS2_4, 2) :-
    CS2_1 = 'N',
    CS2_2 = 'Y',
    CS2_3 = 'N',
    CS2_4 = 'N'.
evaluate_char2(CS2_1, CS2_2, CS2_3, CS2_4, 2) :-
    CS2_1 = 'N',
    CS2_2 = 'N',
    CS2_3 = 'N',
    CS2_4 = 'Y'.
```

```prolog
evaluate_char2(CS2_1, CS2_2, CS2_3, CS2_4, 2) :-
     CS2_1 = 'N',
     CS2_2 = 'N',
     CS2_3 = 'Y',
     CS2_4 = 'N'.
evaluate_char2(CS2_1, CS2_2, CS2_3, CS2_4, 1) :-
     CS2_1 = 'N',
     CS2_2 = 'N',
     CS2_3 = 'N',
     CS2_4 = 'N'.
evaluate_char3(CS3_1, CS3_2, CS3_3, CS3_4, 5) :-
     CS3_1 = 'Y',
     CS3_2 = 'Y',
     CS3_3 = 'Y',
     CS3_4 = 'Y'.
evaluate_char3(CS3_1, CS3_2, CS3_3, CS3_4, 4) :-
     CS3_1 = 'Y',
     CS3_2 = 'Y',
     CS3_3 = 'Y',
     CS3_4 = 'N'.
evaluate_char3(CS3_1, CS3_2, CS3_3, CS3_4, 4) :-
     CS3_1 = 'Y',
     CS3_2 = 'Y',
     CS3_3 = 'N',
     CS3_4 = 'Y'.
evaluate_char3(CS3_1, CS3_2, CS3_3, CS3_4, 4) :-
     CS3_1 = 'Y',
     CS3_2 = 'N',
     CS3_3 = 'Y',
     CS3_4 = 'Y'.
evaluate_char3(CS3_1, CS3_2, CS3_3, CS3_4, 4) :-
     CS3_1 = 'N',
     CS3_2 = 'Y',
     CS3_3 = 'Y',
     CS3_4 = 'Y'.
evaluate_char3(CS3_1, CS3_2, CS3_3, CS3_4, 3) :-
     CS3_1 = 'Y',
     CS3_2 = 'Y',
     CS3_3 = 'N',
     CS3_4 = 'N'.
evaluate_char3(CS3_1, CS3_2, CS3_3, CS3_4, 3) :-
     CS3_1 = 'Y',
     CS3_2 = 'N',
     CS3_3 = 'Y',
     CS3_4 = 'N'.
evaluate_char3(CS3_1, CS3_2, CS3_3, CS3_4, 3) :-
     CS3_1 = 'N',
     CS3_2 = 'Y',
     CS3_3 = 'Y',
     CS3_4 = 'N'.
```

```
evaluate_char3(CS3_1, CS3_2, CS3_3, CS3_4, 3) :-
    CS3_1 = 'Y',
    CS3_2 = 'N',
    CS3_3 = 'N',
    CS3_4 = 'Y'.
evaluate_char3(CS3_1, CS3_2, CS3_3, CS3_4, 3) :-
    CS3_1 = 'N',
    CS3_2 = 'Y',
    CS3_3 = 'N',
    CS3_4 = 'Y'.
evaluate_char3(CS3_1, CS3_2, CS3_3, CS3_4, 3) :-
    CS3_1 = 'N',
    CS3_2 = 'N',
    CS3_3 = 'Y',
    CS3_4 = 'Y'.
evaluate_char3(CS3_1, CS3_2, CS3_3, CS3_4, 2) :-
    CS3_1 = 'Y',
    CS3_2 = 'N',
    CS3_3 = 'N',
    CS3_4 = 'N'.
evaluate_char3(CS3_1, CS3_2, CS3_3, CS3_4, 2) :-
    CS3_1 = 'N',
    CS3_2 = 'Y',
    CS3_3 = 'N',
    CS3_4 = 'N'.
evaluate_char3(CS3_1, CS3_2, CS3_3, CS3_4, 2) :-
    CS3_1 = 'N',
    CS3_2 = 'N',
    CS3_3 = 'N',
    CS3_4 = 'Y'.
evaluate_char3(CS3_1, CS3_2, CS3_3, CS3_4, 2) :-
    CS3_1 = 'N',
    CS3_2 = 'N',
    CS3_3 = 'Y',
    CS3_4 = 'N'.
evaluate_char3(CS3_1, CS3_2, CS3_3, CS3_4, 1) :-
    CS3_1 = 'N',
    CS3_2 = 'N',
    CS3_3 = 'N',
    CS3_4 = 'N'.
evaluate_char4(CS4_1, CS4_2, CS4_3, 5) :-
    CS4_1 = 'Y',
    CS4_2 = 'Y',
    CS4_3 = 'Y'.
evaluate_char4(CS4_1, CS4_2, CS4_3, 4) :-
    CS4_1 = 'Y',
    CS4_2 = 'Y',
    CS4_3 = 'N'.
evaluate_char4(CS4_1, CS4_2, CS4_3, 4) :-
    CS4_1 = 'Y',
    CS4_2 = 'N',
    CS4_3 = 'Y'.
```

```prolog
evaluate_char4(CS4_1, CS4_2, CS4_3, 4) :-
    CS4_1 = 'N',
    CS4_2 = 'Y',
    CS4_3 = 'Y'.
evaluate_char4(CS4_1, CS4_2, CS4_3, 3) :-
    CS4_1 = 'Y',
    CS4_2 = 'N',
    CS4_3 = 'N'.
evaluate_char4(CS4_1, CS4_2, CS4_3, 3) :-
    CS4_1 = 'N',
    CS4_2 = 'N',
    CS4_3 = 'Y'.
evaluate_char4(CS4_1, CS4_2, CS4_3, 3) :-
    CS4_1 = 'N',
    CS4_2 = 'Y',
    CS4_3 = 'N'.
evaluate_char4(CS4_1, CS4_2, CS4_3, 1) :-
    CS4_1 = 'N',
    CS4_2 = 'N',
    CS4_3 = 'N'.
evaluate_char5(CS5_1, CS5_2, CS5_3, CS5_4, 5) :-
    CS5_1 = 'Y',
    CS5_2 = 'Y',
    CS5_3 = 'Y',
    CS5_4 = 'Y'.
evaluate_char5(CS5_1, CS5_2, CS5_3, CS5_4, 4) :-
    CS5_1 = 'Y',
    CS5_2 = 'Y',
    CS5_3 = 'Y',
    CS5_4 = 'N'.
evaluate_char5(CS5_1, CS5_2, CS5_3, CS5_4, 4) :-
    CS5_1 = 'Y',
    CS5_2 = 'Y',
    CS5_3 = 'N',
    CS5_4 = 'Y'.
evaluate_char5(CS5_1, CS5_2, CS5_3, CS5_4, 4) :-
    CS5_1 = 'Y',
    CS5_2 = 'N',
    CS5_3 = 'Y',
    CS5_4 = 'Y'.
evaluate_char5(CS5_1, CS5_2, CS5_3, CS5_4, 4) :-
    CS5_1 = 'N',
    CS5_2 = 'Y',
    CS5_3 = 'Y',
    CS5_4 = 'Y'.
evaluate_char5(CS5_1, CS5_2, CS5_3, CS5_4, 3) :-
    CS5_1 = 'Y',
    CS5_2 = 'Y',
    CS5_3 = 'N',
    CS5_4 = 'N'.
```

```
evaluate_char5(CS5_1, CS5_2, CS5_3, CS5_4, 3) :-
      CS5_1 = 'Y',
      CS5_2 = 'N',
      CS5_3 = 'Y',
      CS5_4 = 'N'.
evaluate_char5(CS5_1, CS5_2, CS5_3, CS5_4, 3) :-
      CS5_1 = 'N',
      CS5_2 = 'Y',
      CS5_3 = 'Y',
      CS5_4 = 'N'.
evaluate_char5(CS5_1, CS5_2, CS5_3, CS5_4, 3) :-
      CS5_1 = 'Y',
      CS5_2 = 'N',
      CS5_3 = 'N',
      CS5_4 = 'Y'.
evaluate_char5(CS5_1, CS5_2, CS5_3, CS5_4, 3) :-
      CS5_1 = 'N',
      CS5_2 = 'Y',
      CS5_3 = 'N',
      CS5_4 = 'Y'.
evaluate_char5(CS5_1, CS5_2, CS5_3, CS5_4, 3) :-
      CS5_1 = 'N',
      CS5_2 = 'N',
      CS5_3 = 'Y',
      CS5_4 = 'Y'.
evaluate_char5(CS5_1, CS5_2, CS5_3, CS5_4, 2) :-
      CS5_1 = 'Y',
      CS5_2 = 'N',
      CS5_3 = 'N',
      CS5_4 = 'N'.
evaluate_char5(CS5_1, CS5_2, CS5_3, CS5_4, 2) :-
      CS5_1 = 'N',
      CS5_2 = 'Y',
      CS5_3 = 'N',
      CS5_4 = 'N'.
evaluate_char5(CS5_1, CS5_2, CS5_3, CS5_4, 2) :-
      CS5_1 = 'N',
      CS5_2 = 'N',
      CS5_3 = 'N',
      CS5_4 = 'Y'.
evaluate_char5(CS5_1, CS5_2, CS5_3, CS5_4, 2) :-
      CS5_1 = 'N',
      CS5_2 = 'N',
      CS5_3 = 'Y',
      CS5_4 = 'N'.
evaluate_char5(CS5_1, CS5_2, CS5_3, CS5_4, 1) :-
      CS5_1 = 'N',
      CS5_2 = 'N',
      CS5_3 = 'N',
      CS5_4 = 'N'.
```

```
evaluate_char6(CS6_1, CS6_2, CS6_3, CS6_4, 5) :-
    CS6_1 = 'Y',
    CS6_2 = 'Y',
    CS6_3 = 'Y',
    CS6_4 = 'Y'.
evaluate_char6(CS6_1, CS6_2, CS6_3, CS6_4, 4) :-
    CS6_1 = 'Y',
    CS6_2 = 'Y',
    CS6_3 = 'Y',
    CS6_4 = 'N'.
evaluate_char6(CS6_1, CS6_2, CS6_3, CS6_4, 4) :-
    CS6_1 = 'Y',
    CS6_2 = 'Y',
    CS6_3 = 'N',
    CS6_4 = 'Y'.
evaluate_char6(CS6_1, CS6_2, CS6_3, CS6_4, 4) :-
    CS6_1 = 'Y',
    CS6_2 = 'N',
    CS6_3 = 'Y',
    CS6_4 = 'Y'.
evaluate_char6(CS6_1, CS6_2, CS6_3, CS6_4, 4) :-
    CS6_1 = 'N',
    CS6_2 = 'Y',
    CS6_3 = 'Y',
    CS6_4 = 'Y'.
evaluate_char6(CS6_1, CS6_2, CS6_3, CS6_4, 3) :-
    CS6_1 = 'Y',
    CS6_2 = 'Y',
    CS6_3 = 'N',
    CS6_4 = 'N'.
evaluate_char6(CS6_1, CS6_2, CS6_3, CS6_4, 3) :-
    CS6_1 = 'Y',
    CS6_2 = 'N',
    CS6_3 = 'Y',
    CS6_4 = 'N'.
evaluate_char6(CS6_1, CS6_2, CS6_3, CS6_4, 3) :-
    CS6_1 = 'N',
    CS6_2 = 'Y',
    CS6_3 = 'Y',
    CS6_4 = 'N'.
evaluate_char6(CS6_1, CS6_2, CS6_3, CS6_4, 3) :-
    CS6_1 = 'Y',
    CS6_2 = 'N',
    CS6_3 = 'N',
    CS6_4 = 'Y'.
evaluate_char6(CS6_1, CS6_2, CS6_3, CS6_4, 3) :-
    CS6_1 = 'N',
    CS6_2 = 'Y',
    CS6_3 = 'N',
    CS6_4 = 'Y'.
```

```
evaluate_char6(CS6_1, CS6_2, CS6_3, CS6_4, 3) :-
     CS6_1 = 'N',
     CS6_2 = 'N',
     CS6_3 = 'Y',
     CS6_4 = 'Y'.
evaluate_char6(CS6_1, CS6_2, CS6_3, CS6_4, 2) :-
     CS6_1 = 'Y',
     CS6_2 = 'N',
     CS6_3 = 'N',
     CS6_4 = 'N'.
evaluate_char6(CS6_1, CS6_2, CS6_3, CS6_4, 2) :-
     CS6_1 = 'N',
     CS6_2 = 'Y',
     CS6_3 = 'N',
     CS6_4 = 'N'.
evaluate_char6(CS6_1, CS6_2, CS6_3, CS6_4, 2) :-
     CS6_1 = 'N',
     CS6_2 = 'N',
     CS6_3 = 'N',
     CS6_4 = 'Y'.
evaluate_char6(CS6_1, CS6_2, CS6_3, CS6_4, 2) :-
     CS6_1 = 'N',
     CS6_2 = 'N',
     CS6_3 = 'Y',
     CS6_4 = 'N'.
evaluate_char6(CS6_1, CS6_2, CS6_3, CS6_4, 1) :-
     CS6_1 = 'N',
     CS6_2 = 'N',
     CS6_3 = 'N',
     CS6_4 = 'N'.
evaluate_iac(Rating1, Rating2, Rating3, Rating4, Rating5,
     Rating6, excellent):-
     Score is Rating1 + Rating2 + Rating3 + Rating4 + Rating5 +
     Rating6, Score = 30.
evaluate_iac(Rating1, Rating2, Rating3, Rating4, Rating5,
     Rating6, good) :-
     Score is Rating1 + Rating2 + Rating3 + Rating4 + Rating5 +
     Rating6,
     Score < 30,
     Score >= 24.
evaluate_iac(Rating1, Rating2, Rating3, Rating4, Rating5,
     Rating6, fair) :-
     Score is Rating1 + Rating2 + Rating3 + Rating4 + Rating5 +
     Rating6,
     Score < 24,
     Score >= 18.
evaluate_iac(Rating1, Rating2, Rating3, Rating4, Rating5,
     Rating6, poor) :-
     Score is Rating1 + Rating2 + Rating3 + Rating4 + Rating5 +
     Rating6,
     Score < 18,
     Score >= 12.
```

```prolog
evaluate_iac(Rating1, Rating2, Rating3, Rating4, Rating5,
     Rating6, inadequate) :-
     Score is Rating1 + Rating2 + Rating3 + Rating4 + Rating5 +
     Rating6,
     Score < 12.
get_char1(CS1_1, CS1_2, CS1_3, CS1_4) :-
     write('Are qualified people with good references hired?
     (Y/N) '),
     read(CS1_1),
     nl,
     write('Are annual vacations required? (Y/N) '),
     read(CS1_2),
     nl,
     write('Are employees in positions of trust bonded (Y/N)
     '),
     read(CS1_3),
     nl,
     write('Is there a conflict of interest policy? (Y/N) '),
     read(CS1_4),
     nl.
get_char2(CS2_1, CS2_2, CS2_3, CS2_4) :-
     write('Has an organization chart been developed? (Y/N) '),
     read(CS2_1),
     nl,
     write('Are record keeping and custody of assets separate?
     (Y/N) '),
     read(CS2_2),
     nl,
     write('Are authorization and record keeping separate? (Y/N)
     '),
     read(CS2_3),
     nl,
     write('Are receiving and purchasing separate? (Y/N) '),
     read(CS2_4),
     nl.
put_iac_rate(excellent) :-
     nl,
     write('The internal accounting controls are excellent.'),
     nl.
put_iac_rate(good) :-
     nl,
     write('The internal accounting controls are good.'),
     nl.
put_iac_rate(fair) :-
     nl,
     write('The internal accounting controls are fair.'),
     nl.
put_iac_rate(poor) :-
     nl,
     write('The internal accounting controls are poor.'),
     nl.
```

```
put_iac_rate(inadequate) :-
    nl,
    write('The internal accounting controls are inadequate.'),
    nl.
get_char3(CS3_1, CS3_2, CS3_3, CS3_4) :-
    write('Is there proper authorization of transactions? (Y/N)
    '),
    read(CS3_1),
    nl,
    write('Are checks signed only with proper support? (Y/N)
    '),
    read(CS3_2),
    nl,
    write('Is a chart of accounts (with definitions) employed?
    (Y/N) '),
    read(CS3_3),
    nl,
    write('Are operating & acctg procedures described in a
    manual?(Y/N) '),
    read(CS3_4),
    nl.
get_char4(CS4_1, CS4_2, CS4_3) :-
    write('Are important documents prenumbered? (Y/N) '),
    read(CS4_1),
    nl,
    write('Have comparative financial statements been developed?
    (Y/N) '),
    read(CS4_2),
    nl,
    write('Has a budget been prepared and compared with actual?
    (Y/N) '),
    read(CS4_3),
    nl.
get_char5(CS5_1, CS5_2, CS5_3, CS5_4) :-
    write('Is access to inventory limited? (Y/N) '),
    read(CS5_1),
    nl,
    write('Are all important records safeguarded? (Y/N) '),
    read(CS5_2),
    nl,
    write('Are cash receipts deposited intact daily? (Y/N) '),
    read(CS5_3),
    nl,
    write('Are paper valuables kept in fireproof containers?
    (Y/N) '),
    read(CS5_4),
    nl.
get_char6(CS6_1, CS6_2, CS6_3, CS6_4) :-
    write('Are bank statements independently reconciled? (Y/N)
    '),
    read(CS6_1),
```

```
    nl,
    write('Are cash receipts prelisted? (Y/N) '),
    read(CS6_2),
    nl,
    write('Is a complete inventory regularly taken? (Y/N) '),
    read(CS6_3),
    nl,
    write('Is an annual audit bye a CPA firm done? (Y/N) '),
    read(CS6_4),
    nl.
controls :-
    get_char1(CS1_1, CS1_2, CS1_3, CS1_4),
    evaluate_char1(CS1_1, CS1_2, CS1_3, CS1_4, Rating1),
    get_char2(CS2_1, CS2_2, CS2_3, CS2_4),
    evaluate_char2(CS2_1, CS2_2, CS2_3, CS2_4, Rating2),
    get_char3(CS3_1, CS3_2, CS3_3, CS3_4),
    evaluate_char3(CS3_1, CS3_2, CS3_3, CS3_4, Rating3),
    get_char4(CS4_1, CS4_2, CS4_3),
    evaluate_char4(CS4_1, CS4_2, CS4_3, Rating4),
    get_char5(CS5_1, CS5_2, CS5_3, CS5_4),
    cvaluate_char5(CS5_1, CS5_2, CS5_3, CS5_4, Rating5),
    get_char6(CS6_1, CS6_2, CS6_3, CS6_4),
    evaluate_char6(CS6_1, CS6_2, CS6_3, CS6_4, Rating6),
    evaluate_iac(Rating1, Rating2, Rating3, Rating4, Rating5,
    Rating6, Iac_rate),
    put_iac_rate(Iac_rate),
    nl.
```

■ SUMMARY

1. Prolog is not a natural language, but one suitable for developing natural language processing applications. It allows a programmer to program logic directly using induction and deduction. Prolog can be programmed to modify itself to simulate human learning. In an expert systems, the goal of Prolog is to describe relationships between data items. Two important features are its ability to incorporate flexible data structures to adapt on the fly every time a change occurs in the type or quantity of information flowing through the program and its ability to handle symbolic information.

2. Unlike LISP, Prolog is nonprocedural and nondeterminant, in that the programmer does not have to direct the flow of control within the program. It contains rules, which are goals to be satisfied, and clauses, which are statements that may represent either facts necessary to the program or rules specifying how to derive facts from other clauses when a program is used. A fact is a fundamental Prolog structure that states a relationship. The predicate is the relationship being defined by the fact. The arguments are the objects of the relationship. A variable is a symbol that represents an atom that is not yet known. Prolog uses these through questions asked by the user. Prolog searches its databases for a match to the user's queries.

3. The basics of Prolog include a database of facts and rules and queries from the user. Something is instantiated when an instance of some fact or rule exists that it matches. Backtracking consists of reviewing what has been done, and attempting to resatisfy the goals by finding an alternative way to meet them. However, this process can be blocked with a cut. A list is an ordered sequence of elements that can have any length.

4. Prolog is not the language to use for "number crunching," because it only contains integer match functions with signed two-byte numbers ranging from $-32,768$ to $+32,767$.

5. Three types of predefined predicates to help debug databases that do not work are tracers, spy points, and leashers. They allow examination and control of program execution so that the programmer may watch each iteration of the four main break points in a Prolog program: the call, the fail, the exit, and the redo.

■ TERMS TO LEARN

Anonymous variable a special type of variable in Prolog that contains an underscore and gives a YES or NO answer.

Arguments the objects of the relationship in fact statement.

Atom noninteger constant in Prolog.

Backtracking a way of satisfying goals in which Prolog reviews what has been done and attempts to resatisfy the goals by finding an alternative way to meet them.

Call an attempt to satisfy a goal has been initiated in which Prolog will try to instantiate the clause.

Clause facts necessary to a program or rules specifying how to derive facts from other clauses.

Cut a goal in Prolog that succeeds and blocks backtracking.

Database a collection of facts and rules.

Empty list a list with no elements.

Exit occurs when a clause is exited after Prolog has either failed or finished all possible instantiations.

Fact a fundamental Prolog structure that states a true relationship.

Fail occurs when instantiation fails or when the goal is satisfied and the solution is printed.

Goal an uninstantiated query in Prolog.

Head the leftmost element in a fact or a rule.

Instantiate something is instantiated in Prolog when an instance of some fact or rule exists about that thing.

Leasher a predefined predicate in Prolog that helps to debug databases that do not work as expected.

List an ordered sequence of elements that can have any length.

Predefined predicate a built-in command that makes it easier for the user to program in Prolog.

Predicate the relationship being defined by the fact.

Redo occurs when Prolog returns to a marked clause for a second attempt at satisfying backtracking.

Rules goals to be satisfied in a Prolog program; fundamental Prolog clauses that define a relationship from which facts may be inferred.

Share when two uninstantiated variables are matched together, they share, meaning that when one is instantiated, so is the other.

Spy point a predefined predicate in Prolog that helps to debug databases that do not work as expected.

Stack a contiguous block of memory containing some memory.

Stack pointer a indicator that tells where the top of the stack is.

Tail everything except the first element in a list or rule.

Tracer a predefined predicate in Prolog that helps to debug databases that do not work as expected.

Variable a symbol in Prolog that represents an atom not yet known.

Appendix ▪ B

VP-Expert: A Tutorial

■ INTRODUCTION

T his tutorial is included as a hands-on supplement to expert systems courses using VP-Expert. It should be a useful and quick reference to help in building expert systems. More details on this inexpensive shell are available in a manual that accompanies the student version of VP-Expert or the developer version. The student version diskette that accompanies this text allows up to 100 rules to a knowledge base.

This tutorial emphasizes the user interface, the use of information stored in database files, and text-based graphics and windows. Examples and illustrations are also included to simplify building expert systems.

■ SETTING UP VP-EXPERT

If your PC has a hard drive, an efficient way to work with VP-Expert is to load it in a directory on the hard drive. At the **C:** prompt, make a directory by typing: **MD VPX**

The response should be: **C:\VPX**

Next, load VPX diskette in the **A:** drive, type **A:,** and then type the command **COPY *.* C:\VPX**
The system will copy the entire diskette into the directory VPX. Once completed, go back to the **C:** drive, load the directory **(CD VPX),** and then type **VPX.** The logo appears on the screen within seconds.

As a precaution, you should "write protect" your original disk (shell and data) to protect against accidental erasures and possible viruses.

■ A FIRST LOOK

With VP-Expert properly installed, you are now ready for a sample consultation. Here is a three-step procedure:

1. At **C:\VPX <ENTER>,** enter **VPX** to load the shell.

2. The response should be a logo Displaying VP-Expert, developer name, copyright date and information, etc.

3. Press any key and Figure B–1 is displayed.

VP-Expert divides the screen into three special-purpose areas, called windows. Notice the options available on the bottom two lines. The first line displays options (Help, Induce, Edit, etc.). The default is Consult. The bottom line indicates the choices available if the consult option is selected.

Checking the Path

The first recommended step, before looking up the knowledge base, is to identify the path; make sure to move the cursor to option 7 (path) to tell the system where to find the knowledge base. When you press **ENTER,** the screen displays the default path. Figure B–2 is an example of the path window usually set in the current VP-Expert session. Enter the proper path, if different. Press **Esc** key to return to the main screen.

Figure B–1

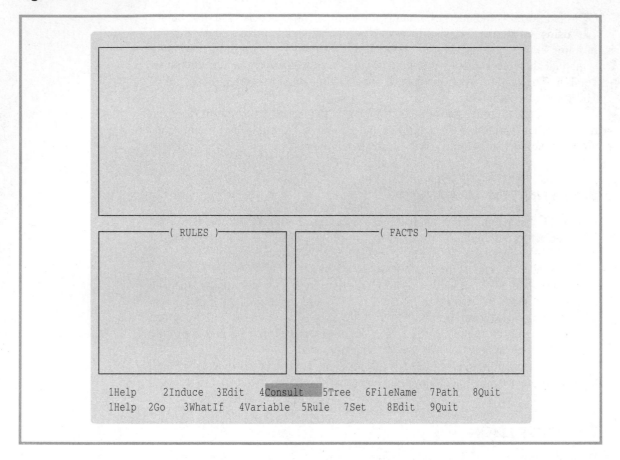

```
                           ┌─────( RULES )─────┐        ┌─────( FACTS )─────┐


    1Help     2Induce  3Edit  4Consult    5Tree  6FileName  7Path  8Quit
    1Help  2Go  3WhatIf  4Variable  5Rule  7Set     8Edit   9Quit
```

Selecting FileName

At the main screen, select option 7 (filename) to display a list of files (knowledge base or KBS) as shown in Figure B–3. If you do not succeed, chances are the system is looking for files in the wrong directory or wrong drive. Press **Esc** and Figure B–2 should reappear. Reselect the path.

■ CONSULTING THE KNOWLEDGE BASE

The **Consult** option allows you to consult the knowledge base. After you have selected the file (via filename), press **ENTER,** and VP-Expert should load the file, automatically highlighting the GO option. After pressing the GO option, VP-Expert displays information in two windows. The Consult window is the upper window that displays the questions with options. The lower left window is the RULES window that provides information on what the inference engine is doing. See Figure B–4.

Figure B–2

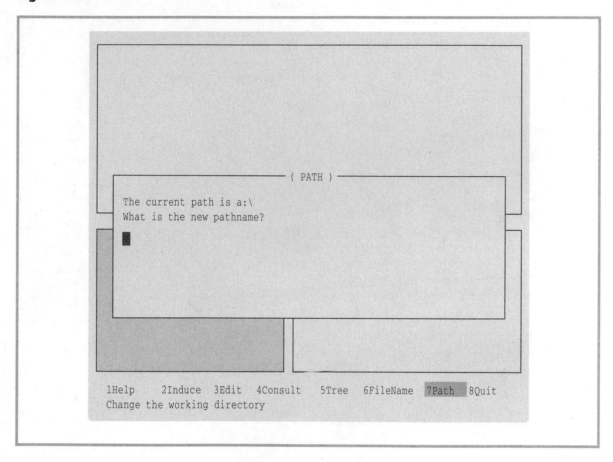

```
                              ─( PATH )─
  The current path is a:\
  What is the new pathname?

  ▮



 1Help     2Induce  3Edit   4Consult   5Tree   6FileName  7Path  8Quit
 Change the working directory
```

▉ CREATING A KNOWLEDGE BASE

Building a knowledge base begins with Edit (option 3) command from the main menu. To update or change an existing knowledge base, press **EDIT.** The knowledge base asks for the filename. Type the name of an existing file or the name of a new file (e.g., TEST). Once completed, VP-Expert will switch to the editor screen. See Figure B–5 on page 554. Note the upper right corner, displaying the name of the file selected. If it is the wrong screen, you may leave the editor screen by pressing **Alt + F8** then type **Y.** To save what you have edited or a knowledge base just completed, press **Alt + F6** and then type **Y.**

Hands-On Use of the Editor

To understand how the editor works, type the following commands, pressing **ENTER** at the end of each line:

```
!Sample knowledge base ⊠
ACTIONS ⊠
CLS ⊠
FIND author_Namy ⊠
```

Figure B–3

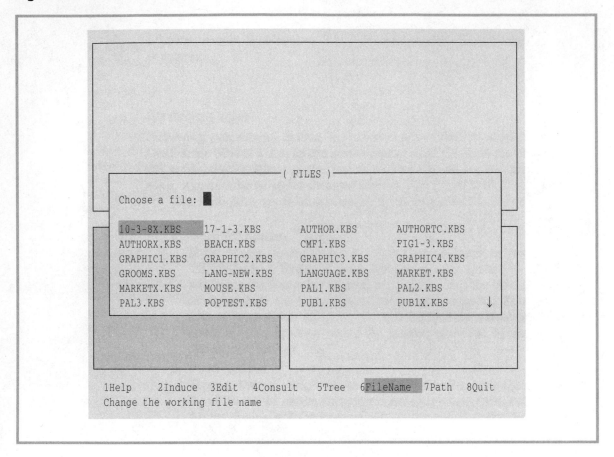

The last word is supposed to be "author_Name". To make corrections, use the ↑ key to move the cursor up one line, press **END** to to the end of the line, then move the ← key once. It should be on top of the character "Y". Use **Del** key to delete "Y" and then type **e.** When you press **ENTER,** the cursor should move automatically to the next line.

On the line after "FIND Author_name", type the following commands:

```
FIND Reviews ⊠
DISPLAY "{Author_Name}, {Response} ⊠
⊠
Press <ENTER> to stop ~"; ⊠
⊠
```

Next, enter the following two rules:

```
RULE GoodBook ⊠
    IF Reviews = good or ⊠
      Reviews = fair
    THEN Response = publish_manuscript; ⊠
```

Figure B–4

```
Ventilation in the area where the equipment
will be cleaned?
   Poor                    Fair                    Good ◀

Does the equipment to be cleaned contain
any rubber components?
   Yes ◀                   No

The safest and most effective cleaning
solvent for the job is Polysol Plus CNF 100.
```

```
──────( RULES )──────          ──────( FACTS )──────
Solvent = Polysol CNF 100      Main_Material = Stainless_Steel CNF 1
Testing 4                      00
RULE 4 IF                      Main_Material = Other_Metal CNF 100
Equipment_Class = Class_1 AND  Equipment Class = Class_1 CNF 100
Ventilation - Good AND         Ventilation = Good CNF 100
Rubber = Yes                   Rubber = Yes CNF 100
THEN                           Solvent = Polysol_Plus CNF 100
Solvent = Polysol_Plus CNF 100
```

```
RULE PoorBook ⊠
    IF Reviews = poor ⊠
    THEN Response = reject_manuscript; ⊠
⊠
ASK author_name "what is the author's name?"; ⊠
ASK reviews "what are the reviewers' comments?"; ⊠
CHOICES Reviews: good, fair, poor; ⊠
```

At this point, you have completed the knowledge base. It should look like Figure B–6.

If the knowledge base is clear of errors, then the next step is to save it. Hold down the **Alt** key and press **F6** at the same time. The following message is displayed.

```
save as "test.KBS" (Y or N)?
```

Assuming you made no typographical errors, pressing Y will save your knowledge base under the current name (in our example, it is test.KBS) and return the system to the main menu. The following message is displayed in the consultation window:

```
Loading File . . .
File Loaded
```

Figure B–5

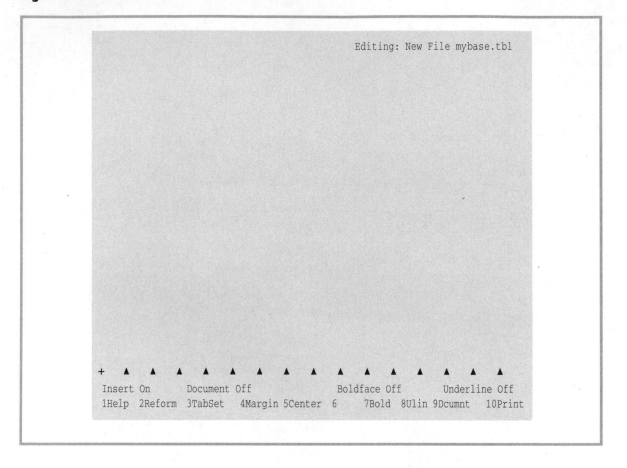

```
                                          Editing: New File mybase.tbl
```

```
+    ▲    ▲    ▲    ▲    ▲    ▲    ▲    ▲    ▲    ▲    ▲    ▲    ▲

Insert On        Document Off              Boldface Off         Underline Off
1Help  2Reform  3TabSet   4Margin 5Center  6    7Bold 8Ulin 9Dcumnt  10Print
```

If you answered "N" to the save choice, the system will ask you "please enter the file where you want to save your test:" You may now enter a new name, and the knowledge base will be saved under the new name.

The next step is to go back to the main menu, press **GO** to start the consultation. You will be asked two questions:

```
1. What is the author's name?
2. What are the reviewers' comments?
good__  fair__  poor__
```

In the first question, you simply add a name; press **ENTER,** and then **END.** For the second question, you make one choice (good, fair, poor), press **ENTER** and then **END.** If you choose good or fair, the response should be "publish_manuscript". This is when "Rule GoodBook" is fired. If you choose "poor," then the response should be "reject_manuscript". In this case, "Rule PoorBook" is fired.

◼ PRINTING A KNOWLEDGE BASE

The F10 key is used to print your current knowledge base. Pressing **F10** should give you a screen similar to Figure B–7. It gives you a chance to set margins,

Figure B–6

```
!sample knowledge base ⊠
ACTIONS ⊠
CLS ⊠
FIND author_name ⊠
FIND reviews ⊠
FIND response ⊠
DISPLAY "{author_name}, {response} ⊠
press <ENTER> to stop ~"; ⊠
RULE GoodBook ⊠
IF Reviews = good or ⊠
  Reviews = fair ⊠
THEN response = publish_manuscript; ⊠
RULE PoorBook ⊠
IF reviews = poor ⊠
THEN response = reject_manuscript; ⊠
⊠
ASK author_name: "what is the author's name?"; ⊠
ASK reviews: "what are the reviewers' comments?"; ⊠
CHOICES reviews: good, fair, poor; ⊠
⊠
```

Figure B–7

```
                        Editing: Old File a:\pub 1
Top margin       6      Bottom Margin        6
Line Spacing     1      Page Offset          10
Lines on Page    66     Continuous Forms?    Y
Page Width       65     Number Pages?        Y
            Next Position:        ENTER or Tab
            Previous Position:    Back Tab
            When All Values Are Set, Press <END>
```

line spacing, and so on, before final printing of the knowledge base. Press **END** when you're ready to print. Press **Esc** if you decide not to print.

STRUCTURE OF A KNOWLEDGE BASE

In VP-Expert, a knowledge base has three major elements:

1. ACTIONS block
2. Rules
3. Statements

Each element is explained briefly here.

ACTIONS Block

The ACTIONS block's main function is to define the problem the knowledge base is trying to solve and identifies the procedure for solving it. This first step is mandatory. The block begins with the word ACTIONS and ends with a semicolon. In between the block are clauses that are executed in the order they are listed. The three most common clauses are

1. **CLS**—clear the screen, may be used anywhere in the ACTIONS block or any time the screen should be cleared.

2. **DISPLAY**—displays information on the screen or writes it to the printer. A display message begins and ends with a double quote marks. Anything in between is displayed exactly as entered. The tilde (~) after "press **ENTER** to stop ~" in the sample knowledge base causes the inference engine to stop and waits for the user to press the **ENTER** key.

3. **FIND**—activates the inference engine to find a value for the variable, following the FIND clause. In our example (Figure B–6), FIND author_name, the inference engine attempts to look for a rule that makes conclusions about author_name or for an ASK statement. Actually, the FIND clause initiates backward-chaining, which is the default chaining process.

Note that other clauses are covered in the VP-Expert manual. Also, VP-Expert is not case-sensitive. Uppercase and lowercase can be used without a problem.

RULES Block

In VP-Expert, a rule has four parts: a rule name, a premise, an action (conclusion), and a semicolon at the end. To explain the "why" question on the main screen, a rule may have an option BECAUSE, which stores the explanation in response to "why" See Figure B–8.

Note that each rule must have a *unique* name that may be up to 40 alphanumeric characters long. If the name is more than one word, underscores link them together.

The Rule Premise

The first part of a rule is called the *rule premise* and begins with the keyword **IF.** It may contain one or more conditions that compare specific variables with values. The relational operators used are

Figure B–8

```
               RULE GoodBook
  Required      IF Reviewer_Comments = good
               THEN response publish_manuscript
  Optional        BECAUSE "good reviews mean professional
                  acceptance of the manuscript as a
                  potentially good book for adoption.";
```

= equal
<> not equal
> greater than
< less than
>= greater than or equal to
<= less than or equal to

Multiple conditions are linked together with logical operators AND and OR. Care should be taken in how you use both AND and OR in one rule premise. For example,

```
RULE GoodBook
  IF Reviewer_comments = good AND
     author_requirements = low OR
     author_reputation = established
  THEN response publish manuscript;
```

VP-Expert considers OR before AND. Rule GoodBook is interpreted as follows:

```
"If reviewer_comments = good AND (author_requirements = low
OR author_reputation = established)
```

It means that if the reviewers' comments are good and either the author's requirements are low or the author has an established reputation, it will result in a publishing commitment. Remember that VP-Expert does not allow the use of parenthesis in its rule format.

The Rule Action

The action part of the rule assigns a value to a variable if the condition of the rule premise is true. A FIND clause activates the inference engine to search for a rule or rules whose conclusions assign values to the goal variable of the FIND clause.

Although any clause may be used in a rule action, FIND and DISPLAY are the most common clauses. For example:

```
RULE GoodBook
  IF reviewer_comments = good AND
       author_requirements = minimum
  THEN possible_publication = high
       FIND possible_publication;
```

This rule suggests that a publication is called *high* if it receives good reviewer's comments and author's requirements are minimum. If "high" is a possibility, then the system should look for (find) publication possibility.

STATEMENTS Block

The third major element of a knowledge base is a statement block. Unlike clauses, statements are independent items, ending with a semicolon. The two most common statements are ASK and CHOICES. If the rules make conclusions about a value for a FIND variable (in the preceding example, it is "possible_publication"), the inference engine will assign a value to that variable. Otherwise, the value will be UNKNOWN. Then, the system would want to ask the user to provide the information, which is done with an ASK statement.

ASK Statement

The syntax of ASK statement is

```
ASK variable: "text";
```

The hands-on example uses the following ASK statement:

```
ASK reviews: "what are the reviewers'_comments?";
```

Note that the text is separated from the variable *reviews* by a colon, and the statement must end in a semicolon.

CHOICES Statement

The CHOICES statement gives the user a specific set of choices from which to select an answer to a question. When an ASK statement is displayed, the corresponding CHOICES are listed following the question. In the hands-on example:

```
ASK reviews: "what are the reviewers'_comments?";
CHOICES reviews: good, fair, poor;
```

In the consult window, the representation looks like the following:

```
What are the reviewers' comments?
good___X___  fair_____  poor_____
```

The cursor automatically waits at the first option. It can be moved to the middle or right option, simply by pressing the arrow key to the right once or twice, respectively.

■ STOPPING A CONSULTATION

VP-Expert provides two ways for a user to stop a consultation before the inference engine reaches the semicolon at the end of the ACTIONS block. If the system is not waiting for a response, you simply press the **Esc** key. Otherwise, press the **/** key, which allows you to select **6Quit** from the GO menu.

■ SETTING THE TRACE FUNCTION

Tracing allows you to see the rules considered during a consultation or situations in which values are assigned to certain variables. It is another way of having VP-Expert keep track of what it does during consultation. To do means setting the TRACE function.

Setting TRACE involves three main steps:

1. From the CONSULT menu, select **6set** option as shown:

```
            1Help    2GO      3WhatIF   4Variable   5Rule      6Set    7Edit   8Quit
Set menu ──▶ 1Help    2Trace   3Slow     4Fast       5Windows   6Quit
```

2. When you press **SET,** it brings up its own menu. The next step is to select **2Trace** to set the TRACE ON. The message "The Trace is ON" is then displayed in the consultation window.

3. After setting Trace On, pick **6Quit** and then run a consultation in a normal procedure.

Viewing a TRACE

A TRACE can be viewed in the next or graphic mode. Assuming your TRACE is ON, viewing a trace in the text mode involves three steps:

1. Terminate the consultation in the normal procedure.

2. Select **8Quit** from the consultation menu.

3. Select **5Tree** from the main menu.

You should see the following tree choices displayed:

```
1Help    2Test    3Graphics    4Quit
Display a text tree
```

Text Mode

To view a TRACE in a text mode, press **2Text.** You should see a trace similar to Figure B–9. You may leave the editor by pressing **ALT** and **F8** and then **Y.**

Graphic Mode

To view a TRACE in the graphic mode, select **3Graphics** from the tree menu. The resulting screen should be similar to Figure B–10. You may zoom the shaded area by pressing the space bar.

◼ IMPROVING THE USER INTERFACE

In addition to developing a reliable knowledge base, a user needs to customize the way information is displayed on the screen. Sometimes, all you need is to incorporate color with proper boxes and layout for an attractive display.

Use of RUNTIME Statement

As you develop experience with VP-Expert, you will find that the *Rules* and *Facts* windows are of little or no use to the ultimate user. Therefore, a user can better benefit from converting the screen into a full-fledged consultation window to accommodate more than one question and answer at a time. Adding a RUNTIME statement after testing your knowledge base eliminates the Rules and Facts windows from the screen. Go back to the sample "Test.KBS" knowledge base and add a RUNTIME statement at the top of the program and an exclamation mark <!> in front of the RUNTIME statement, save the addition, and redo a consultation. What changes do you see?

Exclamation marks are comments that normally appear at the beginning of a knowledge base. Comments may be used to identify the knowledge base, its author, name, and so on. Because they are comments, they are optional for the purpose of knowledge base operation.

Figure B–9

```
                                      Editing: Old File solventZ.trc

Testing SOLVENT2.kbs◄
(= yes CNF 0 )◄
!  Solvent◄
!  !  Testing 1◄
!  !  !  Equipment_Class◄
!  !  ·  !  !  Testing 13◄
!  !  !  !  !  Main Material◄
!  !  !  !  !  !  (= Plastic CNF 100 )◄
!  !  !  !  Testing 14◄
!  !  !  !  Testing 15◄
!  !  !  !  (= Class_3 CNF 100 )◄
!  !  Testing 2◄
!  !  Testing 3◄
!  !  Testing 4◄
!  !  Testing 5◄
!  !  Testing 6◄
!  !  Testing 7◄
!  !  Testing 8◄


+   ▲   ▲   ▲   ▲   ▲   ▲   ▲   ▲   ▲   ▲   ▲   ▲   ▲   ▲

Insert On       Document Off          Boldface Off      Underline Off
1Help 2Reform  3TabSet  4Margin 5Center 6    7Bold 8Ulin 9Dcumnt  10Print
```

Using Windows

In addition to the RUNTIME statement windows and color can be used to enhance the user interface, which is made possible by the BKCOLOR (background color) statement. The following is a list of eight color codes or BKCOLOR statements:

0   black
1   blue
2   green
3   light blue
4   red
5   magenta
6   brown
7   white

A BKCOLOR statement changes the background color to the color based on the number following it. Each color statement represents a window that can be any size, can be next another window, or can be overlapping.

Windows are defined with WOPEN, using the syntax clause:

```
WOPEN window_num, top_row, left_col, num_of_rows,
num_of_cols, bkgnd_color
```

Figure B–10

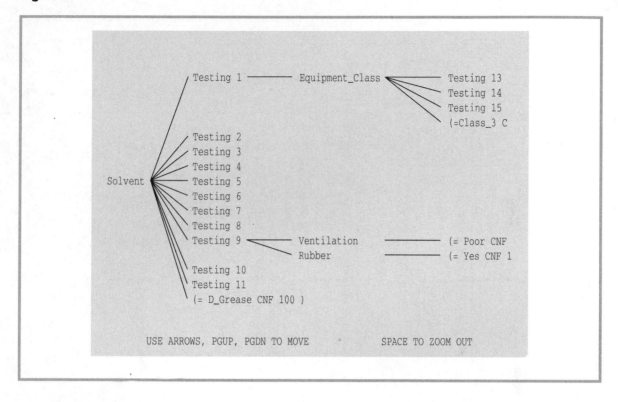

- **Window_num:** the number of windows with a maximum of 9.
- **Top_row, left_col:** define the location of the upper left hand corner of the window.
- **Num_of_rows, Num_of_cols:** define the size of the window. The range is from 2–20 rows and 2–77 columns.
- **BKgnd_color:** sets the background color.

To illustrate, consider the following two windows:

1. WOPEN 1, 3, 6, 8, 70, 1
2. WOPEN 2, 15, 4, 9, 70, 2

The *first* window begins at the third row, sixth column, and has a total of eight rows and 70 columns. Its background color blue. The *second* window begins at the fifteenth row, fourth column, and has a total of nine rows and 70 columns. Its background color is green.

WOPEN allows you to define and draw a window on a screen only. To write information in it, the window must be activated, using the ACTIVE clause. Once executed, all displays are shown in the ACTIVE window. For example, examine the partial program in Figure B–11, which uses WOPEN and ACTIVE:

This example defines two windows: activate the first for an introductory (display) message and activate the second window for the response. Remember that a window continues to be activated until it detects another ACTIVE clause. The COLOR clause (e.g., COLOR = 3) changes the color to be used by future

Figure B–11

```
    .
    .
    .
! define two windows: one for introduction
! and one for dialog
WOPEN 1,3,6,8,70,1
WOPEN 2,15,4,9,70,2
! Activate window 1 and display introduction message
ACTIVE 1
COLOR = 2
DISPLAY   "This Publisher Advisor may be used by a college
          book editor to determine whether a manuscript
          should be published.  For each question, use the
          appropriate choice, press the <ENTER> key,
          followed by <END> key."
!Activate second window for the dialog
ACTIVE 2
ACTIVE 3
FIND Response
CLS
DISPLAY   "Based on all data received, the decision is to
          {response}.  (Press <ENTER> to return to main
          menu)~";
```

DISPLAY clause. See VP-Expert manual for sophisticated details on window design and programming.

▓ ENTERING CONFIDENCE FACTORS DURING CONSULTATION

Normally, the user is expected to select an answer, press **ENTER,** move on to another question, and so on. Sometimes, however, when the choice is not 100 percent certain. VP-Expert allows the user to answer a question by entering a certainty factor or a CNF.

To enter a CNF, first press **ENTER** and then **HOME** instead of **END.** A rectangle appears that allows you to enter the CNF (e.g., 80). After entering the CNF, enter **END** to complete the choice. When in doubt, refer to VP-Expert manual or press **F1** for HELP on how to enter a CNF. Refer to Chapter 11 for calculation of CNF values. To enter CNF in a rule, simply add (CNF + value) after a variable. For example:

```
IF marketability = high AND author_reputation = average
THEN decision = offer contract CNF 75;
```

■ INDUCTION FROM A TEXT FILE

VP-Expert can convert a decision table, a text file, a spreadsheet, or a database file easily into rules. To illustrate, take the following text file:

```
Reviewer_comments    Author_reputation    Marketability    Decision
   good                 established          high            offer_contract
   good                 established          poor            offer_contract CNF 80
   good                 up_n_coming          high            offer_contract CNF 80
   good                 up_n_coming          poor            offer_contract CNF 60
   good                 first_time           high            offer_contract CNF 80
   good                 first_time           poor            reject_manuscript CNF 75
   poor                 established          high            offer_contract CNF 50
   poor                 established          poor            reject_manuscript
   poor                 up_n_coming          high            reject_manuscript CNF 60
   poor                 up_n_coming          poor            reject manuscript
   poor                 first_time           high            reject_manuscript CNF 70
   poor                 first_time           poor            reject_manuscript
```

The first line represents the variable name (conditions). The last variable is the decision or action taken based on the value of the variables in each row. All values must be separated by tabs. To enter the text file, first, choose **2Create** on the induce menu to create a text file before inducing the requisite rules.

■ AN ILLUSTRATION

To illustrate how VP-Expert works, the following expert system advises a book editor whether a manuscript should be accepted for publication. Examine the rules and procedures and determine the areas or ways in which this Publisher Advisor can be improved. A running copy is available on a diskette that accompanies the text.

```
RUNTIME
ENDOFF;
BKCOLOR = 3;
ACTIONS
    WOPEN 3,7,6,9,66,1
    ACTIVE 3
    COLOR = 11
    DISPLAY"
            Publisher Advisor
        Developed by Dong Lee and Daisy Tai
          Press any key to continue.~"
    WCLOSE 3
    WOPEN 1,0,0,9,79,1
    WOPEN 2,10,0,12,79,5
    ACTIVE 1
    COLOR = 11
    DISPLAY "This knowledge base may be used by a publisher to
decide on the adoption of a potential text manuscript.
When you are ready to begin, press any key.~"
```

```
    CLS
    DISPLAY "For each question, type your response or use the arrow
keys to move to the appropriate choice, then press <ENTER>.
If you are not sure about an answer, enter your certainty factor by:
1) Make your selection and press <HOME>.
2) Enter the certainty factor and press <ENTER> twice."
    ACTIVE 2
    COLOR = 0
    FIND Decision
    FIND final;
!---------------------------------------------
RULE R0
IF    Total = (positive)
THEN  Reviews = Strong
BECAUSE "The reviewers' comments on the proposed manuscript are one of the
most important factors to consider while making a publishing decision.";
RULE R1
IF    positivef >= 0.70
THEN  Reviews = Strong
    CLS
    DISPLAY "According to your responses, this manuscript has
received {Reviews} reviews."
    FIND agree
    WHILETRUE Agree = no THEN
        FIND U review 1
        Reviews = (U_review1)
        RESET Agree
    END
BECAUSE "The reviewers' comments on the proposed manuscript are
one of the most important factors to consider while making a publishing
decision. You may override the system's assessment in some special
cases. Especially, if you consider that some reviewers' comments carry
more weight than those of others";
RULE R2
IF    negativef >= 0.65
THEN  Reviews = Weak
    CLS
    DISPLAY "According to your responses, this manuscript has
received {Reviews} reviews."
    FIND agree
    WHILETRUE Agree = no THEN
        FIND U_review3
        Reviews = (U_review3)
        RESET Agree
    END
BECAUSE "The reviewers' comments on the proposed manuscript are
one of the most important factors to consider while making a publishing
decision. You may override the system's assessment in some special
cases. Especially, if you consider that some reviewers' comments carry
more weight than those of others";
RULE R3
```

```
IF     zerof >= 0.70
THEN   Reviews = Mixed
    CLS
    DISPLAY "According to your responses, this manuscript has
received {Reviews} reviews."
    FIND agree
    WHILETRUE Agree = no THEN
        FIND U_review 2
        Reviews = (U_review2)
        RESET Agree
    END
BECAUSE "The reviewers' comments on the proposed manuscript are
one of the most important factors to consider while making a publishing
decision. You may override the system's assessment in some special
cases. Especially, if you consider that some reviewers' comments carry
more weight than those of others";
RULE R4
IF     negativef >= (positivef + zerof)
AND    positivef < 0.40
THEN   Reviews = Weak
    CLS
    DISPLAY "According to your responses, this manuscript has
received {Reviews} reviews."
    FIND agree
    WHILETRUE Agree = no THEN
        FIND U_review3
        Reviews = (U_review3)
        RESET Agree
    END
BECAUSE "The reviewers' comments on the proposed manuscript are
one of the most important factors to consider while making a publishing
decision. You may override the system's assessment in some special
cases. Especially, if you consider that some reviewers' comments carry
more weight than those of others";
RULE R5
IF     negativef >= (positivef + zerof)
AND    positivef >= 0.40
THEN   Reviews = Mixed
    CLS
    DISPLAY "According to your responses, this manuscript has
received {Reviews} reviews."
    FIND agree
    WHILETRUE Agree = no THEN
        FIND U_review2
        Reviews = (U_review2)
        RESET Agree
    END
BECAUSE "The reviewers' comments on the proposed manuscript are
one of the most important factors to consider while making a publishing
decision. You may override the system's assessment in some special
cases. Especially, if you consider that some reviewers' comments carry
more weight than those of others";
```

```
RULE R6
IF     negativef < (positivef + zerof)
AND    positivef < 0.61
THEN   Reviews = Mixed
     CLS
     DISPLAY "According to your responses, this manuscript has
received {Reviews} reviews."
     FIND agree
     WHILETRUE Agree = no THEN
          FIND U_review2
          Reviews = (U_review2)
          RESET Agree
     END
BECAUSE "The reviewers' comments on the proposed manuscript are
one of the most important factors to consider while making a publishing
decision. You may override the system's assessment in some special
cases. Especially, if you consider that some reviewers' comments carry
more weight than those of others";
RULE R7
IF     negativef < (positivef + zerof)
AND    positivef >= 0.61
THEN   Reviews = Strong
     CLS
     DISPLAY "According to your responses, this manuscript has
received {Reviews} reviews."
     FIND agree
     WHILETRUE Agree = no THEN
          FIND U_review1
          Reviews = (U_review1)
          RESET Agree
     END
BECAUSE "The reviewers' comments on the proposed manuscript are
one of the most important factors to consider while making a publishing
decision. You may override the system's assessment in some special
cases. Especially, if you consider that some reviewers' comments carry
more weight than those of others";
!----------------------------------------
WHENEVER RQ0
IF     Decision = Rejected
THEN   Final = Rejected
     CLS
     DISPLAY "According to the data available, the manuscript should
be {#Decision}.
     Press any key to end consultation~";
WHENEVER RQ1
IF     DECISION = Published
THEN   WKS Requirement, c3..c6, lookup
     GETCNF Decision, Publish_CNF;
WHENEVER RQ2
IF     Decision = Published_with_reservations
THEN   WKS Requirement, c8..c11, lookup
     GETCNF Decision, Publish_CNF;
```

```
WHENEVER RQ3
IF      req = no
THEN    Author_req = Acceptable
BECAUSE "In order to make a publishing decision, it is important to
consider the author's requirements. Generally, those requirements are
comprised of grants, royalties, and advances. If your answer is NO, the
system will assume that the author's requirements
are reasonable.";
RULE RQ4
IF      Req = yes
AND     grant <> (Undefined)
AND     Royalties <> (Undefined)
AND     Advance <> (Undefined)
THEN    Max_value = ((grant × .35) + (royalties × 550) + (Advance
        × .10))
BECAUSE "In order to make a publishing decision, it is important to
consider the author's requirements. Generally, those requirements are
comprised of grants, royalties, and advances";
RULE RQ5
IF      Author_req = Excessive
THEN    Final = Rejected
        CLS
        DISPLAY "According to the data available, the manuscript should
be {#Final}.
        Press any key to end consultation~";
RULE RQ6
IF      Author_req = Acceptable
OR      Author_req = (Undefined)
THEN    Final = (Decision)
        CLS
        DISPLAY "According to the data available, the manuscript should
be {#Decision}.
        Press any key to end consultation~";
RULE RQ7
IF      Publish_CNF <= 100
AND     Publish_CNF >= 90
AND     Max_value <= (Requirement[1])
THEN    Author_Req = Acceptable;
RULE RQ8
IF      Publish_CNF <= 100
AND     Publish_CNF >= 90
AND     Max_value > (Requirement[1])
THEN    Author_Req = Excessive;
RULE RQ9
IF      Publish_CNF < 90
AND     Publish_CNF >= 70
AND     Max_value <= (Requirement[2])
THEN    Author_Req = Acceptable;
RULE RQ10
IF      Publish_CNF < 90
AND     Publish_CNF >= 70
AND     Max_value > (Requirement[2])
```

```
THEN   Author_Req = Excessive;
RULE RQ11
IF     Publish_CNF < 70
AND    Publish_CNF >= 50
AND    Max_value <= (Requirement[3])
THEN   Author_Req = Acceptable;
RULE RQ12
IF     Publish_CNF < 70
AND    Publish_CNF >= 50
AND    Max_value > (Requirement[3])
THEN   Author_Req = Excessive;
RULE RQ13
IF     Publish_CNF < 50
AND    Publish_CNF >= 0
AND    Max_value <= (Requirement[4])
THEN   Author_Req = Acceptable;
RULE RQ14
IF     Publish_CNF < 50
AND    Publish_CNF >= 0
AND    Max_value > (Requirement[4])
THEN   Author_Req = Excessive;
!---------------------------
RULE 0
IF   Market = Low AND
     Reviews = Strong AND
     Author = Established AND
     School = A OR
     School = B
THEN  Decision = Published CNF 75
     BECAUSE "The marketability of the proposed manuscript is one of
the most important factors to consider while making a publishing
decision.";
RULE 1
IF   Market = Low
THEN  Decision = Rejected;
RULE 2
IF   Market = Very_high OR
     Market = High AND
     Reviews = Strong
THEN  Decision = Published
     BECAUSE "The marketability of the proposed manuscript is one of
the most important factors to consider while making a publishing
decision.";
RULE 3
IF   Market = Very_high AND
     Reviews = Mixed AND
     School = A OR
     School = B
THEN  Decision = Published
BECAUSE "The institutional affiliation of the author is an important
factor to consider while making a publishing decision.";
```

RULE 4
IF   Market = Very-high AND
      Reviews = Weak AND
      Author = First_Book
THEN   Decision = Rejected
BECAUSE "The reputation of the author is an important
factor to consider while making a publishing decision.";
RULE 5
IF   Market = Very_high AND
      Reviews = Weak AND
      Author = Established OR
      Author = Up&Coming AND
      School = C OR
      School = D
THEN   Decision = Rejected
BECAUSE "The institutional affiliation and reputation of the author are
important factors to consider while making a publishing decision.";
RULE 6
IF   Market = Very_high AND
      Reviews = Mixed AND
      Author = Established AND
      School C OR
      School = D
THEN   Decision = Published
BECAUSE "The institutional affiliation and reputation of the author are
important factors to consider while making a publishing decision.";
RULE 7
IF   Market = Very_high AND
      Reviews = Mixed AND
      Author = UP&Coming AND
      School = C OR
      School = D
THEN   Decision = Published CNF 80
BECAUSE "The institutional affiliation and reputation of the author are
important factors to consider while making a publishing decision.";
RULE 8
IF   Market = Very_high AND
      Reviews = Weak AND
      Author = UP&Coming AND
      School = A OR
      School = B
THEN   Decision = Rejected CNF 80
BECAUSE "The institutional affiliation and reputation of the author are
important factors to consider while making a publishing decision.";
RULE 9
If   Market = Very_high OR
      Market = High AND
      Reviews = Weak AND
      Author = Established AND
      School = A OR
      School = B

```
THEN  Decision = Published_with_reservations CNF 70
BECAUSE "The institutional affiliation and reputation of the author are
important factors to consider while making a publishing decision.";
RULE 10
If   Market = Very_high OR
     Market = High AND
     Reviews = Mixed AND
     Author = First_Book AND
     School = C OR
     School = D
THEN  Decision = Published_with_reservations CNF 70
BECAUSE "The institutional affiliation and reputation of the author are
important factors to consider while making a publishing decision.";
RULE 11
If   Market = High AND
     Reviews = Mixed AND
     Author = Up&Coming OR
     Author = First_Book AND
     School = A OR
     School = B
THEN  Decision = Published CNF 80
BECAUSE "The institutional affiliation and reputation of the author are
important factors to consider while making a publishing decision.";
RULE 12
If   Market = High AND
     Reviews = Mixed AND
     Author = Up&Coming AND
     School = C OR
     School = D
THEN  Decision = Published CNF 60
BECAUSE "The institutional affiliation and reputation of the author are
important factors to consider while making a publishing decision.";
RULE 13
If   Market = High AND
     Reviews = Mixed AND
     Author = Established AND
     School = A OR
     School = B
THEN  Decision = Published
BECAUSE "The institutional affiliation and reputation of the author are
important factors to consider while making a publishing decision.";
RULE 14
If   Market = High AND
     Reviews = Mixed AND
     Author = Established AND
     School = C OR
     School = D
THEN  Decision = Published CNF 80
BECAUSE "The institutional affiliation and reputation of the author are
important factors to consider while making a publishing decision.";
```

RULE 15
If   Market = Moderate AND
     Reviews = Strong AND
     School = A OR
     School = B
THEN   Decision = Published CNF 80
BECAUSE "The institutional affiliation of the author is an important
factor to consider while making a publishing decision.";
RULE 16
If   Market = Moderate AND
     Reviews = Mixed AND
     Author = First_Book OR
     Author = Up&Coming AND
     School = A OR
     School = B
THEN   Decision = Published CNF 60
BECAUSE "The institutional affiliation and reputation of the author are
important factors to consider while making a publishing decision.";
RULE 17
If   Market = Moderate AND
     Reviews = Strong AND
     Author = Established OR
     Author = Up&Coming AND
     School = C OR
     School = D
THEN   Decision = Published CNF 70
BECAUSE "The institutional affiliation and reputation of the author are
important factors to consider while making a publishing decision.";
RULE 18
If   Market = Moderate AND
     Reviews = Mixed AND
     Author = Established AND
     School = A OR
     School = B
THEN   Decision = Published CNF 70
BECAUSE "The institutional affiliation and reputation of the author are
important factors to consider while making a publishing decision.";
RULE 19
If   Market = Moderate AND
     Reviews = Mixed AND
     Author = Established AND
     School = C OR
     School = D
THEN   Decision = Published CNF 60
BECAUSE "The institutional affiliation and reputation of the author are
important factors to consider while making a publishing decision.";
RULE 20
If   Market = Moderate AND
     Reviews = Strong AND
     Author = First_Book AND

```
        School = C OR
        School = D
THEN   Decision = Published CNF 60
BECAUSE "The institutional affiliation and reputation of the author are
important factors to consider while making a publishing decision.";
RULE 21
If   Market = Moderate AND
     Reviews = Mixed AND
     Author = Up&Coming AND
     School = C OR
     School = D
THEN   Decision = Published_with_reservations CNF 70
BECAUSE "The institutional affiliation and reputation of the author are
important factors to consider while making a publishing decision.";
RULE 22
If   Market = Moderate AND
     Reviews = Mixed AND
     Author = First_Book AND
     School = C OR
     School = D
THEN   Decision = Published_with_reservations CNF 60
BECAUSE "The institutional affiliation and reputation of the author are
important factors to consider while making a publishing decision.";
RULE 23
If   Market = Moderate AND
     Reviews = Weak AND
     Author = Established AND
     School = A OR
     School = B
THEN   Decision = Published_with_reservations CNF 80
BECAUSE "The institutional affiliation and reputation of the author are
important factors to consider while making a publishing decision.";
RULE 24
If   Market = Moderate OR
     Market = High AND
     Reviews = Weak AND
     Author = Established AND
     School = C OR
     School = D
THEN   Decision = Rejected
BECAUSE "The institutional affiliation and reputation of the author are
important factors to consider while making a publishing decision.";
RULE 25
If   Market = Moderate OR
     Market = High AND
     Reviews = Weak AND
     Author = Up&Coming OR
     Author = First_Book
THEN   Decision = Rejected
BECAUSE "The reputation of the author is an important
factor to consider while making a publishing decision.";
```

```
!-------------------------------
WHENEVER 101
IF   positive < (total)
THEN  positivef = (positive/total)
BECAUSE "The reviewers' comments on the proposed manuscript are
one of the most important factors to consider while making a publishing
decision.";
WHENEVER 102
IF   positive > (total)
THEN  positivef = 0
      negativef = 0
      zerof = 0
      reviews = 0
      decision = 0
      final = 0
      CLS
      DISPLAY "The system is not able to reach a conclusion because
data are inconsistent.  Number of people who have reviewed the
manuscript: {total} Number of people who would adopt the book:
{positive}
Press any key to restart consultation.~"
BECAUSE "The reviewers' comments on the proposed manuscript are
one of the most important factors to consider while making a publishing
decision.";
WHENEVER 103
IF   positive = (total)
THEN  positivef = 1
      negativef = 0
      zerof = 0
BECAUSE "The reviewers' comments on the proposed manuscript are
one of the most important factors to consider while making a publishing
decision.";
WHENEVER 104
IF   negative < ((total) - (positive))
THEN  negativef = (negative/total)
BECAUSE "The reviewers' comments on the proposed manuscript are
one of the most important factors to consider while making a publishing
decision.";
WHENEVER 105
IF   negative > ((total) - (positive))
THEN  positivef = 0
      negativef = 0
      zerof = 0
      reviews = 0
      decision = 0
      final = 0
      CLS
      DISPLAY "The system is not able to reach a conclusion because
data are inconsistent.
Number of people who have reviewed the manuscript: {total}
Number of people who would adopt the book: {positive}
```

```
Number of people who would not adopt the book: {negative}
Press any key to restart consultation.~"
BECAUSE "The reviewers' comments on the proposed manuscript are
one of the most important factors to consider while making a publishing
decision.";
WHENEVER 106
IF   negative = ((total) - (positive))
THEN  negativef = (negative/total))
     zerof = 0
BECAUSE "The reviewers' comments on the proposed manuscript are
one of the most important factors to consider while making a publishing
decision.";
WHENEVER 107
IF   zero = (total - (positive + negative))
THEN zerof = ((zero)/(total))
BECAUSE "The reviewers' comments on the proposed manuscript are
one of the most important factors to consider while making a publishing
decision.";
WHENEVER 108
IF   zero > (total - (positive + negative))
THEN  zerof = 0
     reviews = 0
     decision = 0
     final = 0
     CLS
     DISPLAY "The system is not able to reach a conclusion
because data are inconsistent.
Press any key to restart consultation.~"
BECAUSE "The reviewers' comments on the proposed manuscript are
one of the most important factors to consider while making a publishing
decision.";
WHENEVER 109
IF   zero < (total - positive + negative))
THEN
     miss = (total - (positive + negative + zero))
     missf = (miss/total)
BECAUSE "The reviewers' comments on the proposed manuscript are
one of the most important factors to consider while making a publishing
decision.";
RULE 110
IF   missf <= .25
THEN  CLS
     DISPLAY "Of the {total} reviewers to whom a manuscript was
sent, {miss} are not accounted for."
     FIND Continue
     WHILETRUE Continue = Yes THEN
     total1 = (total - miss)
     positivef = (positive/total1)
     negativef = (negative/total1)
     zerof = (zero/total1)
     RESET Continue
```

```
    END
    WHILETRUE Continue = No THEN
    zerof = 0
    reviews = 0
    decision = 0
    final = 0
    CLS
    DISPLAY "The consultation has been terminated.
Press any key to start new consultation.~"
    RESET Continue
    END
ELSE   zerof = 0
    reviews = 0
    decision = 0
    final = 0
    CLS
    DISPLAY "The consultation has been terminated because not
enough reviewers have returned their comments.
Press any key to start new consultation.~"
BECAUSE "The reviewers' comments on the proposed manuscript are
one of the most important factors to consider while making a publishing
decision.";
!-----------------------------
ASK Market : "How do you rate the marketability of the proposed
manuscript?";
CHOICES Market : Very_high, High,
Moderate, Low;
ASK total: "How many people have reviewed the manuscript?";
RANGE total: 1, 40;
ASK positive: "How many of those reviewers would adopt the book?";
RANGE positive: 0, 40;
ASK negative: "How many of those reviewers would not adopt the
book?";
RANGE negative: 0, 40;
ASK zero: "How many of those reviewers had mixed feeling on the
adoption issue?";
RANGE zero: 0, 40;
ASK Agree: "Do you agree with the system's assessment?";
CHOICES Agree: Yes, No;
ASK U_review1: "Please, choose your evaluation of the reviewers'
comments?";
CHOICES U_review1: Mixed, Weak;
ASK U_review2: "Please, choose your evaluation of the reviewers'
comments?";
CHOICES U_review2: Strong, Weak;
ASK U_review 3: "Please, choose your evaluation of the reviewers'
comments?";
CHOICES U_review 3: Strong, Mixed;
ASK Author: "How do you rate the author's reputation?";
CHOICES Author: Established, Up&Coming, First_Book;
ASK School: "How do you rank the author's institutional affiliation?
```

```
         A: Premier research institution.
         B: High reputation national university or college.
         C: Moderate reputation national university or college.
         D: Community college.";
CHOICES School: A, B, C, D;
ASK grant: "How much is the grant requested by the author?
(Enter amount without signs or commas (e.g., 15000))";
RANGE grant: 0, 25000;
ASK royalties: "What is the percentage of royalties requested by the
author? (Enter percentage from 10 to 20 (e.g., 15))";
RANGE royalties: 10, 20;
ASK advance: "How much is the advance requested by the author?
(Enter amount without signs or commas (e.g., 2000))";
RANGE advance: 0, 10000;
ASK req: "Does the author have any requirements?";
CHOICES req: Yes, No;
ASK continue: "Do you want to continue the session?";
CHOICES continue: Yes, No;
```

Appendix ▪ C

EXSYS: A Tutorial

▓ INSTALLING RULEBOOK

MS Windows

1. Exit Windows and return to the DOS level.
2. Select the drive to install to by entering the drive letter, for example:

`C:`

3. Create a new directory called RuleBook on your hard disk with the DOS command:

`MD\RuleBook`

4. Make this new directory the default directory by entering:

`CD RuleBook`

5. Copy the contents of all of the disks to the new directory by putting the distribution floppy disk in drive A and entering:

`COPY A:\*.* C:\RuleBook\V`

(Once RuleBook is installed on the hard disk, store the distribution disks in a safe place.)

6. Return to MS Windows.
7. Go to the Program Manager window. Under the *File* menu select *New.*
8. Select *Program Group.*
9. A dialog box will appear. Enter *"RuleBook"* for description and click *OK.*
10. Return to the Program Manager window and select *New* under the *File* menu.
11. This time select *Program Item* and click *OK.* In the dialog that appears enter:

Description: *RuleBook*
Command Line: *\RuleBook\RuleBook.EXE*
Working Directory: *\RuleBook*

Click *OK* and the RuleBook icon should appear in the window

12. From here on, all you have to do is click on the *RuleBook* icon to start the program.

Macintosh

1. Create a new folder called *RuleBook* on your hard disk by selecting *New Folder.*
2. Insert the distribution disks and copy all files and programs on the disks into the *RuleBook* folder. (Once RuleBook is installed on the hard disk, store the distribution disk in a safe place.)
3. From now on, all you have to do is click on the *RuleBook* icon to start the program.

■ THE BASICS ABOUT RULEBOOK

Tree Structure Approach

In RuleBook, the expert system is defined by a set of tree diagrams. To get started, choose a simple problem that has a well defined set of solutions and few alternatives. Even then, the system can be written in variety of ways.

For example, suppose we want to write a system to simulate the publishing advisor problem. First we will make a simple decision tree for the problem.

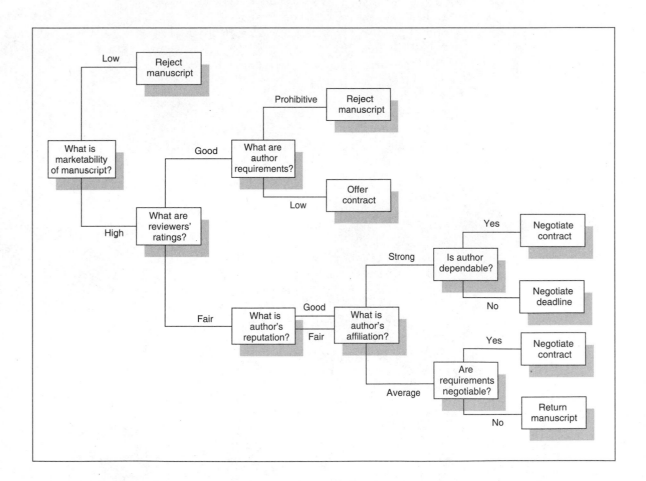

The rules that the tree represents can be easily seen in this example. Each branch of the tree represents a rule. Beginning with the top branch, the rules would be:

```
Rule 1
IF
      Marketability of manuscript is low
THEN
      Reject manuscript - Confidence = 10
```

```
Rule 2
IF
      Marketability of manuscript is high
and   reviewers ratings are good
and   author requirements are low
THEN
      Offer contract - Confidence = 10
Rule 3
IF
      Marketability of manuscript is high
and   reviewers ratings are good
and   author requirements are prohibitive
THEN
      Reject manuscript - Confidence = 10
Rule 4
IF
      Marketability of manuscript is high
and   reviewers ratings are fair
and   author reputation is good
and   author affiliation is strong
and   author is dependable
THEN
      Negotiate contract - Confidence = 10
Rule 5
IF
      Marketability of manuscript is high
and   reviewers ratings are fair
and   author reputation is good
and   author affiliation is strong
and   author is not dependable
THEN
      Negotiate deadlines - Confidence = 10
Rule 6
IF
      Marketability of manuscript is high
and   reviewers ratings are fair
and   author reputation is good
and   author affiliation is average
and   Requirements are negotiable
THEN
      Negotiate contract - Confidence = 10
Rule 7
IF
      Marketability of manuscript is high
and   reviewers ratings are fair
and   author reputation is fair
and   author affiliation is average
and   Requirements are not negotiable
THEN
      Return manuscript - Confidence = 10
```

Backward Chaining

Most expert-system problems are divided into sub-problems which can often be divided further. Writing these small trees to solve the individual problems through sub-goals is much easier. More general trees can be written using the solutions to the smaller problems. RuleBook will automatically use such solutions to derive the information it needs for the overall problem. This ability to automatically invoke the rules needed to derive information is called "backward chaining."

As covered in the text, backward chaining is one of the most powerful aspects of an expert system. Regardless of how the problem is approached, backward chaining will probably be used to obtain information from other rules. Backward chaining may at first seem strange because the program does so much of the work. The expert system does not have to be instructed that rules are available that allow the information to be derived or told which rules to use. If the rules exist, the program will find them and use them. Their order does not matter. If a rule is relevant to part of the decision process, it will automatically be called. It can be added anywhere in the rule set and associated with any tree.

One approach to solving smaller problems is to ask in the broadest terms, how does one solve the overall problem. The answer will probably be "If . . . and . . . then. . . ." Consider if the IF conditions could be made into questions that would be appropriate to ask a user and reliably get a meaningful answer. If the questions are too complex to ask or are stated in terms too general for the end user to be able to answer, then consider how it could be broken down into questions that the intended user would understand.

Terms

Tree

A tree is a branched decision tree that represents all or a portion of the decision making instructions as illustrated below. It is made up of nodes, factors (qualifiers and variables), and choices.

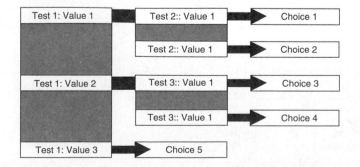

Nodes

A tree is made up of nodes that represent decision branch points and those that are assignments of value. These correspond to IF and THEN condition in a rule.

The IF nodes always have at least 2 values and may have as many as 30. The various values are joined together in a block. In the above figure, Test 1, Test 2, and Test 3 are IF nodes. The node values can be multiple choice text items, ranges of numeric variable or true/false tests of a mathematical expression.

THEN nodes have a single value and assign a value to choice (goal) of the expert system assigned text or numeric data, display a message to the end user, or annotate the tree. THEN nodes have a black triangle on their left side.

Factors

Factors are text or numeric data items that are used to define the nodes. There are two types of factors: Qualifiers and Variables.

Qualifiers   Qualifiers are multiple choice lists. Typically, they are text and can contain up to 30 values.

For example:

What is the color of light?

1. Red

2. Yellow

3. Green

A qualifier condition is a statement in the tree (or rule) made up of the starting qualifier text and one or more of the associated values. A qualifier can be used in the IF part of a tree branch to test a value or in the THEN part to assign a value.

Variables   Variables are numeric variables. A variable value may be any value between its upper and lower bounds. For the purposes of building the tree, the value of the variable is divided into ranges defined by the logical break points in the decision making process.

Numeric - Use this for measurements like:

[pressure] = 37.482
[length] = 5.6

and for financial figures like:

[cost] = 72.00
[U.S. debt] = 4000000000000000

String - Use for anything requiring letters or punctuation like:

[name] = "Epson MX-80F/T"
[address] = "555 Elm St, Bldg. C, Anytown, NM 87000"
[Social Security Number] = "585-21-4444"
[Telephone Number] = "(505)256-8356"
[Note] = "Hi, Nancy, you are doing a great job."

Choices

Choices are the goals that the expert system will decide among. A system to identify types of flowers would have the various species of flower as choices. A system to determine the cause for a failure in a machine would have the possible items that could break as choices. Depending on the Confidence Mode used, a choice may be assigned a confidence value to determine its relative likelihood. Choices can be used in the THEN part of branches only.

For example:

The disease is the mumps - Confidence 70

■ BUILDING EXPERT SYSTEM WITH RULEBOOK

Starting a New Expert System

To start a new expert system, pull down the main menu bar item *File* and select *New.* You will be asked to name the knowledge base you are creating. Enter a file name and, if appropriate for your operating system, drive or path.

Whenever a new knowledge base is created, RuleBook asks the developer to define certain parameters for the new system. These steps are necessary only when a new expert system is created. All parameters except the **confidence mode** can be edited later.

```
┌────────────────────────────────────────────────────────────┐
│ ▬                        Parameters                          │
├────────────────────────────────────────────────────────────┤
│                                                              │
│  Subject:    │                                             │  │
│                                                              │
│  Author:                                                     │
│                                                              │
│  ┌─Confidence Mode:──────────────┐   ┌─Display Threshold:──┐ │
│  │                               │   │                     │ │
│  │   ○  Yes / No                 │   │   │ 1            │   │ │
│  │   ◉  0 - 10       [ Help! ]   │   │                     │ │
│  │   ○  Incr / Decr              │   └─────────────────────┘ │
│  │                               │                           │
│  └───────────────────────────────┘                           │
│                                                              │
│                  [ Starting Text ]      ○  Display Rules     │
│    [   OK   ]    [  Ending Text  ]      ◉  Do NOT Display    │
│                                                              │
└────────────────────────────────────────────────────────────┘
```

Subject

Enter a short subject name for the system being developed. This is required and will be used on the system title screen. The text should be fewer than 200 characters long. RuleBook will not continue past this screen unless a subject is entered.

Author

The program asks for the author's name. Like the subject, the author's name is required and must be less than 200 characters. It is also used for the title screen. Like the subject, RuleBook will not continue past this screen unless an author is entered.

Confidence Mode

Following subject and author, the next step is to select which of the three Confidence Modes to use in the new expert system. Click on the button next to the mode desired. Because this parameter directly affects the structure of the rules, it cannot be edited or changed later.

There are three types of confidence mode available for the user:

1. **YES/NO System**

   If the expert system does not require any estimate of probability, the YES/NO (0–1. System is best. This confidence system is very easy to use, since the first rule that fires for a choice sets the value to 1 for Yes or 0 for No) No intermediate values are assigned. This confidence system is good for selecting choices from a list, automated questionnaire, or other systems where the answers provided by the system are definitely "yes" or "no."

2. **0–10 System**

   This system is compatible with the intuitive knowledge used in the development of an expert system. An assignment of 0 locks the value for the choice at 0 (No) and an assignment of 10 locks the value at 10 (Yes).

   This is the recommended system setting for beginning and intermediate users of RuleBook.

3. **Increment/Decrement System**

   Points are added to or subtracted from the total points for a choice. A rule can add or subtract as much as 100 points from the total for a choice. This system differentiates among possible solutions that would provide similar or identical scores using the 0–10 systems.

Display Rules

When this option is chosen, all rules that fire are displayed immediately after they fire.

Do Not Display Rules

This mode does not display rules when they fire, but will allow the end user to have rules displayed and ask about rules with the HOW and WHY commands. This is the most commonly used system since it allows the end user to fully interrogate the expert system on the basis for the recommendation.

Starting Text

RuleBook provides the option for the developer to write explanatory text which is displayed at the beginning when the knowledge base is run for the end user. To enter starting text, click on the *Starting Text* button and a window will appear. Enter the desired text and click on the *OK* button. This text can be edited later as required.

Ending Text

RuleBook provides the option for the developer to write explanatory text that is displayed for the end user when the knowledge base is run, just before the conclusion is displayed. To enter starting text, click on the *Starting Text* button and a window will appear. Enter the desired text and click on the *OK* button. This text can be edited later as required.

When all the parameters are set, click on *OK* button. The Subject and Author fields *must* be completed before you can proceed. The other parameters are set to their normal default values. You will be able to change most of these parameters later by selecting the *Parameters* menu item from the *Options* menu. As mentioned earlier, the confidence mode *cannot* be changed once you start adding rules, so make sure your selection is correct.

Starting an Existing Expert System

To select an existing system, select the *Open* menu item from the *File* menu, and a list of all of the files with an .Rb1 extension will be displayed. Double click on the desired file, or select a file and click on the Open button.

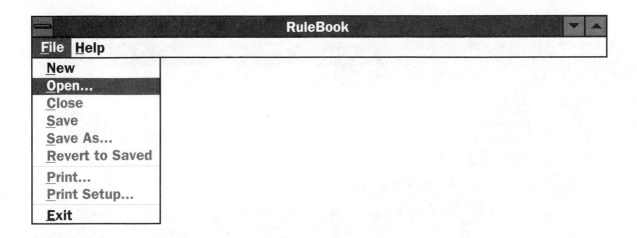

Structure of RuleBook

RuleBook is designed to look like a notebook. Sections are divided with page tabs. When you click on a page table, the program will bring you to the specified window.

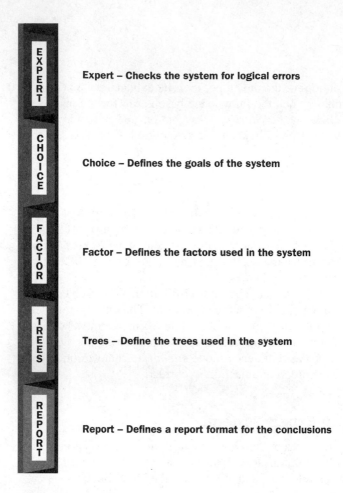

Expert – Checks the system for logical errors

Choice – Defines the goals of the system

Factor – Defines the factors used in the system

Trees – Define the trees used in the system

Report – Defines a report format for the conclusions

These same sections can also be accessed from the main menu under the *Page* menu option.

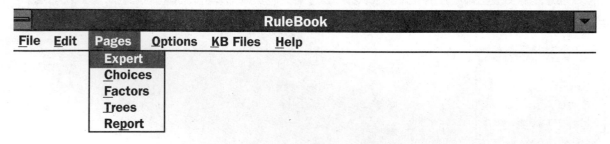

■ SAMPLE PROBLEM

The following demonstration uses the publishing advisor sample mentioned earlier to illustrate the basic RuleBook operations when designing an expert system.

Choices

After all the initial parameters are set (see Starting a New Expert System), RuleBook will automatically lead you to the Choices window.

Click on the *New* button. In the dialog box that appears, enter "Reject manuscript" in the blank. Click on *OK* when done or *Cancel* to cancel the entry. You will be prompted automatically for the next choice. Enter the following choices:

Offer contract
Negotiate contract
Negotiate deadline
Return manuscript

When you have entered all of the choices, click on **Cancel** to exit the entry
dialog box.

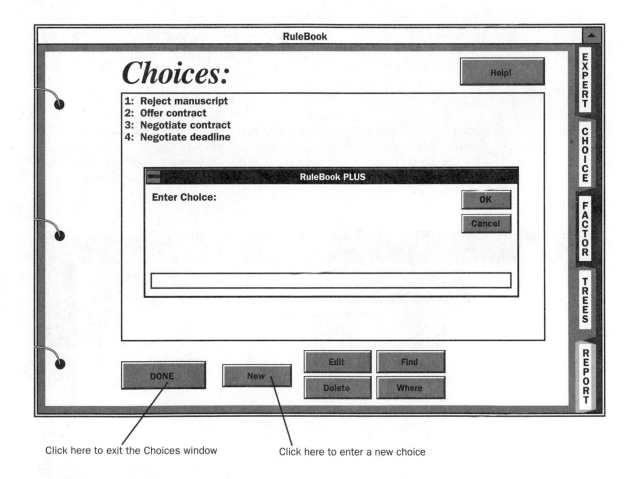

Click here to exit the Choices window   Click here to enter a new choice

When you are done entering the choices, click on the **DONE** button.
You can also delete or edit existing choices as follows.

Deleting a Choice

To delete a choice, click on the choice in the list box. The choice selected will
be highlighted. Then click on the **Delete** button. If the choice is not used in any
of the trees, it will be deleted from the list.

Editing a Choice

To edit a choice, click on the choice in the list box. The choice selected will be
highlighted. A dialog edit box is displayed with the selected choice. Edit the
choice and click **OK.** The edited text automatically replaces all places where the
choice was used.

Finding a Choice

A choice can be selected by clicking on the item in the list box. If there are many choices, an alternative is to click on the *Find* button. A dialog box will appear. Enter the text to search for and click *OK.* The first choice in the list which contains the search string will be selected and highlighted.

Where is a Choice Used in the Trees

Select a choice by clicking on the item in the list box. The choice selected will be highlighted. When you click on the *Where* button, RuleBook displays the tree nodes that use the choice. The tree window is then displayed with the nodes highlighted.

Factors

Factors are the items of data that the expert system uses to decide among the choices. When you enter the Factors window, you will see the window divided into two sections. As shown below, the upper section allows you to enter text factors—qualifiers, and the lower section allows you to enter numeric factors—variables.

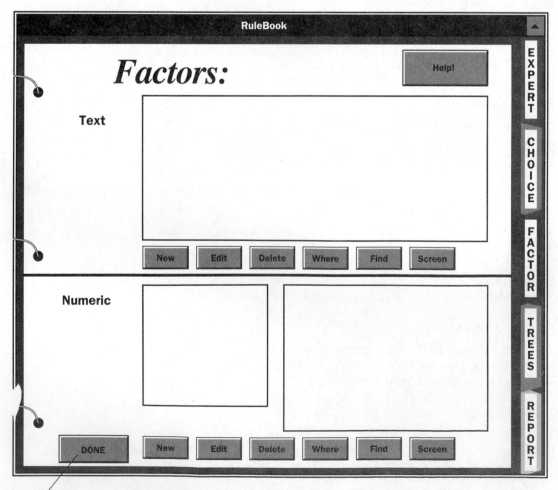

Click here to exit the Factors window

Add/Edit Qualifier

To add a text factor, click on the New button in the upper section of the Factors window. A dialog box appears as shown below.

Add/Edit Qualifier

Qualifier:1   **Name:** [   ]   [Help!]

Qualifier: What is marketability of manuscript?|

Value:

[Edit]   [Replace]   [Undo Edit]   [Add]   [Delete]

1 Low

[OK]   ☐ **Display at end**   [Custom Screen]
              ☐ **Limit input values to:** [   ]

[Cancel]   ☐ **Default value:** [   ]   [Custom Help]

Fill in the first qualifier question in the blank labeled "Qualifier" and type "What is marketability of manuscript?"

Use the tab key to advance to the blank labeled "Value" and enter the first value associated with the question: "Low." Repeat this step for all other values. Click on *OK* when done. You will be taken back to the Factors window. When you are done entering all of your factors, click on the *DONE* button.

Trees

Trees are added and edited from the Main Tree window. To display the Main Tree Window click on the Trees notebook tab or select Trees under the Pages menu.

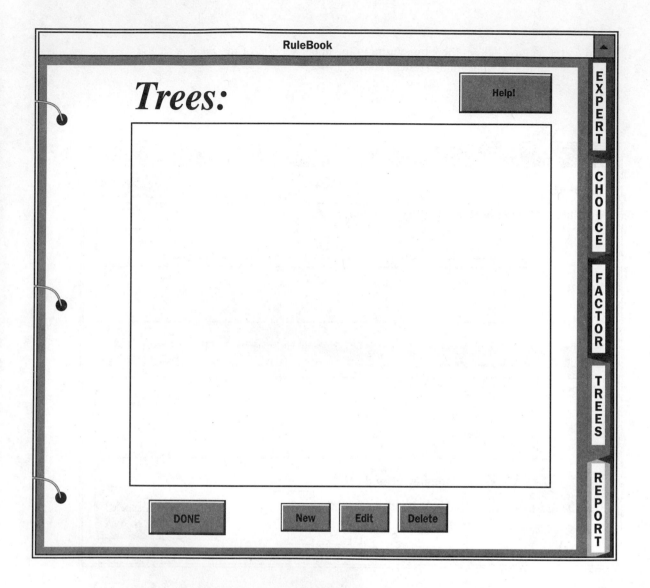

Adding a Tree

To add a tree, click on the *New* button. A dialog will appear asking for the name of the new tree. Enter a name descriptive of the purpose of the tree. The name can be up to 40 characters. Click *OK* and the new tree window will be displayed.

Adding Nodes to a Tree

When a new tree is created, it will only have a terminal node that says "Double Click to Add Factor."

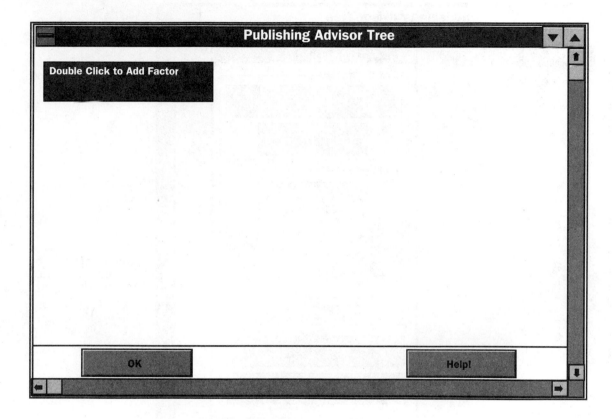

To add the first factor to the tree, double click on the terminal node. A dialog box for adding factors will be displayed.

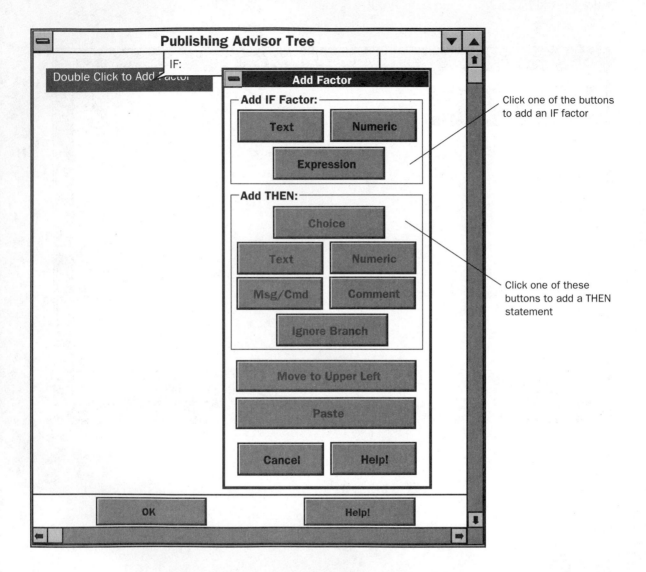

For our sample system, click on the *Text* button. A dialog box containing all the qualifiers you have entered will be displayed.

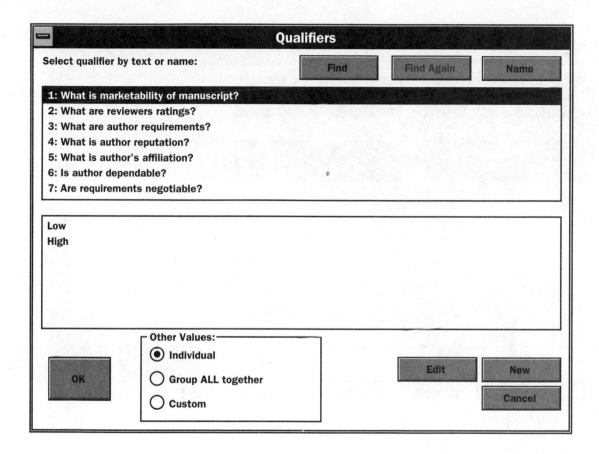

Highlight the first qualifier: "What is the marketability of manuscript?" and "Low," and then click on the *OK* button. The first set of nodes will be added to the tree as shown below.

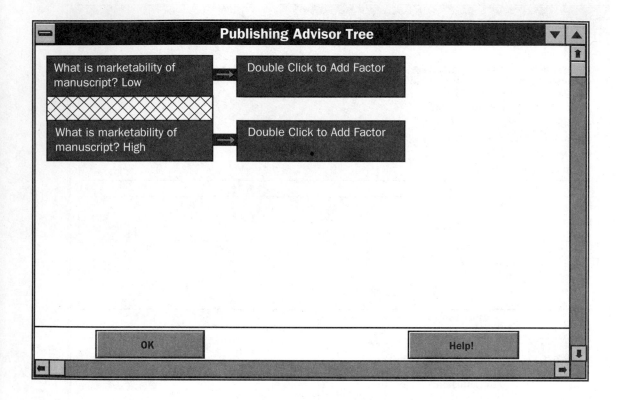

Proceed to add the remaining factors.

When you need to add the THEN statement, double click on the node, and choose *Choice* in the *Add THEN* section.

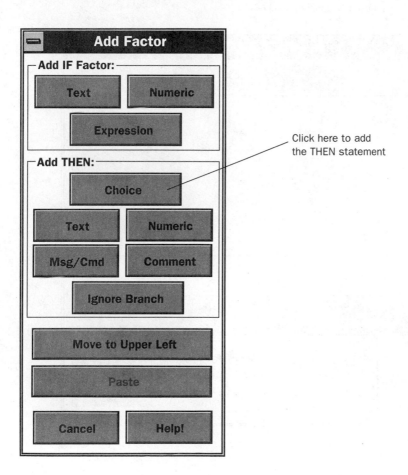

Click here to add
the THEN statement

A dialog box with all the choices you have entered will be displayed. Choose the appropriate choice and the confidence factor and click the *OK* button.

Choose the appropriate choice

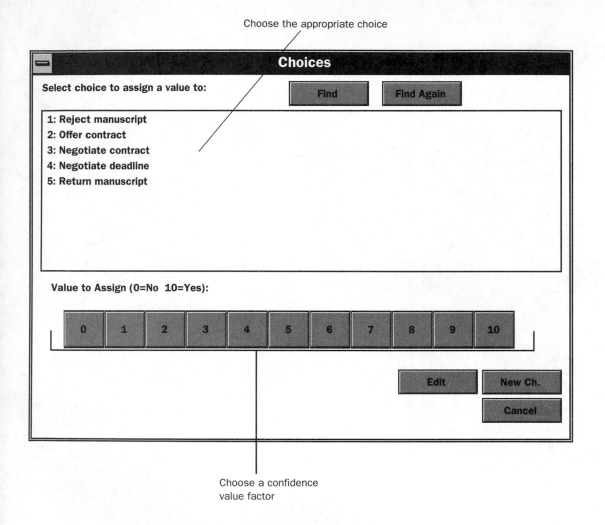

Choices

Select choice to assign a value to:

Find   Find Again

1: **Reject manuscript**
2: **Offer contract**
3: **Negotiate contract**
4: **Negotiate deadline**
5: **Return manuscript**

Value to Assign (0=No 10=Yes):

| 0 | 1 | 2 | 3 | 4 | 5 | 6 | 7 | 8 | 9 | 10 |

Edit   New Ch.

Cancel

Choose a confidence
value factor

Expert

When you are done editing the tree, click the *OK* button to return to the Trees window and click the *DONE* button to exit the Trees window. This will lead to the Expert window.

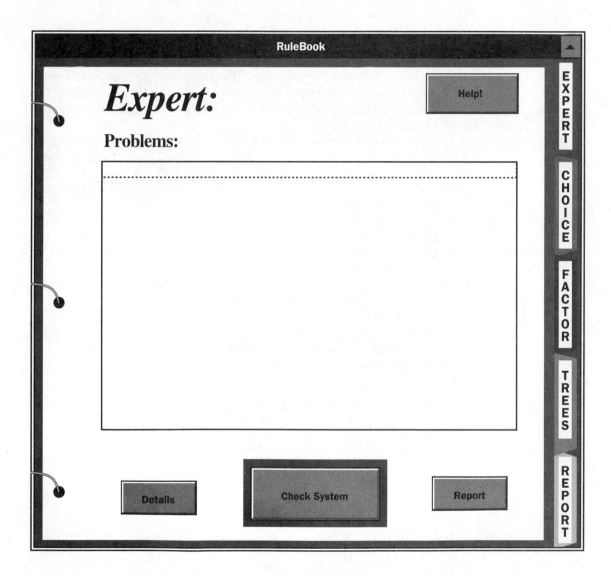

To have the Expert check the system, click on the *Check System* button. If there is a red border around the button, the trees have been changed since the last check and it is time to recheck the system. If there is no red border, the trees have not been changed since the last check. Since checking the system can take some time for large systems, it is a good idea to correct as much as possible after each check.

The Expert does two different checks of the system. The first looks for errors that can be found rapidly. The second part actually runs the rules with all of the combinations of data. Sets of input are systematically generated and used to test the rules. During the test, the Expert looks for various types of errors.

Since the number of possible combinations of input can get very large for some systems, it can take a while to complete the second set of tests.

If an error is found in the first quick check, a dialog will be displayed asking if the second (longer) part of the test should be done. Usually, if an error is found in the quick check, it should be corrected before running the second part of the check.

Report Generator

RuleBook has a built-in report generator. This enables the user to control what data is output to a disk file or printer. The report specification can include the commands to print notes, choice, value or qualifier values, restart the program, and exit to the operating system.

The report output specification is an ASCII file with the same the name as the expert system with an .OUT extension. For example, if you have an expert system named ENGINES, you would have two files on your disk: EN-GINES.RB1 and ENGINES.RB2. A report generator specification would be put in a file called ENGINES.OUT.

The .OUT file is an ASCII file created with a text editor or a word processor that can create ASCII files without additional control characters. By having the .OUT file created and modifiable by text editors, the end user will be able to make modifications to the generated report.

The RuleBook Editor may also be used to create report files. Click on the Report tab or select **Report** from the **Page** menu.

The report file can be edited in the Report window. To save the changes in the file, click on Save File. To delete the current report file, click on Delete File.

For commands used to compose a report, please refer to pages 143–165 in the EXSYS RuleBook User Manual.

▓ CUSTOMIZING THE USER INTERFACE

When an expert system is created with RuleBook, there is a default format for asking questions. This provides the normal RuleBook user interface. For most systems, this interface is appropriate. However, in some cases, it is desirable to change the look of RuleBook. There are a variety of ways to do this.

The customization techniques covered in the EXSYS RuleBook User Manual are:

1. Custom help screens
2. Custom question screens
3. Hypertext
4. Qualifiers with values inserted in the middle.

Custom screens are designed with the screen design program ExDesign. ExDesign can be accessed directly or called from the Factor edit windows for qualifiers or variables.

Create a New Screen

The following menu is used to create a new screen file, load an existing screen file, save a screen file, print, or to exit the program.

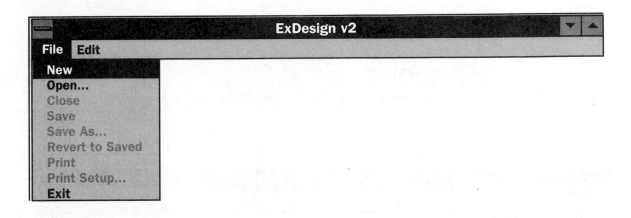

To create a new screen file, select *New* from the *File* menu. A dialog box will be displayed to ask the user to enter a filename.

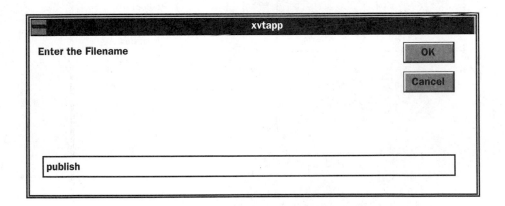

If no file extension is given, the program will provide the default .SCR extension. Clicking on the *OK* button will display another dialog box asking for the screen identifier for the first screen to be created.

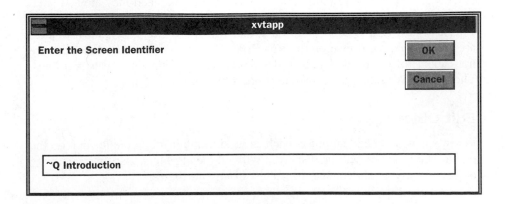

Make sure to use the correct syntax for the screen identifier. Each screen identifier begins with a "~" character.

Create Objects

Once the new screen is created, you can use the *Object* menu to add new objects.

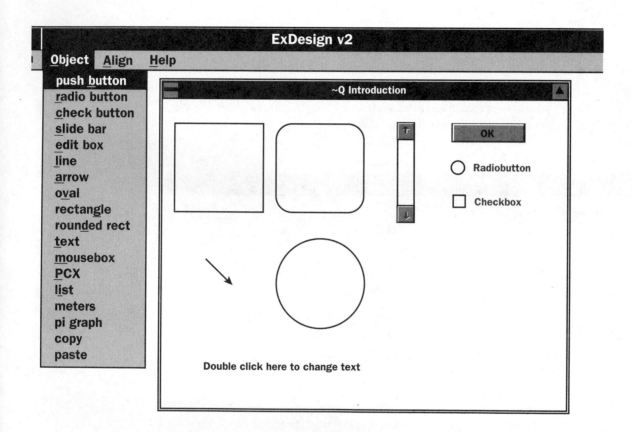

ExDesign provides two types of objects that can be placed on a RuleBook Custom Input Screen. They are control objects and graphical objects. Control objects are capable of sending input data to RuleBook when they are activated during RuleBook run. This category includes Push Buttons, Radio Buttons, Check Boxes, Edit Boxes, Slide Bars, and Mouse Regions. Graphical objects are objects that are drawn on the RuleBook Custom Screen at runtime, but are not capable of returning data to RuleBook, such as rectangles, ovals and lines. The above illustration shows some of the objects.

Edit Objects

When you wish to edit an object such as its size and layout, double click on the object. A dialog box will be displayed with all the attributes associated with the object. Then you can change the values of any attributes.

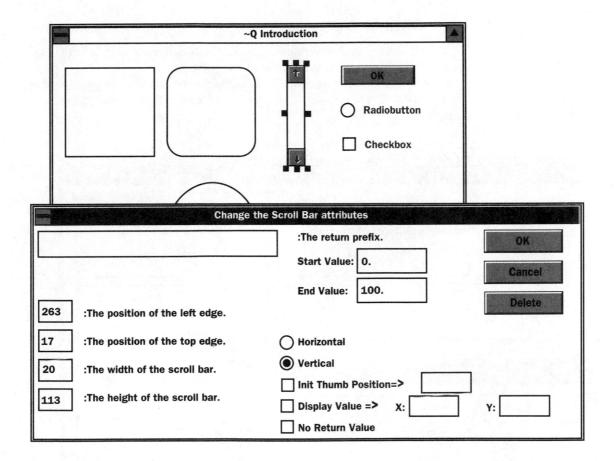

If you want to move an object, click on the object, hold down the left mouse button and drag the object to the desired location.

Other Ways to Create Screens

Customized screens can be created using the **Custom Screen** button in the edit qualifier and edit variable dialog boxes.

In the Factor window in RuleBook, highlight the qualifier or variable you want to create the screen with, and click on the **Edit** button. A dialog box will be displayed.

Add/Edit Qualifier

Qualifier:1   Name: [   ]   [Help!]

Qualifier: [What is marketability of manuscript?]

Value: [   ]

[Edit]   [Replace]   [Undo Edit]   [Add]   [Delete]

1 Low
2 High

[OK]   ☐ Display at end
              ☐ Limit input values to: [   ]   [Custom Screen]
[Cancel]   ☐ Default value: [   ]   [Custom Help]

Click here to customize your screen

When you click on the **Custom Screen** button, you will be led to the screen design window in ExDesign.

You can also create customized screens with a word processor, such as a text editor. The screen definition language file consists of ASCII text. All lines are either commands or text to be echoed to the screen. Lines starting with a ~ are commands. Many screens are stored in a single file and are separated by special commands that indicate the start of a new screen.

Appendix ■ D

Expert Systems Development Software

■ EXPERT SYSTEM SHELLS

Program	Company Address/Tel No.	Knowledge Represented	Inference	Computer Type	Price
ACE	Knowledge Associates, Ltd. 302 W. 259th St. Riverdale, NY 10471-1908	Rule-based	Forward & Backward Chaining		Contact vendor
Under $500					
Arity Expert	Arity Corp. 29 Domino Dr. Concord, MA 01742 (508) 371-1243	Frame-based	Backward Chaining and Induction	IBM-PC and PS/2	$295
Auto-Intelligence 1.26	IntelligenceWare, Inc. 9800 S. Sepulveda Blvd. Los Angeles, CA 90045-5228 (213) 417-8896	Rule-based	Backward Chaining		$490
EXSYS EL	EXSYS, Inc. P.O. Box 11247 Albuquerque, NM 87192 (505) 256-8356	Rule-based, optional frame extension	Forward & Backward Chaining	IBM-PC and PS/2 Unlimited runtime lic. DEC VAX and some UNIX machines	$175 $600 $2,500 and up
Intelligence/Compiler	IntelligenceWare, Inc. 9800 S. Sepulveda Blvd. Los Angeles, CA 90045-5228 (213) 417-8896	n/a	Forward & Backward Chaining, and Inexact Logic	DEC VAX	$495 $7,500
KnowledgerMaker	Knowledge Garden, Inc. 473A Malden Bridge Rd. RD2 Nassau, NY 12123 (518) 766-3000	Table-form	Induction	IBM-PC	$199
Kappa-PC	IntelliCorp 1975 El Camino Real West Mountain View, CA 94040 (415) 965-5500	Rule-based, Frame-based, and Object-oriented	Forward & Backward Chaining	IBM-PC	$495
Level5	Information Builders Inc. 1250 Broadway New York, NY 10001-3782 (914) 347-6860	Rule-based	Backward Chaining	IBM-PC and Macintosh DEC VAX	$295 $19,200
LogicTree	CAM Software 750 N. 200 West, Ste. 208 Provo, UT 84601 (801) 373-4086	Table-form	Induction	IBM-PC and PS/2	$495

Program	Company Address/Tel No.	Knowledge Represented	Inference	Computer Type	Price
MacSMARTS	Cognition Technology Corp. 565 Wheeler St. Cambridge, MA 01238 (617) 492-0246	Table-form	Induction	Macintosh	$195
MacSMARTS Professional	Cognition Technology Corp. 565 Wheeler St. Cambridge, MA 01238 (617) 492-0246	Table-form	Induction	Macintosh	$495
Personal Consultant	Texas Instruments Corp. P.O. Box 1444 Houston, TX 77251 (800) 847-2787	Decision tree	Backward Chaining	IBM-PC Runtime disk	$495 $95
Personal Consultant Easy	Texas Instruments Corp. P.O. Box 1444 Houston, TX 77251 (800) 847-2787	Rule-based	Forward & Backward Chaining	IBM-PC	$495
pLogic	pLogic Knowledge Systems, Inc. 23133 Hawthorne Blvd. Torrance, CA 90505 (213) 378-3760	Table-form	Induction	IBM-PC Runtime disk	$495 $95
Superexpert	Softsync Inc. 162 Madison Ave. New York, NY 10016 (212) 685-2080	Table-form	Induction	IBM-PC and Macintosh	$199.95
VP-Expert	Wordtech Systems, Inc. P.O. Box 1747 Orinda, CA 94563 (510) 689-1200	Rule-based	Forward & Backward Chaining and Induction	IBM-PC	$349

Program	Company Address/Tel No.	Knowledge Represented	Inference	Computer Type	Price
$500–$1,000					
Advisor-2	Expert Systems International 1700 Walnut St. Philadelphia, PA 19103 (215) 735-8510	Rule-based	Forward & Backward Chaining	IBM-PC, DEC, VAX, MicroVAX, Sun, and Apollo workstations	$695
Crystal	Intelligence Environments P.O. Box 388 Chelmsford, MA 01824 (508) 256-6412	Rule-based	Forward & Backward Chaining and Induction	IBM-PC MS-DOS version OS/2 version	$995 $1,995
ESP Advisor	Expert Systems International 1700 Walnut St. Philadelphia, PA 19103 (215) 735-8510	Rule-based	Forward & Backward Chaining	IBM-PC, DEC, VAX, MicroVAX, Sun, and Apollo workstations	$695
ESP Frame Engine	Expert Systems International 1700 Walnut St. Philadelphia, PA 19103 (215) 735-8510	Rule-based	Forward & Backward Chaining	IBM-PC, DEC VAX, MicroVAX, Sun, and Apollo workstations	$695
EXSYS Professional	EXSYS Inc. P.O. Box 11247 Albuquerque, NM 97192 (505) 256-8356	Rule-based	Forward & Backward Chaining, and Optional Frame Extension	PCs Unlimited runtime lic. DEC VAX and some UNIX machines	$995 $1,000 $2,500 and up
Guru First Step	Micro Data Base Systems, Inc. P.O. Box 6089 Lafayette, IN 47903-6089 (800) 344-5832	Rule-based	Forward & Backward Chaining, Mixed Forward & Backward Chaining, and Induction	IBM-PC	$895
KnowledgerPro	Knowledge Garden, Inc. 12 Technology Dr. #8 Setauket, NY 17133-4049 (518) 246-5400	Rule-based	Forward & Backward Chaining	IBM-PC	$595
LASER	Bell Atlantic Knowledge Systems Group 34 Washington Rd. Princeton Junction, NJ 08550 (609) 275-4545	Frame-based	Forward & Backward Chaining	Sun, DEC VAX, RT/IBM-PC, PS/2, IBM 9370, and Macintosh II	$900–$25,00

Program	Company Address/Tel No.	Knowledge Represented	Inference	Computer Type	Price
Level5 Object	Information Builders, Inc. 1250 Broadway New York, NY 10001-3782 (914) 347-6860	Rule-based and Frame-based	Forward & Backward Chaining	IBM-PC and Macintosh	$995
M.4	Cimflex Teknowledge 1810 Embarcadero Rd. Palo Alto, CA 94303 (800) 285-0500	Rule-based	Forward & Backward Chaining	IBM-PC	$995
Nexpert Object	Neuron Data 444 High St. Palo Alto, CA 94301 (414) 321-4488	Rule-based and Frame-based	Forward & Backward Chaining	IBM-PC, Macintosh, DEC VAX, 386 machines, PS/2, Sun, Apollo, HP, and other UNIX platforms	$995–$8000 development system $750 runtime version

$1,000–$2,000

Program	Company Address/Tel No.	Knowledge Represented	Inference	Computer Type	Price
AIM	Abtech Corp. 503 Dale Ave. Charlottesville, VA 22903 (804) 977-0686	Rule-based	Forward & Backward Chaining	IBM and Macintosh	$1,495
Flex	Logic Programming Assoc. Ltd. Studio 4 Royal Victoria Patriotic Trinity Rd., SW 18 3SX UK (44) 81 871-206	Rule-based and Frame-based	Forward & Backward Chaining	PCs	$1,000–$2,000
OPS83	Production Systems Technologies 5001 Baum Blvd. Pittsburgh, PA	Rule-based	Forward Chaining	MS-DOS version OS/2 version UNIX System V version	$1,950 $2,950 $3,950
TIMM	General Research Corp. 1900 Gallows Rd. Vienna, VA 22182 (703) 506-5166	Table-form	Induction	IBM-PC Mainframes	$1,900 $19,000

$2,000–$10,000

Program	Company Address/Tel No.	Knowledge Represented	Inference	Computer Type	Price
1st-Class	Trinzic Corp. 101 University Ave. Palo Alto, CA 94301 (415) 328-9595	Table-form	Induction	IBM-PC and DEC VAX	$2,500
ART-IM (Automated Reasoning Tool)	Inference Corp. 5300 W. Century Blvd. Los Angeles, CA 90045 (213) 417-1243	Rule-based and Frame-based	Forward Chaining	IBM-PC, PS/2	$6,900
Decision Expert	Digital Equipment Corp. 290 Donald Lynch Blvd. Marlboro, MA 01752-4790 (508) 490-8052	Table-form	Induction	DEC VAX	$7,900
Guru	Micro Data Base Systems Inc. P.O. Box 6089 Lafayette, IN 47903-6089 (800) 344-5832	Rule-based	Forward & Backward Chaining, Mixed Forward & Backward Chaining, and Induction	IBM-PC, PS/2, DEC VAX, and Sun workstation single-user systems version LAN versions	$7,000 $9,900
KBMS	Trinzic Corp. 101 University Ave. Palo Alto, CA 94301 (415) 326-9595	Rule-based and frame-based	Forward & Backward Chaining	IBM-PC, DEC VAX, and Sun	$9,000
KDS	KDS Corp. 934 Hunter Rd. Wilmette, IL 60091 (708) 251-2621	Rule-based and frame-based	Forward & Backward Chaining, and Induction	IBM-PC and Apollo workstation	$1,795
KEE (Knowledge Engineering Environment)	IntelliCorp. 1975 El Camino Real West Mountain View, CA 94040 (415) 965-5500	Frame-base and Object-oriented	Forward & Backward Chaining	DEC VAX, Sun, Apollo, Symbolics, micro-Explorer, and Explorer workstations; RT IBM-PC, Compaq 80386, and HP machines	$9,000–$30,000

Program	Company Address/Tel No.	Knowledge Represented	Inference	Computer Type	Price
KES (Knowledge Engineering System)	Software Architecture & Engineering Inc. 1600 Wilson Blvd. #500 Arlington, VA 22209 (703) 276-7910	Frame-based	Forward & Backward Chaining	PCs Sun-4 Apollo and other Sun machines	$4,000 $10,000 $7,000
M.1	Cimflex Technology Corp 1810 Embarcadero Rd. Palo Alto, CA 94303 (415) 424-0500	Rule-based	n/a	PC site licenses	$5,000
ReMind	Cognitive Systems Inc. 220–230 Commercial St. Boston, MA 02109 (914) 347-6860	Rule-based and Frame-based and Object-oriented	Forward & Backward Chaining	IBM-PC	$3,000

■ FUZZY LOGIC DEVELOPMENT TOOL

Name	Address/Tel No.	Computer Type	Price
Boole	URSIC Computing 5210 Trafalger Place Madison, WI 53714 (608) 241-0651	IBM-PC	$95
CubiCalc	Hyperlogic Corp 1855 E. Valley Pkwy Ste. 210 Escondido, CA 92027 (619) 746-2765	IBM-PC	$495
RT/Fuzzy	Integrated Systems Inc. 3260 Jay St. Santa Clara, CA 95054 (408) 980-1500	UNIX and VMS workstations	$5,000
TILShell	Togay Intralogic Inc. 340 Corporate Park, Ste. 107 Irvine, CA 92714 (714) 975-8522	IBM-PC	$3,000

▪ PROLOG

Name	Address/Tel No.	Computer Type	Price
AAIS Prolog	Advanced AI Systems Inc. P.O. Box 39-0360 Mountain View, CA 94039-0360 (415) 948-8648	Macintosh	$298
Active Prolog Tutor	Amziod 40 Samuel Prescott Dr. Stow, MA 01775 (508) 897-5560	IBM-PC	$65
ALS Prolog Professional	Applied Logic Systems P.O. Box 90 University Station Syracuse, NY 13210-0090 (315) 471-3900	IBM-PC and Macintosh 386-Based PCs under DOS or SCO UNIX	$499 $799
Arity Prolog Professional Compiler	Arity Corp. 29 Domino Dr. Concord, MA 01742 (508) 371-1243	IBM-PC	$650
BIM Prolog (SPARC)	BIM Kwikstraat 4 Everbert B-3078 Belgium 01132 (27) 595-925 US Distributor: The Shure Group 1514 Pacific Ranch Dr. Encinitas, CA 92024 (619) 944-0320 (800) 627-6564		$7,500
Cogent Prolog	Amziod 40 Samuel Prescott Dr. Stow, MA 01755 (508) 897-5560	IBM-PC	$199
Delphia Prolog	Delphia 27 Ave. de la Republique 38170 Seyssinet FRANCE c/o Arity Corp	Sun3, SPARC, Apollo, HP 9000, and VAX VMS	$10,000
IF Prolog (SPARAC)	InterFace GMbH Garmischerstr. 4/V Munich D-8000 GERMANY (011) 49 89 510 860	DOS Macintosh and micro-Vax HP SPARC and IBM RS/6000 DEC Station	$1,999 $5,400 $7,200 $6,300 $10,200

Name	Address/Tel No.	Computer Type	Price
PDC Prolog	Prolog Development Center 568 14th St., N.W. Atlanta, GA 30318 (800) 762-2710	n/a	$299–$2,000
Quintus DOS Prolog	Quintus Corp 2100 Geng Rd. Palo Alto, CA 94303 (415) 813-3800	IBM-PC	$325–$1,695
Quintus MacProlog	Quintus Corp. 2100 Geng Rd. Palo Alto, CA 94303 (415) 813-3800	Macintosh	$1,295

Appendix ■ E

Expert Systems on Internet

For those who are in the fast lane on the information superhighway, what follows is a list of list servers, bulletin boards, newsgroups, and user groups to keep you on the cutting edge of Expert Systems and artificial intelligence.

■ GENERAL

- ■ **AI** Artificial intelligence, expert systems, hypertext retrieval, and related topics. **ILINK** ➥ *number* 46
- ■ **AI EXPERT** A supplement to *AI Expert* magazine. Direct AI questions to industry and academic leaders and exchange information with other members. **COMPUSERV** ➥ *go* AIEXPERT
- ■ **Artificial Intelligence** Topics include expert systems, knowledge base design, genetic algorithms, natural language interfaces, and artificial life. **FIDONET** ➥*tag*AI
- ■ **comp.ai** (NG) General discussion of AI from book announcements to discussion questions about techniques. **USENET**
- ■ **comp.ai.fuzzy** (NG)(fuzzy-logic) Discussions of fuzzy-logic applications in AI. **USENET**

■ ARCHIVES

- ■ **DartNet** A Mac-based neural network simulator with tools for building, editing, training, testing, and examining networks. **INTERNET** ➥ *ftp* DARTVAX.DARTMOUTH.EDU ➥ ANONYMOUS/<YOUR EMAIL ADDRESS> ➥ pub/mac/dartnet.sit.hqx
- ■ **UCLA Artificial Life Depository** Series of articles, papers, software and other materials of interest to artificial-life researchers. **INTERNET** ➥ *ftp* FTP.COGNET.UCLA.EDU ➥ ANONYMOUS/<YOUR EMAIL ADDRESS> ➥ pub/alife

■ NEURAL NETS

- ■ **Artificial Neural Network** ANNs are called the "bottom up" approach to developing artificial intelligence. Information here includes resource referrals, code exchange, and problem solving for cognitive and behavior scientists and other researchers. News comes from the Usenet newsgroup COMP.AI.NEURAL-NETS and Neuron Digest list. **FIDO-NET** ➤ *tag* NEURAL_NET

- **C.N.S. BBS**   (BBS) Neural-network-related information. (509) 627-2627

- **comp.ai.neural-nets**   (NG-ML) For people interested in exploring neural networks or neural-network-like structures. **USENET INTERNET** ➤ *email* NEURON- REQUEST@CATTELL.PSYCH.UPENN.EDU *Subscribe by request*

APPLICATIONS

- **AIL-L**   (ML) Devoted to artificial intelligence and law. **INTERNET** ➤ *email* LISTSERV@AUSTIN.ONU.EDU *Type in message body:* SUBSCRIBE AIL-L <YOUR FULL NAME>

- **AI-MEDICINE**   (ML) Devoted to discussing computer-based medical-decision support. **INTERNET** ➤ *email* AI-MEDICINE- REQUEST @MED.STANFORD.EDU. *Subscribe by request*

- **comp.ai.edu**   (NG) Discussions about AI and education, including intelligent computer-aided instruction. **USENET.**

- **Vision-List**   (ML) Forum for artifical-intelligence vision researchers. "Anything related to vision and its automation is fair game." **INTERNET** ➤ *email* VISION- LIST-REQUEST@ADS>COM *Subscribe by request*

Appendix ▪ F

Glossary of Terms

Action a list of commands to be carried out if the premise evaluates to true, or a Boolean expression that evaluates to true whenever the premise does; either conclusions to be drawn with some appropriate degree of certainty or instructions to be carried out.

Action (portion of a rule) the goal; either conclusions to be drawn with some degree of certainty or instructions to be carried out.

Age effect bias against a person due to age.

Agenda/protocol mechanism that controls the order in which rules fire.

Agent also called intelligent agent; a bit of intelligence that represents specific attributes to other agents on a network.

Aggression resistance to expert systems through employee sabotage of the system.

AI see artificial intelligence.

AI programming symbolic approach that uses programming languages to process symbols by analyzing and reaching conclusions on a logical level of knowledge representation.

Ambiguity characterizes a statement that has more than one meaning or is interpreted in more than one way.

Analogies comparing a problem to a similar one encountered previously.

Anonymous variable a special type of variable in Prolog that contains an underscore and gives a YES or NO answer.

Arc a line denoting the relationship between the nodes of a semantic network.

Arguments the objects of the relationship in fact statements.

Artificial imitating or emulating something natural or real.

Artificial intelligence (AI) subfield of computer science; the science of making machines do things that would require intelligence if done by humans; processes analogous to human reasoning processes; the capacity to acquire and apply an understanding gained through experience or study in order to imitate or emulate "natural intelligence"; "the science of making machines do things that would require intelligence if done by man" (Marvin Minsky).

Atom noninteger constant in Prolog.

Automatic programming process in which user requirements are input into the computer, which automatically generates a program that meets the requirements.

Avoidance resistance to expert systems through employee withdrawal from the job or scene.

Axon a neural element that carries signals (output) away.

Back propogation a supervised learning mode, in which an output error signal is passed back through the network changing connecting weights to minimize that error.

Backtracking a way of satisfying goals in which Prolog reviews what has been done and attempts to resatisfy the goals by finding an alternative way to meet them.

Backward chaining goal-driven inference strategy in which the system works backward from the goal to find supporting data; working "backward" through a chain of rules in an attempt to find a verifiable set of condition clauses.

Belief a qualitative judgment about the nature of the statement or the problem under review; measure of the level of credibility.

Blackboard a shared database in which various knowledge sources work together to solve a problem.

Blackboarding experts work together in a common electronic work area to come up with a solution.

Black-box testing testing a system's behavior in a real-life environment; a validation phase.

Brainstorming an unstructured approach by which two or more experts generate ideas about a problem domain.

Call an attempt to satisfy a goal has been initiated in which Prolog will try to instantiate the clause.

Case knowledge at an operational level; episodic description of a problem and its associated solution.

Case-based reasoning (CBR) a methodology that records and documents previous cases and then searches the relevant case(s) to determine their usefulness in solving a current problem; computer systems that solve new problems by analogy with old ones.

Certainty factor (CF) a measurement of belief or a subjective quantification of an expert's judgment and intentions.

Champion individual within the organization who believes the project will benefit the company and is willing to take risks in supporting its development; has credibility with both management and users and has access to key persons.

Chunked knowledge a group of items stored and recalled as a unit.

Chunking grouping ideas or details that are stored and recalled together.

Circular rule a rule that has embedded contradiction in meaning or logic.

Clause facts necessary to a program or rules specifying how to derive facts from other clauses.

Closed question asks for a specific response.

Code of ethics a declaration of principles and beliefs that govern how employees of a corporation are to behave.

Common sense possessing common knowledge about the world and making obvious inferences from this knowledge.

Compilation the way a computer translates the programmer's instructions into machine language.

Computer vision the addition of computer intelligence capability to digitized visual information received from a machine to control machine movement; interpretation of pictures through visual recognition of precise characteristics.

Consensus reaching a clear agreement on the best solution to a problem.

Consensus decision making knowledge engineer conducts the exercise after brainstorming to rally the experts toward one or two alternatives and to convey the impression that all of them are part owners of the alternative(s).

Control expert system manipulates operation of a system's overall behavior; intelligent automation.

Control mechanism coordinates the flow and pattern of the problem solution in a blackboard model.

Corporate knowledge the combined knowledge of decision makers and experts of an organization.

Customer-user a user interested in knowing how to use the system for problem solving on a regular basis.

Cut a goal in Prolog that succeeds and blocks backtracking.

Database a collection of facts and rules.

Data-driven beginning with the evidence and attempting to find the cause or solution; descriptive of forward-chaining.

Data hierarchies organize information in a way that reflects the actual organization of information in the problem domain.

Debugging expert system recommends correction or remedies for malfunction.

Decision-making flow integration matching expert system problem-solving processes with the user's style of thinking.

Decision support systems (DSS) computer-based information systems that combine models and data for solving complex problems with extensive user involvement.

Decision table a list of conditions with their respective values matched against a list of conclusions.

Decision tree a hierarchically arranged semantic network that is closely related to a decision table; composed of nodes representing goals and links that represents decisions or outcomes.

Declarative knowledge surface information that experts verbalize easily.

Deductive inference logically clear and sound; reasoning from general principles or rules to reach specific conclusions.

Deductive reasoning also called exact reasoning, takes known principles (exact facts) and applies them to instances to infer an exact conclusion.

Deep knowledge knowledge based on the fundamental structure, function, and behavior of objects.

Definitional rule a rule in which the inference sets a relationship between terms; a rule that defines relationships among objects in the knowledge base, but doesn't contain any expert knowledge about how to solve a problem.

Delphi method a survey by questionnaires that poll experts concerning a given problem domain.

Demon program a program that "sits" in the background, waiting for an event to occur, and then takes action when the event does occur.

Dendrite a neural element that carries signals (input) into the network.

Deployment physical transfer of the technology to the organization's operating unit.

Design expert systems configures objects into a system based on problem constraints; develops products to specifications.

Diagnostic expert system identifies causes based on the symptoms; estimates defects.

Dichotomous question a question answerable by one of two answers, usually yes or no.

Disclaimer renunciation of a claim or power vested in a person or product.

Distributed artificial intelligence (DAI) a group of agents that form a cooperative unit and communicate directly through messages to solve common problems.

Domain expert a person whose expertise is being modeled in the system; an individual who is widely recognized as having the knowledge and know-how to solve a problem or make a decision in a specific knowledge domain.

Editing facility ensures that the syntax is correctly entered and represented in the knowledge base.

Electronic brainstorming a computer-aided approach to dealing with multiple experts through a network of PCs, which promote live exchange of ideas between experts, and a sorting and condensing of them into an organized format.

Empty list a list with no elements.

Enhancement upgrading the system to meet a new set of user requirements.

Episodic knowledge knowledge based on experiential information chunked as an entity and retrieved from long-term memory on recall; see also deep knowledge.

Episodic memory knowledge of cases based on experience.

ESDLC see expert system development life cycle.

Ethics fairness, justice, equity, honesty, trustworthiness; a subjective feeling of being innately right.

Exact reasoning deductive reasoning.

Exhaustive testing a procedure in which all possible combinations of input values in an expert system are tested.

Exit occurs when a clause is exited after Prolog has either failed or finished all possible instantiations.

Experience the factor that changes unrelated facts into expert knowledge.

Expert company an organization that works smarter by the way it captures human knowledge, represents knowledge in a computer-acceptable form, and uses the resulting program to solve various kinds of ill-structured, focused problems that were once the sole domain of humans.

Expertise the skill and knowledge possessed by some humans that result in performance that is far above the norm; knowledge based on years of specialized experience.

Expert system a sophisticated computer program that applies human knowledge in a specific area of expertise to create solutions to difficult problems.

Expert system consultation environment (ESCE) allows the user to consult a knowledge base.

Expert system development environment (ESDE) allows the knowledge engineer to create a knowledge base.

Expert system development life cycle (ESDLC) the steps through which an expert system project goes before it becomes operational.

Expert system package a ready-to-use program that advises a specific user in a specific industry how to address a specific problem domain.

Explanation facility an inference engine feature that shows the basis for the solution offered by the system.

Explanatory facility the system's capability to display the reasoning behind its solutions.

Explicit priorities a specific order in which certain rules must be fired; usually set by the knowledge engineer.

Express warranty warranty offered orally or in writing by the maker of the system.

Facet the value of an object or a slot.

Face validity testing a system at its face value; comparing human domain expert's value judgment to test results for reliability.

Fact a statement of a certain element of truth about a subject matter or a domain; a fundamental structure that states a true relationship.

Fail occurs when instantiation fails or when the goal is satisfied and the solution is printed.

False representation a statement that incorrectly represents pieces of knowledge, associated with Type I and Type II errors.

Focus control block (FCB) a module or unit of work that allows the knowledge engineer to segment the knowledge base and control the consultation.

Forward chaining data-driven inference strategy in which the system begins with known data and works forward to see if any conclusions can be drawn.

Frame a structure for organizing knowledge; consists of attributes that carry knowledge by associating objects with facts, rules, or values.

Fuzzy inexact knowledge or imprecise reasoning present in the knowledge used by human experts.

Fuzzy logic the approximate rather than exact logic underlying modes of reasoning; allows an expert system to reason with uncertain data.

Fuzzy set a class of elements defined by a membership function.

Gender effect bias against a person based on gender.

Goal an uninstantiated query in Prolog.

Goal-driven a search that starts with the goal and works backward to determine the supporting processes needed to achieve it.

Grid a scale or a bipolar construct on which elements are placed within gradations.

Head the leftmost element in a fact or a rule.

Heuristic a rule of thumb based on years of experience.

Ideawriting a structured group approach used to develop ideas, explore their meaning for clarity and specificity, and produce a written report.

Implementation stage three of the expert system development life cycle; the process of organizing the knowledge and integrating it with the processing strategy (inference engine) for testing.

Implied warranty presumed warranty; certain facts implied in the facts that represent the product.

Incomplete knowledge a statement that represents some but not all pieces of needed information.

Inconsistency rule a rule that has the same input but different results.

Inductive reasoning reasoning from a given set of facts or specific examples to general principles or rules.

Inference engine the "brain" of an expert system; a cluster of computer programs that coordinate through a scheduler the reasoning and inferencing based on the rules of the knowledge base to produce the solution or advice.

Inferencing deriving a conclusion based on statements that only imply that conclusion.

Inheritance an instance of a particular class is assumed to have all the properties of more general classes of which it is a member.

Inheritance mechanism relates objects with similar characteristics within a group.

Injury any wrong or damage done to others, their rights, property, or reputation.

Input stimulation level in a neural network; user's response to questions posed by the expert system.

Instantiate create a frame by filling its slots; something is instantiated in Prolog when an instance of some fact or rule exists about a thing.

Instantiation repetitions.

Instruction/training expert system diagnoses and modifies learning behavior; trains and transfers information.

Intelligence the capacity to acquire and apply knowledge through the ability to think and reason.

Interactive dialogue allows the user to answer requests from the expert system for additional or new information that allows it to arrive at solutions.

Interpretation expert system infers problem description from sensor (real) data; clarifies situations.

Interview a face-to-face interpersonal situation in which a person called the interviewer asks another person questions designed to elicit certain responses about a problem domain.

Job aids screen designs that rely on color to highlight a question or an answer, partitions on the screen to separate one answer from another, and so on.

Job role job function; set of tasks making up a person's expected behavior in a given position.

Justifier explains the action (line of reasoning) of the expert system to the user.

Knowledge understanding, awareness, or familiarity acquired through education or experience.

Knowledge acquisition capturing heuristics from the domain expert; stage one of the expert system development life cycle; corresponds to the system analysis step in the conventional systems development life cycle; a process by which the experts thoughts and experential knowledge are captured and represented (coded) into a knowledge base.

Knowledge analysis tools tools such as semantic networks, scripts, and decision trees that are used in knowledge acquisition during initial knowledge gathering.

Knowledge base a collection of facts, rules, and procedures organized into schemas or models; the assembly of all of the information and knowledge of a specific field of interest.

Knowledge engineer a well-rounded, versatile professional with competency in technical skills involving expert systems tools and methodologies, interpersonal communications, and organization skills; a specialist who captures knowledge from the mind of expert(s) and represents it in a knowledge base.

Knowledge management an approach that allows managers to focus on knowledge content and needs and opportunities associated with a specific operation; a standardized tool for managing knowledge.

Knowledge representation facts or rules represented in a knowledge base; representing the knowledge in such a way that an inferencing program will be able to use it to draw conclusions in a given problem domain.

Knowledge representation scheme a plan that defines how the expert system organizes information and how information is acted upon.

Knowledge-sharing integration integrating the expert system in such a way that it can be accessed by different branches of the company, allowing them to share information.

Knowledge source a unique module that has the knowledge to solve the problem.

Knowledge worker a company employee with experience to do a specialized job, usually using a computerized system with access to information.

Learning knowledge or skill acquired by instruction or study.

Learning by discovery acquiring new ideas by exploring a domain with no advance knowledge of what is being sought.

Learning by example acquiring new ideas based on specially constructed examples or scenarios.

Learning by experience acquiring new ideas based on hundreds of previously stored concepts.

Leasher a predefined predicate in Prolog that helps to debug databases that do not work as expected.

Link represents relationships between word concepts (semantics); connects nodes and descriptors.

LISP(LISt Processor) oldest programming language; symbolic language.

List an ordered sequence of elements that can have any strength.

Logic the study of reasoning; the scientific study of the process of reasoning and the set of rules and procedures used in the reasoning process.

Logic Gem a software package that electronically builds decision tables of any size.

Machine translation translating one language into another; understanding a text written in one language and then generating it in a different language.

Maintenance making necessary corrections so that the expert system continues to meet the initial system requirements.

Malpractice negligence or professional liability of a certified professional related to design defects in systems tailored specifically for professional use.

Matching the values associated with a given entity paired with the slot values of the frames to signify that an instance has occurred.

Membership function relates a grade of membership with each class element.

Membership set a range of values.

Memory the ability to store and retrieve relevant experience at will.

Metaknowledge knowledge about the structure of stored knowledge and how it is used.

Metarules rules that control the usage of other rules.

Metric quantitative measure used for system validations.

Model-based reasoning observed sensor data is received from the machine in operation and is compared with the predicted simulation values, setting off an alarm or transmitting a message whenever the actual value is beyond the predetermined range of tolerance.

Modularity a design in which adding, updating, or deleting a module does not affect other modules.

Modus ponens a common rule for deriving new facts from existing rules and known facts; inference rule type that, from "a implies b", justifies b by the existence of a.

Monitoring expert system determines how close an observation is to expected outcome; compares observations to expected standards.

Monotonic reasoning a process that moves in one direction only, continuously adding additional truths.

Multiple-choice question offers the expert specific answer choices.

Natural language interface provides the user with the capability to communicate with the computer in the user's own natural conversational language.

Natural language programs programs that concentrate on understanding what the user means when the user asks a question.

Natural language understanding a complex process of analyzing natural language sentences and words for making a correct interpretation through syntactic analysis, semantic interpretation, and pragmatic evaluation.

Negligence omission to do something, which a reasonable person, guided by those ordinary considerations that ordinarily regulate human affairs, would do; lack of reasonable conduct and care.

Neural network (NN) an information system modeled after the human brain's network of electrically interconnected processing elements called neurons; a self-programming system that creates a model based on its inputs and outputs.

Neuron a processing element or unit.

Node represents the description of a fact; a single neuronlike processing element in a network.

Nominal-group technique small group meetings in which individual judgment can often be effectively pooled; interface between consensus and brainstorming.

Nonmonotonic reasoning allows new facts to invalidate old facts; holds a set of premises to be true and keeps a collection of contingent beliefs and revises those beliefs when new knowledge is derived.

Novice an individual with skills and solutions that work some of the time but not all of the time.

Object an elementary unit in predicate logic.

On-site observation observing, interpreting, and recording an expert's problem-solving behavior as it occurs in the domain.

Open-ended question asks for general rather than specific responses.

Opportunistic reasoning an inference strategy that uses forward chaining to draw conclusions from existing data and backward chaining to find data that make it possible to generate the solution.

Output sum of inputs multiplied by their respective weights.

Output layer the layer of nodes that produce a neural network result.

Parameters variables; facts about the domain of expertise.

Parent a variable or module that calls another.

Partial knowledge a type of uncertainty.

Participant observation see on-site observation.

Planning expert system determines a course of action in advance; develops goal-oriented schemes.

Predefined predicate a built-in command that makes it easier for the user to program in Prolog.

Predicate a statement about objects, by themselves and in relation to other objects; applied to a specific number of arguments and has a value of either true or false when objects are used as the arguments.

Predicate calculus representing knowledge in finer detail than propositional calculus.

Predicate logic capable of representing knowledge in finer detail than propositional logic.

Prediction expert system infers likely consequences of a given action or situation; intelligent guessing.

Premise a Boolean expression that must be evaluated as true for the rule to be applied; portion of the rule that provides the evidence from which the conclusion must necessarily follow; evaluates the truth or falsehood with some degree of certainty.

Primary question a question that elicits the most important information in one area during the interview; leads to further questions to obtain pertinent details.

Problem domain special problem area in which an expert solves problems very well.

Procedural knowledge instinctively knowing how to perform a repetitive task or procedure.

Procedural rule a rule that describes a sequence of relations relative to the domain.

Production rule knowledge representation method in which knowledge is formalized into rules.

Product liability a tort that makes a manufacturer liable if its product has a defective condition that makes it unreasonably dangerous to the user or consumer.

Projection resistance to expert systems through employee display of hostility toward peers.

Prolog (PROgramming in LOGic), a reasoning or symbolic language.

Proposition a statement that is either true or false.

Propositional logic relies on established truths, followed by logical extensions resulting in new knowledge.

Protocol analysis systematic collection and analysis of thought processes or problem-solving methods; synonymous with the think-aloud technique.

Pupil-user an unskilled worker trying to learn or gain some understanding of the captured knowledge.

Race effect bias against a person due to race.

Ranking scale question asks the respondent to arrange items in a list according to preference or importance.

Rapid prototyping spontaneous, on-the-spot, iterative approach to building expert systems; an iterative process by which the knowledge engineer shows the domain expert what the expert system looks like based on the knowledge captured to date.

Rating scale question a multiple-choice item that offers a range of responses along a given dimension.

Reasoning the process of applying knowledge to arrive at solutions based on the interactions between rules and data.

Redo occurs when Prolog returns to a marked clause for a second attempt at satisfying backtracking.

Redundancy rule a rule that offers a different approach to the same problem; duplication or meaning the same.

Reliability dependability, truthfulness of the response or answer to a given question; credibility; how well the system delivers solutions with consistency, accuracy, or integrity; detecting or removing anomaly.

Repair expert system administers prescribed remedies; automatic diagnosis; plan, debug, and fix.

Repertory grid knowledge acquisition tool by which the problem domain is classified and categorized around the domain expert's own model; a representation of the expert's way of looking at a particular problem.

Response bias bias resulting from the subjective responses of the domain expert to any given question.

Robot an electronic "worker" or a system that combines sensory systems with mechanical movement to perform predetermined tasks.

Role bias an altered attitude resulting from the expert's awareness of his or her importance in the building of an expert system.

Rule a formal way of specifying a recommendation, directive, or strategy, expressed as a premise and a conclusion (IF . . . THEN); in an expert system shell, a relationship between parameters or facts; conditional statement that specifies an action to be taken if a certain condition is true; a formal way of specifying a recommendation, directive, or strategy, expressed as IF (premise) . . . THEN (conclusion); a goal to be satisfied in a Prolog program; fundamental Prolog clause that defines a relationship from which facts may be inferred.

Rule-based system knowledge base built around rules; a system in which knowledge is represented completely in terms of rules.

Rule of inference a deductive structure that determines what can be inferred if certain relations are taken to be true; facts known to be true used to derive other facts that must also be true.

Scenario the formal description of how a situation selected for a knowledge base system development operates.

Scheduler an inference engine program that coordinates and controls the sequence of the rules.

Screens in an expert system shell, custom displays used during knowledge base consultation.

Scribe a person who takes notes during interviews and maintains all the documentation related to the project.

Secondary question a question used to probe for further details or follow up on an area under discussion.

Self-assessment question-and-answer procedure that allows a person to appraise and understand personal knowledge about a particular role; in ethics, to think about ethics and reinforce one's ethical behavior.

Semantic interpretation assigning meanings to words and phrases while interpreting natural language.

Semantic knowledge highly organized, "chunked" knowledge that resides in the expert's long-term memory and represents concepts, facts, and relationships among facts.

Semantic memory knowledge of facts.

Semantic networks, or nets collections of nodes linked together to form a net; graphical method of representing descriptive or declarative knowledge.

Sex effect bias due to one's gender

Shallow knowledge readily recalled knowledge that resides in short-term memory.

Share when two uninstantiated variables are matched together, they share meaning that when one is instantiated, so is the other.

Shell a commercial software package containing a user interface and an inference engine that makes it easy to build a knowledge base; a complete expert system stripped of a knowledge base.

Shell developer a specialist who develops the shell of the inference engine of an expert system.

Short-term memory the part of the human brain that retains information for a short period of time.

Shuttle process the back-and-forth aspect of the knowledge engineer's recollection of an event as it was initially mentally registered to the evaluation of the event at the time of the retrospection.

Slot a specific object being described or an attribute of an entity; stores each fact or value related to a specific object; represents the properties of the object.

Speech understanding the ability of the computer to recognize and understand spoken language.

Spy point a predefined predicate in Prolog that helps to debug databases that do not work as expected.

Stack a contiguous block of memory containing some memory.

Stack pointer an indicator that tells where the top of the stack is.

Stakeholder customer, employee, vendor, or person who has a vested interest in a company, a project, or a system.

Standard programming algorithmic approach that uses a "brute force" method in which standard procedural languages are used to develop the IF . . . THEN rules.

Strict liability a seller is liable for any defective or hazardous products that unduly threatens a user's safety.

Structured interview an approach in which the questions are fixed in advance; used when the knowledge engineer wants specific information.

Subsumption in rules, if one rule is true, one knows the second rule is always true.

Supervised learning learning by reinforcement; associating a set of input patterns with specific output to minimize error.

Support aids automate the time-consuming phase of acquisition, improve the effectiveness of representation, and ensure a usable interface between human and machine.

Symbol a sign or character that represents something else.

Synapse an axon–dendrite connection; an input-output pathway.

System owner a user who will be responsible for maintaining the system after it is installed.

Systems analyst a specialist who gathers information from the user or the user's staff in order to understand a problem and determine alternative solutions and their consequences within conventional information system development.

Tail everything except the first element in a list or rule.

Technical integration integrating an expert system into an existing operation through the firm's local area network environment, resident mainframe, workstations, or other information system applications.

Testing time-intensive verification and validation of expert systems.

Think-aloud technique knowledge acquisition method in which the expert speaks out loud whatever thoughts come to mind while answering a question or solving a problem; synonomous with protocol analysis.

Threshold see transfer function.

Tort wrongful act, subject to civil action; a legal wrong committed upon a person or a property independent of a contract; a wrongful injury to a person, a person's reputation, or a person's property.

Tracer a predefined predicate in Prolog that helps to debug databases that do not work as expected.

Training set pairs of inputs and outputs applicable to a neural network used to train the network before it becomes operational.

Transfer function a limiter that mirrors the input within a given range; a linear function that has been clipped to minimum and maximum values.

Tree establishes a hierarchy and allow the inheritance to occur between frames.

Triple a link in the semantic net.

Turing test a blind evaluation of the relative merit of the solution without a priori knowledge of whether the solutions were generated by a human expert or an expert system.

Tutor-user a user with a working knowledge of the expert system knowledge base and the responsibility for system maintenance.

Type I error a rule is accepted when it should be rejected; a false positive.

Type II error a rule is rejected when it should be accepted; a false negative.

Uncertainty in the context of expert systems, a value that cannot be determined during a consultation; a lack of adequate information necessary to make a decision.

Uniform Commercial Code (UCC) a law drafted by the National Conference of Commissioners on Uniform State Laws that governs commercial transactions.

Unstructured interview an approach in which the questions and the alternative responses are open-ended.

Unsupervised learning adjusting the neural network solely through direct confrontation with new experiences; self organization.

Unusable rule a rule that only fires if the conditions succeed, that never fires, or that has one or more contradictions.

User-attitude survey a survey in which opinions are collected from users to learn how well they like the system and how closely it meets user requirements.

User interface component of a computer system that allows bidirectional communication between the system and its user; all parts of a knowledge-base system that a user sees on the screen and interacts with during a consultation.

Validation a system test to ensure the right system; a system that meets the expert's expectations; black-box testing; beta test or user acceptance test.

Validity the logical correctness of a question, which is worded in order to elicit the information sought.

Variable a symbol in Prolog that represents an atom not yet known.

Verification a system test to ensure the proper functioning of the system; addresses the intrinsic properties of the expert system; white-box testing; alpha test.

Virtual reality worlds with movement where objects react in a manner consistent with a set of rules; immersion and navigation within computer-generated, three-dimensional environments and ability to manipulate objects within space.

Warranty a promise made by the seller that assures certain facts are truly representative of a product or service, subject to certain limitations.

Weight an adjustable value associated with a connection between neurons or nodes in a network; synaptic strength.

White-box testing analyzing the rules for sequence, structure, and specifications; a verification phase.

Workflow re-engineering changes in the workplace or jobs within the problem domain triggered by insights resulting from expert system implementation.

Index